Handbook
for
Marine
NCOs

By the same author

THE DEFENSE OF WAKE

MARINES AT MIDWAY

SOLDIERS OF THE SEA

A DICTIONARY OF MILITARY
AND NAVAL QUOTATIONS

VICTORY AT HIGH TIDE

Co-author

THE MARSHALLS:
INCREASING THE TEMPO

THE MARINE OFFICER'S GUIDE

Handbook for Marine NCOs

Colonel Robert Debs Heinl, Jr.,
U. S. Marine Corps (Retired)

Naval Institute Press
Annapolis, Maryland

vi

For the Brave and Professional
Noncommissioned Officers of the
Marine Corps—Past, Present,
and Future.

"Once a Marine, always a Marine . . ."

Foreword

". . . these squad leaders and section chiefs, and I'm talking about the corporals and sergeants of this regiment, have no less responsibility than I. The only difference in our positions is in the number of Marines we each control."

That's what a Marine regimental commander said of his noncommissioned officers after a hard-won battle during World War I. It's a timeless statement; it would apply at any point in our Corps' proud history. I know it applies now, and I know it will apply in the future, in or out of combat.

To the men under him, the Marine NCO must constantly set an example of professional skill and purpose. To officers, the noncommissioned officer must always be a strong right arm and a partner in leadership. To all Marines, enlisted and commissioned alike, the Marine NCO is the master of Marine know-how and the keeper of our traditions.

If I could give only one sentence of counsel to all the officers of our Corps, I would say: "Help your NCOs, know your NCOs, and trust your NCOs."

If I were equally limited to a single statement of advice to all Marine noncommissioned officers, and to those who aspire to join their ranks, it would be: "Hold high the trust placed in you; know how to be a good NCO."

This book will help fill in the details of that short piece of advice, and it will do more—it will teach you.

I urge you to read this book and use the knowledge you find in it; not once but often in your career as a Marine noncommissioned officer. If you abide by what is set down here, you will better serve your Corps. It will help you fulfill your important position as a Marine NCO. It will aid you as a master of Marine know-how and keeper of our tradition.

L. F. CHAPMAN, JR.
General, U. S. Marine Corps
Commandant of the Marine Corps

Preface

This is a book for and about Marine noncommissioned officers. To help the new NCO (or the new staff NCO), it contains the information and guidance required by a man who plans to make the most of his chevrons and get ahead in the Corps. For the experienced noncommissioned officer, this Handbook is designed to provide ready reference material on the wide variety of subjects every NCO must know.

To achieve these objectives, this Handbook tells what the Marine Corps is and does, and, in addition, provides general information on the Navy, the Defense Department, and the other armed services. It outlines the history and traditions of our Corps, together with military and social customs and usages among Marines and their families. Most important, it endeavors to provide sound information and guidance on all professional matters that affect the individual NCO, his career, and his performance of duty.

Remember, however, that this work is a guide and a digest— especially in such fields as pay, retirement, dependents' benefits, and the like—covering material constantly subject to revision. Such information is difficult to keep current and must be weighed as of the date of publication and against ever-changing regulations and legislation. Consequently, no attempt has been made to present complete texts, special provisos, semicolons, and subparagraphs of every regulation and instruction in "the book."

On the other hand, this Handbook intentionally goes beyond many matters dealt with in official publications, and does everything possible to describe Service custom and usage in matters *not* covered by "the book."

To insure that this work is accurate and complete and meets the needs of the Corps and our noncommissioned officers, it has been reviewed in detail by well-qualified professional Marines, including a panel of senior noncommissioned officers whose extensive individual contributions are acknowledged elsewhere.

While the resulting opinions and assertions are those of the author, and are not to be construed as official or as reflecting the views of the Navy Department or of the Naval Services at large, no effort has been spared to make this handbook as correct and authoritative as such a work can be.

However, because this is the first edition of a wholly new book, readers will be bound to discover mistakes and to think of ways in which future editions can be improved. For example—Is this Handbook correct? Is it complete? Is it useful? Does it answer questions or at least show you where to find answers?

Corrections, comments, and suggestions on any of the foregoing points (or any other aspect of the book) will be welcome and should be addressed to the author, in care of the U. S. Naval Institute.

Only with such help and interest from readers can this Handbook meet the needs of Marine noncommissioned officers and therefore of our Corps as a whole.

R. D. HEINL, Jr.,
Colonel, U. S. Marine Corps (Retired)

Acknowledgments

A work of this kind could not possibly be written singlehanded, and this one is the product of many hands, preeminently those of the senior warrant and noncommissioned officers who have worked so hard to help make this a useful book.

In preparing this Handbook, I have, from the beginning, relied on an advisory panel of five highly qualified Marines: Chief Warrant Officer A. G. Nicholson, Sergeant Major of the Marine Corps H. J. Sweet, Sergeant Major R. F. Lee, Master Gunnery Sergeant D. M. Oeser, and First Sergeant E. P. Bond, Jr. The members of this panel have reviewed every chapter in detail as it was written, some have checked proofs, and all have enriched this Handbook with ideas and improvements. Sergeant Major Sweet had the onerous task of staffing it through Headquarters Marine Corps.

Without the unstinting help and can-do efforts of the advisory panel, this Handbook could never have been completed.

But the work could also never have been completed without continuing support and encouragement from two Commandants, General W. M. Greene, Jr., and General L. F. Chapman, Jr.

Many others, however, have helped this Handbook, and, for ideas, facts, corrections, and all manner of support, I am greatly indebted to: Lieutenant Generals H. W. Buse, J. M. Masters, Sr., and R. G. Weede; Major Generals M. E. Carl, L. E. English, D. J. Robertson, O. R. Simpson, W. G. Thrash, and R. McC. Tompkins; Brigadier Generals Regan Fuller and J. E. Herbold; Colonels D. L. Dickson, J. H. Magruder, III, H. H. Reichner, Jr., W. J. Sims, and J. R. Stockman; Lieutenant Colonels R. E. Campbell, N. E. McKonly, W. E. Riley, and J. I. Sustad; Major J. B. Walker and Lieutenant Commander Edward M. Byrne; Captains J. J. Bruce, K. L. Bourgeois, W. J. Egger, G. W. Keiser, P. E. Tucker, and W. K. Wilsmann; Sergeants Major O. W. Craddock and M. W. Kreuger; First Sergeant E. Johnson, Jr.; Gunnery Sergeant T. M. Sampson; and David Rosenberg, Ruth A. Sandgren, and Betty Wright.

Indexing was done by Chief Warrant Officer A. G. Nicholson.

Photographs are official U. S. Marine Corps, Navy, or Defense Department.

Besides the generous individual contributions already acknowledged, particular thanks go to the editors of *Leatherneck* and the *Marine Corps Gazette* for permission to reproduce various material and illustrations, and to the staff of Headquarters Marine Corps, the Marine Corps Development and Education Command, and the Marine Corps Museum, as well as the Office of the Assistant Secretary of Defense (Public Affairs).

R. D. HEINL, Jr.

Introduction

When I shipped into the Corps, noncommissioned officers learned their business (and learned it well) by example, by word of mouth, by hard study of what little was handy, and by following the traditions established by those who had gone before.

None of the foregoing is any less important today. But when we have a hundred thousand NCO's in the modern Marine Corps, and have had for many years, it has become essential that they have a reference of their own to point them in the right direction and help them make the most of themselves as noncommissioned officers and marines.

The specific aims of this book, as I see them, are:

(1) to enable every noncommissioned officer to do his present job better;

(2) to prepare each NCO for higher rank and more important responsibilities; and

(3) to help nonrated Marines plan and initiate their first steps toward noncommissioned officer rank.

I see this Handbook filling a long-standing need, and I commend it to your reading.

J. W. DAILEY
Sergeant Major, U. S. Marine Corps
Sergeant Major of the Marine Corps

Prefatory Note

In 1917 when I first enlisted in the Marine Corps, and later, after World War I, during the 1920s and 1930s, little need existed for a handbook to teach our old-timers what a Marine noncommissioned officer needed to know. In those days between wars, the pace of promotion was "a rate a cruise," with plenty of time and opportunity to learn on the job, and besides, only one out of every four Marines was a noncommissioned officer at all.

Times have changed and so has the Corps. Promotions come quickly. Today, every other Marine wears chevrons. The turnover of experienced men, especially after the fourth major war the Corps has fought in this century, is enormous.

What this Handbook does is therefore very important. It codifies the wealth of past professional experience and the traditions that have brought the Marine noncommissioned officer where he is today, and passes on that collective experience and our traditions to men who are starting their way up.

This Handbook is no substitute for experience in the Corps as a noncommissioned officer but it is the next best thing.

G. C. THOMAS,
General, U. S. Marine Corps (Retired)

Editorial Note: General Thomas is the only Marine in the history of the Corps who, besides exercising command in combat in both World Wars and Korea, has risen on active duty from private to general.

Contents

Foreword: General L. F. Chapman, Jr., Commandant,
    U. S. Marine Corps   viii
Preface   x
Acknowledgments   xii
Introduction: Sergeant Major J. W. Dailey, Sergeant Major
    of the Marine Corps, U. S. Marine Corps   xiv
Prefatory Note: General G. C. Thomas,
    U. S. Marine Corps (Retired)   xv

Chapters

1. The Noncommissioned Officer   3
2. The Defense Establishment   8
3. The Marine Corps   33
4. The Story of the Marine Corps   64
5. Traditions, Flags, and Decorations   91
6. Uniforms, Clothing, and Insignia   113
7. Posts of the Corps   133
8. The Marine Corps Reserve   160
9. Women Marines   178
10. Individual Administration   186
11. Pay, Allowances, and Travel   212
12. Making Good   235
13. Leadership   261
14. On Watch   288
15. Military Courtesy and Ceremonies   303
16. Notes on Military Law   346
17. Life in the Field   359
18. Service Afloat   371
19. Embassy Guard Duty   425
20. Personal Affairs   433
21. Social Life   465

Appendices

1. Commandants of the Marine Corps   482
2. The Importance of Being Inspected   483
3. Brother Marines   489
4. Marine Veterans' Associations   496
5. Simple Exhibition Drills   498

Handbook
for
Marine
NCOs

Daniel Joseph Daly won his first Medal of Honor as a private
during the defense of the legations at Peking in 1900, and his
second Medal of Honor as a gunnery sergeant in Haiti during the
First Caco War, October 1915.

*Any officer can get by on his sergeants. To be
a sergeant you have to know your stuff. I'd
rather be an outstanding sergeant than just
another officer.*

—Gunnery Sergeant Daniel Daly

1 The Noncommissioned Officer

Noncommissioned officers are the backbone of the Corps.
Try to imagine a Marine Corps without NCOs.

There could be no boot camp because there would be no DIs.
Think of the hundreds of platoons in a Marine division, each platoon
headed by a new lieutenant just out of Basic School with no NCO
standing by to show him the ropes and keep him out of trouble.
The dignity of command, which is essential to discipline, would be
lost without NCOs to "go between." The LDOs and warrant officers,
hand-picked specialists in essential functions of the Corps, would
vanish. The Embassy Guard program would cease to exist. Airplanes
would have no crew chiefs, weapons would rust, property accounts
would become chaotic, there would be no reveille roll call.

In fact, without NCOs, the Corps would be an armed rabble rather
than the strongest, most versatile elite force in the Free World.

It is no accident that, of all the services, the Marine Corps has
always had (and has today) the lowest ratio of commissioned officers
to enlisted strength. This is because Marine NCOs are rewarded with
greater responsibility than noncommissioned officers in other services.

In 1969, for example, the U. S. Army had one commissioned officer
for every 7.7 enlisted men; the Marine Corps had one officer for
every 10.8 enlisted men. What makes this difference, and who takes
up the slack? Obviously, the Marine noncommissioned officer makes
the difference and takes up that slack. He always has and always
will.

The only way a military organization can operate with fewer
officers is to have better NCOs. To accomplish this is an unceasing
job for the Marine Corps and, most of all, for the NCOs themselves.
You are the people who make the difference. Your rewards are
responsibility and respect, both of which must be protected and
defended.

The NCO and His Purpose

101. ORIGINS OF THE NONCOMMISSIONED OFFICER. Noncommissioned officers are as old as war itself.

In the 7th century B.C., the Book of Deuteronomy speaks of "captains of fifties and captains over tens" among the forces of Moses. The smallest tactical unit in the Roman legion was commanded by a *centurion,* who was a kind of Roman gunnery sergeant.

During the Middle Ages, after the fall of Rome, there were no organized armies as the Romans knew them or as we know them today. However, as soon as the first rudiments of modern military organization appeared during the 14th century, the noncommissioned officer reappeared, too.

The *condottieri,* or mercenary French, Swiss, and Italian soldiers —professionals who served under the colors of any state that paid and fed them—were the first modern military units. It was in these companies that the ranks of sergeant and corporal came into being. Sergeant goes back farthest, dating from 1425.

By 1778 when Baron von Steuben, a Prussian adviser, was forging the Continental Army into a professional force, he wrote the following into his *Regulations for the Order and Discipline of the Troops of the United States.*

> The choice of noncommissioned officers is an object of the greatest importance: The order and discipline of a regiment depends so much on their behavior, that too much care cannot be taken . . . Honesty, sobriety and a remarkable attention to every point of duty, with a neatness in their dress are indispensable requisites; a spirit to command respect and obedience from the men, an expertness in performing every part of the exercise, and an ability to teach it, are also absolutely necessary.

Von Steuben's attributes for a noncommissioned officer can be boiled down to *character, attention to duty, loyalty, command presence, professional skill,* and *ability to instruct.* They are as valid today as they were at Valley Forge.

102. THE PURPOSE OF NCOs. The corps of noncommissioned officers exists for five main purposes:

1. To decentralize command authority in an orderly structure down to the smallest element in an organization.
2. To provide links between commanders (as well as officers in general) and the troops.
3. To provide a senior enlisted adviser—a platoon sergeant, a first sergeant, or a sergeant major—for each commander.
4. To afford avenues for advancement whereby enlisted men may realize their full potential as leaders. (Not every Marine can become a general; but with application and attitude every Marine can win chevrons and, in so doing, demonstrate to those around him that the road to the top is always open.)
5. To recognize and reward outstanding technical and military skills.

In other words, we have noncommissioned officers to help a commander lead, train and take care of his people; to enable good men to get ahead; and to make best use of essential skills.

In a broader context, a veteran British officer, Reginald Hargreaves, has written:

> *The NCO exists to teach the soldier the detail of his business and to cushion those contacts between officer and man which would lead to disillusionment on both sides.*

The Marine NCO

103. MARINE NCOs: DIFFERENT AND BETTER. One main reason why the Marine Corps is different and better than any other military organization is that Marine NCOs are different and better.

The history of the Corps is studded with the names of great noncommissioned officers: Hayes, Quick, Daly, Basilone, Diamond, Fisher, Janson, Schriver, Stockham, and Wilson, to name but a few. In addition, many outstanding Marine officers were outstanding NCOs before they were commissioned. Among these are Cukela, Puller, Crowe, Hanneken, Berkeley, Commiskey, and Thomas (the last being the only Marine in the history of the Corps to rise from private to full general on active duty).

Most military histories identify the generals who won battles, but as the names listed above will testify, Marine Corps history has also identified and immortalized the noncommissioned officers who made those victories possible. The Marine Corps recognizes its NCOs as the foundation on which the Corps is built and never forgets them.

104. YOUR CERTIFICATE OF APPOINTMENT. On becoming a noncommissioned officer, you receive a *certificate of appointment,* sometimes still spoken of as your "warrant." This certificate—like the commission every officer is given—is the basis of your authority, rank, status, and responsibilities. An NCO certificate of appointment is shown in Figure 1-1.

The words on a Marine NCO warrant sum up the reasons why the Corps expects its noncommissioned officers to be the best. Nevertheless, as in the case of insurance policies, titles to property, leases, automobile warranties, etc., men often obtain appointments as noncommissioned officers at some cost and effort and then fail to read and understand the full significance of the certificate of appointment.

Special Trust and Confidence is the keynote of your new status. This phrase in the heading certifies that both your commanding officer and the Marine Corps count on you very specially and therefore have chosen you for the rank in question. In this same sentence, your grade and date of rank are also stated.

Following the heading, your certificate of appointment enjoins you to "carefully and diligently discharge the duties of the grade to which appointed by doing and performing all manner of things thereunto pertaining." This simply means that you are to do your best in performing all the duties of your grade. To live up to this injunction,

6   you are expected to consider yourself on duty at all times.

The next sentence in your NCO warrant establishes your authority over all seamen and Marines of lower rank. They must, in the words of the certificate, "render obedience to appropriate orders." Note that word *appropriate*. Your orders must be correct and lawful. Also

Fig. 1-1: NCO Certificate of Appointment.

To all who shall see these presents, greeting:

Know Ye that reposing special trust and confidence in the fidelity and abilities

of   *, I do*

appoint   *in the*

United States Marine Corps

to rank as such from the   *day of*   *, nineteen*

hundred and

This appointee will therefore carefully and diligently discharge the duties of the grade to which appointed by doing and performing all manner of things thereunto pertaining. And I do strictly charge and require all personnel of lesser grade to render obedience to appropriate orders. And this appointee is to observe and follow such orders and directions as may be given from time to time by Superiors acting according to the rules and articles governing the discipline of the

Armed Forces of the United States of America

Given under my hand at **Headquarters United States Marine Corps**

this   *day of*   *, in the year of our Lord nineteen*

hundred and

_____
COMMANDANT OF THE MARINE CORPS

DD FORM 216MC
1 SEP. 54

note that your authority isn't just confined to your own squad, platoon, or company. You are an NCO in the Marine Corps, not the 5th Marines, the 11th Marines, VMF-211, or some other particular unit. You, in other words, *are* the Marine Corps to all immediate subordinates.

Finally, your certificate of appointment requires you to "observe and follow such orders and directions as may be given from time to time by superiors acting according to the rules and articles governing the discipline of the Armed Forces." This is nothing new. Obedience is a Marine's first rule. However, the obedience of a noncommissioned officer must be intelligent obedience and it must also be rendered in such a way as to support his own authority down the line by giving the example.

105. "WHAT THE MARINE CORPS TEACHES . . ." There are many reasons why Marine NCOs are different and better, but few statements of these reasons surpass that by Samuel W. Meek, Jr., who served with the 4th Marine Brigade in France during World War I. Years later, as a leading business executive, Samuel Meek said:

> What the Marine Corps teaches is valuable in all of life. Responsibility, discipline, self-control, self-confidence, co-operation, self-reliance, accuracy, modesty, inventiveness, enthusiasm, decisiveness, devotion to duty are the firm pillars upon which the Marine Corps has been built.

Are you that kind of a noncommissioned officer?

Our country demands a most vigorous exertion
of her force, directed with judgment.

—Lord Nelson

2 The Defense Establishment

The U. S. organization for national security is headed by the President of the United States, who, under our Constitution, is Commander in Chief of the Armed Forces. *The National Security Council (NSC),* which includes the Vice President, the Secretaries of State and Defense, and other designated high officials, advises the President on all problems relating to national security so that the Defense Department, the services, and all other government departments and agencies may cooperate most effectively for the common defense.

Central Intelligence Agency (CIA) is administered under the direction of the National Security Council. The CIA coordinates all intelligence activities of the U. S. Government.

Bureau of the Budget, although its name suggests otherwise, is a civilian general staff for the President. In this capacity, as well as through its fiscal power, the Bureau exercises considerable influence over the Defense Department and the defense policies of the U. S. Government.

Atomic Energy Commission (AEC) administers nuclear research and development, international cooperation, production of atomic energy and special nuclear materials. The Military Liaison Committee of the AEC, made up of representatives of Departments of the Army, Navy, and Air Force, works with the Defense Department on all military applications of atomic energy.

National Aeronautics and Space Administration (NASA) deals with problems of flight in space and in the earth's atmosphere, develops and operates space vehicles, and is charged with the exploration of space.

Selective Service System provides nation-wide machinery for the registration and military induction—in other words, the draft—of individuals with obligated military service. The Marine Corps ordinarily relies on volunteers, but has sometimes been forced by national policy to accept draftees in time of war.

Veterans Administration (*VA*) administers all laws authorizing benefits for former members of the armed forces and their dependent beneficiaries and administers all government insurance programs open to members of the armed forces. For benefits and services of the Veterans Administration, see Chapter 20.

201. NATIONAL OBJECTIVES. The national objectives of the United States affect the military departments and the Armed Forces. While never officially promulgated as such, the statement of national objectives which follows has been compiled from the speeches and other pronouncements of high Government officials.

Our prime national objective is the desire of our people for peace and security, without sacrifice of either the rights of the individual or the present sovereignty we cherish.

While we intend to maintain our political way of life and our form of government in our own country, our national objectives do not demand a similar political way of life or a similar form of government in other countries of the world.

We intend to maintain and to improve our American standard of living.

We desire freedom, peace and security for the entire world, and all the benefits that these conditions can bring to all peoples everywhere.

We will seek and work for an effective world organization under the United Nations, for we believe that world peace is an inseparable part of American peace.

Ultimately, we hope to eliminate any sort of warfare as a means for the resolution of international disputes.

Finally, if war be forced upon us, we intend to win that war and to win it in such a way that it can be followed by a stable, livable, and longlasting peace.

The Pentagon, headquarters of the Department of Defense, is the world's largest office building.

The Department of Defense

The Department of Defense is the largest single agency in the Government of the United States. It spends approximately half the national budget in an ordinary fiscal year and employs nearly 3,500,000 persons (including a million civilians). In two decades since its creation, the Office of the Secretary of Defense has mushroomed from a handful of policy makers (in 1949 the Secretary of Defense had only three special assistants) to one of the major bureaucracies of the Government, staffed by thousands of officers, enlisted men, and civilian employees.

The Defense Department includes the Office of the Secretary of Defense (OSD), the Joint Chiefs of Staff (JCS) and their supporting establishment, the Departments of the Army, Navy, and Air Force, and the four military services (Army, Marine Corps, Navy, and Air Force) within those departments, the unified and specified commands, and such other agencies as the Secretary of Defense establishes to meet specific requirements. The central function of the Department of Defense is to provide for the military security of the United States and to support and advance the national policies and interests of the United States.

202. THE NATIONAL SECURITY ACT. The National Security Act of 1947, as amended, is the controlling military legislation of the United States. The policy section of the Act reads: "It is the intent of Congress to provide a comprehensive program for the future security of the United States and to provide for the establishment of integrated policies and procedures for the departments, agencies, and functions of the Government relating to the national security." In so doing, the Act:

1. Provides three military departments, separately organized, for the operation and administration of the Army, Navy (including naval aviation), United States Marine Corps, and Air Force, with their assigned combatant and service components;
2. Provides for coordination and direction of the three military departments and four services under the Secretary of Defense;
3. Provides for strategic direction of the armed forces, for their operation under unified control, for establishment of unified and specified commands, and for the integration of the four services into an efficient team of land, naval, and air forces, but neither establishes a single Chief of Staff over the armed forces nor an Armed Forces general staff.

Unification has been accomplished by giving the Secretary of Defense authority, direction, and virtual military control over the four military services, although he does not administer the Departments of the Army, Navy, and Air Force. He also has authority to eliminate unnecessary duplication in procurement, supply, transportation, storage, health, and research and engineering. His greatest power of control lies in administration of the military budgets of the Department of Defense.

The Secretaries of Army, Navy, and Air Force no longer enjoy Cabinet status, but each secretary has the right to appeal any matter directly to the President or to make representations direct to the Bureau of the Budget or to Congress; however, he must first inform the Secretary of Defense of his intention to do so.

203. OFFICE OF THE SECRETARY. *The Secretary of Defense,* principal assistant to the President in all matters relating to the Department of Defense, is appointed from civil life by the President with the advice and consent of the Senate. Under the President, the Secretary exercises direction, authority, and control over the Department.

The Deputy Secretary of Defense is responsible for supervision and coordination of the activities of the Department and acts for the Secretary during the latter's absence or disability.

The Armed Forces Policy Council (AFPC) advises the Secretary of Defense on matters of broad policy relating to the armed forces and sometimes serves as a final clearing house or court of appeal for major administrative decisions. The members are Secretary of Defense (Chairman); Deputy Secretary of Defense; Secretaries of the Army, Navy, and Air Force; Director of Defense Research and Engineering; Chairman of the JCS; Chief of Staff of the Army; Chief of Naval Operations; Chief of Staff of the Air Force. The Commandant of the Marine Corps, although not a Council member by statute, regularly attends and participates in meetings.

Various agencies, offices, and positions created by the National Security Act, together with certain other agencies which assist the Secretary of Defense, constitute the primary staff—civil and military—of the Secretary of Defense on matters within their cognizance.

204. THE JOINT CHIEFS OF STAFF. To insure direct access to the President by his principal military advisors, the Joint Chiefs of Staff were organized in 1942.

The Joint Chiefs of Staff comprise a Chairman appointed by the President from one of the four services with the advice and consent of the Senate, the Chiefs of Staff of the Army and Air Force, and the Chief of Naval Operations. When a matter which concerns the Marine Corps is under consideration, the Commandant of the Marine Corps sits with the Joint Chiefs and on such occasions enjoys coequal status with the other members.

The Chairman, who takes precedence over all officers of the Armed Services, serves as presiding officer, provides agenda for meetings, and manages the Joint Staff.

On matters affecting the Marine Corps, the Commandant has the prerogatives of a member of the JCS, and the Marine Corps has representation on the supporting staff agencies of the Joint Chiefs of Staff.

As principal military advisers to the President, the National Security Council, and the Secretary of Defense, the Joint Chiefs prepare strategic plans and provide strategic direction of the military forces; they prepare joint logistic plans and assign logistic responsibilities in accordance with such plans; they establish unified commands in strategic areas; they formulate policies for joint training of the military forces and coordinate the education of members of the military forces; they review major material and personnel requirements of the military forces in accordance with strategic and logistic plans; and they provide United States representation on the Military Staff Committee of the United Nations.

The Joint Staff provides planning and staff assistance for the JCS. It is limited to 400 officers (having expanded four times since it was created in 1947) who are chosen from the Army, Navy, Marine Corps, and Air Force. The Director, Joint Staff, an officer of three-star grade, attends meetings of the Joint Chiefs of Staff and serves in effect as the expediter and coordinator of the JCS organization.

205. OTHER DEFENSE AGENCIES. Other than the unified and specified commands established by the JCS (see below) a number of major agencies and joint service schools come directly under the Defense Department or Joint Chiefs of Staff. Certain of these agencies are of significant stature and perform for the Defense Department major functions which were once considered to be within the operating and administrative purview of the military departments.

Defense Atomic Support Agency (DASA)
Defense Supply Agency (DSA)
Defense Intelligence Agency (DIA)
Defense Communications Agency (DCA)
Defense Advanced Research Projects Agency
National Security Agency (NSA)
Joint Strategic Target Planning Staff.

The Joint Service Schools are three in number, and all come under the Joint Chiefs of Staff, namely, National War College, Industrial College of the Armed Forces, and Armed Forces Staff College. In addition, the United States provides facilities and support for the Inter-American Defense College which is located adjacent to the National War College at Fort McNair, Washington, D.C.

206. UNIFIED AND SPECIFIED COMMANDS. Coming directly under the Joint Chiefs of Staff are unified and specified commands, predominantly located outside the United States and covering areas of greatest strategic importance. A *unified command* is a command with a broad continuing mission, under a single commander, composed of components of two or more services. Representation on the commander's staff usually comes from all services, and the command includes "service component commanders" who command all units from their respective services within the unified command. There are seven unified commands.

Atlantic Command
Pacific Command
U. S. European Command

U. S. Southern Command
Alaskan Command
Continental Air Defense Command

A specified command, like a unified command, has a broad continuing mission, but is normally composed of forces from but one service. There is now only one specified command, Strategic Air Command (SAC).

The Department of the Army

207. MISSION OF THE ARMY. The National Security Act charges the Department of the Army with providing support for national and international policy and the security of the United States by planning, directing, and reviewing the operations of the Army Establishment to include the organization, training, and equipping of land forces of the United States for prompt and sustained combat operations on land.

The Secretary of the Army heads the Department of the Army. He is responsible for all affairs of the Army Establishment. In addition, the Secretary of the Army has certain quasi-civil functions, such as maintenance and operation of the Panama Canal, the Alaska Communications Service, and the Corps of Engineers' civil works program; supervision of U. S. battle monuments; and all aspects of the Federal Civil Defense Program assigned to the Department of Defense.

208. THE STRUCTURE OF THE ARMY. Command channels flow from the President, through the Secretary of Defense and the Secretary of the Army, to Army units and installations throughout the world.

A field army is composed of a headquarters and two or more corps, each of two or more divisions. The division is the smallest unit which contains a balanced proportion of the combined arms and services and which, therefore, is constituted to operate independently. Below division level, units are mainly composed of the separate arms or services of the Army. The company is the smallest administrative unit in the Army.

The Army is made up of the following basic and special branches (See Figure 2-1).

Basic Branches

General Staff (Officers)	Quartermaster Corps
Infantry	Finance Corps
Armor	Ordnance
Field Artillery	Chemical Corps
Air Defense Artillery	Transportation Corps
Corps of Engineers	Military Police Corps
Signal	Intelligence and Security
Adjutant General's Corps	

BASIC BRANCHES

Fig. 2-1: Branch insignia of the Army

GENERAL STAFF
(OFFICERS)

INFANTRY *

ARMOR*

FIELD ARTILLERY*

CORPS OF ENGINEERS*

SIGNAL *

ADJUTANT GENERAL'S
CORPS *

QUARTERMASTER CORPS

ORDNANCE*

CHEMICAL CORPS *

TRANSPORTATION CORPS*

MILITARY POLICE CORPS

SPECIAL BRANCHES

INSPECTOR GENERAL

JUDGE ADVOCATE
GENERAL'S CORPS

CHAPLAINS (CHRISTIAN)

CHAPLAINS (JEWISH)

MEDICAL CORPS *

DENTAL CORPS

VETERINARY CORPS

ARMY NURSE CORPS

WOMEN'S ARMY CORPS *

CIVIL AFFAIRS, USAR*

NATIONAL GUARD
BUREAU (OFFICERS)

OTHER INSIGNIA

ENLISTED UNASSIGNED
TO BRANCH

STAFF SPECIALISTS,
USAR (OFFICERS)

WARRANT OFFICERS

AIDES TO THE PRESIDENT
OF THE UNITED STATE

AIR DEFENSE ARTILLERY*

FINANCE CORPS*

INTELLIGENCE AND
SECURITY*

MEDICAL SERVICE CORPS

ARMY MEDICAL
SPECIALIST CORPS

Enlisted insignia are
mounted on flat
disks.

Special Branches
Inspector General
Judge Advocate General's Corps
Chaplains (Christian)
Chaplains (Jewish)
Medical Service Corps
Medical Corps
Dental Corps
Veterinary Corps
Army Nurse Corps
Army Medical Specialist Corps
Women's Army Corps
Civil Affairs, USAR
National Guard Bureau, Officers
Other Insignia
Enlisted unassigned to branch
Staff Specialists, USAR, Officers
Warrant Officers
Aides to the President of the United States
Enlisted insignia are mounted on flat disks to distinguish them from officer's insignia.

Officers from all branches are detailed to the *General Staff Corps* and the *Inspector General's Department.* Members of the *Women's Army Corps* are detailed to, but not commissioned in, the various branches.

Regular Army. For over a century and a half the Regular Army has been the framework upon which we have built up our wartime armies. It is the duty of the Regular Army to:

1. Perform occupation duties;
2. Garrison the United States and overseas possessions;
3. Train the National Guard, Organized Reserve, and ROTC;
4. Provide an organization for the administration and supply of the peacetime military establishment;
5. Provide educated officers and men to become leaders, in event of war, of the expanded Army of the United States;
6. Expand and record the body of military knowledge so as to keep this country up to date and prepared;
7. Constitute, with the National Guard and units of the Organized Reserve, a covering force in case of a major war;
8. Cooperate with the Marine Corps, Navy, and Air Force in carrying out their missions.

National Guard. The National Guard is the militia of the United States. In time of peace, the National Guard of any state can be called to active duty by the governor of that state to perform emergency duties. Units or individual members of the National Guard can be called to active duty by the Federal Government only during war or national emergency, or with their own consent in time of peace.

In addition to augmenting the Regular Army, the Guard:

1. Trains additional volunteers and assigned selectees;
2. Supplies instructors for schools and training centers;
3. Furnishes cadres of experienced officers and men for new units;
4. Furnishes enlisted men who qualify for officer commissions.

209. WOMEN IN THE ARMY. Women have served in and with the United States Army for many years and in a number of wars, at first as "contract nurses," then in the Army Nurse Corps, the Army Medical Specialist Corps, and the Women's Army Corps as nurses, officers, and enlisted women.

Department of the Air Force

210. MISSION OF THE AIR FORCE. The Department of the Air Force and the United States Air Force were established in 1947 by the National Security Act of 1947. The Department includes aviation forces, both combat and service. It organizes, trains, and equips forces of the Air Force for the conduct of prompt and sustained combat operations in the air—specifically, forces to defend the United States against air attack, to gain and maintain general air supremacy, to defeat enemy air forces, to control vital air areas, and to establish local air supremacy as required. The Air Force has primary responsibility for:

1. Developing doctrines and procedures (in coordination with the other services) for the defense of the United States against air attack;
2. Organizing, training, and equipping Air Force forces for strategic air warfare;
3. Organizing and equipping Air Force forces for joint amphibious and airborne operations, in coordination with the other services;
4. Furnishing close combat and logistical air support to the Army;
5. Providing air transport for the armed forces, except as otherwise assigned;
6. Developing, in coordination with the other services, doctrines, procedures, and equipment for shore-based air defense, including continental United States.

The Secretary of the Air Force heads the Department of the Air Force and is responsible for all matters pertaining to its operation.

211. STRUCTURE OF THE AIR FORCE. As a result of experience during and after World War II, Korea, and in Vietnam, the Air Force has evolved the following basic organizational structure.

FLIGHT. The lowest tactical echelon recognized in the Air Force structure. Flights are not formally designated in the structure, but are subdivisions of combat squadrons. They provide the basis for combat formations and are used for training purposes.

SQUADRON. The basic unit in the organizational structure of the United States Air Force. A squadron is manned and equipped to perform best a specific military function, such as combat, maintenance, food service, or communications.

GROUP. A flexible unit composed of two or more squadrons whose functions may be either tactical or administrative in nature.

WING. The smallest Air Force unit manned and equipped to operate independently in sustained action until replacement and resupply can take place.

AIR DIVISION. An air combat organization normally consisting of two or more wings. Divisions are operational in nature with minimum administrative or logistics responsibilities.

NUMBERED AIR FORCE. The intermediate command echelon designed to control and administer a grouping of combat wings. It is flexible in organization and can vary in size. Usually, a numbered air force has one of three missions—strategic, tactical, or defensive. Its wings may be grouped for operational control under air division or be directly under the numbered air force.

MAJOR COMMAND. A functionally titled command echelon directly below Headquarters USAF, charged with a major responsibility in fulfilling the Air Force mission.

Components of the USAF. The United States Air Force is composed, in its entirety, of the regular Air Force, Air National Guard, Air Force Reserve, and the Air ROTC.

212. WOMEN IN THE AIR FORCE. Women serve in the Air Force as line officers, in enlisted ranks (WAF), and as nurses and medical specialists. Present provisions of law for Air Force women personnel are similar to those for women of the other services.

The Department of the Navy

With 71 percent of the globe covered by water and with 6,000 miles of coastline, the United States has long appreciated the importance for our security of strong naval forces. Essentially, the United States is a maritime power, and American strategy must always be fundamentally maritime. In two world conflicts we have successfully kept war from our shores by superior sea power. Without control of the seas, we could not have transported fighting men, equipment, and supplies to distant battle areas, nor could we ever have projected our fighting power from the seas onto the land as we are doing in Vietnam today where, despite much publicity about U.S. airlift capabilities, over 98 percent of all tonnage for the war arrives by sea.

Today, control of the seas is more important than ever. The United States depends increasingly on overseas areas for raw materials to sustain our growing industrial production. Our security is bound up with the security of friendly powers in many parts of the world. By maintaining control of the seas, we assure that our lifelines to these nations and to our far-flung advance bases will not be broken. More important, we assure control of the seas to assure our ability to use the seas for the offensive operations which victory requires. For all these reasons we must maintain the greatest maritime force in the world—the United States Fleet. In doing this, the basic policy of the Department of the Navy is:

> . . . *to maintain the Navy and Marine Corps as an efficient, mobile, integrated force of multiple capabilities and sufficiently strong and ready at all times to fulfill their responsibilities . . . to support and defend the Constitution of the United States against all enemies, foreign and domestic; to insure, by timely and effective military action, the security of the United States, its possessions, and areas vital to its interest; to uphold and advance the national policies and interests of the United States; and to safeguard the internal security of the United States.*

As you reflect on this policy, remember the words of General Shepherd, 20th Commandant, "Both the functions and the future of the Marine Corps are intimately linked with those of the U. S. Navy."

213. MISSION OF THE DEPARTMENT OF THE NAVY. The responsibilities of the Department of the Navy are expressed as follows in the National Security Act as amended.

> Sec. 206 (a) The term "Department of the Navy" as used in this Act shall be construed to mean the Department of the Navy as the seat of government; the headquarters, United States Marine Corps; the entire operating forces of the United States Navy, including naval aviation, and of the United States Marine Corps, including the reserve components of such forces; all field activities, headquarters, forces, bases, installations, activities, and functions unders the control or supervision of the Department of the Navy; and the United States Coast Guard when operating as a part of the Navy pursuant to law.
>
> (b) The Navy, within the Department of the Navy, includes, in general, naval combat and service forces and such aviation as may be organic therein. The Navy shall be organized, trained, and equipped primarily for prompt and sustained combat incident to operations at sea. It is responsible for the preparation of naval forces necessary for the effective prosecution of war except as otherwise assigned and is generally responsible for naval reconnaissance, antisubmarine warfare, and protection of shipping.
>
> All naval aviation shall be integrated with the naval service as part thereof within the Department of the Navy. Naval aviation consists of combat, service, and training forces, and includes land-based naval aviation, air transport essential for naval operations, all air weapons and air techniques involved in the operations and activities of the Navy, and the entire remainder of the aeronautical organization of the Navy, together with the personnel necessary therefor.
>
> The Navy shall develop aircraft, weapons, tactics, technique, organization, and equipment of naval combat and service elements. Matters of joint concern as to these functions shall be coordinated between the Army, the Air Force, and the Navy.
>
> The Navy is responsible, in accordance with integrated joint mobilization plans, for the expansion of the peacetime components of the Navy to meet the needs of war.
>
> (c) The Marine Corps, within the Department of the Navy, shall be so organized as to include not less than three combat divisions and three

air wings, and such other land combat, aviation, and other services as may be organic therein. The Marine Corps shall be organized, trained, and equipped to provide fleet marine forces of combined arms, together with supporting air components, for service with the fleet in the seizure or defense of advanced naval bases and for the conduct of such land operations as may be essential to the prosecution of a naval campaign. In addition, the Marine Corps shall provide detachments and organizations for service on armed vessels of the Navy, shall provide security detachments for the protection of naval property at naval stations and bases, and shall perform such other duties as the President may direct. However, these additional duties may not detract from or interfere with the operations for which the Marine Corps is primarily organized.

The Marine Corps shall develop, in coordination with the Army and the Air Force, those phases of amphibious operations that pertain to the tactics, technique, and equipment used by landing forces.

The Marine Corps is responsible, in accordance with integrated joint mobilization plans, for the expansion of peacetime components of the Marine Corps to meet the needs of war.

Except in time of war or national emergency declared by Congress after June 28, 1952, the authorized strength of the Regular Marine Corps in enlisted members, excluding retired enlisted members, is 400,000 less the actual strength of the Marine Corps in permanent regular officers other than retired regular officers. However, this strength may be temporarily exceeded at any time in a fiscal year if the daily average number in that year does not exceed it.

214. THE SECRETARY OF THE NAVY (SecNav). The Secretary of the Navy is the head of the Department of the Navy. He is responsible for the policies and control of the Department of the Navy, including its organization (except as otherwise prescribed in law), its administration, operation, and efficiency. As far as practicable, the Secretary discharges these responsibilities through his Civilian Executive Assistants and the other military and civilian assistants. The Secretary, however, retains personal direction over activities relating to legislation and Congress and maintains personal relationships with the Secretary of Defense and other principal Government officials and the public.

The Secretary of the Navy is the principal morale officer of the Department of the Navy and as such directs a continuing effort to promote the welfare and morale of all hands.

The Secretary may communicate directly with any principal official of the Department of the Navy, the Shore Establishment, or the Operating Forces.

The Secretary recommends to the Secretary of Defense and the President, appointments, removals, or reassignments of the legally constituted positions of the Department of the Navy. In his own discretion he controls the selection and assignment of all other principal officials of the Department.

The Under Secretary, Assistant Secretary (Financial Management), Assistant Secretary (Research and Development), Assistant Secretary (Installations and Logistics), Assistant Secretary (Manpower and Reserve), and Special Assistant to the Secretary are the principal Civilian Executive Assistants. They exercise top management coordination over the bureaus and offices of the Navy Department. Each Civilian Executive Assistant oversees areas of responsibility assigned by the Secretary.

The various *Naval Personnel Boards* function under the Under Secretary. These Boards, which promote and safeguard the welfare and rights of Navy and Marine officers and enlisted men, include:

Board for Correction of Naval Records
Board of Decorations and Medals
Naval Examining Board (Line)
Naval Examining Board (Marine Corps)
Naval Examining Board (Medical)
Naval Examining Board (Supply Corps)
Naval Clemency Board
Physicial Review Council
Physical Disability Review Board
Board of Review, Discharges and Dismissals

215. THE NAVAL EXECUTIVE ASSISTANTS TO SecNav. *The Chief of Naval Operations (CNO)*, an admiral, is the senior military officer of the Department of the Navy. He is principal naval adviser to the President and to the Secretary of the Navy on the conduct of war and is naval executive assistant to the Secretary of the Navy on the conduct of the activities of the Department of the Navy. As Navy member of the Joint Chiefs of Staff, CNO is responsible additionally to the President and Secretary of Defense for certain duties external to the Department of the Navy.

The *Commandant of the Marine Corps,* a general and the senior officer in the Corps, commands the United States Marine Corps and is directly responsible to the Secretary of the Navy for its administration, discipline, organization, training, requirements, efficiency and readiness, and for the total performance of the Marine Corps. The Commandant of the Marine Corps has additional responsibility to CNO for the organization, training, readiness, and performance of elements of the operating forces of the Marine Corps assigned to the Operating Forces of the Navy. Also, he is responsible to the Civilian Executive Assistants for matters related to the duties assigned them. In addition, the Commandant's responsibilities include:

1. Planning and determining the support needs of the Corps for equipment, weapons, materials, supplies, facilities, maintenance, and supporting services. This responsibility includes determination of Marine Corps characteristics of materiel to be procured or developed, and the training required to prepare Marines for combat.
2. Development, in coordination with the Army, Navy, and Air Force, of the tactics, techniques, doctrines, and equipment employed by landing forces in amphibious operations.

3. Plans for and determination of present and future needs, qualitative and quantitative, for regular and reserve personnel of the Marine Corps. This includes responsibility for leadership in maintaining a high degree of competence on the part of all hands in necessary fields of specialization through education, training, and equal opportunities for advancement; and for leadership in maintaining the esprit of Marines and the prestige of a Marine Corps career.
4. Planning and determining the needs for the care of the health of Marines.
5. Budgeting for the Marine Corps (except as otherwise directed by SecNav) and supervising the performance of its supporting establishment.
6. Sitting with the Joint Chiefs of Staff when matters which concern the Marine Corps are under consideration, on which occasions the Commandant has coequal status with members of the JCS. The Commandant also regularly attends meetings of the Armed Forces Policy Council.

The Commandant of the Coast Guard when the latter is attached to the Navy pursuant to law is also a naval executive assistant.

216. THE NAVAL SUPPORTING ESTABLISHMENT. The supporting establishment of the Navy consists of several "systems commands," bureaus, offices, and the Shore Establishment.

NAVAL AIR SYSTEMS COMMAND (NAVAIR). This command, similar to the former Bureau of Aeronautics, has cognizance over Navy and Marine aircraft, air-launched weapons systems (including aerial torpedoes and mines), airborne electronics (avionics), airborne underwater sound systems and minesweeping, airborne pyrotechnics, astronautics, aircraft and air weapons targets, photographic gear, meteorological gear, and pyrotechnic gear. The command handles procurement, design, manufacture, maintenance, alteration, and material effectiveness of naval aircraft, as well as the design, construction, and maintenance of aeronautics shore establishment stations.

NAVAL SHIP SYSTEMS COMMAND (NAVSHIP). Like the former Bureau of Ships, this command coordinates all naval shipbuilding; designs, constructs or procures, and maintains active and reserve ships and small craft; has cognizance over surface navigational gear, sonar, and search radar; and is responsible for the Naval Tactical Data System (NTDS), for rescue and salvage systems, and for degaussing and shipborne minesweeping gear.

NAVAL ELECTRONICS SYSTEMS COMMAND (NAVELECS). Separating out electronics functions from the former Bureau of Ships, this command has cognizance over all ship and shore electronics, certain space programs, other radio or electronics programs and gear, and electronic standards and compatibility throughout the Navy.

NAVAL ORDNANCE SYSTEMS COMMAND (NAVORD). In some ways a

virtual reversion to the pre-1959 Bureau of Ordnance, this command has cognizance over all shipboard weapons systems (i.e., fire control radar, fire control gear, guns, weapons launchers, and related items); shipboard sonar; air-launched underwater weapons (i.e., torpedoes and mines); ammunition, explosives, and pyrotechnics; harbor-defense gear; landing force gear; seaborne targets; and explosives research and development.

NAVAL SUPPLY SYSTEMS COMMAND (NAVSUP). Although this is a new title, the basic organization remains that of the former Bureau of Supplies and Accounts and thus coordinates the Navy supply system. This command procures, stores, and issues supplies, provisions, clothing, fuel, and whatever other material the technical bureaus do not procure directly; keeps the property and money accounts of the Navy; and pays invoices and Navy payrolls.

NAVAL FACILITIES ENGINEERING COMMAND (NAVFACENG). Like the Supply Systems Command, this command, too, is a virtually unchanged redesignation of a former bureau—in this case, Yards and Docks. This organization designs, constructs, and maintains public works and utilities at continental and outlying bases; and trains, organizes, and maintains the Construction Battalions (Seabees), which specialize in advance base development and frequently serve with the Fleet Marine Force. The Chief of the Bureau of Yards and Docks was also responsible for maintenance of all Navy shore facilities and plant property, except insofar as Marine Corps installations are concerned; this command has the same responsibilities.

BUREAU OF NAVAL PERSONNEL (BUPERS). Procures, trains, and distributes Navy officers and enlisted personnel; supervises promotion, discipline, and welfare of Navy personnel; administers the Naval Reserve; and operates field personnel establishments. The Chief of Naval Personnel is one of the two bureau chiefs who remain directly under the Chief of Naval Operations rather than under the Chief of Naval Material.

BUREAU OF MEDICINE AND SURGERY (BUMED). Is responsible for the health, sanitation, and medical and dental care of the Navy and Marine Corps. BuMed operates the Medical Department and exercises administrative control over the Medical, Dental, Nurse, Hospital, and Medical Service Corps. The Surgeon General of the Navy heads the Bureau. Like the Chief of Naval Personnel, the Surgeon General (and BuMed) function under direct supervision of the Chief of Naval Operations.

OFFICE OF THE JUDGE ADVOCATE GENERAL (JAG). Handles all legal matters of the Department of the Navy in the field of military, administrative, legislative, and general law. This responsibility covers the entire Naval Establishment, including the Marine Corps.

OFFICE OF NAVAL RESEARCH (ONR). Assures the Navy a well-rounded program by coordinating research throughout the Department of the Navy. In addition, ONR is responsible for protecting the Navy's interests in patents, inventions, and related matters.

The Shore Establishment comprises all field activities of the Department of the Navy, except shore activities assigned to the Operating Forces of the Navy. The Shore Establishment includes those Operating Forces of the Marine Corps which are not assigned to the Operating Forces of the Navy or to a unified or specified command.

The activities of the Shore Establishment are distributed along our coasts where they can best serve the Operating Forces. However, many activities in which such close proximity is not essential (notably air, ordnance, and supply) lie well inside continental United States and territories.

The Shore Establishment includes 15 *Naval Districts* with their headquarters.

1st Naval District: Boston, Massachusetts
3rd Naval District: New York, New York
4th Naval District: Philadelphia, Pennsylvania
5th Naval District: Norfolk, Virginia
6th Naval District: Charleston, South Carolina
8th Naval District: New Orleans, Louisiana
9th Naval District: Great Lakes, Illinois
10th Naval District: San Juan, Puerto Rico
11th Naval District: San Diego, California
12th Naval District: San Francisco, California
13th Naval District: Bremerton, Washington
14th Naval District: Pearl Harbor, Hawaii
15th Naval District: Balboa, Canal Zone
Naval District, Washington, D.C.

Naval districts exercise the functions of public relations, legal, military administration discipline, intelligence, and disaster planning.

Naval districts enable CNO, via the sea frontier commanders, to maintain coordination control over shore activities. District commandants exercise command over certain Shore Establishment activities in their districts—*except* field activities under the Chief of Naval Air Training and the Commander, Naval Reserve Training, and the installations of the Marine Corps Supporting Establishment. Bureaus may delegate to a district commandant control over some of their functional responsibilities in a district. In the role of grassroots public relations, the district commandants perform important service for the Secretary of the Navy. Closely allied to this, district commandants administer the Naval Reserve program in their districts—except activities assigned to the Chief of Naval Reserve Air Training.

Forces of the Navy

217. THE OPERATING FORCES. The Operating Forces of the Navy comprise the fleets, seagoing forces, sea frontier and district forces, Fleet Marine Forces, the Military Sea Transportation Service,

24 and such shore activities of the Navy and other forces as may be
assigned by the President or Secretary of the Navy. The Chief of
Naval Operations commands the Operating Forces of the Navy.
218. THE REGULAR NAVY. Commissioned officers of the regular Navy (and Naval Reserve) are divided among the line and eight
staff corps.

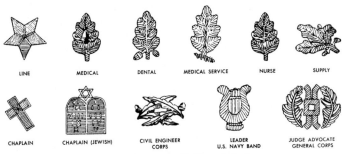

Fig. 2-2: U. S. Navy Commissioned officers' devices.

Line. Line officers exercise military command, are accountable for
the exercise of their authority, and cannot divest themselves of the
accompanying responsibility. Only line officers command at sea.
Among line officers are several types of "line" specialists: naval
constructors, naval engineers, and specialists in such fields as intelligence, oceanography, communications, and public affairs.
Specialists cannot command at sea. In general, only line officers
exercise command ashore, except that members of certain staff corps,
such as Medical, Supply, and Civil Engineer Corps, command shore
activities and units (such as Seabees) under the cognizance of their
respective bureaus. Although of course not eligible to command at
sea or to command a Naval base or station, Marine officers are
nevertheless line officers of the naval service and have been held,
legally, to be naval officers.

Medical Corps (MC). In this staff corps, commissioned graduate
doctors of medicine provide medical services and administer the
hospitals, dispensaries, sickbays, and other medical units of the
Naval Establishment. Medical and dental service for the Marine
Corps is provided by Navy doctors, dentists, and hospital corpsmen.

Dental Corps (DC). Composed of graduate dental surgeons, this
is a separate corps whose members serve at hospitals and dispensaries
and aboard larger ships. The Dental Corps, like the Medical, Nurse,
and Medical Service Corps, comes under the Bureau of Medicine
and Surgery.

Medical Service Corps (MSC). This corps is composed of specialists
in the fields of optometry, pharmacy, or such allied sciences as
bacteriology, biochemistry, psychology, sanitation engineering, or
medical statistics.

Nurse Corps (NC). Navy nurses are commissioned officers in the

Nurse Corps, who serve in hospitals and dispensaries at home and on foreign station and in hospital ships and transports at sea.

Supply Corps (SC). The business branch of the Navy administers the Navy supply system and receives and disburses funds for supply and for pay, subsistence, and transportation.

Chaplain Corps (CHC). Ordained ministers of various denominations, officers of the Chaplain Corps conduct religious services and promote the spiritual and moral welfare of the Navy and Marine Corps. The Chief of Chaplains heads the corps.

Civil Engineer Corps (CEC). Composed of graduate civil engineers, normally restricted to shore duty, CEC supervises buildings, grounds, and plant at shore stations, as well as construction of buildings and the layout of shore stations. This corps conceived, organized, and commanded the naval construction battalions (Seabees), which served so illustriously beside Marines during World War II and in Korea and are now serving in Vietnam.

Judge Advocate General's Corps (JAGC). Established in 1967 this staff corps is composed of law specialists who are graduate lawyers specially certified for legal duties within the Naval Establishment.

Fig. 2-3: U. S. Navy Breast insignia.

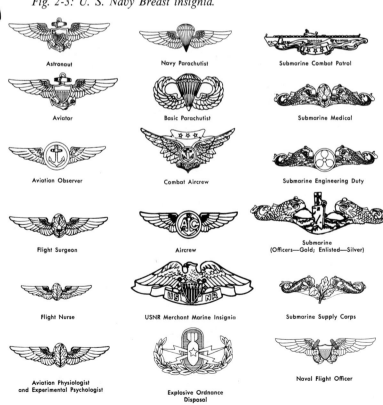

Command at Sea

Astronaut

Aviator

Aviation Observer

Flight Surgeon

Flight Nurse

Aviation Physiologist and Experimental Psychologist

Navy Parachutist

Basic Parachutist

Combat Aircrew

Aircrew

USNR Merchant Marine Insignia

Explosive Ordnance Disposal

Submarine Combat Patrol

Submarine Medical

Submarine Engineering Duty

Submarine (Officers—Gold; Enlisted—Silver)

Submarine Supply Corps

Naval Flight Officer

26   *Warrant Officers.* Navy warrant and commissioned warrant officers possess the most detailed practical knowledge of the complicated mechanisms of our modern Navy and thus provide an invaluable footing of technical know-how for the Fleet. Warrant grade titles include Boatswain and Operations Technicians, Machinist, Electrician, Ship's Clerk, Aerographer, Photographer, Supply Clerk, Underwater Ordnance Technician, Communications and Electronics Technicians, Ship Repair Technicians, Civil Engineer Corps, Band-

Fig. 2-4: Specialty marks of Navy enlisted ratings.

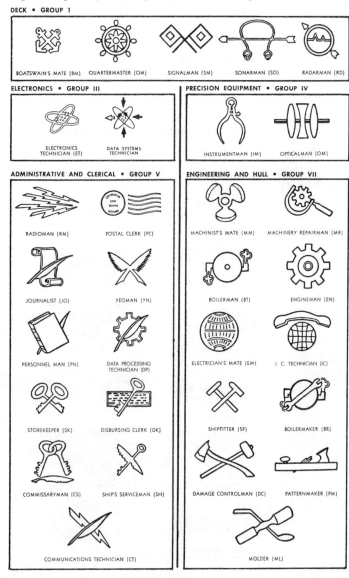

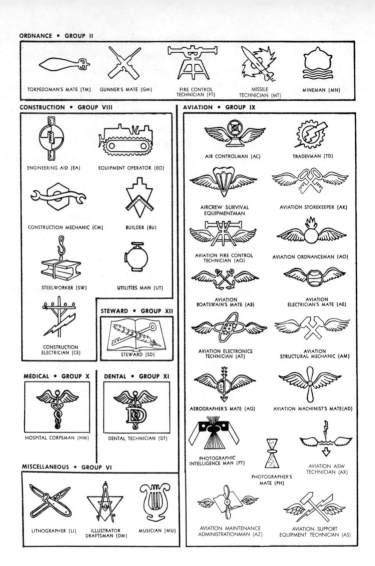

ORDNANCE • GROUP II

TORPEDOMAN'S MATE (TM)	GUNNER'S MATE (GM)	FIRE CONTROL TECHNICIAN (FT)	MISSILE TECHNICIAN (MT)	MINEMAN (MN)

CONSTRUCTION • GROUP VIII

ENGINEERING AID (EA) EQUIPMENT OPERATOR (EO)

CONSTRUCTION MECHANIC (CM) BUILDER (BU)

STEELWORKER (SW) UTILITIES MAN (UT)

CONSTRUCTION ELECTRICIAN (CE)

STEWARD • GROUP XII

STEWARD (SD)

MEDICAL • GROUP X   **DENTAL • GROUP XI**

HOSPITAL CORPSMAN (HM) DENTAL TECHNICIAN (DT)

MISCELLANEOUS • GROUP VI

LITHOGRAPHER (LI) ILLUSTRATOR DRAFTSMAN (DM) MUSICIAN (MU)

AVIATION • GROUP IX

AIR CONTROLMAN (AC) TRADEVMAN (TD)

AIRCREW SURVIVAL EQUIPMENTMAN AVIATION STOREKEEPER (AK)

AVIATION FIRE CONTROL TECHNICIAN (AQ) AVIATION ORDNANCEMAN (AO)

AVIATION BOATSWAIN'S MATE (AB) AVIATION ELECTRICIAN'S MATE (AE)

AVIATION ELECTRONICS TECHNICIAN (AT) AVIATION STRUCTURAL MECHANIC (AM)

AEROGRAPHER'S MATE (AG) AVIATION MACHINIST'S MATE(AD)

PHOTOGRAPHIC INTELLIGENCE MAN (PT) PHOTOGRAPHER'S MATE (PH) AVIATION ASW TECHNICIAN (AX)

AVIATION MAINTENANCE ADMINISTRATIONMAN (AZ) AVIATION SUPPORT EQUIPMENT TECHNICIAN (AS)

master, Medical and Dental Service Warrants, Aviation Boatswain, Air Intelligence and Air Control Technicians, Surface Ordnance and Ordnance Control Technicians, and Aviation Electronics, Maintenance, and Ordnance Technicians.

Enlisted Men. Basic legislation allows 500,000 enlisted men in the regular Navy. During an emergency the actual number depends on the size of the Fleet and Shore Establishment to be maintained.

Enlisted men and women of the Navy and Coast Guard are divided into a dozen rating groups as illustrated in Figure 2-4. Just as we expect Navy people to recognize and identify Marine noncommissioned officers, so a Marine should be able to identify Navy petty officers in the various ratings.

219. THE "TASK FORCE PRINCIPLE." The "task force principle" is the name given to the Navy and Marine Corps system of organizing forces for given tasks while preserving a separate administrative organization for training and housekeeping. This is the fundamental organizational principle of the U.S. fleets.

"Type Organization." All forces in the U. S. Fleets are grouped into the "type organization" of the fleet. As its name implies, the type organization is based on types of ships or forces. Note that the Fleet Marine Force is a type command, since it comprises all Marine Corps tactical units—air and ground—assigned to the fleet.

"Task Organization." The other facet of fleet organization is the "task organization." The task organization exists simultaneously with the type organization. The task organization conducts operations, using units prepared and provided by the type organization. Taking the Atlantic Fleet as an example, it includes several permanent *task fleets* and *task forces*. Certain of these, such as the antisubmarine warfare forces, are task-organized from aviation, surface, and submarine forces to maintain control of the sea. The Second Fleet is a task fleet whose functions are offensive: fast carrier operations and amphibious assault.

Under the above system a flexible structure is provided consisting of fleets further subdivided into forces, groups, units, and elements. Each of these descending subdivisions has a numbered designation and appropriate communication call signs. When a Task Fleet Commander receives a task from higher authority, he can then assign necessary forces under his command to do the job, creating an organization of ships and units as needed. Such a "task organization" is adaptable to any magnitude of organization ranging from the campaigns of entire fleets in general war to a single ship on a temporary mission. For example, an LPH, or helicopter assault ship, of the Amphibious Force might be given a task designation simply to steam across Chesapeake Bay for a Navy Day visit, and, on conclusion of the job, the task designation would cease.

A typical (hypothetical) task fleet numbering system would be one in which the Commander Seventh Fleet would assign his major forces to numbered task forces (TF), such as Striking Force, TF 70; Amphibious Task Force, TF 71; Service Force, TF 72; and so forth.

Within each force he would then assign logical subdivisions of that force as task groups (TG), such as TG 70.1, Carrier Group; TG 70.2, Gunfire Support and Covering Group; and so on.

Within each task group, in turn, would be found task units (TU). For example, TG 70.1, Carrier Group, noted above, might be divided into TU 70.1.1, Carrier Unit, and TU 70.1.2, Destroyer Screen Unit.

Note the fashion in which components of a task organization are designated by addition of decimal separators and successive numbers; this enables you to determine at a glance the chain of operational command in which a given unit may be functioning.

Significance. The simultaneous organization of the fleets by types and tasks is obviously complex. It is, nevertheless, a system which adapts itself precisely to the job to be done, large or small, temporary or permanent. Moreover, it is completely flexible and innately economical of forces.

Fig. 2-5: Enlisted insignia of rank.

SERVICE				
ARMY	**NAVY**	**AIR FORCE**	**MARINES**	
STAFF SGT. MAJOR / COMMAND SGT. MAJOR / SPEC. 9	MASTER CHIEF P.O.	CHIEF MASTER SGT. / CHIEF MASTER SGT. OF THE AF	SGT. MAJOR / MASTER GUNNERY SGT.	E-9
1ST SGT. / MASTER SGT. / SPEC. 8	SENIOR CHIEF P.O.	SENIOR MASTER SGT.	1ST SGT. / MASTER SGT.	E-8
SGT. 1ST CLASS / SPEC. 7	CHIEF P.O.	MASTER SGT.	GUNNERY SGT.	E-7
STAFF SGT. / SPEC. 6	P.O. 1ST CLASS	TECHNICAL SGT.	STAFF SGT.	E-6
SGT. / SPEC. 5	P.O. 2ND CLASS	STAFF SGT.	SGT.	E-5
CORPORAL / SPEC. 4	P.O. 3RD CLASS	SGT.	CORPORAL	E-4
PRIVATE 1ST CLASS	SEAMAN	AIRMAN 1ST CLASS	LANCE CORPORAL	E-3
PRIVATE	SEAMAN APPRENTICE	AIRMAN	PRIVATE 1ST CLASS	E-2
PRIVATE	SEAMAN RECRUIT	BASIC AIRMAN	PRIVATE	E-1

ARMY	AIR FORCE	MARINE CORPS	NAVY	COAST GUARD
GOLD BROWN — W-1 WARRANT OFFICER / GOLD BROWN — W-2 CHIEF WARRANT OFFICER	GOLD SKY BLUE — W-1 WARRANT OFFICER / GOLD SKY BLUE — W-2 CHIEF WARRANT OFFICER	GOLD SCARLET — W-1 (SEE NOTE) WARRANT OFFICER / GOLD SCARLET — W-2 CHIEF WARRANT OFFICER	W-1 WARRANT OFFICER / W-2 CHIEF WARRANT OFFICER	W-1 WARRANT OFFICER / W-2 CHIEF WARRANT OFFICER
SILVER BROWN — W-3 CHIEF WARRANT OFFICER / SILVER BROWN — W-4 CHIEF WARRANT OFFICER	SILVER SKY BLUE — W-3 CHIEF WARRANT OFFICER / SILVER SKY BLUE — W-4 CHIEF WARRANT OFFICER	SILVER SCARLET — W-3 CHIEF WARRANT OFFICER / SILVER SCARLET — W-4 CHIEF WARRANT OFFICER	W-3 CHIEF WARRANT OFFICER / W-4 CHIEF WARRANT OFFICER	W-3 CHIEF WARRANT OFFICER / W-4 CHIEF WARRANT OFFICER
(GOLD) SECOND LIEUTENANT	(GOLD) SECOND LIEUTENANT	(GOLD) SECOND LIEUTENANT	ENSIGN	ENSIGN
(SILVER) FIRST LIEUTENANT	(SILVER) FIRST LIEUTENANT	(SILVER) FIRST LIEUTENANT	LIEUTENANT JUNIOR GRADE	LIEUTENANT JUNIOR GRADE
(SILVER) CAPTAIN	(SILVER) CAPTAIN	(SILVER) CAPTAIN	LIEUTENANT	LIEUTENANT
(GOLD) MAJOR	(GOLD) MAJOR	(GOLD) MAJOR	LIEUTENANT COMMANDER	LIEUTENANT COMMANDER
(SILVER) LIEUTENANT COLONEL	(SILVER) LIEUTENANT COLONEL	(SILVER) LIEUTENANT COLONEL	COMMANDER	COMMANDER

NOTE: ADDITIONAL INSIGNIA FOR THOSE WARRANT OFFICERS DESIGNATED AS MARINE GUNNERS.

The Coast Guard

220. THE U. S. COAST GUARD. The Coast Guard is a military service within the armed forces at all times. Although under the Transportation Department in peacetime, Coast Guard personnel receive the same pay as service personnel under the Department of Defense and are subject to the Uniform Code of Military Justice.

ARMY	AIR FORCE	MARINE CORPS	NAVY	COAST GUARD
COLONEL	COLONEL	COLONEL	CAPTAIN	CAPTAIN
BRIGADIER GENERAL	BRIGADIER GENERAL	BRIGADIER GENERAL	COMMODORE	COMMODORE
MAJOR GENERAL	MAJOR GENERAL	MAJOR GENERAL	REAR ADMIRAL	REAR ADMIRAL
LIEUTENANT GENERAL	LIEUTENANT GENERAL	LIEUTENANT GENERAL	VICE ADMIRAL	VICE ADMIRAL
GENERAL	GENERAL	GENERAL	ADMIRAL	ADMIRAL
GENERAL OF THE ARMY	GENERAL OF THE AIR FORCE	NONE	FLEET ADMIRAL	NONE
AS PRESCRIBED BY INCUMBENT GENERAL OF THE ARMIES	NONE	NONE	NONE	NONE

Fig. 2-6: Commissioned insignia of rank.

Headed by an admiral as Commandant in peacetime, the Coast Guard's rank and rating structure is very similar to the Navy's. The uniform is that of the Navy, with distinguishing insignia. On declaration of war or when the President directs, the Coast Guard operates as a service within the Naval Establishment.

In both war and peace, the Coast Guard performs a wide range of functions, mainly military. In peace, most of these duties center about protecting lives and property on the seas and along the coasts and include manning lifeboat stations, search and rescue centers, lighthouses, lightships, and loran stations; icebreaking, locating icebergs and recommending safe sea lanes in northern waters; enforcing maritime safety regulations; and manning ocean "stations" to obtain weather data, assist aircraft navigation, and render on-the-spot assistance to planes and ships in trouble.

The Coast Guard is also charged with enforcing a variety of laws at sea and in Alaska for other Government agencies. In wartime it performs such duties as escort and antisubmarine warfare, manning transports, port security, and operating landing craft.

The Service has been in continuous operation since 1790, when it was organized by Alexander Hamilton as the Revenue Marine Service. The name was later changed to Revenue Cutter Service and, in 1915, to Coast Guard. Its motto is *Semper Paratus* ("Always Ready").

The Coast Guard in peacetime includes about 30,000 officers and men. Appointments to the Coast Guard Academy at New London, Connecticut are by competitive examination open to civilians and enlisted men from any armed service between the ages of 18 and 22. The four-year course is basically engineering, and cadets receive a B.S. degree on graduation and are then commissioned as ensigns in the U. S. Coast Guard.

I have just returned from visiting the Marines at the front, and there is not a finer fighting organization in the world.

General of the Army
Douglas MacArthur
21 September 1950.

3 The Marine Corps

First to fight . . .
Retreat, hell! We just got here . . .
Gone to fight the Indians—will be back when the war is over . . .
Uncommon valor was a common virtue . . .
The Marines have landed, and the situation is well in hand. . . .
Phrases like these say more about the United States Marine Corps than all the handbooks ever written. As you read, therefore, remember that there is far more to the Marine Corps than can ever be expressed in any manual.

301. WHAT IS THE MARINE CORPS? Beyond the statutes and official definitions, what is the U. S. Marine Corps?

To begin with, the Marine Corps is a military anomaly—"Soldier and sailor, too."

Every world power has an army. Most powers have navies and air forces. But only 23 countries (Argentina, Brazil, Chile, Colombia, Denmark, Great Britain, Korea, Indonesia, Republic of China, the Netherlands, Pakistan, Peru, Spain, Thailand, Turkey, the USSR, Venezuela, South Vietnam, Italy, France, Portugal, Mexico, the Philippines, and the United States), maintain Marine Corps.

In addition, certain other nations maintain units or forces whose functions, primarily in the field of raiding and other light amphibious operations, approximate those of Marines. Among such countries are Albania, Bulgaria, Burma, Cambodia, Ecuador, Iran, Israel, Yugoslavia, Paraguay, Poland, Rumania, and Sweden.

Nowhere but in the United States, however, has any Marine Corps attained the status of our own. This status was not foreseen when the Continental Congress, on 10 November 1775, formed two battalions of Marines. Instead, the Corps gained its unique position through long evolution.

The Corps possesses many individual attributes of its brother services. As a result, you can usually discern something suggestive of the other services in the Marine Corps, and this is only natural in a Corps which has spent most of its time spearheading, supporting, or serving beside the Army, Navy, and Air Force. But you can also see much more which belongs only to the Marine Corps.

Certainly the Marine Corps attitude is peculiar to the Corps.

Fully as important as its attitude, however, is the fundamental mission of the Corps. This primary mission—*readiness*—combined with the Marine state of mind, makes the Corps what it is today: a national force in readiness, prepared in fact, and required by law, to "perform such other duties as the President may direct"—which means "ready for anything."

Most Americans, including some who know little about the Corps, recognize Marines as the national force in readiness. Such tried and true phrases as *"Call out the Marines!"* or *"The situation is well in hand,"* or *"Tell it to the Marines,"* have entered American speech, and voice the country's attitude.

The existence of this nation-wide feeling makes the Marine Corps a national institution.

As a Marine noncommissioned officer, you represent a national institution whose standing and reputation are in your hands.

These professional Marines have each volunteered for Drill Instructor School (see Section 317) that through discipline and esprit de corps they may mold recruits in the tradition of the Marine Corps.

302. WHAT THE MARINE CORPS STANDS FOR. The qualities the Marine Corps stands for have shaped the Corps since 1775, from Princeton to Belleau Wood, from Trenton to Chosin Reservoir and Conthien.

Quality and competence. A Marine has to be good. In the Marine Corps, your best is just the acceptable minimum. It is expected, as a matter of course, that the technical performance of a single Marine or a whole Marine outfit, whether on parade or in the attack, will be the best in sight.

Discipline. Of all the principles of the Marine Corps, its insistence on discipline is the most unvarying and most uncompromising.

Valor. After the seizure of Iwo Jima, Fleet Admiral Nimitz epitomized the performance of the Marines who took the island. *"Uncommon valor,"* wrote the admiral, *"was a common virtue."* More than 240 Medals of Honor have been awarded to U. S. Marines. Valor and courage are the Marines' stock in trade. "Retreat, hell! We just got here," was originally uttered in 1918 by a company commander of U. S. Marines.

Esprit de corps. A Marine is intensely proud of his Corps, loyal to his comrades, and jealous for the good name of the Corps.

Loyalty and faithfulness. *"Semper Fidelis"* ("Always Faithful") is the motto of the Corps. In addition, every honorable discharge certificate from the Marine Corps bears the phrase, *"Fideli certa merces"* ("A sure reward to the faithful"). Marines understand that these are not idle words. Absolute loyalty to the Corps, as well as devotion to duty, are required of every Marine. The Corps has never had a mutiny. Percentages of Marines missing in action or taken prisoner by the enemy are minute. A good Marine places the interests of the Marine Corps at the top of his list.

The individual. The Marine Corps cherishes the individuality of its members and, although sternly consecrated to discipline, has cheerfully sheltered nonconformists, flamboyant individuals, and very distinct personalities. It is a perennial prediction that colorful characters are about to vanish from the Corps. They never have and never will. (If you question this, just take a look at some of the NCOs you've met and served with since you first enlisted.) No Marine need fear that the mass will ever absorb the man.

The volunteer. Despite occasional acceptance of drafted men in times of peak manpower demand, as in the Vietnam war, the Marine Corps is "a volunteer outfit." The Corps relies on men who *want to be Marines.* There is no substitute. In the old phrase, "One volunteer is worth ten pressed men."

Relations between officers and men.
The relation between officers and enlisted men should in no sense be that of superior and inferior nor that of master and servant, but rather that of teacher and scholar. In fact, it should partake of the nature of the relation between father and son to the extent that officers, especially commanding

officers, are responsible for the physical, mental, and moral welfare, as well as the discipline and military training, of the young men under their command . . .

Thus wrote a Commandant of the Marine Corps. His words now stand as an enduring testimony to the comradeship and brotherhood among all Marines, whether officer or enlisted.

Traditions. St. Paul's injunction, "Hold the traditions which you have been taught," could be a Marine motto. Respect for the traditions of the Corps is deeply felt. Every Marine adheres to the traditions which have shaped the Corps. Preserving and carrying on these traditions is a special responsibility of the corps of noncommissioned officers.

Professionalism. The U. S. Marine is a professional who stands ready to fight any time, anywhere, any enemy, that the President or Congress may designate and to do so coolly, capably, and in a spirit of professional detachment. He is not trained to hate, nor is he whipped up emotionally for battle or for any other duty the Corps may be called on to perform. Patriotism and professionalism are his only two "ism's."

Marine Corps Missions and Status

303. MARINE CORPS ROLES AND MISSIONS. THE LAW. The Statutes of the United States include many provisions, which affect the Corps. All these provisions are codified under Title 10 (Armed Forces), U. S. Code.

The "charter" of the Marine Corps, however, has evolved from three laws:

1. The Act of 11 July 1798, "Establishing and Organizing a Marine Corps",
2. The Act of 30 June 1834, "For the Better Organization of the Marine Corps", and
3. The National Security Act of 1947 as amended.

The National Security Act, which unified the armed services, is the controlling military legislation of this country. This act as now amended (see Paragraph 213) makes the following provisions for the Marine Corps.

1. It reaffirms the Corps's status as a service within the Department of the Navy;
2. It provides for Fleet Marine Forces, ground and aviation;
3. It requires that the combatant forces of the Corps be organized on the basis of three Marine divisions and three air wings and sets a 400,000-man peacetime ceiling for the regular Corps;
4. It assigns the Corps the missions of seizure and defense of advanced naval bases, as well as land operations incident to naval campaigns;

5. It gives the Marine Corps primary responsibility for development
of amphibious warfare doctrines, tactics, techniques, and equipment employed by landing forces;
  6. It seats the Commandant of the Marine Corps in coequal status
with members of the Joint Chiefs of Staff whenever matters of
Marine Corps interest are under consideration;
  7. It affords the Marine Corps appropriate representation on various
joint Defense Department agencies, notably the Joint Staff;
  8. It assigns the Marine Corps collateral missions of providing security forces for naval shore stations, providing ships' detachments, and performing such other duties as the President may
direct.

In taking stock of Marine Corps's missions found in law, it is
important not to overlook the short phrase, ". . . *and shall perform
such other duties as the President may direct.*" This phrase, which the
Unification Act quotes directly from the 1834 Marine Corps law,
stems in turn from similar language in the Act of 1798. It validates
in law Marine Corps functions which transcend the Corps's purely
naval missions and allows employment of Marines any time, anywhere, on any service the President directs.

ADDITIONAL MISSIONS OF THE MARINE CORPS. In addition to the
missions expressly assigned by Congress, the Corps also performs
several tasks either assigned by the Department of Defense or in
accordance with long-standing custom.

"The Functions Paper." Originally known as "the Key West Agreement," the Defense Department directive which states the functions
of that Department and of its major components is now usually
spoken of as "the Functions Paper." This directive is essentially a
compilation of inter-service agreements dating from 1948 and later
revised from time to time, as to how the roles-and-missions provisions of the National Security Act are to be implemented. In addition, the directive establishes a number of service relationships and
common functions within the Defense Department, which affect the
Marine Corps equally with the other services.

"Unified Action Armed Forces." (*UNAF*) is a doctrinal publication
which governs the activities of two or more of the armed services
when operating together and prescribes joint procedures and responsibilities which apply to the Marine Corps along with sister
services. Insofar as the Corps is concerned, one of the more important portions of *UNAF* is that which delineates the amphibious and
landing force developmental responsibilities of the Marine Corps.

State Department Guards. Under authority of the Foreign Service
Act of 1946, the Marine Corps has a collateral mission of providing
security guards for American embassies, legations, and consulates.
For this duty, which demands the highest discretion and trust, the
Marine Corps furnishes approximately a thousand officers and men
who are distributed throughout more than 95 State Department
overseas posts. See Chapter 19.

White House Duties. Dating from 1798, the scarlet-coated Marine Band has been styled "The President's Own" because of its privilege of providing the music for state functions at the White House. Similarly, Marines have established and guarded Presidential camps at Rapidan, Virginia; Warm Springs, Georgia; Camp David, Maryland, and elsewhere, while Marine helicopters were the first to carry a President and still routinely do so.

UNWRITTEN MISSIONS. Nowhere do the statute books say that the Marine Corps is *the national force in readiness,* yet our history demonstrates clearly that the fundamental mission of the Corps is just that, and always has been. To quote former Assistant Secretary of the Navy John Nicholas Brown:

> Readiness, the capacity to move anywhere immediately and become effective, is always needed and at the present juncture of events is especially necessary. This is the daily bread of the Marine Corps.

304. STATUS OF THE MARINE CORPS. "The Marine Corps is *sui generis"*("something entirely of its own sort"), once ruled a Federal judge when construing the legal status of the Corps. This is probably the best one-sentence description the Marine Corps ever had.

The Marine Corps is one of the several armed services (Army, Marine Corps, Navy, and Air Force) which, with the Coast Guard (when attached to the Naval Establishment in time of war) comprise the Armed Forces of the United States. It is important that you be aware of this, since you may sometimes hear or read the erroneous term "the three services," which is usually encountered among persons who either think the Marine Corps is part of the Navy or want to exclude it from something.

Side by side with the Navy, the Marine Corps is one of two military services in the Naval Establishment, under direct control and supervision of the Secretary of the Navy. In the words of Representative Carl Vinson, when Chairman of the House Armed Services Committee:

> The fact is that the Marine Corps is and always has been, since its inception 175 years ago, a separate military service apart from the United States Army, the United States Navy, and the United States Air Force.

A final ruling on the foregoing point is in House Report 970, 84th Congress. This is the report by the House of Representatives on the codification of Title 10 (Armed Forces), U. S. Code. This report states:

> The Marine Corps is legally a separate and distinct military service within the Department of the Navy, with individually assigned statutory responsibilities, and the Commandant directs and administers the Marine Corps under the direct delegated command of the Secretary of the Navy.

The status of the Marine Corps can therefore be summed up in three sentences.

1. The Marine Corps is a separate military service possessing statutory roles and missions prescribed by the Unification Act;
2. The Marine Corps is a part of the Naval Establishment (or Department of the Navy) and comes directly under the Secretary of the Navy;
3. The Commandant of the Marine Corps commands the Corps as a whole and is directly responsible to the Secretary of the Navy for the total performance, administration, readiness, discipline, and efficiency of the Corps.

Navy Regulations recognize the foregoing by providing that the Commandant of the Marine Corps is a *naval executive* of the Secretary of the Navy.

As a naval executive, the Commandant reports directly to the Secretary of the Navy in matters pertaining to the Marine Corps, just as the other naval executive, the Chief of Naval Operations, reports to the Secretary in Navy matters. When the Secretary so directs, however, the Commandant may accept orders from the CNO expressly given in the name of the Secretary.

Both *Navy Regulations* and Navy Department general orders summarize the responsibilities of the Commandant.

1. Command, administration, discipline, organization, training, efficiency, and readiness of the Marine Corps;
2. Development of tactics, techniques, doctrines, and equipment used by landing forces in amphibious operations;
3. Provision of technical advice to the Secretary of the Navy and Assistants, in the formulation of naval policies and procedures;
4. Marine Corps representation on the Joint Chiefs of Staff.

Working Relations Between Marine Corps and Navy. Although we have emphasized the separate status of the Marine Corps in the Naval Establishment, don't get the idea that this prevents close and harmonious relations between the Marine Corps and the Navy.

Not only do individual Marines serve with Navy men as part of Navy commands and vice versa, but units are likewise freely interchanged. Every Navy staff of any consequence includes Marine officers and men, while all Marine units and stations have Navy doctors, dentists, chaplains, and hospital corpsmen.

Organization of the Marine Corps

Major General W.S. ("Bigfoot") Brown (who got his start to the top as an NCO) once began a lecture at Quantico with these words, "Well, gentlemen, they've given me the job of describing the organization of the Marine Corps. This surprised me somewhat, because I never knew we had any organization. . . ."

Despite that remark, the Marine Corps does have an organization.

The Corps is made up of land combat, security, and service forces; Marine Corps aviation; and the Marine Corps Reserve. See Figure 3-1. In many ways the organization of the Corps resembles that of

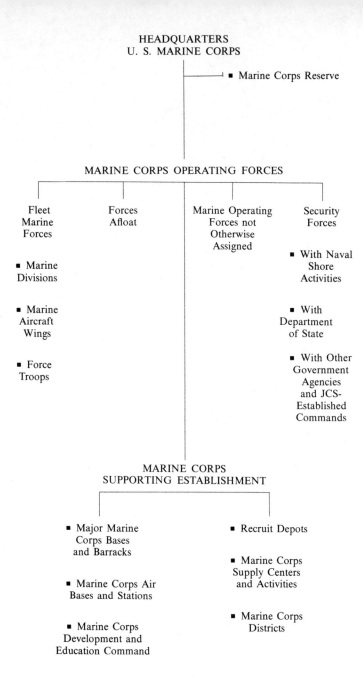

HEADQUARTERS
U. S. MARINE CORPS

- Marine Corps Reserve

MARINE CORPS OPERATING FORCES

Fleet Marine Forces	Forces Afloat	Marine Operating Forces not Otherwise Assigned	Security Forces
■ Marine Divisions			■ With Naval Shore Activities
■ Marine Aircraft Wings			■ With Department of State
■ Force Troops			■ With Other Government Agencies and JCS-Established Commands

MARINE CORPS
SUPPORTING ESTABLISHMENT

- Major Marine Corps Bases and Barracks

- Marine Corps Air Bases and Stations

- Marine Corps Development and Education Command

- Recruit Depots

- Marine Corps Supply Centers and Activities

- Marine Corps Districts

Fig. 3-1: Organization of the Marine Corps.

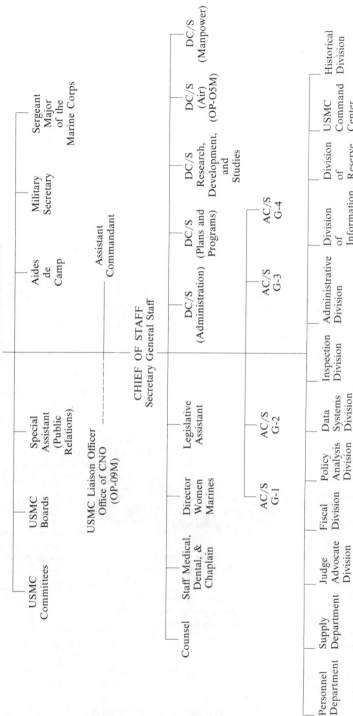

Fig. 3-2: Organization of Marine Corps Headquarters.

the Navy. Like the Navy, the Marine Corps is organized into three principal subdivisions.

Marine Corps Headquarters
Marine Corps Operating Forces
Marine Corps Supporting Establishment (including the Reserve Establishment)

Throughout these components, Marine Corps aviation is included as necessary to carry out the missions of the Corps.

Marine Corps Headquarters

305. HEADQUARTERS, U. S. MARINE CORPS. Marine Corps Headquarters, in Washington, D.C., is the executive part of the Corps. It is located in Arlington Annex of the Navy Department. Headquarters is literally the headquarters of the Commandant and could, in theory, take the field, as it actually did on occasion in the 19th and early 20th centuries. An organization chart of Marine Corps Headquarters appears in Figure 3-2.

The Commandant of the Marine Corps.
I want each of you to feel that the Commandant of the Corps is your friend and that he earnestly desires that you should realize this. At the same time, it is his duty to the Government and to the Marine Corps to exact a high standard of conduct, a strict performance of duty, and a rigid compliance with orders. . . .

In those simple terms, one Commandant defined his responsibilities. Earlier in this chapter (Section 304), you have seen what the Commandant's responsibilities are today, so there is no need to repeat them here.

The Commandant is appointed by the President from among the active general officers of the Corps with the advice and consent of the Senate for a four-year term. He holds the rank of general. The Commandant may be, and frequently has been, reappointed for more than four years. Archibald Henderson, 5th Commandant, who held office more than 39 years, has the record.

The principal duties of the Commandant extend to, but are not limited to, procurement, discharge, education, training (individual and unit), distribution of the officers and enlisted men of the Corps, and all matters of command, discipline, requirements, readiness, organization, administration, equipment, and supply of the Marine Corps. You will find a list of the Commandants in Appendix II.

The Assistant Commandant, a general (when the strength of the Corps exceeds 200,000), discharges the duties of the Commandant during the latter's absence or disability and performs such other duties as the Commandant may direct. The Assistant Commandant—if a lieutenant general—is by law senior to all other lieutenant generals in the Corps.

The Chief of Staff, a lieutenant general, is the Commandant's executive officer. He directs, coordinates, and supervises staff activities of Marine Corps Headquarters.

Deputy Chiefs of Staff. There are five Deputy Chiefs of Staff. The Deputy Chief of Staff (Plans and Programs), a lieutenant general, acts for the Chief of Staff in his absence, coordinates Marine Corps planning, programming, budgeting, and represents the Marine Corps in certain Joint Service matters. The Deputy Chief of Staff (Research, Development and Studies) has cognizance over all Marine Corps R&D matters, while the Deputy Chief of Staff (Air) is responsible for planning, coordinating, and supervising matters pertaining to Marine Corps aviation. In addition, as *ACNO Marine Aviation* (Op-05M), he administers on behalf of the Deputy Chief of Naval Operations (Air), all matters pertaining to Marine Corps aviation in order to assure maximum cooperation with Naval aviation as a whole. The Deputy Chief of Staff (Administration) assists and acts for the Chief of Staff in administrative matters as directed. The Deputy Chief of Staff (Manpower), a lieutenant general, coordinates Marine Corps plans, policies, and administration of manpower.

Military Secretary. The Military Secretary manages the immediate office of the Commandant.

The Sergeant Major of the Marine Corps advises and assists the Commandant in all matters pertaining to enlisted Marines. His duties and functions are described in Section 306.

Secretary of the General Staff. The Secretary of the General Staff assists the Chief of Staff and staff by coordinating staff action and assures that staff matters presented to the Chief of Staff and to the Commandant are complete.

Legislative Assistant to the Commandant. The Legislative Assistant is the Commandant's principal adviser in legal and legislative matters, including liaison with Congress. He prepares comments on legislative proposals referred to or affecting the Marine Corps (except cases in the province of the Fiscal Director).

Director of Women Marines. The Director of Women Marines (the senior woman Marine officer, a colonel) advises the Commandant on matters affecting women Marines, regular and reserve. She not only formulates policy, but also reviews and makes recommendations on policy matters affecting women Marines. Further information on women in the Corps is contained in Chapter 9.

Marine Corps Liaison Officer with the Chief of Naval Operations. To insure that the Commandant and the Chief of Naval Operations are in step with each other, the Commandant maintains a general officer in the Office of the Chief of Naval Operations to provide liaison between the two headquarters. His designation in the CNO organization is "Op-09M."

Assistant Chief of Staff, G-1. The ACofS, G-1 (to give him his short title), is a general officer who heads the G-1 Division of Headquarters. G-1 formulates plans, policies, and programs concerned with military personnel administration and manpower management, including determination of requirements and establishment of allowances, as well as distribution and utilization of all personnel, military and civilian, who are under Marine Corps control.

Assistant Chief of Staff, G-2. The ACofS, G-2, a general officer, heads the G-2 Division. G-2 is responsible for Marine Corps plans and policies for intelligence and counterintelligence and maintains liaison for the Marine Corps with other Government intelligence agencies. He also disseminates intelligence information within Marine Corps Headquarters and the entire Marine Corps.

Assistant Chief of Staff, G-3. The ACofS, G-3, a general officer, heads the G-3 Division. G-3 is responsible for strategic and joint service operational planning, formulates plans and policies, and supervises their execution regarding training, troop movement, and operations of the Marine Corps; organization and employment of the Fleet Marine Force and Marine Corps Reserve; supervision of marksmanship; supervision of Marine Corps bands; and (in coordination with G-4) equipment development, procurement, and allocation policies.

Assistant Chief of Staff, G-4. The ACofS, G-4, a general officer, heads the G-4 Division. G-4 formulates plans and policies on supply, evacuation, transportation, construction, storage, maintenance, salvage, embarkation, mobilization, and supply allowances and replacement factors, and it develops equipment. In coordination with G-3 and G-1, G-4 plans for organization, operations, and training of Marine service units.

Director of the Administrative Division. The Director of the Administrative Division heads the Administrative Division. This division provides management advice and assistance to the Headquarters; controls issuance of general-purpose Marine Corps publications; supervises machine records; administers civilian personnel programs at Headquarters; performs office service functions; performs security control, declassification, and classified records stowage (except historical records and archives which come under the Historical Branch, G-3); and provides communications, mail, and general file services.

Director, Policy Analysis Division. The Director, Policy Analysis Division, examines and evaluates current and projected Marine Corps policy in its broad aspects, giving special attention to continuity, coordination, and timeliness.

Director of Marine Corps History. Prepares official Marine Corps history, maintains historical records and reference library, HQMC.

Director of Information. The Director of Information heads the Division of Information. It is his exacting and sometimes thankless job to represent the Marine Corps to the public. The Director of Information maintains liaison with Defense Department and Government information agencies and with national information and news media. He also supervises Marine field activities which disseminate information.

Director, Data Systems Division, formulates policy and administers Marine Corps automatic data processing (ADP) programs.

Director, Marine Corps Reserve. The Director, Marine Corps Reserve, is responsible for plans, programs, and administration of the Marine Corps Reserve.

Director, Marine Corps Command Center, directs, plans for, and supervises operations of the Marine Corps Command Center—the Commandant's "eyes and ears" in the world operations of the Corps.

Inspector General. The Inspector General heads the Inspection Division. It is the Inspector General's eagle-eyed responsibility to conduct inspections and investigations as directed by the Commandant, to supervise the audit of nonappropriated funds (such as recreation and exchange funds) and to maintain liaison with the inspection agencies of the other services. It is worth comment at this point that, although an "IG Inspection" invariably begets trepidation and soul-searching, the mission of the Inspector General is to help and to improve by constructive inspection.

Director, Judge Advocate Division. A general officer advises the Commandant and takes necessary staff legal action on all matters of military law, general law, legal assistance, and law enforcement.

The Director of Personnel. The Director of Personnel, a general officer, heads the Personnel Department, one of the two Headquarters "departments" which are established by law (the other is the Supply Department).

Of all agencies in Marine Corps Headquarters, the Personnel Department has more to do with you directly than any other.

"Personnel" recruits you, ships you over, controls your promotions, and administers you from the moment of first enlistment until you rest beneath the trees in a National Cemetery. When you become a staff NCO, the Personnel Department controls your assignments, manages your career, promotes you, transfers you to the Fleet Reserve, and ultimately retires you. It maintains your records at Marine Corps Headquarters, as it maintains similar records on every officer and man in the Corps. If you become a casualty, the Personnel Department notifies your next of kin, gives you your Purple Heart, and sees that you get the decorations and medals you have earned. Should you have a claim against the Government, the Director of Personnel adjudicates. And finally, in the form of disembodied statistics, you pass through the Marine Corps Personnel Accounting system in the hands of the Personnel Department.

The Quartermaster General (QMG). The Quartermaster General, a major general, heads the Supply Department. The Supply Department coordinates and supervises the procurement and administration of material and services required by the Corps (except those assigned by the Secretary of the Navy or Secretary of Defense to some other agency), the maintenance of facilities, and the transportation of personnel—you, that is, and your dependents—and household effects.

Fiscal Director. The Fiscal Director heads the Fiscal Division. It is his job to plan and coordinate the Marine Corps budget; to present and justify that budget to other Defense Department agencies and to Congress; to supervise the spending of appropriated funds; to disburse funds for military and civilian pay and general expenses; and to analyze, record, and report on expenditures under the Department of Defense "performance budget" procedure.

306. THE SERGEANT MAJOR OF THE MARINE CORPS. The senior noncommissioned officer at Marine Corps Headquarters and of the Corps as a whole, is the Sergeant Major of the Marine Corps. His billet, with interruptions in this century, dates back to 1801. The Sergeant Major of the Marine Corps advises and assists the Commandant in all matters pertaining to enlisted Marines and particularly to NCOs. As a member of the Commandant's personal staff, he accompanies him on all official trips. He is also a member of the Uniform Board and the Enlisted Performance Board. More important than these formal functions, the Sergeant Major's principal job is to be accessible to the noncommissioned officers of the Corps. If you are in Washington and have a question, a suggestion, or a problem and don't know where to start, knock on the Sergeant Major's door. If you can't get to Washington, he will always answer a letter.

The Marine Corps Operating Forces

307. MARINE CORPS OPERATING FORCES. The Marine Corps Operating Forces fall into four categories.

1. Marine Corps Operating Forces assigned to the Operating Forces of the Navy or unified commands,
2. Marine Corps Operating Forces assigned to shore activities of the Naval Establishment,
3. Marine Corps Operating Forces assigned to the State Department, and
4. Marine Corps Operating Forces not otherwise assigned.

308. MARINE CORPS OPERATING FORCES WITH THE OPERATING FORCES OF THE NAVY. When Marine units are assigned to the Operating Forces of the Navy, they come under operational control of the Chief of Naval Operations, except for administration and individual and unit training, which of course always remain under the Commandant. Marine units so assigned fall into two categories: *Fleet Marine Forces* and *ships' detachments.*

309. FLEET MARINE FORCES. The Fleet Marine Forces, or "FMF," constitute the bulk of the Marines assigned to the Operating Forces of the Navy. Both the Atlantic and Pacific Fleets include Fleet Marine Forces. The FMFs are integral components in the Fleet organization and enjoy status as "type commands" (see Section 219). This Marine expeditionary force integral to the Fleet was created by Major General John H. Russell, 16th Commandant, in 1933.

A Fleet Marine Force is a balanced force of combined arms, including air. It consists of a headquarters, force troops (i.e., non-divisional units which reinforce and support the divisions), service units, one or more Marine divisions or brigades, and one or more Marine aircraft wings. Fleet Marine Forces are organized, trained, and equipped for the following jobs.

1. Service with the fleets in seizure and defense of advanced bases and for land operations related to naval campaigns;
2. Development of amphibious tactics, technique, and equipment;
3. Training the maximum number of Marines for war or emergency expansion;
4. Immediate expeditionary service where, when, and as directed.

In accordance with law, the FMF includes at least three combat divisions and three air wings. Based on combat experience, the ratio of one air wing to support one Marine division is fundamental to the Marine air-ground team.

In addition to the divisions and air wings, Fleet Marine Force troops include extra artillery, engineers, armor, motor transport, amphibious reconnaissance, air and naval gunfire liaison company, service troops, and numerous specialized units which may be required to form balanced task forces for any kind of operations. (See Figure 3-3.)

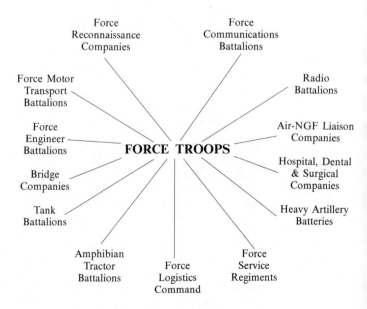

Fig. 3-3: Typical Components of Force Troops.

Tables of Organization ("T/Os") spell out the organization of every FMF unit, right down to the individual Marine, his duties, his rank, his specialist qualifications, and his weapons. *Tables of Equipment* ("T/Es") list the equipment required by each unit, and *Tables of Allowance* ("T/As") give basic allowances of standard items, such as bunks, helmets, and cleaning gear—to cite examples —which vary in direct proportion to the number of men in a unit.

One step in getting ahead is familiarize yourself thoroughly with the T/O of every unit you serve in, and acquire more than a nodding acquaintance with your T/E and T/A and with the organization of other FMF units with which you are in immediate contact.

The *Marine Division* (see Figure 3-4) is the ground fighting organization of the Marine Corps. The division is a balanced force of combined arms and services, but it does not include organic aviation. The division comprises about 21,000 officers and men, more than half of whom serve in the three infantry regiments which are the division's cutting edge. To support these infantry regiments, the Marine division includes an artillery regiment, a service battalion, special teams to control air and naval gunfire support, engineers, shore party, motor transport, medical, signal, and other troops normal for a force of combined arms. During World War II the Corps reached an all-time high of six divisions.

Fleet Marine Force Aviation. The basic tactical and administrative unit of FMF aviation is the squadron. Two or more tactical squadrons plus a headquarters and maintenance squadron and an air base squadron, comprise the *Marine aircraft group.* Two or more groups, with appropriate supporting and service units, make up the *Marine aircraft wing* (Figure 3-5). FMF aviation units whose aircraft permit carrier operations are so trained and serve aboard aircraft carriers of the Fleet. A complete discussion of Marine aviation can be found in Sections 323 and 324.

A *Force Logistics Command* is established to provide close logistic support to each Fleet Marine Force when in combat. Fleet Marine Force, Pacific includes such a command to support operations in Vietnam. For support of FMF units in continental United States, each of the two FMFs has a *force service regiment.*

310. MARINE AIR-GROUND TASK FORCES. For most operations, Marine ground and supporting aviation units are organized into a single integrated landing force under overall command of a single commander. A landing force built around a Marine division and a Marine aircraft wing is called a *Marine expeditionary force* (MEF). A smaller landing force shaped from a regimental landing team (RLT) and an air group (MAG) is designated a *Marine expeditionary brigade* (MEB), while such a force made up of an aviation squadron and a battalion landing team (BLT) is a *Marine expeditionary unit* (MEU). In any case, the aviation component is organized to suit the requirements of the landing force mission and can comprise units and aircraft of any category—helicopter, fighter/attack,

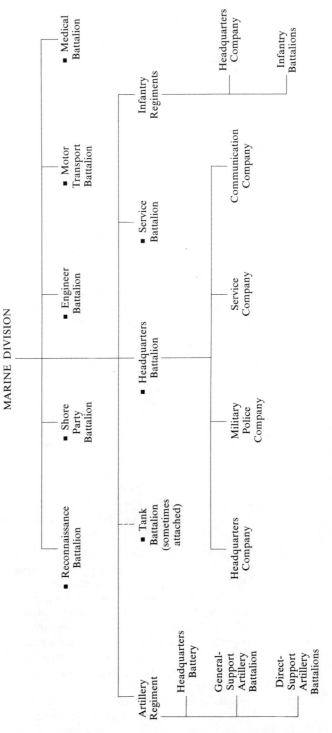

50

MARINE DIVISION

- Reconnaissance Battalion
- Shore Party Battalion
- Engineer Battalion
- Motor Transport Battalion
- Medical Battalion
- Tank Battalion (sometimes attached)
- Headquarters Battalion
- Service Battalion

Headquarters Company
Military Police Company
Service Company
Communication Company

Infantry Regiments
— Headquarters Company
— Infantry Battalions

Artillery Regiment
— Headquarters Battery
— General-Support Artillery Battalion
— Direct-Support Artillery Battalions

Fig. 3-4: Organization of the Marine Division.

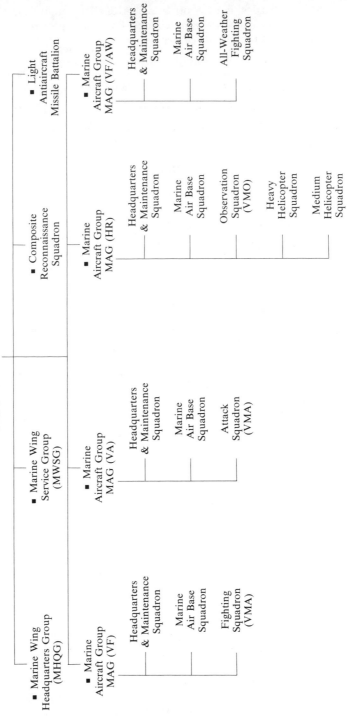

MARINE AIRCRAFT WING

- Marine Wing Headquarters Group (MHQG)
- Marine Wing Service Group (MWSG)
- Composite Reconnaissance Squadron
- Light Antiaircraft Missile Battalion

- Marine Aircraft Group MAG (VF)
  - Headquarters & Maintenance Squadron
  - Marine Air Base Squadron
  - Fighting Squadron (VMA)

- Marine Aircraft Group MAG (VA)
  - Headquarters & Maintenance Squadron
  - Marine Air Base Squadron
  - Attack Squadron (VMA)

- Marine Aircraft Group MAG (HR)
  - Headquarters & Maintenance Squadron
  - Marine Air Base Squadron
  - Observation Squadron (VMO)
  - Heavy Helicopter Squadron
  - Medium Helicopter Squadron

- Marine Aircraft Group MAG (VF/AW)
  - Headquarters & Maintenance Squadron
  - Marine Air Base Squadron
  - All-Weather Fighting Squadron

Fig. 3-5: Organization of a typical Marine Aircraft wing.

52 fixed-wing transport, or others. Similarly, units from Force Troops are added as may be required. For the composition of typical MEFs, MEBs, and MEUs, see Figure 3-6.

> *Note:* When deployed in Vietnam, the air-ground task forces just described are locally designated as Marine *Amphibious* Force, Brigades, etc., with initial "A" replacing the "E" in the standard abbreviations given above.

311. SEAGOING MARINES. Although the FMF naturally has first claim to attention among Marines assigned to the Operating Forces of the Navy, never overlook the ships' detachments, or "seagoing Marines." Every battleship, large aircraft carrier, and cruiser, together with certain amphibious and depot ships, has its detachment of Marines. This is a Marine mission which dates from earliest antiquity—from the fleets of Hiram of Tyre, and of Greece and Rome, where, respectively, Marines were known as *epibatae* or as *milites classiarii.* For more detailed information on seagoing Marines and on sea duty, turn to Chapter 18 ("Service Afloat").

312. MARINE CORPS OPERATING FORCES WITH NAVAL ESTABLISHMENT SHORE ACTIVITIES. Marine forces provide internal security for all major shore stations in the Naval Establishment. At such stations Marine guards perform the predominantly military activities which directly affect the internal security of the base. Many of the oldest Marine Barracks are those at naval shore stations.

Although Marine security forces are part of the naval stations where they serve, they also have the function of providing cadres from which the Fleet Marine Force can obtain additional trained regular Marines in a hurry. In fact, until the FMF was established, Marine Barracks were the only source of troops to form expeditionary forces. The Marine security forces therefore conduct training which is prescribed by Marine Corps Headquarters in order to keep officers and men at each Marine Barracks ready for instant field duty.

313. MARINE CORPS OPERATING FORCES ON OTHER ASSIGNMENT. Since the President may assign Marines to any duty (". . . such other duty as the President may direct"), Marine Corps Operating Forces may be, and frequently have been, detached for service outside the Naval Establishment, under unified commands, independently, or even under other executive departments (such as the Marine embassy guards). Command of Marine units not otherwise assigned by the President or the Secretary of the Navy remains with the Commandant of the Marine Corps. Such forces include units in training, in a standby status, or not specifically assigned elsewhere.

The Marine Corps Supporting Establishment

314. THE SUPPORTING ESTABLISHMENT. The Marine Corps Supporting Establishment provides, trains, maintains, and supports the Operating Forces. The Supporting Establishment includes Marine Corps Development and Education Command; the

Fig. 3-6: Typical Marine Air-Ground Task Forces.

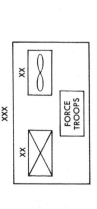

MARINE EXPEDITIONARY FORCE (MEF)

Headquarters
1 Marine Division
1 Marine Aircraft Wing
Force Troops:
  Motor Transport Battalion
  Engineer Battalion
  155 Gun Battery (Self-propelled)
  8" Howitzer Battery (Self-propelled)
  Tank Battalion
  Amphibian Tractor Battalion
  Force Reconnaissance Company
  Force Service Regiment Detachment, Headquarters Company
  Hospital Company

(basically structured on
1 Marine Division/Wing Team)

MARINE EXPEDITIONARY BRIGADE (MEB)

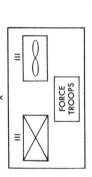

Headquarters
1 Regimental Landing Team (RLT)
1 Aircraft Group
Force Troops Units:
  Tank Company (Reinforced)
  Detachment, Force Service Regiment
  Amphibian Tractor Company
  Detachment, Motor Transport Battalion, FMF
  Detachment, Force Reconnaissance Company

(about 1/3
Marine Division/Wing Team)

MARINE EXPEDITIONARY UNIT (MEU)

Headquarters
1 Battalion Landing Team (BLT)
1 Jet Attack Squadron
1 Helicopter Squadron
Force Troops Units:
  Tank Platoon (Reinforced)
  Amphibian Tractor Platoon (Reinforced)
  Detachment, Force Reconnaissance Company
  Detachment, Force Service Regiment

(about 1/9
Marine Division/Wing Team)

recruit depots; supply installations; reserve activities; certain Marine Corps Bases, Barracks, and Air Stations; Headquarters Battalion, Marine Corps Headquarters; and a number of miscellaneous small activities.

315. MARINE CORPS DEVELOPMENT AND EDUCATION COMMAND (MCDEC). Stemming from World War I courses and training activities at Quantico, and those formally established by General Lejeune in 1920, the Development and Education Command (known for almost a half-century as "Marine Corps Schools") has the following jobs.

1. Development of doctrine, tactics, techniques, and equipment for landing forces in amphibious operations.
2. Support of Marine Corps requirements for long-range planning.
3. Formal education of Marine officers and selected NCOs.
4. Conduct of such other schools and functions as may be directed.

The Marine Corps Education Center conducts 11 subordinate schools of varying duration, including Command and Staff College, Amphibious Warfare School, Communication Officer School, Basic School (where newly commissioned second lieutenants are trained), Officer Candidate School (which trains and screens candidates for commissioned and warrant rank), Ordnance School (which trains officers and NCOs in such specialties as ordnance officer, optical instrument repairman, and the like), Women Officer School (which also runs a Women NCO Leadership Course), Instructor Training School, Computer Sciences School, and Physical Fitness Academy.

Besides the foregoing resident schools, an important agency at Quantico for all ambitious noncommissioned officers is the Extension School—a correspondence school which conducts correspondence courses based on the resident courses. Insofar as possible, each Extension School course uses the same texts as the resident schools, together with supplemental material.

The Marine Corps Development Center performs research, development, test, and evaluation functions, including war gaming for the Marine Corps and for all landing forces.

316. MARINE CORPS RECRUIT DEPOTS. As every non-commissioned officer knows, the recruit depots are the foundation of the Corps. "Boot Camp" converts the average young American into a basic Marine. Recruits from the Eastern States go to Parris Island (PI) while those from the West go to San Diego. In the past, as special conditions have dictated, the Corps has trained recruits at Washington, D.C. (MB, Eighth and Eye Streets), as well as at Quantico and Camp Lejeune.

317. DRILL INSTRUCTOR SCHOOLS. If, as stated above, the recruit depots are the foundation of the Corps, drill instructors are the foundation of recruit depot. The two Drill Instructor Schools, at Parris Island and San Diego, have the job of training carefully selected NCOs as DIs. *There are few more direct and rewarding ways to the top than as a DI.*

Candidates for DI School come from all occupational fields in the Corps in accordance with criteria established by HQMC. Besides having to be over 21, potential DIs must be screened by psychiatrists and by a depot screening team made up of officers and experienced NCOs. After this, an intensive eight-week course takes candidates over every jump, requalifies them with weapons, and, above all, gives them the knowledge, command presence, instructional ability, and leadership which are required before they can don the coveted field hat of a DI.

Note: Successful completion of a tour as a DI demonstrates that you are a superior Marine and thus inevitably brightens your promotion prospects. The precept of each NCO Selection Board convened at HQMC specifically directs attention to former DIs and underscores that they are to be considered as proven and superior in leadership.

318. THE RECRUITING SERVICE. The feeder for the Recruit Depots is the Recruiting Service, which operates under Marine Corps Headquarters, but is decentralized into *Marine Corps districts* which are discussed in Chapter 8. The recruiting service procures enlisted men and women for the regular and reserve establishments. It also maintains liaison in the field with local Selective Service agencies. Thus every town of importance has its Marine recruiters posted beside their "A-signs," who are quick to ship in a likely recruit but also supremely concerned with maintaining the quality of the Corps.

319. MARINE CORPS SUPPLY. The Marine supply services provide logistic support for the Corps. Logistics comprises supply, service, transportation, and evacuation.

The supply establishment procures, stores, distributes, maintains, and repairs all materiel which passes through the Marine supply system. The Quartermaster General heads the Supply Department, HQMC, which coordinates and supervises procurement, stock control, and distribution of materiel.

Supply Organization. The supply organization of the Marine Corps is designed to respond to modern logistic requirements. The Marine Corps supply system (now short-titled, "MUMMS," for "Marine Corps Unified Materiel Management System") heads up what is called an *inventory control point* or "ICP," located at Marine Corps Supply Activity, Philadelphia. There is also an alternate ICP at Marine Corps Supply Center, Albany, Georgia. The main functions of the ICP are centralized procurement of virtually all materiel for the Corps, centralized processing of all requisitions, and stores accounting. In addition, however, MCSA, Philadelphia, performs other vital functions in support of the entire Marine Corps supply system. These functions are:

1. Cataloging. Every item entering the Marine Corps supply system is identified and cataloged and assigned a federal stock number (FSN) in accordance with the Federal Cataloging Program.
2. Provisioning. All major equipment or "end-items" entering the

Marine Corps supply system, particularly for support of the FMF, require repair parts support. The function of "provisioning" (which has nothing to do with food) is the selection and procurement of the thousands of new repair parts required each year for support of new equipment.

3. Technical Services. Users of equipment or maintenance personnel frequently encounter conditions which require engineering or technical assistance. This assistance, which is provided by ICP, Philadelphia, may vary from the relatively minor determination of the exact characteristics of a repair part to development of a major modification or "engineering change."

4. Publications Support. The publications which are the bibles of the supply system are called *Marine Corps Stock Lists*. You should be as familiar with these (at least in general terms) as with the *Marine Corps Manual* and other basic administrative publications.

The principal Marine Corps logistic establishments (those which physically stock the materiel) are called *remote storage activities,* or "RSA." The two principal RSAs of the Marine Corps are the Marine Corps Supply Centers at Albany, Georgia, and Barstow, California. These RSAs store and issue materiel in accordance with instructions from the ICP at Philadelphia, they conduct and supervise stores accounting for post supply outlets and serve as area repair centers. With one supply center at Albany and the other at Barstow, the Marine Corps system has an East Coast Complex and a West Coast Complex.

To facilitate distribution and decentralization within the limits of the system and at the same time to promote responsiveness to supply needs, various smaller supply agencies support certain of the major posts. These smaller supply agencies, formerly known as "Stock Accounts," are now also designated as RSA. Communications and actual processing of transactions between the inventory control point and the remote storage activities is accomplished through a network of electronic transceivers and computers providing immediate response to supply needs.

Sources of Supply. Recent years have witnessed the emergence of the Defense Supply Agency (DSA) as the overall Defense Department manager of materiel. Under DSA, Defense Supply Centers exist for the various materiel categories, such as petroleum, subsistence, medical, industrial supplies, general supplies, communications and electronics, engineer and construction supplies, automotive and ordnance, and others. In addition, the Defense Clothing and Textile Supply Center makes or procures uniforms and clothing for all the services. The Defense Supply Agency and all supply centers are staffed by officers from each of the services, generally in proportion to the requirements of each. Thus, if you enter the supply field, you may reasonably expect to be detailed at some time to one of these joint agencies.

Aviation Supply. To understate—Marine aviation supply is complicated. A Marine in an aviation unit gets his clothing, individual equipment, rations, weapons, and pay from the Marine Corps. From the Naval Air Systems Command, however, he receives his vehicles, his airplane, its armament, his flight gear, and most of his training aids and manuals. His barracks, quarters, and the hangars, runways, revetments, and shops for his airplane come from the Navy's Facilities Engineering Command.

320. MARINE CORPS BASES AND AIR STATIONS. Several Marine Corps bases, camps, barracks, and air stations exist primarily to support other Marine activities. Unlike the barracks for Marine security forces, these stations come under military command of the Commandant of the Marine Corps. These posts are:

Marine Barracks, 8th and Eye Streets, S.E., Washington, D.C.
Henderson Hall, Arlington, Virginia
Marine Corps Base, Camp Lejeune, North Carolina
Marine Corps Base, Camp Pendleton, California
Marine Corps Base, Twentynine Palms, California
Marine Corps Camp Elmore, Virginia
Marine Corps Camp Garcia, Vieques, Puerto Rico
Marine Corps Camp H. M. Smith, Oahu, Hawaii
Marine Corps Camp S. D. Butler, Okinawa
Marine Corps Air Station, Quantico, Virginia
Marine Corps Air Station, Cherry Point, North Carolina
Marine Corps Air Station, Beaufort, South Carolina
Marine Corps Air Station, El Toro, California
Marine Corps Air Station, Yuma, Arizona
Marine Corps Air Station, Kaneohe Bay, Hawaii
Marine Corps Air Station, Iwakuni, Japan.
Marine Corps Air Station (Helicopter), New River, North Carolina
Marine Corps Air Station (Helicopter), Santa Ana, California

In addition to the foregoing major stations, there is an air facility (MCAF) at Futema, Okinawa. (An MCAF is an aviation installation whose primary function is support of helicopter units.)

321. THE MARINE BAND. A unique organization in the Supporting Establishment is the U. S. Marine Band, stationed at Marine Barracks, 8th and Eye Streets, Washington, D.C.

This 113-piece military band is not only the best but the oldest (1798) of the armed forces musical organizations. In length of service to the country, the Marine Band is nearly twice as old as the combined ages of the Army, Navy, and Air Force Bands. It has the privilege of providing music for all White House and official state functions in Washington, in addition to its normal duties in military parades and ceremonials. By long custom, the Leader of the band is *ex officio* musical director of two of Washington's traditional dining clubs, the Gridiron Club (Washington correspondents) and the Order of the Carabao (military and naval). In addition, wearing another hat, the Leader serves as Supervisor, Marine Corps Bands, under the ACofS, G-3, Marine Corps Headquarters. Here he supervises and coordinates band training, procurement of bandsmen, and musical standards and proficiency of all Marine bands.

Not counting rehearsals, the band averages about 1,600 playing engagements per year. These range from military ceremonies to formal concerts with either band or symphonic orchestra instruments, including the band's annual cross-country tour of nine weeks with two concerts seven days a week.

The bandsmen are enlisted for four-year cruises, being selected by audition and previous musical education. (About 90 percent of the members of the band are graduates of a musical college.) On acceptance for the Marine Band, musicians are directly enlisted into the E-5 pay grade, with subsequent promotions as earned, to E-9. The three officers of the band including the Leader (who holds rank equivalent to colonel) are selected either from the musicians of the band or from one of the Marine Corps field bands.

322. THE MARINE CORPS RESERVE. Although separate from the regular establishment, the Marine Corps Reserve (Chapter 8) forms a vital part of the Supporting Establishment.

Marine Corps Aviation

323. THE AIR-GROUND TEAM. The role of Marine Corps aviation in *the air-ground team* is to support Fleet Marine Force operations by close and general tactical air support and to provide air defense. Secondary to this main job, Marine aviation may be called on to provide replacement or augmentation squadrons for duty with the fleet air arm.

Marine aviation forms an inseparable part of the combined-arms team with which the Corps backs up its infantry. Thus the special role of Marines in the air is to support their teammates on the ground. The kind of close air support that Marines are accustomed to demands complete integration between air and ground. Plane captain and platoon sergeant wear the same color uniform, share the same traditions and common fund of experience and went through boot camp side by side. Battlefield and beachhead liaison between air and ground is accomplished by Marine pilots who share frontline foxholes with the riflemen while directing Marine aircraft onto targets just ahead. This makes for maximum reliance by ground on aviation and for maximum desire by aviation to assist the "grunts."

Probably the outstanding demonstration of this tradition in Marine aviation took place during the defense of Wake in 1941. Marine Fighting Squadron 211 provided a heroic air defense of Wake until there were no more airplanes left. Then the officers and men of the squadron calmly donned helmets, picked up their '03 rifles, and went down to glory as infantry. Twenty-four years later, in Vietnam, a handful of aviation mechanics made similar history when a suicide demolition section of 11 Viet Cong fanatics rushed the flight line of MAG-16 at Danang in an attempt to blow up helicopters with satchel charges. As the Viet Cong charged, three mechanics downed tools, seized their rifles, and killed or wounded every attacker in one blast of well-aimed fire.

324. ORGANIZATION OF MARINE CORPS AVIATION. In many respects, aviation is the part of the Corps which most lives up to Kipling's "Soldier an' sailor, too," since Marine aviation is very closely related to Naval aviation. This relationship stems not only from the long partnership between Marine Corps and Navy, but also because the preponderance of Marine squadrons that are organized and equipped for carrier operations and regularly perform tours of duty afloat. In addition, all Marine pilots undergo flight training at Pensacola and win their wings as naval aviators while most noncommissioned officers in Marine aviation go through naval aviation schools and training, as at NATTC, Memphis.

The primary function of Marine Corps aviation is to participate as the supporting air component of the Fleet Marine Forces in whatever operations they may conduct. A collateral function of Marine aviation is to participate as an integral component of naval aviation in the execution of naval functions as directed by the fleet commanders.

The Commandant of the Marine Corps controls the administration, individual training, and organization of Marine aviation. The Chief of Naval Operations, however, prescribes (via the Commandant) the aeronautical training programs and standards for Marine aviation units, and the aviation materiel used by Marine squadrons comes from the same sources in the Navy as does similar materiel for Navy squadrons.

The organization of Marine Corps aviation falls into subdivisions which correspond to the organization of the Corps as a whole.

1. Office of DC/S (Air), Marine Corps Headquarters,
2. Aircraft, Fleet Marine Forces,
3. Aviation Supporting Establishment.

Office of the Deputy Chief of Staff (Air) embodies the headquarters organization for Marine aviation. This office plans and supervises matters relating to the organization, personnel, operational readiness, and logistics of Marine aviation. The Deputy Chief of Staff (Air) is also Assistant Chief of Naval Operations for Marine Aviation. This arrangement insures that the Deputy Chief of Staff (Air), under one hat or another, controls all Marine aviation whether in the Marine Corps Supporting Establishment or under CNO in the Marine Corps Operating Forces (i.e., the FMF). Organized Reserve aviation training is also supervised by Deputy Chief of Staff (Air).

Aircraft, Fleet Marine Forces. Aviation units in the Fleet Marine Force (FMF) comprise the combatant part of the organization. Rather than comprising separate subordinate commands as has been the case in past years, aircraft wings of both Fleet Marine Forces are now under the direct command of the respective FMF Headquarters.

Operations and training of FMF air units are ultimately controlled through fleet chains of command by the Chief of Naval Operations, in whose office the ACNO, Marine Aviation, actually holds the reins insofar as Marine air is concerned.

Aircraft, Fleet Marine Forces, includes fighting squadrons (day, night, and all-weather); attack squadrons; photographic squadrons; observation squadrons (helicopter and fixed-wing); transport squadrons (helicopter and fixed-wing); ground-controlled intercept squadrons; and headquarters, air bases, and maintenance squadrons for the groups and wings. The wing is the basic tactical unit of Marine aviation, just as the division is the basic ground unit. You should remember, however, that the wing is a flexible, not a fixed organization and that different component organizations may be added or deleted.

Aviation is represented in staff and planning billets throughout the ground organization and through the tactical air control parties (or "TACP") which form part of the infantry battalion, regimental, and division headquarters of the Fleet Marine Force.

Aviation Supporting Establishment. The Marine Corps maintains several air stations and base commands in order to support aviation units operating ashore. On each coast, there is a *Marine air base command* which commands all Marine aviation shore establishments that, in turn, support aviation units of the FMF. The east coast command is Marine Corps Air Bases, Eastern Area, with headquarters at MCAS, Cherry Point; the west coast command is Marine Corps Air Bases, Western Area, with headquarters at MCAS, El Toro.

Marine Corps Staff Organization and Procedure

325. MARINE CORPS STAFF ORGANIZATION. The general framework of Marine staff organization corresponds to that employed by the U. S. Army. A complete description of that organization and the staff functions it performs can be found in *Field Manual 101-5, Staff Organization and Procedure.*

To suit differing needs of the Marine Corps (particularly in amphibious operations), we modify some of the staff functions described in *FM 101-5.* Moreover, the Marine Corps has several staff functions peculiar to Fleet Marine Force operations, which do not appear at all in *FM 101-5.* These latter, together with all the staff organization and functions of the Fleet Marine Force, are described in *Marine Corps Command and Staff Action* (*FMFM 3-1*).

Staff Organization. The Marine commander's staff consists of the
following three subdivisions.

The general (or executive) staff,
The special staff,
The personal staff.

As we discuss the staff, one principle should be kept in mind:
regardless of how much help the commander receives from his staff
(who serve as his eyes, ears, and agents), *the commander, and he
alone, is responsible for all that his unit does or leaves undone.* This
is the basic principle of command.

The General (or *Executive*) *Staff* is a coordinating staff group
which plans and supervises all the basic functions of command. In
units below divisional or wing level, it is known as the *executive
staff;* in divisions or higher headquarters, it is the *general staff.* Except for scale, however, the functions and duties of general and
executive staffs are identical.

The basic functions of command are: *personnel, intelligence, operations and training,* and *logistics.* These four functions are referred
to by number, in the order just given—that is, personnel as "1,"
intelligence as "2," operations and training as "3," and logistics as
"4." If the staff is divisional or higher (a general staff, in other
words), these numbers are prefixed by the letter "G"; if the staff
level is below division or wing (an executive staff), its number is
prefixed by the letter "S."

The general staff, which is concerned with these command functions, is headed by a *chief of staff* (or *executive officer* in units smaller
than brigade), who may be assisted by a *deputy chief of staff* and
by a *staff secretary,* who acts as office manager for the commander,
the chief of staff and his deputy. The remaining members of the
general or executive staffs are *personnel officer* (G-1 or S-1), *intelligence officer* (G-2 or S-2), *operations and training officer* (G-3 or S-3),
and *logistics officer* (G-4 or S-4). In addition to the "G's," as the
four assistant chiefs of staff are referred to, the staffs of all major
commands, both FMF and non-FMF, include a *comptroller* or
financial management officer, who is usually considered to be a
member of the general staff.

You will find detailed descriptions of the duties of each of the
foregoing officers both in *FM 101-5* and in *FMFM 3-1.*

The Special Staff. The special staff includes all the staff who are
not members of either the general staff or the personal staff. The
special staff is a body of specialist advisers and assistants to the
commander. The job of the special staff is to provide technical
advice, information, and supervision concerning all important specialized fields of military activity.

Special staff sections may be organized at will by the commander
to fill a particular need, or existing sections may be consolidated
or inactivated. Thus, the following list of special staff officers is

typical rather than fixed (although in point of fact most of these staff sections appear in tables of organization and may therefore be considered "normal" for a major Marine headquarters).

Adjutant	Food director
Air officer (NA)	Headquarters commandant
* Aircraft maintenance officer	Historian
Amphibian tractor officer	Information services officer
Antiaircraft artillery officer	Inspector
Antimechanized officer	Legal officer
Armored amphibian officer	Liaison officer
Artillery officer	Military government/civil
Nuclear, biological, and	affairs officer
chemical officer	Motor transport officer
* Aviation electronics officer	Naval gunfire officer
* Aviation supply officer	Ordnance officer
* Base operations officer	Postal officer
Chaplain (ChC, USN)	Provost marshal
Chief air observer	Shore party officer
Communications-electronics	Special services officer
officer	Unconventional warfare officer
* Crash crew officer	Supply officer
Data processing officer	Surgeon (MC, USN)
Dental surgeon (DC, USN)	Tank officer
Disbursing officer	* Utilities officer
Embarkation officer	* Weather officer
Engineer	* Photographic officer
* Engineering officer	
Exchange officer	
Explosive ordnance disposal	
officer	

*Aviation staff function only.

Commanding officers of attached units with no special staff representation act as advisers to the commander on matters pertaining to their units. Details on the Marine Corps special staff should be obtained from *FMFM 3-1,* rather than *FM 101-5,* since certain Marine special staff functions differ somewhat from apparently corresponding functions in the Army.

The Personal Staff consists of the staff officers whom the commander wishes to coordinate and administer directly, rather than through his chief of staff. The personal staff thus includes such officers as aides-de-camp and, for certain purposes, selected members of the special staff, such as the *information officer* or the *inspector.*

The *sergeant major* is, in a qualified sense, a member of the personal staff, although he has important responsibilities to the chief of staff or executive officer as well.

The relationship between the commander and his personal staff is direct, personal, and confidential. *The personal staff performs only such duties as the commander personally directs.*

326. AVIATION STAFF FUNCTIONS. Because of the inherent differences between ground and air operations and because aviation units perform certain staff functions along naval lines (in order to keep step with Naval aviation), Marine aviation has a few staff functions not encountered in the ground organization just described. These are marked with an asterisk in Section 325. In addition, Marine Corps aviation units embody all the general staff functions covered above.

*No one can say that the Marines have ever failed
to do their work in handsome fashion.*

—Major General Johnson Hagood, USA

4 The Story of the Marine Corps[1]

The history and the traditions of the Marine Corps are as much a part of the individual Marine's equipment as his rifle and his pack. Every Marine should therefore learn as much as possible about the history of the Corps.

As a noncommissioned officer, however, you are expected not only to know the facts, but to be able to explain and pass them on to younger Marines. This is the best possible way to safeguard the quality of the Corps.

401. MARINES IN THE REVOLUTION. The Marine Corps dates from 10 November 1775. On this day the Continental Congress authorized formation of two battalions of Marines.

Samuel Nicholas of Philadelphia was commissioned captain on 28 November 1775 and charged with raising the Marines called for by Congress. Nicholas remained senior officer in the Continental Marines through the Revolution and is properly considered the first Commandant of the Corps.

The initial Marine recruiting rendezvous opened at Tun Tavern, in Philadelphia, and by early 1776, organization had progressed to the extent that the Continental Marines were ready for their first expedition. The objective was New Providence Island in the Bahamas, where a British fort and large supplies of munitions were known to be. With Captain Nicholas in command, 277 Marines sailed from Philadelphia in Continental warships. On 3 March 1776, Captain Nicholas landed his battalion, took the fort, and captured the powder and arms for Washington's army.

For the first time in U. S. history, the Marines had landed, and the situation was well in hand.

[1]For a definitive history of the Marine Corps, see Col. R. D. Heinl, Jr., *Soldiers of the Sea,* (Annapolis, Maryland, U. S. Naval Institute, 1962).

During the succeeding year, Nicholas, now a major, commanded a battalion of Marines who fought with distinction in the Middle Atlantic campaigns of 1776 and 1777, at Trenton, Morristown, Assanpunk, and Fort Mifflin. At sea (notably under John Paul Jones), shipboard Marines played traditional parts as prize crews, riflemen, and landing forces (such as in the Penobscot Bay expedition in 1779).

402. EARLY YEARS, 1783–1811. After the end of the Revolution in 1783, although individual Marines continued to be enlisted for and to serve in the few U. S. armed vessels of the period (such as Revenue Cutters), no Corps organization existed until 11 July 1798, when Congress re-created the Marine Corps as a military service. Major William War Burrows, another Philadelphian with Revolutionary experience, was appointed Major Commandant of the Corps. Archibald Summers, appointed on 1 January 1801, was the first Sergeant Major of the Marine Corps.

During the decade which followed, the Naval War with France (1798–1800) and the campaign against the Barbary pirates (1801–1805)

Tun Tavern, Philadelphia, in 1775 was the birthplace of the Marine Corps; the site of Tun Tavern is now under a Philadelphia freeway.

provided employment for the Corps. Other noteworthy events were the movement of Marine Corps Headquarters to Washington in 1800, the retirement of Major Burrows as Commandant in 1804, and organization of the Marine Band in 1798.

The third Commandant, Lieutenant Colonel Franklin Wharton, found approximately 65 percent of his small Corps on duty in the Mediterranean. Here, in 1805, the assault of the fortress of Derna, Tripoli, by a mixed force including the Marines commanded by First Lieutenant Presley Neville O'Bannon and Sergeant Arthur Campbell, overshadowed many less dramatic but equally important actions. O'Bannon's handful of Marines were the first U. S. forces to hoist the Stars and Stripes over territory in the Old World. The "Mameluke" sword, carried by Marine officers to this day, symbolizes O'Bannon's feat.

While events in the Mediterranean held the spotlight, Marines, together with Army and Navy forces, were active in Georgia and East Florida and in the lower Mississippi, where, in 1804, a 106-man detachment was established at New Orleans.

403. THE WAR OF 1812. During the first two years of the War of 1812 the main American achievements were at sea or on the Great Lakes. Marines distinguished themselves in the great frigate duels of the war, as well as at the Battles of Lake Erie and Ontario.

The outstanding record among seagoing Marines, however, was set by Captain John M. Gamble, captain of Marines in USS *Essex,* the raider which virtually destroyed England's Pacific whaling trade. In April 1813, Gamble, with a crew of 14 Marines and seamen, was placed in command of a prize. After proving himself in a brilliant action against HMS *Seringapatam,* Gamble was promoted to squadron commander of a covey of prizes thinly manned by the U. S. crews and British prisoners. Late in 1813, Gamble was ordered to the Marquesas Islands by Captain David Porter, commanding *Essex,* to establish an advance base for further operations.

The warlike Marquesans began a series of probes which culminated in a pitched battle quelled by Gamble's naval gunfire. No sooner had this been settled, however, than mutiny reared its head among the British captives, who retook *Seringapatam,* captured Gamble, and cast him adrift in an open boat with four loyal men. Gaining one of his ships, Gamble, despite a wound sustained in the mutiny, got her underway with no charts and with a crew scarcely able to sail. He and his men made the Hawaiian Islands, only to be captured in 1814 by a British man-of-war. For all these exploits he was awarded a brevet as lieutenant colonel.

In mid-1813, British forces under Admiral George Cockburn and Major General Robert Ross began a campaign of raids against the Middle Atlantic seaboard. A year later, in August 1814, British soldiers, sailors and Marines advanced on Washington, D.C. On 24 August, after the Government had fled to Frederick, Maryland, American soldiers and militia under Brigadier General Winder of

Sharpshooting Marine riflemen dominate the action between USS *Wasp* and HMS *Reindeer*, 1814.

the Army attempted to halt the much smaller British column at Bladensburg, just east of Washington. Reinforcing Winder's 6,000 soldiers were 114 Marines from Eighth and Eye Streets and a contingent of seamen gunners with five guns under Commodore Joshua Barney of the United States Navy.

Winder's soldiers broke and ran at the first volley from the British, who advanced unconcernedly until they hit a piece of high ground occupied by the Marines and seamen who were standing firm. Marine volleys and Navy gunnery forced the British (seven times stronger) to halt, to deploy, and finally, three times in succession, to charge—at a cost of 249 casualties. After having suffered more than 20 percent casualties the Marines and sailors withdrew in good order, with at least a moral victory to their credit.

The British, having put Washington to the torch, now determined to seize New Orleans.

Although a peace treaty was being signed in Europe, the British expedition forced its way up the Mississippi. On 28 December 1814, the first enemy attack spent itself against an American line with Marines (under Major Daniel Carmick) holding the center. Less than two weeks later, on 8 January, the British tried again. This time, Andrew Jackson had distributed the Marines in small groups across the entire front. Despite a courageous assault by the redcoats, Jack-

From a few years after the War of 1812 until immediately before the Civil War, Archibald Henderson led the Marine Corps through the Indian Wars, the War with Mexico, the "Opening" of China, Central America, and the "Plug-Uglies."

son's main battle position stood unbroken. As the British commander, Pakenham, fell mortally wounded, the attack ebbed, and New Orleans was saved.

404. ARCHIBALD HENDERSON TAKES OVER. The most important event in the history of the Marine Corps following the War of 1812 took place on 17 October 1820, when Archibald Henderson succeeded Lieutenant Colonel Anthony Gale and became fifth Commandant. Gale's term as Commandant had been cut short by a poorly timed row with the Secretary of the Navy, which was followed by a court-martial.

During the 39 years and ten Presidential administrations which followed, Henderson dominated the Corps and gave it the high military character which it holds to this day. Had it not been for Henderson's firmness, reinforced by Congress, the Corps might well have been abolished as a result of President Jackson's attempt in 1829 to transfer the Marines into the Army. Supporting Henderson, Congress in 1834 placed the Corps directly under the Secretary of the Navy—and increased its strength to boot. This was the first instance of Congressional rescue for the Marine Corps—something which has occurred repeatedly since then.

405. ACTIONS AGAINST THE CREEKS AND SEMINOLES, 1836-1842. From 1836 through 1841, the Army, Navy, and Marine Corps attempted to transfer the Creek and Seminole Indians of Georgia and Florida to new reservations. Colonel Henderson, the Commandant, spent part of this time in the field at the head of a brigade of Army troops and a Marine regiment (the first organization of that size in the history of the Corps). At the Battle of Hatchee-Lustee, Florida, in 1837, Colonel Henderson won one of the few decisive victories of the campaign and was thereupon brevetted brigadier general—the first general officer in the Corps. Despite this success, as well as others against the Creeks, the Seminoles continued an obstinate resistance, and, in 1842, the war ended—with most of the Seminoles still in Florida.

406. TO THE HALLS OF THE MONTEZUMAS. The War with Mexico included three distinct campaigns: that against Mexico City and those against California and the west coast of Mexico. Marines took part in all three and were, in fact, the first U. S. forces to set foot on the soil of Mexico proper (at Burrita, 18 May 1846).

A battalion of Marines formed part of General Winfield Scott's column which advanced from Vera Cruz toward Mexico City. The key to the capital was Chapultepec Castle, set on a crag commanding the swamp causeways into the city. In the assault on Chapultepec, the Marines were divided into storming parties to head the attack up the south approach.

Under a hail of fire, the Marines moved out. Major Twiggs, the battalion commander, fell early in the attack, while Captain Terrett, a company commander, pressed home a separate assault toward the city. After a night in the outskirts of Mexico City, the Marines marched into town, at the head of their division—the first U.S. troops to enter—and occupied the palace of the Montezumas. The date was 14 September 1847.

In the Pacific, Marines played important roles in the conquest of California, helping to capture Monterey, Yerba Buena (San Francisco), Los Angeles, and San Diego, while First Lieutenant Archibald Gillespie acted both as confidential agent of President Polk and subsequently as a bold combat leader.

With California uneasily at rest by 1847, Marines of the Navy's Pacific Squadron secured the Mexican west coast ports of Mazatlan, Guaymas, Muleje, and San Jose. Mazatlan was garrisoned by Marines until June 1848, when peace was concluded.

407. BETWEEN THE WARS. The decade which followed peace with Mexico was hardly one of peace for the Marine Corps, despite postwar reduction of the Corps to approximately 1,200.

The opening of Japan in 1853-54 provided a historic setting for the landing of almost one-sixth of the Corps (six officers and 200 Marines, commanded by Major Jacob Zeilin, Mexican War hero and future Commandant). In the best traditions of the Corps, Major Zeilin's Marines were the first to set foot on Japanese soil.

"To the Halls of the Montezumas." The Marine battalion, preceded by General Quitman, enters Mexico City after having stormed Chapultepec Castle.

Hardly as peaceful were the landings at Shanghai (1854) and Canton (1856). In each, the conflicts represented trials of strength between Chinese and the Americans bent on "opening" China. At Canton's "Barrier Forts," 176 Chinese cannon were taken, and 5,000 Chinese put to flight.

A hemisphere away, in Nicaragua, Panama, Paraguay, and Uruguay, Marines were scarcely less active. With discovery of gold in California, the Panamanian Isthmus assumed great importance in 1855, when a rickety U. S. railroad was finally completed across the Isthmus. Soon Panama became a hotbed of disorder, which necessitated several landings by Marines, ultimately including a brigade in 1885. In Uruguay and Paraguay, the story was the same —unsettled times, immature governments, and Marines to keep the peace.

And at home, in Washington, Marines were called out in 1859 to stand off a gang of Baltimore hoodlums who styled themselves the "Plug-Uglies" and carried a loaded brass cannon as a show of force. While Marines and rioters faced each other across a downtown square, an old man, armed only with a gold-headed cane, stepped forward and placed his body across the muzzle of the mob's cannon. It was Brevet Brigadier General Archibald Henderson, 5th Commandant of the Marine Corps, 74 years old. While the thugs milled about the steadfast old man, a squad of Marines rushed the cannon, and that was that.

408. THE CIVIL WAR. For the Marine Corps, the opening shots of the Civil War sounded almost two years before Fort Sumter. On 17 October 1859, shortly after John Harris had succeeded Henderson as Colonel Commandant, 88 Marines were dispatched by the President to Harper's Ferry, Virginia, to recapture the U. S. Arsenal, which had been seized by the insurrectionist, John Brown. The Marine force reported to Colonel Robert E. Lee, the senior U. S. Army officer present. When John Brown refused to surrender, the Marines, led by First Lieutenant Israel Green, smashed their way under fire into Brown's stronghold, wounded the abolitionist, and quelled the insurrection.

After 1861, the Marine Corps—like the regular Army—was never large enough to fill the demands upon it. A Marine battalion fought in the first Battle of Bull Run, and other Marine forces served ashore in the Mississippi Valley and in the defenses of Washington. All along the Confederate seaboard, from Hatteras Inlet to Hilton Head and Fort Pickens, shipboard Marines, sometimes in provisional battalions, executed successful landings which put teeth into the Union blockade. Only at Fort Fisher in 1865 did Marines share with the Navy a bloody defeat.

By and large, the reputation of the Corps did not gain during the Civil War. Its strength was kept small—only 4,167 officers and men. And, as a Corps, Marines were not called on to perform amphibious tasks. As early as 1864 (and again in 1867), attempts were made to disband the Marine Corps and merge it with the Army. Both times, however, Congress stepped into the breach, and the Corps was saved.

409. POST-CIVIL WAR. Although the period from 1865 to 1898 has sometimes been spoken of as one of marking time by the Marine Corps, U. S. Marines landed during those years to protect American lives and property in Egypt, Colombia, Mexico, China, Cuba, the Arctic, Formosa, Uruguay, Argentina, Chile, Haiti, Alaska, Nicaragua, Japan, Samoa, and Panama.

In addition to these and many minor landings, a Marine-Navy landing force was sent, in 1871, in to the west coast of Korea, where, after storming an elaborate system of Korean forts along the Salee River, it captured 481 guns and 50 Korean battle standards. In this fighting two Marines tore down the Korean flag over the enemy citadel under intense fire and consequently were awarded Medals of Honor, the first of many to be won in Korea.

Three able Commandants (Jacob Zeilin, Charles G. McCawley, and Charles Heywood) did much to sparkplug the Corps out of the Civil War doldrums, and despite its small strength (still below 3,000), the Marine Corps was in excellent shape when the United States declared war with Spain in 1898.

410. WAR WITH SPAIN. On the night of 15 February 1898, USS *Maine* was blown up and sunk in Havana Harbor. Twenty-eight Marines were among the 266 casualties. The gallantry of Private William Anthony, the Captain's orderly, in rescuing Captain Sigsbee despite great personal danger, made Anthony the first U. S. hero of the impending war.

On 1 May 1898, little more than a week after declaration of war, Commodore George Dewey destroyed the Spanish squadron in Manila Bay. Two days later Dewey landed his Marine detachments to secure Cavite Navy Yard and settled down for the three-months wait until the Army could get troops to the Philippines.

Just as Marines were first to land in the Philippines, so also were they the first U. S. forces to land and fight in Cuba. On 10 June 1898, an Atlantic Fleet battalion of Marines, commanded by Lieutenant Colonel R. W. Huntington, landed under cover of ships' guns at Guantanamo Bay, Cuba, and seized an advanced base for the Fleet. Four days later, at Cuzco Well, Huntington routed the remaining Spanish forces, destroyed their water supply, and completed the victory. The hero of the day was Sergeant John H. Quick, who won the Medal of Honor for semaphoring, while under U. S. and Spanish shellfire, for an emergency lift of the naval bombardment.

Huntington's battalion was not the conventional ship's landing party of the 19th century, but rather a self-contained Marine expeditionary force which included infantry, artillery, and a headquarters complement of specialist and service troops. The battalion formed part of the Fleet—a miniature Fleet Marine Force whose primary mission was landing on hostile shores to secure an advanced base.

411. "OUR FLAG'S UNFURL'D TO EVERY BREEZE. . . ." Between 1899 and 1916, the Marine Corps participated in eight major expeditions or campaigns: the Philippine Insurrection, the Boxer Uprising, Panama, the Cuban Pacification, Vera Cruz, Haiti, Santo Domingo, and Nicaragua. It was in two of these campaigns (Boxer Uprising and First Caco War in Haiti) that Gunnery Sergeant Daniel Daly won his two Medals of Honor.

At least as important and possibly more so, Marine Corps developments of this period laid the foundation of American amphibious warfare techniques and insured the future survival and growth of the Corps. And all this was accomplished despite sustained Navy and Presidential attempts to get rid of the Corps; Congress finally squelched these attempts in 1909.

Long oppressed by Spain, the Philippines in 1899 sought to make a clean break with colonialism and launched the Philippine Insurrection—or rather transferred their insurrection from the Spanish to the Americans. This three-year campaign included the first modern Marine brigade ever organized, as well as three exploits for which the Corps will be remembered: Major Waller's march across Samar, the storming of Sojoton Cliffs in Samar (where Captains Porter and Bearss won Medals of Honor), and the pacification of the Subic Bay area on Luzon.

As 1900 dawned, China was undergoing one of her periods of antiforeignism—the Boxer Rebellion. In Tientsin and Peking, foreign missions were soon besieged by the bloodthirsty Chinese mob. In Peking, together with other foreign garrisons, U. S. and

The fight at Guantanamo Bay. Huntington's Marines repulse a Spanish attack in 1898. The present Marine Barracks at "Gitmo" is near the site of this repulse.

British Marines linked arms, as so often in the past, this time to defend the beleaguered Legation Quarter throughout the summer of 1900. In the international relief column dispatched to save Tientsin and Peking was a U. S. Marine force commanded by Major L. W. T. Waller and later by Major W. P. Biddle. By midsummer, Tientsin had been relieved, and on 14 August 1900, the Marines stormed the Ch'ien Men, leading into the Tartar City, the oldest and northern section of Peking, and the legations were saved.

At almost the same time, conditions in Panama began to threaten free transit of the Isthmus. In 1903, on orders from President Theodore Roosevelt, a U. S. Marine brigade—led by General Elliott, the Commandant—landed at Colon to protect U. S. rights during Panama's revolt against Colombia. Marines remained in the Canal Zone until the situation became fully routine in 1911, when the Army took over.

First in 1906 and again in 1912, Marine brigades were sent to Cuba to restore order under the so-called "Platt Amendment," by which the United States had the right to intervene in that newly liberated country. Twenty-four towns were occupied in 1906, and 26 in 1912, and considerable fighting took place in eastern Cuba before peace was finally attained.

Marines defend the Tartar Wall, during the siege of the Legations in Peking, 1900.

In 1901 the Marine Corps initiated special training and organization for the seizure and defense of advanced bases. Succeeding years saw increased use of battalions and regiments based in Navy transports as a means of projecting naval power across the shoreline. In 1910, at New London, Connecticut, Major General G. F. Elliott, 10th Commandant, established the Marine Corps Advanced Base School, the first in U. S. history to be devoted exclusively to the unsolved problems of amphibious warfare.

Hand in hand with establishment of the Advance Base School was the organization of the Advanced Base Force, a Marine brigade containing all the necessary combined arms and maintained in readiness for immediate expeditionary service with the Fleet. The Advanced Base Force was the prototype of the Fleet Marine Force.

When President Wilson was obliged to protect American rights, property, and citizens in Mexico in 1914, Marines from the Advance Base Force were the first to land at Veracruz. Army forces followed in due course. Veracruz provided the first field test of the Advanced Base Force, a test which was passed with flying colors.

Early in 1915, Haiti was wracked by revolution. Ships' detachments landed, but Haiti's troubles called for reinforcement by units of the Advance Base Force. The pacification of Haiti proved to be long and arduous. Bandits were firmly established in the north of Haiti, where the rugged country gave them every advantage. Under the leadership of Colonel L. W. T. Waller and Major Smedley Butler, Marines finally brought the bandits to battle in their stronghold at Fort Rivière, in the storming of which Butler won his second Medal of Honor, having won his first at Veracruz. Sergeant Ross L. Iams and Private Samuel Gross were also awarded Medals of Honor for the same feat—that of entering the Caco fort via a slippery masonry drain, more than 15 feet long, with the enemy firing their rifles down it. The resulting victory brought peace to northern Haiti. The Marines undertook military government, and, for the time being, Haiti breathed easily.

In 1916, Marine forces dispatched to restore order in the Dominican Republic again dramatized the ability of the Corps to take effective action on short notice. More than 2,000 Marines landed in Santo Domingo, where, until 1924, a protracted campaign was waged to suppress banditry and enable a Dominican civil government to regain control of the country.

By the end of 1916, the Corps had ended a major era of growth. It had become, in fact, a national force in readiness. In addition, the seeds of Marine amphibious development had been sown, and the leadership of the Corps had been hardened in continual combat and expeditionary experience which was destined to pay off for years to come.

412. MARINES "OVER THERE." Although Marines served faithfully around the globe during World War I and although Marine commitments in Haiti, Santo Domingo, Cuba, and Nicaragua remained little changed, the pre-eminent Marine story of World War I is that of the 4th Marine Brigade in France.

The 4th Brigade was the largest unit of Marines assembled during World War I, or ever before. It was composed of the 5th and 6th Regiments and the 6th Machine Gun Battalion, totaling some 9,444 officers and men. Of the Brigade's succession of notable actions (Belleau Wood, Soissons, Saint Mihiel, Blanc Mont Ridge, the Argonne), Belleau Wood is most significant, not only because it saved Paris from the massive German offensive in June 1918, but because it was the greatest battle up to that time in the history of the Corps. The casualties of the 4th Marine Brigade in assaulting the well organized German center of resistance in Belleau Wood were comparable only to those casualties later sustained in the hardest-fought beach assaults of the Second World War. After Belleau Wood, German intelligence evaluated the Marine Brigade as "storm troops"—the highest rating on the enemy scale of fighting men. It was at Belleau Wood that Gunnery Sergeant Daly, whose platoon was attacking German machine guns in the edge of the woods,

Riflemen of the 5th Marines attack the Hunting Lodge at Belleau Wood in 1918.

shouted, "Come on, you sons of bitches! Do you want to live forever?"

By 11 November 1918, the 4th Marine Brigade and Marine aviation units in France had sustained more casualties in eight months of virtually continuous combat than had the entire Corps in the preceding 143 years. The grim total was 11,366.

413. MARINE AVIATION. Founded in 1914 as part of the Advance Base Force, Marine Corps aviation was still in experimental stages when World War I began. During the war Marine aviation units flew in combat over France and supported the Fleet from an advanced base in the Azores. The spark plug of aviation's participation in the war was Major A. A. Cunningham, the Corps' first pilot. Starting from a strength of seven officer pilots and 43 enlisted men in 1917, Marine aviation, at war's end, mustered 282 officers and 2,180 enlisted men. In the best traditions of the Corps, the 1st Aeronautical Company, destined for the Azores, was the first completely equipped American aviation unit to leave the U.S. for service overseas. The first noncommissioned officer pilot in the Corps was Gunnery Sergeant Archie Paschel, who was designated locally by the CO, Marine Flying Field, Miami, in 1919 and later became the Corp's first NAP when that status was created in 1920.

414. "BEYOND THE SEAS." While the 4th Brigade was gaining immortal victories, the Advanced Base Force remained hard at work in Haiti, Santo Domingo, and Cuba. One regiment, the 8th Marines (later reinforced by the 9th Marines), was held in east Texas to protect the Mexican oil fields should the Germans try (as intelligence indicated they intended to do) to disrupt this source of Navy oil supply.

The 5th Marine Brigade was sent to France, but was refused permission by the Army to enter combat and was instead parcelled out in noncombatant duties—mainly provost marshal and military police in the Army communications zone.

415. EXPEDITIONS BETWEEN WORLD WARS. In addition to continuing commitments in the Caribbean, 1919 found the Corps performing occupation duty along the Rhine.

Marines were also occupying eastern Cuba, which was ultimately pacified in 1922. Two years later, in 1924, six hard-fought, campaigning years in Santo Domingo came to an end, and Marines were finally withdrawn. Haiti meanwhile was at a boil with banditry again in full cry, this time between 1918 and 1920. Following suppression of bandit forces in 1920, Brigadier General John H. Russell, expert in Haitian affairs, was appointed U. S. High Commissioner to Haiti to administer the American protectorate over the troubled republic. It was not until 1934 that the 1st Marine Brigade hauled down its colors in Port-au-Prince and boarded ship for home.

1927 was marked by trouble in both hemispheres—in Nicaragua and China. Naturally, Marines were soon involved.

As early as 1912, Marines had landed in Nicaragua to preserve order, but were withdrawn in 1925. No sooner were they out of the country, however, than the worst civil war in the history of Nicaragua erupted, and Marines (spearheaded by the ships' detachments) were immediately despatched to Nicaragua at the mutual request of the leaders of both warring factions. Marine occupation continued after an uneasy peace and consisted of disarming dissidents, conspicuous among whom was Agosto Sandino, a self-styled "patriot" guerrilla supported from Mexico and neighboring Honduras. A native *Guardia Nacional,* much like the *Gendarmerie d'Haiti* (also Marine-trained), was organized under the Marines to facilitate the hard job of policing a population which included thousands of demobilized revolutionary soldiers.

Marine aviation not only played a leading role in supporting ground operations in Nicaragua, but also pioneered tactical and logistic air support on a scale hitherto unknown. The technique of dive bombing (invented by Marine aviators in Haiti in 1919) was greatly refined. Virtually all the isolated patrols and outposts in the heavily jungled northern area of Nicaragua were maintained by air supply. To evacuate Marine wounded, First Lieutenant C. F. Schilt made ten landings and takeoffs from a village street in Quilali in a fabric-covered scout plane under murderous enemy fire. Lieutenant Schilt was awarded the Medal of Honor.

When the Marines left Nicaragua in 1933, they turned over to the Nicaraguan government a well organized Guardia, a military academy, a system of communications, and a first-rate public health service, plus many less obvious improvements.

As in Nicaragua, Marine embassy guards had been stationed in China for many years before 1927. But here, too, civil disturbances of increasing violence reached a peak in 1927, and additional forces —the 4th Marines to Shanghai, and a brigade to North China—were hurried in. Mainly because of these precautions, the threatening situation eased, and the brigade was withdrawn. The remaining units in Shanghai, Peking, and ultimately Tientsin as well, faced crisis after crisis with Chinese warlords and Japanese until World War II closed the ledger.

416. GUARDING THE MAILS. In 1921 after a series of violent mail robberies in the United States, the President directed the Marine Corps to guard the mails. Within a matter of hours, Marine armed guards were riding mail-cars and trucks, with orders to shoot to kill. Not a single successful mail robbery took place against a Marine guard, and in less than a year the Marines were withdrawn. Five years later, when mail robberies again broke out, Marines were called in a second time, and this time as well, the robberies ended at once.

417. AMPHIBIOUS PIONEERING. In the early 1920s it became clear to Marines that a war with Japan was inevitable and that such a war, to be successful, would require amphibious seizure of a chain of advanced bases across the Pacific, the world's greatest ocean. In 1921, the year after Marine Corps Schools opened at Quantico, the course of a war with Japan was forecast with prophetic accuracy by Lieutenant Colonel Earl Ellis, who subsequently "disappeared" while on an intelligence mission in the Japanese Palaus in 1923.

To Major General John A. Lejeune, 13th Commandant, the prospect of amphibious war was a bleak one. The British failure at

These "Horse Marines" are the detachment stationed in Peking, China in 1938.

Gallipoli had convinced military thinkers that an amphibious operation could not succeed against strong opposition. Despite the discouraging nature of the problem, General Lejeune set the Marine Corps to solving it.

Quantico became the focal point of American amphibious development. Marine Corps Schools attacked the problem and by 1934 had produced the first U. S. manual of amphibious doctrine ever written—*Tentative Landing Operations Manual*. This historic document was adopted intact by the U. S. Navy in 1938, under the title, *FTP-167, Landing Operations Doctrine, U. S. Navy*. In 1941, when the U. S. Army issued its first amphibious publication, Quantico's book was again borrowed verbatim, even down to the illustrations, and appeared this time as *War Department Field Manual 31-5. Tentative Landing Operations Manual* still constitutes much of the basis for publications which are today's amphibious bible.

To deal with materiel aspects of amphibious problems, the Marine Corps Equipment Board was brought into being in 1933. Most notable among the Board's pre-World War II achievements was the amphibian tractor, or LVT, which joined the FMF in 1940.

During these pioneering years, the Advanced Base Force was redesignated in 1921 as the East Coast Expeditionary Force and in 1933 as the Fleet Marine Force, after Major General John H. Russell, 16th Commandant, had persuaded the Secretary of the Navy that Marine expeditionary troops should form an integral part of the U. S. Fleet. The Fleet Marine Force not only constituted a force in readiness, but also performed an invaluable role in testing the doctrines and materiel evolved by Marine Corps Schools and by the Equipment Board. From 1935 on, annual Fleet Landing Exercises enabled the new FMF to shake down as well as to keep the thinkers at Quantico progressing along sound lines.

Because of this pioneering in the 1920s and 1930s, the Marine Corps—ground and aviation—was ready for amphibious war and ready also to train others to wage it, when the opening salvos of World War II rocked the world. Before World War II had run its course, seven U. S. Army divisions (including the first three Army divisions ever to receive amphibious training) were trained in landing operations by the Marine Corps, and the doctrines of Quantico girdled the globe.

418. OCCUPATION OF ICELAND. In 1941 with the 17th Commandant, Major General Thomas Holcomb, in office, the Fleet Marine Force demonstrated its capabilities.

Iceland, garrisoned by British forces, was critical in the Battle of the Atlantic. President Roosevelt, who well knew Iceland's strategic importance, agreed with Prime Minister Churchill that the island should be more adequately secured and that U. S. forces should be employed. After the Army proved unable to provide ready forces for the Iceland mission, the President turned to the Marine Corps. Less than one week later, on 22 June 1941, the 1st Provisional Marine Brigade had been organized, had embarked, and had sailed. On 7 July, more than 4,000 Marines debarked at Reykjavik. Once again first on the spot, the Corps had proved itself the national force in readiness.

419. "UNCOMMON VALOR." At the outset of World War II in 1941, the Marine Corps totaled some 70,425 and was organized into two Marine divisions, two air wings, and seven defense battalions (advanced base artillery units). By 1944, the Corps included six divisions, four wings, and corps and force troops to support the two amphibious corps which were the FMF's highest formations; its top strength was 471,905.

Despite differences in terrain and character of operations, both the South Pacific and Central Pacific campaigns of World War II highlighted Marine Corps attributes—the South Pacific, *readiness;* the Central Pacific, *amphibious assault capability.*

The Guadalcanal campaign (1942) typified not only the South Pacific, but, more important, Guadalcanal dramatized to the American public the function of the Fleet Marine Force.

In 1942 (on the heels of valiant Marine defensive fighting at Wake, Midway, and Corregidor), it became clear that a U. S. advanced base must be established in the southern Solomons. Guadalcanal, where the Japanese were already building an air strip, was the logical target. Despite high-level prophecies of disaster and recommendations that the assault be delayed until the following year, when Army troops could be trained to participate, the 1st Marine Division was given the job of retaking Guadalcanal and adjacent Tulagi. On 7 August 1942, Marines landed.

It was the first U. S. offensive of World War II; the long road back had commenced.

Odds were never more unfavorable during the Pacific War than

81 on Guadalcanal. But by late November 1942 when Army troops began to arrive in strength, battered Henderson Field was firmly secured by U. S. Marine ground and air, and, in the inner councils of Japan, it was already acknowledged that the turning point of the war had passed.

The lesson of the Guadalcanal campaign was that without a ready Marine Corps, the operation could never have taken place. Undertaken as a purely naval campaign by fleet units and Marines, Guadalcanal demonstrated the dependence of sea power on Fleet expeditionary forces, as well as the degree to which the Marine Corps had placed itself in readiness for just such an occasion as this.

On Iwo Jima, as on Tarawa, the fighting ability of the individual Marine came into sharp focus.

From the foxholes of Belleau Wood to the foxholes of World War II, Marines scratched out shallow rifle pits wherever the front lines lay.

If Guadalcanal and subsequent operations in the South Pacific—New Georgia, Bougainville, Choiseul (all in 1943), and New Britain (1944)—proved that the Corps was ready for war, the campaign across the Central Pacific displayed the Marine Corps' capability in amphibious assault.

The succession of Central Pacific battles—Tarawa (1943), the Marshalls, Saipan, Guam, Tinian, Peleliu (all 1944), Iwo Jima and Okinawa (both 1945)—was by hard necessity a series of frontal assaults from the sea against positions fortified with every refinement that Japanese ingenuity and pains could produce. To reduce such strongholds, wrote one historian, was "the acme of amphibious assault."

On Iwo Jima, toward the end, as on Tarawa at the beginning, the fighting ability of the individual Marine came into sharp focus. Each battle was one of frontal assault and close combat against fortified positions. Tarawa was the first combat test of the Marine Corps doctrines for amphibious assault, and Tarawa demonstrated that those doctrines would work. Two years later, at Iwo Jima—largest all-Marine battle in history—Marines reaped the benefit of Tarawa's experience (and the experience of many other hard-fought assaults) in the form of tested, combat-proven assault technique. Without Tarawa, the even greater assault on Iwo would not have been possible. Without the U. S. Marine Corps (and without the years of study, experiment, and development at Quantico), neither Tarawa nor Iwo nor the battles between could even have taken place, let alone have succeeded.

But the record of the Corps in World War II was not only the great record of its seaborne assaults. Beginning on 7 December 1941, at Wake, Marine aviation was also in the war. At Midway, Guadalcanal, Bougainville, the northern Solomons, in the Marshalls, at Peleliu, Iwo Jima, and Okinawa, Marine fliers again helped to forge the concept of the air-ground team. And just as World War II proved the long-studied amphibious assault doctrines of the Corps, so also World War II witnessed the perfection of Marine close air support. In the reconquest of the Philippines, four Marine air groups working with Marine air liaison parties on the ground reached a high point in Marine tactical air support (even though this support was for Army comrades).

By the end of the war, the Fleet Marine Force, air and ground, was poised for invasion of Japan—an invasion rendered unnecessary by U. S. sea power. The Corps which under General Holcomb, 17th Commandant, had mustered 19,354 in 1939, neared 500,000 in 1945, under Holcomb's successor, General Vandegrift of Guadalcanal. The victories in World War II had cost the Corps 86,940 casualties. In the eyes of the American public, the Marine Corps was second to none and seemed destined for a long and useful career. Admiral Nimitz's ringing epitome of Marine fighting on Iwo Jima might very well be applied to the entire Marine Corps in World War II: *"Uncommon valor was a common virtue."*

420. THE MARINE CORPS, POSTWAR. After World War II, although the Corps enjoyed high public prestige and seemed indeed here to stay, the years 1946 to 1949 were devoted to a searching examination into the mission and (in high quarters, behind closed doors) even the need for the Marine Corps. These doubts were inspired, as two Commandants testified before Congress, by the Army General Staff, whose long-term objective since before World War I had been abolition of the Marine Corps, or alternatively its reduction to a minor security and ceremonial unit. The question was firmly—and, Marines hoped, finally—resolved by the National Security Act of 1947, which gave the Corps firm missions and reaffirmed its status as the Service charged with primary amphibious responsibility over landing force tactics, technique, and doctrine. Subsequently the Douglas-Mansfield Bill, enacted in 1952, afforded the Commandant coequal status with the Joint Chiefs of Staff in all matters concerning the Marines and legislated today's organization of the Corps.

While the roles, missions, and status of the Marine Corps were being debated in both executive and legislative branches of government, the Corps maintained occupation forces in Japan and North China, and completed an orderly demobilization unmarred by indiscipline or untoward incident.

The postwar FMF comprised two major forces: Fleet Marine Force, Pacific and Fleet Marine Force, Atlantic—assigned respectively to the Pacific and the Atlantic Fleets. Each force embodied a Marine division and an air wing (both on peace scales) and supporting logistic units.

421. KOREA: "NOT A FINER FIGHTING ORGANIZATION IN THE WORLD." Like the story of the Corps in World War II, the Marines' part in the Korean War is covered by the official histories. This narrative therefore confines itself only to high spots of a gruelling three-year war at the outset of which, to quote Hanson Baldwin, of *The New York Times:*

> The Marines were ready to fight; if they had not been, we might still be fighting in the Pusan perimeter.

On 24 June 1950, when the Russian- and Chinese-supported North Korean communists attacked South Korea, the Corps numbered approximately 75,000. The FMF was deployed in two shrunken divisions at Pendleton and Lejeune. Aviation (which had narrowly missed transfer to the Air Force by Defense Secretary Louis Johnson) was even thinner: eleven squadrons divided into two wings, at Cherry Point and El Toro. The Chairman of the Joint Chiefs of Staff, General Omar Bradley, had predicted publicly, hardly eight months before, that the world would never see a large-scale amphibious landing.

On 2 July, faced with mounting catastrophe, General MacArthur sent his first request to the Joint Chiefs of Staff for help from the Marines: immediate assignment of a Marine regimental combat team (RCT) plus a supporting Marine air group. In the days which followed, General MacArthur sent five more pleas, culminating in one for a war-strength Marine division and a war-strength air wing.

Less than two weeks later, as soon as Navy shipping could be readied, the 1st Provisional Marine Brigade was crossing the Pacific, heading for the Pusan perimeter into which shaken U. S. Army and Republic of Korea (ROK) units were already streaming rearward. On 3 August 1950, Marine F4Us from USS *Sicily* scored first blood for the Corps in an air strike over Inchon; on 7 August, eleven years after Guadalcanal, ground elements of the brigade were in hot action, plugging holes in the Pusan perimeter. And here for the first time helicopters were being flown in battle—by Marines.

To form this spearhead, the 1st Marine Division had been stripped, with only a cadre left behind. Now it was up to the Corps to re-form the division for the amphibious stroke which General MacArthur had visualized from the outset of the war.

For these, and other worldwide commitments, it was obvious that the 75,000-Marine peacetime Corps would not suffice. Ten days after

United States Marines rest in the snow on the march from the Chosin Reservoir.

the 1st Brigade had sailed, the President mobilized the Organized Reserve. The 2d Division, at Lejeune, was stripped of all but headquarters and a cadre; 7,000 men were transferred to Camp Pendleton.

While this administrative nightmare was in progress and the brigade was fighting desperately along the Naktong River, U. S. Marine and Navy planners were in Tokyo, translating into reality General MacArthur's plan to relieve Pusan and retake Seoul by an amphibious assault to be delivered at the Korean west coast port of Inchon. Because of extreme tidal fluctuation, 15 September was the only suitable D-day until mid-October. Within five days after the 1st Marine Division had finally gotten together in one piece in one place and the 1st Wing was fully in business, convoys were sailing for Inchon.

Despite unprecedented haste in preparation and numerous calculated risks of enemy opposition, geography, and hydrography, the Inchon landing was almost anticlimactic in its success. As favorable reports poured in throughout D-day, General MacArthur signalled:

> The Navy and Marines have never shone more brightly than this morning.

On 26 September 1950, 90 days after the communist blitz, Seoul was in the hands of the 1st Marine Division. A week later, with capture of Uijongbu, the Inchon-Seoul campaign was complete. Largely as a result of the amphibious capability and readiness of the Marine Corps, the North Korean army south of the 38th Parallel had been all but destroyed.

The strategic sequel to Inchon was another amphibious flanking maneuver, a right hook up the east coast into Wonsan, and thence northwest—it was intended—to the Yalu. To execute this scheme, the Marines were again chosen.

Although the 1st Division's orders called for a wide-open, free-style push to the Yalu, the Marines, warned by an initial contact with the Chinese Communist Forces near Hamhung on 2 November, made haste slowly. The advance was careful, and the main supply route to the sea was painstakingly developed and secured.

On 25 November 1950 after an eerie lull, Chinese Communists hit the right wing of the Eighth U. S. Army, routed and destroyed at least one U. S. Army division, and launched an entire army group, eight divisions, against the 1st Marine Division.

The blow fell when the division's forward elements were west of Chosin Reservoir, at Yudam-Ni. In face of "General Winter" and of every weapon, artifice, and attack in overwhelmingly superior strength, the 1st Division concentrated promptly, rescued and evacuated surviving remnants of adjacent, unprepared Army formations, and commenced one of the great marches of American history from Chosin Reservoir to the sea.

On 11 December, having brought down its dead, saved its equipment, and rescued three Army battalions, the 1st Marine Division —supported by the 1st Wing—reached the sea with high morale and in fighting order. The division had shattered the Chinese Communist Forces (CCF) 9th Army Group, killed at least 25,000 Chinese, and wounded more than 12,500.

Following amphibious redeployment and a short "breather" cleaning out a North Korean guerrilla division which had infiltrated southeast Korea, the 1st Division spearheaded the IX Corps spring offensive of 1951. At the same time the 1st Wing continued to provide the majority of all close-support sorties nominally credited to the Fifth Air Force, under whose control the wing now operated.

Although overlooked by the publicity accorded other divisions at this time, the Marine division played a stellar role against the Chinese counteroffensive which recoiled on the U. S. IX Corps. The division's defense of Hwachon Reservoir saved the IX Corps from disaster and largely stopped the enemy offensive. Soon after, with initiation of armistice talks, the front stabilized, and the division found itself holding the "Punchbowl" sector on the east coast of Korea. The pattern of inconclusive, savage seesaw fighting in this sector was destined to recur here and elsewhere throughout the rest of the war.

During this time, the feats of the Marine Corps (and Royal Marines) in holding and exploiting offshore islands far up the east and west coasts of Korea began to pay off. Fifteen islands, including seven in embattled Wonsan Harbor, served as springboards for raiding, havens for aircraft in trouble, bases for intelligence skulduggery, and observation posts for Marine shore fire control parties.

In spring, 1952, the 1st Division moved to the arena of its final battles in Korea: the line of the Imjin River, astride the Munsan-Ni corridor to Seoul. Here, holding a frontage greater than any other division in Korea, the division kept Seoul safe, anchored the United Nations' left flank, and overlooked the Panmunjom truce site. From these positions the Marines fought a series of bloody trench-warfare actions of a type and scale unheard-of in the Corps since World War I: the battles for "Bunker Hill" and "The Hook," and the fighting about Outposts "Reno," "Carson," and "Vegas."

And here the armistice found the 1st Marine Division and its valiant supporting Marine air wing, still holding the Imjin.

Korea had tested "the new Marine Corps" in readiness and fighting quality. Neither had been found wanting. Korea demonstrated to doubters in high places and low that amphibious operations were anything but dead. Korea proved, as had World War II before it, the high caliber and readiness of the Marine Corps Reserve. Most of all, in a time of immense changes in military techniques, Korea underscored the fact that the military principles, virtues, and intangibles for which the Marine Corps stood, remained as sound in 1953 as they had been in 1775.

422. AT MID-20TH CENTURY. As there had been no victory in Korea, so there was no demobilization. The Corps continued in the structure of three divisions and three wings which Congress had established in 1952, with one of each on the east and west coasts of the United States and in the Far East (Okinawa and Japan). From these major forces, floating battalions were maintained on station with the U. S. fleets in the Mediterranean and Far East and, from 1960 on, in the West Indies as well. A thorough modernization of the war-tested amphibious doctrines of the Navy and Marine Corps, originally conceived in Quantico in the late 1940s, gave these forces assault helicopters as landing craft and specially designed helicopter carriers as transports. Blending these sophisticated and original methods with the tried and true ones of seaborne assault by landing craft and amtracs, the amphibious assault now had even greater shocking power and flexibility than before. Recognizing imitation as the sincerest flattery, the Marines who had pioneered the tech-

nique of "vertical envelopment" could watch developments with interest when, 15 years later in Vietnam, the Army gave wide publicity to its "airmobile" concept, which was simply a shore-based version of Marine Corps vertical envelopment.

In the decade following Korea it became clear that, despite the everpresent threat of nuclear war, the characteristic pattern of Cold War was one of limited operations, of politico-military guerrilla warfare—in short, the type of small war in which the Marine Corps had become so thoroughly versed during the first 150 years of its existence. In the Far East between 1955 and 1963, Marines landed in the Tachen Islands, Taiwan, Laos, Thailand, and South Vietnam, in countermoves against communist pressure. In the Mediterranean, not only did Marines land at Alexandria to help evacuate U. S. and foreign nationals during the Suez incident of 1956, but, in July 1958 on an appeal from the Lebanese government, secured Beirut against a communist coup. A Marine brigade, subsequently reinforced by Army troops, stood by for ten weeks until peaceful elections had been completed and a constitutional change of government had been duly carried out. In the Caribbean, our October 1962 confrontation with communism saw Cuba ringed with floating Marine landing forces, while other FMF units insured that Guantanamo Bay remained safe and secure against Castro aggression. Soon afterward in May 1963, a Marine expeditionary brigade lay off Port-au-Prince for three weeks in expectation that the regime of Haiti's dictator, François Duvalier, would finally topple. This was not to be, but active service loomed ahead elsewhere on Hispaniola.

423. EXPLOSION IN SANTO DOMINGO. On 24 April 1965, what had started as a military coup escalated into an attempt by Castroite communists to gain control of the Dominican Republic. In a five-day blood bath, the government of Santo Domingo ceased to exist. Foreign lives and property were in extreme danger; the American Embassy (and seven other foreign embassies) came under fire or were actually violated by leftist revolutionaries. In the circumstances, the United States government had no alternative but to step in. In the late afternoon of 28 April, President Johnson ordered the landing of the 3d Battalion, 6th Marines, at Ciudad Santo Domingo, from USS *Boxer* lying offshore. It had been 39 years since U. S. Marines last landed in the Caribbean (at Bluefields, Nicaragua, in 1926).

Quickly augmented to brigade size despite appreciable resistance in some areas, the landing force established a demilitarized international zone protecting the American and other embassies. When Army airborne units arrived, the Marines came under command of the Army and, when pacification of the city had been effected in June, were withdrawn. Noteworthy in this operation—aside from its demonstration that the United States was still ready to intervene when national interest so dictated—was the fact that once again seaborne Marines had reached an objective well ahead of even the fastest moving Army airborne units.

424. WAR IN VIETNAM. Meanwhile, on the other side of the globe, the dragging war in Vietnam—the Nicaragua of the 1960s—heated up. Marine helicopter units (flying half the total sorties and flight hours with 20 percent of the helo-lift in the country) had been in Vietnam since 1962. So had Marine reconnaissance troops and a U. S. Marine advisory mission to train the Vietnamese Marine Corps.

To protect the air base complex at Danang on the north coast, the 3d Marine Division was deployed to that place on 8 March 1965—the first U. S. ground combat unit to enter the war. With it came the 1st Wing. Subsequently, the 1st Marine Division and MAG-36 followed westward, being split between Vietnam and Okinawa. By the end of the year, almost two-thirds of the combat units of the Marine Corps were thus committed to the Vietnamese war.

A Marine gives coordinates of VC position to the Forward Air Controller during Operation Cochise near Da Nang.

Adjacent Marine coastal "enclaves" were established at Danang and Chulai with the objective not only of protecting these important air bases but of pacifying a populous and productive region, using the "oil-stain" tactics originated in this very region by France's master of colonial warfare, Marshal Lyautey. Consolidated under Headquarters, III Marine Amphibious Force (commanded by General Lewis Walt), the Marines soon came to grips with the Vietcong, winning a notable action at Van Tuong near Chulai in August 1965. Subsequently, in making full use of our amphibious capability, a series of surprise landing attacks, code-named *Dagger Thrust,* was executed along the Vietnamese coast by Marines embarked with the Seventh Fleet. During 1966, unlike the Army forces in Vietnam, the Marines in I Corps area concentrated on steady attempts to pacify the area, and an important development was the Combined Action Company (CAC), made up of a handful of Marines to train, lead, and stiffen Vietnamese troops. The success of this program was so notable that, in 1967, the North Vietnamese commenced a succession of brutal, headlong assaults directly across the 17th parallel demilitarized zone (DMZ) in which units of the newly reformed 5th Marine Division distinguished themselves beside veterans of the 1st and 3d Divisions. Still another success of the CACs was that, in the 1968 *Tet* offensive, it was the Marine villages in I Corps that withstood the tide without exception.

America was again at war, and the Marines, as usual, were in the thick of it.

425. THE CUTTING EDGE OF SEA POWER. An important lesson not only in Vietnam but in Santo Domingo and the myriad lesser operations of the late 1950s and early 1960s is that of the ability of maritime expeditionary forces, positioned in international waters, to anticipate trouble and hover indefinitely, if need be, in easy reach of the key points. While airborne forces remained tied to objectives containing major airdromes, cumbered by limits on overflight (as had happened in the Lebanon operation), and dependent even then on seaborne follow-up to give them combat staying power, the ability of the Fleet to go where it pleased, to stay there, and to project its power readily ashore made the Fleet Marine Force a cutting edge of sea power in the Cold War.

Old breed? New breed? There's not a damn bit of difference so long as it's the Marine breed.

—Lieutenant General Lewis B. Puller

5   Traditions, Flags, and Decorations

The traditions of the Marine Corps, its history, its flags, its insignia —*the Marine Corps way of doing things*—make the Corps what it is and set it apart from other military organizations and services.

These traditions give the Marine Corps its spirit and are the reason why the Corps respects its past and its ways of acting and speaking. These things underlie the discipline, valor, loyalty, aggressiveness, and readiness which make the term *Marine* ". . . signify all that is highest in military efficiency and soldierly virtue."

One writer on Marine traditions nailed down their importance in the following words:

> As our traditions, our institutions, and even our eccentricities—like live coral—develop and toughen, so the Corps itself develops and toughens.

And remember: whenever a Marine Corps tradition dies, *you* are generally to blame. Traditions are not preserved by books and museums, but by faithful adherence on the part of all hands—*you especially.*

NCO Ranks and Traditions

The oldest known noncommissioned rank with a standard title and standard function is that of the Roman *centurion.* The centurion commanded a "century" (100 men), which was half of a "maniple," the next higher unit in the legion. Vegetius, the leading Roman military writer, wrote a description of the centurion's duties in 378 A.D. that could apply to any company gunnery sergeant or NCO commanding a platoon or squad.

> He is to be vigilant, temperate, active, and readier to execute the orders he receives than to discuss them; strict in exercising and keeping up proper discipline among his soldiers, in obliging them to appear clean and well dressed and in having their arms constantly polished and bright.

501. STAFF NCO RANKS. The grade of *sergeant major* dates back to the 13th century when that title applied to the chief tenant of a knight's military retinue. The grade is peculiar in that it has at various times been applied to commissioned officers as well as NCOs. In the 16th and 17th centuries, the sergeant major was a field officer below the grade of lieutenant colonel, equivalent to major today, who usually performed duties as adjutant. In mid-17th century England under Cromwell, sergeant major was actually a general officer rank equivalent to today's major general. From the 18th century to the present, sergeant major has become the title of the highest NCO grade.

Whether the grade was that of commissioned or noncommissioned officer, the responsibilities of the rank have always been those of superintendence over the organization's drill, discipline, and administration.

In the Marine Corps, the grade was created by Congress in 1798. The first incumbent was Sergeant Major Archibald Summers. For exactly a century, until the Spanish War in 1898, the Corps had but one sergeant major billet (which is the origin of today's post of Sergeant Major of the Marine Corps).

Although the title of *first sergeant* and therefore presumably the function go back in the Corps to 1833, the actual rank originally held by NCOs serving as first sergeants was that of *orderly sergeant,* a grade which was abolished in 1872 in favor of first sergeant.

Master gunnery sergeant and *gunnery sergeant* both stem from the law that expanded the Marine Corps for the War with Spain in 1898, although the more senior rank was not explicitly created until 1935.

Master sergeant, the newest of the Corps's staff NCO ranks, dates from 1946 when the Marine Corps, for reasons which remain obscure, bodily adopted the existing NCO rank-structure then in force for the Army, master sergeant being one of those grades. *Staff sergeant,* also originally an Army rank, was adopted by the Marine Corps in 1923.

502. JUNIOR NCO RANKS. *Sergeant,* like sergeant major, is a very old rank. The title comes from an Old French word, *sergent,* that derives from the Latin, *servientem,* which has among its meanings, "be in service to, be devoted to, work hard for"—which are good descriptions of many a sergeant's duties for the Corps. The rank of sergeant first appeared in 1425 as a person in military service below the rank of knight. By 1548, in the *condottieri* (see Chapter 1), the sergeant had come to be what he is today, an NCO above the grade of corporal. Curiously, in the Marine Corps, sergeant is an older rate than sergeant major. Throughout the Revolutionary War and until 1798, sergeants were the senior NCOs of the Corps.

Corporal is another old rank, dating back to 1529, from the Italian title, *capporale,* meaning an NCO in charge of a body of troops. In 16th century England, the corporal's command—what today we would call a squad—was known as "a corporalship." In the 17th century, a corporal, entitled "Corporal of the Field," could be a commissioned officer like the sergeant major. A corporal of the field served as an aide or staff officer to the 17th century officer-grade sergeants major. Together with sergeant, corporal is one of the two oldest NCO ranks in the Marine Corps.

Lance Corporal results from a marriage of the French word, *lancepessade,* (literally meaning "broken lance" and hence an old soldier who has broken many a lance in combat) to "corporal". At first the rank was simply *lancepesade,* but soon became *lancepesade-corporal,* from which the present title comes, being first recorded in 1611. The Marine Corps has had lance corporals (and, for a time, lance-sergeants, too) since the 1830s, although the rank went out of use between 1930 and 1958, when it was reestablished.

Marine Corps Traditions and Customs
503. GLOBE AND ANCHOR. When the late Major General Smedley Butler (winner of two Medals of Honor) was a lieutenant in the Philippines in 1899, he decided to get himself tattooed.

> I selected an enormous Marine Corps Emblem [wrote Butler] to be tattooed across my chest. It required several sittings and hurt me like the devil, but the finished product was worth the pain. I blazed triumphantly forth, a Marine from throat to waist. The emblem is still with me. Nothing on earth but skinning will remove it.

Butler was somewhat premature in his last sentence. Within less than a year during the storming of the Tartar Wall in Peking, a Chinese bullet struck him in the chest and gouged off part of his emblem. The rest of it accompanied him to the grave forty years later.

Whether you are a private or general is secondary compared to the privilege you share of wearing the emblem. The Globe and Anchor is the most important insigne you have.

The Marine Emblem as we know it today, dates from 1868. It was contributed to the Corps by Brigadier General Jacob Zeilin, 7th Commandant. Until 1840 Marines wore various devices mainly based on the spread eagle or foul anchor. In 1840 two Marine Corps devices were accepted. Both were circled by a laurel wreath, undoubtedly borrowed from the Royal Marines' badge, but one had a foul anchor inscribed inside, while the other bore the letters *USM.* In 1859 a standard center was adopted—a U. S. shield surmounted by a hunting horn within which was the letter *M.* From this time on, the bugle and letter *M* without the shield or laurel wreath were usually worn by Marines on undress uniforms. This type of bugle was the 19th century symbol for light infantry or *jägers*—so called because they were recruited from the ranks of foresters, game-keepers, and poachers, all renowned as skirmishers and riflemen.

In 1868, however, General Zeilin felt that a more distinctive emblem was needed. He chose another device borrowed from the British Marines: the globe.

94

The globe had been conferred on the Royal Marines in 1827 by King George IV. Because it was impossible to recite all the achievements of Marines on the Corps Color, said the King, "the Great Globe itself" was to be their emblem, for Marines had won honor everywhere.

General Zeilin's U. S. Marine globe displayed the Western hemisphere, since the "Royals" had the Eastern hemisphere on theirs. Eagle and foul anchor were added, to leave no doubt that the Corps was both American and maritime.

The Marine Corps seal, designed by General Shepherd, 20th Commandant, was approved by the President in 1954.

504. THE MARINE CORPS SEAL. The official seal of the Corps, designed by General Shepherd, 20th Commandant, consists of the Marine Corps Emblem in bronze with the eagle holding in his beak a scroll inscribed *"Semper Fidelis,"* a scarlet and blue background for the emblem, and the words, *"Department of the Navy"* and *"United States Marine Corps"* encircling the background.

505. MARINE CORPS COLORS. The colors of the Corps are scarlet and gold. Although associated with U. S. Marines for many years, these colors were not officially recognized until General Lejeune became 13th Commandant. Today you will see scarlet and gold throughout Marine posts—on signboards; auto tags; bands-

men's drums, pouches, and trumpet slings; MP brassards; officers' hat-cords and aiguillettes; and, it sometimes seems, everywhere in sight.

In addition to scarlet and gold, forest green enjoys at least semi-official standing as a Marine color. During the years since 1912 when forest green was adopted for the winter service uniform, it has become standard for such equipment as vehicles, weapons, armor, and organizational chests and baggage. In addition, forest green is today the distinguishing color of Marines throughout the world, being worn as a service uniform by the British, Dutch, Korean, and other corps.

Forest green comes from the same source as the light infantry bugle which was once part of the Corps badge. The costume of 18th century huntsmen was forest green. The riflemen recruited from that calling wore green uniforms—a green which survives not only among Marines but also in the uniforms of Britain's Rifle Brigade (the Greenjackets), of India's Ghurkhas, and of elite units of the Finnish Army.

506. THE MARINE CORPS MOTTO. *Semper Fidelis* ("Always Faithful") is the motto of the Corps. That Marines have lived up to this motto is proven by the fact that there has never been a mutiny, or even the thought of one, among U. S. Marines.

Semper Fidelis was adopted about 1883 as the motto of the Corps. Before that, there had been three mottoes, all traditional rather than official. The first, antedating the War of 1812, was *Fortitudine* ("With Fortitude"). The second motto, "By Sea and by Land," was obviously a translation of the Royal Marines' motto *Per Mare, Per Terram.* Until 1848, the third of the Marine Corps' mottoes was, "To the Shores of Tripoli" in commemoration of O'Bannon's capture of Derna in 1805. In 1848 after the return to Washington of the Marine battalion which took part in the capture of Mexico City, this motto was revised to: "From the Halls of the Montezumas to the Shores of Tripoli"—a line now familiar to all Americans. This revision of the Corps motto in Mexico has encouraged speculation that the first stanza of "The Marines' Hymn" was composed by members of the Marine battalion who stormed Chapultepec Castle.

The Marine Corps shares its motto with England's Devonshire Regiment, the 11th Foot, whose sobriquet is "the Bloody Eleventh" and whose motto is also *Semper Fidelis.*

507. MARINES' HYMN AND MARINE CORPS MARCH. "The Marines' Hymn" is what its name implies, the hymn of the Marine Corps. "Semper Fidelis," one of John Philip Sousa's best known works, is the Corps march. Every Marine knows those words of "The Marines' Hymn," the oldest of the official songs of the armed services, and will sing them at the drop of a field hat. The origin of the Hymn is obscure. The words date back into the 19th century, and the author remains unknown. The music comes from an air, "Gendarmes of the Queen," in Jacques Offenbach's opera, *Geneviève de Brabant,* first performed in November 1859. Regardless

of its origin, however, *all Marines get to their feet whenever "The Marines' Hymn" is played or sung.*

"Semper Fidelis" was composed by Sousa in 1888 during his tour as leader of the Marine Band. "Semper Fi" is habitually rendered for parades, reviews, and march-pasts of Marines.

508. BIRTHDAY OF THE CORPS. The Marine Corps was founded by the Continental Congress on 10 November 1775. The resolution which created our Corps reads as follows:

> *Resolved,* That two Battalions of Marines be raised consisting of one Colonel, two lieutenant Colonels, two Majors, & Officers as usual in other regiments, that they consist of an equal number of privates with other battalions; that particular care be taken that no persons be appointed to office, or inlisted into said Battalions, but such as are good seamen, or so acquainted with maritime affairs as to be able to serve to advantage by sea, when required. That they be inlisted and commissioned for and during the present war with Great Britain and the colonies, unless dismissed by order of Congress. That they be distinguished by the names of the first and second battalions of American Marines, and that they be considered as part of the number, which the continental Army before Boston is ordered to consist of.

Chapter 21 of this *Handbook* tells how we celebrate the Marine Corps Birthday. Although the Marine Corps joins the other services each May in observing Armed Forces' Day, November 10th remains the Marines' own day—a day of ceremony, comradeship, and celebration.

509. MARINE CORPS SWORDS. The swords carried by Marine officers and noncommissioned officers go far back into the traditions of the Corps and are among the oldest weapons in continual use in the U.S. Armed Forces.

The sword that officers carry goes back to the *Uniform Regulations* of 1826. Records of the day, however, indicate that swords of this pattern were worn by Marine officers before the War of 1812.

The Mameluke sword of the officers gets its name from the cross-hilt and ivory grip, both of which were used for centuries by the Moslems of North Africa and Arabia. The Marine Corps tradition of carrying this type of sword dates from Lieutenant O'Bannon's assault on Derna, Tripoli in 1805 when he is said to have won the sword of the governor of the town.

The noncommissioned officers' sword is the U.S. Army model sword which was adopted by the Marine Corps in 1859 and briefly carried by Marine officers as well. When officers went back to the Mameluke pattern in 1875, the Army-type sword was retained as a distinctive model for the corps of noncommissioned officers and has been carried by Marine NCOs ever since.

510. "FIRST ON FOOT, AND RIGHT OF THE LINE." Marines form at the place of honor—at the head of column or on right of line—in any naval formation. This privilege was bestowed on the Corps by the Secretary of the Navy on 9 August 1876.

511. "FIRST TO FIGHT." The slogan, "First to Fight," has appeared on Marine recruiting posters ever since World War I.

Marines have been in the forefront of every American war since the founding of the Corps. Marines entered the Revolution in 1775, even before the Declaration of Independence was signed. Before declaration of the War of 1812, Marines helped to defend USS *Chesapeake* against the British. At the outset of hostilities against Mexico, Marines helped to raise California's Bear Flag. In the Civil War, Marines not only captured John Brown at Harper's Ferry but were among the few U. S. regulars who fought in the first Battle of Manassas in 1861. In 1898, Huntington's Fleet Marines were the first U. S. troops to occupy Cuban soil, and Admiral Dewey's Marines were the first to land in the Philippines. Marines were first to land at Veracruz (1914). In World War I, the 5th Marines formed part of the first American Expeditionary Force (AEF) contingent to sail for France. In the second World War, at Pearl Harbor, Ewa, Wake, Midway, Johnston Island, and Guam, Marines formed the ready forefront of our Pacific outpost line. In the Korean War, the first reinforcements to leave continental United States were the 1st Provisional Marine Brigade. The first American troops to land in the Lebanon in 1958 were Marines. At Santo Domingo, in 1965, Marines were again the first to fight, while, in Vietnam, the first U. S. ground unit to be committed to the war was the 3d Marine Division.

On this record of readiness, "First to Fight" constitutes the Marine's pride, responsibility, and challenge.

512. "LEATHERNECKS." The Marines' long-standing nickname, "Leathernecks," goes back to the leather stock, or neckpiece, which was part of the Marine uniform from 1775 to 1875. One historian has written:

> Government contracts usually contained a specification that the stock be of such height that the "chin could turn freely over it," a rather indefinite regulation, and, as one Marine put it, one which the "taylors must have interpreted to mean with the nose pointing straight up."

Although many justifications have been adduced for the leather stock, the truth seems to be that it was intended to insure that Marines kept their heads erect ("up and locked," the aviators would say), a laudable aim in any military organization, any time.

Descended from the stock is the standing collar, hallmark of Marine blues. Like its leather ancestor, the standing collar regulates stance and posture and thus proclaims the wearer as a modern "Leatherneck."

513. SCARLET TROUSER-STRIPE. Officers and NCOs have worn scarlet stripes on dress trousers ever since the early days of the Corps. It is unsubstantiated, even though oft repeated, that the right to wear scarlet stripes was conferred on the Corps as a battle honor after the Mexican war (actually the initial uniform trousers issued after reconstitution of the Corps in 1798 had scarlet piping).

514. HEADGEAR. Two Marine traditions center about headgear.

The *quatrefoil* (the cross-shaped braid atop officers' frame-type "barracks" caps) has been worn ever since 1859. The design, of French origin, is a distinguishing part of the Marine officer's uniform.

The *field hat* was the rugged, picturesque expeditionary headgear of the Corps from 1898 until 1942 and became a universal favorite. As a result, although the hat became outmoded during World War II, General Cates, the 19th Commandant, authorized its use on the rifle range in 1948 and took steps to issue field hats to all medalist shooters in Marine Corps matches. Subsequently, in 1956, General Pate, the 21st Commandant, directed that field hats be worn by all recruit drill instructors, and the hat has become a symbol of Marine Corps recruit training.

515. COLLAR EMBLEMS. Although officers have worn collar emblems since the 1870s, enlisted Marines did not rate this privilege until August 1918 when Franklin D. Roosevelt, then Assistant Secretary of the Navy, visited the 4th Marine Brigade in France, shortly after Belleau Wood. In recognition of the Brigade's victory, Mr. Roosevelt directed on the spot that enlisted Marines would henceforth wear the emblem on their collars.

516. MARINE TALK AND TERMINOLOGY. The 4th Marine Brigade's admired Army commander at Belleau Wood, Lieutenant General James G. Harbord, USA, was quick to note and record the salty Marine way of saying things:

> In the more than a month that the Marine Brigade fought in and around the Bois de Belleau, I got a good opportunity to get the Marine psychology. . . . The habitual Marine address was "Lad" . . . No Marine was ever too old to be a "lad." The Marines never start anywhere: they always "shove off." There were no kitchens: the cooking was done in "galleys." No one ever unfurled a flag—he "broke it out."

Never feel self-conscious about using Marine terms. Require that subordinates use them. Accept no substitutes.

517. THE CANTON BELL. In Quantico hangs a weathered bronze Chinese bell—the "Canton Bell"—cherished gift from the Royal Marines. This bell was taken by "the Royals" after storming the Canton Forts in South China in 1856 and for years occupied a place of honor in Royal Marine officers' mess at Chatham. When Chatham Barracks was decommissioned after World War II, the officers of the mess voted to present their trophy to the U. S. Marines as a symbol of the comradeship between the two corps during this attack and later.

518. "THE PRESIDENT'S OWN." Founded in 1798 (more than a century before the bands of the other three services), the Marine Band has performed at White House functions for every President except George Washington and was especially sponsored by Thomas Jefferson. Because of its traditional privilege of performing at the White House, the band is spoken of as "The President's Own."

The scarlet-coated Marine Band, "The Presidents Own," has played for the White House as our country's history has been made.

President Kennedy epitomized the band's special position when he remarked in 1962, "I find that the only forces which cannot be transferred from Washington without my express permission are the members of the Marine Band, and I want it announced that we propose to hold the White House against all odds, at least for some time to come."

The Marine Band has been present at many of the most memorable and cherished moments in our nation's history, including the dedication of the National Cemetery at Gettysburg when Lincoln gave his immortal address (and his aide-de-camp was Second Lieutenant H. C. Cochrane USMC). Among the band's many traditions, including leadership for twelve years by John Philip Sousa, is its scarlet, full-dress blouse, the only red coat worn by American forces since the Revolutionary War. (In 1956, the Marine Corps Drum and Bugle Corps was likewise granted the privilege of wearing red coats.)

The Marine Band tours the country each fall and has done so ever since Sousa commenced the practice in 1891, although one section of the band always remains in Washington to fulfill its traditional primary mission: "To provide music when directed by the President of the United States, the Congress of the United States, or the Commandant of the Marine Corps."

519. EVENING PARADE. From May through October, a ceremonial Evening Parade is held each Friday evening after nightfall at the Marine Barracks, Eighth and Eye. This colorful ceremony, executed under searchlight illumination, features the Marine Band, Marine Corps Drum and Bugle Corps, a special exhibition drill platoon, and a battalion of Marines from the barracks. Evening Parades were first held in 1957 after a Marine Corps ceremonial detachment participated in the Bermuda International Searchlight Tattoo, and this parade became a fixed Marine Corps custom following similar participation by a larger Marine detachment in the famed Edinburgh Searchlight Tattoo in Scotland in 1958. Evening Parades are open to the public, and any noncommissioned officer who desires to attend with a reasonable number of guests may obtain seats by telephoning the Marine Barracks (OX-3-4484).

520. "AND ST. DAVID." During the Boxer Uprising (1900), at Tientsin and Peking, the Marine battalion in the international relief column was brigaded with the Royal Welch Fusiliers (23d Foot), one of Britain's most renowned regiments. The resulting fellowship between the two organizations is symbolized each year on St. David's Day (1 March, the Welsh national holiday), when the Commandant of the Marine Corps and the Colonel of the Fusiliers exchange by dispatch the traditional watchword of Wales: ". . . *And St. David."*

521. THE COMMANDANT'S LICENSE PLATE. If, in Washington, D.C., you ever bump a car bearing license "1775," climb out of the wreckage at attention. That license plate is set aside for the official sedan of the Commandant of the Marine Corps.

522. RUM ON NEW YEAR'S DAY. Every New Year's Day since 1804, the Marine Band serenades the Commandant at his quarters and receives a tot of hot buttered rum in return. This occasion marks the last surviving issue of "grog" in the armed forces.

523. SHIP'S BELL. All Marine posts (and even some camps in the field) have their ship's bell, usually from a warship no longer in commission. This bell is mounted at the base of the flagpole, and

"Corporal" Chesty III, an English bulldog, holds the billet of Marine Corps mascot.

the field music of the guard has the duty, between reveille and taps, of striking the bells—and also of keeping the bell in a high polish.

524. LAST TO LEAVE THE SHIP. Marines are always or should be the last—other than the ship's captain—to leave a ship being abandoned or put out of commission. Although the tradition is an old one, it first appears in *Navy Regulations* of 1865:

> When a vessel is to be put out of commission, the Marine officer with the guard shall remain on board until all the officers and crew are detached and the ship regularly turned over to the officers of the Navy Yard or station.

525. SWAGGER STICKS. The swagger stick (which may be carried optionally by all officers and NCOs) originated in the British Army and goes as far back as 1790. In the Marine Corps, the stick came into vogue in the later 19th century and was virtually a required article of uniform until World War I. The origin of the swagger stick lay in the whips or batons carried by mounted officers of the 18th century.

526. MARINE CORPS MASCOT. The English bulldog has become a traditional Marine Corps mascot. This image probably dates from World War I when it is said that German soldiers referred to Marines as "Devil Dogs." The phrase was used in the press as a soubriquet for Marines from Belleau Wood on. After the war, an English bulldog, named "Sergeant Major Jiggs", was presented to General Lejeune, 13th Commandant. From that time on, an English bulldog, assigned rank as earned, has served at Eighth and Eye and participated in ceremonies as mascot of the Corps. The present incumbent's name of "Chesty" not only refers to his bulldog build but, of course, to a distinguished, hard-fighting retired general officer who gained his stars from the ranks.

527. "TELL IT TO THE MARINES!" In his book, *Fix Bayonets!*, Captain John W. Thomason, Jr. gives the generally accepted version of the origin of "Tell it to the Marines!."

> They relate of Charles II that at Whitehall a certain sea-captain, newly returned from the Western Ocean, told the King of flying fish, a thing never heard in old England. The King and court were vastly amused. But, the naval fellow persisting, the Merry Monarch beckoned to a lean, dry colonel of the sea regiment, with seamed mahogany face, and said, in effect: "Colonel, this tarry-breeks here makes sport with us stay-at-homes. He tells of a miraculous fish that foresakes its element and flies like a bird over the water." "Sire," said the colonel of Marines, "he tells a true thing. I myself have often seen those fish in your Majesty's seas around Barbados—" "Well," decided Charles, "such evidence cannot be disputed. And hereafter, when we hear a strange thing, we will tell it to the Marines, for the Marines go everywhere and see everything, and if they say it is so, we will believe it."

This yarn (for such it is) was for many years credited to Samuel Pepys, although scholars disclaimed it. On the other hand, the phrase, "Tell it to the Marines," is an old one and can be found in print as early as 1726.

528. AT DIVINE SERVICE. When attending divine service in uniform, or present in uniform at an occasion when prayer is offered (as at a military funeral), uncover (if not already done) and assume the *old* pre-1939 position of "Parade Rest without Arms," i.e., right foot carried six inches to the rear, left knee slightly bent, weight equally distributed on both feet; hands clasped without constraint in front of the center of the body, left hand uppermost—and in the case of prayer, head slightly bowed. This position enables you to appear reverent and military at the same time, and was used as the traditional position for prayer at sea throughout the Old Navy.

529. CONDUCT IN ACTION. Over and above the competence, resolution, and courage which are expected of every Marine in battle, it is particularly expected that no wounded or dead Marine will ever be left on the field or unattended, regardless of the cost of bringing him in. As for surrender, the Marine Corps code is that expressed by Napoleon:

> There is but one honorable mode of becoming prisoner of war. This is, by being taken separately; by which is meant, by being cut off entirely, and when we can no longer make use of our arms.

In the Korean War, whereas many thousand American troops surrendered, only 221 Marines were taken by the enemy. Their steadfast, disciplined, and faithful behavior in communist prison-camps earned the Corps special commendation in the Senate's 1956 investigation of Korean prisoner-of-war scandals.

530. MARINE CORPS MUSEUMS. "The scrapbook of the Marine Corps," as it is sometimes described, is the Marine Corps Museum at Quantico. No summary of the traditions of the Corps would be complete without mention of this collection of awards, battle honors, historical flags, and other objects of lasting sentimental significance to the Marine Corps. The Museum collection documents Marine Corps history from 1775 to the present day. On display are uniforms, weapons, artifacts, equipment, prints, and paintings giving tangible substance to the proud traditions of the Corps. Included among numerous historical flags, for example, are the famous Colors raised by the 28th Marines atop Suribachi Yama on Iwo Jima. The weapons collection is one of the finest in the world and is backed up by over 55,000 documents covering design, patent data, and test reports on machine guns and automatic weapons alone. Every Marine should be thoroughly familiar with this museum, which ranks among the best military and naval museums in the United States. In addition to the museum at Quantico, there is an excellent Post Museum at Parris Island, and in Philadelphia, in New Hall, a restored building from pre-Revolutionary days, may be found an outstanding collection of material dealing with the early days of the Corps and its origins in Pennsylvania.

531. MARINE CORPS MEMORIAL CHAPEL, QUANTICO. The Post Chapel at Quantico serves, in addition to its regular functions, as the Memorial Chapel of the Marine Corps. Here is kept a "Book of Remembrance" listing the name, rank, and date of death for Marines and members of the Navy serving with the Marine Corps who have given their lives in action. For the time being, the Book of Remembrance begins with Vietnam, but it is planned to extend it back, eventually to include by name every Marine or eligible Navy man recorded as killed in action since the Revolution.

Colors, Flags, and Standards

532. COLORS, FLAGS, AND STANDARDS. A recruit once asked his drill instructor, "Sergeant, who carries the Flag in battle?"

Came the unhesitating reply, "Son, *every* Marine carries the Flag in battle!"

As the soldier's proverb says, "The Flag is a jealous mistress," and any Marine will fight and die rather than permit the National Colors or a Marine Corps Color to be dishonored.

Colors or standards must never fall into enemy hands. If capture seems inevitable, they should be burned. Unserviceable colors or standards, or those from disbanded units, are delivered to the Marine Corps Supply Activity, Philadelphia. The latter in turn forwards flags of historical value to the Marine Corps Museum, which is the Corps repository for historical flags, as well as for flags and war trophies captured by Marines. Soiled, torn, or badly frayed flags, if not historical, are destroyed privately by burning.

533. TYPES OF FLAGS. Marine Corps terms which deal with flags are precise and particular. As a noncommissioned officer, you must learn to distinguish the various kinds of flags and to speak of them in the correct terminology.

National Color or Standard: This is the American flag. When the flag is displayed over Marine or Navy posts, stations, or ships, its official title is the *National Ensign.* The national flag carried by Marine organizations is made of silk or nylon and is called the *National Color* (*except* when borne by a mounted, mechanized, motorized, or aviation unit, when its title becomes the *National Standard*). This technical distinction between a *color* and a *standard* also applies to the battle colors and organization colors described in the following paragraphs.

The National Color is carried on all occasions of ceremony when two or more companies of a unit are present. When not in the hands of troops, the National Color is entrusted to the adjutant. With the Marine Corps Color (discussed below), the National Color is usually displayed in the office or before the tent of the commanding officer. Whenever the National Color is carried in the open, it is escorted by a *color guard* composed of selected Marines, and the Color itself is borne by an outstanding NCO, the *color sergeant.*

The national Ensign, displayed over ships and shore stations, comes in three sizes. These are:

1. *Post flag:* size 10 by 19 feet, flown in fair weather except on Sundays and national holidays;
2. *Storm flag:* size 5 by 9 feet 6 inches, flown during foul weather;
3. *Garrison flag:* size 20 by 38 feet, flown on Sundays and national holidays as provided in the *Marine Corps Flag Manual* (but never from a flagpole shorter than 65 feet).

For more information on display of the National Color or Ensign, turn to *Navy Regulations,* and *Marine Corps Flag Manual.*

Marine Corps Colors and Standards: The Commandant issues to every major Marine unit or organization a distinguishing flag which is carried beside the National Color. These unit flags are called *Marine Corps Colors* (or Standards). A Marine Corps Color bears the emblem and motto of the Corps and the unit title and follows the color scheme of the Corps, scarlet and gold.

The Marine Corps Color of a Fleet Marine Force unit is called the unit *Battle Color;* the Color authorized for an organization in the Supporting Establishment (such as a Marine Barracks) is called the *Organization Color.* No unit smaller than a separate battalion or regiment receives a Battle Color, nor does a temporary or provisional unit receive one unless specially authorized by the Commandant.

Certain organized units of the Marine Corps Reserve are likewise authorized to carry Organizational Flags of the type just described, but bearing a Reserve designation.

Guidons: These are small rectangular flags, made in the Marine Corps colors, carried by companies, batteries, or detachments, or used as marker flags for ceremonies. *Organization guidons* carry the Marine Corps emblem and the title of the unit. *Dress guidons* (used as markers) simply bear the initials "USMC."

A COMPANY, SECOND MARINES

H&S COMPANY, SECOND BATTALION, EIGHTH MARINES

A COMPANY, HEADQUARTERS BATTALION, HQMC

RST GUARD COMPANY, MARINE BARRACKS, GHTH AND I STREETS, WASHINGTON, D.C.

MARINE BARRACKS, ANNAPOLIS

MARINE DETACHMENT, USS *SPRINGFIELD*

Fig. 5-2. Lettering and design of typical organizational guidons.

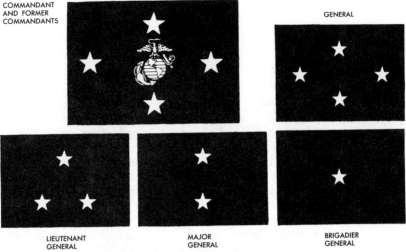

Fig. 5-3: General officers' distinguishing flags.

Personal Flags: Every active general officer in command displays a *personal flag.* Marine Corps personal flags consist of a scarlet field with white stars according to the general officer's rank, arranged in the same manner as the stars on Navy personal flags. Regulations governing personal flags are in *Navy Regulations* and *Marine Corps Flag Manual.*

Miscellaneous Flags: In addition to the ceremonial flags just described, the Corps employs several miscellaneous flags and pennants described in *Marine Corps Flag Manual.* Examples are:

Geneva Convention flag	Sanitary cordon flag
Church pennant	Recruiting flag

534. APPURTENANCES OF FLAGS. The appurtenances of Marine colors, standards, flags, and guidons are:

Streamers	Tassels
Bands	Staff ornaments
Cords	

Streamers denote participation in combat or award of a collective citation or decoration conferred on the unit as a whole.

A *silver band* is attached to the staff of a Marine Corps Color or Standard for each streamer awarded.

When the unit or organization does not rate streamers or bands, a *cord and tassel,* woven in the Corps colors, is substituted.

The heads of staffs bear the following *staff ornaments:*

Colors and standards:	silver lance head
Personal flag:	silver halberd
Guidon:	plain silver cap

535. BATTLE COLOR OF THE MARINE CORPS. The Corps as a whole has one Battle Color entitled *The Battle Color of the Marine Corps*. This Color is entrusted to the senior post of the Corps, Marine Barracks, Eighth and Eye Streets, Washington. Attached to it are all the battle honors, citations, battle streamers, and silver bands which the Corps has won since 1775. Up to July of 1969, these honors were the following:

Presidential Unit Citation Streamer with four silver stars and one bronze star
Navy Unit Commendation Streamer with five silver stars and two bronze stars
Army Distinguished Unit Streamer with four oak-leaf clusters
Revolutionary War Streamer
War of 1812 Streamer
Indian Wars Streamer
Mexican War Streamer
Civil War Streamer
Marine Corps Expeditionary Streamer with eleven silver stars, four bronze stars, and one silver "W"
Spanish-American War Streamer
Philippine Campaign Streamer
China Relief Expedition Streamer
Cuban Pacification Streamer
Nicaraguan Campaign Streamer
Mexican Service Streamer
Haitian Campaign Streamer with one bronze star
Dominican Campaign Streamer
World War I Victory Streamer with one silver star
Army of Occupation of Germany Streamer
Second Nicaraguan Campaign Streamer
Yangtze Service Streamer
China Service Streamer with one bronze star
American Defense Service Streamer with one bronze star
Asiatic-Pacific Campaign Streamer with eight silver stars and one bronze star
American Campaign Streamer
European-African-Middle East Campaign Streamer with one silver star and four bronze stars
World War II Victory Streamer
Navy Occupation Service Streamer with Asia and Europe Clasps
National Defense Service Streamer with one bronze star
Korean Service Streamer with two silver stars
Armed Forces Expeditionary Streamer with one silver and one bronze star
Vietnam Service Streamer with one silver star and four bronze stars.
Philippine Defense Streamer with one star
Philippine Liberation Streamer with two stars
Philippine Independence Streamer

French Croix de Guerre Streamer (Fourragère) with two palms and
one gilt star

Republic of Korea Presidential Unit Citation Streamer.

Decorations, Medals, and Unit Citations

536. DECORATIONS AND MEDALS. "A soldier will fight long
and hard for a bit of colored ribbon," said Napoleon, who originated
the awarding of personal decorations.

Napoleon's conqueror, the Duke of Wellington, in turn introduced
all-hands campaign medals, the first of which went to British troops
who fought at Waterloo.

Both Wellington and Napoleon realized that decorations and
medals not only express national gratitude to individuals but stimu-
late emulation and *esprit* in battles to come.

Today, Marine Corps awards fall into three classes: personal and
unit decorations; commemorative, campaign, and service medals;
and marksmanship badges and trophies. The *Navy and Marine Corps
Awards Manual* gives details on all these, together with guidance for
anyone who wishes to originate a recommendation that an award
be made.

537. PERSONAL AND UNIT DECORATIONS. The United
States, despite the limitations in Article I, Section 9, of the Constitution, confers numerous military decorations. These range from the
Medal of Honor at the top to the Naval Reserve Medal in junior
position. In order of precedence, these personal or unit decorations
are:

★ Medal of Honor (Navy)
★ Medal of Honor (Army and Air Force)
‡★ Marine Corps Brevet Medal
★ Navy Cross
★ Distinguished Service Cross (Army)
★ Air Force Cross
  Distinguished Service Medal (Navy)
  Distinguished Service Medal (Army and Air Force)
★ Silver Star Medal
† Legion of Merit
† Distinguished Flying Cross
* Navy and Marine Corps Medal
* Soldiers' Medal (Army)
* Airmens' Medal (Air Force)
† Bronze Star Medal
† Air Medal
  Joint Services Commendation Medal
† Navy Commendation Medal
† Navy Achievement Medal
† Commendation Medal (Army and Air Force)
  Purple Heart
  Combat Action Ribbon
‡ Specially Meritorious Medal

★ Presidential Unit Citation
★ Distinguished Unit Emblem (Army and Air Force)
† Navy Unit Commendation
Meritorious Unit Commendation
* Gold Lifesaving Medal (Treasury Department award)
* Silver Lifesaving Medal (Treasury Department award)
Marine Corps Reserve Special Commendation Ribbon
Marine Corps Good Conduct Medal
Navy Good Conduct Medal
Army and Air Force Good Conduct Medal
Coast Guard Good Conduct Medal
Organized Marine Corps Reserve Medal
Naval Reserve Medal

(★) Awarded for heroism only.
(†) Awarded for either heroic or meritorious acts.
(*) Awarded for heroism not in combat.
(‡) No longer awarded.

Among the foregoing, the *Medal of Honor* rates special mention. The Medal of Honor is the highest decoration conferred by the United States. Ordinarily, you can win it only for gallantry and intrepidity in combat, at the risk of your life, above and beyond the call of duty. Since the Civil War, when the award was created, more than 250 Medals of Honor have been won by U. S. Marines.

On attaining the age of 40, winners of the Medal of Honor are eligible for a special pension of $100 per month. In addition, if you hold the Medal of Honor, you are entitled to have your son(s) appointed to Annapolis, to West Point or to the Air Force Academy. You may also travel without charge in U. S. armed forces aircraft. It is a tradition (though not officially recognized) that all hands salute a Medal of Honor man, regardless of rank.

538. UNIT DECORATIONS. All U. S. unit decorations, or "unit citations," as well as several foreign unit citations, have been won by Marine Corps units. If you are a member of an organization when it wins a collective citation, you are thereafter entitled to wear the citation ribbon or device as a personal decoration.

The *French Fourragère* is the senior unit award (and first collective award) won by Marines. The Fourragère dates from Napoleon's time; it was awarded to the 4th Marine Brigade in 1918 in lieu of awarding all hands the Croix de Guerre. The green and scarlet cord of the Fourragère may still be seen on the left shoulders of members of the 5th and 6th Marines, and of a few remaining Marines who were present when the 4th Brigade won the award.

The *Presidential Unit Citation* is the highest Navy and Marine Corps unit award. It was also the first American collective award, having been personally instituted by President Franklin D. Roosevelt as a citation for the defenders of Wake (1st Defense Battalion and Marine Fighting Squadron 211) in December 1941. The Presidential

Unit Citation is considered to represent unit attainments which would warrant award of the Navy Cross if the recipient were an individual.

The *Distinguished Unit Emblem* is the Army and Air Force collective citation roughly equivalent to the Presidential Unit Citation. The Distinguished Unit Emblem has been awarded to several Marine ground and aviation units on detached service with the Army or Air Force.

The *Navy Unit Commendation* ranks next, in the naval service, after the Presidential Unit Citation. Unlike the latter, however, the Navy Unit Commendation may be won by extremely meritorious service in support of, but not participation in, combat operations. When awarded for combat performance, the Navy Unit Commendation is comparable to the Silver Star Medal for an individual; for noncombat meritorious service, this commendation is comparable to the Legion of Merit for an individual.

The *Meritorious Unit Commendation* ranks after the Presidential Unit Citation and the Navy Unit Commendation. It is awarded only for meritorious, as distinct from heroic, unit performance.

539. CAMPAIGN MEDALS. Campaign or service medals are issued to all hands who take part in particular campaigns or periods of service for which a medal is authorized. In addition to medals for specific campaigns, Marines may be awarded the *Marine Corps Expeditionary Medal* for service ashore on foreign soil in operations against opposition, for which no other campaign medal is authorized, such as the one for Cuba (3 January 1961 to 23 October 1962) and the one for Thailand (16 May 1962 to 10 August 1963). Or, for similar joint operations in which the Army or Air Force may be involved, the *Armed Forces Expeditionary Medal* may be substituted. Campaign medals are often embellished by clasps or bronze stars which denote participation in specific battles or phases of the campaign.

In addition to campaign and service medals, certain *commemorative medals* have been struck to commemorate noncombat but notable achievements, such as polar and antarctic expeditions or pioneer flights.

540. INITIATING AN AWARD. One of your responsibilities as a combat leader is to see that your men are promptly recommended for awards you believe they have earned. During active operations, it is usual for every FMF unit, from battalion up, to maintain a *board of awards*. The board evaluates and passes on recommendations for decorations which originate within the organization, but you must see that the board of awards receives recommendations promptly and that the recommendations are accurately stated in whatever form may be required by standing operating procedure for awards.

Few leadership derelictions are more reprehensible than failure to submit proper recommendations for awards. To see the award fail because you were too lazy to recommend it in the right form and with the detailed information required is one sure way of destroying the morale of your people.

Standard Marine Corps procedure for initiating awards is described in the *Navy and Marine Corps Awards Manual*. Before you make a recommendation, check this reference, especially the article which tells how to use Marine Corps *combat award recommendation cards*.

541. WEARING YOUR DECORATIONS AND MEDALS. The Marine Corps has strict rules which govern the wearing of decorations and medals. These rules are in the *Marine Corps Uniform Regulations*.

Subject to regulations, you may now accept awards from foreign nations. (Until 1966, such acceptance was prohibited except by special Congressional authorization.) However, as in the past, awards worth more than $50 still must be turned over to the Commandant of the Marine Corps, for retention by the Department of State pending Congressional approval. Also, persons on duty in connection with the military assistance program may not accept awards from foreign host countries.

When medals are prescribed instead of ribbons, all unit citations and other ribbons for which a medal has not been struck will be worn centered on the *right* breast.

Marines with eight or more ribbons of any type should wear them in rows of four rather than three, thus avoiding a top-heavy stack. Ribbons are worn one-eighth inch above top edge of pocket (one-eighth inch above badges when worn); the left edge of ribbon bars must always be in a true vertical. Large medals may not be worn more than seven per single row; and miniatures, not more than 10.

With every U. S. decoration (and many foreign ones, too) you receive a lapel device for wear with civilian clothes. This may be worn in the left lapel of your civilian suit when you think fit.

Decorations and medals are part of your uniform and must be worn, *except* that, when ribbons are prescribed for the shirt, you are only required to display personal decorations and unit citations; the wearing of campaign ribbons is optional.

Marksmanship badges may be prescribed for any uniform, but it is not customary to wear these badges when medals are prescribed. Nor can you wear *any* ribbon (such as Navy marksmanship ribbons) in lieu of a marksmanship or gunnery badge. Incidentally, you are limited to a ceiling of three badges of your choice, if you rate more than three.

When soiled, faded, frayed, or otherwise unserviceable, the ribbons of decorations and medals should be destroyed by burning, not thrown away, because burning prevents reuse by unauthorized persons, and because these ribbons symbolize the bravery, devotion, and sacrifice of U. S. Marines.

Even though entitled to wear foreign decorations or medals, you must always display at least one U. S. medal or award at the same time. And remember that foreign awards take precedence *after* U. S. awards.

In heraldry, the senior, and therefore most honored, of colors is blue. This means that in the Presidential Unit Citation the blue stripe is always up, and on the ribbon for the Navy and Marine Corps Medal the blue stripe is inboard (i.e., on the wearer's right).

The precedence, from right to left and top to bottom in which classes of decorations and medals are worn is:

Personal U. S. military decorations
U. S. unit awards
Personal U. S. nonmilitary decorations
U. S. campaign medals
Personal foreign military decorations
Foreign unit awards
Foreign campaign or service medals.

A well dressed soldier has more respect for himself.

—Joseph Joubert, 1754–1824

6   Uniforms, Clothing and Insignia

Marines have long been known for their soldierly appearance, military smartness, and distinctive uniforms. What has maintained that reputation has been unceasing emphasis on correct wearing of the uniform, careful supervision (by noncommissioned officers especially), and the pride of individual Marines.

It is up to you, as a noncommissioned officer, 24 hours a day, on duty and off, to help uphold the Marine Corps reputation for smart, soldierly appearance.

Marine Corps Uniform Regulations is the bible on uniforms, insignia, and grooming. You must:

Know those *Regulations,*
Set the example by rigid compliance, and
Enforce them meticulously.

In addition to *Uniform Regulations, Individual Clothing Regulations* list the articles of uniform which every enlisted Marine must maintain at all times. Figure 6-1 of this *Handbook* provides a table showing the types and combinations of uniforms authorized for enlisted Marines.

History of the Uniform

601. EARLY MARINE UNIFORMS. When the Continental Marines were organized in 1775, the uniform consisted of green coats with white facings, white waistcoats, white breeches, short black gaiters called "spatterdashes," and round felt hats. Every Marine, officer and enlisted, wore a leather stock, or neckpiece, from which we still have our nickname "Leathernecks." In 1798 after the Corps was re-formed, Marine uniforms were Army surplus clothing remaining after disbandment of Wayne's Legion—blue coat, scarlet vest, tight blue trousers called "overalls," with thin scarlet stripes.

The sergeant of 1825 wore a blue coatee (blouse) with yellow stripe and scarlet collar and white (summer) or gray (winter) trousers.

In 1804, the first *Uniform Regulations* were issued, providing again for white trousers and changing the headgear to the shako with pompon worn during the War of 1812. The importance of non-commissioned officer supervision of uniforms in "The Old Corps" is shown in this extract from the 1804 regulations.

> Each NCO charged with a Squad shall be held responsible for their Dress and good appearance & that the men may appear on Parade clean and properly dressed & in good uniform, and a Non Com. Officer is appointed to each Room who half an hour before the Parade is to turn the men out of their rooms, their hair dressed and powdered, their clothing and accoutrements clean, their arms in good order. The Sergeant Major is then to inspect; he is not to suffer a man to go on Parade who is not fit for the inspection & it is expected he will report those NCOs who are negligent in this duty.

The flour used to powder the troops' hair for inspection was apparently no treat for users, as an 1805 requisition calls for "1 barrel of *sour* flour for powdering."

It was not until 1822 that NCO chevrons were introduced; until 1830 captains and lieutenants wore chevrons, too. Four years later, the handsome blue, white, and scarlet uniforms were shelved for green coatees with buff facings and for grey trousers with buff stripes for officers and NCOs. This color combination lasted only a few years, however; and, in 1839, the traditional Marine colors of blue, white and scarlet were restored.

The 1839 uniform was a blue coatee with red piping, standing collar and leather stock, and white crossbelt. In summer troops wore white trousers; in winter, sky-blue trousers (with scarlet stripes for officers and NCOs). Then as now, the Marine Band rated red coats, as did all field musics. Except for changes in cut and of course in headgear and accessories, the 1839 uniforms are the blues of today.

During the Civil War, Marines made up in uniform what they lacked in numbers. While the service uniform was virtually a copy of the Army's, the dress uniform was an eye-catcher. Even privates wore gold epaulettes, white crossbelts, and high-crowned round hats complete with scarlet pompon and dress-cap emblems as big as salad plates. This uniform lasted until 1875, when not only was the leather stock abolished (after exactly 100 years) but the Corps shifted over to blue or white spiked helmets, an all-white tropical uniform with standing collar, and the first field uniform, made of coarse grey material called "cheesecloth," to be worn with Army-pattern blue flannel shirts.

602. TWENTIETH CENTURY UNIFORMS. When war was declared on Spain in 1898, it was obvious that dress blue blouses and spiked helmets were not appropriate for field service in Cuba and the Philippines. Within three weeks after outbreak of war, the

The NCO sentry of the 1850s wore his dress blues with standing collar, light-blue trousers, and scarlet trouser stripes.

Depot of Supplies at Philadelphia had designed and produced sufficient brown linen khaki uniforms to fit out the Corps and had obtained from the Army, brown felt campaign hats. After the war, a less hastily designed version of this combination, with standing collar, became the standard field uniform of the Marine Corps, while, in 1912, a forest green uniform was adopted for winter field service. Though somewhat different in cut and with very large NCO chevrons almost twice today's size, the dress uniforms of this period were, in general, those we still have today.

During World War I, the Marines who went to France were required to wear Army OD uniforms and wrapped cloth spiral puttees. Once back home, however, they resumed the standard combinations of blues, khakis, and greens. Khaki, the standard field uniform, was that in which the Corps campaigned in Haiti, Nicaragua, and Santo

The Sergeant Major of the Marine Corps in 1859 wore his full-dress blues.

Spiked helmets were the standard headgear for Marines from 1875 on. The first sergeant is wearing today's NCO sword.

Domingo. In fact, khaki was the field uniform for most of the Marine units which fought in the Pacific after outbreak of war in 1941. By the end of 1942, the green utility uniform and field shoes had been adopted, and both khaki and the felt field hat were superseded.

With the arrival of utilities (and, during the Korean War, of special winter clothing for cold-weather service), the basic outfit of Marine Corps uniforms had reached, by 1950, virtually what it is today, except for the requirement imposed on the Corps during the 1960s to change to black leather from its traditional cordovan brown. These uniforms are well adapted to all types of service at sea, in the field, and in garrison ashore. They have served Marines well and are widely recognized and admired by the American public. So is the Marine inside them.

In 1912, the field, khaki, cold-weather, and undress uniforms looked like this.

603. GENERAL RULES. Here are important rules which govern wearing of uniforms:

1. Uniforms designed to be buttoned *will be worn buttoned.*
2. Wear headgear whenever under arms or on watch, except when in a space where a meal is being served or divine service is being conducted, when in quarters (if on watch), or when specifically excused from remaining covered. Remain covered at all times when out-of-doors or on topside spaces aboard ship.
3. "Mixed uniform" (components of two different uniforms, worn simultaneously—blue blouse and utility trousers, for example) is strictly forbidden unless specifically authorized in *Uniform Regulations.*
4. *Blue Dress A* (*Blues with medals*) is prescribed for parades, reviews, and ceremonies or official social occasions of formality, importance, or high honor. *Blue Dress B* (*Blues with ribbons*) is required when a man reports for duty at sea or when the commander so prescribes, for the ceremonies and occasions listed above. In addition, Blue Dress B is always the preferred liberty uniform for any U. S. Marine. Dress uniforms should be worn on formal evening occasions when civilian full dress is prescribed (such as the Marine Corps Birthday Ball) or worn on semiformal evening occasions. Dress A or B as appropriate will be prescribed for official or military-sponsored affairs, either formal or semiformal. Any evening function which you attend as a representative of the Corps is one for dress uniform. Blues should always be prescribed for evening affairs when foreign military personnel, visiting noncommissioned officers of other services, or distinguished civilians are to be present.

Note: Neither "white-blue-whites" are authorized for social occasions, leave, or liberty; nor is Blue Dress C ("Seagoing").

5. *Service Uniform,* as appropriate to the season and location, will be worn when reporting for duty ashore and on such other occasions as prescribed. Winter Service C (greens without blouse) and Summer Service B (cotton khaki) are essentially duty uniforms and will not be worn off-post except for the purpose of going to and from home. Neither may be worn on liberty, except that hospital patients may wear Summer Service B if no other uniform is immediately available.
6. Utilities may be worn only in field work, or when it is obviously impracticable to wear service uniform. *Utilities may not be worn between home and place of duty, off Government reservations, except as specified in local regulations.*
7. You must obtain and maintain in good condition all articles of clothing prescribed in *Individual Clothing Regulations.* However, because noncommissioned officers must set a very high example of military bearing, neatness, and appearance, you should

118

Fig. 6-1: Types and combinations of uniforms for enlisted Marines.

Uniform (l)	Headgear	Blouse	Belt (Blouse)	Shirt
Blue Dress A	Dress	Blue	Blue White (a)	—
Blue Dress B	Dress	Blue	Blue White (a) (f)	—
Blue Dress C ("Seagoing")	Dress	—		Khaki Tropical (g
Blue/White Dress A	Dress	Blue	White	—
Blue/White Dress B	Dress	Blue	White	—
Winter Service A	Service or Garrison (i)	Green	Green	Khaki (h) (j)
Winter Service B	Service or Garrison (i)	—	—	Khaki (h) (j)
Summer Service A	Service or Garrison (i)(trop)	—	—	Khaki Tropical (h) (m)
Summer Service B	Garrison (cotton)	—	—	Khaki Cotton (h) (m)

a. Dress white belt always worn with blues on occasions of duty or ceremony and may be prescribed for liberty.
b. With web trouser belt and brass buckle.
c. Black leather gloves will always be worn or carried with overcoat or raincoat in winter months.
d. May be prescribed.
e. Dependent on weather.
f. Commanders may prescribe white belt for wear with blues on leave or liberty.
g. During summer, COs may prescribe khaki shirt, quarter-length sleeve, with blue trousers as uniform of the day. This combination will not be worn in ceremonies, parades, on leave or liberty, or other occasions when the blouse would be appropriate.
h. With field scarf and clasp.
i. As prescribed in *Uniform Regulations* and in local orders.
j. Either cotton or tropical garrison.
k. Green scarf is an optional item for wear with the overcoat or raincoat.
l. Black shoes and socks will be worn with all uniform combinations prescribed herein.
m. Khaki shirt with quarter-length sleeve may be prescribed.

Trousers	Gloves	Raincoat Overcoat	Emblems	Medals	Badges	(n) Ribbons	Sword
Blue	White Black (c)	Raincoat Overcoat (d) (e)	Dress	Large	(i) (o)	—	(d)
Blue	White Black (c)	Raincoat Overcoat (d) (e)	Dress	—	(d) (o)	yes	(d)
Blue (b)	(c)	Raincoat Overcoat (d) (e)	Dress	—	(d) (o)	yes	(d)
White	White	Raincoat Overcoat (d) (e)	Dress	Large	(d) (o)	—	(d)
White	White	Raincoat Overcoat (d) (e)	Dress	—	(d) (o)	yes	(d)
Green	(c)	Raincoat Overcoat (d) (e)	Service	—	(d) (o)	yes	(d)
Green (b)	(c)	Raincoat Overcoat (d) (e)	—	—	(d)	(d)	(d)
Khaki Tropical (b)	—	Raincoat (d) (e)	—	—	(d) (o)	yes	(d)
Khaki Cotton (b)	—	Raincoat (d) (e)	—	—	(d)	(d)	(d)

n. Aviation parachutist insignia will be worn as prescribed in *Uniform Regulations.*

o. Optional

Note: As of this printing, khaki summer service uniforms are being phased out. Staff NCO white mess and blue evening dress jackets are being phased in. Detailed instructions as to resulting new uniform combinations will be provided in the next edition of this Handbook.

Effective 1 May 1972, staff-NCO ornamented waist-plate required with dress white belt for staff sergeants and above.

possess enough extra uniforms to allow for frequent changes in some circumstances as often as several times a day. All uniforms must be serviceable, that is, no frayed collars or cuffs on shirts, no spots or visible mending on any part of the uniform, no patches; clothing should be properly fitted, and the trousers should be of correct length. You must keep your full assignment of uniforms with you at all times except when in the field.

8. All staff NCOs have the privilege of wearing officer-type summer and winter service uniforms on leave, on liberty, and in garrison, but not in formation with troops. Sergeants major and master gunnery sergeants may wear such uniforms at all times, however; and those who maintain officer-type uniforms do not have to maintain equivalent issue uniforms.

9. The law prohibits anyone not in the armed forces from wearing the uniform or any distinctive part thereof (Act of 3 June 1916, Sec. 125 as amended). This does not apply to honorably discharged Marines, who may continue to bear the title and, on occasions of military ceremony, to wear the uniform of highest rank held during war service.

10. Wearing of the uniform by discharged or retired Marines is specifically prohibited in connection with nonmilitary business or commercial activities, at meetings or demonstrations of any organization on the Attorney General's subversive list, and under any circumstances that would bring discredit to the uniform or the Corps.

11. No Marine (including retired or reserve personnel) may wear uniform while attending (unless in a duty capacity) or participating in a demonstration, assembly, or activity the purpose of which is furtherance of personal or partisan views on political, social, economic or religious issues. In other words, *demonstrations and the Marine Corps uniform don't mix.*

If after retirement or transfer to the Fleet Reserve you are employed by a military school or the Marine Corps Junior ROTC as an instructor, you may wear your Marine Corps uniform and rank insignia, but no school or other unauthorized insignia, patches, etc., may be worn. To qualify for this privilege, however, you must have written permission from the Commandant of the Marine Corps (Code AJB).

604. UNIFORM ACCESSORIES. The following rules concern the wearing of uniform accessories.

1. *Belts* are worn with buckle centered. Belt buckles and brass tips (except on 782 equipment) must be brightly polished. On the web belt, the tip must extend two to four inches past the buckle; on the green cloth belt, the tip must extend $2\frac{3}{4}$ to $3\frac{3}{4}$ inches.

2. *Leather gloves* may be worn or carried with the winter service uniform, without overcoat or raincoat, at the option of the indi-

vidual. Gloves are required with winter service when wearing overcoat or raincoat. Local commanders designate whether gloves will be worn by troops in formation.

3. With the exception of staff NCOs, all enlisted men must wear issue *footgear*. Dress shoes are worn with all uniforms except utilities. Staff NCOs are required to wear issue footgear when in formation, but may wear officer-type black dress shoes (but not chukka or monk straps) at other times. No double soles or taps are permitted. You should possess at least two pairs of *combat boots*—one highly shined for inspections and ceremonials, the other for PT and field work.

4. *Chevrons* should be positioned so that the tip or point is up and should be centered on the outer half of the sleeve, four inches from the shoulder seam (three inches for SgtMaj/MGySgt and 1stSgt/MSgt), except on the short-sleeve shirt where it is midway between the shoulder and the bottom edge of the sleeve. *Hashmarks* should be centered on the outer half of the sleeve, one-half inch above the point of the cuff (overcoat and blouse) at an angle of 30 degrees.

5. Marines may not wear *jewelry, fobs, pens, or pencils* exposed on the uniform, except:

   Wrist watch
   Regulation tie-clasp
   Rings (conservative pattern)
   Sunglasses (conservative design—but may not be worn in line with troops).

6. You wear the regulation black *mourning band* on your left arm between shoulder and elbow:

   When a pallbearer or a body escort or when attending a military funeral in an official capacity,
   During prescribed official mourning, and
   For family mourning (optional).

7. *Swords* may be prescribed only with dress or service uniforms and must be carried in line with troops in dress uniforms. Swords are worn with dress uniforms by staff NCOs and worn by sergeants, if in charge of troops on occasions of ceremony. When winter or summer service uniforms are worn, swords may be prescribed for sergeants or above for drill, parades, reviews, and ceremonies.

605. NAVY PETTY OFFICERS SERVING WITH THE MARINE CORPS. Navy enlisted men serving with the Marine Corps are issued Marine service and field uniforms for wear when prescribed. On service uniforms they wear blue Navy rating badges; with utilities, they wear a bronze specialty mark (Hospital corpsmen wear a caduceus) on the left collar and, on the right, a bronze miniature of their rate. *U. S. NAVY* will be stenciled on utility coat pocket. Marine Corps emblems, however, are worn in the usual way on blouse and headgear when in Marine service uniform, except that on headgear chief petty officers wear the bronze CPO cap device instead of the Marine Corps emblem.

Uniform Fit and Marking
606. FIT OF UNIFORMS.

1. *Blouses.* The service blouse is intended to be only semiform-fitting and should not be altered to present too tight an appearance. Conversely, the dress blouse should be formfitting, and you should alter or fit yours accordingly. The skirt on your blouse should extend one to two inches below the crotch.
2. *Trousers* should be cut so that the front of the trouser breaks slightly over the front of the shoe and rear of trouser so that it comes to the junction of where the heel and the shoe meet. Measurement is taken with the waist of the trouser slightly above the hip bone. It is most important to get a good fit in the seat; remember that the waist can always be altered.
3. *Shirts.* Avoid the skintight ("cut-down") shirt. The sleeve length should be measured from your spinal column to where the wrist joins and the hand widens. A one-half inch tolerance is acceptable.
4. *Shoes.* Shoes should hold your feet securely but not too tightly. With the right fit, a shoe allows room for each part of the foot to function normally and easily with no strain or pressure to cause discomfort or even foot injury and with no slipping at the heel. No double soles or taps are permitted.

607. MARKING OF CLOTHING. Except for items issued on memorandum receipt, all clothing must be marked with your name (black on light-colored articles, white on dark). Markings should not be visible when the clothing is worn, except in the case of utilities. You may use marking machines, stencils, or stamps, but sewn-on or embroidered name-tags or name tapes are nonregulation on utilities. Articles to be marked, and where, are:

Belts (except trouser belts): Center of underside, parallel to top, six inches from plate or buckle.
Belt, trouser, web: Center of underside, parallel to top, one inch from buckle, on one side only.
Blouse and overcoat: Right sleeve lining, near shoulder.
Cap, frame: Sweatband, at right side, parallel to edge.
Cap, garrison and utility: On the inside.
Cover, cap: Inside the band, on right side of the double edge.
Drawers: Near the front (plain waistband); near front, immediately under waistband (stretch-type waistband).
Gloves: Inside at wrist, parallel to edge. Tape may be used.
Liners, raincoat and overcoat: Inside neckband.

Scarf, field: On inside of neckloop.

Seabag: On outside of bottom of bag.

Shirts: In the center of inside neckband (except utility); on utilities only, outside, centered one-half inch above left breast pocket.

Shoes and boots: Inside near top, parallel to upper edge.

Socks: Near top, except that stretch socks will be stamped on center of right side of sole, parallel to bottom edge when folded (name tapes may not be used).

Trousers: Inside right waistband.

Undershirt: Across center of back, inside, one-inch below neckline seam.

Care and Maintenance of Uniforms

Proper care and maintenance insure long life and usefulness for your uniforms and also insure that they may be worn with the justifiable pride that should distinguish any Marine noncommissioned officer in uniform. No uniform will continue to look its best unless you care for it when you wear it as well as when you stow it. Put on uniforms carefully, keep them buttoned, and keep large or heavy articles out of pockets, so the shape won't be destroyed. Use wooden hangers shaped to fit shoulder contour, with locking trouser bars. Always have shoe trees, which save you money by prolonging shoe life and make shoes easier to shine. When uniforms are stowed in seabags, fold them carefully to preserve their original shape.

608. DRESS AND SERVICE UNIFORMS. When possible, hang your uniforms in well ventilated areas and have them periodically cleaned and mothproofed. To avoid deterioration and wear along creases, occasionally press out old creases and reform them very slightly to either side of the previous crease. Check your sleeve cuffs and trouser hems for wear and, if material permits, turn them.

When sending uniforms to be cleaned, send them as sets—in the case of greens, with blouse and trousers together; in the case of khakis, with trousers, shirt, and field scarf together. This can be facilitated by putting a small number inside shirt tail, inside trouser pocket, and on field-scarf neckband. By sending uniforms as sets to the dry cleaner, you obtain exactly the same rate of fading.

Pressing. Before pressing, brush away lint and dust, preferably with a flat brush rather than a whisk broom. For woolen materials, use a damp cloth between the iron and the fabric when pressing. For cotton khakis or utilities, dampen the fabric and iron directly. Don't get your iron too hot.

To shrink baggy trouser knees, spread trouser legs on your ironing board, dampen bulges, cover with a cloth, and press. After the areas are dry, match outer and inner leg seams, and crease with iron. Press the inside of the leg first, then the outside.

Don't press over buttons, press around them; otherwise they will be pressed into the fabric and may become malformed.

To press the sleeve of a blouse, place it so the fold of one edge lies over the ironing board, then move the iron slowly almost to the other fold but never over it. This smoothes the sleeve without creasing it. Before you press the shoulder and top of a sleeve, slip a rolled towel into the armhole so as to have a firm surface.

If you have to press a field scarf, cut a stiff piece of cardboard to the shape and size of the large end of the scarf and slip it in between the two layers of cloth. The cardboard should be thick enough to prevent creasing at edges. Put your pressing cloth over the scarf, dampen, and iron. Be sure to keep straightening the material with your other hand, as you press ahead.

To get or improve a trouser crease when an iron isn't available, moisten creases slightly with damp cloth or sponge, place trousers inside a folded blanket, and sleep on them. Next morning, you will have a crease that can get by.

Folding Blouses. To fold a blouse for stowage in footlocker or seabag, first lay the blouse flat, collar out and inside down. Then, turn back sleeves so that cuffs reach the shoulders. Next, fold bottom of the blouse halfway up and then fold right half of the blouse over the left.

Folding trousers. Fold each leg to the outside just below the pockets, about mid-thigh. Bring ends of trouser legs together so that NCO stripes are in line with and touching each other. Then fold both legs in same direction over top of waist. Adjust folds to fit locker-box, seabag, or suitcase. This preserves crease and eliminates harsh original folds.

609. CARE OF FOOTGEAR. Unless you work steadily on footgear, it won't last its full life and may be hard on your feet, too. Keep shoes clean at all times, as sand, dirt, and grit cause deterioration on shoe threads and leather. Work over the uppers, occasionally with saddle soap. After saddle-soaping or washing with heavy soap lather, wipe shoes dry; never dry leatherwork by strong heat, hot sun, or fire. Avoid use of dubbing, as this dressing seals pores and causes excessive sweating. Sweating is not only bad for shoes, but also for feet. Sprinkle foot powder in liberally to help control perspiration.

Break in new shoes or boots before using them for any full day or march. If you have any choice, don't wear the same pair of shoes on two successive days.

Shoes should be taken to the cobbler for repair when you note any of the following conditions.

Cracked soles
Outer sole worn thin or start of a hole
Heels more than one-quarter inch worn down
Rips in sole or upper leather stitching
Upper or sole pulling loose from welt
Shank (narrow part of sole) worn or cracked.

610. UNIFORM ACCESSORIES. Bronze emblems will not be polished. If the finish wears thin, coat the emblem with protective coating as sold in the Marine Corps exchange.

Dress buttons and other brightwork are issued with a lacquer coating. This can be removed for higher shine and more military appearance by submerging the article for not over two minutes in straight ammonia (above this time, a black deposit may result). Remove any residue with brightwork polish.

Enlisted dress buttons, issued with a very thin layer of gold plate, can also be stripped down for polishing by working over with women's nail-polish remover. This gives a button that can be brought to a fine, high polish with jeweler's rouge or any good-quality brightwork polish compound.

When not in use, the blade of your NCO sword should be dried and coated with a film of light oil or, even better, petroleum jelly thinly applied. The leather part of the scabbard should be cleaned with saddle soap and polished, while the brightwork fittings should be treated as other brass.

611. REMOVING STAINS, SINGES AND "SHINE".

Blood. First, brush dry to break up and remove as much of the caked blood as possible. Soak in cold water at least an hour (avoid hot water, which tends to set bloodstains), then follow with regular washing. If any trace remains, clean with solution of ammonia.

Chocolate. Cover stain with borax and wash with cold water. Then pour boiling water on the stain and rub vigorously between the hands. When spot is dry, sponge with naphtha, carbon tetrachloride, or benzine.

Food Stains. Sponge thoroughly with cold water. If a grease mark persists, sponge with naphtha, carbon tetrachloride, or benzine.

Grease or Oil. Scrape with dull knife, then wash the spot with hot soapy water. If you rub road oil or tar with lard or shortening before washing, it will help. Some oil or grease stains can be rubbed out with a woolen cloth saturated in carbon tetrachloride or benzine. To remove grease spots from 782 web equipment, dip gear completely in gasoline or very heavy suds of laundry soap. Rub the soiled area in clean water.

Kerosine. Wash in warm soapy water.

Ink. Ink stains are quite difficult to remove. Commercial inkspot removers usually do the best job.

Mildew. For recent mildew, simply use cold water. Old mildew is practically impossible to get out. White articles should be bleached.

Lipstick. Gently pat the smear with some petroleum jelly on a handkerchief and allow it to pick up the lipstick's wax base and pigment. Then go over the area with carbon tetrachloride to work out the jelly.

Paint. For fresh paint, put a clean cloth under stain and apply carbon tetrachloride, benzine, or benzol on the stain and tamp it,

126 driving paint into the absorbent material underneath. If stain is heavy, shift cloth to a clean place and flush again with solvent. (This is also effective with oil or grease stains). Old, hard paint stains are very difficult to remove except sometimes by a good dry cleaner. Soaking for at least an hour in turpentine may sometimes soften up the paint so it can be broken away with a teaspoon, following which it should be gone over as for a fresh stain.

Paraffin and Wax. Place a blotter over the spot and iron over with very hot iron. Repeat with clean blotting paper until the spot disappears.

Shine. To lift out the shine from greens or blues, steam area to be treated by laying a wet cloth over it and pressing with a hot iron. Then rub gently with "00" sandpaper or emery cloth. This should preferably be done by a qualified tailor.

Singe. Rub vigorously with the flat side of a silver coin.

612. SEWING. Not only in garrison, but more especially in the field, every Marine should be able to make minor repairs to clothing such as sewing on buttons, darning socks, and mending tears.

Basic Sewing. Cut off a length of thread about 24 inches long and thread your needle. Tie a small knot by passing the thread around tip of your forefinger and crossing it. Then, using thumb, twist the crossed end over the bight and pull from the needle end to tighten the knot.

When sewing, hold needle between thumb and forefinger, and push it forward into fabric by the middle finger (on which you place the thimble). Keep your middle finger crooked. In this fashion you guide the needle with three fingers for greater precision.

A *running stitch* (an under-over stitch) is made as follows. Run from six to eight stitches, then pull through. A *back stitch,* highly desirably because of its strength, is made by first sewing a running stitch through both thicknesses of the material. Then bring needle through to the top again. Next, going back, insert needle down again through the same hole where it went down before. Underneath, the needle goes two stitches ahead each time; on top, it goes one stitch back.

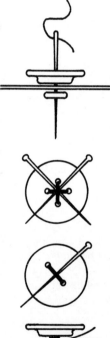

SEWING ON
BUTTONS

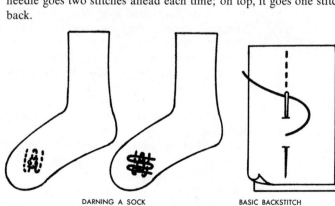

DARNING A SOCK   BASIC BACKSTITCH

Fig. 6-2: Darning and sewing.

At the end of any seam of sewing, take three or more small stitches, one over the other on the under side, to anchor the thread. After completion of work, slip free end of thread under the last loop on the spool so that thread won't unwind and tangle.

Darning Socks. Use an old light bulb as a darning egg. Hold in one hand and slip sock over it. Sew frayed edges into the darn. First anchoring your thread to the sock (rather than knotting it to the needle) by three or four small stitches, sew in a weaving fashion. Run threads of double-strand darning cotton in one direction, carrying them beyond the hole and frayed area. Then run threads crosswise, alternately under and over the others. Leave a little slack at each end of stitching to take care of thread shrinkage.

Patches. Patches are required when tears or holes are too large for darning. First, trim the hole square. Then cut a square patch about an inch or more larger in all directions than the hole. Pin to under side of material, then fix in place by large stitches (basting) to hold patch in place. Remove pins and sew the patch in place with small backstitches.

Tears, Rips, and Frays. To close a tear, bring the two edges together on the back (inside) side of the material and sew together. To repair frayed edges, turn under and sew. For ripped seams, place the edges together and sew with small stitches aligned with the original stitches.

Civilian Clothes

As a noncommissioned officer, you are expected to maintain the same high standard of appearance in civilian clothes, whether you are wearing them on leave or liberty, or, as authorized, in lieu of a duty uniform. At certain civilian schools or on embassy guard duty in certain countries, for example, civilian clothes may be prescribed. In any case, you must take the same care of yourself in civilian clothes as you would in uniform and must no more tolerate eccentricities in civilian clothes then in uniform.

613. GROUND RULES ON CIVILIAN CLOTHING. You are authorized to wear civilian clothes when off duty in the United States, but are subject to local regulations regarding on-base wear.

You may not keep civilian clothes aboard ship except as authorized by the captain, and you may not make liberty in civilian clothes, if serving aboard ship, without authorization from the captain.

In foreign countries, you wear civilian clothes only when authorized by the local commander, when required by local law, or when political conditions render civilian clothing desirable.

When traveling on leave in foreign countries, you should normally wear civilian clothing.

If you are required to wear civilian clothes on duty, you will be issued appropriate clothing and will receive an allowance for its upkeep.

614. MARINE CORPS TIES AND BLAZERS. *Neckties.* The Marine Corps has two distinctive mufti (civilian clothes) neckties, one regimental-striped, the other club-type. Either of these may be worn with civilian clothes by all Marines, regular and reserve; by former Marines; and honorarily, by any member of another service who has served as a member of a Marine Corps organization. The Corps neckties mark you as a Marine when in civilian clothes. They are particularly appropriate for social functions, and you should have at least one of them in your civilian wardrobe.

The so-called *regimental tie* is made up of the three Marine Corps colors, scarlet, gold, and green. It may be obtained from Bolognese, Inc., at Quantico.

The *club tie* consists of tiny Marine Corps emblems woven against an optional background of rifle green or Navy blue. It can be obtained from Brooks Brothers, 346 Madison Avenue, New York City, 10017.

Although no official pattern is prescribed or authorized for *Marine Corps blazers,* such coats are frequently encountered. If you desire to have one, it should be of navy blue, single-breasted, with a Marine Corps emblem placed on the left breast pocket. Although plain silver buttons are appropriate, certain tailoring firms carry suitable buttons with a small emblem mounted or engraved thereon. One word of caution: do not silver-plate regulation uniform buttons and use them on blazers; this practice is forbidden. To convert a standard blue blazer, some tailoring firms stock a kit containing a woven pocket emblem and buttons of the type mentioned above. (Any reputable tailor can help you on this.)

Grooming and Spit-and-polish
615. GROOMING.

1. All Marines must keep their hair neatly and closely trimmed. While three inches is the maximum permissible length, *no non-commissioned officer should ever be seen with hair longer than two inches.* In fact the best rule of all is the old one of no hair longer than the length of a wooden matchstick. Remember Field Marshal Wolseley's saying: "Hair is the glory of a woman, but the shame of a soldier." Get a haircut once a week without fail.

2. Boots and shoes should reflect your pride in yourself and in the Corps. Never be the kind of man who shines just the toe. Welt, heel, and sole should also be outstanding. Shoelaces are cheap; always wear new ones rather than ones ragged or frayed. However, if you lose the metal tip of a lace, twist the end into a point and dip it into clear nail polish, or press melted wax around the end and work into a point. Always keep shoelaces drawn tight, as very little, if any, of the tongue should show.

3. When you put on a clean uniform, put on a clean belt with it. Since the web trouser belt has considerable shrinkage in it, belts

should be washed at least three times before being cut to length. To prevent excess shrinkage after laundering, stretch belts when wet. Duty belts, either leather or web, should never sag, as this looks highly unmilitary. A duty belt should ride the hips firmly, even with the weight of pistol or sword.

Note: In wearing the web pistol belt, the trouser belt buckle, being out of sight, can and should be buckled on the right hip so as to eliminate unnecessary bulge in front.

4. Whenever a field scarf is worn, wear a collar stay.
5. White gear should always be snow-white. Never wear yesterday's belt or cap cover.
6. The field scarf should of course be spotless. When correctly tied, the large end of the scarf should just cover the last shirt button, or should be one and one-half to two inches above belt buckle. There should be no dimple in the knot, and the knot should be small and trim.
7. Buttons on shirts should always be sewn on the same way (something to check before you purchase). On blue or green blouses, the wings of the eagle on the button should always be right-side up.
8. When your barracks cap is not being worn, secure a rubber band from side post to side post so as to retain a good shape for cap and cover. Insert pennies under the keepers to hold the chin strap taut when not dropped. Always wear a cover slightly smaller than the grommet. This prevents "salad-bowl" effect and eliminates sloppy wrinkles. A properly fitted cover will be stretched tight with no wrinkles.
9. When the chin strap on a cap is worn on the chin (as for color-guards, etc.) the strap should be worn on the point of the chin, not down on the Adam's apple.
10. Always wear new, fresh ribbons to show pride in your awards and medals. The lowest ribbon row should be exactly one-eighth inch above the pocket seam, the equivalent of two pennies placed side by side.
11. Although your uniforms contain many pockets, the safest rule is to carry nothing in them. Specifically, you should never place anything in exterior pockets of a dress or service uniform (exceptions: pencil out of sight in a shirt pocket; notebook in hip pocket; wallet, cigarette case, and handkerchief kept flat in trouser pockets).
12. At least a fortnight before the seasonal change from summer to winter uniform and vice versa, break out the forthcoming uniform, have it cleaned and pressed, check it for completeness, repair, and fit.
13. In uniform combinations without blouse, the "gig line" should be straight, i.e., button line, belt buckle, and zipper line should be in a straight line, and the "gig line" should also bisect pistol, or cartridge belt buckle when worn.

14. Outer corners of shirt pockets, both corners of blouse pockets, and cloth belt tips can be tacked down neatly by dress snaps on the underside.

15. When worn by troops, bayonet scabbards should always be perpendicular, never forward like a ceremonial dagger, and centered over the trouser seam. The same applies to the NCO sword.

616. SPIT AND POLISH.

SHOES. *To spit-shine new shoes,* follow these instructions:

Put shoe trees in new shoes and remove laces.

Apply one coat of black dye to shoes, including sides of heels and soles, for six successive days. Let each coat of dye dry 24 hours.

After six coats of dye have been applied, *rub* polish into shoes on four successive days. Rubbed-in polish fills the pores and provides a base from which to build up the spit-shine.

To spit-shine, use a clean, old, white handkerchief of good quality. Soak it in water and wring it out until the handkerchief is barely damp, then tighten it around the first two fingers, and apply small amounts of polish. Work with strokes, back and forth, across the shoe until a good shine begins to appear and then change to a circular rubbing motion until handkerchief is completely dry. If shoes appear cloudy, you have applied too much water.

Do not use excess polish. Remember that every bit of polish must be *worked in.* Always wash out handkerchief after each use to get rid of residue, dirt, grit, etc. The more you wash the handkerchief, the better it will work.

To retain the most brilliant shine, after spit-shining with polish, as above, apply a *very thin* coating of an oil-base paste wax. Apply as you would polish, in a small amount. The wax protects the leather, and your shine will last longer.

Periodically, dab an old toothbrush in polish and run it around between the upper and the sole. This cleans as well as polishes in the crevices.

To spit-shine old shoes.

Put shoe trees in shoes and remove laces.

Remove all excess polish by scrubbing with a wet sponge and saddle soap. After excess polish is worked off, let shoes dry in the air for 24 hours.

Then proceed with spit-shining, as described above.

Occasionally shoelaces should be washed and ironed flat. When they fade, replace or re-dye them.

CAP AND ACCESSORIES. *Visor.* Before attempting to shine a visor, place a protective band of scotch tape around the base of the cap frame above the visor. Dye the visor as in the case of shoes and rub in small amounts of polish until you have built up your base, then proceed to spit-shine. Use of paste wax as described above is highly recommended.

Chin Strap. Remove chin strap from cap frame and place on a locker-box. Separate the two parts of the strap and secure to the locker-box by putting a thumbtack through each screw-post hole, then dye and shine as outlined above.

Alcohol spit-shine. Certain ceremonial units that require visors, holsters, and chin straps to be truly outstanding use plain rubbing alcohol instead of water for spit-shining. Visors so shined will resemble patent leather. In addition, they will not blister or spot permanently if caught in the rain. However, *do not use an alcohol shine on shoes, as leather will crack in short order.*

BUTTONS AND MEDALS. Buttons. Any noncommissioned officer who wishes to present a truly military appearance in blues should strip the gold off one set of dress buttons (see section 610). "Buffed buttons" take a brilliant polish which is far more military than gold plate, need never suffer from corrosion, and set a fine example to junior Marines. *If you don't have a set of buffed buttons, attend to this now, not tomorrow.* One tip: If you know any retired noncommissioned officer (or have a friend who has just made Gunner) who may have a set of buffed buttons, see if you can talk him out of them. Aside from other advantages, if you are a young NCO, the well-polished old buttons will give you a salty appearance unattainable with brand-new gold plate.

Medals. Ceremonial units, ships detachments, etc., can, *as units,* strip the dull bronze finish off medals, buff and polish them, and coat with clear lacquer such as is used for band-instrument finish. This gives medals a brilliant glitter and makes the troops look like Eight and Eye itself, whether in blues or greens.

HOLSTERS. When you draw a new holster, soak it overnight in a bucket of water, let it dry 24 hours, and then dye and shine. The soaking and drying process will harden the leather and make it easier to bring to a high shine.

BONING LEATHER. "Boning" leather footgear, belts, or holsters can, if done with sufficient patience, produce the ultimate in smooth finish and is therefore the ideal preliminary on which to build a spit-shine as previously described.

Boning is simply the process of rubbing the leather surface absolutely smooth with a piece of bone or some bone-like substance. When carried out properly, boning erases all scratches, mars, gouges, or surface irregularities on a piece of leather.

To bone an article, first scrub with saddle soap and allow it to dry 24 hours. A very suitable "bone" is the grip of a bone-handled hunting knife or, if the former is not available, a good toothbrush handle. Commence rubbing the surface firmly with regular, fluid strokes until all scratches, etc., are removed and the leather is completely smooth. This will require patience and time: about four hours' boning, over a week's time, will usually suffice for one shoe. However, once the desired surface has been obtained, you will be able to build a superb shine.

132

Note: Don't try to bone cap visors. The leather is too thin and the process is hard on the shape.

617. YOUR OWN BLUES. Every Marine noncommissioned officer should have his own suit of blues, even if he has never served at sea or in an organization authorized blue issue uniforms. For leave, liberty, Birthday Ball, and many other social occasions, blues are essential. Also, if you are known to have your own blues, your professional reputation will be that much better.

Obtaining Blues. Blues are not expensive, even if tailor-made. However, the best practice is to obtain them through the Marine Corps clothing system.

If you are stationed at one of the 30-odd, large- or medium-sized posts which has a Retail Clothing Outlet, you can buy your blues over the counter as a cash purchase of clothing. Should a Retail Clothing Outlet not be accessible, you can obtain blues by mail order from MCSA, Philadelphia, using the order blank NavMC-10710 if you are a stock size. If you are not a stock size, you must enclose with the NavMC-10710 a copy of the Special Measurement Form. Most important of all, you must in any case enclose the price of the blues, as this transaction is considered to be a cash sale only.

Note: Phase-in of blues to the entire Corps is scheduled to commence in 1973. In the interim, the Commandant of the Marine Corps specially encourages noncommissioned officers to obtain and wear the blue uniform.

*Our flag's unfurl'd to every breeze, from the
dawn to setting sun . . .*

—The Marines' Hymn

7 Posts of the Corps

Only the globe itself—trademark of Marines—limits the number of places where you, as a Marine, may serve.

Here, however, we are going to take a look at the permanent posts and stations of the Corps. These are the places where, between wars and expeditions, you spend much of your career. In addition, this chapter will describe the organization, facilities, services, accomodations, and general conditions as a typical post.

701. POSTS OF THE CORPS. A number of major bases, posts, or air stations form part of the Marine Corps Supporting Establishment and are maintained exclusively for Marine Corps forces. Marines in the security forces man more than 80 Marine Barracks and shore-based Marine Detachments at home and abroad.

Except for posts with missions directly reflected in their titles (such as Marine Corps Development and Education Command or the Recruit Depots), the Corps has the following kinds of stations.

Marine Corps Bases (MCB) and Marine Barracks (MB) are the basic permanent posts for support of ground units of the Corps. Both are administratively autonomous and self-supporting. Marine Corps Bases and Camps are usually devoted to field training and support of major tactical units, whereas most (but not all) Marine Barracks perform security missions.

Marine Corps Air Stations (MCAS) are the aviation counterparts of Marine Corps Bases. Like MCB, air stations are also permanent, autonomous, and self-supporting. All MCAS have a common mission: support of Marine aviation units. *Marine Corps Air Stations (Helicopter)* support Marine helicopter units. *Marine Corps Air Facility (MCAF)* is an aviation installation whose primary (though not necessarily exclusive) function is the support of helicopter units.

702. HOW A POST IS ORGANIZED. Making allowances for different missions and locations, most posts follow the same organization. Figure 7-1 shows the organization of a hypothetical post.

Command. The commanding officer (CO) (if a general, called "the commanding general") commands the post. In the fateful words of *Field Service Regulations,* he is "responsible for all that his command does or leaves undone."

The executive officer is the line officer next junior in rank to the CO. He relieves the commander of administrative detail and succeeds to command in the latter's absence. The extent and character of his duties vary somewhat according to the policies and peculiarities of "the Old Man." On a post commanded by a general, the executive is entitled "chief of staff," and the latter, in turn, may be assisted by a deputy. In either case, the commander has the *post sergeant major* as a member of his immediate staff.

Staff. Just as in tactical units, a post commander is assisted by an executive and special staff much like those described in Chapter 3. The executive staff includes a *personnel officer* (S-1), *operations and intelligence officers* (S-2 and S-3), and *post supply officer* (S-4). In addition, on larger posts, the *fiscal officer* or *comptroller* occupies a status comparable to that of members of the executive staff.

The typical post special staff includes certain billets identical with those found in the FMF special staff, such as:

Communication officer	Inspector
Chaplain (ChC, USN)	Legal officer
Adjutant (on small posts, acts as S-1)	Mess officer
	Motor transport officer
Dental officer (DC, USN)	Special services officer
Disbursing officer	Surgeon (MC, USN)
Exchange officer	

In addition to the foregoing, most posts have a few special staff functions which differ materially in scale or scope from similar FMF staff jobs, where housekeeping is not quite so important as on a post.

PROVOST MARSHAL: This is the post "chief of police" or "sheriff," responsible for public safety, traffic control, criminal investigation, internal and external security, regulation of servants and pets, and law and order in general. Frequently the provost marshal acts as *fire marshal* and thus also becomes responsible for fire protection. Law-abiding members of the post usually encounter the provost marshal in connection with licensing of vehicles or pets and obtaining passes for guests, dependents, and servants.

MAINTENANCE OFFICER: This officer is responsible for minor construction, repair, and upkeep. On small posts, the maintenance officer may also be *police officer* and thereby responsible for the cleanliness and shipshape appearance of the post.

PUBLIC WORKS OFFICER (CEC, USN): On large stations, this is a

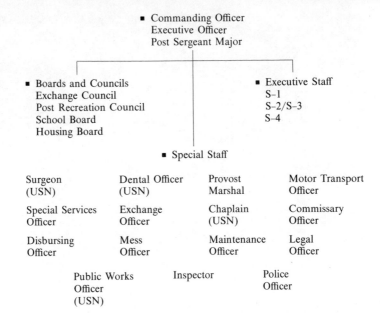

■ Commanding Officer
Executive Officer
Post Sergeant Major

■ Boards and Councils
Exchange Council
Post Recreation Council
School Board
Housing Board

■ Executive Staff
S-1
S-2/S-3
S-4

■ Special Staff

Surgeon (USN)	Dental Officer (USN)	Provost Marshal	Motor Transport Officer
Special Services Officer	Exchange Officer	Chaplain (USN)	Commissary Officer
Disbursing Officer	Mess Officer	Maintenance Officer	Legal Officer
Public Works Officer (USN)	Inspector	Police Officer	

Fig. 7-1: How a typical post or base is organized.

Navy (CEC) officer who supervises new construction, improvements, and plans for post development.

Boards and Councils. To supplement the staff, most stations include one or more standing boards or councils. Some are required by regulations, while others exist to meet local needs. Typical examples are:

Exchange council
Recreation council
School board
Athletic and sports council
Housing board.

703. FACILITIES AND SERVICES. In many ways a post resembles a small community. Most if not all the facilities and services you could expect in such a town have counterparts on a Marine post. Also like small towns, however, stations of various age, locality, and mission exhibit considerable local disparities. Thus what you may find on one post may not exist, or hardly exist, at another. Accordingly, your family fund of service information should include "the word" on conditions at the widely separated stations where you may find yourself.

704. MEDICAL AND DENTAL CARE. Every Marine post includes medical installations for the health and sanitation of the command. These may range from a *dispensary* ("sick bay") to an *infirmary* (dispensary with limited facilities for inpatient care) or,

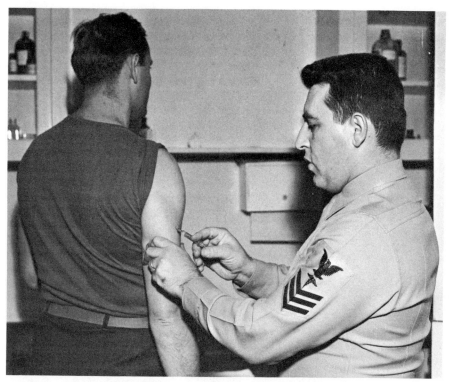

With preventative medicine the Medical Department is able to cure sickness and disease even before they strike.

on the largest posts, a *naval hospital* which can handle any medical or surgical emergency. Routine treatment and consultation are afforded daily at "sick call"—a fixed time of day when the sick bay is fully manned. Emergencies, of course, are dealt with at any time, day or night.

705. DEPENDENTS' MEDICAL CARE. Family medical care for service dependents and for retired dependents is provided by the Government under the *Dependents' Medicare Program.* This program permits civilian medical care and hospitalization, as well as service medical care. A small percentage of the total annual cost of civilian medical expenses and hospitalization is borne by the individual. This program is also known as CHAMPUS, *C*ivilian *H*ealth *a*nd *M*edical *P*rogram *U*niformed *S*ervices.

Eligibility. Virtually all dependents (spouse and unmarried children under 21—subject to a few exceptions) of Marines on active duty are eligible for civilian medical care and care in service medical facilities. Retired Marines and their dependents likewise have such eligibilities, but under differing provisions (see Chapter 20). If you die, whether on active duty or after retirement, your surviving dependents remain eligible for care at Armed Forces or U. S. Public

Health Service medical facilities (subjects to availability of space and staff), as well as for certain civilian medical care and hospitalization.

Civilian Medical Care. Civilian semiprivate hospitalization, outpatient care by civilian facilities, routine doctor visits, prescribed medicines, laboratory and X-Ray tests, rental sickroom equipment, artificial limbs and eyes, etc., are available to active-duty dependents on a cost-sharing basis whereby, in general, you pay only the first $50 per year per person (but not over $100 for the entire family) and 20 percent of the remaining cost; the Government pays the remaining 80 percent.

A program of financial assistance is also provided for active-duty personnel whose spouses or children are mentally retarded or physically handicapped. This program authorizes diagnostic services, treatment, and use of private nonprofit and nonmilitary institutions for such handicapped dependents, with you (the sponsor) paying a varying amount according to rank ($30 per month, for example, by a staff sergeant) and with the Government paying the remaining portion of the cost up to a maximum of $350 per month.

> *Note:* Two provisions will be of special interest to your wife: (1) All care received during and for a pregnancy that results in hospitalization is considered, for payment purposes, as part of that hospitalization and (2) oral contraceptives are considered to be prescription drugs.

Medical Care at Service Facilities. When medical staff, space, and facilities are available, the Navy Medical Department will provide the following care for your dependents:

Diagnosis
Treatment of:
    Acute medical conditions
    Surgical conditions
    Contagious diseases
    Acute emergencies of any kind.
Immunization
Maternity and infant care.

Out-patient service, essentially of free-clinic character, is given dependents (including parents, if in fact dependent upon you, and your widow) at any naval dispensary, infirmary, or hospital which has dependent facilities. Virtually all medical installations on posts in the continental United States and outlying stations have dependent outpatient service. Transports which carry dependents are likewise staffed and equipped to provide full dependent medical care as required.

The extent and quality of dependent medical services vary widely with the limitations of local dispensaries, infirmaries, or hospitals, and with the medical workload as a whole. Isolated outlying stations usually have more self-sufficient medical and dental services.

On Outlying Stations, in addition to the service medical care noted above, dental care can frequently be provided to dependents, subject to limitations of workload and facilities, so long as adequate civilian dental services are not available. Also, by legislation passed in 1965, the Government will, in appropriate cases, provide transportation for dependents from outlying stations where medical care is inadequate to centers where proper care can be provided (with round-trip expenses for attendants when found to be required).

A few cautionary words are in order on the subject of dependent medical care:

First and foremost, the medical needs of military personnel are the *primary* concern of the Medical Department. This means that care for dependents takes second place and always gives way, when conflict arises, to military medicine functions.

Second, although members of the Marine Corps and Navy are entitled to free dental care, dependents are not (except when overseas or on stateside bases declared to be "remote"). As this edition of the *Handbook* goes to press, legislation is under consideration to extend dental care to dependents on a general basis, but firm details are not available.

Third, to receive medical assistance from any Navy (or armed forces) establishment, your dependent must possess and present a Dependent Identification Card (see Section 706 below). Obtain one of these cards and have your wife carry it with her.

Finally—although the professional qualifications of Navy doctors and nurses are of the first rank, care for service dependents remains necessarily at last priority. If you wish, and can afford, the more personal attentions of a private practitioner and civilian hospital, you are free, at your own expense—even when ineligible under the Medicare program—to obtain such services.

> *Note:* By memorandum of 27 April 1964 the Defense Department authorizes military medical facilities to fill prescriptions written by licensed civilian physicians and dentists for military personnel, retirees, and dependents, in reasonable quantities of items stocked routinely.

706. DEPENDENTS' IDENTIFICATION AND PRIVILEGE CARDS. The Department of Defense issues (on application) a standard *Identification and Privilege Card* (Form DD 1173) for dependents (except children under ten) of all active-duty personnel. This card is an essential item to enable your dependents to obtain the use of medical facilities, commissary, exchange and post theaters. It is honored not only on Marine and Navy posts and stations, but on those of the other services as well. As soon as you acquire eligible dependent(s), you are required to apply to your commanding officer for their identification and privilege cards.

707. COMMISSARY. The military equivalent of the supermarket is the sales commissary. There, at prices equal to or occasionally slightly lower than those charged by grocers ashore, you may buy foodstuffs from Government supplies. The privilege of making purchases is limited to regular and retired personnel, to reservists on active or training duty for longer than 72 hours, and to certain Government civilians. Dependents of anyone entitled to commissary privileges may also use the commissary. Needless to emphasize, the

sales commissary is a privilege, not a right, and all purchases must be for your own use and that of your household.

Everyone entitled to commissary privileges must be prepared to identify himself. Active personnel not in uniform, as well as retired personnel, are identified by the ID Card, dependents by the identification and privilege card.

Stock and services available in commissaries vary somewhat according to the size of the post and the availability of adequate civilian facilities off post. In some localities, where one service maintains a large commissary, members of other services stationed nearby may use this. Washington, D.C., where the Army provides commissary facilities for all four services, is an example.

> *Note:* Commissaries now accept U. S. Department of Agriculture food stamps. If you are a junior NCO or have a large family, you may be eligible. To see if you qualify, obtain information from your local city or county government.

708. MARINE CORPS EXCHANGES. Marine Corps Exchanges ("post exchanges" or "PX," as they are known) are maintained by all posts and by almost all FMF units of any size. Any regular Marine Corps organization may, with the approval of the Commandant, establish its own exchange.

Post exchanges go far back into U. S. military history. During the 19th century, when the Army pushed our frontier westward, each isolated post had its "post trader" or sutler, authorized to keep store at the post. One of the trader's perquisites was the right of trading with Indians, trappers, and hunters; and from this practice arose the title "post exchange." After the frontier vanished, the name remained, carrying over from the Old Army into the Old Marine Corps. In early times, the perquisite of keeping the post trader's stores at the various Marine Barracks was awarded to the widow of some officer or senior NCO. The modern post exchange system was established by General Heywood, the 9th Commandant.

Today's exchange is the post general store. On large stations, it approximates a small department store, but the extent of what an exchange offers depends markedly on its volume of business—which in turn stems from the size of the post and the accessibility of civilian shopping centers.

The missions of Marine Corps Exchanges are: (1) to afford service personnel (including dependents), at reasonable prices, articles necessary for health, comfort, and convenience and (2) through reasonable profits, to afford Marines means for recreation and amusement. The latter mission is realized through donation of exchange profits to unit recreation projects and to the *Marine Corps Exchange Fund,* a nonappropriated fund maintained by Marine Corps Headquarters for the entire exchange system and for welfare or recreation.

Typical, though by no means exclusive, of goods and services obtainable in a medium-sized exchange are the following: confectionery and tobacco; toilet articles; periodicals; luggage; photographic supplies; uniforms and accessories; household supplies; soda fountain, beer hall, and lunchroom; check-cashing facilities (up to $50 in any given day for personal checks by any member of the armed forces); barber (and, for ladies, beauty shop); cobbler and tailor; bowling alleys and poolroom. The exchange recognizes the existence of the fair sex—both women Marines and dependents—by stocking many items of primary usefulness to women only.

Eligibility to use the exchange, like the commissary, is a privilege which extends only to active or retired service personnel, to their dependents and widows, and to reservists on active or training duty. The *Marine Corps Exchange Manual* gives the various classes of individuals and their eligibility for exchange privileges. If in civilian clothes when making a purchase, be prepared to show either your ID Card or an Exchange Identification Card (obtainable from the exchange steward).

709. WELFARE ACTIVITIES. In addition to welfare services provided by the chaplain, special services officer, and legal assistance officer, most large posts have representatives of the American Red Cross, Navy Relief Society, and Navy Mutual Aid Association. The assistance furnished by these groups is described in Chapter 20.

710. EDUCATIONAL FACILITIES. Many posts have their own public schools for the children on the post. Because of wide variations between post school systems, however, you should investigate carefully before you assume that you will find schools at the post which meet your needs. If overseas where U. S.-owned school facilities are not available, you may claim a modest schooling allowance for each child you place in a local private school of approved standards.

Every post has a free library, open to Marines and dependents. Marine Corps Headquarters and the Bureau of Naval Personnel provide the books. A few large posts have museums—notably the Marine Corps Museum at Quantico.

711. RECREATION. Many posts include excellent on-station recreation opportunities. Some of these, such as sports facilities (golf courses, boating, athletic facilities, etc.) and hobby shops, are open to all ranks. The focus of much of your recreational and social activity, as a noncommissioned officer, however, is the noncommissioned officers' mess (see Chapter 21).

At a medium-sized post, you may expect to find at least the following: NCO club or mess, small-bore range, swimming pool, and other athletic facilities as space and demand permit.

712. PUBLIC QUARTERS. As you know, the availability of quarters for married NCOs varies from post to post. For this reason, be careful to ascertain the local situation before you decide to live off-station and make arrangements to rent. The reason is that the Defense Department requires a utilization rate of 98 percent for all adequate housing. Your orders must accordingly be endorsed as to nonavailability of quarters before you agree to rent off-station;

otherwise you may find yourself involuntarily assigned on-station and lose your BAQ.

> *Note:* If you are ordered to independent duty in the vicinity of certain posts or bases of the other services, you may be able to obtain public quarters if a housing surplus exists.
>
> Lists of such installations are periodically published.

Major Posts and Stations

713. MB, EIGHTH AND I STREETS, S.E., WASHINGTON, D.C., 20003. "Eighth and Eye" is the senior post of the Corps, both because of its age and because it houses the Commandant. The post has been a Marine Barracks since 1801 and has quartered Marine Corps Headquarters throughout its first century. It is the spit-and-polish post of the Corps, famous for its weekly Evening Parades, and constructed about a traditional barracks square in the heart of old Washington.

The Barracks provides ceremonial troops for official occasions in the nation's capital; it supports the U. S. Marine Band, the Marine Corps Drum and Bugle Corps, and the Marine Corps Institute (see Chapter 12); and its officers and men are assigned to certain special security duties in and about Washington.

The barracks square of Eighth and I has been the parade ground for the red-coated Marine Band, the Drum and Bugle Corps, and the Commandant since 1801.

TRANSPORTATION. *Rail.* Pennsylvania; Baltimore & Ohio; Richmond, Fredericksburg, & Potomac; Chesapeake & Ohio; Seaboard Coast Line. (Commuter service available via B&O between Washington and Baltimore; rapid-transit system, including subway, under development in the 1970s).

Bus. Greyhound; Trailways; Red Star; Virginia Stage Line.

Airports. Washington National Airport; Dulles International, Chantilly, Virginia (35 miles); Friendship International (also serving Baltimore), 35 miles; Andrews AFB (military traffic).

QUARTERS. Naval housing is available at Bolling AFB, Anacostia (Navy Housing Office located in Washington Navy Yard). Ample single dwelling, duplex, and apartment rentals are available at reasonable rates on the local market.

SCHOOLS. In addition to a metropolitan school system, Washington has numerous private and parochial schools at any social level, price range, and quality. Suburban public schools are adequate, with those in Montgomery County generally being considered best.

MEDICAL FACILITIES FOR DEPENDENTS. Washington area medical facilities are outstanding. These include National Naval Medical Center, Bethesda (with associated National Institutes of Health), Walter Reed Army Hospital, and cross-service medical support depending on where you live (including USNH, Annapolis and the Army hospital at Fort Belvoir). Limited dependent dental care is obtainable at Fort Meade, Maryland.

RECREATION. In addition to the Barracks gymnasium, "Eighth and Eye" has a Staff NCO Club, the "1600 Club" for sergeants and below, and special services amply stocked with all sports equipment including camping trailers and fishing gear. Bolling AFB handball courts and swimming pools are also open to Marines.

Besides the foregoing military recreation, Washington of course includes many national and private institutions of great interest, such as the Smithsonian Institution, National Archives, Library of Congress, etc., together with well-preserved historic sites and extensive parks. For lighter entertainment, New York is only a high-speed train ride or shuttle plane trip away.

COMMISSARY AND EXCHANGE. Commissary privileges are available at any of four Army commissaries in the Washington area. Excellent Marine Corps and Army exchanges are at Henderson Hall and Forts Myer and McNair, in addition to the small exchange located at Eighth and Eye.

NEIGHBORING MARINE ACTIVITIES. The Washington area includes Marine Corps Headquarters in Arlington Annex, Navy Department; and Henderson Hall, Arlington, Virginia, which supports Headquarters Battalion, HQMC.

713a. MARINE CORPS DEVELOPMENT AND EDUCATION COMMAND, QUANTICO, VIRGINIA, 22134. "MCDEC" or "Quantico" is in many ways the show place of the Corps. It is a large

(91 square miles) well-developed station on the Potomac River, approximately 35 miles south of Washington, D. C. Marine Corps Development and Education Command is comprised of three major subcommands—the Marine Corps Base, the Education Center, and the Development Center.

The Command also includes a Marine Corps Air Station and a Naval Hospital. Because of its educational and developmental roles, Quantico is the brains of the Corps.

TRANSPORTATION

Rail: Richmond, Fredericksburg and Potomac.

Bus: Greyhound.

Airports: Civilian Aircraft: Washington National Airport and Dulles International Airport (both more than 30 miles distant)

Military Aircraft: Marine Corps Air Station, Quantico

Highway. U.S. 1 and Interstate 95.

QUARTERS. Government quarters are available for all ranks, although the number is insufficient to accommodate all eligible personnel. Off-base housing is available in the surrounding area from Woodbridge south to Fredericksburg, with rapid and seasonal turnover and rentals, though still high, not as bad as in past years. Transient family accommodations are available in the Hostess House. Permanent bachelor SNCO quarters are available in Shuck Hall and Shuck Hall Annex.

SCHOOLS. At Quantico the excellent Dependents' School System includes all grades, kindergarten through high school.

MEDICAL FACILITIES. The U.S. Naval Hospital provides general clinical and hospitalization services for all active-duty service personnel and their dependents. Services include both inpatient and outpatient care in general medicine, general surgery, orthopedic surgery, opthalmology, obstetrics and gynecology, pediatrics, dentistry (military personnel), laboratory and pathology, radiology, pharmacy, and physiotherapy.

RECREATION. Quantico's recreational opportunities often cause it to be called "The Country Club." They include Diamond Hall (the SNCO Club); sergeants' section of Daly Hall (the Enlisted Club); golf (18 holes); sailing (Potomac River); fishing boats and motors (Lunga and Breckinridge Reservoirs); picnic and camping areas; playgrounds; horseback riding; bowling leagues; youth activities; adult recreational classes; Aero Club; Rod and Gun Club; Skeet Club; Sky Diving Club; Hi-Fi Stereo Tape Club; Quantico Players (theater group); hobby shops; tennis courts and swimming pools for all ranks; Larson Gymnasium; Marine Corps football, basketball and track teams; Little Hall (theater and bowling alleys); Marine Corps Museum; and two fine libraries (James C. Breckinridge Memorial Library in Dunlap Hall and Technical and Post Library in Little Hall).

COMMISSARY AND EXCHANGE. Excellent.

714. MARINE CORPS SUPPLY ACTIVITY, PHILADELPHIA, 19146. For more than 170 years, under various designations, the Marine Corps Supply Activity (MCSA) at Philadelphia, birthplace of the Corps, has provided logistic support for the Marine Corps. Originally organized in 1798 by the Secretary of the Navy as "an establishment in Barracks for making and mending clothes for the Marine Corps," and the first 20th century expeditionary supply depot of the Corps, "Eleven Hundred South Broad Street," as it is generally known, has provided uninterrupted service as a key installation in the Marine Corps supporting establishment. Today, MCSA serves as the inventory control point for the Marine Corps, stores and distributes publications and publicity material, and performs certain disbursing functions.

TRANSPORTATION. *Rail.* Pennsylvania; Reading.
Bus. Greyhound and Trailways.
Airport. Philadelphia International Airport.

QUARTERS. There are a limited number of Navy Capehart Units available through the Navy Housing Office at the Philadelphia Navy Yard but a long waiting period is usually required. There is, however, a housing referral office at the Navy Yard which handles all requests for individual or family housing. Since Philadelphia is the fourth largest city in the United States, there is an almost unlimited range of choice in apartments, town houses, or in suburban developments in nearby New Jersey or Pennsylvania. There are no barracks at the Supply Activity and due to limited space in the Marine Barracks in the Navy Yard, only Marines of the rank of Corporal or below are quartered therein. Remaining individuals, single or married, live on the economy.

SCHOOLS. Philadelphia has a metropolitan public school system together with every level of private and parochial school readily available.

RECREATION. The Navy Yard has a theater, gymnasium, and indoor and outdoor swimming pools. There are several public golf courses available at nominal charge through special services. Philadelphia enjoys other cultural and athletic facilities which characterize all our large cities. Among the museums, is the Marine Museum at New Hall, a colonial restoration. While there is no Staff NCO Club available, there is a Chiefs' Club at the Naval Base.

COMMISSARY AND EXCHANGE. There is a small Marine Exchange at the Marine Corps Supply Activity and Navy Exchange and Commissary at the Naval Base.

NEIGHBORING MARINE AND NAVAL ACTIVITIES. The U. S. Naval Base, Philadelphia, located on League Island at the foot of Broad Street, is headquarters of the 4th Naval District and one of the most important East Coast navy yards. The base includes MB Philadelphia, one of the senior Marine barracks in the Corps.

DEPENDENTS' MEDICAL CARE. U.S. Naval Hospital, Philadelphia.

715. MARINE ACTIVITIES IN THE NORFOLK AREA
(Navy ZIP code, 23511) Although the Norfolk-Hampton Roads area includes no major Marine Corps post, it is the location of Headquarters, FMFLant and of its supporting Camp Elmore; of Landing Force Training Command, Atlantic Fleet, at Little Creek; and of MB, Norfolk Naval Shipyard—one of the oldest barracks in the Corps—and MB, Naval Base (Hampton Roads), Norfolk. In addition, as Norfolk is the primary East Coast base of the Atlantic Fleet, many Marines serve in the area for that reason. Thus Norfolk and the surrounding area can be considered as a Marine Corps station of importance.

TRANSPORTATION. *Rail.* Chesapeake & Ohio; Norfolk & Western; and Seaboard Coast Line Railroad

Bus. Greyhound; Trailways

Highway. U.S. 13, Chesapeake Bay-Bridge Tunnel; 17; 58; 60; and I-64.

QUARTERS. There are relatively few Government quarters available for NCOs at Camp Elmore. There is, however, a wide range of private housing available in the Norfolk area.

SCHOOLS. Norfolk has good public and parochial schools and a few, moderately good, private schools.

RECREATION. There are numberous clubs in the area for both senior and junior NCOs. Recreational facilities are excellent.

COMMISSARY AND EXCHANGES. Excellent.

DEPENDENTS' MEDICAL CARE. U.S. Naval Hospital, Portsmouth, Virginia, together with certain dispensaries which also handle dependents.

716. MCAS, CHERRY POINT, NORTH CAROLINA, 28533.
Commissioned in September 1942, Cherry Point is the largest Marine air station in the world and home of the 2d Marine Aircraft Wing. It is an all-weather station and operates a Class A overhaul and repair facility.

TRANSPORTATION. *Rail.* Seaboard Coast Line (nearest main-line stop, Rocky Mount, N.C.).

Bus. Seashore Lines.

Airport. Simmons-Nott Airport, New Bern (19 miles).

Highway. U.S. 70.

QUARTERS. *Staff NCOs* are assigned Capehart MEMQs, on-station with three and four bedrooms, according to date of detachment from last duty station or of entry into CONUS (excluding Hawaii). Sergeants major, master gunnery sergeants, first sergeants and master sergeants have preference for assignment except for the first three places on the waiting list. Price is BAQ allowance, and utilities are furnished. Some furniture is available. All MEMQ Capeharts are single-dwelling units. Elementary school is within walking distance, and bus service is provided for other students. Station service areas are about a 10-minute drive. Units are equipped with central heating and air conditioning and serviced by a master television antenna.

Sergeants and corporals (over four years' service) are assigned to Slocum Village and Fort Macon Housing, off-station, with one-, two-, three- and some four-bedroom units available. Price is BAQ allowance, and utilities are furnished. Some furniture is available. All are multiple-dwelling units. Elementary school is within walking distance of Slocum Village, and High School and Junior High School are within walking distance of Fort Macon Housing. Havelock shopping centers are convenient to both, and station service areas are a 10- to 15-minute drive.

Delays in quarters availability sometimes run as much as several weeks after reporting; therefore, it is wise to write the Joint Reception Center before planning to arrive with your family. A few off-station interim rentals are usually available ashore, but long-term lease-rentals are scarce. The Hostess House is also available for military personnel, dependents, and guests, as temporary housing after transfer or while awaiting quarters assignment. Reservations should be made two to three weeks in advance.

SCHOOLS. Post kindergarten and nursery. There are four public elementary schools, junior high, and high school as well as a Roman Catholic parochial grade school. The quality of the North Carolina public schools in this area is, in general, mediocre. East Carolina College operates a junior-college resident center for Cherry Point Marine and naval personnel, dependents, and local civilians.

RECREATION. Staff NCO Club; NCO Club; movies; hobby shop; bowling; sailing and boating; swimming pools; golf; numerous recreational clubs in special fields of interest.

COMMISSARY AND EXCHANGE. Excellent.

DEPENDENTS' MEDICAL CARE. U.S. Naval Hospital, Cherry Point.

717. MCB, CAMP LEJEUNE, NORTH CAROLINA, 28542.

Camp Lejeune is the East Coast base for the ground units of the FMF. It can accommodate a Marine division plus units of Force Troops and adjoins MCAS, New River, at Peterfield Point, which is virtually an air station for Camp Lejeune. Its neighboring community is Jacksonville, N.C.

TRANSPORTATION. *Rail.* Rail connections nearest to Camp Lejeune are Wilson, Wilmington, Fayetteville, Burgaw, and Rocky Mount, all in North Carolina and all on the Seaboard Coast Line. From these points rail service can be obtained to Atlanta and Washington, where transcontinental connections can be made. Sleeper service is available between Washington and Wilmington.

Bus. National Trailways from both Camp Lejeune and Jacksonville.

Airports. Nearest commercial airports are New Bern, Kinston, and Wilmington; all are served by Piedmont Airlines. Connections may be made with major lines at Raleigh or Charlotte, both in North Carolina, or at Washington, D.C.

Highways. U. S. 17 and N.C. 24. U. S. 258 originates at Jacksonville and runs north into Virginia.

QUARTERS. Housing at Camp Lejeune is made available after reporting aboard, but there is usually a waiting list which varies with rank, date of detachment from last duty station, and type of quarters for which eligible. All eligible personnel reporting to Camp Lejeune are subject to involuntary assignment to adequate family housing. Eligible personnel refers to all NCOs with four or more years' service. Personnel regularly assigned to units at Camp Lejeune who have dependents officially recognized for BAQ purposes are eligible for family housing. Despite the fact that there is housing available, you should, before bringing dependents to Camp Lejeune, write to the Director, Housing and Quarters, for information. Off-base housing varies in availability, although in times of national emergency it is at a premium. Staff NCO quarters are available and are applied for through the Director, Housing and Quarters, the same as married personnel are required to do. There is usually a waiting list, except for the two top pay grades, which are given priority.

Three- and four-bedroom Capehart housing is available for staff NCOs with a total of 607 units. For corporals with four years service and above, there are 1506 one-, two- and three-bedroom units available in Tarawa Terrace.

A Hostess House for enlisted personnel, regardless of rank, is located in the center of Camp Lejeune. Reservations may be made in advance by writing to the Manager (the earlier you write, the better your chances of getting accommodations).

SCHOOLS. Post schools from kindergarten through high school are open to children of service families residing on Federal property. A private kindergarten is available for nominal fees. Families not on Federal property must rely on county or other local schools. East Carolina College operates a branch and an extension division at Camp Lejeune, while a junior college exists at Wilmington.

RECREATION. Camp Lejeune has five staff NCO clubs, an NCO club and 11 service clubs. The Hadnot Point Staff NCO Club is the largest. The NCO club is divided into two rooms; one for NCOs under 21 who are authorized only beer and the other for NCOs who are of age to purchase mixed drinks. There is also a package store available to the latter. Food is served at all clubs at a reasonable price. In addition to the foregoing clubs (and some of the best mess halls in the Marine Corps), Camp Lejeune recreation also includes: 11 post theaters, hunting, fresh and salt water fishing, swimming pools, surf bathing, golf (two 18-hole courses); boating and sailing, and equitation.

COMMISSARY AND EXCHANGE. Excellent.

DEPENDENTS' MEDICAL CARE. U. S. Naval Hospital, Camp Lejeune.

718. MARINE CORPS RECRUIT DEPOT, PARRIS ISLAND, SOUTH CAROLINA, 29905. Parris Island, or "PI," is the larger and older of the two recruit depots. It trains most recruits from east of the Mississippi River. In addition to recruit training, there are numerous schools aboard the Depot, including Personnel Adminis-

tration School with a Basic Personnel Administration Course, Administrative Chiefs Personnel Administration Course, and the First Sergeants' Personnel Administration Course, Recruiters' School, and Drill Instructors' School.

TRANSPORTATION. *Rail.* The nearest main-line station is Yemassee, S.C., on the Seaboard Coast Line, 28 miles away. The SCL has fast sleeper service with Washington, New York, and other East Coast points.

Bus. Greyhound.

Airports. Civilian: Nearest commercial air facilities are at Savannah, Georgia, 50 miles distant. Charleston Municipal Airport is 85 miles away. Military: MCAS, Beaufort, South Carolina.

Highway. U. S. 17 to junction with U. S. 21, which leads to Beaufort, S.C., the neighboring community. From Beaufort follow State 281 to the Main Gate at Horse Island.

QUARTERS. Bachelor and married quarters are available. All bachelor quarters are aboard the Depot, while some married quarters are on the Depot and some are in nearby Laurel Bay, S.C. (10 miles). For bachelor drill instructors assigned to the Recruit Training Regiment, there are two barracks units with complete mess and recreation facilities.

A bachelor staff NCO mess is available. There are 50 one-man rooms with an augmented mess system and recreation facilities. Some transient staff NCO quarters are available here.

For married NCOs there are 127 units.

Additionally, there are 114 trailer sites on the Depot and 47 permanent units to house senior staff NCO's.

At Laurel Bay, 271 quarters are available for staff NCOs.

For temporary residence (7 days), the Hostess House has 28 rooms.

Civilian housing is available in nearby Beaufort.

SCHOOLS. Depot schools are from kindergarten through the eighth grade. There are two grade schools at Laurel Bay. The public high school in Beaufort accepts children from the Depot. On the Depot, there is a circus house and nursery school available for child care.

RECREATION. Staff NCO Club (with swimming pool); NCO Club; swimming; golf (18 holes); saltwater fishing, sailing, and boating; bowling; movies; tennis; skeet; hobby shop; recreational clubs in special fields of interest. There are fine ocean beaches in the nearby area. Picnic facilities on Parris Island are available at both Elliott's Beach and Horse Island.

COMMISSARY AND EXCHANGE. Excellent.

NEIGHBORING ACTIVITIES. Parris Island's most important Marine Corps neighbor is MCAS, Beaufort. In addition, the USNH, Beaufort, is about three miles from the Parris Island main gate.

MEDICAL AND DENTAL FACILITIES. Dental care for military personal and dependents is available at the Depot. Medical care for military personnel and emergency treatment for dependents are available at the Depot with U. S. Naval Hospital in Beaufort the support activity. Medical care for dependents is available at the Naval Hospital.

719. MCAS, BEAUFORT, SOUTH CAROLINA 29902. MCAS, Beaufort (pronounced "Bewfort") is a major jet air base capable of supporting two Marine aircraft groups and associated service units. It is close aboard Parris Island and provides military air services therefor.

TRANSPORTATION. *Rail.* Seaboard Coast Line to Yemassee, S.C., 26 miles northwest, is the most convenient mode to or from northern or eastern points.

Bus. Southern Greyhound.

Airports. Savannah, Georgia (50 miles) and Charleston (76 miles) are the nearest commercial airports.

Highway. U. S. 17, thence by U. S. 21 to Beaufort.

QUARTERS. There are some bachelor staff NCO quarters at the Air Station but NCOs will be quartered in barracks. 154 units of married NCO quarters are on the Air Station. Staff NCOs will be housed in one of the 532 units at nearby Laurel Bay, three miles from the Air Station gate. Civilian housing is available in the Beaufort area.

SCHOOLS. There are two Federal Government grade schools (grades 1 through 6) at Laurel Bay, open to children of families occupying government quarters. The Air Station provides bus service for children attending public schools in Beaufort. A nursery/ kindergarten is operated at the Air Station for children in government quarters. Also at the Air Station is a child care center, operated at nominal costs, for children six months to ten years old.

RECREATION. NCO and staff NCO clubs are provided, as well as a swimming pool, hobby shop, fishing, hunting, boating, golf (at Parris Island) and nearby ocean beaches.

COMMISSARY. Although commissary facilities at the Air Station are limited, those at Parris Island are excellent. The Marine Corps Exchange is excellent.

MEDICAL AND DENTAL FACILITIES. Dental care for both military personnel and their dependents is available at the Air Station. Medical care for military personnel and for emergency treatment of dependents is available at the Air Station, with the U.S. Naval Hospital, Beaufort the support facility. Medical care for dependents is available at the Naval Hospital.

720. MARINE CORPS SUPPLY CENTER (MCSC) ALBANY, GEORGIA, 31704. The Albany Supply Center is one of the newer posts of the Corps, meticulously designed and planned for modern supply operations. Its mission is to receive, store, repair, and supply materials and equipment for the East Coast complex, which includes all Marine Corps forces and establishments east of the Rockies and in the Atlantic theater. It also stores and controls certain items for the Defense Supply Agency. The Center has more than 3,800,000 square feet of closed storage space in its 19 warehouses, and more than 7,700,000 square feet of concrete, asphalt, and gravel open-storage lots.

TRANSPORTATION. *Rail:* Seaboard Coast Line; Central of Georgia; Georgia Northern; and Albany and Northern. The Center is served by one of the largest rail complexes in the southeast.

Bus: Tamiami (National) Trailways.

Airport: Eastern Air Lines and Southern Air Lines. Naval Air Station, Albany (formerly Turner AFB), three miles distant, is used by all military flights connected with the Center.

Highways: U. S. 82 and U. S. 19, and Georgia State Routes 3, 50, 62, 91, 133, 234, and 257.

QUARTERS: Modern (air conditioned) married quarters are available in adequate numbers to meet the requirements; most of the quarters have two and three bedrooms, while a few have four. There is a modern (on-base) trailer park adjacent to the married quarters area. Barracks living is considered to be excellent.

RECREATION: Staff NCO Club (equipped with swimming pool and bachelor quarters); NCO Club; golf course (9 holes); swimming pools; tennis; bowling; skeet and pistol ranges; magnificent hunting and fishing.

COMMISSARY AND EXCHANGE: Excellent.

DEPENDENTS' MEDICAL CARE. General facilities at Dispensary, NAS, Albany.

721. MCAS, YUMA, ARIZONA, 85364. The newest Marine Corps air station in the United States, MCAS, Yuma, was taken over from the Air Force in 1958 and commissioned as a Marine Corps Air Station in July 1962. It has a 13,300-foot main runway—the second longest in the Naval Air Establishment—an instrumented special-weapons delivery range, and the finest flying weather to be found. MCAS, Yuma, is the home of the most elaborate Naval Air Weapons Training Facility in the United States. It is also the home port for Marine Corps Training Group 10 consisting of VMAT-101, VMFT-102, and VMT-103, as well as the 5th Light Antiaircraft Missile Battalion and Marine Air Control Squadron One.

TRANSPORTATION.

Rail. Santa Fe at Yuma

Bus. Greyhound

Airport. Yuma International Airport

Highway. U. S. 80

QUARTERS. A total of 58 housing units are currently available for staff NCOs, including 40 Capehart and 18 Towne House quarters. Some civilian housing is available in Yuma. A staff NCO barracks is also available. Soon to be completed are an additional 330 units of enlisted housing which will accommodate sergeants and above.

SCHOOLS. The Station has only a kindergarten. Other children attend public and parochial, elementary and high schools in Yuma.

RECREATION. Staff NCO club; riding stables; craft shop, garage; gymnasium; bowling alley; swimming pool; tennis and handball courts; MARS radio station; picnic area; golf driving range; two golf courses available in Yuma; Lake Martinez Recreational Area with camping, fishing and boating.

COMMISSARY AND EXCHANGE. Modern and adequate.

DEPENDENTS' MEDICAL CARE. No inpatient facilities are available on Station for dependents—all prenatal and inpatient care is handled at Parkview Baptist Hospital, Yuma, under Medicare. Dependents requiring consultation at the U. S. Naval Hospital, San Diego, are flown to San Diego once a week.

722. MCB, TWENTYNINE PALMS, CALIFORNIA, 92278. With its area of 932 square miles, twice the size of Los Angeles and big enough to encompass Pendleton, Lejeune, and Quantico with room to spare, Twentynine Palms is not only the largest post in the Corps but also a primary training and experimental center for Marine artillery and guided missiles. It has facilities for the major part of Force Troops, FMF Pacific.

TRANSPORTATION. *Rail.* Southern Pacific (Indio); Santa Fe (Amboy). Connection service is poor.

Bus. Local bus to Banning twice daily for connection with Greyhound. Weekly special services liberty bus to Los Angeles.

Airport. Palm Springs (55 miles) has connecting flights with major air lines. Car rentals available.

Highway. U. S. 66 to Amboy, thence by county highway to Twentynine Palms.

QUARTERS. Nearly 300 sets of staff NCO quarters and over 250 units for sergeants and corporals (over four years' service) are available.

SCHOOLS. The base has a nursery school for children from three to six, as well as a child care center. The town of Twentynine Palms has elementary, junior high, and senior high schools together with a parochial grade school (through 8th grade).

RECREATION. Staff NCO club and sergeants' club; swimming; bowling; skeet; hunting and fishing; tennis; golf (nine holes); hobby shop. The base is almost at the center of the southern California recreation area, and practically any kind of outdoor or indoor recreation is available. Joshua Tree National Monument has camping and picnic facilities.

COMMISSARY AND EXCHANGE. Excellent.

DEPENDENTS' MEDICAL CARE. An excellent base hospital is available for normal dependent medical care. Due to the remote location of Twentynine Palms, limited routine dental care on-base is authorized for dependents (contingent on dental officer availability).

723. MCSC, BARSTOW, CALIFORNIA, 92311. The Marine Corps Supply Center at Barstow, with an annex at Yermo, is located on the Mojave Desert, where excellent outdoor storage conditions are possible because of low humidity and small amount of rainfall, thus limiting mold, rust and mildew to equipment. Another ad-

vantage is its geographic location with reference to transportation. The ten-acre Repair Shop, largest building of its kind in the Marine Corps, is located in the Yermo area. The Center's responsibility is to receive, store, maintain, repair, issue and/or ship material as directed by the Inventory Control Point in Philadelphia, Pennsylvania, without regard to geographic location of customers.

TRANSPORTATION. *Rail.* Santa Fe; Union Pacific; and Southern Pacific (coastwise).

Bus. Greyhound and Continental Trailways.

Airports. Los Angeles International and McCarron Field, Las Vegas.

Highways. Interstates 40 and 15; State Highway 58

QUARTERS. Government housing is available for married military personnel and their families at both the Nebo and Yermo areas, plus additional space at Yermo for 12 privately-owned mobile homes. The waiting period for housing varies, depending on rank and the size and composition of family. There are 310 public quarters for all noncommissioned grades including corporals with over four years' service (as well as for those with less service). An off-base Housing Referral Service operates as part of the Housing Office at the Center. Military personnel must check with the Housing Office before executing any commitments for private housing.

SCHOOLS. Public schools located in the towns of Barstow, Yermo, Daggett, Hinkley, and Newberry are available to children of military personnel attached to the Center. Elementary schools are located in all the above listed towns, as well as East Barstow School adjacent to the Center. There are two high schools and a junior college. There are also two parochial schools. Public school buses provide transportation.

RECREATION. There are the staff NCO club and enlisted club. Because of its desert location and proximity to metropolitan areas, the Center offers numerous off-duty and recreational facilities. Special Services offers a variety of trips to special events for military personnel and their dependents. Other recreational features operated by the Center include swimming pools, a nine-hole golf course, softball fields, tennis courts, handball courts, a completely equipped gymnasium, an intramural athletic program featuring year-round sports competition, two theaters, libraries, automotive and body-fender hobby shops, wood and ceramic shops, bowling alley, ham radio station, skeet and trap range, and stables. Obregon Park at Yermo is a popular spot for year-round outings and picnics.

COMMISSARY AND EXCHANGE. Excellent.

MEDICAL CARE. The Center has a well-equipped 40-bed dispensary which provides inpatient and outpatient care, as well as related treatments, such as immunizations and physical examinations. The Outpatient Department ministers to dependents on an appointment-only basis. Emergencies are taken care of at any time.

DENTAL CARE. The Dental Section provides dental services to all military personnel of the Center, as well as retired military residing in the area. An active preventive dentistry program is in effect for military, and also dependent children of active-duty military personnel. X-rays are provided for dependents of active-duty personnel upon presentation of a prescription from their civilian dentist.

724. MARINE CORPS RECRUIT DEPOT, SAN DIEGO, CALIFORNIA, 92140. The primary mission of the Recruit Depot is the training of recruit Marines, but it is also the home of West Coast Sea School and Communication-Electronics School. The Depot recruits come from the 8th, 9th, 12th and portions of the 4th Marine Corps Districts. The Depot is located in northwest San Diego on Highway 101.

TRANSPORTATION. *Rail.* Santa Fe.

Bus. Greyhound, Santa Fe Trailways, and Continental Trailways.

Airport. San Diego International Airport.

Highways. U.S. 5, 8, and I-101.

QUARTERS. Except for a limited number of bachelor staff NCO quarters, there are no Government quarters for married enlisted personnel on the Depot and no Hostess House. Married SNCOs and NCOs with dependents are eligible for Navy Housing, Capehart and Rehabilitated Wherry—operated by the 11th Naval District under agreement with the Depot. The waiting period depends on the size of the quarters required and on the type desired. SNCOs and NCOs with dependents must report to the Navy Public Works Center, San Diego, for an endorsement of quarters availability prior to authorization of quarters allowance.

SCHOOLS. No Depot schools, but San Diego has excellent public, private, and parochial primary and secondary schools. Also, there are three major colleges in the city plus numerous junior colleges.

RECREATION. Southern California supplies virtually every type of recreation from swimming to skiing. The staff NCO club is one of the finest in the Corps.

COMMISSARY AND EXCHANGE. There are three Navy commissaries in the San Diego area. MCRD has an outstanding Marine Exchange.

DEPENDENTS' MEDICAL CARE. U. S. Naval Hospital, Balboa, San Diego.

725. MCB, CAMP PENDLETON, CALIFORNIA, 92055. "Pendleton" is the largest amphibious training base in the Corps. It serves as the major West Coast base for ground units of the Fleet Marine Force and provides facilities and support for a Marine division and some units of Force Troops. In addition, Camp Pendleton includes Edson Range, the weapons training center for the San Diego Recruit Depot. The base has a Naval Hospital, on the shores of Lake O'Neill, named for one of the most redoubtable and courageous Navy medical officers to serve with the Marine Corps.

At Pendleton, recruits who have successfully graduated from San Diego receive advanced individual combat training and basic specialist training. Training conducted by the 2d Infantry Training

Camp Pendleton is surrounded by California hills.

Regiment includes Individual Combat Training, Basic Specialist Training for the infantry MOSs; Weapons Indoctrination Courses for Navy personnel; and Predeployment Training for Marines en route to combat areas. Basic Specialist Training for MOS other than infantry, Formal Schools Training, and Specialized Predeployment Training are conducted by the Schools Battalion. As during the Pacific and Korean Wars, Pendleton is the training "funnel" through which the majority of Marine battle replacements pass on their way to Vietnam.

Camp Pendleton covers 125,000 acres of terrain which includes three mountain ranges and 17 miles of coastline.

TRANSPORTATION. *Rail.* Santa Fe, at Oceanside, California, the adjacent civilian community.

Bus. Santa Fe Trailways, Greyhound, and American Bus Lines. (Rail and bus require local taxi or bus transportation from Oceanside to the base.)

Air. San Diego International Airport; Marine Corps Auxiliary Landing Field (MCALF) at Pendleton.

Highways. Interstate 5 and U. S. 395.

QUARTERS. Located aboard Pendleton are about 1300 sets of two- to four-bedroom quarters for married corporals and above with over four years of service. In addition, there are about 600 one-, two-, and three-bedroom units for married corporals and below with under four years of service. Private housing ashore is available in Ocean-side, Carlsbad, Vista, Fallbrook, and San Clemente.

Before bringing dependents to Camp Pendleton, it is nevertheless advisable, as in the case of Lejeune, to write the Base Housing Office for information. This office can post you on the quarters situation and can, if necessary, help you in finding and forecasting available civilian housing, through the Off-Base Housing Referral Office. There are ample transient bachelor accommodations, and transient NCOs with families may stay at the Hostess House, up to two weeks, by advance reservation.

There are presently 336 rooms with an average occupancy of 500 bachelor SNCOs. Gunnery sergeants and above are provided single rooms when available.

SCHOOLS. Educational facilities for Camp Pendleton Marines and their dependents are excellent. Public, parochial, and some private schools, together with Mira Costa and Palomar Junior Colleges in the immediate vicinity, offer courses for qualified Marines and their families, as do other colleges in the San Diego area. Chapman College has an on-base program offering undergraduate and graduate courses leading to baccalaureate and advanced degrees. Oceanside High School offers evening classes for Marines desiring a high school diploma.

RECREATION. Recreational activities include a surfing beach, riding stables, championship 18-hole golf course, skeet and trap, picnicking, boating and sailing at the Lake O'Neill Recreation Center, field archery range; scuba diving, bowling, tennis, and freshwater and saltwater fishing. In addition, libraries, movies, and live entertainment round out the list of things to do with free time. Various clubs provide outlets for diversified interests such as judo, rock hounds, surfing, skydiving, flying, archery, and square dancing. Youth activities for dependent children include Little League, junior league baseball, football, learn-to-swim programs, and organized playground activities. In addition, there are nine branches of the staff NCO club and five branches of the NCO club located throughout Camp Pendleton.

DEPENDENTS MEDICAL CARE. Inpatient and outpatient medical care to dependents is provided by a Naval hospital. The Civilian Health and Medical Program of the Uniformed Services (which provides for expanded civilian medical care for dependents of active duty personnel) is administered through the Dependents Outpatient Clinic.

COMMISSARY AND EXCHANGE. A modernized commissary is available in the main area of the base, with annexes in the northern section and in the Sterling Homes area, located in Oceanside. The exchange is modern and complete.

726. MCAS, EL TORO (SANTA ANA), CALIFORNIA, 92630. El Toro is the West Coast base for aviation units of the FMF. The base houses and supports a Marine air wing.

TRANSPORTATION. *Rail.* Santa Fe (with connections to Los Angeles).

Bus. Greyhound; Rapid Transit District (RDT) buses to Los Angeles.

Highway. U. S. 101.

Airports. Orange County Airport (jet service) with connections to Los Angeles International Airport.

QUARTERS. Newly renovated SNCO Barracks; public quarters (waiting list three-four months). Housing in Santa Ana, Costa Mesa, El Toro, Mission Viejo, Tustin, Orange, and Laguna Beach is scarce and expensive.

SCHOOLS. Kindergarten through sixth grade available on base. Grades seven to eight attend Urvine Junior High, grades 9 to 12 attend Mission Viejo. Parochial schools are available in Santa Ana.

RECREATION. SNCO club; swimming pool; golf course; riding stables, and theater.

COMMISSARY AND EXCHANGE: Excellent.

DEPENDENT MEDICAL CARE: The dependents' clinic is equipped and staffed to care for dependents. Hospitalization of dependents is accomplished through admission to the U. S. Naval Hospital, Camp Pendleton or through military medicare.

727. MARINE ACTIVITIES IN THE HAWAIIAN AREA. The island of Oahu includes several permanent Marine Corps installations with diverse missions. The headquarters and nerve center of all Fleet Marine Force Pacific activities is at Camp H. M. Smith, overlooking Pearl Harbor from the site of the World War II Aiea Naval Hospital. In addition to Camp H. M. Smith, there is MCAS, Kaneohe, on the windward side of the island, home station in normal times of the 1st Marine Brigade and one of two Marine Corps air stations outside continental United States; here both ground and air units of the FMF train and operate as an integrated air-ground team. The Pearl Harbor Marine Barracks, together with smaller barracks at Barber's Point NAS and at Naval Ammunition Depot, Lualualei, perform security missions. Because of its superb site and outstanding facilities, Camp H. M. Smith was chosen by Commander-in-Chief, Pacific, for his headquarters, which is a tenant activity. Camp Smith is thus the only Marine Corps station which also serves as the headquarters of a unified command. Other Marines serve at the Makalapa headquarters of Commander-in-Chief, Pacific Fleet.

QUARTERS. Bachelor quarters for NCOs/SNCOs are available at all Marine Corps activities on Oahu. Married quarters at Kaneohe are on station, while Camp Smith's main housing area is about six miles from the camp. All noncommissioned officers with more than four years' service are eligible for assignment to public quarters. Waiting periods vary greatly in length. The Armed Services Community Housing Office (ASCHO) has the responsibility of assisting all incoming personnel in obtaining private rentals. Adequate housing on the economy is scarce and expensive, but temporary lodging allowance is available for qualifying personnel for a reasonable period until permanent housing is acquired. Up-to-date information on housing availability and policy is mailed to incoming personnel prior to their departure from their old duty station.

SCHOOLS. In most areas, both public and parochial schools of acceptable quality are located on Government property or in or near housing areas. Public high schools are also conveniently located while excellent private and parochial high schools are to be found in Honolulu which, although some distance from the various Marine bases, is accessible by bus.

RECREATION. Oahu and its naval and military installations afford some of the best all-around recreation and liberty in the Marine Corps. In addition to several excellent clubs and messes, Hawaii provides opportunity for virtually every sport or taste.

COMMISSARY AND EXCHANGE. All services maintain adequate commissaries and exchanges on Oahu, although prices are generally higher than in California.

DEPENDENTS' MEDICAL CARE. Dependents' medical care is available at the dispensary operated at the command to which the sponsor is attached. Cases requiring hospitalization or specialized treatment are referred to the Tripler Army General Hospital.

728. CAMP SMEDLEY D. BUTLER, OKINAWA. For the operation of all Marine Corps facilities on Okinawa, where a Marine division and part of an aircraft wing are normally garrisoned, Camp Smedley D. Butler, with headquarters in south-center Okinawa, has the job of providing logistic and administrative support.

TRANSPORTATION. Chartered commercial aircraft use Kadena AFB, while commercial airlines use Naha International Airport. Marine Corps Air Facility, Futema, handles military traffic for Marine Units and installations on Okinawa.

QUARTERS. No dependents' quarters are available.

RECREATION. Noncommissioned Officers' Messes; fishing; aquatic sports; skin diving; hobby shops; movies.

COMMISSARY AND EXCHANGE. Army and Air Force garrison units have large, excellently stocked commissaries and exchanges open to Marines.

729. MCAS, IWAKUNI, JAPAN. Iwakuni, for some time an MCAF, is now the Marine Corps's newest air station and the only such west of the Hawaiian area. While the station has some quarters, its future development cannot be forecast.

TRANSPORTATION. *Rail.* Japan National Railways has outstanding fast service to all points.

Airport. Nearest international airport is Itami (Osaka). Military traffic, of course, flies directly into Iwakuni.

RECREATION. Noncommissioned Officers' Mess.

COMMISSARY AND POST EXCHANGE. Adequate.

Smaller Posts

730. "FROM THE DAWN TO SETTING SUN . . . " In addition to the large posts just described, the Corps maintains more than 80 Marine Barracks or Detachments at home and abroad, together with handpicked embassy guards throughout the world. If you should be ordered to any of these posts, seek out some NCO who has recently returned, or write the adjutant for local information.

731. POSTS IN THE CONTINENTAL UNITED STATES. Here are the most important smaller Marine Corps stateside posts.

California:
MB, NAS, Alameda; MB, Fallbrook Annex, Fallbrook; MB, NAS, North Island, San Diego; MB, NSY, San Francisco (Hunter's Point); MB, Naval Weapons Station, Seal Beach; MB, Naval Weapons Station, Concord; MB, NB, Long Beach (Terminal Island); MB, Vallejo (Mare Island); MB, NAS, Moffett Field; MB, NS, San Diego; MB, NS, Treasure Island, San Francisco; Landing Force Training Command, (LFTC) NAB, Coronado; MCAS (Helicopter), Santa Ana; MB, NAS, Lemoore; MAD, Naval Missile Center, Pt. Mugu.

Connecticut:
MB, Submarine Base, New London.

Florida:
MB, NAS, Jacksonville; MB, NAS, Sanford; MB, NB, Key West; MB, NAS, Cecil Field; MAD, NABTC, Pensacola; MAD, NATTC, Jacksonville.

Georgia:
MAD, NATTC, Glynco.

Illinois:
MB, Naval Training Center, Great Lakes (Chicago).

Maine:
NB, NAS, Brunswick.

Maryland:
MB, NS, Annapolis; MB, Fort Meade; MAD, NAS, Patuxent River.

Massachusetts:
MB, NB, Boston (Charlestown).

Nevada:
MB, Naval Ammunition Depot, Hawthorne; MB, Lake Meade, Las Vegas.

New Hampshire:
MB, NSY, Portsmouth; MD, Naval Disciplinary Command, Portsmouth.

New Jersey:
MB, NAS, Lakehurst; MB, Naval Ammunition Depot, Earle.

New York:
MB, NB, Brooklyn.

North Carolina:
MCAS (Helicopter), New River (Peterfield Point).

Oklahoma:
MB, Naval Ammunition Depot, McAlester.
Pennsylvania:
MB, NB, Philadelphia.
Rhode Island:
MB, NB, Newport; MB, NAS, Quonset.
South Carolina:
MB, NB, Charleston; MB, Naval Weapons Station, Charleston.
Tennessee:
MB, Clarkesville; MAD, NATTC, Memphis.
Texas:
MAD, NATTC, NAS, Corpus Christi.
Virginia:
MB, NSY, Norfolk (Portsmouth); MB, NB, Norfolk (Hampton Roads); MB, Naval Weapons Station, Yorktown; Landing Force Training Command (LFTC), NAB, Little Creek.
Washington:
MB, NAS, Whidbey Island; MB, Naval Ammunition Depot, Bangor; MB, Bremerton.

732. OVERSEAS POSTS. Marines serve in the overseas states and possessions of the United States, as well as in foreign countries (not including the embassy guards), as follows:

Alaska: MB, NS, Adak; MB, NS, Kodiak.
Bermuda: MB, Naval Station.
Canal Zone: MB, 15th Naval District Activities, Rodman.
Cuba: MB, NB, Guantanamo Bay.
England: MD, London.
Hawaii:
MB, NAS, Barber's Point; MB, Naval Ammunition Depot, Oahu; MB, Pearl Harbor.
Iceland: MB, Naval Forces, Iceland.
Italy:
MB, Naval Support Activity, Naples.
Japan:
MB, NAS, Atsugi; MB, Fleet Activities, Sasebo; MB, Fleet Activities, Yokosuka.
Marianas Islands: MB, Guam.
Morocco: MB, Kenitra (Port Lyautey).
Newfoundland: MB, NS, Argentia.
Okinawa:
MCAF, Futema; MB, NAF, Naha.
Philippine Republic: MB, NB, Subic Bay.
Puerto Rico: MB, NS, Roosevelt Roads; MB, San Juan.
Spain: MB, Naval Activities, Rota.

*In its outstanding service to our Corps, the
Marine Corps Reserve has earned the right to
be called our "Secret Weapon."*

—General L. C. Shepherd, Jr.

8 The Marine Corps Reserve

In many ways the Marine Corps Reserve is the backbone of today's
Marine Corps. Without a high-quality ready Reserve, the Marine
Corps could not retain its position as the national force in readiness.
The Reserve has this mission:

> To provide a trained force of qualified commissioned, warrant and enlisted
> personnel and/or trained units to meet requirements for the initial ex-
> pansion of the regular Marine Corps in time of war or national emergency.

Two wars (World War II and Korea) have tested the Reserve, and
in each it fulfilled its mission to the hilt.

801. HISTORY OF THE RESERVE. The Marine Corps Reserve
came into being in 1916 with an initial strength of three officers and
33 enlisted men. Despite its eventual importance, the Reserve played
no significant role in World War I. In fact, it nearly died on its feet
in the early 1920s as a result of fiscal starvation. But for the loyalty
of pioneer reservists of that decade, there might not be a Marine
Corps Reserve.

Following enactment by Congress of the Naval Reserve Act of
1925, the Marine Corps Reserve began to come into its own. This
legislation for the first time permitted individual training duty with
pay, as well as the organization of drilling units in pay status. Training programs were instituted, and units sprang up in 1927. This
prosperity was short-lived, however, for the depression years of 1929
to 1933 found the Reserve again without funds. During those lean
years most units continued to drill and train without pay—even
buying their own uniforms—and thus again the Reserve was saved.

It was 1935 before the Reserve was finally able to stand on its
own feet. The year 1935 saw these developments.

1. Appropriations for training an organized and volunteer Marine Corps Reserve (ground and aviation) totaling almost 10,000 officers and enlisted Marines;
2. Inauguration of Platoon Leaders Class in order to obtain a steady input of well-trained, carefully selected junior Reserve officers from colleges not participating in Army or Naval ROTC;
3. Dawn of the Reserve pilot program for Marine Corps aviation —an extra dividend of the Naval Aviation Cadet Act of 1935.

In 1938 the 1925 Naval Reserve Act was brought up to date by Congress; the most important aspect was the provision, for the first time, of a charter of rights and benefits for the Reserve. Among these milestones were hospitalization, death and disability benefits, equitable promotion, retirement with pay for active service, and the right to participate in formulation of Reserve policy. Under the Naval Reserve Act of 1938, the Marine Corps Reserve has twice accomplished its job of providing a trained force in readiness.

The solid success of the peacetime Reserve was proven in 1939 (when individual reservists were brought to active duty after President Roosevelt's proclamation of limited national emergency in September of the year), and a year later, when mobilization of the remainder of the Reserve brought 15,138 additional Marines to the Colors. The extent to which the Reserve found its place in the Corps was proven, in 1945, by the fact that, of the 471,000-man Corps, largest in 170 years, approximately 70 percent were reservists.

Much of the Reserve's effectiveness throughout World War II resulted from the philosophy behind its mobilization, a philosophy which today is stronger than ever. Although the 1940 Reserve was built around 36 hometown battalions and squadrons, each with its local associations and comradeship, General Holcomb, then Commandant, believed that no Marine, regular or reserve, while on active duty, should claim any home but the Corps. Thus, as Reserve units reached mobilization points, they disbanded, and their members simply became individual Marines headed for service in the expanding regular units of the Fleet Marine Force. To drive home this point and to emphasize that every man wearing the Globe and Anchor was a Marine, no more and no less, General Holcomb decreed that, except where required by law for administrative purposes the word *Reserve* and its corresponding abbreviation, *R,* following the *USMC,* would not be used. All hands, reserve and regular, were Marines.

That policy remains in effect and has become a tradition of the Corps.

Following World War II, the postwar buildup of its Reserve was one of the great achievements of the Corps. Through good leadership (regular and reserve), through willingness to invest capable personnel in the Reserve program, and because of the unflagging loyalty of former Marines—*"Who ever saw a sorehead ex-Marine?"* asked a

162   prominent journalist—the Reserve was in unmatched readiness to
back up the regular Corps when the Korean War flamed up.

In the field in Korea, as in Pacific battles before, it was impossible
to distinguish reservist from regular. Once again, as always, all hands
were Marines. Among those who had originally started as reservists,
however, it is worth noting that in World War II and Korea some
57 in all won Medals of Honor.

Mobilized by President Truman, this Organized Reserve battalion from
Washington, D.C. marched off to Korea. Without a high-spirited combat-
ready Reserve, the Inchon landings would not have been possible.

Soon after the end of the Korean War, Congress passed the Reserve Forces Act of 1955 which has exercised and will continue to exercise a profound effect on the reserve components of all the Armed Forces, including the Marine Corps. This law (see Section 802 for details), among other features, provided for the so-called "Six Months' Training Program" whereby young men, after receiving six months of hard training with and by regular forces, then enter the Organized Reserve for a prescribed period of years of obligated service. At the time of writing, more than two-thirds of the Organized Reserve includes personnel with some form of legally obligated

service, with a background of professional basic training and therefore with a degree of readiness which has been greatly increased even over that readiness traditional in earlier days. Reflecting this heightened capability, the Reserve was reorganized on 1 July 1962, to provide a unit mobilization structure, embodied in the 4th Marine Division, 4th Marine Aircraft Wing, and added Force Troops units. These can be mobilized and employed as units; however, the Organized Reserve still maintains additional units whose function is to provide trained individual Marines for fleshing-out Regular and Reserve units. This extensive reorganization attests the truth of a statement by a recent Commandant:

> Never before has our dependence upon the Reserve been so great and never before has our Reserve been more worthy of that dependence.

Organization and Composition

802. ORGANIZATION OF THE MARINE CORPS RESERVE. The Marine Corps Reserve today is organized and maintained under the Armed Forces Reserve Act of 1952, which superseded the 1938 Naval Reserve Act. This law incorporated the basic principles of its predecessor, but modernized the Reserve by adding features essential under the increasingly important role which the Reserve has assumed in plans for national defense.

Since the Reserve is a component of the Marine Corps as a whole, command and administration of the Reserve stem directly from the Commandant. Thus the departments and offices of Marine Corps Headquarters bear the same relationships and responsibilities toward the Reserve as they do toward the remainder of the Corps.

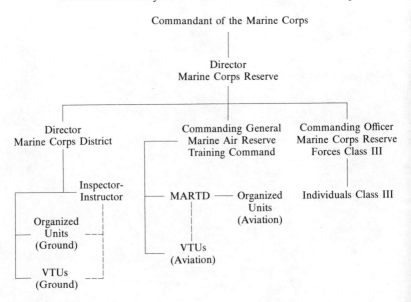

Fig. 8-1: Organization of the Marine Corps Reserve.

803. DIVISION OF RESERVE. The Division of Reserve, headed by the Director, Marine Corps Reserve, a general officer, supervises and coordinates the activities of units and members of the Reserve. The Director, Marine Corps Reserve, advises the Commandant and staff on matters pertaining to the Reserve and directs and exercises control over the Reserve through the several *Marine Corps District directors* and Commanding General, Marine Air Reserve Training Command. The duties and functions of the foregoing agencies are described in the following sections.

804. MARINE AIR RESERVE TRAINING COMMAND. Organized Reserve aviation units are supervised by the Commanding General, Marine Air Reserve Training Command, whose headquarters is at Naval Air Station (NAS), Glenview, Illinois (near Chicago). CG. MARTC, as this commander is short-titled, comes under the military command of the Commandant, but, like all Marine aviation, receives certain logistic support from the naval air establishment—in this case, from the Chief of Naval Air Reserve Training.

805. MARINE CORPS DISTRICTS. The Marine Corps divides the continental United States into seven Marine Corps districts for administration and coordination of reserve affairs, recruiting, and officer procurement.

Each district is headed by a Marine district director, administratively independent and directly responsible to the Commandant. The district director supervises and coordinates the training of Reserve ground units within the district. The district director is responsible, insofar as the Reserve is concerned, for the procurement, administration, discipline, instruction, and mobilization readiness of all reservists under his command. In addition to these duties, district directors maintain liaison with corresponding reserve and recruiting agencies of the other three services, state adjutants general, other Federal agencies (particularly field offices of the Veterans Administration), schools and colleges, and veterans' associations and military societies.

Each district bears a number which corresponds with the naval district in which its headquarters are located. Since a number of the original naval districts have been merged or modified and certain Marine Corps districts consolidated, you may notice gaps or seeming inconsistencies in the numbering of Marine Corps districts. The headquarters and numbers of the respective districts are:

District Number	Headquarters at	
First	New York, N.Y.	
Fourth	Philadelphia, Pa.	
Sixth	Atlanta, Ga.	
Eighth	New Orleans, La.	
Ninth	Kansas City, Mo.	
Twelfth*	San Francisco, Calif.	
Fourteenth	Pearl Harbor, Hawaii	* Includes Alaska

The *Marine Corps Automated Service Center,* at Kansas City, automates and centralizes all Reserve records and disbursing. To facilitate rapid mobilization, the MCADSC can, if necessary, have orders in the mail activating every single Reserve unit and reservist within 18 hours.

If you are a member of the Reserve but not affiliated with a unit or if you live in a locality without a local unit, the district director's office can help you maintain contact with the Corps. If you wish to join the Reserve but have no hometown unit, your district director can help you in this, too.

Marine Reserve affairs outside the United States are administered by the CO, Marine Corps Reserve Forces, Class III.

If you live outside the territorial jurisdiction of the United States and are a member of the Reserve, or desire to be, write to the CO, Marine Corps Reserve Forces, Class III, 1500 East Bannister Road, Kansas City, Missouri, 64131.

806. MARINE CORPS RESERVE UNITS. To a greater extent than many Marines realize, the Corps entrusts its readiness to the units of the Organized Reserve. They are the backbone of the Reserve and constitute the mobilization backbone of the Corps.

The Organized Marine Corps Reserve has been patterned on the MEF (see Chapter 3). Hence you will find ground and aviation units similar to those of the regular establishment. The 4th Marine Division Headquarters nucleus is established at Camp Pendleton, while the staff of MARTC doubles as Headquarters, 4th Marine Aircraft Wing.

Since Organized Reserve units follow the Fleet Marine Force pattern, the administration and functions of these units are carried on in the same way as in similar units in the regular establishment.

Organized ground units are commanded by reserve officers who have been selected for their professional experience and background. Like all commanding officers, they must administer, train, and maintain the readiness of their commands. In addition, however, they must conduct whatever recruiting is needed to keep their units up to strength.

Organized aviation units, like ground units, are commanded by reserve officers whose responsibilities are much like those of ground unit COs in the Organized Reserve.

Because of the large amount of technical training, the paramount requirement for safe flight operations, and the quantities of expensive materiel (including airplanes) which an aviation reserve unit requires, the inspection-instruction organization for reserve aviation outfits differs from that used with ground units.

At the home station of each Organized Reserve aviation unit, a parent Marine Air Reserve Training Detachment is located. This detachment is commanded by a regular Marine Corps aviator, usually a field grade officer with assistant instructors and maintenance crews to support the reserve squadron. The reserve unit's commanding officer comes under the command of the CO of the Reserve Training Detachment.

Staff Groups permit drill pay and Organized Reserve status for senior reserve officers for whom mobilization requirements exist, but who cannot train with other Organized Reserve units. Staff Groups attend paid drills and annual field training.

Volunteer Training Units (VTUs) are not part of the Organized Reserve but afford training in staff and command functions, ground and air, for reserve officers and NCOs ordinarily not associated with an organized unit, who want to stay with the Corps, keep up professional training, and amass credits for reserve retirement.

A Volunteer Training Unit may be made up of six or more members (men or women, officer or NCO) of any military specialty or combination of specialties. Most VTUs train under a specified syllabus provided by Marine Corps Schools, but some specialize in given fields when all members hold the same or related military occupational specialties. Each VTU is assigned an adviser by the CG, MARTC, or District Director. The adviser is usually the nearest I & I (see Section 809) or commanding officer, MARTD.

807. COMPOSITION OF THE RESERVE. The Marine Corps Reserve includes different individual classes for mobilization planning and assignment which vary according to the preferences and background of the reservist. Thus the reserve affords varying opportunities for activity which can usually be adjusted to the desires of anyone qualified to be a Marine.

Fleet Marine Corps Reserve (Class I). Usually short-titled "the Fleet Reserve," Class I is composed entirely of former regular enlisted Marines who enter this status under various laws which, in general, allow transfer to the Fleet Reserve after 20 years active service. Thus the Fleet Reserve provides a backlog of experienced noncommissioned officers who may be employed without further training when the bell rings for full mobilization. Fleet reservists remain in Class I (which in peacetime amounts practically, if not legally, to semiretirement on retainer pay) until they complete 30 years' combined regular and reserve service. Then they are eligible for retirement.

Organized Marine Corps Reserve OMCR (Class II). As you have seen earlier, the Organized Reserve comprises over 45,000 officer and NCO members of organized units which can be immediately assimilated into the FMF. For this reason Organized Reservists must measure up to physical and professional standards comparable to those required of regulars. Today, the majority of the men in the Organized Reserve are young, intelligent, highly motivated six-month trainees with a six-year military obligation; the balance are prior-service noncommissioned officers who provide the necessary hard-skill experience and seasoned leadership. Members of the Organized Reserve attend semimonthly or monthly drills, go to camp for annual training with their unit, and get paid for the drills and training they perform. If you wish to become a Class II reservist (over and above required individual standards), you must be able to attend the regular drills of your unit at its home station. This does not ordinarily present too serious a problem, however, since more than 175 U. S. cities and towns boast organized units of the Marine Corps Reserve. Today, the bulk of the members of Organized Reserve units are Marines with obligated service, and Class II of the Reserve includes only personnel in the category of the "Ready Reserve" (see Section 808).

Volunteer Marine Corps (Class III). Class III, effectively speaking, includes all physically qualified Marine reservists not assigned to Classes I and II. The mission of the Volunteer Reserve is to provide the Marine Corps with personnel for complete mobilization in time of war or emergency.

The Volunteer Reserve is composed of individuals who are classified as either Ready Reservists or Standby Reservists. In order for a Class III reservist to be assigned to active duty for training or to participate in a Volunteer Training Unit (see Section 806), he must be a Ready Reservist.

The Volunteer Reserve gives an opportunity for Marine Corps membership to many men and women whose personal commitments might otherwise preclude this, and the Reserve program includes voluntary training opportunities designed to suit almost any combination of individual convenience or specialization which may apply to you.

Women Reservists. Women reservists fall into the Fleet, Organized, or Volunteer Reserve according to their individual circumstances and qualifications and the policies prescribed by the Commandant (see Chapter 9).

808. RESERVE CATEGORIES FOR ACTIVE DUTY. The reserve establishment is also broken down into three categories, in descending order of availability and of eligibility to perform active duty.

Ready Reserve. Members of the Ready Reserve may, in time of national emergency, be required to serve on active duty for a period not longer than 24 months. In time of war or national emergency declared by Congress, this service may be extended for the duration of the war or national emergency, plus six months thereafter. The Ready Reserve includes about 100,000 Marines.

Standby Reserve. In time of war or national emergency, Marines of the Standby Reserve may be ordered to active duty for its duration and for six months thereafter. This cannot be accomplished without their consent, however, unless the Director of Selective Service has determined that they are available for active service. Members of the so-called "Inactive Status List" cannot be ordered to active duty under these provisions unless the Secretary of the Navy determines that inadequate numbers of active-status personnel are available.

Retired Reserve. These reservists who have attained retirement cannot be ordered to active duty without their own consent, even in event of war or national emergency, unless the Secretary of the Navy determines that there are insufficient reservists in an active status. The tour of duty, as above, is for the duration plus six months.

Reserve Training

809. THE INSPECTOR-INSTRUCTOR. To insure that the Reserve has the benefit of coordinated and professional up-to-date training, certain advisory personnel from the regular Marine Corps are detailed to duty with the Reserve.

Each organized ground unit has a regular Marine officer (with a small staff) whose title is *"Inspector-Instructor."* This title describes the job exactly. The "I & I," as he is known, must, as instructor, provide training assistance and general guidance to the unit. As inspector, however, he must make certain that the unit is up to the standards set by Marine Corps Headquarters. Inspector-Instructors are under the direct command of their respective Marine Corps district directors. As we have seen in paragraph 806, functions com-

During summer active duty the reserve Marine can sharpen up his bayonet training.

parable to those of the I & I are performed for aviation reserve units by the CO, reserve training detachment.

810. NONCOMMISSIONED I & I STAFF. The backbone of the I & I team is a cadre of specially selected regular noncommissioned officers who conduct training, keep unit administration on the track, and, most important, set the Marine Corps example.

A typical I & I group of NCOs would be headed by a first sergeant. Under him might come a gunnery sergeant, a supply sergeant, a motor transport NCO, a communication chief, clerical and administrative NCOs, and added noncommissioned officers according to the size and military specialty of the supported unit.

811. HINTS FOR I & I NCOs. Your job (and for that matter, any duty in connection with the Reserve or ROTC) calls for demonstrated leadership, imagination, and tact. Your responsibilities are heavy (a lot heavier than they look on paper). Although your job is a big one, it can give you corresponding rewards. In most cases you alone represent the active Marine Corps in your community. By your conduct and example and loyalty to what the Corps stands for, your fellow townsmen form their impression of the whole Marine Corps.

DO'S AND DON'T'S. Dress as well as your pocketbook will permit, but don't be extreme in your civilian clothes, which of course you will wear more often than when on line duty. Coat and tie is always the safest rule. Own and wear the Marine Corps club and regimental ties (see Chapter 6).

When in uniform, take care to be *absolutely perfect* (see Chapter 6). Always carry gloves with winter service. Wear blues on social or other occasions when representing the Corps.

Answer all questions, but always be sure you know what you are talking about. The proper answer to any question whose answer you don't know is never, "I don't know," but rather, "I'll find out."

Always be restrained in manner and language. The civilian environment is made up of many differing points of view on every possible issue. Be prepared for give-and-take in every situation. Avoid overassertiveness.

If there are cliques or factions in the supported reserve unit, avoid taking sides and demonstrate that such pettiness is inappropriate among Marines.

812. TRAINING OPPORTUNITIES IN THE RESERVE. Every Organized Reserve unit has to complete a carefully worked out annual training cycle. In addition to this unit training program, you, as an individual reservist, may avail yourself of a wide selection of courses, volunteer periods of training duty, and gratis home study courses (both Marine Corps Schools Extension Courses and Marine Corps Institute—see Chapter 12). This selection of training activities affords something for every individual's interests and opportunities.

Organized Reserve Training. Training of the average OMCR unit consists of 48 paid drills or flying periods, each consisting of at least four training hours and two weeks' annual active-duty training. Certain units, such as Staff Groups and Marine Air Reserve Groups, are only authorized 24 paid drills and their two-week period of active-duty training.

Reserve training is as meaningful as human effort can make it. By holding "multiple drills" at which two or more paid drills are consolidated consecutively, Organized Reserve units now train two full days a month, frequently on a single weekend. This permits realistic field training including overnight problems. The amount of air-ground and combined arms training is considerable, with two or more neighboring units joining in weekend exercises. Organized Reserve artillery units (which in general are located near Army or Marine Corps bases with range facilities) conduct live firing throughout the year.

The hometown Organized Reserve training cycle culminates annually in two weeks' training by the unit at a Marine Corps station. It follows a cycle to include desert, mountain, jungle, amphibious, air-ground, combined arms, and specialist training. When possible, the Marine Corps arranges the movement of Organized Reserve outfits to and from annual training by Marine airlift or in amphibious shipping. This increases the adaptability, professional know-how, and experience of the unit concerned.

As a member of the Organized Reserve, you receive "drill pay" for each drill you attend, as well as for summer camp, and this pay can provide a welcome augmentation for your income.

Volunteer Reserve Training. If you are in the Volunteer Reserve, you do not have to attend drills, but may be required to perform training duty not exceeding 15 days a year. (NCOs in certain categories must perform 30 days' active duty annually.) Many opportunities are open to you to train with Organized Reserve units or Volunteer Training Units on your own initiative with or without pay. If you aim to maintain your professional proficiency and to accrue credits for reserve retirement with pay (see Section 819), you can keep up-to-date by periodic spells of training duty and through the medium of MCS Extension School or MCI correspondence courses.

813. CATEGORIES OF RESERVE TRAINING AND IN-STRUCTION. All training which you perform as a reservist falls into one of the following categories.

Regular drills are performed only by the Organized Reserve; they must last at least four hours, must be regularly scheduled, and must be carried out in uniform.

Equivalent instruction or *equivalent duty* is a substitute period, performed on some other day, for a regular drill which has been or will be missed. Only members of the Organized Reserve perform equivalent duty.

Appropriate duty is any type of duty or training authorized for you as an individual by the Commandant, as appropriate to your rank and military qualifications.

Administrative duty, over and above regular drills, is performed by Organized Reserve COs in connection with the discipline, administration, or maintenance of Government property of an organized unit. If in the Volunteer Reserve, you may perform administrative duty without pay, but thereby accrue credit toward reserve retirement.

Annual training duty is performed by Organized Reserve units only, and lasts 15 days. It is usually conducted at a Marine Corps post, and concentrates on the mobilization mission of the unit.

Active duty, although technically not training duty, enables many reservists, especially Volunteers, to obtain much valuable training. Active duty may be either for a stated period (by contract or "Standard Written Agreement"), or of indefinite duration. Except in war or national emergency, no reservist may be called to active duty except by his own request.

Active duty for training (with or without pay) differs from active duty in that the avowed purpose of the duty is training. Active duty for training may be performed with or without pay, according to your request and to the state of the Marine Corps budget.

Repeated training duty without pay may be performed by any reservist. This category of duty confers authority to perform repeated training-duty periods (such as aerial flights or participation in rifle or pistol matches) but without pay.

Extension courses are open to you from the Extension School at Quantico and from the Marine Corps Institute (MCI) in Washington. You can find out about these in Chapter 12.

814. OBLIGATED SERVICE AND TRAINING. The Reserve Forces Act of 1955, mentioned earlier, provides new alternatives to the draft (including new ways to obtain deferment) and changes future military obligations of American young men. The most important part of this Act is the "six-month" special enlistment training program whereby you can go on active duty for six months and then complete your military obligation by serving five and one-half years in the Ready Reserve. In general, the six-month program is open to young men between the ages of seventeen and twenty-six.

Once you have entered this program and have completed your six months of training with and by the regular Marine Corps (including boot camp at San Diego or Parris Island), you must remain in the Organized Reserve and complete 48 drills per year and attend up to 17 days' active duty for training, or lose your draft deferment.

If you are eligible for and interested in the Marine Corps "six-month" program, you can obtain necessary detailed information from your nearest unit of the Organized Reserve or from the Director of Reserve, Marine Corps Headquarters.

ROTC Duty

The Reserve Officers Training Corps, or ROTC, is a system for training selected college and high school students to qualify for commissions in the Marine Corps Reserve and (if they measure up and so desire) the regular Marine Corps. At college level, the Marine Corps participates in the Naval ROTC program, by providing officer and noncommissioned officer instructors. In addition, certain high schools throughout the country have been designated for Marine Corps Junior ROTC Units, in which students receive the basic training that affords them advanced standing in college ROTC.

815. NONCOMMISSIONED OFFICERS WITH THE ROTC. Each Naval ROTC Unit has a Marine officer and a senior NCO assistant, both regulars on the active list. The NCO instructor usually acts as unit drill instructor, rifle team coach, weapons instructor, exhibition drill team instructor, and as "guide, philosopher, and friend" to the "Marine options" (i.e., midshipmen who have opted for Marine rather than Navy commissions).

MARINE JUNIOR ROTC. Unlike the college-level NROTC Units, the high school Junior ROTC Units are staffed by retired officers and by NCOs from the FMCR or retired list. Such personnel remain in inactive status, but wear the uniform as appropriate, and draw full pay and allowances for the rank in which retired. Each unit has two or more NCOs, who perform much the same duties as the NCO assistant instructors at NROTC Units. Fleet Reserve or retired NCOs interested in detail to the Junior ROTC program should apply to CMC (Code AF).

816. HINTS FOR ROTC DUTY. In addition to the hints contained in Section 811, all of which apply fully to ROTC duty, bear in mind the following.

ROTC Units are, at best, only semimilitary. Just because the midshipmen or cadets wear uniform doesn't alter the fact that they are still young civilians—and civilians over whom your main authority stems from enthusiasm, persuasion, and example.

Keep abreast of world, national, local, and campus developments. *Read.*

Maintain and develop warm personal relationships, but keep them a little formal, too.

Address all midshipmen as "Mister."

Don't drink with midshipmen except at unit functions and receptions and drink only when a substantial part of the unit staff is present.

Miscellaneous

817. TRANSFER INTO THE MARINE CORPS RESERVE. The Armed Forces Reserve Act permits certain members of reserve components of the armed forces to transfer from one service to another. Thus, if you are a member of another reserve component and desire to complete your obligated military service in the Marine Corps Reserve, it may be possible for you to do so.

Generally speaking, if you are not on active duty, but do have a period of obligated service in your reserve component, you may

A Marine, whether Reserve or Regular, takes great pride in Marine blues and globe and anchor and wears his NCO sword and insignia most proudly.

be discharged to accept an appointment in the Marine Corps Reserve. The director of the Marine Corps district in which you live (see Section 805) can advise you on your eligibility for transfer and can assist you in the administrative paperwork.

818. PRIVILEGES AND PERQUISITES OF THE MARINE RESERVIST. A Marine recruiting poster alleged to date from Revolutionary War days tells the privileges and perquisities of the Marine of 1776:

> You will receive *seventeen dollars bounty,* And on your arrival at Head Quarters, be comfortably and genteely clothed—And spirited young boys of a promising Appearance, who are Five Feet Six Inches high, *will receive ten dollars,* and equal advantages of *provisions* and *clothing* with the Men. In fact, the Advantages which the *marine* possesses, are too numerous to mention here, but among the many, it may not be amiss to state—That if he has a *wife* or aged *parent,* he can make them an Allotment of half his *pay;* which will be regularly paid without any trouble to them, or to whomsoever he may direct; that being well Clothed and Fed on Board Ship, the Remainder of his *pay* and *prize money* will be clear in Reserve, for the Relief of his Family or his own private Purposes. The Single Young Man, on his Return to Port, finds himself enabled to cut a Dash on Shore with his *girl* and his *glass,* that might be envied by a Nobleman . . .

Of course times have changed somewhat.

Today, the preeminent privilege which you gain as a member of the Marine Corps Reserve is the right to wear the Globe and Anchor and call yourself a Marine. But you do have other substantial privileges and perquisites, which are summarized below.

Pay, a short but important word, is certainly a perquisite of the reservist. For each regular drill or equivalent, you draw one day's pay, according to rank. This also applies to all active or training duty, unless you elect to perform these in nonpay status. Moreover, regardless of whether you are Volunteer, Fleet, or Organized, you accrue "fogies" (longevity credits) for *all* time spent as a member of the Reserve, active or inactive, just as if you were a regular.

Uniforms worn by reservists are, of course, regular Marine Corps uniforms. They are worn, or may be prescribed, during and when going to and from drills and instruction, and on other appropriate occasions, such as military ceremonies, parades, military dinners or dances, and the like. The uniform may not be worn for any commercial or political purpose, or in connection with any demonstration.

Every reservist must possess the required uniforms (which Marine Corps Headquarters lists from time to time), but you may in addition buy blues (see Section 617) if you want them and have occasions on which you can properly wear them.

It goes without saying that the right to wear Marine Corps uniforms is a privilege which members of the Reserve have always treasured. While you wear that uniform, you are accountable to every high standard of the Corps and its discipline.

Clubs and messes (see Chapter 20), extend a hearty welcome to the Marine Corps Reserve noncommissioned officer, whether active or inactive. Thus you will always find a friendly greeting (and, likely as not, old comrades) in the NCO Club at the Marine Corps or Navy station nearest your home.

Exchange and commissary privileges extend to reservists on a limited basis if on duty for less than 72 hours. If your period of duty exceeds 72 hours, you rate the same exchange and commissary privileges as a regular Marine. The same policy applies to purchases from Marine Corps supply agencies.

Promotion opportunities afford reservists the chance to enhance prestige and responsibility and, of course, to be eligible for increased retirement pay (for information on reserve retirement, see Section 819 below).

Decorations and medals are awarded to Marine reservists as to all other Marines—strictly as earned. They are worn on the uniform or, on certain occasions, with civilian clothes, in the same way as by regulars (see *Marine Corps Uniform Regulations*).

In addition, however, the Marine Corps Reserve boasts three special awards of its own.

1. *The Reserve Special Commendation Ribbon* goes to any officer who, over a period of four years between 1930 and 1940, exercised successful command, in a meritorious manner, of an Organized Reserve battalion or squadron, and who has had at least 10 years' service in the reserve.

2. *The Organized Marine Corps Reserve Medal,* with bronze stars for succeeding awards, goes to members of the Organized Reserve who maintain excellent records over a four-year period and who, during this time, attend four annual training periods with their units, plus at least 80 percent of all scheduled drills.

3. *The Marine Corps Reserve Ribbon* is awarded to each reservist who completes a 10-year period (excluding peacetime active duty) in any class(es) of the Reserve, *providing* this time has not been counted for award of the Organized Reserve Medal.

The Marine Corps Association, which publishes the professional magazine of the Corps, the *Marine Corps Gazette,* is open to membership by officers and NCOs of the Reserve. So also is the U. S. Naval Institute, which publishes the *United States Naval Institute Proceedings,* the professional journal of the Naval Services.

Employment protection. The Universal Military Training and Service Act (P. L. 632, 86th Congress), as amended, protects reservists against loss of seniority, status, pay, and vacation while they are away from their jobs on reserve training duty. Also, if you should unfortunately become disabled while training and can no longer perform the duties of your civilian job, you are entitled to reemployment on other jobs whose duties you may be able to perform. If you are hospitalized incident to training duty, you may delay reemployment application for a period up to one year. On the other hand, the law requires that you request leave of absence from your employer before going on training duty and that you must report back to work immediately on completion of training.

In addition to the foregoing, Federal employees, if in the reserve, rate up to 15 days' extra leave with pay per year to cover periods spent on training duty, and they are protected by law against "loss of time, pay, or efficiency rating" while availing themselves of this additional leave for training. Government employee reservists ordered to active duty must, by law, be restored to the job held before being called up.

819. RESERVE RETIREMENT. Retirement, both honorary (without pay, that is) and with pay, can be earned by members of the Marine Corps Reserve. In general, leaving out the Fleet Reserve, the fundamental prerequisite for reserve retirement with pay is 20 or more years' active service (not necessarily consecutive), or 20 years' "satisfactory Federal service," not all of which need be active.

Although Reserve retirement may be effected under several provisions of law, the principal one affecting most reservists is a section of Public Law 810, 80th Congress (now incorporated in Chapter 67, Title 10, U.S. Code), which makes retirement pay available to all Marine reservists who accumulate sufficient "retirement points" (credit points earned by service and training). The number of retirement points you chalk up also determines the amount of retired pay you may earn.

Without going into excessive detail, here is a brief description of the retirement system just mentioned:

To qualify for reserve retirement, you must earn at least 50 points a year for a minimum of 20 years, but these years need not be consecutive.

If you served in the reserve before 1 July 1949, you automatically accrue 50 points for each such year (other than years spent on active duty).

You get one point for each day of active duty (including training duty) served as a member of the armed forces before 1 July 1949.

After 1 July 1949, you must earn at least 50 points a year in order to have that year count toward Reserve retirement. The amount of retired pay you get (see below) is determined by the total number of points you accumulate. The number of points you earn depends largely on the amount of effort you care to put into training, home study courses, and other kinds of equivalent instruction. It's up to you; the more you give as a reservist, the more you get back in retirement.

You must serve the last eight qualifying years of your 20 years as a reserve member of the armed forces.

After you have met all the requirements, you become eligible for reserve retirement pay the first month after your 60th birthday.

Your retirement pay is computed as follows: Divide by 360 the sum of *all* points earned. Then multiply this by $2\frac{1}{2}$ percent. Then multiply the result by the combined annual base pay and longevity pay you would get if on active duty in the highest grade, permanent or temporary, satisfactorily held by you during your 20 years' service. The answer will be the amount of reserve retired pay you will be eligible to receive each year on attaining the age of 60.

In addition to all the foregoing, physical disability retirement rules which govern regular Marines extend with equal force to reservists who incur service-connected disabilities.

820. ADDITIONAL INFORMATION ON RESERVE MATTERS. The Director, Marine Corps Reserve, Marine Corps Headquarters, Washington, D.C., 20380, can supply more detailed information on the Reserve, not only to Marines, but to potential reservists and friends. The Division of Reserve is always more than glad to answer individual queries and to assist reservists in solving professional problems. However, before you write Marine Corps Headquarters, look under "United States Government" in your local telephone directory, and see if there is a local Marine Corps activity, either regular or reserve. Your local Marine Officer—be he inspector-instructor, recruiter, NROTC instructor, or district director—will always be ready to help you find out what you want to know.

The aim of every woman is to be truly integrated in the Corps. She is able and willing to undertake any assignment consonant with Marine Corps needs, and is proudest of all that she has no nickname. She is a "Marine."

—Colonel K. A. Towle, USMC

9 Women Marines

Although the traditional wartime mission of Women Marines was expressed in the World War II slogan, "Free a Marine to Fight!", Women Marines today perform whatever duties meet the needs of the Corps.

It is the policy of the Secretary of the Navy, as well as that expressed in Congress' charter for women in the service (Women's Armed Services Integration Act of 1948), that Women Marines train for and perform duties in Marine Corps tables of organization; also, that their qualifications for such duties shall be in line with standards applicable to male Marines in similar jobs.

In general, Women Marines are subject to the same rules and regulations as other Marines. The military authority exercised by Women Marines on duty is the same as that authorized for male personnel of the same rank.

The professional objective of all Women Marines is thus well stated in the quotation heading this chapter: " . . . *to be truly integrated in the Corps."*

901. HISTORY OF WOMEN MARINES. In August 1918, the first women ever to wear the Globe and Anchor enlisted in the U. S. Marine Corps as "Reservists (F)." They totaled 305 in all and were immediately nicknamed "Marinettes," an obvious derivative of the Navy's contemporary "Yeomanettes." Although the duties and scope of action of a Marinette (whose top possible rating was sergeant) were much more limited than those of today's Woman Marine, the spirit of the two was the same. The staying power of the original Marinettes is attested by the fact that seven women who wore the Marine uniform in 1918–1919 stayed on as civil servants at Marine Corps Headquarters until retiring decades later from key supervisory or executive jobs.

"She is proudest of all . . . that she is a Marine."

The "new" women's component was organized in February 1943, when Lieutenant General Thomas Holcomb, 17th Commandant, authorized creation of the Marine Corps Women's Reserve. The first officer and enlisted women were trained beside Navy Waves in existing Naval schools for women. By May 1943, 75 women had completed officer training, in a special course at Mount Holyoke College, and 722 had weathered recruit training. July 1943 saw establishment of the Women Reserve Schools at Camp Lejeune. Here at Lejeune was centralized recruit and officer candidate training, together with a number of specialist schools for the 18,000 enlisted women and 821 officers of the Women's Reserve, or "WR," as it was soon short-titled.

It was an emphatic tradition of the new branch of the Corps that there would be no trick nicknames for the group. As far as Women Marines were—and are—concerned, any cute, coy, or punning sobriquet, official or otherwise, would merely demean the Marine Corps Emblem which they proudly wore. Today, this tradition is stronger than ever.

Much of the initial tone and standard of the Marine Corps Women's Reserve was set in ordinary course by the parent Corps, but quite as much if not more was owing to the ability and effort of the first Director of the Women's Reserve, Colonel Ruth Cheney Streeter. Colonel Streeter made it her objective to integrate the women reservists into the framework of the Corps. It was her vision which lifted the World War II women from clerical specialization (the World War I role of Marinettes) into more than 200 separate occupational specialties and billets at every major Marine Corps post in continental United States and ultimately overseas.

At the end of World War II, save for about 100 women officers and enlisted women retained on duty at Marine Corps Headquarters, under Major Julia E. Hamblet (later to become a Director of Women Marines), the Women's Reserve went home. In 1948, however, Congress passed the Women's Armed Services Integration Act, and a new chapter opened. Henceforth, each service would have a career cadre of regulars, in addition to the reservists.

To head the regulars ("WM," they now became), General Cates, 19th Commandant, chose Colonel Katherine A. Towle, former Assistant Dean of Women at the University of California and wartime successor of Colonel Streeter. On 12 June 1948, the Women's Reserve went out of existence, and on the succeeding 4 November, the Women Marines came into being. Members of the former Women's Reserve were reenlisted into the Marine Corps Reserve, and many became members of the Organized Reserve. Like the remainder of the Organized Reserve, the women found themselves mobilized only days after the onset of war in Korea, with 13 Organized Reserve women's platoons responding to the call. If there had to be a fight, the Women Marines wanted to be in it, too. As the rest of the Reserve was released, so were the women, but the regular Women Marines continue as an important portion of the Corps and today are again filling many key billets which release other Marines for field service in Vietnam.

902. ORGANIZATION AND COMPOSITION OF THE WOMEN MARINES. Present law limits the strength of the enlisted Women Marines to not more than two percent of the authorized active enlisted strength of the Corps as a whole. The woman officer strength in turn may not exceed ten percent of the woman enlisted strength, or a theoretical two-tenths of one percent of the authorized enlisted strength of the Marine Corps. As this is written, the actual strength of the WM, in round figures, is about 2,600.

Women Marines are headed by the Director of Women Marines, who is a member of the Commandant's Staff and colonel in the regular Marine Corps. She advises the Commandant and staff agencies of HQMC on all matters concerning women in the Marine Corps and Marine Corps Reserve. Her functions are to:

1. Initiate policies and make recommendations on all matters affecting Women Marines.
2. Advise cognizant staff agencies in the execution of approved policies affecting Women Marines.
3. Advise regarding the detail of Women Marines.
4. Visit and assist in the inspection of activities where Women Marines are stationed.
5. Maintain liaison with directors of women in the other services and represent the Marine Corps on the Defense Advisory Committee on Women in the Services.

In less official language, it may be said that the Director of Women Marines protects, fosters, and sets the tone of the women in the Corps. To borrow Lejeune's phrase, she is indeed the Women Marines' "natural friend and protector."

In keeping with the Women Marines' desire to be fully integrated into the Corps, officers and enlisted women are assigned individually to the jobs they can best fill. At certain posts where WMs serve, they are grouped into a company or detachment commanded by a woman officer. These women's units ordinarily compose part of the headquarters troops of the post where they are stationed. At some other stations, WMs are quartered in women's barracks, but not grouped in a WM unit. Finally, WM noncommissioned officers may be assigned independently to a group of posts with no unit and no women's barracks.

In addition, two other regular Women Marine units exist; a recruit training battalion at Parris Island conducts "boot camp" for enlisted women, and the Women Officer School at Quantico conducts the WM Noncommissioned officer course.

903. DUTIES OF WOMEN MARINES. More than 100 military jobs can be or are performed by Women Marines; and WMs are assigned military duties which include administration, communica-

Women Marines perform more than 100 military jobs alongside male members of the Marine Corps.

tions, supply, intelligence, drafting and surveying, disbursing, electronic training devices, logistics, food services, lithography, transportation, illustration, data processing, public information, photography, flight operations and air control, aerology, instructing, post exchange, and personnel administration (including company officer and non-commissioned officer duties).

WMs serve at every major Marine Corps post and station in the continental United States, in Europe (London, Stuttgart, Brussels, and Naples), in Hawaii, Panama, the Philippines, Okinawa, Japan, Vietnam, Santo Domingo (where, during the 1965 revolt, a WM earned the first combat campaign medal awarded to a Woman Marine), and in various cities throughout the United States.

904. WOMEN RESERVISTS. During World War II, all Marine women were members of the Marine Corps Women's Reserve, the famous "WR." Today, however, women are members of the same Marine Corps Reserve classes as all other Marines, described in Chapter 8.

Women Marine reservists serve in peacetime as citizen Marines while living in their home communities. They are given the opportunity to prepare for military service, should their country need them, by their membership in an organization which does not interfere in peacetime with normal civilian life.

Women veterans of all services are eligible for membership in the Marine Corps Reserve, provided they were not discharged for medical reasons and possess an honorable discharge. Women who have served in any of the armed forces other than the Marine Corps may be appointed to their former rank up through corporal if found qualified.

There are two classes for membership for women in the Reserve—Organized and Volunteer. The woman reservist may request assignment in the Organized Reserve and participate in a drill pay status with male units under restricted conditions. Women with no prior military service are no longer recruited directly into Organized Reserve units. A woman reservist may request assignment to two weeks active duty for training each year. Women members of male units will be permitted to attend annual field training with the unit provided appropriate facilities are available at the training activity. Where the training activity does not have appropriate facilities for women, the woman so concerned may request orders for two weeks' on-the-job training at an appropriate training activity. She may further her military career through correspondence courses and may join Volunteer Training Units located in her home community.

Women reservists, Volunteer or Organized, are subject to the same regulations as male reservists. In the event of war, Organized reservists are mobilized to meet the needs of the Marine Corps. During the Korean emergency, only those Volunteer women reservists were mobilized who specifically requested active duty and whose qualifications were in demand.

Unlike Volunteer reservists, women members of Organized Women Marine Reserve Platoons were mobilized in 1950 with male units to which their platoons were attached. They served at posts and stations in the United States throughout the Korean crisis, releasing men for duty in the combat zone.

905. WOMEN NONCOMMISSIONED OFFICERS. In general, the Marine Corps makes minimum differentiation between women and male NCOs. Women noncommissioned officers compete directly with all other Marine NCOs for promotion vacancies; for example, a woman 0141 or 4021 is strictly a Marine when her jacket goes before a selection board. One of the best statements of the criteria for women noncommissioned officers of any rank is contained in a memorandum furnished to a selection board which had the job of picking the Sergeant Major of Women Marines. Any woman Marine NCO can well measure herself by these following attributes.

1. In personal appearance, an outstandingly representative woman Marine for her age and grade. Feminine in mannerism and person; impeccable in uniform and knowledgeable in presenting an appearance in civilian clothing appropriate to any social occasion.

2. *Poised and mature in military presence; socially aware and approachable; tactful and capable of achieving a nicely balanced relationship with officers, senior staff NCOs, and Marines of lower grades, men and women.*

3. *Possessed of an excellent ability to communicate orally and in writing; particularly well qualified to speak before a sizable audience.*

4. *A Marine Corps career of widest possible experience, particularly in regard to billets in the women's program and in contrast to assignments limited solely to duty in her MOS.*

906. WOMEN IN THE TOP TWO GRADES. Because there are only a limited number of sergeant major or first sergeant billets (at the time of writing, about 16) for women Marines, it is not in the best interests of the individuals, or of the WMs as a whole, that a handful of women NCOs should be restricted to such billets. For this reason, women in the two top grades are rated master gunnery sergeant or master sergeant only. When selected for a sergeant major/first sergeant billet, the individual receives a temporary appointment in the grade in question. This appointment terminates with transfer to any billet not calling for the rank of sergeant major or first sergeant. The top enlisted billet among women Marines is that of the *Sergeant Major of Women Marines,* at HQMC. The Sergeant Major of Women Marines is selected on the basis of the criteria and attributes just listed in Section 905. She is the principal enlisted assistant of the Director of Women Marines.

907. WOMAN NONCOMMISSIONED LEADERSHIP. The fundamentals of leadership are the same for women as for men; these may be found in Chapter 13. However, there are a few special points that women NCOs would be wise to bear in mind.

Be a Lady. By gracious ways, by high standards of conduct, by wholesome outlook, by avoidance of quarreling and squabbles, and by essentially ladylike ways of counseling, guiding, and instructing, you will typify all that is best in the traditions of women in the Marine Corps.

> *Note:* Remember the old definition of a lady as "a woman who makes the men around her willingly act like gentlemen."

Be Polite and Gracious. A gracious manner is one that acknowledges and returns all courtesies. A gracious temper is even and good-humored.

Counseling. As a noncommissioned officer, you will be asked for advice on many personal problems: lonesomeness, occasional disillusionment, worry over conditions at home, male fickleness, homesickness, etc. The main thing is to be a good listener with human sympathy. If you spot real trouble, you should of course let your commander know, so that the expert help of psychiatrists and chaplains can be mobilized. The main rules of sound counseling are:

Never betray a confidence,
Be a good listener,
Keep your sense of proportion and balance,

Think constructively,
Don't brush aside other people's problems,
Don't jump at conclusions.

908. REFERENCES. In keeping with the premise that women are an integral part of the Corps, most of the administrative instructions and information pertaining to women are embodied in corresponding or analogous material applicable to Marines of either sex. For example, much information regarding personnel procurement and entrance into the Corps appears in Chapter 2, *Marine Corps Personnel Manual.* Promotion and reduction of Women Marines are covered by Chapter 6 of the same manual, while retirement, discharge, and civil readjustment are discussed in Chapter 13. *Marine Corps Uniform Regulations,* however, contains much information expressly applicable to women.

Finally, when all printed sources fail, the Director of Women Marines stands ready to provide information, guidance, and policy, or any needed combination thereof.

Paper work will ruin any military force.

—Lewis B. Puller, 1962

10 Individual Administration

Although a few administrators may try to tell you differently, there is nothing inherently complicated or mysterious about individual administration. This term merely comprises a number of administrative matters that concern you personally: your record, rank, promotions, reenlistment, retirement, official correspondence, and leave and liberty. Pay, allowances, and official travel, closely related, are covered in Chapter 11.

Records and Returns

1001. YOUR OFFICIAL RECORD. Throughout your career, correspondence which concerns you accumulates at Marine Corps Headquarters. Adverse matter may not be placed on record without your knowledge, but, whether favorable or unfavorable, correspondence once rightfully included in your record cannot be removed without authorization by the Commandant of the Marine Corps.

The vital importance of your official record to you and your career cannot be overstressed. The entries in your record form the basis of your service reputation. Without vicious intent, many a young noncommissioned officer, by carelessness or ignorance, has written into his record an accumulation of minor lapses which prove detrimental to his service reputation.

Your record (or "jacket") in Washington consists of a file folder with four subdivisions as follows.

1. *Correspondence/Orders:* Copies of orders (and modifications thereto) issued to or concerning you by Marine Corps Headquarters.
2. *Service Summary:* This section, which really gives a picture of your military history, includes enlistment contracts and extensions; awards, citations, and commendatory matter; school certificates, diplomas, etc.; certificates of appointment (promotion warrants); MOS changes; reports of disciplinary action; reports of separation; reserve retirement credits.

3. *Fitness Reports:* All fitness reports rendered on you and also related correspondence.

4. *Service Record Books:* your successive SRBs.

Access to Record. The only persons who enjoy access to your record are you yourself (on personal application to the Files Unit); your personal representative, armed with proper proof; designated Headquarters personnel; and when authorized by the Secretary of the Navy, the courts. No person (including you or your agents) without proper authority may withdraw official records and correspondence from the files or destroy them.

Make it a habit to review your record every time you find yourself in Washington.

1002. YOUR STAFF RETURNS. Your staff returns are the administrative records which accompany you, as distinct from those filed in Washington. Staff returns comprise your *Service Record Book,* your *Military Pay Record,* and your *Health Record.*

Your *Service Record Book* is designed to provide a running record of your military history from enlistment to discharge. It is used by your CO to determine duty assignments, record promotion data, show eligibility for sea or foreign shore duty, and reflect basic civilian and Marine Corps personnel data. It is made up of standard pages to record events which happen to most Marines, as well as a documents section which includes such papers applicable to you as security clearance, clothing record, VA insurance forms, etc. When you complete an enlistment, die, or are discharged, your service record book goes to Marine Corps Headquarters and thence into your jacket.

Your *Pay Record* is a card on which your pay and allowances are credited and which shows the paymaster how much pay you are entitled to at any moment. Most armed forces disbursing officers will honor a military pay record. A new record is opened each 1st of July and January. Loss or mutilation of a pay record can entail serious consequences where they hurt most—in your pocketbook. See Chapter 11 ("Pay, Allowances, and Travel").

Your *Health Record* is opened by the Navy's Bureau of Medicine and Surgery and very literally contains your life history, your physical description, and the medical history of every ailment which befalls you. One of the health record's most important everyday functions is to keep a record of all the shots and inoculations which every Marine must take.

1003. YOUR PERSONAL FILE. The day you become a staff NCO, or sooner if necessary, you should start a personal file, which contains, in one folder, all original travel orders; in another, all official correspondence from, to, and concerning you. In addition, remember that some unofficial letters you write or receive are just as important to your career as the official ones.

1004. FITNESS REPORTS. Fitness reports are the periodic efficiency reports rendered on all NCOs of the rank of sergeant and above (except for bandsmen in the Marine Band). Broadly speaking, your fitness reports present a composite judgment of your military character and relative merits compared with other noncommissioned officers of the same rank and comparable experience. Fitness reports assist selection boards to determine which NCOs are best fitted for promotion, and these reports provide the Detail Branch with information as to each NCO's qualifications for various types of duty.

The Marine Corps fitness report consists of a statement of the duties you perform and your preference for future assignment; an evaluation of your personal characteristics; an estimate of your value to the Service and your professional acceptability to your reporting senior; and a concise evaluation of your character, performance of duty, and promotability. See Figure 10-1.

The fitness report section of your jacket at Headquarters thus presents a running record of your performance of duty under a number of seniors in various types of service.

TYPES OF REPORTS.

1. *Regular reports* are rendered semiannually, also whenever you are detached, whenever your reporting senior changes, and whenever you are discharged, retire, or are appointed to warrant or commissioned rank. Your entire career must be covered by an unbroken sequence of consecutive regular reports. If any period is omitted, your record is incomplete, and therefore you cannot normally be considered for promotion until the missing period is covered.
2. *Concurrent reports* are in addition to regular reports and cover additional duties performed under someone other than your regular reporting senior. Concurrent reports cover only specific periods of additional duty and need not be consecutive nor submitted for less than 30 days. Completed concurrent reports are sent to your regular reporting senior to assist him in rating your regular report. He then forwards them to the Commandant.
3. *Academic Reports* cover periods of duty at a military or civilian school while under instruction. An academic report covers the entire period of the course (if not longer than 12 months), and permits normal semiannual regular reports to be dispensed with.
4. *Letter reports* are fitness reports in letter form rather than on the standard printed form. Letter reports are rendered only when prescribed.
5. *Special fitness reports* are required whenever a noncommissioned officer:
   Distinguishes himself in battle;
   Performs an outstanding act of valor or devotion to duty;
   Displays extraordinary courage, ability or resource in time of peril or great responsibility;
   Is guilty of serious misconduct or marked inefficiency.

In addition to the foregoing, a special fitness report may be submitted at the discretion of the reporting senior whenever the individual's performance of duty—good, bad, or extraordinary—is such that Marine Corps Headquarters should be specially advised.

REPORTING SENIORS. Ordinarily, your reporting senior is your immediate commanding officer or the head of the staff section to which you may be attached. It is your responsibility to submit a signed fitness report, with certain entries completed, to your reporting senior, at the prescribed times. Then he fills out the remainder of the report which, unless of an unsatisfactory character (see below), is sent to the immediate superior in command or to other designated higher authority, for review and, if the latter deems appropriate, comment.

Although not in themselves classified, fitness reports are considered as "private official," and are handled with utmost administrative privacy. If, however, any classified papers are attached, the fitness report must be safeguarded as required for that classification.

ADVERSE OR MARGINAL REPORTS. An adverse or marginal report is one that contains any expressly unsatisfactory or below average rating in items 16, 17, or 19 (see Figure 10-1); a "Prefer Not to Have" entry in item 18; or an unfavorable remark in Section D. If you should be so unfortunate as to receive an unsatisfactory report, your reporting senior is obliged to refer it to you for statement (if you wish to make one) before the report goes forward. You may attach any written statement you choose, providing it is pertinent, is temperate in language, is factual, and does not contain any accusations (See *Navy Regulations,* article 1404 in this connection). After completing and attaching your statement, sign Section F and return the report to your reporting senior. If you do not desire to make a statement (which is in effect a concession that you accept the report and that there are no mitigating or extenuating circumstances), sign the notation to this effect in Section F.

If you do submit a statement, *be extremely prudent in language* and assertion. Before you put it in, check the *Navy Regulations* article cited above, and be sure that you have not forged a weapon which may turn in your hand. Many a statement dashed off in wrath or humiliation has proved more damaging than the original report.

YOU AND YOUR FITNESS REPORT. Always see that your reporting senior has at least one spare report with Section A signed by you; this covers both you and him in an emergency. But never sign Section F in advance. When your next fitness report comes due, ask yourself, "What are my strong points? Where am I weak? What must I do to enhance my favorable characteristics and eliminate the bad ones?"

Whenever you visit Marine Corps Headquarters, take the opportunity to review the fitness report in your jacket. Look for trends and see yourself as others see you. You may be able to fool some reporting seniors some of the time, but . . .

NONCOMMISSIONED OFFICER FITNESS REPORT (1611)
U.S. MARINE CORPS
NAVMC 10233   (REV. 8-62)

SECTION A.

EMBOSSED PLATE IMPRESSION *(Name, Grade, Service No., MOS's)*	EMBOSSED PLATE IMPRESSION *(Organization)*
DALY,JOHN H. 1234567 **GYSGT 0369/E511/0000 00 13213 1**	**A COMPANY** **1STBATTALION 9THMARINES** **3RD MARINE DIVISION** **FPO SAN FRANCISCO 96602**

*1. NAME *(Last)*	*(First)*	*(Middle initial)*	GRADE USMC____	SERVICE NO.

*2. ORGANIZATION

*3. PRIMARY MOS   ADDITIONAL MOS'S

4. OCCASION FOR THIS REPORT *(Check appropriate box)*

☐ SEMIANNUAL   ☒ TRANSFER OF NONCOMMISSIONED OFFICER REPORTED ON *(Enter unit or station to which detached, below)*   ☐ CHANGE OF REPORTING OFFICER   ☐ OTHER *(Explain below)*

5. PERIOD COVERED: FROM *(Day, month, year)*	TO *(Day, month, year)*	MONTHS
1 Jan 70	5 May 70	5

6. PERIODS OF NONAVAILABILITY (30 DAYS OR MORE) *(Explain)*

None

7. DUTY ASSIGNMENTS DURING PERIOD COVERED: A. REGULAR *(Dates, descriptive title, and duty MOS)*

1 Jan 70 - 5 May 70: Company gunnery sergeant (0369)

B. ADDITIONAL *(Descriptive title and number of months)*

None

8. WIFE'S ADDRESS

Not married

9. NAME, AGE, RELATIONSHIP OF DEPENDENTS REQUIRING TRANSPORTATION

None of record

10. NONCOMMISSIONED OFFICER'S PREFERENCE FOR NEXT ASSIGNMENT *(1st choice)*
Sea duty (cruiser, Pacific Fleet) (Y14)

(2d choice)	*(3d choice)*
MB, NB, Yokosuka, Japan (362)	MCRD, San Diego, California

SIGNATURE *(Noncommissioned officer reported on)* *John H. Daly*	DATE 5 May 70

SECTION B. *(To be completed by reporting officer)*

11. NAME AND GRADE OF REPORTING OFFICER	12. DUTY ASSIGNMENT
Charles G. Lejeune, Captain USMC	CO, A/1/9, 3dMarDiv, FMF

13. RECOMMENDATIONS FOR NONCOMMISSIONED OFFICER'S NEXT DUTY ASSIGNMENT
Sea duty as requested

14. DURING THE PERIOD COVERED BY THIS REPORT:

	YES	NO	
(a) Has the work of this noncommissioned officer been reported on in a commendatory way?	☒	☐	*If YES in (a) or (b), and a report has NOT been submitted to the CMC, attach separate statement of nature and attendant circumstances. If a report has been submitted to the CMC, reference such report below:*
(b) Was this noncommissioned officer the subject of any disciplinary action that should be included on his record?	☐	☒	Awd Bronze Star Medal 21 Mar. 69

15A. ENTRIES ON THIS REPORT ARE BASED ON *(Check appropriate box)*

☒ DAILY CONTACT AND CLOSE OBSERVATION OF THIS NCO'S WORK   ☐ FREQUENT OBSERVATIONS OF THIS NCO'S WORK   ☐ INFREQUENT OBSERVATIONS OF THIS NCO'S WORK

15B. TO BE COMPLETED ON ORGANIZED RESERVE NCO
ATTENDED_____ OF _____ SCHEDULED DRILLS

* If embossed plate impression is used, do not complete items 1, 2 and 3.

Fig. 10-1: Noncommissioned officer fitness report.

Promotion, Reduction, and Precedence

1005. THE MARINE CORPS ENLISTED PROMOTION SYSTEM. The system by which enlisted Marines are promoted is designed so that NCOs within each grade, and generally within each

SECTION C. *(To be completed in ink by reporting officer)*

Considering the noncommissioned officer reported on in comparison with all other noncommissioned officers of the same grade whose professional abilities are known to you personally, indicate your estimate of this noncommissioned officer by marking "X" in the appropriate spaces below.

16. PERFORMANCE OF DUTY *(Based on fact)*	NOT OBSERVED	UNSATISFACTORY	BELOW AVERAGE	AVERAGE	ABOVE AVERAGE	EXCELLENT	OUTSTANDING
(a) REGULAR DUTIES							X
(b) ADDITIONAL DUTIES	X						
(c) ADMINISTRATIVE DUTIES					X		
(d) HANDLING ENLISTED PERSONNEL							X
(e) TRAINING PERSONNEL							
(f) TACTICAL HANDLING OF TROOPS *(Unit appropriate to noncommissioned officer's rank)*						X	

17. TO WHAT DEGREE HAS HE EXHIBITED THE FOLLOWING?							
(a) ENDURANCE *(Physical and mental ability for carrying on under fatiguing conditions)*							X
(b) PERSONAL APPEARANCE *(The trait of habitually appearing neat, smart, and well-groomed in uniform or civilian attire)*							X
(c) MILITARY PRESENCE *(The quality of maintaining appropriate dignity and soldierly bearing)*							X
(d) ATTENTION TO DUTY *(Industry; the trait of working thoroughly and conscientiously)*							X
(e) COOPERATION *(The faculty of working in harmony with others, military and civilian)*							X
(f) INITIATIVE *(The trait of taking necessary or appropriate action on own responsibility)*							X
(g) JUDGMENT *(The ability to think clearly and arrive at logical conclusions)*							X
(h) PRESENCE OF MIND *(The ability to think and act promptly and effectively in an unexpected emergency or under great strain)*							X
(i) FORCE *(The faculty of carrying out with energy and resolution that which is believed to be reasonable, right or duty)*							X
(j) LEADERSHIP *(The capacity to direct, control, and influence others and still maintain high morale)*							X
(k) LOYALTY *(The quality of rendering faithful and willing service, and unswerving allegiance under any and all circumstances)*							X
(l) PERSONAL RELATIONS *(Faculty of establishing and maintaining cordial relations with military and civilian associates)*							X
(m) ECONOMY *(Effective utilization of men, money and materials)*						X	

18. Considering the possible requirements of service in war, indicate your attitude toward having this noncommissioned officer under your command.

Would you— | NOT OBSERVED □ | PREFER NOT TO HAVE? □ | BE WILLING TO HAVE? □ | BE GLAD TO HAVE? □ | PARTICULARLY DESIRE TO HAVE? ☒

19. (a) Indicate your estimate of this noncommissioned officer's "General Value to the Service" by marking "X" in the appropriate box:

NOT OBSERVED	UNSATISFACTORY	BELOW AVERAGE	AVERAGE	ABOVE AVERAGE	EXCELLENT	OUTSTANDING
□	□	□	□	□	☒	□

(b) Show distribution of all Item 19 (a) markings awarded noncommissioned officers of his grade for this reporting occasion:

SECTION D. *(To be completed by reporting senior in pen and ink. This space may be used to record additional information that would further classify the noncommissioned officer's performance and qualifications.)*

GySgt Daly is a professional Marine of the best type. He is collected, resolute, + aggressive under fire, and a fine example to all hands in this company. With an opportunity to devote more time to administrative skills, he will be well fitted for 1st Sgt.

SECTION E. *(To be completed by the reporting Senior)*

I CERTIFY that to the best of my knowledge and belief all entries made hereon are true and without prejudice and partiality.

(Signature of reporting senior) _(Date)_

SECTION F. *(To be completed when required)*

I have seen this completed report. *(Check one)*
□ I HAVE NO STATEMENT TO MAKE
□ I HAVE ATTACHED A STATEMENT

(Signature of noncommissioned officer reported on) _(Date)_

SECTION G. *(To be completed by reviewing officer)*

NAME AND GRADE OF REVIEWING OFFICER **DUTY ASSIGNMENT**

US _____ INITIALS _____

U.S. GOVERNMENT PRINTING OFFICE : 1967 O—273-681

occupational field, compete among themselves for promotion to the next higher grade. *Every promotion must positively contribute to the high standards of leadership and military proficiency which are expected of the Marine Corps.*

The objectives of the NCO promotion system are twofold: (1) to maintain the actual strength in each grade at maximum readiness to go into combat, by promoting the best men in each occupational field; and (2) to give every eligible NCO full and fair opportunity for promotion. Details of promotion procedures will be described in the sections that follow.

In summary, promotion to or within staff NCO ranks is effected by the Commandant on the basis of recommendations by an HQMC selection board. Promotion to sergeant and below is effected locally by any CO having special court-martial jurisdiction, as well as certain other designated commanding officers. Promotions to sergeant are based on Corps-wide vacancies, while those to corporal are made as intra-unit vacancies arise. To make sergeant, you must attain a satisfactory "composite score" as described below. Corporals are promoted as a result of local evaluation.

The "distribution" of noncommissioned officers (i.e., the percentage of NCOs in each grade) results from the number of authorized billets for such grades and thus determines the number of vacancies. As of 1968, Marine NCO distribution was as follows.

SgtMaj/MGySgt	1.0%
1stSgt/MSgt	3.4%
GySgt	8.1%
SSgt	14.2%
Sgt	28.5%
Cpl	44.8%

1006. CUTTING AND COMPOSITE SCORES. Since promotion to sergeant is governed by Corps-wide vacancies, the competing candidates have to be measured by the same standards throughout the Marine Corps. In addition, candidates have to complete a minimum amount of service as corporals, which is established from time to time by the Commandant.

Your composite score is a mathematical evaluation of all your military and personal qualifications for promotion, on the basis of which you can be compared with all other noncommissioned officers eligible for promotion. This score gets its name because it is a mathematically weighted composite of your scores and progress in subjects prescribed under Individual Training of Enlisted Men (ITEM)—which has replaced the General Military Subjects Test (GMST)—of your grade for proficiency in rating, of your conduct marks, and of factors based on your length of time in grade and your total length of service.

Cutting scores for each MOS are in turn assigned by the Commandant. If you are otherwise eligible and if your composite score is equal to or higher than the cutting score for your MOS, then you can be promoted by your commanding officer.

Here is an example of how a composite score is calculated:

Corporal John H. Diamond, 1995601/0311 (date of rank, 15 February 1971, cutoff date, 30 September 1972) hopes to make sergeant. His proficiency marks average out at 4.3. His conduct marks average

4.4. His time in grade is 19 months, 15 days, rounded off as 20 months. His time in service is 33 months, 14 days, rounded off as 33 months. His composite score is computed like this:

Element	Score		Multiple		Subtotal
Proficiency (combined average)	4.3	×	18.0	=	77.4
Conduct	4.4	×	8.0	=	35.2
Months in grade	20.0	×	0.5	=	10.0
Months' service	33.0	×	0.2	=	6.6
COMPOSITE SCORE					129.2
			(rounded off as)		129

If the current cutting score for the 03 field is 129 or lower, Corporal Diamond is administratively qualified for his third chevron.

1007. STAFF NCO PROMOTIONS. Promotions to and within the staff NCO grades are controlled by Headquarters Marine Corps, with the number of promotions determined by Corps-wide vacancies in each occupational field.

To be promoted to staff sergeant or gunnery sergeant, you must have completed the prescribed minimum service in grade, must have attained the proficiency required under ITEM for the grade in question, for your MOS and unit mission, and, most important, you must be selected by your board at HQMC.

To be advanced to first sergeant/master sergeant or to sergeant major/master gunnery sergeant, you must have eight years total service (1stSgt/MSgt) or ten years, (SgtMaj/MGySgt); must have completed required minimum time in grade (administratively established as two years); and must be recommended by your selection board.

1008. STAFF NCO SELECTION BOARDS AND PROCEDURES. Selection boards for sergeant major/master gunnery sergeant and for first sergeant/master sergeant are normally composed of one colonel, nine lieutenant colonels, and eight majors. Boards for gunnery sergeant and staff sergeant habitually include two sergeants major and two master gunnery sergeants. Every board has a recorder and as many assistants as the work load requires. Occupational specialties of each board represent the three types of organizations in the Marine Corps operating forces (see Chapter 3), i.e., combat arms, combat support units, and combat service support units, both air and ground. Whenever reserve NCOs on extended active duty (EAD, see Chapter 8) are considered, the board includes at least one reserve officer. Similarly, when women candidates are under consideration, a woman officer member will be added.

The precept for the board is a letter from the Commandant to the senior member, which is read to the entire board at its first meeting. The precept gives the board its general guidance, reminds them of Marine Corps policies, and acquaints them with the Commandant's personal desires regarding the corps of noncommissioned officers. After the precept is read, representatives of G-1 and the Director of Personnel brief the board on salient features of the precept and give certain background information which will help in arriving at decisions. Examples of matters covered at this time are Marine Corps promotion policies and objectives, requirements for promotion, present situations within the grades and occupational fields concerned, and procedural matters. Then the senior member instructs the members concerning procedures for reviewing each case, the order in which occupational fields will be reviewed and presented, and such other related matters as possible selection of otherwise qualified men for retraining and promotion in fields with critical shortages.

After all the foregoing preliminaries, the members begin reviewing the individual jackets of NCOs under consideration. This is done by occupational field (OF) or sometimes by MOS, and selections are likewise so made, in the following manner.

All jackets in a given OF or MOS are distributed among all members. Each member is responsible for evaluating his share of jackets and for briefing the entire board on those candidates (in a sense, you might say that the officer who draws your case is your "lawyer" before the board). Before making his evaluation, each member reviews the *MOS Manual* in order to be fully up to date on the professional requirements for the MOS or OF in question. Then, to be doubly sure that all board members have the picture, there follows a board discussion of the MOS or OF in question, with the members who are experienced in that field taking the lead so that all hands know the special skill requirements involved, special attributes that are desired, etc.

After members have finished evaluating their respective cases, each presents an initial briefing to the board, recommending names which he believes should be eliminated from further consideration. Typical reasons for such adverse recommendations might be:

Poor fitness reports, with comparatively short time in grade or in the Marine Corps
Poor fitness reports without other sufficient evidence to justify such low performance
Unfavorable conduct or disciplinary problems.
Correspondence on record indicating indebtedness or financial irresponsibility of any kind.

However, if any member believes that a candidate should still be considered despite an adverse recommendation, he can so recommend, and, if supported by a two-thirds vote of the board, that man's case will be retained for further consideration.

Following this preliminary screening, the board reviews in detail the records of NCOs whom individual members will nominate to fill the vacancies allocated to the board by CMC. After all cases have been briefed, the board prepares to vote. All names recommended are put on a roster. On this, each member checks the number of names equal to the total vacancies allocated. This done, the senior member reads down the roster and calls for votes of individual members. Any candidate who gets two-thirds of the votes of the board on the first ballot is selected. Then the senior member runs down the roster again in the same fashion, for a second ballot. Again, NCOs receiving two-thirds of the vote are selected and taken off the list. This process is repeated until all vacancies have been filled.

After the board has finished its selections, the recorder determines the relative seniority of the selectees, based on dates of rank in their lower grade. This precedence list determines not only seniority in the new rank but also the order in which promotion warrants will be issued after the Commandant has approved the board's recommended list. This roster also becomes the waiting list from which CMC will promote, usually once a month.

> *Note:* Although this procedure is not mandatory, most NCO selection boards are directed by CMC to set aside informally, for further review by HQMC, the cases of any NCOs who obviously appear to have fallen below the standards of performance and/or conduct expected of Marines of their rank and seniority.

1009. BASIC QUALIFICATIONS FOR NCO PROMOTION. When a staff NCO selection board convenes and operates as described above, it is furnished with a set of basic qualifications for NCO promotions, prepared by Headquarters Marine Corps. Naturally, these qualifications are for guidance only, and the Commandant's specific precept to the board and, in the last analysis, the board's judgment, take first place. However, you would be wise to measure yourself against the following qualifications, which were furnished to a recent selection board.

Requisite Service. When basic requirements are met and all other things are equal, preference is given to men with longer time-in-grade and, secondarily, to those with longer time in the Corps.

Achievement. Performance of regular and additional duties. Decorations and awards (including marksmanship). Letters of commendation/appreciation and Meritorious Mast. Specific achievements (such as, inventions, development of systems, constructive recommendations, money-saving ideas, etc.). Special honors (e.g., DI of the Year). Educational work completed (high school, trade school, college courses, USAFI material). Off-duty military training (MCI and MCDEC Extension courses). Class standing in formal schools and courses. Activities that bring public credit to the Corps. Recommendations for special personnel programs (e.g., OCS or warrant officer).

Leadership. Evidence in fitness reports (Leadership, Handling Enlisted Personnel, Tactical Handling of Troops, and, in particular, reflection of favorable performance in combat). Successful performance of duty requiring high order of leadership, such as DI, recruiter, or member of an I&I staff. Successful performance of independent duty or other duty involving heavy responsibility. Record of performance in unusual or emergency situations. Lack of personal or disciplinary problems. Leadership remarks in Section D of the fitness report.

Experience. Combat. Varied assignments. Special responsibilities. Demanding assignments calling for high order of leadership, imagination, or initiative.

Growth Potential. Estimated ability to perform in next higher rank. Self-improvement efforts. Scholastic record: military and civilian. Performance of duty remarks in Section D of the fitness report.

Motivation. Initiative. Volunteering for critical or important duty (combat, overseas in undesirable areas; DI, Recruiter, State Department) Correspondence courses in military skills.

General Military Proficiency. Marksmanship qualifications and those in swimming and other military skills. GMST scores (when in effect).

Physical Condition. Fitness reports. General appearance as evidenced by photograph in record. PULHES.

Special Qualifications. Language skills. Ability to speak in public and to instruct. Ability as an athletic team player or coach. Community activities.

How nearly do the above qualities fit you?

1010. SPECIAL PROMOTION PROVISIONS. In addition to all that has been explained about the normal promotion system for Marine NCOs, certain special provisions are summarized briefly as follows.

Meritorious Promotions. On receipt of commanding officers' recommendations reporting really exceptional, noteworthy, or commendable performance of duty by an NCO, the Commandant may promote men so recommended, or refer the recommendation for consideration by the next regular board. However, meritorious promotions will not be made into the two top pay grades.

> *Note:* During hostilities in Vietnam, the Commandant granted special promotion authority to Fleet Marine Force Pacific for meritorious battlefield promotions primarily aimed at but not restricted to NCOs at the small-unit level. Similarly, HQMC has solicited special recommendations (by dispatch, if necessary) for expeditious consideration of NCOs for battlefield promotion to staff and gunnery sergeant ranks.

Temporary Appointments for WMs. Any WM master gunnery sergeant or master sergeant who is temporarily assigned to an authorized sergeant major or first sergeant billet may be temporarily appointed to that billet's grade by CMC. See Chapter 9.

Promotion of POWs and Missing. On return to U.S. control, former POWs or NCOs formerly carried as missing will receive promotion consideration for the period during which they were not under U. S. control.

Remedial Promotion. Marines restored to full duty after Physical Evaluation Board action are afforded appropriate remedial promotion opportunity covering the time in non-duty status. Likewise, if for any reason (such as an administrative slipup, or because an NCO has been fully cleared in some pending investigation or disciplinary proceeding which might have reflected adversely on him), his CO feels that he should be considered for remedial promotion, a recommendation for such special consideration may be sent in to CMC. The main purpose of remedial promotion is to deal fairly with every Marine.

Marine Bandsmen. Musicians of the Marine Band are promoted by the Commandant as vacancies occur within the Band.

You Cannot Be Promoted if:

Under orders to appear before a Physical Evaluation Board
Awaiting transfer to retired status
On the inactive list of the Reserve
A student in any officer candidate program (except NESEP)
Convicted by general court-martial within previous twelve months
Convicted by special court-martial within previous six months
Convicted by summary court-martial within previous three months
In probationary status as a result of court-martial or CO's Office Hours
Awaiting or undergoing trial by court-martial
An interested party in any type of investigation or formal pretrial proceeding that might result in trial by court-martial or in any type of administrative separation from the Corps
Awaiting results of administrative board that might result in administrative separation or reduction in rating.

1010a. REDUCTIONS IN RANK. Since this *Handbook* is aimed at noncommissioned officers on the way up, the subject of reduction will be treated only briefly. There are three types of reductions: (1) Nonpunitive (when it is necessary for CMC to reduce the total number of Marines in grade); (2) Punitive (by court-martial or at Office Hours, *but* it is Marine Corps policy that staff NCOs will not be reduced by Office Hours action; see Section 1605 to 1607); (3) Incompetence. Further details on reduction may be found in *Marine Corps Personnel Manual,* Chapter 6.

1011. PRECEDENCE AMONG NONCOMMISSIONED OFFICERS. Precedence is your right of seniority over other noncommissioned officers, based on rank and on the date of your promotion within a grade. The rank and precedence of first and second pay grade NCOs on active duty is shown in numerical order in the *Lineal Precedence List* for the top two grades. Your date of rank is also shown on your NCO warrant (see Chapter 1).

Serial and social security numbers. Effective 1 January 1972, your individual social security number replaces, for all purposes, the familiar serial number which every Marine received in the past on initial enlistment. In addition to your social security number, you also have, if in the two top grades, a *number in grade,* which is your number, in order of precedence, in the Lineal Precedence List. Your number in grade gives an exact indication of your precedence.

Reenlistment

The basic Marine Corps policies on reenlistment or extension of noncommissioned officers are as follows.

1. To be eligible for reenlistment or extension, you must have demonstrated the high standards of leadership, professional competence, and personal behavior required to maintain the dignity and authority of a Marine NCO.
2. No Marine may reenlist to serve beyond 20 years without CMC approval. Applications for such reenlistment from sergeants and below will not be considered. Staff NCO requests will be weighed on the basis of individual records and past performance.
3. The only exceptions to the above policy are staff NCOs selected for promotion whose obligatory two years extend past 20 years' service, and Marines currently on over-20 contracts, who will be allowed to fulfill them.
4. Reenlistments by sergeants and above must be approved by CMC.

1012. CLASSES OF REENLISTMENTS. Reenlistments in the Regular Marine Corps are classed as follows:

Immediate. Reenlistment within 24 hours of the time of discharge, Sundays or legal holidays not counted. Unless you reenlist immediately, you lose your date of rank or seniority and commence with a new date of rank as of reenlistment.

Continuous. Reenlistment within 90 days or less (but longer than 24 hours) since discharge.

Broken. Any reenlistment in which the NCO has been "on the outside" for more than 90 days. The penalties of broken service in terms of rank are that, as is also the case even for a continuous reenlistment, you face serious loss of rank.

For example, if a first sergeant stays out longer than six months, he is normally reenlisted as a staff sergeant. A gunnery sergeant who stays out for two years comes back in as a corporal. The moral is obvious—*immediate reenlistment pays.*

1013. EXTENSIONS. Should you wish to extend an enlistment rather than ship over, you may do so for three, six, or nine months or for one, two, three, or four years. Normally, you may not extend a single enlistment more than twice, nor for a total time exceeding four years. Prior to its actual commencement, your extension may be cancelled if you misbehave, if you change your mind and desire to reenlist, or if it turns out that benefits contingent on an extension

199   are not to be provided. However, once a legal extension has begun, it cannot be cancelled.

You may be involuntarily retained or extended:

For duration of war (or national emergency when Congress is not in session)
While undergoing or awaiting trial
While at sea (awaiting arrival at next port or arrival in CONUS).
While undergoing medical treatment.

> *Note:* If you finally decide not to ship over in the regular Marine Corps, it will be very much to your advantage to reenlist in the Marine Corps Reserve, as you will normally be able to accrue points for Reserve retirement and will of course continue to build up longevity, or "fogies," for pay purposes.

Retirement and Separation

> *Note:* The subject of discharges, separation, transfer to the FMCR, and retirement is complex, technical, and often legalistic. Detailed information may be found in Chapter 13, *Marine Corps Personnel Manual,* which should be consulted in case of doubt. Naturally, your first sergeant or CO are always available for further counseling.

Like death and taxes, it is inevitable that your Marine Corps career will eventually end with retirement or separation from the Service. The sections which follow analyze retirement and separation procedures for regular noncommissioned officers.

1014. BASIC DEFINITIONS. *Retirement* is removal from active duty after completion of certain service and longevity requirements, after which the retired NCO receives retired pay. Although a retired noncommissioned officer is no longer on duty, he remains a member of the Marine Corps, retains his rank and status as an NCO, and may under certain conditions be recalled to active duty.

Discharge is an absolute termination of military status.

Release from active duty is termination of an active-duty status and transfer or reversion to a reserve component (to the FMCR, for example) not on active duty. Note, however, that an NCO does not *retire* with less than 30 years' service. After 19 years and six months and with less than 29 years and six months' service, he is in the FMCR and thus *inactive,* but nevertheless not retired. This is a technical, but an important distinction.

Separation, a general term, includes either discharge or release from active duty.

An *honorable discharge* is a separation from the Marine Corps with honor.

A *general discharge* is separation under technically honorable conditions, but is nothing a Marine could ever be proud of.

An *undesirable discharge* is an administrative separation under conditions other than honorable, such as unfitness, misconduct, or security reasons.

A *bad-conduct discharge* is a separation by sentence of a court-martial, under other than honorable conditions.

Dishonorable discharge is separation from the Marine Corps by sentence of court-martial, under conditions of disgrace. It is the most shameful punishment that can be inflicted on a Marine.

The reasons for discharge from the Marine Corps are:

Expiration of enlistment
Convenience of the Government
Own convenience
Dependency or hardship
Minority
Disability
Unsuitability
Unfitness
Misconduct
Sentence of court-martial
Security
Order of the Secretary of the Navy.

1015. TRANSFER TO THE FLEET MARINE CORPS RE-SERVE. Any regular or reservist who has completed 19 years, six months and less than 29 years, six months, on active duty in the armed forces may request transfer to the Fleet Marine Corps Reserve (see Chapter 8). Your request will be approved or disapproved according to the requirements of the Marine Corps at the time. In the Fleet Reserve, you are, for most purposes, effectively retired. You receive *retainer pay,* which is $2\frac{1}{2}$ percent of the basic pay you were receiving when transferred, multiplied by number of years you had on active duty in the armed forces. If you have been credited by the Secretary of the Navy with extraordinary heroism in line of duty, your retainer pay is increased by 10 percent, but in no case can it exceed 75 percent of your active-duty base pay.

Your application to the Commandant for transfer to the FMCR should be submitted not earlier than 180 days before you wish to transfer and not later than 90 days. This allows time for administrative processing as well as for the thorough medical examination which you get prior to transfer, both to correct minor defects and also to make sure that you are not entitled to physical disability retirement.

After HQMC approves your request, you are normally transferred on the last day of the current month. Copies of your transfer orders go to the Marine Corps District where you will live and on whose rolls you will be carried. Your obligations to the Marine Corps are as follows:

You must keep fit for active service if recalled:
You must keep the following informed of your current *home mailing*

address: CMC; DirMarCorDist; and CO, MCRDSC, Kansas City;
You must promptly answer all official correspondence;

You must inform your District Director immediately of any health change that would render you unfit for service at sea or in the field.

At the conclusion of ten years in the FMCR, your retirement is processed and effected by the Marine Corps District maintaining your records, and in due course you are placed on the regular Marine Corps retired list.

1016. PHYSICAL RETIREMENT. Physical retirement is governed by Title IV of the Career Compensation Act of 1949. Its important provisions are summarized below.

A *temporary-disability retired list* exists in each service to which are transferred individuals whose physical condition prevents proper performance of duty, but who may recover. Persons with less than 20 years service whose disability is less than 30 percent may be discharged with severance pay. Pay on the temporary-disability retired list may be either $2\frac{1}{2}$ percent of active-duty pay per year for the number of years' service, *or* the percentage of disability fixed; but retired pay may not be less than 50 percent or more than 75 percent of active-duty pay. Physical-disability retired pay is tax-exempt.

If on the temporary-disability retired list, you must have a physical examination at least every 18 months, for not more than five years. If during that time your disability has become permanent and is 30 percent or more, you go off the temporary-disability retired list and are permanently retired for physical disability. If, upon examination, you are again found physically fit during that time, you may, at your own consent, be reappointed to the active list in a rank not below that held when you went on the temporary-disability retired list. If you do not wish to return to active duty or are not qualified for duty but are still rated less than 30 percent disabled, you may be separated from the service with severance pay.

If you are hospitalized for more than three months, a clinical board (or board of medical survey) at the hospital considers your case and usually recommends that you be (1) returned to duty; (2) given further treatment; (3) ordered to limited duty and reexamination after a stated period; (4) given sick leave and reexamination thereafter; or (5) ordered before a Marine Corps physical evaluation board.

You may waive the right to appear in person, but *should be very chary of this* unless the medical evidence in your case is uncomplicated and the result certain.

Appearance before the board requires less than a day; final action is taken by the Secretary of the Navy. If you are incapacitated and if continued hospitalization is not required, you may take leave or be assigned to temporary duty. If found qualified for continued active duty, you are discharged from hospital and ordered back to your original organization or to the nearest Marine Corps activity for further assignment. If retired, you must complete travel home within one year from the date of retirement in accordance with *Joint Travel Regulations.* You may choose any residence desired, without regard to your current address of record in Headquarters.

The report of a physical evaluation board is extensively reviewed in the Navy Department. The final reviewing authority is ordinarily the Judge Advocate General of the Navy. Retirement takes effect on the first day of the month after the Secretary approves.

Note: On retirement (*not* transfer to the FMCR) you are promoted to the highest rank, commissioned or noncommissioned, which you have held on active duty and in which you have performed satisfactorily.

Correspondence and Messages

1017. OFFICIAL CORRESPONDENCE. Both Marine Corps and Navy employ the same forms and procedures for official correspondence. These are prescribed in Chapter 16, *Navy Regulations,* in the *Navy Correspondence Manual;* and in Chapter 1, *Marine Corps Manual.* The term "correspondence" embraces letters, endorsements, speedletters (short-cut, urgent letter communications which do not require telegraphic or radio transmission), and memoranda. Correspondence is filed in accordance with the *Navy Filing Manual.*

As an individual, you may originate official correspondence which pertains to you personally (including, however, any recommendations for improvement or innovation which may benefit the Marine Corps). Correspondence which affects a command as a whole can be originated only by, or in the name of, the commanding officer.

Except for speedletters, official correspondence must be conducted through official channels and must be promptly forwarded. Failure to forward an official letter (if in proper form and language) is a very serious dereliction.

Correspondence with civilians or with other Government agencies should be particularly prompt, courteous, complete, and accurate.

Avoid unnecessary, long-winded, vague correspondence. Joseph Pulitzer's rule for the staff of the old New York *World* applies to military correspondence: *"Accuracy, brevity, accuracy!"*

During the past few years Marine Corps correspondence has grown less precise and less military. Vague expressions and superlatives have become commonplace and, in many cases, have replaced clear and understandable military terms. Complex language is used, not because it contributes to the usefulness of correspondence, but because of habit or custom. To permit correspondence to become diluted by unmilitary expressions or unnecessary language is consistent neither with the character of the Marine Corps nor with the efficient conduct of its affairs.

1018. OFFICIAL LETTERS. According to the nature of the correspondence, official letters may follow either the *naval form* (which is used throughout the Naval Establishment) or the *business form.*

Examples and detailed instructions covering both forms can be found in the *Navy Correspondence Manual.* Speedletters, however, may follow the abbreviated form and language employed in dispatches and naval messages.

Hints for Official Letter-Writers. Until you are quite familiar with the prescribed forms for official correspondence, do your writing within arm's reach of the *Navy Correspondence Manual.* See that your unit clerks do likewise. Keep an up-to-date dictionary at hand (*Webster's New Collegiate Dictionary* is excellent).

Avoid pointless letters. Correspondence should be confined to specific requests, reports, and concrete recommendations.

One letter should deal with one subject only. Cover separate subjects to the same addressee by separate letters. Answer official letters by letter, not by an endorsement on the letter received, unless you are specifically directed to do so.

Write in terse, unadorned, direct, and clear language. Use short sentences. Psychological tests show that any sentence longer than seventeen words may stump some readers. Avoid the passive voice. Don't be afraid to use the first person. Remember Pascal's line, "I have made this letter longer than usual because I lack the time to make it shorter."

Be as temperate and courteous in correspondence as you would be in discussing the subject face to face with your correspondent.

Organize your facts and ideas before you write. The standard sequence for a staff study is a good one for almost any kind of official correspondence:

Statement of the problem	Conclusions
Facts bearing on the problem	Recommendations
Discussion	

Intraunit and intraheadquarters correspondence should be by memorandum. Marine usage sometimes omits the closing phrases customary in the Navy, "Very respectfully" or "Respectfully."

Block out important official letters in double-spaced rough draft. This permits you to make legible corrections and interlineations. It is good practice to compose rough drafts on a distinct color of stationery used for no other purpose.

Always capitalize the word "Marine." Avoid the word "member" where "Marine," "officer," "noncommissioned officer," or "enlisted man" can be used. Don't write "personnel" in lieu of "Marines" or "all hands." In expressing time, use the Navy 24-hour system, and never add the superfluous word, "hours"—write "1230," never "1230 hours."

Here is a random list of gobbledygook, canned language, and trite jargon excerpted from a sampling of official correspondence. We would all be better off if most of these were never seen again:

. . . pursuant to . . . in conformance with . . . pertinent facts . . . unprecedented—*as a substitute for unusual* . . . thorough and complete investigation . . . infeasible of accomplishment . . . screening . . . at the earliest practicable moment . . . rendered mandatory . . . materially impaired effectiveness . . . in light of the foregoing . . . above-named personnel . . . management—*as a substitute for* command *or* leadership . . . considered opinion . . . VIP . . . firm up . . . formalize . . . outload . . . offhand . . . onload . . . stage in . . . stage out . . . effectuate . . . definitive— *where* definite *is meant* . . . maximize . . . as appropriate . . . finalize . . . logisticswise . . . personnelwise . . . appraise— *where* apprise *is intended* . . . forward—*as a garble for* foreword . . . marshall—*as a misspelling of* marshal

Finally, how would you answer the following questions about yourself as a letter writer?

1. Are most of your letters less than a page long?
2. Is your average sentence less than 17 words?
3. Do you try for short paragraphs—less then ten lines?
4. Do you prefer active verbs (please make the following arrangements) to passive verbs (it is requested that the following arrangements be effectuated)?
5. When you have a choice, do you choose short words (pay, help, mistake) or big ones (compensation, assistance, inadvertency)?
6. Are your letters free of officialese and jargon?

1019. OFFICIAL MAIL. Official correspondence may be mailed postage-free in what are still described as "penalty envelopes," that is, envelopes bearing an official return address and the notation, *"Official Business"* in the upper left hand corner, and, in the upper right, the phrase, *"Postage and Fees Paid, Navy Department."* As a noncommissioned officer you are entitled to use such envelopes for correspondence which clearly involves Government business and for Government parcels within prescribed weight limits. Be scrupulous in exercising this privilege. Remember you also are a taxpayer.

1020. PERSONAL CORRESPONDENCE. Due to the fact that you change station every few years, keeping correspondents advised of your correct mailing address can be quite a problem. To help out, the Navy Department has change-of-address cards which you can get in any quantity from your mail clerk or station post office. Each time you are transferred, send these to all your regular correspondents and to publications to which you are a subscriber. Should you or anyone wish to write a Marine, but not know his present address, simply address the letter as follows:

c/o Directory Service,
Marine Corps Headquarters,
Washington, D.C., 20380.

Note: For guidance of your family or parents at your permanent home address, Postal Laws and Regulations permit postage-free forwarding of any class of mail addressed to a member of the armed services, if

Fleet Post Office (FPO). Mail may be sent, at domestic postage rates, via the Fleet Post Offices, New York, San Francisco, or Seattle, as appropriate, by or to any officer or enlisted man serving beyond the continental limits of the United States on board any ship, shore station, or FMF unit. This privilege is important not only because it saves you and your correspondents appreciable money in postage (especially on publications and parcel post) but because the Fleet Postmasters keep track of the movements of mobile units and dispatch mail accordingly. A comparable system, used by the Army and Air Force for their units and stations and for some locations overseas where there is a bulk of U.S. correspondence, is that of "APO"s, via the same cities as above. Generally speaking, if a ship or unit is on the East Coast, in the Atlantic, the Caribbean, or Europe or Africa, its mail goes via FPO, New York. Mail for West Coast, Pacific, or Asiatic Station mainly goes via FPO, San Francisco, except for a few destinations, which are routed via Seattle.

All units or stations including those which previously had Navy number designators for mail or APO numbers now have ZIP code numbers assigned, and these should always be used when known. Here is a typical FPO address:

1stSgt Ollie M. Schriver,
3d Battalion, 9th Marines,
3d Marine Division,
FPO San Francisco 96601.

"Free" Mail. Members of the armed forces serving in the Vietnam combat zone are presently entitled to send first-class mail (i.e., letters) without postage, simply writing (printing or typing not permitted) the word, "FREE" where the stamp would be. This frank entitles mail from field post offices to travel first-class air mail. When you avail yourself of this privilege, you must place your name, rank, file number, unit, and FPO/APO address on the upper left-hand corner of the envelope. This privilege is virtually always extended to the services by Congress during major hostilities.

1021. PERSONAL RADIO TRAFFIC. If you are serving at sea or at a station outside the continental limits of the U. S. where there are no commercial cable services, you may file personal traffic for stateside addresses via what is known as "Class E Messages." In this system your message is transmitted by naval communications to the nearest Naval Communication Station in the United States, which relays your message to its ultimate addressee via commercial telegraph. You pay for the cost of commercial relay only. If you want to send a Class E message, see your communications officer.

Security of Information

When you enlisted, you took your oath of allegiance to defend the United States against all enemies, foreign and domestic. Now that you are a noncommissioned officer, more than ever before, you receive access to information not generally available to civilians. One of your most important responsibilities then becomes the safeguarding and discreet use of this information in such a way that it may never fall into the hands of enemies of the United States. Remember that, war or peace—and especially in today's era of the Cold War—the battle for information goes on continually. Our success in this battle will determine whether the odds of physical combat are on our side or our enemies'.

Indiscreet conversation and personal letters constitute great menaces to security. Guard against unthinking discussion of classified shoptalk, even with your family and friends. Avoid loose talk in public places. On the telephone, you can never tell who may be listening. Automatic self-censorship is a responsibility of all Marines.

Self-censorship—i.e., silence—is a negative weapon. To accompany it, there must be the positive weapon: *the habit of alertness.* Every noncommissioned officer should therefore cultivate his powers of observation.

Every Marine is responsible for safeguarding all classified information, gear, or devices entrusted to him (or, for that matter, any such within his observation or knowledge). During the Quebec Conference in 1943, a Marine sergeant major noticed a scrap of paper lying about. On picking it up, he discovered that it contained notes by one of the planners giving the D-day for the Normandy landings, a rough troop list, and parts of the air support plan. He immediately turned in this find and thus single handedly prevented the compromise of one of the most important military secrets in the history of the United States.

Alertness also means that you keep foolish young Marines from loose talk, that you immediately advise higher authority when you have reason to believe or suspect that there has been a breach of classified information, and that you observe and report the behavior of any person acting suspiciously.

Finally, in the words of an excellent Marine Corps *Gazette* article by Major R. M. Head, in February 1954, *do not confirm or deny.* Even when you read something in the papers which appears to disclose classified information, don't make the enemy's job easier by confirming that it is so (or worse still, telling somebody which part of the article is right and which part is wrong).

1022. SECURITY OF CLASSIFIED MATTER. Classified matter is anything—either information or material—which, in the public interest, must be safeguarded against unauthorized or improper disclosure. Chapters 15 and 16 of *Navy Regulations,* as well as the *Navy Security Manual for Classified Matter* and the *Registered Publications Manual,* contain detailed instructions which must be followed to the letter when you handle classified matter. The security of classified matter is the security of the United States.

Classifications. The categories of security classification are *Top*

Secret, Secret, and *Confidential.* In addition, certain information regarding nuclear weapons and related subjects is classed as *Restricted Data;* do not confuse this term with the former classification, "Restricted," which you may see on older publications but which has been replaced by "For Official Use Only." It is up to the originator of matter that should be classified to assign it the appropriate classification, and he, as well as higher authorities in the chain of command, may reclassify it when appropriate. Reclassification may involve either "upgrading" or "downgrading."

Handling of Classified Matter. The precautions regarding preparation, marking, custody, handling, transmitting, stowage, disclosure, control, accounting for, and disposal of classified matter may be found in the references at the beginning of this section, and of course these precautions must be followed to your utmost. If, however, you find yourself in a situation where you cannot physically comply with certain of these rules, you are bound simply to do your utmost, in common sense and zeal, to safeguard whatever may be entrusted to you. Should you have reason to believe classified information has been compromised, through your fault or anyone else's, you must advise your commanding officer at once.

No one, regardless of rank or position, is automatically entitled to knowlege or possession of classified matter. Such information goes only to those who *need to know.*

Leave and Liberty

1023. LEAVE OF ABSENCE. Subject to the needs of the service, leave of absence provides time off for mental and physical relaxation from duty, and gives you opportunity to settle your affairs when the time comes for change of station. Every Marine on active duty accrues leave at the rate of 30 days a year (that is, $2\frac{1}{2}$ days per month).

Without jeopardizing the readiness of the command, your CO sometimes cannot grant every Marine (himself included) all the leave he rates. Whatever leave is not taken "goes on the books" until you have a maximum of 60 days' unused or accrued leave. Earned leave accrued above 60 days must be automatically dropped on 30 June each year and when you retire. As you approach retirement, it is a good idea to let leave accrue to the 60-day maximum, since you receive a lump-sum payment for such accrued leave when you retire. Short of final years, however, take leave as you can; the days that are dropped each 30 June can never come back.

> *Note:* Men who have served at least 120 days in a hostile-fire area may accumulate up to 90 days' leave, rather than the usual 60. The extra 30 days, however, will be lost unless used before the end of the fiscal year following the one in which service in the combat area ends.

Leave of absence describes authorized vacation or absence from duty, as distinguished from *liberty,* which is merely authority to be away from your place of duty for short periods and is not charged to leave.

Accrued leave is the unused leave to your credit, "on the books," each July 1st. You cannot bank up more than 60 days' accrued leave.

Annual leave is leave taken as routine vacation from duty. Annual leave is limited to your total accrued leave plus 45 days' advance leave, but may not exceed periods of 60 days.

Sick leave is given to convalescents on recommendation of the medical authorities or to repatriated prisoners of war. Sick leave does not count against accrued leave.

> *Note:* The Marine Corps will provide transportation or reimburse you with mileage, for home travel when on convalescent leave resulting from wounds in action or illness or injury incurred when you were eligible to receive combat pay. The travel for which you are reimbursed must be between your hospital and home, however, except as otherwise authorized by the Secretary of the Navy.

Emergency leave may be granted to help alleviate some personal emergency, such as death or serious illness in the immediate family. Emergency leave is charged against accrued leave and may not exceed 105 days.

Excess leave is leave in excess of all your accrued leave plus 45 days' advance leave. Avoid taking excess leave when you can possibly do so, since your pay and allowances are checked while you are on excess leave.

Earned leave is the term used to describe the leave potential of an individual at any given date during the fiscal year. Earned leave may be calculated as follows: From the amount of accrued leave, subtract whatever leave has been taken since the outset of the fiscal year to the date in question. To that remainder add the amount of leave earned since the beginning of the fiscal year. Earned leave may exceed 60 days during the fiscal year, but will always be cut back to 60 days at the beginning of the new fiscal year. Note that time in confinement or as an unauthorized absentee or deserter does not count for accrual of leave.

Advance leave is an accounting term to describe leave granted in advance of accrual.

Delay in reporting is leave authorized to be taken after detachment from one permanent station and before reporting to another.

1024. COMPUTING LEAVE AND DELAY IN REPORTING. No small amount of bookkeeping and finger-counting centers about the computations of leave and delay. Here is how to do it.

Your day of departure on leave, whatever the hour, counts as a day of duty (and hence is not charged as leave).

If you return after the beginning of working hours on shore station, or after the hour of 0900 aboard ship, the calendar day of return counts as a day of leave. If, however, you return before working hours, or before 0900 aboard ship, the calendar day of return is a day of duty.

If you are reporting aboard after authorized delay, rather than from leave, you must report before midnight on the final day allowed.
To illustrate:

Amount of leave or delay	Date of departure	Must return and report not later than
10 days' annual leave	10 April (day of duty, not leave).	21 April (before forenoon quarters [0900] or beginning of working hours).
20 days' delay, with 5 days' travel time, and 4 days' "proceed" time (permanent change of station).	1 August (date of detachment, day of duty).	30 August, *before 2400* (without delay, you would be due 10 August; add 20 days' delay, making it 30 August).

Subject to the qualifications just explained about reporting before quarters or working hours, the rule to memorize is: *"Day of departure is a day of duty; day of return is a day of absence."*

One precaution: if you report back from leave or delay, outside of working hours, be sure your return is logged in by the Officer of the Day, organization duty officer, or duty NCO.

Address While on Leave. It is your responsibility to keep your commanding officer apprised of your address at all times while on leave. If your plans change, advise him by letter or telegram. If you are touring, set up a number of check-in points, such as hotels where you expect to stay, American Automobile Association offices, or homes of friends. You have no leg to stand on if, while on leave, your commanding officer tries to communicate with you and cannot reach you.

Your Leave Record. Every Marine has a leave record on which all leave taken is debited and all leave earned is credited each year. This record is contained in your service record book.

1025. FOREIGN LEAVE. Marine Corps Headquarters encourages Marines to take foreign leave, and will assist you in passport arrangements (if required). Noncommissioned officers going on foreign leave may travel, on space-available basis, in Government aircraft. Unless you are authorized by the Commandant to wear a uniform while on foreign leave, you must wear civilian clothes. You should, if possible, check in at the American Embassy or Legation of the country you are visiting, reporting your presence to the NCO-in-Charge of the Marine Security Guard, who will ascertain whether the Naval Attache desires to see you. Likewise, whenever you are in a city where there is an American Consulate, you should unfailingly register your presence with the Consul. Aside from your obligations just stated, the practice of checking in gives you many potential conveniences and local information, as well as a secure forwarding address for mail and messages.

Permission to visit foreign countries while on leave must be granted by the Commandant, except for visits to certain foreign areas specified from time to time in current directives, for which blanket authorization is granted.

1026. LIBERTY. Liberty, as you know, does not count as leave. It may be granted at any time for up to 48 hours. If the period includes a legal holiday, any commanding officer can extend a "forty-eight" to a "seventy-two." If the period includes a weekend, commanding officers so authorized by the Commandant may grant 96-hour liberty; this privilege is reserved for remote areas in which "forty-eights" and "seventy-twos" might be inadequate. But liberty may not be used as a device to extend leave.

Unless you have specific permission to the contrary, while on liberty you must remain within the general vicinity of your post. All posts and units have standing orders which designate "liberty limits" beyond which ordinary liberty does not extend. The purpose of liberty limits is to prevent Marines from going so far afield that they cannot count on returning within the prescribed time.

Off-duty Employment

The basic policy of the Marine Corps regarding off-duty employment by Marines is that the Corps will not prevent any enlisted man from holding a respectable, ethical job which in no way conflicts with his responsibilities toward the Marine Corps or impedes his ability to be a Marine 24 hours a day when so required.

1027. SPECIFIC PROVISIONS. Because of the fact that, even off-duty, you represent the finest military organization in the world, certain specific restrictions govern any off-duty work you may engage in.

If you receive pay from a U. S. Government agency, the total pay you receive, cannot exceed $2,000 a year.

> *Note:* The foregoing limit *does not apply* to wages from nonappropriated funds, such as post exchanges, officer and NCO messes, etc.

Bandsmen may not work for pay as musicians outside military reservations.

You may not work for an organization involved in either a strike or lockout. Should either occur, you must terminate such employment until the conclusion of strike or lockout.

You may not represent any commercial company selling insurance, mutual funds, investment plans, commodities and services on any military reservation, whether for pay or not.

You may not make any commercial solicitation or sales to any member of the armed forces who is junior to you in rank. This does not apply to onetime sales of your own personal property, auto, house, etc.

You may not be employed as a civilian policemen. However, you may work as a private civilian security guard if the nature of your job makes it clear that you are not a law-enforcement officer. In any case, you may not be armed in connection with any such job.

Identity Devices

1028. "ID CARD." The "ID Card," or Marine Corps identification card, is the most important identifying document you have. It identifies you as a Marine and thus must be safeguarded with great care. Regular and active-duty Reserve Marines have the green card whereas inactive reserve personnel carry the red card. All retired Marines are issued a grey card. Loss of an ID card is a serious matter and must be reported immediately. Carry it at all times, and never surrender it.

The ID card, however, is not a pass, but an identifying device.

1029. IDENTIFICATION TAGS. Every Marine on active duty is issued two "dog tags" to identify him should he be killed or wounded in action. These tags are items of equipment. When not required to be worn, they must remain in your possession.

Note that when tags are required, *both* tags must be worn.

1030. GENEVA CONVENTION CARD. This is a white card which is carried by personnel in combat or whenever capture is possible. It is designed to be turned over to a captor, should you be taken prisoner, and thus provide officially authenticated information required by the capturing power in preparation of his POW rolls. When not required to carry the Geneva Convention card, turn it in for stowage attached to your record.

1031. DEPENDENTS' ID CARDS. Your wife and each dependent over 10 years of age are entitled to an Armed Forces Dependent's Card, as described in Chapter 7. Dependents under 10 are covered by your wife's card. This card, like your ID Card, is an identity device and does not in itself entitle the bearer to anything. It ordinarily serves, however, to establish identification for medical care, post exchange, and similar privileges extended to dependents.

*As to pay, I beg leave to assure the Congress
that, as no pecuniary consideration could
have tempted me to accept this arduous
employment at the expense of my domestic ease
and happiness, I do not wish to make any
profit from it.*
—George Washington (to Congress, on his
appointment as Commander-in-Chief, 16 June 1775)

11 Pay, Allowances, and Travel

Note: Since the subject matter presented here is precise, extensive, and liable to change, this chapter is written in general terms. In case of doubt, always consult your paymaster.

It is related that, during the early days of World War II, a lofty-minded civilian visited Guadalcanal. During his tour, war aims were mentioned. Addressing Lieutenant Colonel L. B. Puller, one of the most professional Marines on the island, the visitor inquired, "And what, colonel, are *you* fighting for?"

Colonel Puller paused, reflected for a moment, and answered, "$549 a month."

Whether you incline to this view or to the sentiments of George Washington quoted in the heading, the importance of knowing about pay and allowances is obvious.

The pay and allowances of Marines (and of the other armed services) are fixed by the Career Compensation Act of 1949, as amended by subsequent pay legislation.

Every member of the service is paid monthly or twice monthly, based on his rank and length of service. Regardless of whether your rank is temporary or permanent, you are paid at the rates prescribed for that grade.

The monthly basic pay of enlisted personnel of the Marine Corps, Navy, Coast Guard, Army, and Air Force may be found in current pay tables and is the same, grade for grade, in all of the services.

The sums you receive as "pay" in the civilian sense of the word include:

Basic pay
Allowance for subsistence
Allowance for quarters (under prescribed conditions)

In addition, when and if you qualify, there are numerous additional compensations that can be classed as pay, such as family separation allowance, flight pay and flight-deck pay, jump pay and other hazardous-duty pay, clothing allowance, foreign shore-duty pay, proficiency pay, combat pay, reenlistment bonus, overseas station allowances, responsibility pay, etc.

1101. SERVICE CREDITABLE FOR PAY PURPOSES. In determining your length of service for pay purposes, you receive credit for all service, active or inactive, in the Marine Corps, Navy, Army, Air Force, Coast Guard, and reserve components thereof. In addition, full time is allowed to Women Marines for service in the Army Nurse Corps, the Navy Nurse Corps, the nurse corps of the Public Health Service, and reserve components thereof. Full time is also allowed for service as deck officer or junior engineer in the Coast and Geodetic Survey. Active service in the appointive grade as aviation cadet and service as an enlisted aviation cadet may be counted as service for pay purposes. Further, captains and lieutenants with over four years active duty (including active duty for training) as enlisted men receive a separate, slightly higher rate of pay.

Service not creditable for longevity increases (or "fogies") is service in inactive National Guard, or in State, Home, or Territorial Guard; service in ROTC; time spent in fraudulent enlistment or unauthorized absence; and time lost due to own misconduct.

You count, in the computation of basic pay, the total of all periods authorized to be counted in any of the services.

1102. DEPENDENTS. Certain of your allowances vary according to whether or not you have dependents. The law defines dependents as:

1. Your wife (whose dependency is presumed).
2. Unmarried children under 21, over 21 if handicapped and incapable of self-support, or up to 23 if enrolled full-time in an accredited college.
3. A parent (or one who has stood *in loco parentis*—legal Latin for "in the place of a parent"), if chiefly dependent on you for support.
4. The husband or children of a woman Marine, if they in fact depend on her for more than half their support.
5. Stepchildren and adopted children, if dependent.

Except in the case of your wife or unmarried minor children, you must be able to prove dependency in excess of 50 percent, of any persons for whom you claim allowances. Divorce automatically terminates dependency of a wife, but not necessarily of children.

In the uncommon but not unheard-of situation of families in which both husband and wife are in uniform, neither can usually claim the other as a dependent, each being eligible for a without-dependents quarters allowance, if they live off-base.

1103. SUBSISTENCE. Basic Allowance for Susistence or "BAS," as it is known, goes to an enlisted Marine only when not furnished meals, for example, when given permission to eat at home or when assigned duty where messing facilities are not available. The rate of BAS changes annually to reflect the varying computed cost of the ration.

Where a mess is available but you are authorized *commuted rations*, you receive the commuted money value of the daily ration and have to pay out of pocket for any meals you take in the mess hall. Some noncommissioned officers, however, receive higher subsistence allowances if there is no government mess available or if (like recruiters and other people on independent duty) they must get certain daily meals in commercial restaurants.

If you are not furnished rations in kind, you may be granted *leave rations* (equal to the value of commuted rations) when on leave.

1104. QUARTERS ALLOWANCE (BAQ). You are in general eligible for Basic Allowance for Quarters "BAQ," whenever the Marine Corps fails to provide you with quarters. *If unmarried*, however, you do not draw quarters allowance while in the field or in the hospital. There are two sets of BAQ rates, one for men with dependents and a lower scale for those without dependents.

Corporals and below (under four years service), with dependents, don't receive their quarters allowance directly. Instead, by means of the so-called Q Allotment, a sum, consisting of the man's BAQ plus a $40 deduction from his pay, goes directly to his wife. This arrangement formerly applied to senior noncommissioned officers but no longer does.

If assigned quarters which are inadequate (and have officially been so declared by the local command), you receive your quarters allowance but pay the Government a "fair rental" for the quarters. If the fair rental value exceeds your quarters allowance, you pay only the BAQ.

If serving overseas with dependents in situations where rentals and real estate prices are out of sight, your BAQ may be augmented by a special "station allowance" to help make up the differential.

Note: If you are a corporal considered to be "career-designated" (i.e., serving on a six-year obligation, with more than two but less than four years' service), you are eligible for several benefits, such as shipment of household effects on permanent change of station, previously available only to sergeants and above. Consult your first sergeant for details.

1105. HAZARD AND INCENTIVE PAY. Current law provides various types of "incentive pay" for hazardous duty (some not usually applicable to Marines), as well as two separate categories of "special pay," also for hazardous duty.

INCENTIVE PAYS. The following are some of the hazardous duties which currently rate extra monthly incentive pay: Frequent and regular participation in aerial flights, other than as a crew member; inside observer in high or low pressure chamber; parachute jumping; demolition of explosives as a primary duty, including training for such duty; duty involving intimate contact with lepers; duty as human acceleration or deceleration experimental subject; duty as a human test subject in thermal stress experiments; duty involving flight operations (flight-deck duty) aboard an aircraft carrier (*not* including LPH) or in an aviation unit operating therefrom.

The President may suspend incentive pay in wartime. Finally, you may not receive incentive pay for more than two purposes at the same time.

SPECIAL PAYS. *Combat Pay* (technically termed "Hostile Fire Pay") is provided for all military personnel who serve within geographic limits established by the Secretary of Defense during hostilities and who meet certain criteria of exposure to hostile fire or enemy action. This pay ($65 a month) is the same for all ranks and is taxable to the same extent as other pay. Your disbursing officer can advise you as to eligibility.

Hostile fire pay may be paid in addition to any other categories of hazard pay.

Diving Pay. Although we usually think of diving as a Navy monopoly, the Marine Corps has certain diver billets. To qualify for diving pay, you must be a rated diver, must occupy a diver billet, must maintain your qualifications, and of course must be detailed to diving duty.

1106. ADVANCE PAY. Advance pay, known as a "dead horse," is designed to help pay for transportation, temporary storage of household effects, excess shipping charges and living expenses, and securing new living accommodations. Except when absolutely necessary, avoid drawing a dead horse, as it is usually difficult to repay it once it is used—and liquidation is required within six months.

All NCOs may draw advance pay any time after receipt of orders involving detachment from permanent duty station until 30 days after reporting to a new permanent station, provided the orders are not incident to separation from the service or trial by court martial. Temporary duty en route is no bar to drawing a dead horse. The amount advanced normally does not exceed one month's pay, but as much as three months' basic pay (less income tax, deduction for social security, SGLI, and indebtedness to the Government for a previous advance of pay) may be drawn. Whatever the extent of the advance you draw, however, you must have enough time left on current enlistment to pay the money back. The only possible advantage of a dead horse is the melancholy one that, should you die before it is paid back, your death gratuity cannot be checked to liquidate the overpayment, and your estate is that much ahead. This is worth considering before transfer to combat or before extensive air travel.

1107. SERGEANT MAJOR OF THE MARINE CORPS. The Sergeant Major of the Marine Corps receives $150 per month in proficiency pay.

1108. CLOTHING ALLOWANCES. An initial in-kind clothing allowance is granted to each enlisted man and enlisted woman. Six months after assignment to active duty, a monthly Basic Clothing Maintenance Allowance accrues to each enlisted person for the first three years of service; thereafter an increased Standard Clothing Maintenance Allowance continues while the individual remains on active duty. For noncommissioned officers required to wear civilian clothes, for certain men in the State Department Security Guard program, and for musicians in the Marine Band, special supplementary allowances are provided.

1109. FOREIGN DUTY PAY. For most types of duty aboard ship or beyond the continental limits of the United States and in places designated by the Defense Department, you receive foreign shore-duty (FSD) pay or sea-duty pay ranging from $8 to $22.50 per month depending on your grade.

> *Note:* FSD pay does not become effective until you actually report to your duty station, even though you may be within the designated area previously. For example, if you drive to Alaska (which rates FSD pay) taking 15 days delay en route, your pay doesn't commence until you report aboard. Because of this, if you can arrange it, you would be wiser to report first and take leave after reporting.

1110. OVERSEAS ALLOWANCE. Separate from foreign shore duty pay, overseas allowances are designed to offset higher living costs abroad. Specific allowances are established and monitored by the Defense Department.

There are four categories of overseas allowances.

Cost-of-living allowance (COLA) compensates for overseas costs of food, clothing, and other living expenses determined to exceed comparable costs in the United States. Rates vary of course with geographic area and with the recipient's rank and family size, if any.

Station housing allowance (HOLA) is for families not occupying government quarters, for unaccompanied or single men not in quarters, and for field officers and above who do not elect to occupy quarters.

Temporary lodging allowance (TLA) is given to tide over an initial house-hunting period (not over 60 days) in which you may be required to live in a hotel and eat in restaurants.

Interim housing allowance (IHA) is for persons who are required to locate and obtain housing before dependents' travel is authorized and who thereby have to pay rent for unused space pending arrival of family. This allowance starts on the day housing is secured and runs (but not longer than 60 days) until dependents arrive.

> *Note:* As you can realize, the subject of overseas allowances is complex. For the last and most up-to-date word, consult your disbursing officer and *Joint Travel Regulations.*

1111. SEPARATION ALLOWANCE. "Family Separation Allowance" (FSA) is intended to reimburse married enlisted Marines for the expenses of having to maintain what amounts to two sets of quarters when away from home and family.

Like quarters allowance, FSA is nontaxable. It comes in two categories.

FSA-1 equals your regular quarters allowance *without dependents* and is payable to you when overseas (Hawaiian area doesn't count) without your family if you are not occupying Government quarters. Even if you are already receiving quarters allowance for your family, you still qualify for FSA-1 if you are (1) not in quarters; and (2) overseas.

FSA-2 is a payment of $30 a month which you rate when you are separated more than 30 days on permanent change of station or temporary duty in the U. S. or overseas. This type of separation allowance has three subdivisions (but all paying the identical $30) according to whether:

1. Your dependents' transportation is not authorized at Government expense, and they aren't near or at your permanent station (FSA-R).
2. You are on sea duty aboard a ship away from home port continuously for more than 30 days (FSA-S).
3. You are absent on temporary duty continuously for more than 30 days, and your dependents don't reside near or at your temporary-duty station (FSA-T).

This young noncommissioned officer tests electronic components of the Hawk missile to earn his proficiency pay.

FSA-2 is limited to noncommissioned officers only, with four or more years' service.

While detailed regulations as to when separation allowances stop are somewhat complex, the basic rule is that FSA usually stops when the condition that justified payment ceases to exist.

1112. PROFICIENCY PAY. About one out of every 14 noncommissioned officers, who is proficient in a scarce or particularly demanding military skill, receives, as of 1970, proficiency pay in rates varying from $50 to $100 a month. To be eligible for proficiency pay, you must, in addition to your skill, be a regular Marine who has served at least six years or who has that much obligated service. Thus, proficiency pay, as differentiated from variable reenlistment bonus, described below, is aimed at persuading experienced Marines to stay on in the Corps and in their essential specialties.

There are two categories of proficiency pay: *specialty pay* and *superior performance pay*. The former rewards technical skills while the latter compensates noncommissioned officers in such highly demanding duties as drill instructor, recruiter, and career planner.

A basic prerequisite for proficiency pay is that you be recommended for it by your commanding officer. If at any time he feels you have failed to maintain skill or performance, he can terminate the pay, which is likewise terminated should you be reduced for inefficiency or punishment.

1113. REENLISTMENT BONUS. There are two types of reenlistment bonus—regular and variable. The former is a simple inducement to ship over; the latter is intended to persuade specially skilled men on their first cruise to make the Marine Corps their career.

The *regular bonus* goes to any Marine who, within three months after discharge, ships over in the regular Marine Corps or voluntarily extends for at least two years. The maximum cumulative bonus payable to any individual is $2,000. Payments are computed as follows:

1st reenlistment: one month's base pay for each year of new enlistment or extension.
2d reenlistment: two-thirds of a month's base pay for each year of new enlistment or extension.
3d reenlistment: one-third for each year.
4th and subsequent reenlistments: one-sixth per year.

There are several rather technical restrictions and qualifications to the foregoing general rules. For example, no bonus is payable to privates or privates first class after discharge from second enlistment. A third or later bonus is not payable to any man discharged below the rank of lance corporal. Further, if you fail to complete the reenlistment for which you received your bonus, whether because of misconduct or for voluntary reasons, you must refund a proportionate part of the bonus.

Variable bonus, as its name implies, is a special shipping-over bonus whose amount varies according to the criticality of the skill in question, *at the time you reenlist.* Skills are rated in terms of "multiples" from one to four. A "multiple one" skill means that, in addition to your regular bonus, described above, you receive an added bonus equal to the regular one. A "multiple four" bonus equals a bonus four times the regular one. This is the top bonus and means that you get what amounts to five regular bonuses—but not, in any case, more than $10,000. The variable bonus is paid in a lump sum, if approved by the Marine Corps, otherwise in installments. If you ship over in the tax-free Vietnam area, all installments are tax-free, regardless of where you may later receive the balance.

If paid by installments, you draw your regular bonus when you ship over, then divide the variable bonus by the number of years in the new cruise, and, on each anniversary of reenlistment, you receive that fraction.

Once authorized, your variable bonus remains the same regardless of future rank changes, nor can installments be cut off because of a lapse in your skill or a change in criticality of the skill in question. Further, should you die with part of the bonus unpaid, it goes to your estate.

Finally and most important—*the variable bonus is payable only for your first reenlistment.*

1114. SEVERANCE PAYMENTS. When you are discharged (honorably, of course) or transfer to the FMCR, you receive all basic pay and allowances you may have on the books, receive compensation for unused leave up to 60 days, and are reimbursed for travel mileage to your home of record. In addition, if discharged for physical disability less then 30 percent, you receive severance pay rather than retirement—*except* that, if you have more than 19 years and 6 months service, you are retired anyway.

Unused leave compensation amounts to basic pay for the number of days in question, plus $.70 per day subsistence allowance, plus $1.25 per day quarters allowance (for sergeants and above with dependents—no quarters credit is allowed below that rank). Since leave compensation can add up to a tidy sum, it is obviously to your advantage to keep the maximum amount of leave on the books as separation approaches.

Separation travel pay is six cents a mile, whether you actually perform the travel or not.

If, when separated, you owe the Government money, this amount is deducted from your final settlement, *except* that your travel mileage cannot be checked to liquidate indebtedness.

1115. RETIRED AND RETAINER PAY. *Retired pay* is pay received by a Marine on the retired list. *Retainer pay* goes to members of the Fleet Marine Corps Reserve (FMCR).

In either case, the retirement equity which you gradually amass during years of service is large and important. For each year you serve on active duty in the Corps, you add 2½ percent to this equity, i.e., with seven years' service, you have 17½ percent equity. *But*—unless you serve at least 19 years and 6 months—you can never collect on this equity.

In 1963, an actuarial study, based on the then prevailing pay scales, found that *it would cost $46,000 cash for a gunnery sergeant with 20 years' service to purchase a commercial lifetime annuity equal to his retainer/retired pay at this point.* Just imagine how hard it would be, in *any* job, to save $46,000 in 20 years ...

Computation. As stated above, retainer and retired pay is computed by multiplying your basic pay in grade by total years of active service by 2½ percent. In no case, however, can it exceed 75 percent of your base pay. Allowances are not included in this computation or in retainer/retired pay.

Although retired pay used to increase whenever active-duty pay increased, this is no longer so. Today, your retired pay is geared to rises in the Government's consumer price index (CPI). Whenever the CPI rises 3 percent or more, and stays at that level for three months, retired pay goes up by the same percent. It cannot be reduced, however, should the CPI revert down.

Miscellaneous provisions. Income tax continues to be deducted from retainer/retired pay, except to the extent waived for physical disability. Allotments in effect when you transfer to the FMCR may be continued, except Class Q allotments. However, once you discontinue an allotment, you may not reestablish any not authorized in DODPM. Change in name of beneficiary or in amount is considered a discontinuance.

Travel and Transportation of Military Personnel

1116. TRAVEL EXPENSE AND MILEAGE. The law provides travel expenses for military personnel on a mileage or per diem basis, by rail, private conveyance, steamer, or aircraft, the allowances for travel not to exceed:

a. Transportation in kind, reimbursement therefor, or a monetary allowance in lieu of cost of transportation not above seven cents a mile based on distance in official mileage tables.

b. The allowance in (a) plus a per diem in lieu of subsistence.

c. For travel within continental United States, a mileage allowance not exceeding 10 cents per mile according to current mileage tables.

The actual rates of reimbursement are discussed in Section 1120. These rates and the regulations governing issuance of transportation are contained in the *Joint Travel Regulations* and *Navy Travel Instructions.*

1117. TRAVEL ORDERS. *Travel Status* is travel away from your duty station under orders of official business.

When you apply for reimbursement for travel performed or for transportation for travel to be performed, you must have travel orders.

Basic authority to issue travel orders rests with the Commandant, who delegates this authority to certain commands.

All travel orders contain the same basic information and must:

Address the Marine by name
Reference authority to issue orders if originating from other than the Commandant
State the place or places to which the Marine is ordered to travel
State the date on which he will proceed
State the delay authorized in reporting, if any
State the modes of transportation authorized*
State the duty (official/public) to be performed
State to whom he shall report (if so required)
Give accounting data for cost of travel
State that travel is necessary in the public service*

* Not required under certain conditions.

Omission of any of these items may at least delay reimbursement and may cause rejection of a travel claim as invalid. Be sure you understand your orders before departure and be sure you carry them out exactly.

"PROCEED" TIME. The dates when you must comply with travel orders and when you must report, depend on certain phraseology which always appears in orders. Always check to see which of the following expressions appears, and then govern yourself accordingly.

"*Proceed.*" If your orders have no limited date and no haste is required in execution, you are directed simply to "proceed." Married men up through the grade of corporal, and sergeants or above, with or without dependents, are allowed four days' "proceed time" before commencement of travel (unless granted delay in reporting, as described in Chapter 10).

"*Proceed Without Delay.*" When haste in execution is demanded, you are directed to "proceed without delay." You are allowed only 48 hours' "proceed time" before commencement of travel.

"*Proceed Immediately.*" When maximum haste is required, orders are worded "proceed immediately." In this case you rate only 12 hours' "proceed time" before commencement of travel.

A number of additional ground rules apply to computation and availability of "proceed time" when travel orders require temporary or temporary additional duty (TAD) or travel orders are received while on such duty. For these rules, consult Chapter 5, *Marine Corps Personnel Manual.*

TYPES OF ORDERS. There are four types of travel orders.

Permanent change of station. This includes transfer from one permanent station to another; travel to first duty station after appointment; call to active duty; change in home port or home yard of a ship (for dependents); travel home from last duty station upon retirement, separation, or relief from active duty.

Temporary duty. This is duty at a place other than permanent station, under orders which direct further assignment to a new permanent station. While on temporary duty—as distinguished from temporary *additional* duty—you have no permanent station.

Temporary additional duty (TAD). This includes travel away from permanent station, performance of duty elsewhere, and return to permanent station.

Blanket or repeat orders. These are temporary additional duty orders issued to individuals for regular and frequent trips away from permanent duty stations in connection with duty.

1118. HOW TO COMPLY WITH TRAVEL ORDERS. Here is what you do when you receive a set of orders. (This is written to apply specifically to temporary additional duty [TAD] orders as described above, as they are the most frequently encountered.)

1. On receiving your orders, read them through and check the following points.

Correct rank, name, serial number, and MOS
Departure date
Place or places to be visited
Whether or not you are to report to a given headquarters or command
Mission you are to accomplish
Security clearance
Modes or options of transportation
Are the orders signed
First (receiving) endorsement completed.

If your orders appear basically incorrect or if it appears that you cannot carry them out as directed, return them immediately to the issuing authority with an explanation of the apparent difficulty.

2. Check out before departing and check in on return with your first sergeant during working hours or with the Officer of the Day/Duty NCO at all other times.

3. If your orders so direct, you will have to report to some other headquarters or unit (these are known as "reporting orders"—those not requiring you to report to anyone are known as "nonreporting orders"). When your TAD is completed at the distant place or station and before departing, be sure your orders are endorsed and signed, stating the time and date you reported, the date your TAD was completed, and the availability or nonavailability of quarters and messing facilities.

4. If your orders *do not* direct you to report (i.e., are "nonreporting"), if you intend to claim full per diem, and if your TAD at a place is 24 hours or longer, you *must* obtain a certificate or endorsement from the CO of the post, station, base, camp, etc., to the effect that Government quarters and mess were not available for your

occupancy while there on TAD. This entitles you to higher per diem.

5. If, while away from your parent unit, you find you cannot carry out your orders as written without incurring additional expense or if some unforeseen contingency arises, not provided for in the orders, request instructions by message or telephone (which can be reimbursed at Government expense) before proceeding further. Reimbursement for unauthorized additional expenses or unauthorized travel will not be paid.

6. If orders specify travel by Government aircraft where available, you must use Government air unless you obtain a certificate or endorsement from a transportation officer to the effect that Government air transportation is not available. Under current regulations, Government air is considered "available" if there is a *scheduled* Government plane departing for your destination within 48 hours of the time you plan to leave. If no special mode of transportation—or some other option—is specified in your orders, take your choice.

7. Keep an accurate itinerary and a record of authorized travel expenses for which you can claim reimbursement (see Section 1122).

8. Turn in your orders complete with itinerary, to your unit adjutant, on the first working day after your return to home station.

1119. TRAVEL TIME. Depending both on the type of travel directed by orders and on the mode used, you have several possible ways to compute allowable travel time. There are four classes of travel time:

Commercial land travel time (includes rail, bus, and air)
Air travel time (Government and commercial when specifically directed)
Government and commercial vessel travel time.

Commercial Land Travel Time, though including bus and air, is based on railroad travel. When you go by this mode, you get one day's travel time for each 720 miles or additional fraction thereof. *This mileage must be over the shortest usually traveled route.* Thus, if you are ordered to a new station 1,500 miles away via the shortest usually traveled route, you would be allowed three days' travel time if proceeding by rail.

Private Conveyance Travel Time is usually authorized on permanent change of station only, at a rate of 350 miles per day (or more than 150 miles for an additional day) over the shortest usually traveled route, if you actually make the trip by private auto.

Air Travel Time (either Government or commercial) is based on the fact that you can ordinarily travel anywhere within the United States by air in less than 24 hours. Thus, when going by air (and when this mode of travel is specifically *directed* in your orders) you rate only one day's travel time, unless you can prove that, for reasons other than your own convenience or preference, it actually took longer.

Government and Commercial Vessel Travel Time is the actual time required to complete the trip.

Proceed, delay, and travel time are covered in detail in Chapter 5, *Marine Corps Personnel Manual.*

1120. REIMBURSEMENT. *On permanent change of station,* except when performing group travel or with troops, you may choose one of the following optional allowances for travel within the United States:

1. Mileage at six cents per mile (if a Government transportation request, or "T/R," is not used; but if you travel by private vehicle, you must obtain a certificate that this mode of travel is advantageous to the Government);
2. Transportation in kind, plus per diem;
3. Transportation by Government T/R, plus per diem;
4. Reimbursement for the cost of the mode of travel authorized (if a T/R is not available at the time and place required) plus per diem. When you travel under these circumstances, you may choose between this allowance or mileage as described in 1 above, but you must make your choice before payment of an advance or upon termination of travel.

Mileage is computed via official common-carrier distance or official highway distance, depending upon the mode of transportation used. These distances are given in the Official Table of Distances.

For temporary duty (TD), reimbursement for travel is the same as for permanent change of station as shown above.

On temporary additional duty orders (TAD), which permit per diem reimbursement, transportation is furnished in kind or by transportation request, and reimbursement is at the specified per diem. If you choose to pay your own travel expenses rather than use a T/R, you will be reimbursed at five cents per mile for the official distance. If travel by private automobile is authorized and used—as more advantageous to the Government—you get seven cents per mile plus a per diem allowance. On this mode of travel, you are authorized travel time and per diem for the actual time necessary to make the trip. If the orders authorize you to travel by private conveyance, you are authorized travel time at 350 miles per day, but your per diem will be based on common-carrier schedules, not to exceed time actually used. When orders direct a specific mode of transportation, but you are authorized to perform travel, *for your own convenience,* via another mode, including privately owned conveyance, you will be entitled neither to reimbursement for cost of transportation nor to the monetary allowance in lieu of transportation, unless the authority responsible for furnishing the transportation requests certifies that T/Rs were not available or that the mode of transportation directed was not available at the time and place required in time to comply with the orders. Travel time in excess of that authorized by the directed mode is chargeable as annual leave.

1121. PER DIEM ALLOWANCES. These are designed to cover hotel, meals, tips, taxi fares (other than to and from the station), laundry, and other incidental expenses. You get per diem for temporary additional duty or temporary duty, including periods of necessary delay while awaiting transportation and at ports during permanent change of station.

In the United States. Per diem rates within the United States are given in *Joint Travel Regulations.* Where Government quarters or mess are available, the allowance is reduced proportionately. If you claim maximum per diem, you must secure a certificate from the local commander that Government quarters and/or mess were not available.

Outside the United States. Per diem allowances vary widely from country to country and are subject to frequent change. They are discussed in *Joint Travel Regulations,* Chapter 4.

> *Note:* No per diem will be paid for any round trip involving less than 10 hours' absence from your home station on the same day. In other words, to warrant per diem, your absence, within a single day, must be longer than 10 hours.

1122. REIMBURSABLE EXPENSES. Certain travel expenses (in addition to per diem) are separately reimbursable. These include:

1. Taxi fares or other local transportation between places of abode and terminals, and between terminals when free transfer is not included; also taxi fares between terminal and place of duty;
2. Tips to Pullman and baggage porters; fees for checking baggage; excess baggage, when approved;
3. Tolls for bridges, roads, ferries, tunnels, etc. (when traveling by Government conveyance or "special conveyance" as defined by JTR).
4. *In Government aircraft:* cost of fuel, repairs, nonpersonal services, guards and storage at other than Government fields;
5. *In Government auto:* storage charges, tolls, repairs, fuel, when Government facilities are not available;
6. Telephone and telegraph charges incident to duty and arrangement of transportation, but not hotel reservations;
7. Registration fees at technical, professional, or scientific meetings, etc., when attendance is authorized;
8. Passport and visa fees, including cost of photographs and birth certificates required in connection therewith.
9. Entry fees, port taxes, and embarkation or debarkation fees upon arrival or departure from foreign countries.

On all the foregoing items, except tips, you may be required to produce receipts in order to support claims in excess of $15. If in doubt on any point, consult *Joint Travel Regulations* as well as your disbursing officer.

1123. TRAVEL ADVANCE. Before departure under orders on permanent change of station, you may, if you request, draw an advance on mileage allowance, known as *Travel Advance*. An advance of per diem on temporary duty or TAD orders is also considered a Travel Advance. Do not confuse these advance payments with a "dead horse," described in Section 1106 above.

1124. TRAVEL REIMBURSEMENT. After reporting at your new station and getting your orders endorsed, present your pay record and original orders with one complete copy, to the disbursing office. The disbursing office will help you prepare your claim for mileage and per diem on your orders.

1125. TRAVEL IN GOVERNMENT CONVEYANCE. Travel by Government aircraft or any other Government conveyance is travel in kind. You rate per diem for meals and accommodations. On extended navigational flights for proficiency purposes, if authorized at your request, no per diem is payable.

1126. TRAVEL HINTS. Before departure, compute the exact time by which you must report at the next duty station (see Section 1119).

Commercial air is fast, but not always comfortable or convenient. Some financial advantage may result from traveling with your family in slack times when airlines allow reduced rates for spouses. Coach travel on *established* airlines is less expensive and no great hardship. If traveling with small children, the rapid completion of the trip is one of air's main appeals.

Rail travel is extremely comfortable and allows good opportunity to see the countryside. Families going by rail may consolidate individual tickets, at no additional cost, to obtain a compartment, which many regard as the best mode of travel. Most railroads also have special family rates.

Travel by private automobile usually results in considerable saving, both in your transportation and that of the car; also it permits a family vacation en route, and lets you pick your own route for scenery and visits. You can take advantage also of the leisurely travel time allowed for this mode of transportation (see Section 1119).

Keep a running itinerary as you travel, including dates and local times of arrival at and departure from each stop. You will need this for your travel claim.

On temporary additional duty, jot down reimbursable expenses (see Section 1122) as you go along, even small ones; they mount up and are otherwise usually overlooked.

Last but not least—*don't mislay your original orders.* Without them your reimbursement will not only be long delayed, but you will find yourself in bad odor with your new command.

1127. LOST ORIGINAL ORDERS. If your original travel orders get lost, you can still settle your travel—with some delay—for the mileage involved.

However, no payments for TAD pay or per diem may be authorized without at least one copy of the basic orders and endorsements.

If you receive a travel advance and then lose only your original orders but still have a complete copy, the disbursing officer holding your pay record with the travel advance posted on it may (upon your settlement of a claim in accordance with instructions) settle your travel or TAD only for the mileage involved.

If you cannot find any copy of your orders, a certificate with your travel itinerary may be filed by you and forwarded for settlement and approval by your disbursing officer. This may, however, entail two or more months before payment is approved.

Never throw away or destroy original orders after settlement has been made, but keep them in an orders folder so that you can have them to present for any subsequent claims or entitlements.

1128. TRAVELING WHILE ON LEAVE. If you need help, advice, or information while traveling on leave, look for the *Travelers' Aid Society,* which has desks in virtually all major rail, air, and bus terminals. In addition the armed services maintain *Military Information Desks* at:

Chicago (O'Hare International Airport)
Washington, D.C. (National Airport)
Jacksonville, Fla. (Imeson Airport)
Atlanta (Municipal Airport)
St. Louis (Lambert Field)
Dallas (Love Field)
San Francisco (International Airport)
New York (Kennedy International Airport).

Travelers' Aid or the above Military Information Desks can help you with:

Selection of alternate modes of travel or destination when unable to obtain a flight
Obtaining local ground transportation
Information on local services, such as USO, YMCA, police, medical aid, etc.
Contacting duty station when it appears you may be prevented from reporting or returning on time.

In addition to the above, local recruiting offices and local Marine Corps or Navy activities can provide much the same type of assistance. Recruiters and posts or activities are listed in the phone book under "U. S. Government."

Space-Available Military Air Travel. Marines may travel at no cost, on "space-available" basis, on Military Airlift Command (MAC) aircraft and on Naval and Air Force aircraft. Highest priority for such spaces goes to personnel on emergency leave.

At most military air bases there is a desk (usually at or near base operations) which processes requests for military space-available travel. Other than duty travelers and emergency-leave cases, applications are handled first-come, first-served. Usually, little advance information is available as to flights, destinations, or possible seating spaces, so you cannot make firm plans in advance. You can, however, obtain military flight information by telephoning base operations and identifying yourself by name and rank. Base telephone numbers can be found in the "U. S. Government" listing of the phone book.

Travel by Commercial Air. Most scheduled airlines offer varying discounts to Marines on what is termed *standby air travel.* To qualify for this rate, you must be traveling at your own expense on leave or within seven days after discharge; you must be in uniform when you get your ticket and travel; and you must have a validated DD Form 1580 (Authorization for Commercial Air Travel). Since standby air travel is on a space-available basis, *you cannot make advance reservations*—something you should bear in mind if thinking of holiday travel. Before boarding, you will be told to what point you have been cleared to travel. Up to this point you cannot be "bumped" and receive the same treatment as a full-fare passenger, including baggage allowances and handling.

Military standby travelers get three classes of priority: (1) emergency leave; (2) convalescent and combat leave; and (3) regular leave or travel within seven days after honorable discharge.

Travel by Train. Far more comfortable and interesting than air travel, rail transportation is available on *furlough rates,* good for coach travel at 50 percent discount. You must travel in uniform and have leave papers with you. In addition, virtually all railroads have attractive *family plan rates* for both coach and Pullman travel.

Bus Travel. Certain bus lines offer reduced fares for military travelers. To determine what special rates you may be entitled to, check at the local bus terminal.

Transportation of Dependents and Household Goods

1129. TRANSPORTATION OF DEPENDENTS ON PERMANENT CHANGE OF STATION. Costs of transporting dependents on permanent change of station are paid by the Government.

If you are not traveling by private vehicle, it is simplest to obtain dependents' tickets by Government Transportation Request. You may, however, transport dependents at your own expense and claim reimbursement afterward at 6 cents per mile for dependents over 12 years old (not to exceed two), and 3 cents for additional dependents over 12 years of age, and for children between 5 and 12. *Maximum mileage reimbursement for all your dependents* is 18 cents per mile. Distances are given in Section 1119.

Claims for reimbursement must be signed by you unless you are in a casualty status. When dependents' travel is incident to your having been reported as a casualty, the claim will be signed by the senior dependent.

1130. SHIPMENT OF HOUSEHOLD GOODS. *Household goods* include baggage, clothing, personal effects, and professional books, papers, and equipment. *Not* included, however, are vehicles and boats, wines and liquors, pets, and articles for nonmembers of your family.

Shipment can be made (including crating and drayage) at Government expense on permanent change of station, within weight allowances, for corporals with over four years' service and above, under the following circumstances:

Orders to sea or duty overseas where dependents may not follow;
Permanent change of station orders while on active duty;
Orders to duty under instruction of 20 or more weeks' duration;
Orders to or from *prolonged* hospitalization;
Honorable separation or retirement;
Death on active duty, or reported dead, missing, or interned;
Transfer between ships having different home ports and/or yards;
Orders changing home port and/or yard of ship to which attached;
Transfer between ship and shore station, where shore station is not
   ship's home port or yard.

Shipment cannot be made:

Before receipt of orders, unless specially authorized by competent
   authority;
If separation is other than honorable, or if transfer is incident to
   trial;
For change of station by reservists on duty for less than 6 months;

1131. WEIGHT ALLOWANCES. Current tables of weight allowances show the maximum weight of household goods which may be shipped by you on either permanent or temporary change of station.

On permanent change of station, you may ship "by expedited mode" (in most instances, simply a phrase for express shipment) up to 1,000 pounds net weight of personal property classified as *unaccompanied baggage.* This shipment should include only high-priority items necessary to permit you to carry out your duties or to prevent undue hardship to you or your dependents, and the net weight is charged against your total weight allowance. This type of shipment is invaluable for uniforms and effects required immediately after reporting.

Household goods in excess of weight allowance may be shipped, but excess costs will be charged to you. However, remember that weight allowances shown are net, i.e. they do not include packing materials.

1132. STORAGE OF HOUSEHOLD GOODS. *Nontemporary Storage.* There are at present some 17 various situations under which you may be entitled to "nontemporary" storage of household effects, not exceeding prescribed weight limitations. Since the length of

230 storage at Government expense varies under different circumstances and since you are subject to excess costs for storage beyond the authorized time limit, you should check with the freight transportation office holding your effects so that you will be sure where you stand. Among the most common situations under which you are entitled to nontemporary storage are the following:

Temporary duty pending detail overseas
Change of station from within U. S. to outside U. S.
Permanent change of station with temporary duty en route
Retirement, discharge with severance pay, or reversion in inactive
    duty with readjustment pay (up to one year's storage allowed)
Assignment to government quarters.

Temporary Storage. You are entitled to temporary storage at Government expense for up to 90 days in connection with any authorized shipment of household goods. Under certain conditions arising from circumstances beyond your control—such as unavailability of quarters at new station, arrival of your effects before you do, early surrender of quarters, etc.—competent authority may authorize an additional 90 days' storage. This added time in storage is not automatic; to arrange it, you should consult your traffic management office.

Prohibited Articles. Whether in temporary or nontemporary storage, effects stored may not include automobile, inflammables, weapons, ammunition, or liquor.

1133. DISLOCATION ALLOWANCE. When a noncommissioned officer with dependents has completed a permanent change of station, he gets a *dislocation allowance* to help pay the numerous extra expenses of moving. This allowance is equal to one month's quarters allowance for his rank; it is payable only once in any fiscal year, except by special authorization or when ordered to or from a course of instruction. It is not payable on orders to or from active duty.

1134. TRAILER ALLOWANCE. On a permanent change of station you are entitled to a *trailer allowance* for transportation of a "house trailer," if you own one, within the United States, for use as living space. A trailer allowance therefore is intended for the moving or transporting of a trailer at Government expense or subject to reimbursement. If you elect to claim trailer allowance, you cannot claim dislocation allowance (see Section 1133 above) or transportation of household goods.

Note: Always consult your transportation or supply office, and your disbursing office, before taking any action in transporting your trailer. It will be to your advantage.

1135. TRANSIT INSURANCE. The liability which the Government will accept for a lost or damaged shipment of household goods will not exceed $10,000. In addition, the carrier's liability for loss or damage varies from ten to sixty cents per pound on the actual weight of the shipment, but collection of claims against a carrier is a complicated, frustrating, and often fruitless process. Thus, where the value you set on your household goods exceeds the Government's liability (i.e., over $10,000) you may be wise to purchase additional protection in the form of a commercial *transit insurance policy*.

Should you take out such a policy, be careful to find out exactly what type of coverage you are getting. It is well to note, for example, that most such policies expire when your effects are delivered. Thus, when effects are delivered by van to a warehouse for temporary authorized storage (as in Section 1132 above), your policy will very likely expire as soon as the goods are accepted by the warehouse unless you have made special arrangements to extend your coverage. Further, reimbursement on such policies is computed on the ratio of the declared value of your shipment to the amount of insurance taken out. For example, if you state your effects to be covered are worth $4,000 but only insure for $2,000, and an item worth $100 is lost or broken, the insurance company will pay only $50.

1136. SHIPMENT OF PETS. On overseas permanent change of station, either to or from a United States port of embarkation, you may be able to arrange shipment of household pets aboard an MSTS transport providing no cost to the Government is involved. Certain fixed conditions must be met, and all arrangements must be made by you in advance. Your supply office can advise you as to these important details and as to any local restrictions which might complicate the situation.

Despite the pleasure and affection which we get from our pets, the bother, restrictions, and incidental expenses involved in their transportation and entry into certain overseas areas should be carefully weighed before you decide to bring a pet along. Among the most troublesome difficulties sometimes encountered are lengthy required periods of quarantine on arrival; during such isolation periods the pet may well be miserable, and of course the expenses of boarding will have to be borne by you.

1137. CHECK-OFF LIST FOR SHIPPING HOUSEHOLD GOODS. Here is a summary of things you should do and think about when you ship household goods.

Have enough certified copies of your orders (usually seven copies for each shipment). Then see your shipping office at least 10 days before you plan to move.

If you plan to reach your new station before your household goods are shipped, leave or send your wife enough certified copies of orders to initiate shipment; also leave her a power of attorney or written authority to make the shipment.

If you have valuables to be shipped, inform your shipping officer in order that special arrangements may be made.

Get all possible information about your housing situation at the new station before you request shipment of your goods.

Request storage at point of origin (i.e., your old station) whenever you are in doubt as to where to ship your goods.

If goods go by van, be sure to get a copy of the inventory sheet from the driver. *Never* sign a blank "certificate of packing" which he may present you with.

If your orders are modified or cancelled, or a change of destination of the shipment is desired, notify your shipping office immediately.

Get from your shipping office the ETA (estimated time of arrival) of your goods at destination.

Be at home on the day of the expected move. If Marines or Marine supervisory personnel are expected, have some cold beverages on ice; moving is hot work.

Make arrangements for receipt of your household goods at destination. If you can't be there yourself, check with your shipping office to find out whether storage is authorized. In cases of direct delivery by van, you or your representative must be at the new home to receive it.

If possible, turn over all your household goods for the same destination at the same time, except items of special value or items to be shipped by express.

Let the movers know about fragile items, such as chinaware and delicate glassware.

Keep groceries and food supplies together in one place for proper packing.

Unload drawers in furniture intended for packing and crating. However, if furniture is to go by van, lightweight linens and clothing may be left in the drawers.

Arrange to have your telephone and utilities disconnected.

Label each box, showing its general contents.

DONT'S:

Don't request shipment to some place other than your new station without finding out first how much it will cost you.

Don't contract for shipment with commercial concerns unless you have been authorized in writing to do so by your shipping office.

Don't be upset if the movers don't show up at your quarters at the exactly appointed hour. It is hard to schedule a move by the minute.

Don't try to get special services from the carrier until after you have checked with your shipping office.

Don't pack dishes or bric-a-brac yourself. Leave this to professional packers. Usually commercial firms won't pay claims on items they didn't pack.

Allotments and Taxes

1138. ALLOTMENTS. As you know, you may make allotments of your pay for certain purposes. When you make an allotment, your pay is checked that amount, and the Marine Corps mails it monthly to the designated recipient. To start or stop an allotment, see your first sergeant.

You may grant allotments to a bank for support of your family, for a checking account, or for savings, and you may make allotments for purchase of U. S. Saving Bonds. You cannot grant allotments to repay indebtedness, *except* for life insurance premiums on your life, for repayment of emergency loans from Navy Relief or the Red Cross, or for repayment of indebtedness to the Government.

Allotment checks are mailed on the last day of the month of checkage.

You should register an allotment for support of your family as soon as you are ordered overseas so that your dependents can rely on uninterrupted support. This is especially important if you are headed for combat.

Savings Deposits. Akin to savings allotments, money may be deposited by all Marines overseas, as a pay-record checkage. Such deposits pay 10 percent interest as long as you are overseas and for 90 days thereafter—a highly attractive opportunity.

1139. INCOME TAX. Your pay is taxable income and is subject to withholding tax at its source. The following, however, are not taxable: quarters and subsistence allowances, disability retired pay, and mustering-out pay. Tax exemptions for personnel serving in combat zones during hostilities are covered in Section 1141.

Marine Corps withholding tax procedure provides that the paymaster establishes your withholding rate, based on your rate of pay; this rate changes when your pay changes. Tax deductions are checked on your pay record in the same fashion as allotments. At the end of the year, the paymaster furnishes you a withholding statement to be filed with your income tax return. You in turn must inform the disbursing officer of your tax-exemption status so that he can apply the correct rate.

When hospitalized in a naval hospital for more than 30 days, you may commence excluding up to $100 a week of your pay (not including allowances) for each week you remain hospitalized. This is considered "sick pay" under Federal tax laws. Note, however, that this privilege does not begin until you have spent 30 days in the hospital, and you may not exclude any pay earned during this initial 30-day period. To substantiate deductions for time hospitalized over 30 days, obtain a certificate from the hospital administrative office.

Additional tax tips regarding your personal income tax problems, responsibilities, and exemptions, will be found in Chapter 20 (Personal Affairs).

1140. SOCIAL SECURITY TAX. Social security coverage extends to Marines on active duty, and this requires the withholding of social security deductions from your pay. These taxes are computed on your base pay for grade and length of service and are deducted at rates prescribed by law.

234 The amount subject to withholding and the amount of tax withheld are reflected on the Internal Revenue Service Form W-2 furnished you by your paymaster at the end of each year.

Note: By virtue of your social security coverage as a Marine, you also receive a social security number, which must be used by you in all Federal income-tax matters, returns, or correspondence. This is recorded in your service record book.

1141. TAX EXEMPTIONS. Income tax exemption for officers and men serving in combat areas may be placed in effect (as has been done in the case of Vietnam) by executive order of the President. This exemption extends to all military pay of enlisted men and warrant officers; and to the first $500 per month of taxable income received by commissioned officers. Here again, your disbursing office can advise you as to eligibility and the precise provisions of the effective executive order. Note that the geographic areas of this tax exemption bear no relation to, and do not necessarily coincide with, the combat pay geographic limits mentioned above.

When duty calls, or danger, be never wanting there.

—Old hymn

12 Making Good

This chapter covers a variety of subjects which are important to a noncommissioned officer who is on the way up: MOS, assignment, schooling and study, technique of instruction, opportunities to become an officer, and relations with the public. Besides these, however, there is another special secret to making good, as revealed in the following little story, which happens to be true.

A boot second lieutenant, newly assigned to his first outfit, had the feeling that things were not quite as they should be, so he sought advice of the first sergeant, a veteran of five cruises and many campaigns.

"First Sergeant," said the lieutenant, "I don't think I'm getting along with the Old Man. You always stay one jump ahead of him. How do you do it?"

"The answer is simple, Lieutenant," replied the "Top." "I find out what the old son of a bitch wants—*and I give it to him*!"

1201. A BALANCED CAREER. If you aim for the top, you must have a balanced career. A rounded career, within your primary and additional occupational fields (if any), ripens you professionally and gives you judgment, steadiness, and practicality as you near the top. Raw material for these qualities comes in average quantities among most NCOs. But the extent to which you *develop* those characteristics results largely from the career you pursue.

Among the key ingredients of a balanced career are:

Troop-leading experience
School training
Combat experience
Administrative experience
Sea and foreign shore duty.

These ingredients season a noncommissioned officer. Keep them in mind. And as you go from duty to duty, remember that, while it is the Commandant who ultimately controls your assignment, it is still *your* career. Be alert to make the most and best of it.

1202. CLASSIFICATION AND MOS. The Marine Corps needs to know and to be able quickly to identify the military skills and experience-level of every Marine. This is accomplished by means of classification system, which is designed to insure that round pegs go into round holes rather than into square ones.

Military skills are grouped into what are called *occupational fields* (OFs). Some of the principal occupational fields are:

Personnel Administration: OF 01
Intelligence: OF 02
Infantry: OF 03
Field Artillery: OF 08
Engineer/Shore Party: OF 13
Armor/Amphibian Tractor: OF 18
Ordnance: OF 21
Communications: OF 25
Electronics: OF 28
Supply: OF 30
Food Services: OF 33
Disbursing: OF 34
Motor Transport: OF 35
Band: OF 55
Radar and Data Systems: OF 59
Aviation: OF 62-71

Within each occupational field, specific skills and experience-levels are further identified. The occupational field in which a Marine is trained and qualified and his specific skill are indicated by his MOS (or "military occupational specialty"). The MOS, as you know, is a four-digit number in which the first two digits are those of the occupational field and the last two of the specialty for which the Marine is qualified. For example, MOS 0341 = (occupational field 03, infantry) + (41, mortarman).

Every Marine has a *primary MOS,* and many noncommissioned officers have up to two *additional MOSs,* which indicate possession of skills other than those described by your primary MOS.

Thus the MOS system provides the Marine Corps with a running inventory of its talent and shows at a glance the professional background and qualification of every Marine. Obviously, your MOS and the skills it represents are extremely important to you. It ultimately controls where you go and what you do, because every billet in the Marine Corps carried the MOS most appropriate to that billet. This information is shown in tables of organization, which are described in Chapter 3.

Details of the rules and procedures whereby your MOS may be changed or revoked or how you may be retrained in a different MOS or a new occupational field are found in the *Marine Corps Personnel Manual.* Generally speaking, you acquire a broader and higher-level MOS through formal school training or through demonstrated ability and qualifications. As you pick up a higher MOS, through training or promotion, you drop the lower MOS previously held. Again, in broad terms, changes in a primary MOS held by noncommissioned officers are controlled by the Commandant, either specifically or in accordance with CMC policy directives. Should you feel that you are no longer correctly classified in accordance with your present skills or experience, or should you wish to qualify in a new field, you may so request of your commanding officer, who, *if he approves,* will institute action or correspondence to effect the change. Contrary to common opinion, no individual may initiate any correspondence toward the end of reclassification.

Some final words of caution:

Your MOS is not the last word. Reputation has a way of preceeding you. The Corps is still a sufficiently small and tight organization that it behooves every aspiring Marine to *make every thought and act count for the good of the Corps.* Such a reputation, once earned, takes precedence over any MOS or technical qualification, however high.

Furthermore, although your MOS labels you for certain jobs and patterns of assignment, never let that MOS act as a set of blinders. Remember that every Marine, regardless of MOS, must always be ready to fight as an infantryman. Leadership is the only universal MOS of *all* Marine noncommissioned officers.

1203. ASSIGNMENT. Once you have your primary MOS, you will, to the maximum possible extent, be assigned to billets calling for that MOS, or at least in the same occupational field. If you gained your MOS by formal schooling, you can expect to be assigned for at least one year thereafter in a billet specifically carrying that MOS.

If you are a sergeant or higher, you will be assigned by name, by Headquarters Marine Corps. Corporals and lance corporals are generally detailed by quotas within particular MOS, rather than by name. In general, HQMC assigns noncommissioned officers, by name or by quota as just explained, to commands reporting to or programs directly supervised by the Commandant. Such commands in turn make further assignments as required. Obviously, there are other criteria for detail to particular jobs, stations, or programs, than possession of the appropriate MOS. Among these are length of obligated service, security clearance, educational level, conduct markings above specified levels, etc. It is up to the Enlisted Assignment Section, HQMC, as well as to personnel sections in subordinate commands, to weigh each man against each job and come out with an answer which is best for the Marine Corps—and usually best for you.

1204. SEA AND FOREIGN SHORE DUTY, COMBAT DUTY, AND FMF OVERSEAS. As of 1970, the normal tour of sea duty is 24 months, while tours for combat duty, FMF units overseas, and other foreign shore duty, vary according to local conditions and the existing Marine Corps personnel situation. Tour-lengths are periodically announced in Marine Corps Orders.

In general, priority of assignment of enlisted Marines to overseas duty is as follows:

1. NCOs eligible for overseas duty as a shipping-over incentive
2. Volunteers
3. Men with no prior overseas duty
4. Marines who have served longest in the U. S. since last unaccompanied foreign shore duty.

Subject to the foregoing, as of 1970, no noncommissioned officer will be involuntarily detailed to a *second* unaccompanied tour of duty overseas before completing six months in continental United States ("CONUS") since his last return from overseas. (The date of such return—an important date for you to keep track of—is known as your *overseas control date*.) In addition, the following rules govern assignment to "WestPac" (all FMF units in the Far East and any non-FMF duty in Vietnam):

You will not be assigned to a second tour until every NCO of your rank and MOS has completed an initial tour.

Nor will you be shipped out for a second tour until you have had 24 months in CONUS or an accompanied billet (or have had at least 6 months CONUS duty since a non-WestPac unaccompanied tour).

Despite the foregoing, you can always volunteer.

1205. INDEPENDENT DUTY AND SPECIAL PROGRAMS. *Independent Duty* includes all duty on the inspector/instructor staff of a reserve unit (see Chapter 8), with the Naval ROTC, or as a recruiter. The tour of independent duty is 36 months. Among the special programs or types of duty open to noncommissioned officers are duties as drill instructor, in the State Department's Marine security guards, with MAAGs (military assistance advisory groups) or missions, etc.

Assignment to any of such programs or to independent duty requires that you meet specific criteria and undergo individual screening. In general, only outstanding noncommissioned officers are selected for duties of this type, and successful completion of tours in these categories is a bright mark on your record.

1206. GETTING YOUR PREFERENCE FOR DUTY. We all know that some duty is better than others, and we all have geographic preferences relating to family ties, home ownership, and so on.

While it is the job of Marine Corps Headquarters to try to cross-match your desires with the needs of the Corps *and* with billets which may be open at any given time, it is up to you to express your preferences clearly. The place to do this is on your NCO fitness report. Each time you come up for assignment, your "monitor" (officer making assignments in your occupational field) looks to see what you have requested so that, if the right spot is open, he can put you in it. You make his job harder—and lose your chance to get the assignment you want—if you are content to fill in item 10 on your fitness report with some meaningless phrase like "As directed" or "No preference." *Always state your preference.* This far from guarantees getting it, but without such an indication, your monitor is in the dark.

Your fitness report is not only the best way for preference for duty, but in most cases, it is the only proper way. Letters asking for particular assignments are discouraged, unless you have some unusual justification, or humanitarian reasons for the detail in question. If so, you should include these reasons in your letter. From time to time, however, Marine Corps Headquarters will ask for applications for schools, independent duty, or special programs, and of course your reply would then be by letter.

A good rule is not to request a modification of orders, not to request any particular assignment—or, for that matter, not to write *any* official letter—unless you have good and valid reasons. Otherwise, you are wasting your own time and the time and effort of Marine officers and NCOs who must consider and screen out requests which merit attention by the Commandant.

Schooling and Study

Whether you are on the imparting or receiving end, three things cannot be overemphasized in the career of a noncommissioned officer who wants to make good: training, instruction, and schooling.

There are few surer ways to the top than to become equally capable as student and as instructor. This section of the *Handbook* covers professional schooling, off-duty educational opportunities, and how to study.

1207. FORMAL SCHOOLS. Formal schooling is a gateway to advancement in rank, in skill level, and in MOS. Marine noncommissioned officers are eligible to attend more than a hundred formal or resident courses conducted not only by the Marine Corps but by the Navy, Army, and the Air Force. These courses, their location and duration, the MOS for which they train, their entrance requirements, their frequency, and their prerequisite requirements are listed in *Marine Corps Formal Schools Catalog.* Courses such as these enable you to benefit from the hard-won experience of others. Their successful completion, especially with high class standing (see note below), will obviously exercise immediate leverage on your career.

> *Note:* It is a Marine Corps tradition that, when you attend a school conducted by another service, you are expected to stand at or very near the top of the class. Anything less is unworthy of the Corps.

1208. CORRESPONDENCE COURSES. Two Marine Correspondence schools are open to you: the Extension School at Quantico, and the Marine Corps Institute (MCI) in Washington. If the MCI cannot meet your needs, you may, on payment of prescribed fees, enroll in the U. S. Armed Forces Institute (USAFI). All Marine Corps correspondence schooling, as distinct from USAFI, is free of charge to Marines and Navy personnel serving with the Corps.

Extension School, MCDEC. The Extension School parallels by correspondence the tactical instruction in the resident schools of the Marine Corps Development and Education Command. The Extension School also serves as a clearing house for applications by Marines to enroll in correspondence courses conducted by the other services.

The courses of the Extension School are open to all Marines, regular, retired, or reserve, but the course most frequently taken by and most useful to mid-career NCOs is the Officers' Basic Extension Course. There is nothing to prevent your going further, as some highly motivated NCOs have done, and completing the Junior and even the Senior Officers' Extension Courses. Successful completion of MCS extension work accrues credit toward Marine Corps Reserve retirement and should be carefully considered by every reserve noncommissioned officer.

All texts and written assignments are furnished by the Extension School, whose staff grades and returns your papers as you submit

In South Viet Nam, a few miles from the demilitarized zone, a Marine works on a Marine Corps Institute course for his professional development.

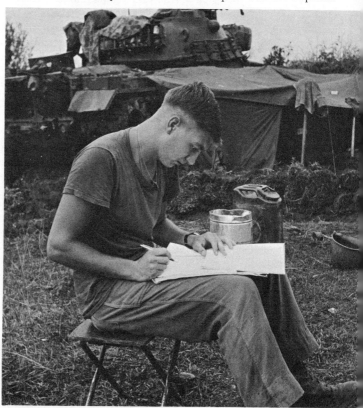

them. In addition, if you have professional questions relating to the study material issued, the School staff will be glad to help you find your answer.

You may enroll in the Extension School by written request, via your commanding officer, to the Director, Extension School, Marine Corps Development and Education Command, Quantico, Va. Before enrolling, you should discuss your plans with your commanding officer, and, if your unit is so provided, with your educational officer. Such discussion will enable you to select the course best suited to your needs and capabilities and to the time available.

The Marine Corps Institute (MCI) located at Marine Barracks, 8th and Eye Streets in Washington, is the oldest correspondence school in the armed forces, having been founded in 1920 to permit World War I Marine veterans to complete interrupted education. Over the years, the MCI has changed from a general, semiacademic correspondence school to one which focuses on the professional development of enlisted Marines.

Today, the MCI has a dual mission of correspondence training and of testing. As a training activity, the Institute administers all correspondence courses in technical and general military subjects. In its testing capacity, the Institute prepares, distributes, and grades the general military subject tests (GMST) which, though suspended incident to the Vietnam war, normally assess your general military proficiency.

The following personnel are eligible for enrollment in the Marine Corps Institute:

Marines of any rank on active duty

Marines of any rank in the Organized and Volunteer Reserve (provided that the courses requested are commensurate with the rank of, and are appropriate for, the individual reservist)

Retired Marines, members of the Fleet Marine Corps Reserve, and disabled former Marines

Eligible members of other armed services (as determined by the service concerned)

Civilian employees of the Marine Corps who, in the opinion of their military supervisors, would improve their efficiency and service to the Marine Corps by completing a Marine Corps Institute course related to their specific duties.

You may apply for an MCI course through your commanding officer or, if retired, directly to: Director, Marine Corps Institute, Marine Barracks, Box 1775, Washington, D.C. 20013.

In all, the Marine Corps Institute has some 150 courses, in which there are approximately a hundred thousand enrollments yearly.

Other Service Courses. If you want to take a correspondence course offered by the Army, Navy, or Air Force, for which the Marine Corps does not have an equivalent, apply through official channels to the Director, Extension School, MCDEC, Quantico. The Extension

School will then process and forward your application. This does not include USAFI courses.

U. S. Armed Forces Institute (*USAFI*), opened in Madison, Wisconsin in 1942, has today taken over the civilian, nonmilitary correspondence schooling with the Marine Corps pioneered more than twenty years earlier via the MCI.

USAFI is a permanent educational institution of the Defense Department. Besides its home station at Madison, USAFI has branches in Alaska, the Caribbean, Europe, Hawaii, and Japan. These schools offer some 200 correspondence courses in elementary, high school, college, and technical subjects including business, English, literature, languages, mathematics, science, and social sciences. After you complete the required assignments, you get a final examination and—if you pass—a certificate and appropriate credits, which are permanently recorded for you in USAFI records.

College and university correspondence courses are also available to Marines through USAFI from over 40 accredited institutions. In these courses, the Marine Corps pays for the lesson service, while you pay for texts, study materials, and certain administrative costs.

> *Note:* An ambitious NCO on his way up can and should make it his habit always to be enrolled in some type of correspondence course, professional or civilian.

1209. TUITION ASSISTANCE AND INSTRUCTOR-HIRE PROGRAM. This program is designed to encourage Marines to take, in classrooms, off-duty courses offered by accredited secondary schools and colleges.

Under the Tuition Assistance Plan, you may enroll in courses presented by accredited civilian schools on campus, at extension centers, or on Marine Corps installations. Where the station is designated as an "isolated area," the Marine Corps may pay accredited institutions a portion of instructors' salaries in order that classes may be held on-station.

The Government pays up to 75 percent of the tuition fees for each university-, college- or high school-level course, not to exceed certain monetary ceilings. You pay all other charges, such as for texts and supplies.

To form a class in an isolated area, at least 15 eligible persons must agree to enroll. In addition to Marines, eligibility extends to military dependents and civil service employees of the Navy Department who are employed by the base.

1210. HINTS ON STUDYING. A large part of the professional and technical information you require as a noncommissioned officer can only be found in texts, manuals, and other reference works. Whether as a student in a formal school or while taking a correspondence course, you should know how to study efficiently so that you can hoist in the maximum amount of information, and then retain it.

As a starting point, *form good study habits.*

Set aside certain periods for studying and stick to your schedule. Find a quiet spot and make that your place of study. When study time comes, start work in a businesslike frame of mind and *really turn to.* Read completely through your study assignment to get a general idea of the lesson content. Don't skim by passages or paragraphs you don't clearly understand. If necessary, go through the study assignment a second time, underlining important facts or sentences so you can go back to them later when reviewing. Don't try to cram in too much information at a single sitting. If you find yourself getting drowsy or inattentive, get up, stretch, breathe some fresh air, and drink a cup or two of coffee.

When you have the reading assignment in hand, you can turn to on the written lesson. First, read all directions before answering questions. Next, go through *all* the questions before you start writing your answers. If you are working on a correspondence lesson, attach notes to your paper requesting instructor assistance on points you don't understand. When a written assignment comes back, go over it to discover your mistakes, and then learn the correct answer—and (most important) learn *why* it is correct.

In preparing for examinations, review all lessons, taking note of previous mistakes and paying special attention to important passages you may have marked in your textbooks. Treat each exam as if you were firing for record. Rest up the night before, don't get the shakes, read questions carefully, and check your "dope," and you will surely "qualify."

Learn to read rapidly and efficiently.

Many people read too slowly. Train yourself to read phrases not words and then to look for ideas not phrases. Every paragraph has a key sentence, usually near the beginning, that states the key idea. Learn to spot this idea and move rapidly along.

Obviously a field manual or a set of technical instructions has to be read more closely than an article in *The Leatherneck,* but even official publications contain key facts and key points, and these are, in effect, the "key terrain features" you must seize and hold.

When you start to read or study a book, make a reconnaissance; that is, look at the table of contents and see what the book is about and how it is organized. Then, scan the pages, observing chapter headings and diagrams and illustrations which present important information. Almost all textbooks and military manuals begin with a summary of the book's purpose and main contents in the first chapter and a similar roundup at the end; look these over so you know what the objective is going to be.

Finally, don't guess at the meaning of new words. Look up unfamiliar terms, using a military dictionary or glossary if necessary. Remember that in the Service we often give special meanings to words. For example, "site" means one thing to a civilian and something quite different to an artilleryman.

1211. PROFESSIONAL READING. Nobody expects every staff sergeant to be a deep student of the theories of war, but every professional noncommissioned officer can benefit himself and learn many interesting things, if he forms the habit of professional reading. Professional reading goes beyond field manuals and TMs. For a Marine NCO it means regular reading of professional magazines, of books dealing with the history and traditions of the Corps, of biographies and reminiscences of famous Marines, and of other works on war and soldiering.

As an up-and-coming NCO, besides subscribing to *The Leatherneck,* you should read *Navy Times* to keep up on current events, and also look through *All Hands,* the Bureau of Naval Personnel's highly readable Navy monthly. When you make gunnery sergeant, join the Marine Corps Association and thus subscribe to the Marine Corps *Gazette.*

Any or all of the following books are highly recommended for readability, interest, and profit; you can find them in any post or station library, or order them at discount prices through *The Leatherneck.*

Asprey, Robert, *At Belleau Wood* (the Marines' greatest fight in World War I)

Davis, Burke, *Marine!* (life of LtGen "Chesty" Puller)

Fehrenbach, T. R., *This Kind of War* (the Korean War)

Geer, Andrew, *The New Breed* (Marines in Korea)

Griffith, S. B., *The Battle for Guadalcanal*

Heinl, R. D., *Victory at High Tide* (the Inchon landing, Korea)

Heinl, R. D., *Soldiers of the Sea* (history of the Marine Corps)

Kersh, Gerald, *They Die with Their Boots Clean* (life in the British Brigade of Guards)

Leckie, Robert, *Strong Men Armed* (Marines in the Pacific War)

Masters, John, *Bugles and a Tiger* (campaigning with the Ghurkas)

McMillan, George, *The Old Breed* (1st Marine Division in World War II)

Montross, Lynn, *The United States Marines* (pictorial history)

Sherrod, Robert, *History of Marine Corps Aviation*

Smith, H. M., *Coral and Brass* (life of General "Howling Mad" Smith)

Stallings, Laurence, *The Doughboys* (Marines and Army in France, World War I)

Thomas, Lowell, *Old Gimlet Eye* (life of General Smedley Butler)

Thomason, J. W., *And a Few Marines* (Marines in France, Haiti, Nicaragua, and China).

Thomason, J. W., *Fix Bayonets!* (4th Marine Brigade in France, World War I)

Wise, F. M., *A Marine Tells It to You* (life of Colonel "Dopey" Wise, renowned Marine Corps character)

As an instructor you should "tell, show, and do." If the student doesn't know and cannot do, you should review your preparation, plan, and delivery of instruction.

How to Instruct

One of the basic jobs of every noncommissioned officer is teaching and training the Marines entrusted to his charge. *Until you become a proficient instructor, you cannot call yourself a proficient NCO.*

This section—though by no means exhaustive—will give you the principles of instructing, how-to-do-it pointers on preparation and delivery of instruction, and useful tips on training aids.

1212. THE LEARNING PROCESS. Military instructors must know and apply several general principles which form the basis of instructional methods and techniques.

Ability to communicate to your men is your essential prerequisite. No matter how well you know a subject, if you cannot transmit your knowledge in understandable fashion, you fail. In other words, *if your students fail to get your message, you fail as an instructor.*

An essential first step in communicating is to *get men's attention.* In the words of a wise and seasoned master gunnery sergeant, "A mule responds better after he knows you are around. Hit him with a two-by-four."

Men must desire to learn. In war they are more eager than in peace because they recognize that what they are learning may save their lives. In either case it is up to you to motivate them.

Men learn through the senses. To help your people grasp a subject, you should register on as many of the senses as possible. Psychological tests tell us that, on the average, we acquire 75 percent of our learning through *sight,* 13 percent through *hearing,* 6 percent by *touch,* 3 percent through *taste,* and 3 percent by *smell.*

Men learn by doing. There can be no learning without some activity in response by the Marine. The best activity is to give him an opportunity—field-stripping a weapon or mechanism, for example—to practice what has been taught.

Explanation, demonstration, application, are the central steps in military instruction (i.e., "tell, show, and do"). When appropriate, *examination* and *critique* may be added, especially for formal instruction.

1213. PREPARATIONS FOR INSTRUCTION. Lack of preparation practically guarantees that an instructor will fall down, if only from stage fright. Even the most experienced instructor, going over material he knows well, habitually checks off certain preliminaries before he steps up in front of the troops.

As soon as you are scheduled to conduct instruction or training, you should take certain steps as follows:

Determine the lesson objective, i.e., know from the start exactly what you intend to put across, and see to it that everything you do or say in the presence of your class contributes to that objective.

Determine the following information:

When and where the instruction is to be conducted
Length of the lesson
Who is to be instructed
Uniform and equipment
Availability of training aids and instructional material.

Prepare (or obtain) a lesson plan (see Section 1214).

If time permits, *rehearse your instruction.*

Check final arrangements. This essentially means a reconnaissance of the classroom or the training area to guard against conflicts, to see that training aids or exhibits are in place and ready, that transportation, if required, is scheduled, and that supplies (such as paper and pencil) or reference materials (such as firing tables or maps) are on hand and in proper quantities.

1214. THE LESSON PLAN. A lesson plan is a written digest and outline of how you are going to teach a given lesson. It shows what material to teach, in what order you teach it, and how you are going to proceed. For most basic subjects, ready-made lesson plans may be obtained in a company office or from S-3 files. These ready-made lesson plans are merely guides, however; you should study them and then formulate your own plan in your own words and way.

A lesson plan has two parts. Part One summarizes *information the instructor needs to know* or decide on in advance, for example,

247   Subject to be presented
Method of instruction (lecture, demonstration, etc.)
Time allotted
Who will receive instruction
Required equipment and materials
Personnel requirements (assistant instructors, range guards, etc.)
Training aids
References and study assignments
Class uniform and equipment
Demonstration or other troop requirements
Transportation requirements.

Part Two, *the lesson outline,* lists the subject matter, methods, and training aids, used in each stage of instruction. Here is a sample outline for an hour's instruction on maps and conventional signs:

LESSON OUTLINE (*Start class: 0730 sharp*)
1. Introduction (*five minutes*)
   a. Importance of having maps and being able to read them.
      Q. Why learn to read a map?
      A. (Develop answer by class discussion.)
         1. To help find your way.
            (Display ordinary road map to illustrate point.)
         2. To help stay alive.
         3. To keep the men you are leading safe in combat.
         4. To be able to locate and attack the enemy.
   b. Purpose of this period of instruction.
      1. To introduce you to military maps.
      2. To familiarize you with standard conventional signs and military symbols.
2. What *IS* a map? (*three minutes*)
   a. It's a picture of the land and the things people have built on the land.
   b. It's a view of things from directly above; compare to viewing football game.
   c. It's a picture, but it's not a photograph.
3. What's *ON* a map? (*five minutes*)
   a. Explain purpose of signs and symbols.
   b. Illustrate on blackboard similarity between the marks on a map and the diagram of a football play.
4. What's a conventional sign? (*fifteen minutes*)
   a. Why, how, and when they are used.
   b. Illustrate on blackboard conventional signs those resembling the real object—buildings; those accenting one feature of the object—barbed wire fence; those using an associated idea—church; those not similar to the object—intermittent stream.
   c. Organize class into equal groups each with an assistant instructor and a tactical map. Direct instructors to have individuals locate and identify on map the features just illustrated on blackboard, and then to explain to group and have individuals

248 locate all of the other common conventional signs.
(Stretch break—light smoking lamp.) (*two minutes*)
5. What's a military symbol? (*fifteen minutes*)
   a. Explain why, how, and when they are used.
   b. Draw common military symbols on blackboard and explain
      how they can be remembered by an association of ideas.
      (Erase blackboard.)
   c. Redraw symbols one at a time; call on a Marine to identify
      symbol as it is drawn.
      (Erase blackboard.)
   d. Direct class to use pencil and paper; call out a symbol by
      name, have Marines draw it on paper; assistant instructors
      check each man's work
6. Summary (*five minutes*)
   a. Clarify any points that you believe were not understood by
      class.
   b. Closing statement: Remember, a map is a picture. It isn't a
      puzzle and it isn't hard to read. In combat you must know
      how to read and use a map if you want to stay alive. Conven-
      tional signs and military symbols make a map easier to read
      and use. This morning, you were introduced to military maps
      and familiarized with standard conventional signs and mili-
      tary symbols. You have completed the first step in learning
      how to read and use a map in combat. During the next period
      we will cover map coordinates, distances, and scales.
      (*Dismiss class: 0820.*)

1215. APPLICATORY INSTRUCTION. Application is learning
by doing. To learn to do something, students must be told *what* to
do, shown *how* to do it, and then *participate in doing it,* until they
are able to do it correctly. Although you can use application at any
suitable point, it logically comes—as pointed out earlier, after the
two preliminary steps of explanation and demonstration.

Here are several methods of applicatory instruction:

Controlled practice. All hands in a class do the same thing, at the
same rate and at the same time, in the same steps, under supervision
of the instructor. ("By-the-numbers" is a very simple illustration of
controlled practice.)

Independent practice. Here the student works at his own rate of
speed and performs the operation as a whole until, through practice,
he establishes the skill and makes it automatic. The Marine works
without control but with supervision.

Coach-and-pupil. This method is used for teaching students who
have already mastered the basic fundamentals of a skill. Men pair
off and alternate as coach and pupil under supervision of the instructor and his assistants. Properly guided, the coach-and-pupil method
makes students think as well as do. It also begins to bring out rudi-
mentary NCO leadership traits such as power of observation and
ability to give directions and commands.

Team practice. Here students are first trained as individuals and then are made to perform their individual functions as part of a team such as a rifle squad, a howitzer section, or a tank crew.

1216. TRAINING AIDS. Training aids include everything that assists in training, such as blackboard, sand table, motion pictures, film strips, recordings, charts, posters, transparencies, slides, models, cutaway mockups, and synthetic trainers. Training aids are invaluable tools for a good instructor, if only because almost all of them rely on the sense of sight, through which we absorb 75 percent of what we learn. However, don't get carried away by a training aid for its own sake. A training aid *must* contribute to the object of the instruction; otherwise it is merely distracting.

Here are a few rules to help you get the most out of training aids:

Keep aid covered when not in use.
Introduce it to the class and explain what it is.
Be sure all students can see it.
Don't obstruct the view of the aid by standing in front of it.
Talk to your class, not into the aid.
Use a pointer.
Remove or cover aid as soon as you are finished with it.

THE BLACKBOARD. The most widely used and available training aid is the old-fashioned blackboard. It can be used out-of-doors or indoors, it can be improvised in the field, and—especially if you can get hold of a few pieces of colored chalk—it is the most versatile training aid of all.

You can make a blackboard from almost any kind of smooth-surface wallboard or plywood, painting it with several coats of waterproof flat paint (nonoil) or, if you can get it, special commercial blackboard paint. In addition to ordinary white chalk, the best colors are the bright ones: red, yellow, orange, and bright green.

HOW TO USE THE BLACKBOARD

1. CHECK ON EQUIPMENT TO BE USED.
2. CHECK FOR GLARE.
3. KEEP BLACKBOARD CLEAN.
4. PLAN YOUR WORK IN ADVANCE.
5. KEEP MATERIAL SIMPLE AND BRIEF.
6. PRINT AND DRAW LEGIBLY.
7. USE COLOR FOR EMPHASIS AND VARIETY.
8. DON'T CROWD YOUR WORK.
9. ERASE UNRELATED MATERIAL.
10. PREPARE COMPLICATED ILLUSTRATIONS BEFOREHAND.

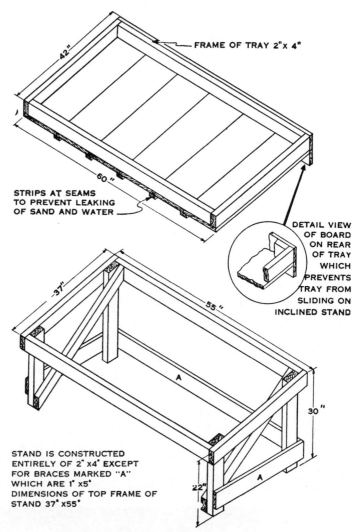

FRAME OF TRAY 2"x 4"

42"

60 "

STRIPS AT SEAMS
TO PREVENT LEAKING
OF SAND AND WATER

DETAIL VIEW
OF BOARD
ON REAR
OF TRAY
WHICH
PREVENTS
TRAY FROM
SLIDING ON
INCLINED STAND

37"

55 "

A

30 "

STAND IS CONSTRUCTED
ENTIRELY OF 2" x4" EXCEPT
FOR BRACES MARKED "A"
WHICH ARE 1" x5"
DIMENSIONS OF TOP FRAME OF
STAND 37" x55"

22"

A

Fig. 12-1: How to build a sand table.

THE SAND TABLE. A training aid which is not so frequently encountered in the Marine Corps is the sand table—a sandbox so arranged and mounted that terrain can be modelled and displayed. Besides being invaluable for indoor instruction during foul weather, the sandbox lends itself particularly to training in terrain appreciation, map reading, tactics, scouting and patrolling, and ship-to-shore movement.

Description. A sand table consists of a sturdy, shallow tray (which, in use, is filled with dampened sand simulating terrain) and a stand. The bottom of the tray should be painted blue so that stream lines and beachlines can be indicated in areas not covered by sand. Accessories for the table include sand, shovel, rake, sprinkling can, water bucket, bucket for mixing water and sand, thumbtacks, string, ruler, green and blue chalk, sieve for powdering chalk, wood blocks of various sizes to represent structures, and toy military equipment (vehicles, tanks, guns, landing craft, assault shipping, control vessels, etc.)

Building a sand table. Figure 12-1 shows the design of a practical-sized sandbox. Stand and tray are separate for ease of moving, and the stand is sloped up so that students can see it from the side.

Using the sand table. Moisten sand so it will hold its shape in the tray. Spread a bag of sand in the tray, and level it with the edge of a board. Using your finger, mark out stream lines; clear sand away from beachline and offshore sea area. Using remaining sand, build up hills and ridges between the main stream lines. Now trace in roads or airstrips (you can level these with the edge of a ruler and can sprinkle with dry, lighter-colored sand so that they stand out). Next come minor stream and drainage lines. Powder green chalk using your sieve and dispense it through a saltshaker so as to simulate ground vegetation (you can also use sawdust previously dipped in green dye). Trees can be represented by sponges dyed green (use a darker shade of green than ground vegetation so trees will stand out in contrast). Finally, locate structures, bridges, etc., and other works of man, as desired.

Whenever possible, it is a good idea to mount vertically a contoured sketch map to the same scale as the terrain layout, immediately behind the sand table. This helps students to think simultaneously on map and terrain.

1217. DELIVERY OF INSTRUCTION. Effective delivery of instruction consists of knowing and applying the principles of good public speaking and of following certain other commonsense rules. Some hold that the ability to instruct is a magic gift, bestowed on some but denied to others. This is far from true. Instructing, like shooting a rifle, can readily be, and has to be, *learned.* True, aptitude varies; some will never be brilliant speakers, others will be. But everyone—you included—can improve his speaking technique with application and practice. *Good speakers are made, not born.*

THE QUALITIES OF AN EFFECTIVE SPEAKER. What are the qualities of effective military speakers?

Be purposeful. You must have a clear view of your objective—of what you are trying to put across. You must be able to balance the time spent against achievement of your objective. Avoid irrelevancy.

Know your stuff. You must have a thorough grasp of your subject. This grasp should be backed up, if possible, by practical experience. Conversely, avoid matters in which you lack experience.

Take pains. Even if you have all the knowledge, skill, and experience needed to put your subject across, there is no short cut in preparation. Choose the right approach and method of presentation;

arrange your material in logical phases, each one followed by a summary; if you are instructing, use visual aids to help your audience *see* your points.

Be enthusiastic. Enthusiasm is as catching as boredom. It is the driving force of a good speech or lecture. Your enthusiasm must be *balanced* and *seasoned.* If you make your hearers feel that you are a nut with a wild gleam in his eye, they will discount what you say and will soon become bored.

Cultivate dramatic sense. Don't be content with dull, stodgy presentations; cultivate what show business calls "sense of staging." Get in touch with your hearers. Use variety of pace, surprise, and dramatic appeal to drive home your points. If you can tell a funny story well, don't be afraid to use it. But don't indulge in a gag just for the gag's sake. Remember that there are usually more effective ways to introduce a subject than by telling an irrelevant "funny" story.

Have a confident, easy manner. Give your hearers confidence in what you say by having that confidence yourself. Speak clearly and distinctly. Remember that distinct speech stems from distinct ideas.

Exploit your voice and body. Voice is your basic weapon. To exploit your voice, develop *power, distinctness,* and *variety of delivery.* Your body supports your voice through erect, confident *posture,* natural *movement,* meaningful *gesture,* and *eye contact* with every listener. Make it a rule to look every hearer in the eye while you speak to a group.

THINGS TO AVOID:

Cheap humor and vulgarity. Don't play the clown to get a cheap laugh. Vulgarity cheapens you and the Marine Corps.

"Big words". Overuse of technical terms or of long and involved constructions wraps your subject in a fog. Five-dollar words used merely for effect do not impress your listeners with anything but your desire to show off.

Sea stories. Don't bore students with personal experiences, except when introduced as firsthand information to emphasize specific points in your lesson plan.

TIPS FOR INSTRUCTORS. Here are some practical rules which will help you avoid pitfalls and become a better instructor.

Locate your class out-of-doors, if possible. A small draw or cup-shaped slope is ideal, with students on the hillside. Avoid a noisy location or one where a lot of distractions are in sight, such as passing vehicles, aircraft landing and taking off, etc.

Be sure all students can see and hear you. It is essential that you be able to look every student in the eye as you instruct. Eye contact, as this is called, is psychologically important because it makes a direct contact between you and every man in your group. Making yourself heard is basic. If possible, do so without a public-address system and try to train your voice so that you can speak to a large group on your own power. Don't try to compete with passing noises, such as low aircraft; wait until the interruption is over and then go on. Don't try to talk into the wind. Similarly, never have students looking into the sun.

Have a squared-away classroom. A sloppy, disorderly classroom in poor police suggests equally sloppy instruction. Windows should be to the sides and rear of students, never facing them. Have the room well ventilated so men can keep awake (if you see many people nodding or yawning, stop the instruction and get everyone on his feet for a stretch break).

Control nervousness. Every instructor feels nervous before he takes the platform. This isn't undesirable if you can control it; in fact, this sense of being keyed-up makes you think and react more quickly and gives intensity and drive to your instruction. The thing you must learn is to make your nervousness work for you rather than against you. The best way to do this is to be thoroughly rehearsed and prepared, especially in your opening and closing remarks.

Don't memorize mechanically and don't read from a script. Either is a sure way to put your troops to sleep. On the other hand, keep your lesson outline (see Section 1214) or a well-prepared set of notes and cues where you can see them.

Becoming an Officer

The decision to try for commissioned or warrant rank is one of the biggest ones a noncommissioned officer ever makes. The Marine Corps has several programs by which—if you are really qualified—you can become an officer. Some of these programs (such as for limited duty officer or warrant officer) apply and appeal to more senior NCOs, while others (such as the Naval Academy or the Navy Enlisted Scientific Program) are for the young and junior.

The Marine Corps was the first of the U. S. Armed Services to open the doorway of its officer corps to enlisted men and to keep that door always open. The basic and traditional policy of the Marine Corps in this respect remains exactly what it has been since early years of this century—to keep the door always open, but to be very choosy about who gets through it. It also means that, no matter what your origin, once you qualify for a Marine commission, you stand on equal footing with every other officer candidate, regardless of source or education.

1218. GENERAL REQUIREMENTS TO BECOME AN OFFICER. To be eligible for a commission in the Marine Corps, you must be a U. S. citizen, morally, mentally, and physically qualified, and your application must be approved by Headquarters Marine Corps. If you are already a veteran, you must of course have an honorable discharge; and if you are a member of the reserve component of any other service, you must obtain a conditional release from that organization.

1219. ROADS TO YOUR COMMISSION. To obtain a commission in the Marine Corps, an enlisted man may follow any one of

Fig. 12-2: Avenues to commissioned or warrant rank

Program	Age Limit
U.S. Naval Academy	Have attained your 17th birthday and have not passed 21st birthday during year of appointment
Navy Enlisted Scientific Program (NESEP)	Be at least 20 and not more than 26 at time of entering college
Meritorious NCO	Be at least 20 and less than 30 years old on 1 July in year in which commissioned
Limited Duty Officer	A. *WO applicants* must be under 46, have over 10 years service. B. *NCO applicants* must have at least 15 but not over 23 years' service.[4]
Combat Commission (Outstanding Leader)	Over 20 and not over 37 by end of fiscal year in which nominated
Warrant Officer	Be less than 46 years old on 1 July of year in which nominated (WM applicants must be able to complete 20 years' total active service by age 55)
Woman Officer Candidate Course (WOCC)	Be at least 21 but less than 29 years old on 1 July of year in which commissioned; be and remain unmarried until commissioned

several roads summarized in the table above and subsequently described.

Notes:

1 All candidates go to U. S. Naval Preparatory School, Bainbridge, Maryland or (NESEP only) Naval Training Center, San Diego.
2 USNA graduates may be appointed as ensign, USN, or 2dLt, USMC; preference for Marine Corps appointments goes to former Marines and sons of Marines.
3 Initial commission in USMCR with opportunity to augment (integrate) in regular Marine Corps if qualified and selected.
4 LDO program falls into two categories depending on whether you

Education Requirements	Open To	Leads To
High school graduate or possess sufficient credits to complete high school while at Naval Academy Prep School[1]	Single USMC enlisted men with combined GCT-ARI score of 118 or higher	2dLt USMC[2]
High school graduate in upper half of class (those with three years' high school accepted if scoring in 90th percentile GED); pass NESEP exam[1]	Corporals or above (WM included) with GCT 120 or higher and six years' obligated service	2dLt USMC (w/B.S. degree in science, engineering, or mathematics)
B.A. or B.S. degree or high school graduate with passing score on Officer Selection Test	Corporals or above with GCT or Aviation Selection Test Score at least 120, and two or more years' previous service	2dLt USMCR[3]
Minimum GCT 110	Temporary officers, warrant officers, temporary WOs, and NCOs GySgt or higher; applicants must have current assignment in designated MOS.	A. WO Applicants: 1stLt USMC;[5] B. NCO Applicants: 2dLt USMC[5]
Minimum GCT 110	Pfc or above with clear record, specifically recommended for commission for outstanding combat leadership under fire.	2dLt USMC (temporary)
(for WO Candidates but not direct appointees): Complete WO Screening Course	Corporals or above with 6–12 years' active naval service; COs may recommend waivers for preeminently qualified NCOs with service not exceeding 14 years.	Warrant Officer (W-1) USMC[6]
A. or B.S. degree or have GCT 115 and passing score on Officer Selection Test	Enlisted WM, any grade	2dLt USMCR[3]

    are applying from warrant officer status or noncommissioned status.

5 Applicants of warrant rank appointed as 1stLt with terminal rank of LtCol; NCO applicants appointed as 2dLt with terminal rank of Capt.

6 Qualified applicants who so desire may apply for flight training and designation as helicopter pilots.

Note: The above programs and requirements are current as of 1970, but, due to the conflict in Southeast Asia, are subject to modification at any time. To insure that you are up to date on any given program, consult your first sergeant.

U. S. NAVAL ACADEMY. Each graduating class from the Naval Academy at Annapolis includes a quota of midshipmen who have been selected for Marine Corps commissions. Since competition for these appointments is keen, preference is given to midshipmen who have held enlisted rank in the Marine Corps and to sons of Marines. Entrance into the Naval Academy is open each year to 85 enlisted men of the Navy and Marine Corps, and 85 from the Naval and Marine Corps Reserve. These appointments are by the Secretary of the Navy who, in the case of the active-duty candidates, makes his selection from successful graduates of the U. S. Naval Preparatory School, Bainbridge, Maryland. Quotas for this school are promulgated annually. Twelve percent of each Naval Academy graduating class are commissioned in the Marine Corps. All USNA graduates have a five-year service obligation after being commissioned.

> *Note:* If you should receive a Congressional or other type of appointment to Annapolis or, for that matter, to West Point or the Air Force Academy, the Marine Corps will arrange for you to attend the appropriate academy preparatory school of the service in question.

NAVY ENLISTED SCIENTIFIC EDUCATION PROGRAM (NESEP). This program—one of the finest opportunities open to young Marines—provides qualified noncommissioned officers with a four-year college education specializing in science, mathematics, industrial management, or engineering. If selected for this program (which requires passage of NESEP screening and College Entrance Examination Board scholastic aptitude tests), you are then sent either to the Naval Preparatory School, Bainbridge, or to San Diego, where you will receive ten weeks' intensive preparatory instruction in English, mathematics, physics, and chemistry. Once at college, you remain on year-round duty at the campus to which assigned, with summer courses, except that, during sophomore summer, you attend OCS at Quantico. All NESEP graduates have a minimum four-year service obligation after being commissioned.

MERITORIOUS NONCOMMISSIONED OFFICERS (corporal or above) who are within specified age limits and meet educational requirements may, if qualified, be sent to OCS at Quantico and, if successful, are then commissioned and put through Basic School. Although these officers receive initial commissions in the Marine Corps Reserve, they have the opportunity to integrate (augment) in the regular Marine Corps.

LIMITED DUTY OFFICERS. Limited duty officers (LDO) are former warrant or noncommissioned officers who are commissioned for duty in the particular occupational fields in which they have specialized. Today, there are two categories of LDOs:

1. Those appointed from permanent warrant rank. These LDOs are initially commissioned as first lieutenants (temporary) and hold temporary rank until attaining the grade of major (temporary), at which time they are reappointed as permanent captains (LDO). This

category may eventually attain the top LDO rank of lieutenant colonel.

2. Those appointed when staff noncommissioned officers are initially commissioned as second lieutenants (temporary). These LDOs have a terminal rank as captain. When an officer in this category completes 20 years' active Naval service, at least 10 of which are as a commissioned officer, he has the option of retiring or of reverting to permanent enlisted rank.

WARRANT OFFICERS. Today's warrant officer program stresses early recognition and selection of potential warrant officers. Noncommissioned officers may apply between their sixth and twelfth year of service (with waivers open for preeminently qualified people of up to 14 years' service). The selection board determines your warrant officer MOS, based on your general qualifications and potential; if necessary, you will eventually be sent to school after selection if that is thought necessary to get you up to the mark in your new MOS.

When selected, you will be sent to the Warrant Officer Screening Course at Quantico. When you successfully complete this course, you receive your appointment as warrant officer W-1 and then go to Warrant Officer Basic Course at Basic School. If you meet current qualifications and so volunteer, you may also be assigned a 7399 MOS and be sent to flight training for qualification as a helicopter pilot.

WOMAN OFFICERS CANDIDATE COURSE (WOCC). Unmarried women noncommissioned officers who on July 1 of the year in which commissioned, were over 18 and less than 29 years of age may attend WOCC. There they may obtain commissions in such fields as company officer, supply, communications, public relations, administration, aviation, and others.

OFFICER CANDIDATES SCHOOL. Most of the routes by which a noncommissioned officer becomes an officer lead through Officer Candidates School (OCS) at Quantico. The courses at this school are among the most rigorous in the Marine Corps—tougher even than boot camp.

In applying for warrant or commissioned rank, you should be fully aware of what you are getting into as you enter OCS. Although you may be an outstanding NCO with wide experience and the highest qualifications, once you enroll at OCS, you are just another "candidate," pursuing a course which is booby-trapped for men who think they have the experience and can coast through. Although the top spots in OCS classes are often occupied by noncommissioned-officer candidates, it is worth pondering that about ten percent of all enlisted men who come to OCS eventually drop out *at their own request*—the main reasons being lack of physical and psychological preparation (i.e., discovery that OCS is no picnic).

In other words, it is not enough to be officer material; as in the case of any other material, you must go through the forge before becoming the finished product.

The future success of the Marine Corps depends on two factors: first, an efficient performance of all the duties to which its officers and men may be assigned; second, promptly bringing this efficiency to the attention of the proper officials of the Government, and the American people.

—*John A. Lejeune*

1220. PUBLIC RELATIONS. Intelligent and candid relations with the public form an important part of every Marine's career, from private to general. For a noncommissioned officer on independent duty, public relations is the key to a successful tour.

Do not confuse "public relations" with public information. Public information is the technical term for the segment of public relations which has to do with the press, radio, and other information media. Public relations transcends public information.

The keystone of good relations with the public is to deserve the public's esteem. As long as the Marine Corps, seen through the citizen's unsparing eye, measures up to high standards of discipline, devotion to duty, individual smartness, and valor, which are traditional with the Corps, our relationship with the public will be what it should be.

The Marine Corps has never depended on any publicity apparatus except the heartfelt pride and loyalty of every Marine toward his Corps. The best advertisement the Marine Corps displays is the individual Marine. *Have you ever seen a soreheaded ex-Marine?*

In season and out, the Corps has drawn its strength and its support from the American public. Deal truthfully, pleasantly, and respectfully with every member of that public, and Marine Corps public relations with continue to take care of themselves.

Pointers for Professionals

1221. DO'S, DON'TS, AND POINTERS. By the fact that you are a Marine—especially in the high visibility of uniform—you represent the entire Corps. For this reason you must always try to conduct yourself with dignity, courtesy, and self-restraint when in the public eye.

Don't take yourself too seriously, even if you are now wearing chevrons. Just remember those famous last words: "You can't lock *me* up. I'm a sergeant!"

On joining a new outfit you will be closely looked over by all hands, officer and enlisted. The first impression can make (or break) you. Be prompt, punctilious, squared-away in uniform and deportment, keeping your mouth shut and your eyes open.

Avoid the habit of complaining or griping and avoid those who do. Don't criticize unless you are ready and able to provide a better solution. By the same token, cultivate the habit of optimism.

Be attentive to duty and don't be afraid of work. (Remember the old saying, "The harder I work, the luckier I get".) Don't be the kind of man who quits cold on the first note of recall. Remember that the Marine Corps is a 24-hour profession, and govern yourself accordingly.

Cultivate your powers of observation. The best noncommissioned officers are the observant ones. Akin to observation, cultivate the habit of forethought and forehandedness.

Learn to control and to hide your feelings. A poker face can be useful in a lot of other places besides a card game.

Be alert. Almost as important, always try to *look alert.*

Whatever you do, do thoroughly, and do it enthusiastically. Apply your imagination to every job. Don't confine yourself to doing only exactly what you are told to do; try to do a little more than you are told to do.

If you are asked a question and don't know the answer, *don't bluff.* And don't reply, "I don't know." The right response is, *"I'll find out."*

Don't procrastinate. When you have a job, do it at once. If you have several things to accomplish, *do the important thing first.* If you are stymied, don't report back that you are licked; try some other way and keep on trying. What matter in the Marine Corps, as you know, are *results.* If you get the reputation of a "can-do" NCO, you are on your way to the top.

Whether you are a senior or a junior NCO, miss no opportunity to keep the Corps shaped up as a tight outfit—details like haircuts, posture, correct wearing of uniforms by the privates, and a hundred other things. These so-called "little things" make the Corps better than any other service, and they are the very things that noncommissioned officers are paid to attend to.

Keep in shape. Avoid fat. Stand straight. Keep your hands out of your pockets and see that the Marines around you do the same. Never chew gum when in uniform.

Avoid cheap, flashy civilian clothes. A clean white shirt and a conservative necktie and a dark suit will take you almost anywhere.

Among your fellow NCOs, stay out of factions. If there is bad feeling between others, don't take sides. Don't gossip. Only say things about other Marines that you would say to their faces.

Especially as a new noncommissioned officer (or at any time, for that matter) particularly avoid the practice of "tearing down" more senior NCOs or any of your officers. One of your most important jobs is to support your seniors, not to undercut them.

Be alert to help and support the new lieutenants. Some of our finest officers owe their success and insight to the help and practical lessons imparted to them in their youth by loyal noncommissioned officers. Don't overlook that the fresh-caught lieutenants of today are the company commanders of only a few years ahead.

Always try to keep at least one step ahead of your immediate superior. Put yourself in his place and try to think the way he would think and act in a given situation. By the same token, train the younger men under you to do the same thing as far as you are

260 concerned. Once you have them trained your way, you will have a going concern.

At every step, keep preparing yourself for the next rank, not only in professional qualifications, but by trying constantly to be worth that next chevron—for the sake of the Corps.

Don't hesitate to make suggestions. There is always a way to do something better. (*Note:* The Navy Department's Beneficial Suggestion Program has actually paid cash awards as high as $25,000; you are just as eligible as the next Marine.)

Never speak ill of the Corps, your own outfit, or the Armed Services—that is, don't foul your own nest—in the presence of civilians or people from the other services. And be careful not to criticize other units or services, at least in public.

Always keep your eyes open for likely recruits. Individual recruiting of new Marines by loyal old Marines is one of the best ways to keep the Corps the way we would like it.

Know where to find information. Start out methodically—even if it's dry work—to read *Navy Regulations, The Marine Corps Manual, The Marine Corps Personnel Manual,* and of course all the field and technical manuals relating to your job and organization. By doing this you will not only learn where to find important information, but will also acquire other information that lazy NCOs say isn't covered in any of the books.

Avoid getting into debt and *live within your means.* One indebtedness letter in your file at Marine Corps Headquarters can prevent your promotion for years.

Be very slow to marry. Play the field for a few years, say, until you make staff sergeant. You will be less likely to plunge carelessly into a mighty serious business, and your undistracted bachelor years will permit you to become a highly trained, professional Marine.

Avoid financial transactions with fellow Marines. "Neither a borrower nor a lender be" is golden advice.

Draw a sharp line between yourself, as a noncommissioned officer, and all nonrated men. Never make liberty with privates, nor allow undue familiarity on their part toward you or any NCO.

If the trumpet give an uncertain sound, who shall prepare himself to the battle?

—I Corinthians 14:8.

13 Leadership

Leadership has passed from Marine to Marine since the founding of the Corps. It is the art of influencing and directing men so as to obtain their obedience, respect, confidence, and loyal cooperation.

Leadership is mainly acquired by observation, experience, and example. Working with other Marines is the Marine leader's school. Although some men possess greater gifts of leadership than others, anyone can sharpen his leadership faculties if he tries.

This chapter discusses attributes common to most successful Marine Corps leaders. It also covers techniques, procedures, and situations which contribute to or demand effective leadership by noncommissioned officers in garrison and in combat.

As you read this chapter (or any other writings on leadership) remember that the best way to become a leader is not to read, but rather to *lead.*

The Marine Leader

1301. PRINCIPLES OF LEADERSHIP. Douglas Southall Freeman, biographer of Lee and Washington and master of war history, used to say that leadership boils down to three fundamentals:

Know your stuff.
Be a man.
Look after your men.

Dr. Freeman's fundamentals are simple and inclusive. They can be expanded into 11 principles:

1. Be tactically and technically proficient.
2. Know yourself; improve yourself.
3. Know your men and look out for them.
4. Keep all hands informed.
5. Set the example.

6. Insure that every task is understood, supervised, and accomplished.
7. Train your people as a team.
8. Make sound and timely decisions.
9. Develop a sense of responsibility among your subordinates.
10. Employ and handle your men in accordance with their capabilities.
11. Seek responsibility and accept it for all that you or your unit do or leave undone.

1302. ATTRIBUTES OF A MARINE LEADER.

The young American responds quickly and readily to the exhibition of qualities of leadership. Some of these qualities are industry, energy, initiative, determination, enthusiasm, firmness, kindness, justness, self-control, unselfishness, honor, and courage.

The above quotation, by General John A. Lejeune, 13th Commandant of the Marine Corps, sums up an impressive list of the leadership traits he considered most important. While Lejeune's list can hardly be improved, it can be enlarged.

The contagion of example was General Lejeune's central thought. It is not enough for you to merely know a leader's qualities; you must exhibit them. To exert discipline, you must have learned self-discipline. When you demand attention to duty, you cannot afford to neglect a single detail, and so on. When asked to sign a long-winded order on leadership, George Crook, one of the Army's ablest 19th century Indian-fighting generals, remarked, *"Example is the best general order."*

Much of the power of example stems from "command presence," or the kind of military appearance you make.

Command presence results from dignity; military bearing; neat, well-fitting uniforms; squared-away equipment; firm, plain, and direct speech; and self-control. Here are ways in which you can develop the command presence of a leader:

Learn to control your emotions; don't let them control you.
Speak firmly, simply, and directly. Avoid sarcasm and profanity.
Observe and study the bearing and demeanor of experienced leaders.
Know and adhere to regulations, thus setting an example of self-discipline.
Remember that "spit and polish" is the immediate advertisement of a good Marine.

Professional competence may not make everybody like you, but it will earn everyone's respect. If you know your job and show it, your Marines will quickly get the word. On the other hand, they will be just as quick to see through a bluff. Remember the old saying, "You can't snow the troops." To improve your professional competence, study and follow the advice in Chapter 12.

Resolution and determination to carry out any task or mission are the fuel of leadership. Never be ashamed to get the reputation of a "hard charger" and—if you are lucky enough to earn this reputation—be proud of it.

Courage is the physical and moral control of fear which enables you to face danger with firmness and presence of mind. It gives you control over yourself and enables you to act in a dangerous situation.

There is an old saying, "Some men fear nothing because they see nothing." When a drunk takes unbelievable chances, we don't describe him as courageous. When in shock or panic a man overcomes great physical odds, we don't ascribe it to his courage. Courage involves full recognition of danger and demands bravery that overcomes fear.

Courage can be *physical* or *moral.* Physical courage is usually spectacular. But moral courage sometimes requires more strength. Moral courage means knowing and standing for what is right, regardless of whether people like it or not. It also means being man enough to admit your own mistakes. By virtue of moral courage a good noncommissioned officer can make or impose unpopular decisions when required.

Few men are born with great courage. Most of us develop courage from effort, application, and experience. You can train yourself to attain courage in these ways:

Always put duty ahead of every personal desire or inclination.
Force yourself to speak and act calmly in every situation, no matter how you feel inside.
Prepare yourself mentally for emergencies and combat conditions. *Know in advance what you should do.*
Know your job inside out.
Remember that you are a Marine and that the good name of the Corps depends on you.

Endurance is akin to courage because it demands that you withstand physical and mental strain. Endurance is the ability to keep going and see a job or a battle through to the end. *Physical readiness,* though not an end in itself, is the main foundation of endurance. To develop physical and mental stamina:

Keep physically fit and avoid excesses.
Undertake and complete hard physical tasks.
Finish every job, regardless of fatigue or obstacles.
Whenever you feel tired and sluggish, make yourself do at least one more task and do it well.

Adaptability, the ability to roll with the punches, marks a seasoned noncommissioned officer. Don't let new or unforeseen situations shake you up. As the pressure rises, stay loose.

Dependability is the quality which leads Marines above and below you to rely on your ability to produce. Dependability results from a high sense of duty and responsibility combined with knowledge of your job. One of the best attributes of the Marine Corps is that, in general, we can depend on fellow Marines to produce. This, of course, means you.

Initiative means seeing what has to be done and then doing it without being ordered to. Initiative is a sure indication of an NCO who is a comer. *Resourcefulness*—the traditional Marine spirit of *"can-do"* and *"make-do"* and doing the best you can with what you have—is closely related to initiative, as are the traits of promptness, cheerfulness, and self-confidence. The world is divided into "can-do" and "can't-do" types. Be sure you are in the former class.

To develop initiative:

Continually look ahead for what needs to be done and do it without being told.
Think ahead.
Be alert.
Always try to find a better way to do something, and don't hesitate to make constructive suggestions whether to juniors or seniors.

Decisiveness is one of the most important qualities a noncommissioned officer can have. Sometimes called "decision," it is the ability to reach sound decisions promptly and to announce them forcefully, briefly, and clearly—and make them stick. The central ingredient of decisiveness is *good judgment.*

Decision mainly results from practice, experience, and mental habit. Here are ways in which you can develop your powers:

In any situation (even if you are only a bystander), ask yourself, *"What would I do?"*. If the final decision differs from yours, ask yourself why.
Learn from your own mistakes. Still better, learn from the mistakes of others.
Be careful to take an all-around look at any situation; do so calmly and methodically.
Get all the facts before you make up your mind.
Force yourself to make decisions. Practice decisiveness.

Loyalty, both upward and downward, distinguishes Marine Corps leaders. This is what *Semper Fidelis* really stands for. Loyalty downward means loyalty to protect your subordinates, to assume responsibility for their actions (their mistakes, too), and to see that they receive all credit due them. Above all, *loyalty downward means looking out for your people.*

Encouragement of subordinates is a tradition of Marine leadership. Give subordinates all the initiative and latitude they can handle. Encourage them in professional studies and reading. Make them seek professional schooling.

Fairness and justice are among the most essential qualities of every leader. An unfair NCO is worthless. Whom do you send on liberty, and who makes the working parties? It takes a long time to build a reputation for fairness. One thoughtless error, one injustice, one act of prejudice, can knock down a reputation it took you months to earn.

To be fair, you must understand people and you must understand yourself. You must learn to tune out your own prejudices, emotions such as uncontrolled anger, and personal likes and dislikes.

To acquire the habit of fairness:

Learn to be impersonal, especially when administering punishment or reprimand.
Be absolutely impartial between men.
Search out the facts in every case.
Study people.
Be honest with yourself, know yourself, and be willing to criticize yourself.

Integrity and honor, uprightness, absolute truthfulness, and honesty mark the best leaders. As you well know, Marines have no confidence in a man who will lie, and there is no place in our Corps for a man who steals. It isn't enough to be *usually* upright or truthful. A noncommissioned officer must be square and straight, clean through.

Devotion to the Marine Corps (esprit de corps) on your part, as a noncommissioned officer, will make your men devoted to the Corps. Take the Marine Corps and its laws and ways and traditions with utmost seriousness, and so will your men.

Military Discipline

1303. THE OBJECT AND NATURE OF DISCIPLINE. Effective performance by men in combat is the direct result and primary object of military discipline. Discipline may be defined as prompt and willing responsiveness to orders and unhesitating compliance with regulations. Since the ultimate objective of discipline is efficient performance in battle, discipline may spell the difference between life and death (or, more important to the Marine, between victory and defeat). It is that standard of deportment, attention to duty, example, and decent behavior which, once indoctrinated, enables men, alone or in groups, to accomplish their missions.

Discipline is the ingredient that keeps the finely tuned machinery of the Marine Corps running more smoothly and effectively, at less cost, than any other military organization in the United States.

To many persons, discipline simply means punishment, that is, something to be afraid of. In fact, discipline is a matter of people working well together and getting along well together, and—even if there be a lack of harmony among them—discipline is a means of cementing them as a fighting organization. In the Marine Corps, as in any military organization, it is necessary for people to do certain things in prescribed ways and at given times. If they do so, we say they are well disciplined; if not, we say they are badly disciplined.

Discipline in everyday life is what causes people to obey traffic lights, pay greens fees, go in through entrances and out through exits, return on the expiration of liberty, and knock before entering. Nevertheless, military discipline differs fundamentally from the disciplines of civilian life. No one is less deluded by the claim that civilian personnel techniques can be used as a basis for military discipline than the man who has had military experience in command. Basically, the difference between the discipline of a Marine and that of a worker in industry is that the former, having accepted certain duties and responsibilities on oath, cannot quit tomorrow and—once having fully embraced the true inner spirit of discipline —would not want to quit tomorrow.

1304. THE BASIS OF DISCIPLINE. The best discipline is self-discipline. Self-discipline amounts to the Marine having control of himself and doing what is right because he wants to. To be really well disciplined, a unit must be made up of men who are self-disciplined. In the ultimate test of combat the leader must be able to depend on his men to do their duty correctly and voluntarily whether anyone is checking on them or not. If time and the situation permit, you should make known to your men the reasons for a given order, since this knowledge will increase the desire of your people to do the job and will enable them to do it intelligently. You must know what you want of your men, let them know, and then demand it of them. Their discipline in response to your leadership must be based on knowledge, reason, sense of duty, and loyalty.

1305. CHARACTERISTICS OF EFFECTIVE DISCIPLINE. Until men are severely tried, there is no conclusive test of their discipline. Troops remain relatively undisciplined until physically and mentally conditioned to unusual exertion (a factor which shapes much of the program in recruit training). No body of men could possibly enjoy the dust, the heat, the blistered foot, and aching back of a road march. Nevertheless, hard road marching is a necessary and sound foundation for the discipline of fighting troops. The rise in spirit within any unit, which is always marked when the men rebound from a hard march or after a record day, does not come from a feeling of physical relief but from the sense of accomplishment of a goal.

Another key factor in sound discipline is consistency and firmness. You cannot wink at an infraction one day and put a man on the report for the same offense tomorrow. You must establish and make known your standards of good discipline and must be consistent every day.

Discipline imposed by compulsion and fear of punishment will inevitably break down in combat or any other severe test. If you threaten your men, discipline will also break. Discipline will not break, however, under the stress of testing demands, for troops will endure hard going when it serves an understandable end.

Military discipline is tangible in terms of its results. It allows no room for familiarity, which truly breeds contempt. On the other hand, honest comradeship is a by-product of discipline and a pillar of unit *esprit.*

The noncommissioned officer is concerned primarily with the leadership of small groups. He lives and works close to his men and leads them by direct contact. He is not only the leader of his men but also their teacher and their comrade. His relations with his men are usually personal and informal. He is a link between them and their officers. He gives them much of their training "on the job." He helps them live together, settles their disputes, looks after their interests, and encourages them to pull together. It is to him that they turn first for leadership, guidance, and help.

1306. THE NONCOMMISSIONED LEADER. As a noncommissioned officer you have already demonstrated, to an extent, that you are a leader. You handle men, you direct their work and training, and you keep them in line. You have ability and ambition, or you wouldn't have earned your chevrons. You also have responsibilities.

Every leader in the chain of command must carry his responsibilities if his unit (and therefore the Marine Corps) is to succeed in its mission. No Marine is "just a corporal." A corporal who fails to see that the brakes are working on a vehicle under his responsibility, who fails to see that the men in his fire team have unloaded their weapons at the end of an exercise, who fails to enforce safety regulations around high explosives or at a fuel dump, or who hesitates in combat, may be taking the lives of fellow Marines. A misfiled letter, a garbled radio message, or an unfilled requisition rarely cost a life, but any such mistake can hurt a unit or an individual Marine.

Because of this, every noncommissioned officer has to be sure that his men are doing their jobs completely and correctly. He must practice and demand "zero defects" in everything he does or is responsible for. This is your established function as an NCO in the chain of command.

1307. THE CHAIN OF COMMAND. All orders and instructions from higher echelons to lower echelons should be issued through the chain of command as far as practicable. An individual or unit must have but one immediate commander from whom all orders and instructions related to a given function are received.

For example, an order from a company commander goes from him to his platoon leaders, to the section leaders, to the squad leaders, and then to the corporals and privates of the squads. This is known as the chain of command. It also operates in reverse order. For example, the private wants to see his platoon sergeant. First he would see his fire team leader, then his squad leader and finally his platoon sergeant. Each subordinate commander at any level in the chain of command has only one immediate commander; thus the chain provides the unity of command that must exist if a unit is to operate effectively.

1308. DECENTRALIZING AUTHORITY. When you pass some of your duties down the chain of command to more junior noncommissioned leaders, you hold the latter responsible for producing.

At the same time, you delegate to each subordinate the authority he needs to carry out his duty. In this way, each level of command, from division or air wing down to fire team, receives authority equal to its responsibilities; and each level carries out its mission under direction and supervision of the next higher level.

Although you can delegate authority to your subordinates, you always carry the ultimate responsibility for all that your unit does or leaves undone. You can't simply delegate away authority to the point where you retain no control, and you must also be sufficiently specific in delegating authority that your subordinates know where they stand.

Delegation of authority by seniors is the main way of developing the capacity of juniors—the very juniors who must be prepared to inherit your place as you go up the line.

1309. THE NCO's ROLE IN THE CHAIN OF COMMAND. A company commander cannot crawl from man to man in combat in order to give each man his orders and direct each man's efforts. The company is divided into platoons, squads, and fire teams each with its own mission. Thus, if company B is to attack Hill 362, the captain calls together his platoon leaders and certain noncommissioned officers. He explains the situation and the company mission and assigns each platoon leader a platoon mission. Each platoon leader then calls his squad leaders together, explains the situation and platoon mission, and assigns missions. The squad leaders assign missions to their fire-team leaders, and the fire-team leaders in a similar manner to their men. Each subordinate leader in the chain of command is responsible for the company mission. Each leader is therefore responsible directly to the next senior leader in the chain of command.

All leaders in the chain of command assist in supervision of the commander's orders. The squad leader cannot assume that, once he has given an order to his fire-team leaders, the chain of command will function automatically from that point on. Having given his orders, he follows up by observing, supervising, and correcting. He has time to do this properly only if he has used his subordinate leaders properly; they handle their units, and the squad leader is able to handle the squad as a whole and to insure that his fire teams are accomplishing their missions. By giving the squad leader responsibility for his squad mission, the platoon leader has provided himself the opportunity to observe, inspect, and direct his platoon more effectively.

1310. THE NONCOMMISSIONED OFFICER'S SUPERVISORY FUNCTION. Supervision is one of the most important things an NCO does. Many noncommissioned officers, such as a platoon sergeant or platoon guide, have no commands of their own, but are needed to assist the platoon leader in supervising his orders. Naturally, their specific duties vary with the situation, especially in combat. For example, as a platoon sergeant in combat, you are primarily concerned with general supervision and coordination of the whole platoon, and, as second-in-command, you are prepared to take over the platoon if the lieutenant falls. You usually have no specific post, but go where your duties require. As the platoon guide, you would usually be charged with discipline, administration, supply, and evacuation, and, like the platoon sergeant, you would also be backing up the platoon leader in supervising and directing the platoon as a whole. You would also be prepared to replace the platoon sergeant, a squad leader, or the platoon leader if required. As a squad or fire-team leader, you have no assistant because your unit is small enough for you to supervise by yourself. Thus, the NCO finds his place in the chain of command either as a leader of a smaller unit or as a supervisory assistant to the officer in command of a larger unit.

In your supervisory capacity, you are essentially *a link between the commander and his men.* Much of your commander's time is spent in studying and implementing orders from higher authority and in coordinating the several units of his own command. On the other hand, the time and effort of the NCOs are mainly taken up with implementing and supervising execution of the commander's instructions within each subordinate unit. Since, as a noncommissioned officer, you work with smaller groups and live closer to the men, you can quickly discover their needs and can quickly correct minor infractions or lapses on the spot. You are also in a position to help the men understand the "why" in a given situation, to make discipline understandable, and thus to avert many problems before they ever happen.

1311. DEVELOPING LEADERSHIP TECHNIQUES. Early in this chapter, 11 principles of leadership have been listed. These are short and simple, not unlike the statement that all you have to do to shoot expert is to "hold 'em and squeeze 'em." We all know that the latter principle is true, but it calls for considerable application. So do the leadership principles just mentioned.

In the following paragraphs we review the 11 leadership principles and suggest ways of application by which they can become effective leadership techniques of your own. Naturally, each NCO will have a different personal style because personalities differ. But by following the hints given here, you will have a basis for adapting these principles to your manner and style.

BE TACTICALLY AND TECHNICALLY PROFICIENT.
What this means in three words is, "Know your job." Give it everything you have; learn it inside out. It also means that you must prepare yourself for the jobs ahead and for more and higher responsibilities. To achieve all these things, follow the advice in Chapter 12 of this *Handbook.*

KNOW YOURSELF; IMPROVE YOURSELF.
This principle is closely akin to the preceding one, but it relates to you rather than the way you handle your job. To know yourself,

watch how others react to you, and try to learn your weak and strong points. Be prepared to accept friendly criticism and guidance; even teasing or kidding directed your way usually reveals some tender spot that others recognize. Get a blank copy of the Marine Corps NCO fitness report. Look over every item and trait and try to mark yourself, not necessarily as you would want the report to look, but as you truthfully think it would if it reflected *you as you are.*

To improve yourself, besides the suggestions given in Chapter 12, observe the successes and failures of others. Ask yourself in each case, why? Profit from the experience of others, remembering that Benjamin Franklin once said, "Experience keeps a dear school, but a fool will go to none other."

KNOW YOUR MEN AND LOOK OUT FOR THEM.

In the final analysis, the essence of Marine leadership is looking out for your people.

For the sake of your men, you must be tireless, you must be imaginative, you must be willing to shoulder responsibility. Their good must be your first preoccupation. Their interest and advancement must be always on your mind.

Are they comfortably clothed, housed, and sheltered?
Are they well fed?
Are they getting their mail?
If sick or wounded, can they rely on help?
Are they justly treated?
Are they getting the recognition they deserve, both individually and as a unit?
Are you available to every man who needs counsel?
Are you alert to help each one better himself in his career?

As a noncommissioned officer, you demand a great deal of your men. But they in fact demand much more of you. If you let down one of your Marines, you are letting down the entire Corps.

KEEP ALL HANDS INFORMED.

When someone fails to get the word, it is just as much a reflection on his squad leader as it is on the man. One of your main jobs as an NCO is to spread the word. In this you also see that they are up to date on regulations, orders, and policies that affect them or the unit as a whole. One simple way to do this is to insure that everyone reads the bulletin board and that the board is kept alive rather than cluttered with dog-eared dead material.

In combat, it is vital that every single man know the unit mission, and it is highly desirable that he know generally how the campaign is going and where. Stopping wild rumors is an important job for all NCOs, as is publicizing our own successes.

SET THE EXAMPLE.

Early in this chapter a section has already been devoted to the contagion example. Just remember General Crooks' famous statement: *"Example is the best general order."* If you steer by this, you won't go wrong. One of the best examples you can set is to be th type of noncommissioned officer who is more concerned over discharging his responsibilities than in enjoying his rights and privileges.

INSURE THAT EVERY TASK IS UNDERSTOOD, SUPERVISED, AND COMPLETED.

The first essential in this is that any order you give is necessary and that it is clear enough for all hands to know what you expect the result to be. When time permits, encourage your men to ask questions on anything that may not be clear to them. Follow up the progress of work through subordinate NCOs and by getting around for yourself, too. When you see something going wrong or some obstacle that has arisen, make immediate correction or take immediate action to keep things moving ahead. Finally, never forget the order by "Fighting Joe" Hooker, of Civil War fame, *"No one will consider the day as ended until the duties it brings have been discharged."*

TRAIN YOUR PEOPLE AS A TEAM.

Develop a sense of comradeship, mutual trust, and confidence among all your subordinates—a feeling that they will never be let down and thus can never let the others down. See that every man learns the job of each other man with whom he habitually functions. Try to see that every man is trained to assume the duties of the next higher grade and of his immediate leader. Encourage your people to make liberty together and to stand by each other.

MAKE SOUND AND TIMELY DECISIONS.

To make a sound decision, you should know your mission, what you are capable of doing to accomplish it, what means you have to accomplish it, and what possible impediments or obstacles exist (in combat, these would be enemy capabilities) that might stand in the way. Timeliness is almost as important as soundness. In many military situations a *timely,* though inferior, decision is better than a long-delayed one even though theoretically correct.

DEVELOP RESPONSIBILITY AMONG YOUR SUBORDINATES.

A noncommissioned officer who is sure of himself will delegate authority to junior NCOs whenever he can. This develops their capabilities and prepares them for advancement. Be quick to recognize and praise their work when they display initiative. Correct their mistakes in a way which encourages them to keep on trying. And always be on the alert for an opportunity to give earned praise—and mean it.

EMPLOY YOUR COMMAND IN ACCORDANCE WITH ITS CAPABILITIES.

This means that you should not ask the impossible and that, on the other hand, you should see that your unit has what it needs to do a given job. If the means are insufficient, let your immediate superior know and ask for what you think you need.

SEEK RESPONSIBILITY AND ACCEPT IT FOR ALL THAT YOU OR YOUR UNIT DO OR LEAVE UNDONE.

A foresighted, ambitious noncommissioned officer will seek a variety of assignments so as to broaden his service experience and fit him for greater responsibilities. As a man on the way up, you should welcome every opportunity to take on a big job.

As long as you are in charge of a job or a unit, you—you alone—are responsible for all that your unit does or leaves undone. Never try to dodge this responsibility or to pass it off onto subordinates.

You and Your Subordinates

1312. DEALING WITH SUBORDINATES. A noncommissioned officer must always support and back up his subordinates. A fire-team leader will soon lose his initiative and quit trying if you, as his squad leader, don't back him up. Even if he is in fact wrong, you should not let this appear, but should privately get him back on the track and let him correct the situation himself.

Remember the story of the sea lawyer in a ship's detachment who approached the detachment commander with a complaint; at the end, he said, "Sir, can Corporal Boatspace do this to me?" To which the commander simply replied, "Go ask the corporal."

Thus, your first duty toward your subordinates is to back them to the hilt. They will turn to you for encouragement, guidance, and material support. Never let them down. Nothing should ever be "too much trouble" if it is needed for your men or your outfit. Protect, shelter, and feed them before you think of your own needs.

Demand the highest standards and never let those standards be compromised.

Live, lead, and exercise command "by the book." Let this be understood by your men.

Keep *responsibility* centralized—in *you*. Decentralize *authority*. Give subordinates wide authority and discretion. Tell them what results you want, and leave the "how" to them. Never oversupervise.

Avoid overfamiliarity of manner. If you have feet of clay—and most humans do—overfamiliarity with subordinates is the surest way to advertise it.

Develop genuine human interest in your men as individuals. Study each man's personality. Seek out his background from his service record. Learn his name, and address him by it. A man's own name is usually the sweetest sound in the English language to him. Never let any Marine picture himself as "a mere cog" in the machine. No Marine is a cog.

In your daily exercise of command, avoid the "hurry-up-and-wait" tendency which characterizes ill-run commands. That is to say, think twice before you apply pressure to speed up something if the net result is simply that your people will have to stand around waiting at some further stage. Don't get them out unduly ahead of time for formations and parades, especially if every other echelon has added its few minutes of anticipation, too.

1313. PERSONAL RELATIONS WITH SUBORDINATES. Besides your official relations with your men, you have personal relations with them, almost 24 hours a day. You may be a personal, as well as an official, friend to them. But, as a leader, you must establish personal and comradely contact, without giving away an inch of your prestige and authority. This doesn't mean that you should be completely aloof, but neither does it mean that you can play poker with the privates or have money transactions with them.

Remember that your prestige can only be lost by you. If you are going to maintain your position as a leader and maintain discipline, you can't join with subordinates in growling about regulations or a superior. If you come upon a group of men complaining about a mannerism of or decision by an officer or the first sergeant, you should either avoid the conversation entirely or point out the true situation or—as a last resort—shut them up, explaining that such bulkheading is unbecoming to Marines.

It is highly unmilitary for privates to call their first sergeant or other noncommissioned officers by their first names. For a noncommissioned officer to encourage his men to do so is to embarrass them, if they are properly indoctrinated. All noncommissioned officers should treat other leaders, particularly the more senior ones, with respect in their conversations in front of their men. For example, you should never speak of another sergeant as "Jones," let alone by his first name, but rather as "Sergeant Jones."

> *EXAMPLE:* Corporal to Sergeant: "What's your first name?"
> Sergeant to Corporal: "My first name is Sergeant."

To increase the spirit of teamwork and cooperation in his unit, the noncommissioned officer should encourage his men to know each other better, to do things together, and to go on liberty together. He should join with them on group parties, picnics, and excursions. However, generally speaking, he should make his own liberties with other noncommissioned officers, not with his men. You cannot drink with your juniors all night and expect respect for your orders the next morning.

The noncommissioned officer should always be available and accessible to his men. He should never be too busy to listen to them and to help them with their problems.

1314. GETTING THE RIGHT MAN IN THE RIGHT PLACE. A considerable part of your duties will be concerned with assigning men to jobs or recommending that they be assigned. To do this well, you must know the requirements of the job and the capabilities and limitations of your men. You should also consider the personalities and desires of each man when you give him an assignment. As far as practicable, be careful not to assign two men to a common task when friction is known to exist between them. A big, naturally aggressive man probably will be better with a flamethrower, whereas a small, reticent man might be best with the mortar squad. When a man likes his job, he usually does it better and requires less supervision than if he dislikes it or is indifferent. A man who wants to be a machine gunner may be a poor clerk; a Marine who wants to drive a truck may be a lazy cook.

But the needs of the unit must take priority over individual desires. No matter how eager he is to become a sniper, a good cook who is fat and only shot marksman on the last record day, should stay in the galley.

Besides having the right man in the right place, you should have a trained replacement for every key man. When an automatic rifleman falls in battle, another properly trained Marine must be able to take over his duties. You must be prepared to lose key men by transfer, promotion, illness, or expiration of enlistment. Thus, you must keep ahead of the situation at all times. As for yourself, you should be prepared and trained to be a replacement for the next higher leader.

1315. ORGANIZING WORK. As a noncommissioned officer, you must organize the work of your unit so that,

Every man knows what to do,
Every man has enough to do,
Every man knows where he is going,
Every man knows where the leader is,
Every action taken contributes to accomplishment of mission.

1316. COMMANDS AND ORDERS. There is an important distinction between a *command* and an *order*. A command must be obeyed immediately and automatically; it permits no deviation, delay, or discretion. An order directs that something be done (the "what") but leaves the method of compliance (the "how") up to the subordinate. "Prepare for inspection!" is a command. When the command is given, the unit opens ranks, dresses right, and stands at attention. "Second Platoon, be prepared for an inspection at 0800 tomorrow," is an order.

COMMANDS. A command must be *positive*. Your tone of voice should be clear, loud, and authoritative. You should say, "Get off the skyline!" not "If I were you, I'd stay off the skyline."

A command should be *definite* and express exactly what is intended. Don't command, "Keep down!" when you mean "Get off the skyline!"

You should *look at, indicate, and address directly* the man, men, or unit to whom you give a command. Use names ("Corporal Witek, take your detail to the clothing room.") or unit designations ("First Squad, stand fast."). When singling out a man in a group for a specific job, call him by name and rank ("Private Fisher, run this message over to the Range Officer.").

Make commands brief. A long-winded command is harder to understand, more complicated to obey, and more likely to be forgotten.

ORDERS. An order allows more leeway than a command. Within certain limits, you may permit an order to be interpreted or even questioned. For example, if you issue an order to your squad which is inadvertently conflicting with a simultaneous commitment for the platoon, one of your fire-team leaders could properly remind you of the conflict.

Orders should be given to the subordinate in charge. This squarely gives him the leadership responsibility for seeing that the order is fulfilled.

When time permits, it is usually wise to explain the "why" behind an order unless the reason is self-evident.

Remember that the recipients of your orders are serving the Marine Corps, not you. There is no need for you to be harsh, arrogant, or overbearing when you give orders.

In carrying out an order or in passing it on to the unit, do so in the spirit of "we will..." *not* "you people will..." If you have a detail unloading a ration truck, you should be out supervising them, not drinking coffee in the galley with the mess sergeant. As you move about, when it doesn't interfere with your supervisory role, lend a hand here and there.

1317. ISSUING AND ENFORCING ORDERS.

Promulgation of an order represents not over 10 percent of your responsibility. The remaining 90 percent consists in assuring through personal supervision on the ground, by yourself and your staff, proper and vigorous execution.

So wrote General George S. Patton on the subject of orders. Issuing and enforcing orders comprises one of the main functions of a noncommissioned officer.

Before you issue an order, ask yourself if it can be reasonably carried out. If an order cannot be executed as given, it should not be given.

Never give an unlawful order, that is, an order which contravenes law or regulations or which demands that your subordinates break the rules. A good test of a lawful order is, "Could a subordinate be court-martialed for failing to comply?"

Issue as few orders as necessary. Keep them concise, clear, and unmistakable in purpose. Anything that can be misunderstood will be.

Never contravene the orders of an officer or another NCO without clear and pressing reason. If possible, make this reason evident when you countermand the order in question. If orders to you conflict, obey the last one. In obeying your last order first, be sure to explain the conflict, but never protest the order.)

When you have once given an order, be sure it is executed as you gave it. Your responsibility doesn't end until you have assured yourself that the order has been carried out. Never tolerate halfhearted, perfunctory compliance. "If anyone in a key position appears to be expending less than the energy that could properly be demanded of him," wrote the German Field Marshal Rommel, "that man must be ruthlessly removed."

Never give an order that you wouldn't be willing to carry out yourself, particularly one involving danger. Never send men anywhere you aren't prepared to go yourself.

An order received from above should be passed on as *your* order and should be enforced as such. Never evade the burden of an unpopular directive by throwing the blame on the next higher echelon.

It cannot be too often repeated that when you issue an order, make it clear what you want done and who is to do it—but *avoid telling subordinates how it is to be done.* Remember the old promotion-examination question for lieutenants, in which the student is told that he has a ten-man working party, headed by a sergeant, and must erect a 75-foot flagpole on the post parade ground. Problem—How to do it?

Every student who works out the precise calculations of stresses, tackle, and gear, no matter how accurately, is graded wrong. The desired answer is simple: The lieutenant turns to the sergeant, and says, *"Sergeant, put up that flagpole."*

1318. PUBLIC PRAISE AND PRIVATE REPRIMAND. The basic rule of praise and reprimand (which are two sides of the same coin) is *praise in public and reprimand in private.*

Public praise is a reward to a good man, and it inspires every other Marine to seek similar praise and emulate a good example. Public reprimand, however deserved, wounds a man's pride and often embarrasses the Marines around him. Anything that destroys a man's pride—besides engendering resentment—also destroys the self-confidence he needs to correct himself.

In particular, a subordinate noncommissioned officer should never be called down before nonrated men. If a squad leader stands up a fire-team leader in front of his men and says, "Fassett, you have no more idea how to get your people across a clearing than a ringtail ape," he has undercut the entire authority of the fire-team leader. He has likewise damaged or possibly even destroyed the fire team's collective confidence in the man who must lead them. The fire-team leader could be criticized quite sharply in private for his shortcomings and still be able to lead his unit with his head up.

Both punishment and reward, however, have definite limitations. Fear of punishment means very little in battle. When a man is dodging bullets, he doesn't worry about deprivation of liberty (of which there isn't any) or of loss of pay when all his money is on the books. On the other hand, a "seventy-two" or a case of beer isn't enough to make a rifleman charge across an open clearing to close with a pillbox when the air is full of lead. At such a time, it is discipline, sense of duty, esprit de corps, and confidence in his leaders and fellow Marines, that get him on his feet and moving forward.

1319. REPRIMAND. One basic rule of reprimand has already been stated—*do it in private.*

A second rule is found in a favorite saying of the late Lieutenant General Leroy P. Hunt, "Never give a man a dollar's worth of blame without a dime's worth of praise."

And avoid collective reprimands, let alone collective punishments. Nothing so rightly infuriates an innocent man as to be unfairly included in an all-hands blast or all-hands punishment.

Before you issue reprimand or censure, be sure than an offense or dereliction of some kind has been committed. This is basic. You cannot call down a Marine just because you don't like the color of his eyes. Before telling off any individual, ask yourself if what he has done, pushed to the limit, would sustain charges under any article in the *Uniform Code of Military Justice*. This circumspection can save you much embarrassment and injured innocence at the hands of sea lawyers, while it sometimes cuts the other way to protect a subordinate against hasty rebuke when not warranted.

Know what you intend to say before you launch into reprimand. A sputtering, inconclusive rebuke only makes a noncommissioned officer look silly.

Avoid uncontrolled anger, profanity, or abuse. Many experienced Marines know how to valve off anger into indignation. Make this your object, but at all costs avoid "acting tough." *Being tough,* which comes naturally, is something quite different.

Never make a promise or threat which you are not capable of fulfilling or which you do not intend to fulfill. Never bluff, or someone will call your bluff in short order.

Like reward, the effectiveness of reproof is in direct proportion to its immediacy. When you spot something amiss, take corrective action at once. Never let a wrongdoing Marine slide by with the thought, "Well, he's not one of *my* men. Let his own outfit handle it." *Every* U. S. Marine is one of *your* men.

If you have occasion to call down a Marine not under your command, find out who he is and see that his command knows about it. At the same time, direct the man to report the matter to his company or battery first sergeant as soon as possible. This will be appreciated by his unit, which is just as anxious to have its Marines up to snuff. Moreover, the derelictions of an individual are the responsibility of his immediate senior. A Marine with a dirty rifle is a black eye for his fire-team leader; a man in your squad who fails to salute is a discredit to your leadership. Napoleon's dictum, "There are no bad regiments—only bad colonels," applies with equal force to fire teams, squads, platoons, companies, and battalions as well.

You and Your Seniors

Your relations with your seniors are important to you in several ways—not least is the practical one that they are the persons who determine your assignments and promote you.

But there are other reasons. To be a good leader, you must be a good subordinate. To learn how to lead, one of the best ways is to observe experienced leaders. To learn more about the Marine Corps and your job, one of the best sources is a more experienced, more senior Marine.

1320. RELATIONS WITH SENIORS. Here are a few rules to guide you in your relations with seniors, whether they are officers or NCOs.

The first task a noncommissioned officer should undertake is to *win the confidence of his seniors*. Until they feel you have earned their complete confidence, you cannot function effectively. This underscores *the importance of making a good first impression*. A good first impression results from:

Smart, well-fitting, and immaculate uniform
Squared-away manner and bearing
Mouth-shut, eyes-open, and alert attitude
Immediate readiness to turn to
Obvious professional knowledge and capability.

Study your seniors closely. Remember the little anecdote with which Chapter 12 of this *Handbook* opens. Find out what they want and then give it to them. Adjust to their special ways of doing things and even to their eccentricities, if any. *Be wary of judging your seniors and even more wary of voicing judgments.* Rarely will you have all the facts and information that permit a fair and balanced judgment. Remember that the man on top, looking down, sees many things that another man, still looking up, cannot see.

Instead of judging your seniors, you should observe and *mentally note their strengths and weaknesses as leaders.* In doing this, try to put yourself in your senior's place (which of course is a way to rehearse yourself for the day when you will be there). If there is some question of adjusting, remember *it is up to you, the junior, to adjust.* On one occasion the officers and staff noncommissioned officers of a rifle company held a conference to discuss the qualifications of two or three corporals and to decide which one to recommend for promotion to sergeant. In discussing one corporal, his platoon sergeant said, "Oh, he's all right; he'll put out if you treat him right." The first sergeant's immediate reply was, "You shouldn't have to treat an NCO right."

You should *cultivate your seniors in a friendly way* because all Marines, of whatever rank, should be friends. This doesn't mean "ear banging", which will quickly be recognized not only by your seniors but also by your own people. By establishing a good relationship with an immediate senior, you also establish mutual professional confidence, which is important to both parties.

Remember that *you are wearing your chevrons to solve problems and get results,* not to present problems to and ask for solutions from your seniors. You should avoid taking your troubles to your boss and should concentrate on finding ways to solve problems on your own. When you do have to present a problem to your seniors, you should always present a recommended solution and, if applicable, an alternate possible solution.

On the other hand, you should take pains to *keep seniors advised* as to what is going on, progress being made, results achieved, and requirements that arise. When you are on watch as corporal of the guard, you may have to call the sergeant of the guard in case of some unforeseen contingency, but you can't ask him to stand your watch for you.

Avoid making excuses. There may be reasons for deficiencies, but, in the Marine Corps, there are never excuses. Results are what count, and results are what your seniors expect of you. *If you consistently get results, there is no limit to your opportunities.*

Leadership Indicators

The levels of morale, discipline, esprit de corps, and military proficiency in any organization indicate the quality of leadership within that organization, especially and particularly that of the leader himself. This section lists indicators of the above qualities. It also discusses inspections, which are one of the most important ways in which the condition of a unit is measured and tested.

1321. INDICATORS OF UNIT MORALE. Morale is the state of mind of the individual Marine—how he feels about himself, his comrades, the Corps, and his own basic needs. High morale naturally results from good leadership and results in feelings of confidence and capability on the part of all hands. Morale is never static: it is either rising or sinking. Here are specific indicators you should watch in evaluating morale:

Rate of unauthorized absences
Requests for transfer
Sick-call rate (including malingering)
Rate and kinds of offenses
Avoidable loss of or damage to equipment
Appearance of troops (haircuts, for example)
Personal hygiene
Professional proficiency
Attention during and attitude toward training
Military courtesy
Compliance with orders and directives
Condition of equipment and weapons
Condition of quarters and unit areas
Adequacy of mess and rations
Use of recreational facilities
Prevalence of rumors
Troop quarrels or evident ill-feeling
*Care of casualties and dead
*Stragglers
*Self-inflicted wounds.

(*) Under combat conditions

1322. INDICATORS OF UNIT DISCIPLINE. Discipline is the military quality which maintains order in a unit and results in prompt obedience to command by action. Self-discipline enables a Marine to act resourcefully and correctly in combat or in emergency without having to be told to do so. Many indicators of discipline are the same as or similar to the indicators of morale. In fact, the two qualities are closely linked, for it is virtually impossible to discover high morale in the absence of good discipline. Here are danger signals which suggest poor discipline:

Indifferent compliance with orders and directives
Unwarranted turnout for sick call or malingering
Untidy or uncleanly conditions
Poor saluting, and inattention to military courtesy
Careless performance of any kind
Unauthorized absence
Offenses or misbehavior by men on leave or liberty
Insubordinate attitudes
Quarrels and fights
Disrespect for NCOs.

1323. INDICATORS OF ESPRIT DE CORPS. The Marine's esprit de corps is the highest in the armed services. Esprit de corps has been defined as having the highest possible opinion of your own corps and looking down on all others. Among Marines esprit de corps shows itself in loyalty to Corps and unit, and in pride and willingness to fight and die for its honor.

Esprit de corps held the Marines steady at Bladensburg (when others ran away), took Belleau Wood, put the Colors on top of Mount Suribachi, brought the 1st Marine Division down from the Chosin Reservoir, and held Khe Sanh.

Here are some indicators of the esprit de corps which every Marine unit should possess:

Pride in the traditions and history of Corps and unit
Belief that this is the best outfit in the Corps
Good reputation among other units
Strong competitive spirit
Good teamwork and readiness of men to stand by each other
Pride in wearing of the uniform
Excellence in ceremonials and close-order drill.

1324. INDICATORS OF MILITARY PROFICIENCY. Proficiency results from training, the efficacy of which in turn stems in great part from morale, discipline, and esprit de corps. Supervising training forms a major part of your duty as a noncommissioned officer. You will get proficiency only by demanding the highest possible standards in every detail and exercise. Here are indicators of a unit's military proficiency:

Condition of weapons and equipment

Appearance and physical condition of troops
Troop-leading ability of junior leaders
Businesslike functioning of the unit
Absence of confusion and of unnecessary commands, orders, or
   signals
Willing acceptance and discharge of responsibility by subordinates
Promptness and accuracy in relaying orders and instructions
Promptness and accuracy in reporting and disseminating information
Effective use of communications
Level of marksmanship qualification.

A Commandant of the Marine Corps inspects a rifle.

1325. INSPECTIONS. Inspection is one of the most important
tools of command. Throughout your Marine Corps career you will
continually be inspected or inspecting. Inspections serve two purposes: first, to enable commanding or superior officers to find out
conditions within an organization; and second, to impart to an
organization the standards required of it.

There are several types of inspection, varying from inspection of personnel in ranks to inspections of materiel, supplies, equipment, records, and buildings. Each inspection has a particular purpose which the inspecting officer will keep foremost in mind. Thus it is up to you to ascertain or forecast the object of the inspection and to prepare yourself and your command accordingly. For example, if the inspection is to deal with the crew-served weapons and transportation in your unit, it does no great good to emphasize clean uniforms and haircuts at the expense of materiel upkeep. On the other hand, good-looking vehicles do not excuse greasy, worn clothing at a personnel inspection.

1326. PREPARE FOR INSPECTION. Once you know the purpose of an inspection, you must prepare your outfit. The best way to do this is to put yourself in the inspector's shoes. Be sure your subordinate leaders also understand the "why" of the inspection so that they can cooperate intelligently in getting tuned to concert pitch. Many an inspection crisis has been averted by a quick-witted, loyal subordinate with a ready answer.

While your unit prepares for inspection, move about your area. This preliminary inspection enables you to see that preparations are what you want, and it reminds your men that you have direct interest in the hard work they are engaged in. It also lets you discover weak spots in good time.

Time the preparation for inspection so that everything is ready about 30 minutes before the appointed hour. This gives your men a final opportunity to get themselves ready. It also gives you a margin to handle last-minute emergencies.

Ten minutes beforehand, have your responsible subordinates standing by their respective posts or, if the inspection is to be in formation, have your unit paraded, steady and correct. You should be at your place in formation or at the entrance to your area, poised to meet the inspecting party. Your company commander or platoon leader will indicate which noncommissioned officer he wants to accompany him during the inspection. Platoon sergeants and first sergeants should have pencil and notebook ready to take notes. The police sergeant should have a flashlight. All rooms, compartments, sheds, etc., should be unlocked and open. Tents should be rolled, unless the weather is foul.

When the inspecting party arrives, salute and report your unit prepared for inspection. Post yourself at the left rear of the inspecting officer and follow along with him. Answer questions calmly and with good humor. Avoid alibis. Do not reprimand your men during inspection for shortcomings the inspection brings out. It is *your* outfit; the shortcomings are *yours.* Be alert for the inspecting officer's comments. These forearm you for the next inspection.

Afterward, if results have been notably good or notably poor, assemble your people and tell them about it. Give every man a personal stake in the success of each inspection.

1327. INSPECTION FOLLOW-UP. An inspection loses value if you fail to follow it up. This is the main reason for keeping careful notes on the comments of the inspecting officer.

Inspection notes should be broken down into items for corrective action and disseminated to everyone concerned so that they can serve as a checklist. When you reinspect, review previous inspection notes as a guide for follow-up. On the receiving end, you can use past notes to prepare for future occasions. *It is a grave reflection on you as a leader if the same defects continue to show up on consecutive inspections.*

1328. INSPECTION DO's AND DON'T's. When your relief, fire team, squad, or platoon are being inspected, you should strive to look even better than your people. You should be the outstanding-looking Marine in the unit.

During an inspection, never ask a Marine of yours anything that will not bring out a constructive answer.

See that every man and every area are covered by the inspection. Nothing so annoys Marines as to prepare for inspection and then not be inspected. Conversely, a completed inspection, when successful, is a strong morale booster.

In any given unit, *all hands should be inspected.* Messmen, working parties, etc., should be carefully inspected, too, even if a second special inspection is required.

When inspection notes have been disseminated, as stated above, assemble your people for a critique. In some instances—possibly in most—it is good practice to hold an immediate, informal critique while the inspection is still uppermost in everyone's mind.

Combat Leadership

This *Handbook* is not a tactical manual, nor is it so intended. Nevertheless, no chapter on noncommissioned officer leadership would be complete without mention of certain special principles, factors, and problems of combat leadership in small units, together with a summary of the so-called "troop-leading steps" which are standard in the Marine Corps.

All basic principles of Marine Corps leadership hold good in combat. In fact, they take on even greater importance there than at any other time. Therefore, as you read this section of the *Handbook,* remember that combat is no time to "throw away the book" but rather to apply intensively all you have previously learned.

1329. SPECIAL FACTORS IN COMBAT LEADERSHIP. The paramount consideration in combat leadership is *attainment of the objective.* Everything else is secondary. *Aggressiveness*—the desire to close with the enemy and destroy him, or the will to fight—is the primary moral factor that makes men take their objectives. *Firepower* is the material (as distinct from moral) factor that gets assault troops into close combat with the enemy and sustains them on the objectives they have taken. *Coordination and control of fire and movement* is the principal responsibility of small-unit leaders from the fire team up. Another leadership responsibility which is almost as important is to *keep the unit structure and chain of command intact,* no matter what casualties are sustained. This means that leader positions must be kept filled, that fire teams and squads must be reorganized and, where necessary, consolidated, and that weapons must be kept in action.

Every noncommissioned officer must prepare himself for leadership in combat.

1330. TROOP-LEADING STEPS. Closely associated with the principles of combat leadership are certain troop-leading procedures that help you to formulate your plans of action in tactical situations.*

DISCUSSION. The Marine rifle squad, properly organized and equipped and forcefully led, is a striking force to be reckoned with on any battlefield. Leading such a squad in battle is a task of great responsibility. You will very likely have such an opportunity during your career as a Marine, and it is important that you prepare yourself for the task.

Under stress and excitement, a mind trained to follow well-defined procedures will function effectively and arrive at logical solutions to problems which confront it. Most combat problems arise when a unit is under fire or in close contact with the enemy; so, as a squad leader, you do much of your work under conditions of extreme stress. To face a difficult, dangerous situation in combat, evaluate it and arrive at a solution.

Troop-leading procedure, a logical checklist of actions to follow in solving a tactical problem, will help you in carrying out your tactical functions as a unit leader. While not meant as a substitute for effective, logical thinking, troop-leading procedure provides a ready guide for a pattern of actions which insure consideration of all pertinent aspects of a combat situation.

"METT". One of the central processes in all combat decisions is arriving at an *estimate of the situation.* Only when you have logically considered the various factors which can help or hinder you in a particular situation can you decide upon a logical plan of action. At most times, you will have several possible courses of action open to you. To determine which you should follow, you consider the advantages and disadvantages of each in light of:

Mission
Enemy strength and dispositions
Terrain and weather
Troops and fire support available.

This list is referred to as "METT", the word formed by the first letters of each of the foregoing yardsticks.

SUMMARY OF TROOP-LEADING STEPS. The six troop-leading steps which follow can form the basis of action by a troop leader performing a tactical mission. They are organized in a logical sequence so as to cover all (and only) the important factors in solution of a tactical problem.

   I. Begin Planning
      A. Plan the use of available time.
      B. Begin the estimate ("METT").

---

*This section is a condensation of similar material contained in *The Marine Noncommissioned Officer* (MCI 03.3d), prepared by the Marine Corps Institute, to which this entire chapter owes much.

      1. Analyze terrain from map, sketch, or aerial photograph for:
- a. Key terrain features
- b. Observation and fields of fire
- c. Cover and concealment
- d. Obstacles
- e. Avenues of approach

      2. Analyze enemy strength, locations, disposition, and capabilities.

   C. Make preliminary plan. (Announce planning guidance to subordinates.)

  II. Arrange for Reconnaissance and Coordination

   A. Movement of Unit (Where, when, how).

   B. Reconnaissance (Select route, schedule, persons to take along, use of subordinates).

   C. Coordination (Adjacent and supporting units).

 III. Make Reconnaissance. (Examine the ground. If necessary, change preliminary plan.)

 IV. Complete Plan. (Receive recommendations, complete estimate, change preliminary plan as needed, announce concept, prepare order.)

  V. Issue Order. (Include orientation on terrain, if possible.)

 VI. Supervise

1331. MAXIMS OF LEADERSHIP AND COMMAND

¶ *Learn to obey before you command.—Solon*

¶ *Respect yourself and others will respect you.—Confucius*

¶ *The superior man is firm in the right way, and not merely firm.—Confucius*

¶ *An army of deer led by a lion is more to be feared than an army of lions led by a deer.—Philip of Macedon*

¶ *He that ruleth over men must be just.—II Sam.* 23

¶ *Everyone is bound to bear patiently the results of his own example.— Phaedrus*

¶ *Be swift to hear, slow to speak, slow to wrath.—James* 1:19

¶ *The wise man, before he speaks, will consider well what he speaks, to whom he speaks, and where and when.—St. Ambrose*

¶ *You may pardon much to others, nothing to yourself.—Ausonius*

¶ *Reason and calm judgment, the qualities specially belonging to a leader, —Tacitus*

¶ *Self-confidence is the first requisite to great undertakings.—Samuel Johnson*

¶ *Never to repent and never to reproach others, these are the first steps to wisdom.—Diderot*

¶ *Impossible is a word that I never utter.—Colin d'Harleville*

¶ *Nothing gives one person so much advantage over another as to remain always cool and unruffled under all circumstances.—Thomas Jefferson*

¶ *There are no bad regiments—only bad colonels.—Napoleon Bonaparte*

¶ *Correction does much but encouragement does more. Encouragement after censure is as the sun after a shower.—Goethe*

¶ *To the timid and hesitating, everything is impossible because it seems so.—Sir Walter Scott*

¶ *This world belongs to the energetic.—Emerson*
¶ *The man who trusts men will make fewer mistakes than he who distrusts them.—Conde di Cavour*
¶ *Death is light as a feather; duty, heavy as a mountain.—Emperor Meiji of Japan*

A Marine on duty has no friends.

—Marine Corps proverb

14 On Watch

One of the most stirring guard orders ever received by U. S. Marines was issued on 11 November 1921 by Navy Secretary Edwin Denby, himself a former Marine.

The nation was in the grip of a crime wave which had been highlighted by armed robberies of the U. S. Mails. Four days before Secretary Denby wrote his letter of instruction, the President had directed that the Marine Corps take over the job of safeguarding the mails, and 53 officers and 2,200 enlisted Marines were already on watch in post offices, railway mail cars, and postal trucks throughout the country. *"To the Men of the Mail Guard,"* wrote Edwin Denby:

I am proud that my old Corps has been chosen for a duty so honorable as that of protecting the United States mail. I am very anxious that you shall successfully accomplish your mission. It is not going to be easy work. It will always be dangerous and generally tiresome. You know how to do it. Be sure you do it well. I know you will neither fear nor shirk any duty, however hazardous or exacting.

This particular work will lack the excitment and glamor of war duty, but it will be no less important. It has the same element of service to the country.

I look with proud confidence to you to show now the qualities that have made the Corps so well beloved by our fellow citizens.

You must be brave, as you always are. You must be constantly alert. You must, when on guard duty, keep your weapons in hand and, if attacked, shoot and shoot to kill. There is no compromise in this battle with the bandits.

If two Marines, guarding a mail car, are suddenly covered by a robber, neither must hold up his hands, but both must begin shooting at once. One may be killed, but the other will get the robber and save the mail. When our men go in as guards over mail, that mail must be delivered or there must be a Marine dead at the post of duty.

To be sure of success, every Marine on this duty must be watchful as a cat, hour after hour, night after night, week after week. No Marine must drink a drop of intoxicating liquor. Every Marine must be most careful with whom he associates and what his occupations are off duty. There may be many tricks tried to get you, and you must not be tricked. Look out for women. Never discuss the details of your duty with outsiders. Never give up to another the trust you are charged with.

Never forget that the honor of the Corps is in your keeping. You have been given a great trust. I am confident you will prove that it has not been misplaced.

I am proud of you and believe in you with all my heart.

/s/ Edwin Denby

Mail robberies declined and ceased within a matter of days after Secretary Denby penned his order, and not a single piece of mail was lost to a robber while Marines stood watch.

Marine mail guards protected the United States mails from banditry in 1921 and 1926. Not a piece of mail was lost while Marines stood watch.

1401. WATCHSTANDING. THE IMPORTANCE OF GUARD DUTY. In the Marine Corps and Navy, the safety and good order of the entire command depend on those who stand guard. Thus, watchstanding is your strictest routine duty.

The importance of guard duty is underscored by the fact that sleeping on watch can be punished by death in time of war and in peace by heavy penalties.

In addition to combat missions, the Marine Corps is the security force for the Naval Establishment, as well as for the Department of State and for certain high-security establishments of the Department of Defense. The Corps is thus not only responsible for the good order and protection of its own posts, but also of all stations and ships where Marines are assigned. As a Marine, you are therefore expected to be an authority on watchstanding and guard duty, as well as a model watch-stander ashore or afloat.

Semper Fidelis never demands more than when you are on guard.

TYPES OF GUARDS. Marines maintain three kinds of guard:

Exterior guard ashore
Interior guard ashore
Ship's guard afloat

In addition, Marines frequently perform armed forces police and shore patrol duties for the regulation and assistance of Marines and seamen on liberty.

An *exterior guard* is maintained only in combat or when danger of attack exists. An exterior guard protects the command against outside attack. An exterior guard is organized and armed according to the tactical situation, in line with the principles laid down in *Field Service Regulations* (*FM 100-5*) covering security in combat.

Interior guards have the threefold mission of protecting life, preserving order and enforcing regulations, and safeguarding public property. In addition, the interior guard sometimes operates the brig.

Ship's guards carry out the same general missions afloat as interior guards do ashore, but differ in details of organization and duty because shipboard conditions and routine differ from those ashore. See Chapter 18.

STATUS OF MARINES ON WATCH. *Any Marine on guard, whether officer or enlisted, represents the commanding officer.* In the execution of orders or the enforcement of regulations, his authority is complete. When you receive a lawful order from a member of the guard, comply without hesitation and ask your questions afterward. Remember that a sentry has full authority to *enforce* his instructions.

The Interior Guard

1402. THE INTERIOR GUARD. You will find detailed instructions covering interior guard duty in the *Landing Party Manual, U. S. Navy.* Remember that these instructions, although similar in many respects to those prescribed for the Army in various manuals

291

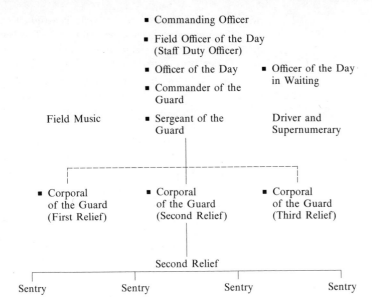

Fig. 14-1: Organization of a typical interior guard. There are as many sentries in each relief as there are posts. On a small station, the field officer of the day or staff duty officer may be omitted.

which you may encounter, nonetheless differ in a number of essentials. The *Landing Party Manual* is the bible on Marine Corps guard duty.

The interior guard—established to preserve order, protect life and property, and enforce regulations—derives its authority directly from the commanding officer. Figure 14-1 shows the organization of a typical interior guard. The guard is composed of a *main guard* and, when needed, *special guards* and *brig guards*—or "chasers."

1403. DUTIES OF THE GUARD. The duties of the guard (and the CO's responsibilities in connection with the guard) are as follows:

The Commanding Officer establishes the guard and sees that it functions properly. Either the CO or his representative (usually the executive officer or adjutant) receives the daily reports from and relieves the officers of the day, examines the guard book, and issues whatever special instructions may be needed.

The *Field Officer of the Day* may be required on a large post where subordinate commands maintain separate guards. The field officer of the day coordinates subordinate guards and acts for the post commander in emergency. On many stations, the field officer of the day is entitled "staff duty officer."

The *Officer of the Day* (*OD*) supervises the main guard (and, when directed, the brig guard), executes all orders that pertain to the guard, and is responsible that his guard performs effectively. On many small posts, where there are only a few officers assigned, staff noncommissioned officers may be assigned duty as officer of the day. If so detailed, you are the direct representative of the commanding officer. Your duties are discussed in Sections 1407-1411.

The *Officer of the Day in Waiting* is the officer next on the roster for duty as officer of the day. He must be prepared to relieve the OD should the latter become ill or for any reason be unable to continue his watch.

The *Commander of the Guard,* an officer (or NCO) junior to the officer of the day, is responsible for the proper instruction, discipline, and performance of the guard. A commander of the guard is usually required only for a large guard or required to afford new officers practical experience before detail as officers of the day. Duties of commander of the guard are covered in Section 1410.

The *Sergeant of the Guard,* whatever his actual rank, is the senior NCO of the guard. The sergeant of the guard assists the commander of the guard or, if the guard does not include one, performs the latter's duties. The sergeant of the guard supervises the enlisted members of the guard and is responsible for Government property charged to the guard.

Nonrated members of the guard are organized into three *reliefs,* each of which includes a sentinel for each post and is commanded by a *Corporal of the Guard.* The corporal of the guard instructs and supervises his relief, which takes its successive turn on guard throughout the tour of duty.

1404. DUTIES OF SENTINELS. A sentinel's duties are to carry out the *general orders for a sentinel on post,* as well as special orders applicable to his particular post.

In addition to routine sentry duties, non-rated members of the guard are assigned to certain special duties.

Guardhouse Sentinel (Post No. 1): When assigned, he assists the corporal of the guard in carrying on guardhouse routine and takes charge of prisoners in the brig (if administered by the guard). Your guardhouse sentinel should be picked for his intelligence, reliability, and smartness.

Main Gate Sentinel: He insures that only authorized persons enter or leave the post through the main gate; he also directs traffic and assists visitors. Your main gate sentry stands his watch in the showplace of the station; therefore select him for soldierly appearance, judgment, and thorough knowledge of the post. *The main gate is a spot for outstanding Marines.*

Field Music: The field music stays at the guardhouse. He sounds the prescribed bugle calls, strikes the bells, and acts as "timekeeper" and officer of the day's messenger. The music also polices the quarters of the officer of the day and officers of the guard.

Supernumerary: One additional man stands by as a supernumerary to replace any man who must be relieved. Like the music, the super-

Making the bells is the traditional duty of the field music of the guard who also acts as messenger.

numerary can be kept busy as a messenger and general factotum in the guardhouse.

Orderlies: When orderlies are needed, they are selected from outstanding privates of the guard on the basis of soldierly appearance and correct performance of duty. When selected as an orderly, a Marine is relieved of routine guard duty and reports to the officer to whom assigned.

Driver: A motor transport man is assigned to the guard to drive the guard truck. Always insure that the drivers (as well as other nonwatchstanders of the guard) maintain their personal appearance up to the standard expected of a Marine guard.

Color Sentinel: Whenever the unit Colors are broken out for airing—usually each Sunday and national holiday—a color sentinel is posted over them. If the Colors can be seen directly and close at hand from the guardhouse, a color sentinel is not mandatory, *if* the guardhouse sentinel can keep them under observation. The color sentinel guards the Colors, cases and protects them if the weather turns inclement, and acknowledges salutes rendered to the Colors (See Section 1511).

1405. DAILY GUARD ROUTINE. The daily routine of an interior guard varies somewhat according to the wishes of the commanding officer and the size and missions of the post. But, in the main, guard duty runs as follows.

The normal tour is 24 hours. Anyone detailed for guard duty must be on board and fit for duty at least four hours before commencement of his tour. No man going on watch should partake of alcoholic beverages during the preceeding eight hours.

Details for guard duty should be published well in advance, by written order, and should specify uniform and equipment which will be needed, together with any other information not covered in standing orders. *Persons detailed for guard duty must be notified in person or by written order, preferably both.* This is the adjutant's responsibility. He also keeps the officer-of-the-day roster.

A tour on guard begins with *guard mounting,* when the old (outgoing) and new (incoming) guards are paraded and inspected. Guard mount usually takes place immediately after Morning Colors. After guard mount, old and new officers of the day and sergeants of the guard relieve each other. Thereupon the officers of the day report

At guard mounting, the old and new guards are paraded and inspected.

to the commanding officer, and the new officer of the day assumes duty.

The guard's routine includes execution of Colors, posting and relief of sentinels, supervision of working details of prisoners (when a separate brig guard is not maintained), supervision of meal formations, and rendition of honors to the commanding officer, visiting officers, or civilian dignitaries.

1406. CHALLENGING AND COUNTERSIGN. *"Halt! Who goes there?"*, the traditional challenge, has been employed by Marines since 1775. You should know exactly how to challenge and reply, since a faulty challenge or reply may not only embarrass you, but in combat can cost someone his life.

The *challenge* is used at night or in low visibility to identify anyone approaching a sentinel.

On hearing any suspicious noise, the sentinel brings his weapon to a ready position, and commands, *"Halt! Who goes there?"* The person challenged halts and then identifies himself either by a password or by some such answer as *"Friend,"* or *"Officer of the Day."* The sentinel replies, *"Advance, Friend, and be recognized."* The person is allowed to approach near enough to the sentinel to be recognized and is halted again, at which time the sentinel examines him. When satisfied, the sentinel commands, *"Pass, Friend";* or, if being visited by the officer of the day, reports, *"Post Number . . . secure, Sir."*

It is extremely important, not only as military etiquette, but for your own safety, to reply audibly and promptly when challenged and to comply exactly with the sentry's orders. The sentry is the man behind the gun. You are *in front* of it.

Challenge and countersign (sometimes called the "password") are used to distinguish between friend and enemy. In the use of this procedure, which takes place only when prescribed by the commanding officer, the person or party approaching a sentry is challenged in the usual way, as described above. Then, after he has advanced the person for recognition, the sentry repeats the secret challenge, an agreed code word to which the person being challenged must respond with the countersign, a second code word which validates the reply. Challenge and countersign change daily and must be kept from the enemy at all costs. For detailed instructions on this important subject, see Chapter 5, section II, *Landing Party Manual.*

OD and Commander of the Guard

1407. OFFICER OF THE DAY AND COMMANDER OF THE GUARD. Since commander of the guard duties will take up much of your energies, you must be thoroughly familiar with Section II, Chapter 5, *Landing Party Manual,* as well as post standing orders which deal with guard duty.

1408. DUTIES OF THE OFFICER OF THE DAY. Should you be assigned as Officer of the Day (and therefore the CO's personal representative), you must be ready to act promptly and sensibly in any contingency not covered by the letter of your orders. This paragraph gives a listing of routine duties and responsibilities that you, as OD, will be expected to perform or meet.

Inspect each relief of the guard by visiting sentinels at *least once* while that relief is on post. *One inspection must take place between midnight and reveille.* When visiting sentinels, cover the following points:

Verify that the sentinel is on his post, alert, in correct uniform, and correctly armed and equipped.

Question the sentinel on his special orders and check particularly that he knows:

The limits and designation of his post,

Location of fire-fighting gear on the post, and how to sound a fire alarm,

Any recent changes in special orders for his post,

The reason why the post is required (his mission as a sentinel), and

Restrictions, if any, on use of his weapon.

Verify that he knows verbatim and understands the general orders for sentinels. Make him repeat several of these and explain them in his own words.

Supervise and coordinate the inspections to be made by your commander of the guard and sergeant of the guard. See that these do not conflict with or duplicate yours.

Take immediate steps, in an emergency, to protect life and public property and to preserve order. As soon as the situation permits, report what has happened and what you are doing about it to the commanding officer (or to the executive officer or to the staff duty officer if your post has one).

Always inform the guard where you can be reached when not in the guardhouse. If possible, leave a telephone extension.

Abstain from alcohol throughout your tour.

Unless otherwise authorized, remain fully clothed at all times. This enables you to turn out immediately in case of fire or other fast-moving emergency. Nothing can get an OD into more trouble than arriving late and drowsy at the scene of trouble.

Inspect galleys and messes, in accordance with local orders, at each meal during your watch. When you do this, look out for:

Cleanliness and sanitary conditions of the galley, messhall, and immediate areas outside (don't forget the garbage house),

Personal cleanliness (clothing, haircuts, fingernails) of cooks and messmen,

Quality and sufficiency of meals,

Adequacy of food service, and

Good order and proper uniform of troops being fed.

If the brig is under control of the guard, inspect the brig and prisoners. Before you do this, review the *Navy Brig Manual.* This contains the important rules for brig administration. Brigs and prisoners are "dynamite." Take care that every regulation is complied with. Give each prisoner an opportunity to make complaints. Do not sanction or hesitate to report to the commanding officer any violation of required brig procedure.

At guard mount, see that prisoners (other than general court-martial prisoners) whose sentences expire that day are released. Also report to the CO any prisoners confined with no record of charges against them.

Review the guard book before guard mount and correct any mistakes. In it, log the times when you visited sentries, together with any other information you think proper to place on record. Then attest the correctness of the entire report by signing the guard book.

1409. RELIEVING AS OFFICER OF THE DAY. After guard mount, old and new officers of the day inspect the guardhouse together and verify the count of prisoners (if under control of the main guard). After that, both report to the commanding officer for relief and posting.

March in, at attention, covered, and wearing side-arms and halt in front of the commanding officer (old OD on the right). You both salute together. Thereupon the old officer of the day says, "Sir, . . . reports as old officer of the day" and hands the guard book to the CO. The latter reads the guard report, asks any questions which come to mind, and comments as he thinks necessary. Then he informs the old officer of the day, "You are relieved." Thereupon the old OD salutes and withdraws. Then the new officer of the day again salutes, and says, "Sir, . . . reports as new officer of the day." The commanding officer gives the new officer of the day his instructions, whereupon the latter salutes and withdraws. All movements during relief and posting as officer of the day are carried out at attention and in cadence. If an emergency strikes between guard mount and the time when you report to the CO, the senior of the two ODs takes charge of both guards, old and new.

1410. DUTIES OF THE COMMANDER OF THE GUARD. The duties of commander of the guard are carried out by the sergeant of the guard if no commander of the guard is detailed. Regardless of whether performed by an officer or NCO, the following constitutes a useful checklist by which you can insure that your guard is running smoothly.

Inform your officer of the day of any orders which have come to you from anyone other than the OD. Pass on to your own relief all instructions and current information.

See that your guard is properly instructed and that it performs properly.

Make certain that all inspections (yours and the sergeant of the guard's) are carried out on time and as directed by the OD.

See that sentinels are relieved, Colors executed, the proper bugle calls sounded, bells struck, and guard routine followed.

Insure that legible copies of general and special orders for each post are mounted both in the guardhouse and under shelter on each post.

Inspect guardhouse and brig thoroughly at least once during your tour.

Inspect each relief of the guard while it is on post. Follow the procedure described in Section 1408. Like the officer of the day, you must make one inspection of sentinels between midnight and reveille.

Parade the guard for inspections as required. In an emergency, turn out the guard, sound the appropriate call or alarm, and promptly notify your officer of the day.

If any sentry calls, *"The Guard!"* send help immediately. This is the SOS for a sentinel on post. If he is in serious danger, he may fire his piece three times.

Like the officer of the day, you must keep the guard informed of your whereabouts whenever you leave the guardhouse—if possible, by a telephone number.

Report to the officer of the day if any member of the guard takes sick, quits his post, or has to be relieved for any reason.

It is up to you to keep the guard in prescribed uniforms and equipment.

Make up the details to execute Morning and Evening Colors and attend Colors to be certain that this ceremony is correctly performed. Insure that the Colors are properly stowed and are handled only in performance of duty. Finally, report to the OD if a set of Colors is unserviceable. See Sections 1517-1518.

Detain any suspicious persons and report the circumstances to the OD.

You are responsible for prisoners if held by the guard. This means that you must:

See that corporals of incoming and outgoing reliefs verify the prisoners,

Insure adequate search and medical examination of anyone being confined,

Report all confinements to the OD, and

Administer the brig in accordance with the *Brig Manual.*

Write your report in the guard book and, at the end of your tour, present the guard book to the OD.

1411. HINTS FOR THE OFFICER OF THE DAY. Of all Marines on the station, you are the one who can least tolerate any discrepancy, or violation of orders. *Never overlook a dereliction or infraction, however minor.* Be especially alert for:

Unmilitary behavior

Men out of uniform
Traffic offenders
Safety hazards
Unsanitary, unusual, or unsightly conditions
Improper safeguarding of or undue leniency toward prisoners
Security of restricted areas.

Keep closely posted on the movements and whereabouts of the commanding officer, the executive officer or a visiting senior officer. Try to see the post as it would appear through their eyes and act accordingly.

Be meticulous in bearing and conspicuous by your neatness, when on watch. A neat OD has a well turned-out guard. Keep your leather shining. Polish your brightwork and sword. Wear your best uniforms. Set an example for the whole command.

No matter how many times you have stood watch before, review the guard orders as soon as you take over. Changes have a way of sneaking in without warning. "That isn't the way it used to be," is no excuse for a bobble.

Prevent your guard from idling. See that they are instructed in guard orders and routine and especially in safety precautions. More so-called accidental discharges of firearms take place during guard duty than anywhere else. Sad but true, the overheads of many guardrooms are pockmarked by .45 caliber bullet-holes.

See that reliefs and sentinels are posted in military fashion, by the book.

Keep an eye on the Colors. Such avoidable fumbles as Colors unwittingly hoisted upside down have, on occasion, provided the hapless OD with several days' enforced leisure. Never allow Colors to become fouled or snarled about the pole or halyards.

Visualize every emergency which could happen during your watch. Decide *now* what you will do. What if fire breaks out? A prisoner escapes? A serious automobile accident occurs? Electric power or utilities fail? Disaster in nearby community? Be forehanded. Know your answer in advance.

Visit the main gate during rush hours. Let yourself be seen and let the main gate guards know you are on hand to back them up.

Be unfailingly courteous, especially to civilians and visitors. The good name of the post is in your hands when you are on watch.

Avoid gumshoeing. It is one of your main functions to be seen.

Enforce orders to the hilt. If an order is unwise, impractical, or out of date, the best way to get it modified is to enforce it and to report that you are doing so. Never slough over an order because *you* think it is a "dead letter."

See that enlisted members of the guard deal with drunks. This is important because it may save the drunken man from some offense that would be more serious if done toward an officer. Never allow a drunk to be roughly treated and, above all, *never confine a supposed drunk without medical examination.* It is easy to confuse seeming intoxication with the symptoms of serious head injury.

Be immediately accessible at all hours. Don't let members of the guard, however well-meaning, interpose themselves between you and any sober caller, whether in person or by telephone. You never know who may be calling.

Finally, run your guard the way you know it should be run. You have the responsibility, backed up by almost unlimited authority. If the guard is below standard, you have only yourself to blame.

Charge-of-Quarters

1412. DUTIES OF CHARGE-OF-QUARTERS. The *Charge-of-Quarters,* as you know, performs duties in a company or battery or separate platoon, which are comparable at that level to those of the officer of the day for a larger command. The charge-of-quarters is simply the duty noncommissioned officer of a small unit. His primary job is to insure orderly functioning of the unit routine at times when the company office is secured. His specific duties will vary according to the unit's circumstances and the desires of the commanding officer and first sergeant.

The charge-of-quarters is detailed by roster, usually from among the sergeants of a company, except that in headquarters or other special-type companies or batteries with a high proportion of staff NCOs, junior SNCOs may be so assigned, though this is undesirable. The tour of duty is normally 24 hours, with charge-of-quarters on standby status in the company area during normal working hours when the company office is manned.

After working hours, the charge-of-quarters maintains a telephone watch in the company office, except when required to absent himself on other duties. His duties may include but are not limited to:

Inspect and check liberty men in and out,
Maintain fire watch in unit area,
See that storerooms and offices are properly secured,
Turn standing lights on and off as required by unit routine,
Carry out bunk checks,
Verify the presence of PALs and restricted men,
Insure that men assigned extra police duties carry out their tasks,
See that unit routine and special orders are meticulously executed and complied with,
Wake up messmen or any other special-duty men or details as required,
Provide bunk space and, if necessary, arrange hot meal for men joining after working hours,
Report to higher authority and take necessary action on any emergency or unusual occurrence, and
Maintain charge-of-quarters log.

Like the officer of the day, the charge-of-quarters should remain fully clothed at all times and, needless to say, may not partake of alcohol at any time while on watch.

The first sergeant posts and relieves the charge-of-quarters, receiving any special reports, verifying the log, and issuing special instructions as necessary to the new charge-of-quarters.

Military Police and Shore Patrol

1413. MILITARY POLICE AND SHORE PATROL. Whenever troops go ashore on liberty, it is customary to provide military police (MPs), whose job is:

To assist the civil authorities in dealing with men of the armed forces,
To maintain discipline and good behavior among Marines and blue-jackets ashore, and
To aid and safeguard liberty men in every possible way.

This duty is described as "military police" when performed by a Marine organization; when a ship or Navy shore station provides such a guard, it is known as "shore patrol." Shore patrol routine and duties are covered in the *Navy Shore Patrol Manual*. In a few places where large military populations are present from all services, a joint patrol is organized with the title, "Armed Forces Police Detachment."

Where permanent need exists, the military police or shore patrol are organized about a full-time cadre of specially selected officers and enlisted men. A permanent MP detachment is usually administered by a provost marshal and is known as a "provost guard," whereas a corresponding Navy unit is called the "permanent shore patrol" and is headed by a "senior patrol officer," either a Navy or Marine officer.

Although local conditions vary markedly, MP and SP detachments generally perform the following tasks:

"Town patrol" of areas frequented by liberty men. This patrol is made up of noncommissioned or petty officers who work in pairs. When both bluejackets and Marines are on liberty, one patrolman should be a Marine NCO, and the other a Navy petty officer. This permits offenders to be dealt with by members of their own services.

Maintain close liaison with municipal authorities—primarily, the police, but not overlooking the other emergency services and the prosecuting attorney.

Operate aid stations where liberty men may obtain emergency medical treatment and venereal prophylaxis.

Supervise boat landings and patrol transportation points used by military and naval personnel.

A footnote on dealings with the military police or shore patrol: Never resist, obstruct, or fail to cooperate with a shore patrolman or MP, even if he comes from the Army or Air Force. Under joint regulations, MPs and SPs have all-service authority, with power to enforce any lawful acts or instructions. If you have any complaints, make them via military channels to the proper superior authorities.

1414. HINTS ON MP AND SP DUTY Military police or patrol duty carries the same kind of problems and responsibilities as guard duty, and, in general the instructions in Sections 1408 and 1410-1411 (the last section especially) apply, at least in spirit, to MPs and SPs. Even at the expense of repetition, however, the following points should be kept firmly in mind:

When on patrol, make yourself a model Marine in every respect —outstanding in dress, irreproachable in bearing and conduct, and courteous but firm in execution of your orders. "Fair, firm, and formal" are the "three Fs" of a successful watch officer, MP, or sentry.

Remember that you are a *military* policeman. Don't permit your men to assert police authority over civilians. That is a job for the civilian police.

Never imbibe alcohol while on MP or SP duty. It is a long-standing Naval custom that the least evidence that an MP or SP has partaken of alcohol while on duty demands a court-martial. The temptations of military policy duty are manifold; the least failing is fatal.

Make yourself and your men conspicuous to liberty men and townspeople alike. This helps to hold down violations and gives assurance to all that the situation is well in hand. Insure that your men are outstanding in every respect. Bear down on them.

If possible, have medical assistance ready at hand. Should your patrol not include a doctor or corpsman, know where you can get medical aid and how to get it without delay.

Get on easy working terms with the local police. Cooperate sincerely with them and they will do the same with you. *Be unfailingly courteous toward civilians.*

If in a foreign port, obtain a trustworthy interpreter who knows the local customs. Try to select men who know the language.

For reasons given in Section 1411, try to keep drunks out of contact with officers. Be sure to give a medical examination to any seemingly intoxicated prisoner.

Handle prisoners "by the book." Allow no undue force, "third degree," or abusive behavior toward a prisoner, no matter how he provokes you. Unauthorized treatment is not only unworthy of the Marine Corps but a sure road to trouble.

Avoid disorderly public scenes, prolonged disputes, or heated brawls. Get troublemakers, noisemakers, or contrary-minded "ferninsters" back to headquarters, out of the public eye, and deal with them in private.

Know your orders, *Navy Regulations,* and *Uniform Code of Military Justice,* down to the last comma.

Above all, exercise common sense and tact. It is your job to prevent trouble as well as to quell it. When you see a Marine or bluejacket in difficulty, ask yourself, *"How can I help this man?"*

Law, order, duty and restraint, obedience, discipline . . .

—Rudyard Kipling, M'Andrew's Hymn

15 Military Courtesy and Ceremonies

Military Courtesy

Military courtesy is the traditional form of politeness in the profession of arms. Though sharing many elements with courtesy in civilian life, military courtesy stems firmly from a traditional code of rules and customs. Just as courtesy in general is said to be "the lubricant of life," so military courtesy helps to ease us along well-worn, tried, and customary paths. Since by its nature, the life and discipline of the service is formal, so the form of courtesy used by military men must be formal, too.

Military courtesy embraces much more than the salute or any other ritual, important as these are. *Courtesy is a disciplined attitude of mind.* It must be accorded to all ranks and on all occasions. Courtesy to a senior indicates respect for authority, responsibility, and experience. Courtesy toward a junior expresses appreciation and respect for his support and for him as a fellow Marine. Courtesy paid to the Colors and to the National Anthem expresses loyalty to the United States and to the Constitution which we are sworn to uphold and defend, as well as pride and respect for the principles for which those symbols and our country stand.

Military courtesy is a prerequisite to discipline. It promotes the willing obedience and unhesitating cooperation which make a good outfit "click." When ordinary acts of military courtesy are performed grudgingly or omitted, discipline suffers. Discipline and courtesy alike stem from *esprit de corps*. Both are essential factors which help to transform civilians into Marines.

The best fighting outfits can be readily recognized by their standards of military courtesy. The Marine Corps has always stood at the top among the services by full and willing observance of the twin virtues of soldierly courtesy and discipline.

1501. CONDUCT TOWARD MEMBERS OF OTHER SERVICES. The details of military courtesy vary little from service to service, and from nation to nation. As a Marine (and therefore, as a *professional*), you must learn the meaning and traditions behind the badges, insignia, and titles of the officers and enlisted men of other military services, both American and foreign.

When you go to duty with another Service or in another country, make it a particular point to know and defer to the customs and traditions of that service or country. On the other hand, *never forget that you are a Marine,* never feel self-conscious about holding fast to Marine Corps standards of uniform or to the Marine way of doing and saying things. Remember that in every action, great or small, you represent the Corps.

1502. MILITARY TITLES, PHRASEOLOGY, AND ADDRESS. Every Marine should know, use, and enforce the use of the correct Marine Corps terms and phrases for things. In these days of unification, Marines should also be very careful not to pick up inappropriate terms and phrases from other services, even if we do serve alongside them. (This, of course, does not apply to the Navy, which is our partner in the Naval Establishment.)

Addressing Officers. It is an old-time soldierly tradition that, when you address an officer, you speak in the third person; for example, "Would the Lieutenant care to check these rifles now?" or "Sir, Sergeant Major Janson reports for duty," or "If I were the Lieutenant, I'd look out. Here comes the Captain."

Speaking to Juniors. To promote subordination and respect among your juniors, address them by name *and* rank. Avoid casual use of first names or nicknames. Formality in speaking to a subordinate is never wrong whereas informality may compromise your position. In particular, never permit disrespectful reference to an absent officer or NCO on the part of a junior.

Although both first and second lieutenants may, by regulation, be spoken of as "Mr.", the fine point of distinction between the two ranks is to speak of and to a second lieutenant as "Mr." while reserving "Lieutenant" for a first lieutenant. In the presence of junior enlisted men, however, it is best to speak of any lieutenant (first or second) as "lieutenant."

Navy officers below commander are also addressed as "Mr." Although some lieutenant commanders like to be called "Commander," this is not only not required but is wrong. On the other hand, lieutenant colonels should be addressed as "Colonel."

Generals and admirals, of whatever grade are spoken to as "General" or "Admiral."

Where the male officer is addressed as "sir," a woman officer may be addressed as "ma'am," or by rank, as "Yes, Major," or "Good morning Lieutenant." Women warrant officers and company grade officers may be addressed informally as "Miss" (or "Mrs."), as may nurses below the grade of commander.

Medical and dental officers below the rank of commander may be addressed as "Doctor."

Chaplains of any rank should preferably be addressed as "Chaplain," except that Roman Catholic chaplains (and Episcopal chaplains who so prefer) should be addressed as "Father."

While the first sergeant of a unit may be *privately* addressed by officers of the unit as "Top," he should always be spoken to and of as "First Sergeant" by all other enlisted Marines (as well as by officers in public or on formal occasions). The Army title, "top sergeant," should not be used at any time by Marines.

Any NCO above corporal may be informally addressed as "sergeant," but it is better to give him his exact rank. Similarly, when an enlisted man speaks of himself or to or of another enlisted man, he should do so by rank—"*Lance Corporal* Daly," not just "Daly."

Drummers and trumpeters (but not bandsmen), regardless of rank, are addressed as "Music" and are spoken of collectively as "field musics."

Navy chief petty officers are habitually spoken to as "Chief."

Hospital corpsmen of rank equal to yours, or junior to you, may be addressed as "Doc."

TERMS AND USAGES TO BE AVOIDED. In recent years as a result of unification, certain undesirable terms from outside the Marine Corps and Navy have been picked up by a few individuals and used instead of the authentic Marine Corps way of talking. Here are several that you should avoid in your own conversation and keep junior Marines from using:

Trooper: Do not speak of Marines as "troopers." This is an Army term going back to the horse cavalry or, today, to the paratroopers and airborne, or the state highway patrol. Marines should be referred to collectively as "Marines" or, less formally, in the Marine usage going back to Tun Tavern, as "people." (Example: "You people better square yourselves away before the Old Man gets here" or "Corporal Stevenson, what in hell are your people up to over there?")

ZI: Use "Conus" or just "the United States."

GI: Say "squared-away" or "regulation". *Never* refer to another Marine as "a GI."

EM: Just say "enlisted man." Even better, say "Marine."

Member: Do not use when referring to any person in the Marine Corps or Navy. No Marine is ever "a member."

TDY: Although this Army/Air Force abbreviation appears on many joint forms, you should always use the correct Navy/Marine abbreviation, "TAD."

Hitch: Say "cruise" or "enlistment." "Hitch" is another Army term going back to the horse cavalry.

"The Military": Avoid this unflattering civilian term for anybody in uniform. Speak and think of yourself as being in "the Service," never "the military."

E-4 (or other similar ways of speaking of rank). Never speak of a Marine or sailor as "an E-3" or "an E-6," etc. This is as bad as

Fig. 15-1: Correct forms of address for naval and military personnel.

Person Addressed or Introduced	To Military Personnel		To Civilian	
	Introduce as:	*Address as:*	*Introduce as:*	*Address as:*
MARINE, ARMY or AIR FORCE OFFICER (Capt. or above)	Major (or other rank) Smith	(same)	Major (or other rank) Smith[1]	(same)
NAVAL OFFICER (Comdr. or above)	Captain (or other rank) Smith	(same)	Captain (or other rank) Smith[1]	(same)
MARINE, ARMY or AIR FORCE OFFICER (First Lieutenant or below)	Mr. Smith	(same)	Lieutenant Smith[1]	Mr. Smith
NAVAL OFFICER (Lt. Comdr. or below)	Mr. Smith	(same)	Lt. Comdr. (or other rank) Smith, Dr. Smith	Mr. Smith / Dr. Smith[3]
WOMEN OFFICER (Capt. USMC, or Comdr. or above)	Capt., Comdr. (or other rank) Smith[2]	(same)	Capt., Comdr. (or other rank) Smith[2]	(same)
WOMAN OFFICER (First Lieutenant, or Lt. Comdr. or below)	Lieutenant Smith Warrant Officer Smith, etc.	Miss (Mrs.) Smith / Miss (Mrs.) Smith	Warrant Officer (or other rank) Smith[1]	Miss (Mrs.) Smith
NAVY STAFF CORPS OFFICER (Comdr. or above)	Comdr. Smith[3] / Chaplain Smith[3]	(same) / (same)	Comdr. Smith[3] / Chaplain Smith[3]	(same) / (same)
COAST GUARD AND COAST AND GEODETIC SURVEY OFFICER	Same as for the same rank in the Navy[4]	(same)	(same)	(same)

	(cut off)	(cut off)	(cut off)	(cut off)	(cut off)
OFFICER (M.D. or D.D.S.)				Dr. Smith of the Public Health Service	Dr. Smith
U.S. PUBLIC HEALTH SERVICE OFFICER (Sanitary Engineer)	Mr. Smith[4]		(same)	Mr. Smith of the Public Health Service	Mr. Smith
COMMISSIONED WARRANT OFFICER[5]	Chief Warrant Officer Smith[5] or Chief Marine Gunner Smith		(same)[5] or Gunner Smith	Warrant Officer Smith[5] or Chief Marine Gunner Smith	Mr. Smith[5] or Gunner Smith
MIDSHIPMAN OR CADET	Midshipman (or Aviation Cadet) Smith.		Mr. Smith	Midshipman (or Aviation Cadet) Smith	Mr. Smith
WARRANT OFFICER[5]	Warrant Officer Smith[5] or Marine Gunner Smith		(same)[5] or Mr. Smith	Warrant Officer Smith[5] or Marine Gunner Smith	Mr. Smith[5] or Gunner Smith
STAFF NCO[6] OR CHIEF PETTY OFFICER	Sergeant Major Smith,[6] Chief Machinist's Mate Smith		Sergeant Major Smith[5] or Chief	Sergeant Major Smith,[6] Chief Machinist's Mate Smith	(same)[6]
NON-COMMISSIONED OFFICER OR PETTY OFFICER	Corporal Smith, Smith, Gunner's Mate, Second		Corporal or Smith	Gunner's Mate Smith, Corporal Smith, or Petty Officer Smith	(same)
PRIVATE OR SEAMAN	Private (or Seaman) Smith		Private Smith or Smith	Private Smith or Seaman Smith	(same)
ENLISTED WOMAN	Corporal (or Yeoman) Smith		(same)	Corporal (or Yeoman) Smith	(same)

[1] When not in uniform, an officer should be introduced as "of the Navy" or "of the Marine Corps" to distinguish his rank from similar-sounding ranks in the other armed services. Suggested phraseology: "This is Lieutenant Smith of the Marine Corps. Mr. Smith is now stationed at Camp Pendleton." Such a form of introduction indicates the officer's rank, service, and how to address him. (But see paragraph 1502 on the distinction in address between first and second lieutenants.)

[2] When status of a woman is not clear, add "of the Medical Corps," "of the Navy Nurse Corps," "of the Women Marines," etc.

[3] Add "of the Medical Corps," "of the Civil Engineer Corps," or other corps, when helpful to indicate status of officer. If a senior officer of the Medical Corps prefers to be addressed as "Doctor," such preference should be honored. Some senior members of the Chaplain's Corps prefer to be addressed by their rank, but it is always correct to address a Chaplain of any rank as Chaplain. See paragraph 1502.

[4] In any case where there is reason to believe that the officer's insignia might not be recognized, it is correct to add, "of the Public Health Service," "of the Coast Guard," or "of the Coast and Geodetic Survey."

[5] Male Marine Corps warrant officers appointed in Line occupational fields bear the title of (Chief) Marine Gunner.

[6] All staff NCOs are addressed by their particular titles, e.g., "Gunnery Sergeant Hays," "Master Sergeant Wodarczyk," "Staff Sergeant Basilone," etc.

calling him "a member." Give people their correct ranks. You can be an E-7 in the Army or Air Force, but only a Marine can be a gunnery sergeant, and only a bluejacket can be a chief boatswain's mate.

"Career" (as in "career NCO"). Just say "Regular," and don't forget that capital *R*.

Medic or Aid Man. These are other Army/Air Force terms for a hospital corpsman. Always say "corpsman," *never* "Medic" or "aid man."

Hours. The Commandant has expressly prohibited the Army practice of suffixing the unnecessary word, "hours," after each indication of the time of day. Say or write, "1200," never "1200 *hours.*"

1503. POINTERS ON MILITARY ETIQUETTE. This section compiles a miscellany of Marine Corps and Navy customs, courtesies, and points of etiquette, some written, others unwritten—but all important for you to know and observe.

The CO's "Wishes." When your commanding officer says, "I wish," "I desire," "I would like," or similar expressions, these have the force of a direct order and should be complied with on that basis.

Accompanying a Senior. The position of honor for one's senior is on the right. Therefore, in company with a senior, you walk, ride, and sit on the left. When entering a vehicle or a boat, you embark first and take the less desirable places in the middle or on "jump" or front seats (or forward in a boat); when debarking, the senior leaves first, while juniors follow in order of rank.

When a senior is inspecting, he is followed by the immediate commander of the unit being inspected, who remains on the senior's left, one pace to the rear—*except* that, during inspection of troops in formation, the immediate commander remains on the *right* of the inspecting officer and *precedes* him while inspecting in ranks. For other pointers on inspections, turn to Chapter 13.

Acknowledging Orders. When a Marine receives orders or instructions from an officer, he replies, "Aye, aye, sir." This phrase, which descends from the earliest days of the Marine Corps and Navy, is used in both services. It means: *"I understand the orders I have received and will carry them out."* Never permit a Marine to acknowledge an order by "Very well," "All right," "Yes," or "OK."

Mounted Juniors dismount before addressing or reporting to seniors, except when in the field. Even then, however, dismount if practicable. This applies to vehicles as well as horses.

When You Meet a Senior Indoors, either in a passageway or on a stairway, give way smartly and promptly. If he is a general or a flag officer, halt and stand at attention with your back to the bulkhead until he has passed. Enlisted men should halt at attention until any passing officer is clear.

When Sent for by a Senior, juniors must report immediately and in correct uniform. If in the field, on the drill field, or on parade ground, it is customary for juniors to proceed and report at the double.

When an Officer enters a room or passes close aboard unorganized groups either indoors or outside, the senior NCO of the group or groups commands "Attention!" All hands come to attention and remain so until the officer has passed. If out of doors and covered, all hands salute.

Uncovering Under Arms. The only exception to the rule that Marines under arms never uncover, is at divine service, such as a wedding, when officers and NCOs may wear swords and still uncover. You do not unsheathe your sword inside a church, however, unless express authority is granted by an appropriate religious functionary.

Permission to Speak to Senior Officers. When one of your people wishes to speak to the company or detachment commander, he first obtains the first sergeant's permission. If he desires to speak to an officer of still higher rank or position, he must in turn have his company or detachment commander's permission. When permission has been duly granted, the Marine reports, "Sir, Private Quick has the first sergeant's (*or* Captain McCawley's) permission to speak to the company commander (*or* to the battalion commander)."

The reasoning behind this procedure is that the first sergeant or CO can probably solve the problem satisfactorily by himself without the matter having to go higher.

Entering an Office. Men entering any office should be required to observe the following procedure, regardless of whether an officer is in the office or not:

1. Knock;
2. Enter and stand at attention immediately inside doorway, uncovered (unless under arms);
3. Identify himself by name and rank, and state business.

   Note: Never enter an office while you are smoking, and do not smoke inside unless invited to do so by the senior person in the office. This applies even if other office personnel are smoking at their desks.

Delivering Messages. When you are given a message to deliver, you should always follow the customary forms of address (even, for example, if a new officer who entrusts you with the message or the reply, forgets to do so).

The originator of a verbal message should always include "compliments" to any junior officer and "respects" to a senior. *Examples:*

1. The company commander, a captain, sends a message to one of the platoon leaders: "Music, my compliments to Lieutenant Gale, and will he please . . . "
2. The lieutenant replies, "Runner, present my respects to Captain Biddle, and report that . . . "

After a message has been delivered, the messenger should report that fact to the officer who sent the message; for example, "Sir, your message has been delivered. Captain Zeilin presents his respects. The guard will be paraded at 1000."

On the Telephone. Use moderate and respectful tones and identify yourself and your organization. Be brief. For example, in answering a call: "Company B, 5th Marines, First Sergeant Osborn". *Never* "Hello."

When using a field telephone, always be sure to ring off at the end of a conversation.

Except in emergency or when specifically ordered to do so, you should not telephone an officer, but should present yourself in person. It is the senior's privilege to phone someone more junior.

Arrival and Departure of the CO. If you are the first sergeant or sergeant major, you should, unless specifically excused, be on hand when the CO leaves or returns to the command, day or night.

On a Ladder or Stairway. When you encounter any senior, officer or NCO, on a stairway, in a passageway, or in a doorway, you should always give way. If you encounter an officer on a stairway, you should halt and remain at attention until the officer passes.

During Training or Exercises. When drilling or instructing your people on the parade ground or in a training area and when closely approached by an officer, you should come to attention, salute, and advise the officer what you are doing—"Battery F, 15th Marines, sighting and aiming exercises, Sir."

Similarly, on the drill field, never cut across the front of a unit commanded by a senior, thus causing him to halt or mark time, even if you may feel you have the right-of-way.

Salutes and Saluting

1504. THE MILITARY SALUTE. *Marines and the Salute.* It is a matter of pride among Marines, from general to private, to salute willingly, promptly and proudly.

Especially since World War II (when saluting was misguidedly de-emphasized in some of the services), the good Marine has stood out among the other services by his smart, correct, and cheerful salute, which is as much a hallmark of the Corps as the Globe and Anchor. When you salute or receive a salute, you mark yourself as a Marine who has pride in himself and in his Corps. Moreover, the hand salute is perhaps the most difficult movement to execute *right;* so the sharp, correct salute indicates to all that you are a Marine and therefore a professional.

As a noncommissioned officer you must recognize and teach that the salute is a privilege enjoyed only by military men and is a mutual acknowledgement of comradeship in the profession of arms.

ORIGINS OF SALUTING. Over the centuries, men-at-arms have rendered fraternal and respectful greetings to indicate friendliness. In early times, armed men raised their weapons or shifted them to the left hand (while raising the empty right hand) to give proof of amicable intentions. During the Middle Ages, knights in armor, on encountering friendly knights, raised their helmet visors in recognition. If they were in the presence of feudal superiors, the helmet was usually doffed. In every case, the fighting man made a gesture of friendliness—the raising of the empty right hand. This gesture survives as today's hand salute, which is the traditional greeting among soldiers of all nations.

Like the original hand salute and doffing of the cap, the discharge of weapons, presentation of arms, and lowering of the point of the sword were all intended to signify good will. In every case, the one so saluting, in good faith, momentarily rendered himself incapable of using his weapon offensively. The descendants of these earlier gestures are the modern sword salute, present arms, and gun salutes.

WHOM TO SALUTE. All military men must salute when they encounter and recognize any person who rates a salute, under circumstances in which the salute is required. An individual with the true soldierly instinct never misses an opportunity to salute a senior. *Those entitled to salutes are:*

1. All commissioned and warrant officers of the Army, Marine Corps, Navy, Air Force, and Coast Guard; of the Reserve components of those services; and of the National Guard.
2. Officers of friendly foreign powers.
3. In addition, by service custom though not by regulation, we salute any high civilian official who is entitled to honors by *Navy Regulations;* and ladies, on occasions when, if in civilian clothes, the hat would be raised or tipped. *Never tip your headgear when in uniform;* substitute a salute.

Officers of the same rank exchange salutes on meeting. The first one to recognize the other initiates the salute.

Enlisted men salute other enlisted men only in formation when rendering reports. However, it is most proper for any military man, regardless of rank, to exchange salutes with any other, since the salute is a shared soldierly greeting of all hands, regardless of rank. Prisoners may not salute or wear the Marine Corps Emblem.

DEFINITIONS. The following definitions apply to Marine Corps saluting procedure:

Out-of-doors means "In the open air; or the interior of such buildings as drill halls and gymnasiums when used for drill or exercises of troops; or on the weather decks of a man-of-war; or under roofed structures such as lanais, covered walks, and shelters open at one or both sides to the weather." It is synonymous with "on the topside," when used afloat.

Indoors means "The interior of any building ashore, other than a drill hall, gymnasium, or armory."

Between decks means "Any shipboard space below a weather deck, other than officers' country."

312   *Covered* and *uncovered* means "When and when not wearing headgear."

Under arms: A Marine is under arms when he has a weapon in his hand, is equipped with sidearms, or when he is wearing equipment pertaining to an arm, such as a sword sling, pistol belt, or cartridge belt. Any Marine wearing an "MP" or "SP" brassard is considered under arms.

Saluting distance means "The maximum distance within which salutes are rendered and exchanged," prescribed as 30 paces. This figure is considered to be one within which recognition of insignia is possible and to be approximately that within which friends or acquaintances can recognize and greet each other. The salute should be rendered when six paces from the person (or Color) to be saluted. If the person or Color to be saluted obviously will not approach within this distance, the salute is rendered at the point of nearest approach.

1505. HAND SALUTES. *Significance.* In some services, the hand salute has been de-emphasized almost to the vanishing point, based on an erroneous belief that rendition of a salute, rather than being an act of courtesy and soldierly recognition, signifies inferiority and subservience. Nothing could be further from the truth. As in civil life, "on the outside," where you render courtesy to older or more important persons, so, as a junior Marine, you salute first. In returning your salute, the senior in turn salutes you as a brother in arms. Thus, the exchange of hand salutes is a two-way street.

The manner and enthusiasm with which you render or receive a salute indicate the state of your training, your individual *esprit,* the discipline of your outfit, and your quality as a Marine.

Correct saluting habits characterize a good Marine.

How to Execute the Hand Salute. Salute at quick time only. If you are at the double and must salute or receive a salute, slow to quick time. Stand or walk at attention: head up, chin in, and stomach pulled in. When halted, come to attention distinctly as a preliminary motion to the salute; bring your heels together audibly. Look directly at the person or Color you are saluting. If walking or riding, turn your head smartly toward the person being saluted and catch his eye. Execute the first movement, holding position until the salute is acknowledged or until you see that it is not going to be, then complete the salute by bringing your hand down smartly. When doing this, keep your fingers extended and joined, your thumb streamlined alongside. In returning a salute, execute the two counts at marching cadence.

In the Marine Corps and Navy it is customary to exchange a greeting with a salute. The junior should always say, "Good morning (or evening), sir," and the senior should unfailingly reply in the same vein—with a smile.

In the Marine Corps and Navy one does not salute when uncovered—that is, when not wearing headgear. The only exception to this rule is that the salute *may* be rendered uncovered when, in a special circumstance, not to salute might cause misunderstanding. For example, when serving with the Army or Air Force (who *do* salute uncovered), you may, if you wish, depart from the Naval procedure but beware of contracting the habit.

If carrying a swagger stick during receipt or rendition of a salute, hold the stick snugly under your left arm, large end forward, exactly parallel to the deck, with your left arm in normal position at your side, not swinging.

How Not to Salute. A sloppy, grudging salute, or a childish pretence not to notice anyone to whom a salute is due, indicates unmilitary attitude, lack of pride in self and Corps, and plain ignorance. Evasive, unmilitary saluting betrays the amateur; a sharp, keen salute distinguishes the professional.

Have you ever seen a Marine who amounted to anything who was ragged in his saluting?

Never salute with pipe or cigarette in your right hand or your mouth. If you are chewing tobacco or gum, bring your jaws to rest during the exchange of salutes. As under any other circumstances, it is highly unmilitary to be caught saluting with one hand in your pocket, your blouse unbuttoned, or your cap not squared.

Avoid—and, as a noncommissioned officer, *never tolerate*—trick salutes. The commonest faults are:

Right wrist bent
Left elbow stuck out at exaggerated, unnatural angle
Palm turned inward, knuckles kept forward
Fingers of right hand bent and flexed inward
Right thumb extended away from fingers
Hips thrust forward and shoulders swayed back.

When you find a Marine doing any of these things, no matter how hard he seems to be trying, correct him on the spot, and see that he knows and practices the correct way to salute.

1506. RIFLE SALUTES. The rifle salute, as you know, may be executed from the following positions:

Right or left shoulder arms
Order arms
Trail arms
Present arms

Any individual under arms with the rifle salutes by one of the foregoing rifle salutes. The only occasion where a hand salute is executed by a man with a rifle is when the rifle is at "sling arms."

In its four forms, the rifle salute is rendered as follows under the conditions given:

Right or left shoulder arms—when out-of-doors, at a halt or at a walk
Order arms—when at a halt, either indoors or out-of-doors.
Trail arms—when at a walk, indoors or out-of-doors.

Fig. 15-2: Rifle salutes at: A right-shoulder arms; B order arms;

Presenting arms is a special compliment, as a Marine at present arms
represents the authority of the nation. The privilege of saluting
by presenting arms is reserved for troops in formation and for
sentinels on post.

Marines armed with a slung weapon use the hand salute only and,
when so saluting, carry the piece at sling arms, with the left hand
grasping the sling to steady the weapon.

1507. SWORD SALUTES AND MANUAL. You will find the
manual of the sword described in Chapter 2, the *Landing Party
Manual,* while further information on the sword is given in Section
1515-1516. Every Marine Officer and NCO takes pride in being pre-

C trail arms;   *and D present arms.*

cise, dexterous, and at ease with his sword.

When armed with the sword, you render or return salutes in the following ways:

RENDERING THE SALUTE:

1. *If your sword is sheathed* and you are not in formation, execute the normal hand salute.
2. *If your sword is drawn and you are halted,* either in or out of formation, execute present sword as prescribed in the manual of the sword. If commanding a formation, which will usually be the case when your sword is drawn, bring your troops to attention before you do so.

3. *If your sword is drawn and you are underway in formation,* execute the sword salute, having first brought your command to attention, if necessary.

WHEN YOU ARE RETURNING A SALUTE:

1. *If your sword is sheathed,* acknowledge by the hand salute.
2. *If your sword is drawn,* acknowledge by the sword salute.

1508. INDIVIDUAL SALUTING ETIQUETTE. *Whether to Salute Once or Twice.* After an officer has been saluted initially, if he remains nearby and no conversation takes place, no further salutes are required.

When a junior is spoken to by or addresses a senior officer, he salutes initially, and again when the conversation ends or the senior leaves. Throughout the conversation, the junior stands at attention unless otherwise directed by the senior.

Reporting, Indoors. When you report indoors to an officer senior to you, unless under arms, you uncover, place your cap (visor forward) under your left arm, knock, and enter when told to do so. Two paces in front of the senior, halt and report, "Sir, Gunnery Sergeant Jansen reports to Major Russell." Remain at attention unless told to carry on or to be seated. On being dismissed, take one backstep, halt, then face about, and march out. If under arms, remain covered and salute on reporting and again on being dismissed. The latter salute is rendered after completion of your backstep.

After entering, do not report until recognized by the officer and until he has completed whatever business he may have in hand.

Enlisted Men Not in Formation. When an officer approaches enlisted men who are not in formation, the first to recognize him calls the group to attention as soon as the officer comes within ten paces. Out-of-doors, if covered (as they should be), all men salute when the officer is within six paces. The salute is held until returned. The men remain at attention until the officer has passed or until he commands, "Carry on."

Overtaking. When you overtake an officer proceeding in the same direction, draw abreast on the left, coming to the salute as you do so, and say, "By your leave, Sir." The officer acknowledges the salute and replies, "Granted."

When you overtake a Marine junior to you, pass on the right.

Indoors. Marines not under arms do not salute indoors. When an officer is present, enlisted men uncover in lieu of saluting. See Section 1504. *In an office,* however, men need not cease work when an officer enters unless called to attention. When addressed by an officer, the person so addressed should rise.

In the Mess Hall. Men at meals do not rise when called to attention, but stop eating and keep silent. If spoken to by an officer, an enlisted man gets to his feet and stands at attention. If not under arms, be sure to uncover when you enter a galley, mess hall, or ship's messing compartment.

At the Pay Table. Men not under arms uncover before approaching the pay table, and do not salute. A Marine under arms salutes the paymaster when front and center of the pay table, and again after receiving his pay before moving off. The paymaster, being occupied, does not acknowledge.

In Vehicles. Officers in vehicles are saluted as if afoot, except when aboard public conveyances, such as street cars, busses, and trains. The driver of a motor vehicle does not salute if the car is in motion. If the vehicle is not underway, he salutes without rising. Other passengers salute or return salutes as necessary, remaining seated.

When Mounted. Mounted persons salute in the same manner as if on foot, but salutes are not rendered by anyone standing to or leading a horse. A mounted junior always dismounts before addressing a senior who is not mounted; this rule applies to vehicles as well as horses.

During Games. Games are not interrupted at the approach of an officer. Spectators do not rise or salute unless individually addressed by an officer.

In Plain Clothes. Marines in civilian clothes salute officers as usual. Officers wearing plain clothes salute and are saluted, if recognized, as if they were in uniform.

ON GUARD.

1. *When armed with the rifle,* sentries salute by presenting arms. A sentry walking post halts, faces the officer being saluted, and comes to the present. If then spoken to by the officer (or by any other person), the sentry executes port arms and holds this position throughout the conversation. If speaking with an officer, he does not interrupt the conversation to salute another officer, unless the officer with whom he is speaking likewise salutes; if so, the sentinel presents arms. At the end of the conversation, the sentry presents arms again. During hours of challenging, the first salute or present arms is rendered when the officer has been duly advanced and recognized.

2. *When not armed with the rifle,* a sentry renders hand salutes in the usual way. A sentry armed with submachine gun, pistol, or (in other services) the carbine does not salute during hours for challenging. While challenging, a sentry armed with the pistol remains at raise pistol; one armed with submachine gun or carbine remains at port arms.

If circumstances are such that payment of compliments interferes with a sentry's performance of duty, he does not salute.

Prisoner Guards ("Chasers"). Prisoner chasers do not salute except when addressed by an officer. If marching his prisoners, the chaser halts them and takes necessary precautions for their security before rendering the salute. If armed with the rifle, a chaser executes rifle salute, but does not present arms. Prisoners may not salute at any time.

> NOTE: *Never pass between a guard and his prisoners,* and be sure to correct any guard who permits you or any other person to do so.

On Board Ship. Saluting procedure aboard a man-of-war is that described in the preceding paragraphs and in Chapter 18.

When in Doubt. If you are uncertain as to whether a salute is required, always salute. For a properly trained Marine, there should never be any doubt. Should a doubtful situation arise, however, do not go out of your way to avoid saluting. Having made up your mind to salute, do so properly and smartly. Never give a hesitant, half-hearted salute which suggests only too plainly that you really don't know the score. *Remember, it is better to render five unnecessary salutes than to omit one which you should give.*

Fig. 15-3: In group saluting, the NCO-in-command brings his people to attention and executes the hand salute.

1509. GROUP SALUTING ETIQUETTE. *Troops in Formation.*
Troops in formation salute on command only. Officers and NCOs
in command of formations render salutes for their respective units.
Before rendering a salute, the person in command brings his unit
to attention. Individuals armed other than with a rifle (and officers
and NCOs whose swords are not drawn) execute the hand salute.

If an officer speaks to an individual in ranks, when the unit is
not at attention, the person spoken to comes to attention. At the
end of the conversation, he resumes the position of the remainder
of the unit.

Troops at Drill and on the March. Troops drilling do not render
compliments. The person in command renders salutes for his unit.
An officer in a formation is saluted only if he is in command of
the entire formation, and he alone returns all salutes. NCOs in
charge of detachments or units do not exchange compliments with
other units so commanded, except at guard mounting, when the
old and new guards do exchange compliments.

Troops marching at ease or route step are called to attention on
the approach of a senior entitled to a salute.

Marine units always begin and end a march at attention. March
your unit at attention while within barracks and central areas and
on main roads of your post. No matter how tired you are after a
day or a night in the field, bring your outfit home with a short,
snappy step, with pieces aligned, in dressed ranks, at regulation
cadence, and at attention. That is the Marine way.

Formations in Vehicles. Members of formations embarked, *as units,*
in military vehicles do not salute individually. The senior person
in each vehicle renders and acknowledges salutes. Only the hand
salute is employed.

Working Parties. The NCO in charge renders salutes for the entire
detail. Individuals come to attention and salute if addressed by an
officer, but do not interrupt work at the approach of any officer
unless the detail is called to attention.

While Honors are Being Rendered.

1. During ruffles and flourishes by the band or field music, while
   honors are being rendered, the guard presents arms to the recipient of honors. All persons in the vicinity come to attention and
   salute, following the motions of the guard (for example, hand
   salute on present arms; terminate salute on order arms).
2. If ruffles and flourishes are followed by a gun salute, persons in
   the vicinity but not in formation stand fast at attention until the
   last gun has fired.
3. On board ship, all hands on the quarterdeck salute while an officer
   is being piped over the side. If the guard is paraded, follow the
   motions of the guard in your hand salute.

At Military Funerals.

1. The basic rule for saluting at a military funeral is, *salute each*

time the body bearers move the coffin, and during volleys and "Taps." If you are wearing civilian clothes, uncover and hold your headgear over your left breast.

2. During prayers, stand at the pre-1939 position of parade rest without arms (described in Section 528), with head bowed. During the firing of volleys, come to attention and salute.

3. Body bearers remain covered, both indoors and outdoors, when carrying the coffin. When the remains are lowered into the grave, body bearers stand at attention, hold the flag waist-high over the grave. The officer in charge of the escort presents this flag to the next of kin, after the ceremony.

4. When a military funeral cortege passes, all hands come to attention and salute the remains, using the hand salute if in uniform and uncovering in the civilian salute if wearing civilian clothes.

Note: For general information and procedure regarding military funerals, see Section 1513.

1510. SALUTING THE NATIONAL ANTHEM. When the National Anthem is played or "To the Colors" or "Retreat" (Evening Colors) is sounded, all military personnel come to attention, face toward the music, and salute. You hold your salute until the last note of the music, but remain at attention until "Carry On" is sounded. If the anthem or call is being played incident to a ceremony involving the Colors, face toward the Colors rather than the music.

Troops in Formation. Troops in formation are halted (if on the march) and brought to attention, and the commander salutes, facing in the direction of his unit's original front. If participating in a ceremony which includes rendition of the National Anthem or "To the Colors" or "Retreat" (Evening Colors), troops present arms.

Personnel in Vehicles. During the playing of the National Anthem, all vehicles within sight or hearing of the ceremony stop. Passengers do not debark, but remain seated at attention and do not salute. If the passengers comprise a military detail in an official vehicle, the person in charge debarks, faces toward the flag or music, and salutes.

Mounted Personnel halt and salute without dismounting.

Sentries halt, face in the direction of the flag or music, and render the hand salute or present arms as appropriate (see Section 1508).

In Civilian Clothes. If wearing plain clothes, come to attention, remove your headgear, and hold it over your left breast with your right hand.

Indoors. When the National Anthem is played indoors, you come to attention and face the music. Only men under arms salute.

Foreign National Anthems. Accord the national anthems of friendly foreign powers the same courtesies as our own.

1511. COURTESY TO THE FLAG. This section confines itself to the courtesies which apply to the National Color (or National Ensign). You will find additional information dealing with flags, colors, and standards in Chapter 5, and Section 1518 in turn covers execution of Morning and Evening Colors, the daily ceremonies which take place when the flag is raised and lowered.

Saluting the Flag. Except at Morning and Evening Colors and on board a man-of-war at anchor, the flag is not saluted when displayed from a mast or flagstaff, nor is any flag saluted unless it is a National Color or Standard as defined in Chapter 5. When Colors are encased in a protective cover (and said to be "cased"), they are not saluted.

Colors and Standards not cased are saluted when either you or they approach or pass within six paces. Hold your salute until the Colors have passed or been passed by that distance.

In the field or in camp, it is customary to display the National Color and unit Battle Color in front of the commanding officer's tent. According to his wishes, this may be done every day or only on Sundays and national holidays. All hands who approach within saluting distance (six paces) execute a hand or rifle salute as appropriate, holding the salute until six paces beyond. If a Color sentinel is posted, he acknowledges salutes rendered by enlisted men; when officers salute the Colors, he holds his own salute or present arms until the officer has completed his.

Motor Vehicles Passing Colors. When passed by an uncased National Color, all persons embarked in a vehicle remain seated at attention. Vehicles approaching and passing Colors, reduce speed; embarked personnel remain seated at attention but do not salute.

Individuals Not in Formation. At the approach of Colors, persons not in formation come to attention, face the Colors, and salute when within saluting distance. Construe this distance liberally. Hold your salute and keep your head and eyes turned smartly toward the Colors until they have passed or been passed by six paces. In civilian clothes, render the civilian salute with headgear held over your left breast. If mounted, bring your horse to a walk and salute without dismounting.

Dipping the Battle or Organizational Color. In military ceremonies Battle and Organizational Colors (See Chapter 5) are dipped in salute during the playing of the National Anthem, "To the Color," or "Retreat" (in place of the National Anthem), or "Hail to the Chief"; during honors rendered to the organizational commander or individual or higher rank; and, during military funerals only, on each occasion that the funeral escort presents arms.

On these occasions, when passing in review, the Battle Color or Organizational Color (but never the National Color) is dipped when six paces from the individual receiving the salute, and it remains dipped until six paces beyond.

Dipping the National Ensign. The National Color or Ensign is never in any circumstances permitted to touch the ground or deck. At sea, however, it is customary for merchantmen to dip their Colors when passing close aboard a man-of-war, and, in reply, the warship runs her Ensign halfway down and then back up again. This is the only time when a National Color or Ensign may be dipped.

1512. POINTERS ON SALUTING. All salutes received must be returned unless the recipient is uncovered or has both hands fully loaded or occupied. If you are uncovered or in any circumstance in which you cannot render a salute, you should, if standing still, come to attention; if underway, you should turn your head and eyes smartly (as in "Eyes Right") toward the person or Color being saluted, in a noticeable movement, holding your arms steady by your side.

When wearing civilian clothes and covered, render and return salutes as if in uniform, except that the civilian salute (headgear held over left breast, in lieu of hand salute) should be used for:

Salutes to the Colors
Salutes to the National Anthem
Salutes during military funerals.

If salutes are to be properly exchanged, both junior and senior must be alert. The junior must spot the approaching senior, and the senior must respond with alacrity.

In saluting, *do:*

Begin your salute in ample time (at least six paces away).
Hold your salute until it is returned or acknowledged.
Extend the same military courtesy to women officers as to male officers.
Look squarely at the person or Colors being saluted.
Assume the position of attention.
Have thumb and fingers extended and joined.
Keep hand and wrist in same plane, not bent.
Incline forearm at forty-five degrees.
Hold upper arm horizontal while hand is at salute.
Bring your heels together audibly.
Place swagger stick smartly under left arm, cutting away the hand before saluting.

Do not:

Salute with blouse or coat unbuttoned.
Salute with cigarette, pipe, or cigar in mouth.
Have anything in your right hand.
Have your left hand in a pocket.
Salute when in ranks, at games, or part of a working detail.
Salute at crowded gatherings, in public conveyances, or in congested areas unless addressing or being directly addressed by a senior.
Salute when to do so would physically interfere with performance of an assigned duty.

Note: One of the most unmilitary habits encountered among some Marines, both while saluting and even in ranks, is the ludicrous habit of leaning over backwards (literally) in an effort to stand straight. This swaybacked stance, with stomach and pelvis thrust forward, jaw jutting out, and shoulders too far back, is a caricature of the position of attention. A Marine at attention should stand straight as an arrow, not bent like a bow.

Military Funerals

1513. GENERAL INFORMATION ON FUNERALS. Navy and Marine Corps funerals are conducted in accordance with *Navy Regulations* and the *Landing Party Manual,* both of which you should check carefully if you are to take an official part in a military funeral. Chapter 20 of this Handbook contains administrative information on funerals and burials.

Classification. Military funerals fall into the following classes:

By size of escort (depending on rank of deceased) and type of ceremony, i.e., full honors, simple honors, or modified.

By location of military ceremony, i.e., church or chapel service (remains received at church and escorted to gravesite); transfer (remains received at station, airport or cemetery gate and escorted to gravesite); gravesite (remains conveyed to gravesite by civilian undertaker, military participation and ceremony at gravesite only).

Uniforms and Equipment. If the organization providing the funeral escort is authorized blues, uniform should be dress blue A or dress blue/white A, according to season. Otherwise the uniform should be seasonal service dress with large medals instead of ribbons, if blouse is worn.

Body bearers should not wear bayonets or scabbards.

For difficult terrain, mud, or foul weather, units and individuals —such as body bearers, music, and firing party—who must leave paved areas may wear shined boots instead of dress shoes.

Officers of funeral escort wear mourning band and mourning sword knot, as do pallbearers; noncommissioned officers armed with the sword wear mourning sword knot only (except if acting as pallbearer, when mourning band will also be worn).

When sanctioned by the denomination concerned (as in the case of the Episcopal Church), the officiating clergyman, if so entitled, should wear military ribbons on his vestments.

Dependents' Funerals. Military honors (i.e., firing of volleys and sounding of "Taps") are reserved for deceased military or former military persons. For the funerals of Marine dependents, body bearers may be assigned and, if desired, the funeral service will be conducted by a Navy chaplain.

Type of Ceremony, as classified above, depends on the rank of the deceased and, subject to that consideration, on the wishes of the next of kin. Some next of kin may wish only gravesite honors or a reduced escort; some may not wish the firing of volleys. Such wishes of course govern.

Musical Honors, if prescribed by Navy Regulations, are rendered during each transfer of remains into and from hearse or caisson to church (or vice versa) and from hearse or caisson to gravesite. Next of kin should have an opportunity to select hymns or funeral music to be played by the band, but the Navy Hymn, "Eternal Father, Strong to Save," should always be included.

Rehearsals and Reconnaissance. Unit rehearsals obviously cannot be conducted at church or gravesite, although the various evolutions can be adequately rehearsed on the parade ground. Careful but unobtrusive reconnaissance should, however, be conducted by the adjutant (who acts as officer-in-charge unless otherwise prescribed, by the escort commander, and by the parade sergeant-major or other leading noncommissioned officer of the escort. All Marines assigned to funeral details—especially firing party and body bearers—must have attained the necessary high standards of individual proficiency in their duties for these occasions.

Rules for Saluting by those attending military funerals are found in Section 1509.

1514. FUNERAL ESCORTS. OFFICERS' FUNERALS. The basic escort for a deceased officer consists of:

Escort commander (same rank as deceased, if possible)
Staff (colonels and general officers only)
Band
Color guard
Body bearers
Firing party (eight riflemen with NCO-in-charge)
Field music
Personal flag bearer (general officers only).

Troop escort for:

Major General or Senior: Three ceremonial companies (two platoons of three eight-man squads each).
Colonel or Brigadier: Two ceremonial companies composed as above.
Major or Lieutenant Colonel: One ceremonial company composed as above (escort commander commands company and has no staff).
Company and Warrant Officers: One ceremonial platoon (three eight-man squads, escort commander serves as platoon leader and has no staff).

ENLISTED MARINES' FUNERALS. The funeral escort for a deceased enlisted Marine consists of a noncommissioned escort commander (same rank as deceased, or senior), body bearers, firing party (eight riflemen), field music, and, in the case of gunnery sergeants or above, troop escort consisting of a 14-man rifle squad.

SIMPLE-HONORS FUNERALS. When next of kin does not desire full honors, the simple-honors funeral escort, for all ranks, consists of an escort commander (not above rank of captain), body bearers, firing party, and field music.

Note: For military funerals when troop strength is limited, the *Landing Party Manual* contains a special procedure requiring only eight enlisted men and an officer or NCO-in-charge.

1515. THE NCO SWORD. Although not specifically mentioned in uniform regulations until 1840, swords for Marine noncommissioned officers were carried and issued much earlier. These were probably of the same pattern as those worn by Army NCOs (i.e., the so-called "Starr Swords," models of 1813 and 1818). In 1840 (and again in 1859) Marine Corps uniform regulations prescribed the Army sword, which by this time was the model of 1840, patterned on a French model, with straight blade and cast bronze hilt. During the Civil War, senior Marine NCOs began to wear a sword of the same type as the Army infantry officer's sword, and in 1875 this pattern was made official and continues to the present. (The model

Fig. 15-4: Standing at ease with sword drawn and at parade rest.

326

Fig. 15-5: A Carry sword; B carrying sword when not in formation;

1840 sword, superseded by this change, was worn for many years afterward by bandsmen and field musics.)

Slight design changes in the pattern of the NCO sword were effected after World War I, as was the requirement that the blade be etched with the Marine Corps Emblem and the legend, "United States Marines."

Swords (other than those individually owned) are organizational equipment. They are worn by staff NCOs when blues or white-blue-whites are worn. Sergeants may, when prescribed, wear the sword for drill with troops, parades, reviews and ceremonies. Instructions regarding the sword are found in Chapter 2, *Landing Party Manual.* The various positions for correct manual of the sword for Marine NCOs are shown in illustrations herein.

1516. MANUAL OF THE SWORD. This is shown in Chapter 2, *Landing Party Manual.* Even though the illustrations depict a Navy officer (whose sword, accessories, and rigging differ from those of the Marine Corps), it is correct. In addition to the manual just mentioned, however, two additional positions are sometimes used.

Standing at Ease. When it is desired to stand at ease or at rest but with sword drawn (as distinct from "Parade Rest"), for quick return to the carry for the purpose of giving commands, the old

C present sword;   *and D eyes right.*

(Naval) position formerly used at rest is both military and convenient. Simply stand with the feet apart, as in "Parade Rest," but with the sword blade carried horizontally without constraint across the front of the body, hilt in the right hand and lower blade in the left. See Figure 15-4.

Carrying Sword When Not in Formation. As your sword is not a fishing pole, a hoe, or a golf club, it should be carried and handled in a military way even when you are not in formation and the sword is unrigged. The proper way to do this is to crook your left arm at right angles across the front of your body and to place the sword (sheathed in its scabbard) in the crook, curve of the blade downward and hilt rearward. The sword will ride easily here as long as you hold your forearm steady, and the appearance will be formal and soldierly.

Displaying the Flag

1517. DISPLAYING THE FLAG. *General.* Throughout the Navy and Marine Corps, the National Ensign is displayed from 0800 to sunset (except in ships underway, which fly the Ensign continuously). On shore the flag is flown near post headquarters or at the headquarters of the senior, when two or more commands are located so close together that separate flags would be inappropriate. Outlying commands or activities display the National Colors in order to make clear their governmental character.

Except when intentionally lowered to half-mast, the flag must be "two-blocked" at all times—that is, it must be hoisted and secured at the *very top* of the staff or gaff, since any flag not so secured is technically considered to be at half-mast. Display of the flag at half-mast indicates official mourning. On Memorial Day, the flag is half-masted until completion of the required gun-salute or until noon, if no salute is fired.

The position of half-mast is midway between the peak (or truck) and the base of the flagstaff, except when the latter has yardarms or is supported by guys, stays, or shrouds, in which case half-mast

Fig. 15-6: Correct ways in which to display the national ensign.

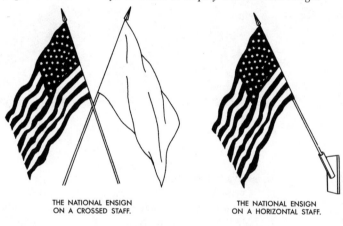

THE NATIONAL ENSIGN
ON A CROSSED STAFF.

THE NATIONAL ENSIGN
ON A HORIZONTAL STAFF.

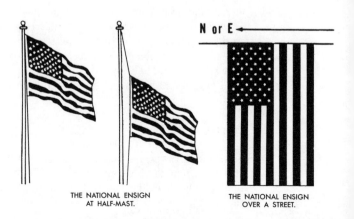

THE NATIONAL ENSIGN
AT HALF-MAST.

THE NATIONAL ENSIGN
OVER A STREET.

is halfway between the truck and the yardarm or the point at which guys, stays, or shrouds join the staff.

The church pennant is the only flag ever flown above the Ensign. It is hoisted at the sounding of "Church Call" for divine services, and the National Colors are lowered to a position just under the church pennant. When divine services have concluded, the church pennant is hauled down and the National Colors two-blocked.

Colors must never be allowed to become fouled. It is an important responsibility of the guard to prevent this. To avoid fouling, they should be raised or lowered from the leeward side of the pole. Should it become necessary to exchange a set of Colors already hoisted, a new set is first run up on a second halyard (that is why flagpoles have two sets of halyards), and the original set is lowered as soon as the new one has been two-blocked.

It is a recognized international *distress signal,* afloat or ashore, sanctioned by law, to fly the National Ensign upside down.

In Battle. It is a very old tradition, although no longer prescribed by *Navy Regulations,* that, on joining action, ships break out National Ensigns at the trucks of all masts. The spirit of this tradition should be observed on shore. Any position under attack, at which Colors are normally flown, should keep those Colors flying throughout action, night and day, just as the original Star Spangled Banner flew through the night over Fort McHenry at Baltimore (where Marines formed one of the defending units).

Half-Masting the Flag. First, two-block the flag at the truck of the staff, and keep it at the truck until the last note of the National Anthem or "To the Colors" and then lower it to the half-mast position. In lowering the flag from half-mast, hoist it smartly to the truck at the first note of the music and then lower it in the regular manner, as described in Section 1518.

Displayed with Other Flags. The National Colors are always on the right (to your left as you face the displayed flags). If other flags are flown from adjacent poles, the American flag will be the first one raised and the last one lowered.

When displayed from crossed staffs, the National Colors are on the right, and the staff is in front of the staff of the other flag with which it is crossed.

When displayed over a street, the blue field (or "union") of the flag should point north on a street running east-west and should point east on a street running north-south.

When used to drape a coffin, the flag should be placed so that the union would cover the head and left shoulder of the body within.

Foreign Flags. Except in cases of official ceremonies, the carrying of foreign flags by members of the U. S. Armed Forces is not authorized. An example of an official ceremony would be the arrival or departure of a foreign head of state. Rulings as to whether given events may be considered official ceremonies should be obtained from Headquarters Marine Corps.

1518. MORNING AND EVENING COLORS. Colors are the most important ceremonies of the working day and must be conducted with precision and ceremony. Executing Colors is the responsibility of the guard of the day and should be personally supervised by the commander of the guard (see Chapter 14). Honors to be rendered by individuals and formations are described in Section 1510.

RAISING THE FLAG (MORNING COLORS).

The *color guard,* a noncommissioned officer and two privates, forms at the guardhouse, with the NCO (carrying the folded Colors) in the center. The color guard marches to the flagstaff, halts, and bends on the flag to the halyards. Although elementary, one of the most important habits a color-guard NCO can cultivate is to verify absolutely that the "union" or blue field of the flag is bent onto the snap link (toggle) of the top or uppermost end of the halyard. The halyards are manned by the two privates, and the NCO holds the flag until it is hauled free of his grasp. He must see that the Colors never touch the ground. At precisely 0800 the signal to execute Colors is given from the guardhouse by the corporal of the relief on watch. The field music then makes eight bells, after the last stroke the music begins, and the flag is hoisted smartly. When the flag is clear, the NCO comes to hand salute. As soon as the flag is two-blocked, the privates manning halyards likewise come to hand salute and hold this position throughout the National Anthem or "To the Color," after which the halyards are triced. In saluting during Colors, *members of the Color Detail should avoid looking up at the Colors and should salute in the normal manner and stance.*

The *guard of the day and band,* or field music, parade facing the flagpole. At Morning Colors, following the last stroke of eight bells, attention is sounded by bugle, followed in turn by the National Anthem (if a band is present) or "To the Color" (by field music). The guard is brought to present arms on the call to attention. If friendly foreign forces are present, the band renders prescribed honors to foreign ensigns after playing the U. S. National Anthem. Hand salutes and present arms terminate on the last note of the music, after which "Carry On" is sounded.

In the absence of a band, "To the Color" is sounded by field music. If no music is present, the signals for attention, hand salute, and carry on must be given by whistle, which is most undesirable. *Even if your outfit does not rate or include a music, you should make every effort to obtain a bugle and train a nonrated man to sound the calls required for Colors.* This is where initiative, enterprise, and spirit of "make-do" can show.

LOWERING THE FLAG (EVENING COLORS)

Evening Colors is executed by the same guard details as Morning Colors, and the ceremony is virtually a reverse performance of the latter. The flag is lowered precisely at sunset, the exact daily time of which should be kept in a table in the guardhouse. Beginning with

331

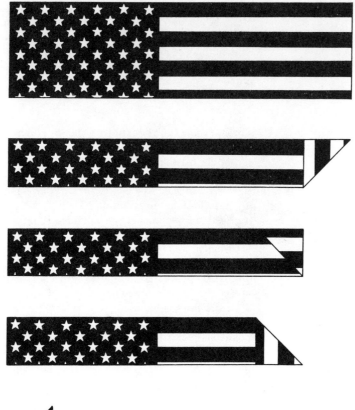

Fig. 15-7: Folding the national ensign.

the first note of the music, the flag is slowly lowered, in time with the music, so that it will be in the hands of the NCO of the color guard as the last note sounds. In the absence of a band, "Retreat" is sounded by field music.

After being lowered, the flag is folded in the shape of a cocked hat. The correct procedure for folding a set of Colors may be found in the *Marine Corp Flag Manual* and should be followed. (See Figure 15-7).

Standing lights (such as street lights, aircraft obstruction lights, etc.) throughout the post should be turned on after the last note of Evening Colors.

Honors and Honor Guards

1519. RENDERING HONORS. Military honors consist of certain salutes, ceremonies, parading of honor guards, and other marks of official deference to the individual being honored. These honors are prescribed in law and regulations and are quite complicated. A single table giving the honors for all dignitaries, officers, and others so entitled, may be found in Chapter 18, *Marine Officer's Guide.*

As a noncommissioned officer, your first contact with honors will probably occur aboard ship or possibly ashore or when you find yourself detailed in some capacity in an honor guard.

Here are some basic terms:

Guard of the Day: For rendering honors, *Navy Regulations* provide that the "guard of the day" (normally not part of the interior guard, except aboard ship) shall be not less than one rifle squad.

Full Guard: Not less than one rifle platoon.

Guard of Honor: Any guard, not part of the interior guard, which is paraded ashore for rendition of honors. When the interior guard turns out in compliment to an individual, it is spoken of as *the guard,* not as a guard of honor.

Compliment of the Guard: This honor consists of an interior guard turning out and presenting arms, as a compliment to visiting officers or civilian dignitaries. During an inspection in garrison by the CO or CG, the guard is turned out when the inspecting party approaches or passes the guardhouse.

Shipboard Compliments: In addition to honors by a guard, shipboard compliments may include any or all of the following elements, which are dispensed with ashore:

Manning the rail on weather decks by the ship's company
Piping alongside and over the side
Sideboys.

Since Marines in a ship's company are fully occupied with other elements of rendering honors to visitors, these shipboard compliments are performed only by Navy officers and enlisted men.

Honors. Arrangements for rendering honors ashore are usually coordinated by the commanding general's aide. On a post or unit not commanded by a general officer, arrangements are made by the adjutant.

Ashore and afloat, we render the same salutes, honors, and ceremonies, insofar as practicable, at Marine Corps posts and stations and on Naval ships and stations. Wherever Marines are present, they provide the honor guard. You will find detailed pointers and procedures on honors in Section 1520.

Troops paraded as honor guards must be the *best.* See that your guard is correct, snappy, and immaculate—a reflection of the Marine Corps at its smartest.

Note: *Marine Corps Uniform Regulations* specify the correct uniform combinations for honor guards on all occasions.

1520. PROCEDURE AND POINTERS ON RENDERING HONORS. *Preparations.* The general's aide (or the adjutant) and the sergeant major virtually always have advance notice to prepare for an official visit which requires honors and to notify those concerned.

When detailed to organize an honor guard, you should immediately report to the sergeant major and obtain all possible information. Check with the bandmaster on the timing of ruffles and flourishes and with the NCO in charge of the saluting battery. If the saluting guns are remote from the honor guard's parade, see that absolutely foolproof communications are established between the parade and the saluting battery. It is elementary, but vital, that the saluting battery knows how many guns are to be fired and also that a standby piece and spare rounds are in instant readiness to fire in the event of hangfire or malfunction of a saluting gun.

> *Note:* If for any reason your saluting battery doesn't have a stopwatch for timing the rounds (or if the watch stops permanently), the NCO-in-charge may obtain the correct interval between rounds by repeating, "If I wasn't a gunner, I wouldn't be here—Fire One (two, three, etc.)." This is a trick that dates back to early days in the sailing Navy.

Make a personal reconnaissance of the honor guard's parade and know exactly where the guard and band and the recipients of honors are to be posted. Determine what markers and guidons are required and who will supply and locate them. If possible, platoon leaders and leading NCOs should have an opportunity to look over the ground. If you are going to provide an escort of honor, verify the route of march.

As to the guard itself, spare no effort to make it the finest in the Marine Corps. See that every man is immaculately turned out, that the guard is perfectly sized, and that the entire formation, if possible, is adequately rehearsed. If troops for the guard come from units other than your own, have no hesitation in returning substandard men to their units, reporting that you have done this (and why) to the adjutant.

> *Note:* An underrehearsed honor guard quickly reveals itself in a weak manual at the halt and in a march-past which is barely adequate, if that. Rehearse several times: two points to emphasize, (1) have men hit their pieces *audibly* during manual, and (2) keep the hands closed, with fist clenched and a pronounced arm-swing, when marching.

Procedure for Honors on an Official Visit Ashore. The following general procedure can serve as a guide for rendering honors ashore. (Remember, however, that almost every post has its ground rules and standing operating procedures, and be sure to consult these when preparing to render honors.)

1. Well before the time of arrival of the visiting official, complete the preparations discussed above. Guard and band are paraded, while the Color detail stands by to break or haul down personal flags involved, and the saluting battery remains manned and

ready. If possible, especially on a large post, there should be communications which can apprise you, up to the last moment, of the visitor's movements and approach (field radio equipment is ideal).

2. When the recipient of honors arrives and debarks from boat, train, car, plane, or helicopter, "Attention" is sounded by bugle. The local commander (or whoever is receiving him) greets the dignitary and conducts him to his post front and center of the guard.

3. When the official takes post, the commander of the honor guard brings the guard to present arms. All hands in the vicinity but not in formation come to hand salute, following the motions of the guard.

4. When the guard has been presented and the commander has executed his salute, the band sounds off with ruffles, flourishes, and other musical honors. The personal flag or National Color, as specified for the individual in question, is broken on the first note of the music. When national anthems are prescribed for arrival and departure ceremonies, the foreign anthem is played first, followed by "The Star Spangled Banner."

5. The guard is brought to the order after the last note of music or if there is no music, when the commander of the guard has exchanged salutes with the official. If a gun salute is rendered, the first gun is fired immediately after the last note of the music, and the guard remains at present arms throughout the salute, as do all hands in the official party, holding their salutes throughout the gun salute. Persons not in the official party but in the immediate vicinity, remain at attention during the gun salute. If the National Color or a foreign flag or ensign is to be displayed during the gun salute only, it is broken on the first gun and hauled down on the last.

6. On completion of the musical honors or the gun salute, if fired, the honor guard commander brings his guard to order arms, executes present sword to the person being honored, and reports, "Sir, the honor guard is formed." If the personage desires neither to inspect the guard nor to receive the pass-in-review, the honor guard remains at attention. For the procedure to be followed for marching the guard in review or for its inspection by the personage, see *Landing Party Manual,* Chapter 3.

Honors on Departure from an Official Visit Ashore. In general, departure honors reverse those given on arrival.

1. Departure honors commence when the visiting official has completed his personal leave-taking from the senior officer present. Either the latter officer himself or the aide will signal this to the commander of the guard.

2. Gun salutes, if rendered on departure, must begin before the individual actually leaves (that is, while he is within earshot). His personal flag, or any national ensign displayed, is hauled down on the last gun.

335 3. An honor guard is not normally inspected on departure. Hold the guard on parade until the official is out of sight.

Honors are dispensed with under the following circumstances:

When the visiting officer is in plain clothes or visits the post unofficially.

Between sunset and 0800 (except that foreign officers may be rendered honors at any time during daylight).

During meal hours for the troops (except in the case of foreign officers).

When a ship is engaged in maneuvers and general drills, is undergoing overhaul in a navy yard, or is in action.

When a unit or post ashore is carrying on tactical exercises or emergency drills.

On Sundays or national holidays (except in the case of foreign officers).

For ships with a complement of less than 180 seamen.

Honors in the Field. Despite the rigors of field service, Marine units make every effort to render appropriate honors when so serving. The spirit, if not the letter, of the preceding paragraphs must be faithfully observed. It is the distinguishing mark of really professional troops that in face of handicaps and obvious obstacles to smartness, they nevertheless remain smart and military and do the best they can with what they have. Marines in the field may well remember what was said of England's Brigade of Guards: "They die with their boots clean."

For rendition of honors in the field, the most important points are that:

Men be in clean, homogeneous uniforms

Equipment (especially weapons) be in first-class, evident serviceability

Individuals be smart, keen, and cleanly

The place for rendering honors be not subject to enemy shelling or observation

Military readiness or combat operations be not interrupted.

Ceremonies

1521. TYPES OF CEREMONIES. The Marine Corps and Navy have eight military ceremonies which may be performed on shore. These ceremonies are in form prescribed by Chapter 3, *Landing Party Manual* and may only be modified when the nature of the ground or exceptional circumstances require that change be made.

The title and a brief description or discussion of each ceremony are given below.

A review is a ceremony at which a command or several commands parade for inspection by and in honor of a senior officer, a distinguished visitor, or a civilian dignitary. In a review, the individual

Kings and other heads of state have reviewed the troops at Marine Barracks, Eighth and Eye.

being honored passes on foot or in a vehicle throughout the formation, which is then marched past him.

Presentation of decorations is the ceremony at which decorations are presented. This ceremony follows, in part, that prescribed for a review; it is noteworthy in that, regardless of rank, the individuals who have been decorated receive the review side by side with the reviewing officer. In modified form, this ceremony can be adapted for such occasions as presentation of commissions or enlisted warrants, commendations, and so forth

A parade is the ceremony at which the commanding officer of a battalion or larger unit forms and drills the entire command and then marches them in review. The battalion parade is the most common form of periodic ceremony and, under normal garrison conditions, is usually performed each Saturday morning. Together with guard mounting, described below, the parade is probably the most important ceremony for you to know by heart. "Memorize every comma in it!" Captain Lewis ("Chesty") Puller used to enjoin his Basic School lieutenants.

Escort of the National Color is known less formally as "Marching on (or off) the Colors." That is, when the Colors are to take part in a ceremony, to be presented to a unit, or to be turned over to some institution or person for safekeeping, they are ceremonially received and escorted from their place of safekeeping (usually the CO's headquarters), and are similarly returned, by a picked escort. The ceremony for this occasion corresponds somewhat to portions of the famous British ceremony, *Trooping the Color,* and is derived from that.

Escort of Honor is the ceremonial escorting of a senior officer or other dignitary during an official visit or on arrival or departure.

Military funerals are covered in Chapter 3, *Landing Party Manual,* as well as elsewhere in this chapter of the *Handbook.* The ceremonials followed in military funerals are among the most longstanding in the profession of arms; some parts, such as the firing of volleys (originally to frighten evil spirits) can be traced, in one guise or another, to pagan times.

Inspections, as you have seen from Chapter 13, run to all types. The ceremonial inspection of troops in ranks has as its object the general military appearance and condition of individual uniforms and equipment within a command. If headed for sea duty, note that personnel inspection on board ship follows considerably different lines and frequently varies from ship to ship. Be sure you know your own ship's ground rules and inspection procedure.

Guard Mounting is the ceremony whereby a guard is organized from guard details, is inspected before assuming the guard, and then relieves an outgoing or "old" guard. This is a very old ceremony, portions of which antedate the Revolutionary War and go back to the British Army. Guard mounts may be *formal* or *informal,* according to weather, size of guard, availability of music, or local conditions. Most commands in garrison perform at least two formal guard mounts weekly; the ceremony is relatively tricky and is one which you must learn thoroughly. Ability to run a formal guard mount is the mark of a well-drilled NCO.

Morning and Evening Colors, although sometimes regarded as parts of the daily routine, should be considered ceremonies, if only out of respect to the significance of the daily raising and lowering of the National Ensign. You will find the execution of Colors discussed in Section 1518 of this *Handbook* as well as by Chapter 3, *Landing Party Manual.*

In addition to the foregoing eight ceremonies of general character, we employ specific ceremonial forms on the occasion of *change of command,* on *relief of the sergeant major,* and for celebration of the *Marine Corps Birthday.* All these are covered in the *Landing Party Manual,* while additional information on the observance of the birthday of the Corps may be found in Chapter 21 of this *Handbook.*

Another form of ceremony not covered in any official regulations is the *tattoo* (sometimes called "searchlight tattoo"). A tattoo is an evening parade conducted under floodlights or searchlights; embellished with traditional, historic, or display drills and special musical features; and usually climaxed by lowering of the Colors and by playing of "Taps" and sometimes a traditional evening hymn. Evening parades at 8th and Eye, though not so entitled, are in fact a form of tattoo which was inaugurated on the basis of experience by Marine ceremonial detachments which took part in the Bermuda International Tattoo (1957) and the Edinburgh Tattoo and Brussels Expositions in 1958.

1522. TRADITIONAL ELEMENTS AND TERMS IN A MARINE CORPS PARADE. With the exception of guard mount, parades and reviews are the most commonly encountered and best known ceremonies. They both embody military traditions and traditional terms and elements which date far back in the history of the Corps and of the profession of arms.

Parade. In its original sense, a "parade" was simply a prepared ground, the military application of the word being to the courtyard of a castle or any enclosed, level plain, suitable for holding troop formations or drills. From the practice of "parading" troops at such places, the ceremony has acquired the name of parade.

Adjutant and Sergeant Major. In Chapter 5 you have already seen the origin of the sergeant major's rank and function. That of the adjutant, which is conspicuous on parade, goes back to the days when the latter was the principal staff officer (and also executive) of the commander. The adjutant's duties have been traditionally associated with mustering, inspecting, and training troops; superintending drill and discipline (along with the sergeant major, his enlisted counterpart); and forming parades and lines of battle. Until recently, the adjutant also gave special attention to training and instruction of junior officers.

Sound Off. This custom goes back to the Crusades. Soldiers selected or volunteering for expeditionary duty on a Crusade would form on the right of the line. They would then be honored by having musicians march and countermarch in front of their select group only. The three chords or drum-rolls of "Sound Off" symbolize the three cheers of the assembled populace during the ceremony.

Publication of Orders. In the 18th and 19th centuries, when there were no typewriters, mimeographs, or public-address systems, a daily parade was held, which not only provided opportunities for troop inspection and drill, but also published routine or special orders to all hands, such as daily guard details, etc. This custom survives in publication of the O.D.'s detail whenever we hold a parade.

Drums and Bugles. Drums and bugles and flutes have been used to keep troops moving in step, to control and change formations, to carry out special evolutions, and to initiate or terminate parts of the daily routine, ever since the days of ancient Greece and Rome. Until the beginning of this century (when deployments became so extended that control had to be exercised by semaphore, heliograph, and finally radio), armies fought their battles by fife, drum, and bugle, with hundreds of calls and combinations to cover every possible movement or action. The stirring drum roll and trumpet call heard at a Marine Corps parade when bayonets are fixed is the old-time musical command to fix bayonets and stand by to charge.

Officers Center. The origin of "Officers Center" also is found on the battlefield. When a unit was formed either in an assembly area, or in line of battle preliminary to action, the commander called his officers together for final instructions. The presence of guidons enabled the commander and adjutant quickly to distinguish between the unit commanders and be sure all were present. In latter times, it gives the CO a brief chance to critique the conduct of the ceremony or to order it done over again.

1523. PRECEDENCE OF FORCES IN PARADES OR CEREMONIES. To avoid conflicts at parades or ceremonies, the places of honor are allocated in order of service seniority. Since you may readily find yourself at the head of a Marine detachment in a parade or ceremony, you should know your own place and those of other components relative to your own. As prescribed in law (*Federal Register,* volume 14, 19 August 1949, page 2503), the precedence of

340 U. S. forces in parades or ceremonies is as follows (reading from the head to rear of column or from right to left in line):

1. U. S. Corps of Cadets (U. S. Military Academy)
2. Midshipmen, U. S. Naval Academy
3. Cadets, U. S. Air Force Academy
4. Cadets, U. S. Coast Guard Academy
5. United States Army
6. **United States Marines**
7. United States Navy
8. United States Air Force
9. United States Coast Guard
10. Army National Guard of the United States
11. Organized Reserve Corps, U. S. Army
12. **Marine Corps Reserve**
13. Naval Reserve
14. Air National Guard of the United States
15. Air Force Reserve
16. Coast Guard Reserve
17. Other training organizations of the Army, **Marine Corps,** Navy, Air Force, and Coast Guard, in that order.

When the Coast Guard is serving as part of the Navy, in time of war or emergency, the precedence of Coast Guard units and personnel shifts to position immediately after Navy units and personnel.

Bear in mind, as a Marine, that although the Air Force is one of the three larger Services, it is nevertheless junior in precedence to the Marine Corps. Never accede to erroneous assignment of fourth or junior place to Marines, following Air Force units, as is sometimes carelessly done on the basis of size.

Since the place of honor is the head of column or right of the line, foreign units should be assigned that post of honor in any ceremony or procession. Where several foreign units of mixed nationality are present, they should be placed in alphabetical order, ahead of any U. S. forces, if the ceremony is conducted by U. S. forces or on American soil.

The official who organizes and coordinates a street parade or procession is entitled the *grand marshal* or sometimes, the *marshal.* If your unit is misplaced, he is the official who should rectify the mistake.

1524. GENERAL APPEARANCE OF TROOPS AND UNITS. The Marine Corps has long enjoyed a worldwide reputation for smart appearance and soldierly performance of every task. This reputation has been enhanced by continually demonstrating to the American public that our execution of peacetime functions is excelled only by our performance in battle.

During peacetime the reputation of the Corps is maintained to a considerable degree by creating favorable, highly military impressions in parades, ceremonies, and other functions. It is therefore a responsibility of every Marine concerned that marching units in the public eye fully meet the standards by which the Marine Corps is measured. Men in key positions must have perfect posture, troop leaders must excel in command presence, and uniforms and equipment must be in outstanding condition and appearance. All such public appearances should be preceded by ample drill and specific rehearsal as needed. Here is where you, as a noncommissioned officer, can make yourself felt and can give unremitting attention to the fine points which make a good Marine organization shine on parade.

There is a mistaken tendency today for some NCOs to say, "I'm not a parade Marine," or "I'm a field Marine;" this tendency is sometimes reflected in units which, as soon as they hit the field, live, look, and act like pigs, on the theory that this demonstrates how tough and salty they are. The hallmark of the world's great fighting organizations—the Roman legions, the Spanish *Tercios,* the Foreign Legion, Britain's Brigade of Guards, and many others—is that *they are as good on parade as they are in the field or in the attack.* Most outfits can be good at some single aspect of their duties; only the elite excel at everything, and that is what the Marine Corps expects of every Marine. It should be a matter of professional and personal pride to you, as a noncommissioned officer, for example, not only to shoot expert every year and be a capable troop leader, but to know every trick and detail and fine point of the ceremonies and drill at which past generations of Marines have earned the Corps the special reputation *you* now have to uphold.

1525. POINTERS FOR THE COLOR GUARD. The Colors and color guard are a focal point in every ceremony. In order to honor the Colors properly as well as to have them smartly displayed and carried, a really well-drilled, carefully selected color guard, under an outstanding color sergeant, is essential.

The most important aspect of a good color guard is that it looks and acts like one man, not four individuals. For this reason, color guards should be carefully selected for height and should use balanced rifles.

Color guards always march at close interval and should always *carry Colors absolutely vertical* (except as required when dipping organizational colors during honors, etc.). Wear the sling low, and always wear the belt over the sling correctly to prevent riding up. If you wear the sling up in your stomach, you will have far less control of the flag, especially on a windy day.

A color guard never fixes bayonets (to prevent tearing or ripping the Colors). All members of the guard should have two chin straps on their barracks caps. The second chin strap is always worn down (on the point of the chin); its purpose is to prevent the Colors or wind from whipping off a cap. It is also very military in appearance. Finally, don't forget that the two outboard men (the extreme right

342

A good color guard looks like and acts as one man.

and left files) are always, respectively, at right and left shoulder arms, and they must be drilled to execute these opposite movements simultaneously and correctly according to which side they are on.

1526. POINTERS ON CEREMONIES. *Know Your Parade Ground.* If possible, not only make a personal reconnaissance of the parade ground or area where a ceremony is to be held, but conduct a rehearsal on the ground. At a minimum, be sure your leading NCOs and unit guides know the layout of the ground and how the field is to be marked.

Markers. Dress guidons mark the boundaries and the reviewing point for a parade ground. In addition, it is sometimes customary to place small metal discs on the ground to mark the posts of unit guides and other key personnel. The adjutant places markers and guidons, but every officer and NCO must know the system and layout of markers. In addition, guides and leaders should know the lineup of landmarks adjacent to and visible from the parade ground, so as to be able to march in exactly straight lines and columns without wavering or falling off to right or left. Guides and leaders should keep their heads up and their lines of sight directly to the front and well out, so as to be able to "navigate" on guidons, markers, and landmarks.

Photographers. Photographers, both official and otherwise, can do more to detract from the formality and solemnity of a military ceremony than anyone else. Keep them under strict control, preferably in a suitably located, enclosed vantage point, from which they can get good pictures but cannot mar the occasion by capering about at will.

Marching and Cadence. Marching correctly is very much like Latin American dancing: you move from the *hips down,* snapping the *knee* and *ankle* in unison with the other men in ranks. The regulation cadence is 120 steps per minute, and this is the "tempo" at which a military band plays marches. That is, the bass drummer hits his drum 120 times per minute, with a heavier downbeat or thump on the first and succeeding alternate beats. For parades or ceremonies, it makes for smarter appearance to have a short, snappy step and, if possible, a slightly accelerated cadence that should never fall below 120. When the band is not playing, individual foot movements during a ceremony, notably those by the adjutant and guides when taking post, are traditionally executed at markedly accelerated cadence, with short, quick steps.

Officers Center is an evolution which should be gone over until all concerned are *letter perfect.* Every individual participant is on display, and this evolution comes at a high point of the parade. As in the case of color-guard movements, a properly executed "Officers Center" should appear to be the movement of a single man rather than of several. Manuals of the sword and guidon count here as at no other time. If you are weak on either, work on them.

Use of Public-Address Systems and Amplifiers. Except for the largest ceremonies and under special conditions, it is most unmilitary to employ a public-address system for commands or other purposes incident to military ceremonies. Sergeants major, first sergeants, gunnery sergeants, and drill instructors, in particular, and all noncommissioned officers in general, should pride themselves on their *voice of command* and should, if necessary, practice to strengthen and increase its carrying power.

Stepping off in Time with the Music. Units must step off on the left foot, as is well known, and must accomplish this on command of the leader, *and* on the first beat of the music—a combination which you as a Marine must be prepared to lick.

One method of achieving this result—which requires briefing your men and some rehearsing, but is well worth it—is to give your preliminary command just in advance of the music and have all hands drilled to step off automatically on the first note of the music, without any command of execution from you; in other words, to *let the first note of the music be the command of execution.* This is particularly effective on parade, after the preliminary commands have been given to pass in review.

For guard mounting and for many other ceremonies where units march onto their parades to music, troops must be brought to right shoulder arms at the first note of Adjutant's Call and marched off at the first note of march music. This, too, requires coordination by leader and unit. A recommended sequence for these evolutions—"by the numbers"—has been published by Master Sergeant G. P. Finn in *The Marine Corps Gazette,* and is summarized as follows:

1. Bear in mind that "Adjutant's Call" is a 16-beat call, and the "first note of march music" will therefore be count 17.
2. The signal for the first note of "Adjutant's Call" is given by the drum major, who brings down his baton. This signal can be seen by all hands.
3. Give your commands in time with "Adjutant's Call," on successive beats as shown in this diagram, in which numbers correspond to beats in the call:

1	2	3	4
RIGHT	SHOUL-	DER	ARMS
5	6	7	8
	(troops execute the movement)		
9	10	11	12
	(pause)		
13	14	15	16
FOR-	WARD	(pause)	MARCH

4. Rehearse this a few times with a field music and "You've got it made."

Command of Mixed Detachments of Seamen and Marines. When a mixed (or composite) detachment of seamen and Marines is formed for a parade, the Marines occupy their post of seniority and honor at the head of column or on right of line, *but* the senior line officer present, of the Marine Corps or the Navy, according to date of rank, commands the entire detachment. This rule does not apply when Navy and Marines form separate detachments. It usually occurs when a ship parades her landing force as a unit (of which the Marines form part).

Close-order Drill. The object of drill is to teach troops by exercise to obey orders and to do so immediately in the correct way. For this reason, slovenly drill is harmful. Close-order drill is one foundation of discipline and *esprit de corps.* Well executed, confident, precise, ceremonial close-order drill is therefore the foundation of success in ceremonies.

Uniform for Inspections, Parades, and Ceremonies. Where possible, dress or undress uniforms (i.e., blues or white-blue-whites with ribbons or medals) should be prescribed for inspections, parades, and ceremonies. Additionally, swords should be worn on such occasions in preference to pistols and belts. If blues are not authorized for the command, large medals may be prescribed on ceremonial occasions for wear with the service blouse.

Music Played During "Sound Off." At a review or parade, when a foreign visitor or officer of another service is being honored, the march played during "Sound Off" should if possible be one traditional to his country or branch of the service. At ceremonies conducted by Marine artillery units, "The Caisson Song" is normally played during "Sound Off." For a parade on the occasion of a Marine's retirement, it is a pleasant and appropriate courtesy to ascertain whether there is any particular march he would like to have played on "Sound Off." When several individuals are being so honored, the senior, of course, gets his choice.

Law is a regulation in accord with reason, issued by a lawful superior, for the common good.

—Thomas Aquinas, Summa Theologica

16 Notes on Military Law

Military law governs individual conduct and performance of duty in the Naval Services. It also provides means for enforcing the rules; that is, the courts-martial system and the nonjudicial powers of commanding officers. The prime essential, however, is always to insure justice in every case.

This chapter contains a general description of the system of military law in force in the armed services. *What you read here, however, is merely in the nature of orientation. For authoritative information on any given point of law or discipline, you should turn to your immediate commanding officer, who can either give you the answer or will know where to find it.**

Military law has two basic purposes. It is designed to protect individuals from unjust treatment. More important, however, it is designed to provide means to insure that the military organization can be made to function under any circumstances, and to protect the Marine Corps against those who do not desire to, or cannot, discipline themselves.

As a noncommissioned officer, you should know the sources and legal extent of your authority and you should also be able to furnish general, nontechnical explanations of the Marine Corps disciplinary system to nonrated men.

1601. SOURCES OF MILITARY LAW. The written sources of military law include the Constitution (based on the authority of Congress "to make rules for the government of the land and Naval forces"), the Uniform Code of Military Justice (known as "UCMJ"), other acts of Congress, and some state laws covering conduct not

---

**Military Law: A Handbook for the Navy and the Marine Corps,* written by Lieutenant Commander Edward M. Byrne, JAGC, U. S. Navy and published by the U. S. Naval Institute, Annapolis, Maryland, is a handbook and a textbook on military law and covers courts-martial, UA and larceny, nonjudicial punishment, Military Justice Act of 1968, *Manual for Courts-Martial, 1969,* and many other topics a Marine NCO should be aware of.

governed by the foregoing sources. The Uniform Code of Military Justice leaves its administration up to the President and the military secretaries. Pursuant to this authority, the President promulgated the *Manual for Courts-Martial,* (cited in this chapter as *"MCM"*), and the Secretary of the Navy published the *Manual of the Judge Advocate General of the Navy* (cited as *"JAG Manual"*). These two publications, plus *Navy Regulations* and certain general orders, constitute the sources of written military law as it applies to the Navy and Marine Corps.

The other sources of law include decisions of the courts, directives of the President, directives of the Secretary of Defense and Secretary of the Navy, opinions of the Attorney General and the Judge Advocate General of the Navy, court-martial reports, and customs and usage of the Service.

1602. CIVIL AND MILITARY LAW. In addition to being subject to the federal and state laws which bind all citizens of the United States, members of the armed forces are subject to a third body of law which governs the armed forces. This includes the statutes and regulations setting forth the rights, liabilities, powers, and duties of officers and men in the military services. Thus, members of the armed forces may be brought before either civil or military tribunals. As a general rule, courts-martial may try military personnel for offenses that are service-connected, are minor in nature, or occur in a foreign country. Breaches of the peace and other minor offenses by service personnel which violate both civilian and military law will often be tried by court-martial, although this does not exclude exercise of civil jurisdiction as well. Just as civil courts may not interfere with military courts (other than by writ of *habeas corpus*), neither do military authorities have power to interfere with civil courts.

A member of the Marine Corps accused of an offense against civil authority may, upon proper request, be delivered to the civil authority for trial. Regulations promulgated by the Secretary of the Navy covering this are found in the *JAG Manual.*

1603. UNIFORM CODE OF MILITARY JUSTICE ("THE CODE"). On May 5, 1950, the Uniform Code of Military Justice (hereafter cited as the Code) was approved by President Truman.

Instructions and Publication. Certain articles of the Code must be carefully explained to every enlisted Marine when he begins active duty, then again after six months, and also when he ships over; and a complete text of the Code must be available to every person on active duty in the Armed Forces of the United States.

At frequent intervals the "punitive articles" (those dealing mainly with offenses and punishments) must be published to troops, to the crew of a Naval vessel, and to the personnel of shore stations. This is known—in the old Navy phrase—as "reading the Rocks and Shoals."

THE PUNITIVE ARTICLES. Articles 77-134 of the Code ("the Rocks and Shoals") divide punishable offenses into three general groups,

First, crimes common to both civil and military law, such as murder, rape, arson, burglary, larceny, sodomy, and frauds against the United States; *second,* purely military offenses, arising out of military duties and having no counterpart in civilian life, such as desertion, willful disobedience of lawful orders of superior officers and noncommissioned officers, misbehavior before the enemy, and sleeping on watch; and *third,* a general group of offenses based on two articles which do not specify any particular acts of misconduct but cover a variety of transgressions harmful to the service in general terms. Article 133 applies only to officers and midshipmen. It makes punishable "conduct unbecoming an officer and a gentleman."

Article 134 applies to all persons who are subject to military law. Offenses punishable under this article include: Disorders and neglects prejudicial to good order and discipline; conduct tending to bring discredit upon the armed forces; crimes and offenses covered by Federal laws other than the Uniform Code of Military Justice. This general article insures that there will be no failure of justice simply because an offense is not specifically mentioned in an article of the Code.

Among the foregoing punitive articles, those most violated are as follows:

83: Fraudulent enlistment
85: Desertion
86: Unauthorized absence
87: Missing ship or unit movement
92: Disobedience of orders
93: Maltreatment
107: Knowingly signing false return, record, etc.
108: Unlawful disposition of Government property
111: Drunken or reckless driving
113: Drunk or asleep on watch, or quitting post without proper relief
121-3: Theft or misappropriation
128: Assault
134: General article (conduct to prejudice of good order and discipline; scandalous conduct).

Jurisdiction. All persons in the armed forces are subject to the Code. Reciprocal jurisdiction between services is provided, but the exercise of jurisdiction is in accordance with regulations prescribed by the President and is resorted to only when an accused cannot be brought before a court-martial of his own service. For the purpose of these regulations, the Navy and Marine Corps are considered to be "the Naval Services."

Rights of the Accused. In addition to the constitutional rights which are enjoyed by all American citizens (excepting those expressly or by implication inapplicable to the armed forces), the most important rights of an accused person under the Code are as follows: the right to be warned before interrogation if suspected of an offense; the right to consult counsel in advance and to have counsel present during the conduct of interrogation; the right to a preliminary investigation before trial of a serious offense; the right to challenge members of the court, both for cause and peremptorily; the right to have the findings and sentence of the court made known to him as soon as determined; the right, if convicted, to testify under oath or to make an unsworn statement to the court as to matters in extenuation and mitigation; the right to forward a brief of matters which should be considered in review of the case; and the right to counsel, either a line officer or an officer lawyer, at specified stages of the foregoing proceedings.

Review and Appeals. The Code establishes elaborate machinery and channels for review and appeal of courts-martial. In addition to review by various officers in the chain of command, courts-martial may be scrutinized by *Courts of Military Review* (composed of three or more officers or civilian lawyers qualified to practice before Federal courts or before the highest court of a state); by the *Judge Advocate General of the Navy;* and by the *Court of Military Appeals.* This last tribunal, in Washington, is composed of three civilian judges, appointed for 15 years, with the same qualifications as other Federal judges.

OFFICERS PERFORMING LEGAL DUTIES. *Staff Judge Advocate:* The senior Marine officer lawyer, certified in accordance with the UCMJ, performs the staff legal duties of a command.

Judge Advocate: A Marine officer lawyer certified in accordance with the UCMJ, to perform duties as trial and/or defense counsel. In addition, he is authorized to review trial records of summary and non-BCD special courts-martial.

Military Judge: A judge appointed by the Judge Advocate General of the Navy, who serves on general and special courts-martial in the same capacity as that of a civilian judge. If the accused requests and the military judge consents, a military judge may sit as a one-officer court-martial to determine the issue of guilt or innocence and adjudge sentence if found guilty.

Legal Assistance Officer: An officer designated by the commander to give legal advice to members of the command on personal legal problems and problems involving civilian law generally.

Legal Officer: An officer (nonlawyer) designated by a commanding officer to perform legal duties, of purely military nature, within the command. This officer does not render legal assistance (see above), but can answer questions regarding UCMJ.

1604. AUTHORITY OF NONCOMMISSIONED OFFICERS. The authority you need is well established. Among the sources of this authority are: your warrant (see Chapter 1); and Chapters 12 and 13, *Navy Regulations,* for example:

Art. 1211: "All persons in the Naval Services are required to obey readily and strictly, and execute promptly, the lawful orders of their superiors."

Art. 1335: " . . . petty officers and noncommissioned officers shall have, under their superiors, all necessary authority for due performance of their duties, and they shall be obeyed accordingly."

In addition to the foregoing sources of authority, Article 7, UCMJ, provides that,

" . . . petty officers and noncommissioned officers shall have authority to quell all quarrels, frays, and disorders among persons subject to this code and to apprehend persons subject to this code . . . upon reasonable belief that an offense has been committed."

Nonjudicial Punishment

1605. NONJUDICIAL PUNISHMENT (CO'S OFFICE HOURS). Legally speaking, a "commanding officer" is one who is authorized to award summary punishment and/or courts-martial at Office Hours (called "Captain's Mast" in the Navy). In general, the following are recognized in naval law as commanding officers: COs of any Navy or Coast Guard ship, shipyard, base, or station; COs of any Marine brigade, regiment, battalion, or corresponding unit; COs of any Marine barracks, aircraft group, squadron, station, base, auxiliary airfield; CO of any separate or detached command or group of detached units placed under a single commander for legal purposes; CO of any independent Marine Corps unit or organization where members of the Corps are on duty. If, instead of being officially designated as "commanding officer," the officer exercising command has the title, "officer-in-charge," he may nevertheless inflict nonjudical punishment.

In addition, nonjudicial punishment may be imposed by any officer possessing general court-martial jurisdiction or by any officer senior in the chain of command to one otherwise so authorized.

Nonjudicial punishment under Article 15, UCMJ, is intended to take care of offenses too serious to be dealt with by a mere rebuke, but not serious enough to warrant court-martial.

Preliminary Report and Investigation. The customary procedure for putting a man on report is as follows:

An officer submits a report against an enlisted man directly to the executive officer or adjutant of the command concerned. When a *noncommissioned officer* makes the report to the first sergeant of the offender, the offender is brought before the commanding officer by the first sergeant. If the company commander decides that the facts warrant action on a higher level, a written report is submitted to the battalion commander or the adjutant, giving the name of the offender, the offense charged, the name of the NCO making the charge, and any witnesses.

The executive officer or adjutant makes a thorough investigation of the charges or causes one to be made by the offender's company commander, the provost marshal, or other responsible officer.

Each morning the executive officer or adjutant informs the commanding officer of the enlisted men placed on report during the preceding day.

1606. OFFICE HOURS. Office Hours, as we have seen, is the Marine Corps equivalent of Captain's Mast. Like Mast, Office Hours can be, and frequently is, devoted to nondisciplinary matters such as praise, special requests, and the like. The Marine Corps has two nonpunitive types of Mast: Meritorious Mast and Request Mast. Both are handled at Office Hours. Office Hours, like any ceremony, should be dignified, disciplined, especially set apart in the daily routine, and carefully planned.

Office Hours should be:

Held at a set time, in a set place, usually the office of the commanding officer.

Attended by immediate commanding officers and first sergeants of men required to appear, whether for praise, reproof, or request.

Supervised by the adjutant and sergeant major if at battalion or barracks level, otherwise by the company first sergeant.

Held in full, immaculate uniform of the day.

If one of your men is up, take a careful look at his service record book and talk with his squad leader. Assure yourself that he is in tip-top condition as to uniform, cleanliness, and military demeanor.

Here is a typical Office Hours procedure:

1. Ten minutes before the scheduled time, the field music sounds "First Sergeants' Call," and the sergeant major assembles all men who are to appear, together with any enlisted witnesses and the respective first sergeants, who bring the men's service record books (if these are not already in the hands of the sergeant major). At the same time, immediate COs and any officer witnesses report to the adjutant, who conducts the officers into the commanding officer's office, where they are then seated.

2. At the appointed time, the adjutant stands on the left of the commanding officer with the service record books (obtained from the sergeant major); these should be opened, already tabbed appropriately for ready reference. First sergeants stand in a group to one side. The sergeant major conducts in the first man and reads aloud the charge or report against him, while the adjutant places his service record book before the commanding officer. The man stands uncovered and at attention throughout, one pace in front of the commanding officer's desk.

3. After the charges have been read by the CO, he must warn the accused, "Private————, you have the right to consult with a lawyer before being interrogated, and you do not have to make any statement regarding the offense of which you are accused or suspected. I must warn you that under Article 31, UCMJ, any statement made by you may be used as evidence against you in a trial by court-martial. Also that, if you so desire, you have the right to trial by court-martial rather than accept nonjudicial punishment here at Office Hours. *What have you to say?*"

This gives the accused a chance to tell his side of the case if he wishes to do so. Witnesses may be called—usually the reporting officer and witnesses to the offense. The accused must not be compelled to make a statement; he does not have to admit guilt or produce evidence.

4. After all explanations have been heard and the commanding officer has considered the report of preliminary investigation, the CO has four courses of action:

He may dismiss the accused, either accepting the explanation or giving a warning.

He may award nonjudicial punishment.

He may order the accused to be tried by special or summary court-martial (or he may recommend such trial, if he himself is not authorized to convene these courts).

For a very serious offense, he may order or recommend that an investigation be conducted under Article 32, UCMJ, to determine whether or not the accused should be tried by general court-martial. An Article 32 or pretrial investigation must be conducted before a case can be referred to a general court-martial.

5. At the conclusion of the hearing, the sergeant major commands, "1. About. 2. FACE. 3. Forward. 4. MARCH." On the command "MARCH," the man marches out of the office, and the process is repeated in the next case.

When meritorious cases (such as presentation of Good Conduct Medals, promotions, or special commendations) are involved, disciplinary cases should be paraded in the rear of the CO's office to watch the proceedings. They are then marched out by the sergeant major and individually brought in again as described above.

1607. LIMITS OF NONJUDICIAL PUNISHMENT. At Office Hours the commanding officer, in addition to or in lieu of admonition or reprimand, may impose one or certain combinations of the punishments prescribed under Article 15, UCMJ.

The Code gives anyone punished under Article 15 the right to appeal to the next superior commander in the chain of command, who may suspend, set aside, or remit any part of the punishment. In addition, any person not attached to or embarked in a ship now may elect trial by court-martial—prior to the award of punishment—rather than accept Office Hours' punishment.

While the law permits reduction of two grades for NCOs and petty officers above pay grade E-4 (corporal), Navy Department regulations provide that no such person can be reduced more than one grade. And, even more important as far as Marines are concerned, *no staff NCO may be reduced nonjudicially at Office Hours under Article 15, UCMJ except by the Commandant himself, as he is the only one who has the authority to promote a staff NCO.*

Office Hours punishment is not considered as a conviction insofar as the offender's record is concerned. Remember, also, that under no circumstances may an offender who is awarded extra duty be placed on guard to work it off.

The Commandant of the Marine Corps favors resort to nonjudicial punishment whenever justice and discipline may be attained by its use. Proceedings are brief and direct, and punishment is prompt, which in turn is far more conducive to discipline than punishment long-deferred. The accused's rights are protected as he has a right to appeal to the next higher authority in the chain of command.

Naval Courts-martial

1608. SUMMARY COURTS-MARTIAL. Summary courts-martial, originally called deck courts, may be convened by any person who may convene a general or special court-martial, that is, the commanding officer of a ship, naval station, or Marine Corps post and the commanding officer or officer-in-charge of any other command, when empowered by the Secretary of the Navy.

A summary court-martial consists of one commissioned officer, whenever practicable, not below the rank of captain, USMC, or equivalent; when practicable, this officer should have at least six years' commissioned service. When only one officer is attached to a command, the commanding officer himself shall be the summary court-martial, in which case no convening order is required. The summary court-martial officer is not sworn, but performs his duty under overall sanction of his oath of office.

The reporter—if one is required—may be any person who is competent to keep the record of the case.

Witnesses testify under oath. Examination is conducted by the summary court-martial (deck court) officer.

Objection to Trial by the Accused. An accused must signify his willingness to be tried by summary court-martial by signing a statement to that effect. If he objects, it is possible that he may be tried by a general or special court-martial, as appropriate.

Record. The record of a summary court-martial is customarily printed or typed on a standard summary court-martial charge sheet (if the accused pleads not guilty, a summary of testimony should be appended thereto). The accused is informed of the findings (and sentence if convicted) in the course of trial. An entry reflecting trial by summary court-martial is also made in the man's service record book. The case is then reviewed by higher authority. Action taken on the case subsequent to that by the convening authority must be communicated to the convening authority for implementation and notation in the accused's service record book.

1609. SPECIAL COURTS-MARTIAL. Special courts-martial may be convened, insofar as the Marine Corps is concerned, by an officer with general court-martial authority: commanding officer of any Marine brigade, regiment, detached battalion, or corresponding unit; commanding officer of any aircraft group, squadron, station, base, Marine barracks, or auxiliary airfield; the commanding officer of any independent Marine Corps unit or organization where members of the Corps are on duty; and any other CO or OinC when so designated by the Secretary of the Navy. A special court-martial may try officers or enlisted persons for any offenses (except capital) which the convening authority deems appropriate.

A special court-martial is composed of not less than three members, who may be commissioned officers, warrant officers, or (if the accused is an enlisted person and so requests) enlisted men.

The senior member of the court, usually a captain or higher, is the president. The trial counsel conducts the prosecutor's case; the defense counsel acts as defense attorney for the accused. In the Naval Services, a reporter transcribes the testimony and keeps the record under guidance of the trial counsel. The orderly acts as guide and messenger, and, if need be, escorts the accused.

Fig. 16-1: Sample seating arrangements for a special court-martial.

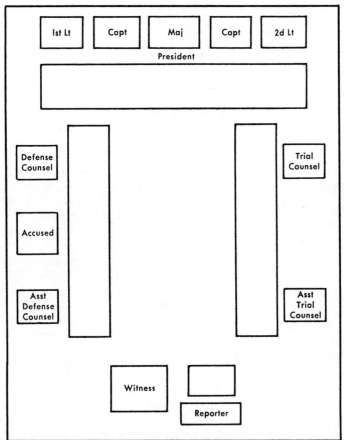

If an accused enlisted man requests in writing that enlisted members be included in the special court-martial trying his case, at least one-third of the members must be enlisted, unless that many cannot be obtained. Enlisted members cannot be from the same unit as the accused. When enlisted members cannot be obtained, the trial may still be held, but convening authority must give the reasons in writing. No member of a court-martial should be junior to the accused, and warrant officers or enlisted men may not under any circumstances sit as members for the trial of an officer.

No special legal qualifications are required for special court-martial counsel, but the accused must be advised of his right to a military lawyer to defend him. Specifically, if the trial counsel is a lawyer, the defense counsel must be so qualified. Lawyer defense counsel must be provided for an accused facing charges on which a BCD may be awarded.

Investigation. The convening authority must conduct a thorough preliminary investigation, unless the charges have already been thoroughly investigated and the accused was present at the investigation (as when appearing before an Investigation or Court of Inquiry). This preliminary inquiry is usually informal. It may be conducted by the commander or a member of his command. It may consist only of an examination of the charges and the summary of expected evidence which accompanies them; in other cases it may involve interview of witnesses, the search of barracks, quarters, or other places, or the collection of documentary evidence. In the Marine Corps, Office Hours often serves as the preliminary inquiry.

Punishments Authorized. Special courts-martial may adjudge any punishment not forbidden by the Code *except:* death; dishonorable discharge; dismissal; more than six months' confinement; more than three months' hard labor without confinement; loss of pay exceeding two-thirds pay per month, for a period exceeding six months. Bad-conduct discharge may not be adjudged unless a complete record of proceedings and testimony has been made, a lawyer defends the accused, and a military judge is detailed.

Review. After the record has been written up and signed by the president and examined and receipted for by the defense counsel, it is reviewed by the convening authority and the officer exercising general court-martial jurisdiction over the accused.

1610. GENERAL COURTS-MARTIAL. *General.* The highest Naval court, the general court-martial, may be convened by the President; the Secretary of the Navy; the Commandant of the Marine Corps; the commanding generals of the Fleet Marine Forces; the commanding general of any corps, division, aircraft wing, or brigade; the commander-in-chief of a fleet; the commanding officer of a naval station or Marine Corps post or large shore activity beyond the continental limits of the United States; any general officer or his immediate successor in command of a unit or activity of the

Marine Corps, and such commanding officers as may be authorized by the President and the Secretary of the Navy. General courts may try anyone who is subject to the Code.

Composition. A general court-martial is composed of not less than five members (one-third enlisted, *if* an enlisted accused so requests). A qualified military judge serves with each general court-martial. The president must, if practicable, be at least a captain or equivalent, but Navy Department policy requires that he must be a senior officer. For the trial of a Marine or a Navy staff corps officer, at least one-third of the members of the court should be of the same corps as the accused. Unless unavoidable, all members should be senior to the accused. The detailed trial and defense counsel must both be military lawyers.

The military judge of a general court-martial must be a member of the bar of a Federal court or of the highest court of a state and be certified for duty by the Judge Advocate General. The military judge advises the court on points of law. He has no vote in the deliberations of the court.

Investigation of Charges. Charges may not be referred to a general court-martial unless they have been formally investigated. This investigation may be ordered by the immediate CO of the accused or by the CO of a higher unit. The officer conducting the investigation should be of field grade and should possess legal training and experience. His job is neither to build up nor to whitewash a case, but simply to ascertain the facts thoroughly and impartially.

In a formal pretrial investigation, such as must precede a general court-martial, the accused has a right to be represented by a lawyer certified by the Judge Advocate General as competent to act as either trial or defense counsel. If the accused does not desire such counsel, he must waive this right, and his written waiver must be enclosed with the investigating officer's report and recommendations.

The investigation should be dignified and military, as brief as is consistent with thoroughness and fairness and should be limited to the issues raised by the charges and to the proper disposition of the case. Recommendations of an investigating officer are advisory only. After investigation, the convening authority must refer the charges to his staff judge advocate for consideration and advice.

Should the convening authority decide that a general court is not warranted, a lower court may be awarded, or the charges dismissed. But if it is decided that the accused should be brought to trial, the court is assembled, and the trial proceeds as soon as practicable. Proceedings are conducted with maximum formality.

1611. APPEARANCE AS A WITNESS. As a noncommissioned officer, you will very likely have to give evidence, for either prosecution or accused, at all types of courts-martial.

When appearing before a court or an investigation or at Office Hours, you must take care to wear your best uniform, have a haircut, and make the most military appearance possible.

Remember that you have been ordered to appear before the court to provide information that may determine whether or not an accused is guilty—whether he should be punished or set free. What you say and the way you say it, will help to determine whether the court makes a proper decision.

Present your testimony slowly, audibly, and distinctly, giving definite answers to questions. Tell the facts as you know them from observation, and do not state an opinion unless asked to do so.

No matter how you may be provoked, do not lose your temper. A witness who becomes angry is apt to become confused, to contradict himself, and, to say things he does not mean.

If a question is not clear, ask that it be repeated. Then think before you speak. The court wants a complete and accurate answer and will appreciate your efforts to give a well-considered statement when asked for one.

No matter how strong your convictions may be as to whether an accused is guilty or innocent, strive to keep an impartial attitude when you testify. Be fair, but, on the other hand, do not lean backward to give any party an undeserved "break." If you believe strongly that the accused is guilty, it is especially important that you do not allow your feelings or wishes to influence your statements. The court will give greater weight to your testimony if you state without bias all that you know. You are not there to decide guilt or innocence; that is the mission of the court.

If necessary, and you are permitted to do so, you may refresh your memory from notes, if made shortly after the occurrence about which you are speaking. The notes, however, may not be offered as evidence. You should not refer to notes except when absolutely necessary, and you may not read directly from them.

1612. ACCUSED AS A WITNESS. An accused has three courses open to him: he may remain silent, in which case the court may not hold his silence against him; he may, *at his own request only,* take the stand in his own defense and be sworn like any other witness; he may (after the findings) make a statement, in person or through counsel, or in both manners.

The accused has an absolute right not to testify if he so desires, and he should not be permitted to testify except at his own request. Failure of the accused to testify must not be used as the basis for any inference against him. An accused may at his own request be permitted to testify as to only one or more of the several offenses for which he is being tried; such testimony constitutes a waiver of his privilege against self-incrimination, but only as to information that relates to the offense or offenses concerning which he testified on direct examination or that is relevant to his credibility, which is of course in issue.

If the accused takes the stand as a witness, he becomes subject to rigorous cross-examination upon the offenses concerning which he has testified and upon the question of his credibility. Once an accused has been convicted, he may make either a sworn or an unsworn statement. This statement must be considered by the court in its determination of the sentence awarded. He cannot be cross-examined on an unsworn statement.

Fig. 16-2: Court-martial punishments.

Type of Punishment	General Court-Martial	Special Court-Martial	Summary Court-Martial
Admonition	Yes	Yes	Yes
BCD (Enlisted Only)	Yes	Yes	No
Confinement	Yes	Yes (not in excess of 6 months)	Yes (only enlisted below 5th paygrade; not in excess of 1 month)
Bread and Water*	Yes	Yes	Yes
Death	Yes	No (not in excess of 6 months)	No (not in excess of 1 month)
Detention of Pay (Enlisted only)	Yes	Yes	Yes
DD (Warrant Officer and Enlisted Only)	Yes	No	No
Dismissal (Officers Only)	Yes	No	No
Fines	Yes	Yes	Yes
Forfeiture	Yes	Yes (not in excess of ⅔ pay per month for 6 months)	Yes (not in excess of ⅔ of 1 month's pay)
Hard Labor (without confinement—enlisted only)	Yes (not in excess of 3 months)	Yes (not in excess of 3 months)	Yes (not in excess of 45 days) (only enlisted below 5th paygrade)
Life Imprisonment	Yes	No	No
Loss of Rank, Promotion, Seniority	Yes (Seniority only)	No	No
Suspension from Rank, Command Duty	No	No	No
Reduction of Officer	No	No	No
Reduction to Lowest Enlisted Grade	Yes	Yes	Yes (only enlisted below 5th pay grade)
Reprimand	Yes	Yes	Yes
Restriction to limits	Yes (not in excess of 2 months)	Yes (not in excess of 2 months)	Yes (not in excess of 2 months)

* May be awarded by any court-martial, and by COs under Article 15, in accordance with paragraph 125, MCM-1951, dated January 1963.

Henceforth, in fields of battle, the tents shall be our home.

—Old Hymn

17 Life in the Field

Life in the field or under canvas takes up a good share of the normal Marine Corps career, and what you make of it is largely up to you. An experienced soldier can, as you know, be comfortable, clean, and well fed under conditions which seem miserable to the recruit. This chapter gives a few facts and tips which will make field service more livable for you and the Marines under you.

1701. MAKE CAMP. The steps in making a camp are much like the steps involved in reconnaissance, selection, and occupation of a tactical position. In fact, for a tactical camp, the principles are identical.

Reconnoiter for a good campsite. Do this in person, if possible; if not, at least make a thorough map reconnaissance. You will find information on the details of a campsite in Chapter 6, *Landing Party Manual.* Keep this manual with you when detailed to a quartering party or to build a camp or bivouac. Look for a site which is tactically sound (or one which supports your mission, if not tactical); one which is sheltered from the weather, well drained, easy of access, moderately level, and convenient to a good source of water.

Organize your advance detail. It is the advance detail's job to lay out the camp, build as much of the camp as time and manpower permit, and guide the main body into camp. The advance detail includes: artificers for camp construction, engineer equipment operators, mess personnel, hospital corpsmen, communicators, motor transport men, and a small labor force. Depending on the size of the camp, your advance detail may have no more than a set of pioneer tools, or you may need surveying instruments, heavy engineer equipment, earth-moving gear, and demolitions. Be sure, above all, that the advance detail contains energetic, resourceful noncommissioned officers, and at least one corpsman.

Occupy the campsite. First, make camp for the advance detail.

360   Make every step count toward the finished camp. Start from the beginning with a well-defined and orderly camp plan in mind. Give sanitation first priority as you approach each task. Chapter 7 of the *Landing Party Manual* contains the basic information you will need, together with a wealth of practical tips. *Field Manual 21-10, Military Sanitation,* is also an excellent reference. Establish water points for drinking and for washing; dig heads immediately and mark them plainly; locate your galley on the side of camp away from the heads and close to the water point; and dig a garbage pit.

Establish communications and open your message center. Develop and mark access roads and the camp road net. Destroy as little timber and vegetation as you can, for the sake of shelter and for camouflage. From the outset, establish a regular camp routine. Make full use of your field music. Remember, the bugle was used to control armies thirty centuries before the public-address system and radio were invented. If one can be obtained, get a ship's bell to strike the hours and sound the alarm. As the camp nears completion and occupancy, generate competitive spirit as to who has the best tent area, best-looking motor pool, etc.

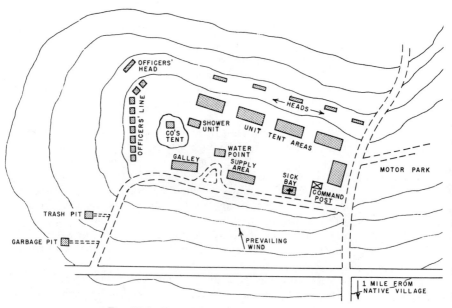

Fig. 17-1: Typical nontactical camp layout.

Be prepared for emergencies. Never neglect tactical security; establish a camp guard; promulgate a fire bill; know your sources of outside help; keep your fuel dump secure against fire and theft; establish liaison with your military and/or civilian neighbors. To supplement camp illumination, spot vehicles with headlights bearing on essential areas (such as sick bay, communications shack, ammunition stowage, gates, guard tent, etc.) in case generators should fail.

Finally, work your men hard, but take good care of them. Give them an opportunity to bathe and, if possible, to swim each day. Feed well, and waste no time in getting an effective galley and mess into operation. Get all hands a beer ration, and insure availability of exchange supplies.

P.S.—Don't forget a good tall flagpole for the Colors!

1702. LIVING UNDER CANVAS. "Under canvas" covers everything from life under a shelter half to a squad tent. Even so, the fundamentals are the same.

To be comfortable under canvas, you must:

Keep dry. This means erecting your tent properly, ditching it to prevent being flooded out, making sure your tent is leakproof, and not allowing branches or heavy brush to touch the surface of the tent. Though a tent should be taut in the first place, it can collect water under heavy rain. Do *not* push the water off by pushing up from the inside; if you do so, the canvas will leak where you touch it. It only takes a little rain to kill a night's sleep and make you miserable. In humid conditions, put a blanket between your sleeping bag and air mattress, to collect condensation.

Sleep soft. Make your bed before dark. Select a level spot, free from rocks or roots. If you have an air mattress, inflate it; if not, hollow out a hip-hole or form-fitting depression about three-inches deep, where you expect your hips to be when you lie down (this is most important for comfortable sleeping on the ground).

Cheat the insects. Dust your bedding with insecticide. Rig a mosquito net carefully before dark, and take good care of your net to prevent holes or rips. A mosquito net with a hole in it merely serves as a mosquito trap, with you as live bait. If possible, get the hospital corpsman to spray down your tent area, and use an insecticide "bomb" if you can get one. If nothing else is available, rub all exposed areas of skin with insect repellent.

Keep clean. Wash and shave, using your helmet as basin and bucket. You can rig a washstand by resting the helmet inside three tent pegs or sticks in triangular formation driven upright into the ground. Keep a small steel mirror with your toilet articles. If you are going to be in camp longer than overnight, get hold of an expeditionary can to provide water storage for your tent.

Keep warm. If the weather is cold, winterize your tent by throwing dirt around the bottom edges and packing it to keep drafts from blowing under. Any kind of insulating layer between ground and sleeping bag will help you to sleep warm. Use your poncho, a blanket, even your parka. You can pile layer after layer on top without doing much good, whereas insulation between you and the ground will keep you snug. If you are in a semipermanent setup with canvas cots, a few layers of newspaper or magazines make a fine underpinning for a warm bunk. If you camp in one site for a while, fluff your sleeping bag each day; this prevents matting underneath and consequent loss of insulation.

Make a deck. If you can find scrap boards, make a deck for your tent. Even if you have only one piece of plank, use this beside your bunk as a footing to keep your feet out of the dirt and off the ground when you dress or undress. If you have footlocker or seabag, be sure to rest it on trestles or duckboards so as to permit circulation of air underneath and to avoid the damp, which will rot anything in contact with the ground. If you have a tent deck, beware of snakes nesting under it (or, for that matter, crawling into warm parts of your tent at night).

Make a light. Always have a flashlight handy and in working order. If you can, obtain a gasoline pressure-lantern such as comes in the standard Marine Corps illuminating chest. Possibly you may have a pressure lantern of your own. If so, keep a few spare mantles handy. *Never forget a dry supply of matches.*

Keep safe. If in an area subject to enemy attack or air raid, dig a foxhole immediately. In the rainy season (*if* drainage permits), dig your foxhole inside your tent or under a shelter half. Arrange your gear inside the tent so that your weapons, ammunition, and equipment avoid direct contact with the ground and stay free from dust, mud, or rain. Learn the location of guy lines so you won't trip over them in the dark or when diving for your fighting hole. On squad tents with metal stakes, put tin cans on the stakes to prevent people from injuring themselves in the dark.

1703. SANITATION. The first and best hint on field sanitation is to make yourself thoroughly familiar with Chapter 7, *Landing Party Manual,* already mentioned. This manual is readable, complete, and practical. Every officer and NCO should be well acquainted with it.

The fundamentals of field sanitation, both for individuals and units, are:

Personal cleanliness
Disposal of waste (trash, garbage, excrement, and urine)
Control of insects and pests
Disease-free food service and water supply.

In the Spanish-American War, the U. S. Army sustained more than four deaths from disease for every man killed in action. Approximately 50 percent of the Army in Cuba became casualties to yellow fever, malaria, and enteric disease. A substantial fraction of these appalling nonbattle casualties could have been averted by sanitary techniques known even then—*plus* effective leadership. By comparison, the U. S. Marine battalion which served in Cuba throughout the war suffered only two percent sanitary casualties and had no nonbattle deaths at all. *Today, there is no excuse for casualties resulting from bad sanitation. Poor sanitary conditions and the inevita-*

ble casualties which result are a direct reflection of poor leadership, weak discipline, and inadequate supervision.

1704. INDIVIDUAL HYGIENE. *Keep as clean as you can.* As a minimum, bathe feet, hands, and private parts. If possible, change your underwear and socks after bathing.

Change your underwear and socks at least twice a week. If you cannot wash your clothing, crumple it, shake it out, and hang it outside in the sun, turned inside out, for at least two hours.

Get out of wet clothing as quickly as you can. This is particularly important in cold-weather operations.

Drink only water which has been purified. *Regard every water source as contaminated until you know otherwise.* Drink plenty of water, but do not drink large amounts at one time. In warm weather, increase your intake of salt, if necessary by salt tablets from your sick bay. Use your own canteen or cup only.

Inspect your body frequently for lice. If you cannot wash, dust with insecticide.

Carry toilet paper and keep it dry. Inside your helmet liner is a good place. *Relieve yourself only at prescribed heads and urinals.*

Have a short, regulation haircut and keep your fingernails short and clean. Brush teeth at least once daily.

Avoid direct contact with damp ground, especially when hot or perspiring. Likewise avoid drafts.

Keep your mess gear scrupulously clean. Wash mess gear in hot, soapy water and rinse it in boiling water, before and after each meal. Be sure no garbage, grease, or food particles adhere to mess gear between meals.

Take care of your feet. This means properly fitted shoes and socks, daily washing, toenails trimmed straight across, use of shower clogs when in garrison, and correct treatment of blisters and corns.

Use your mosquito net and keep it in good condition. Scrupulously observe any antimalarial instructions which the surgeon may prescribe.

As a noncommissioned officer, set an example of personal cleanliness and sanitary discipline to your men. Wash and shave daily. Observe all the precautions just described, and require that your people do likewise.

1705. CAMP AND UNIT SANITATION. *Lay out and build camps and bivouacs around the sanitary plan.* Make sanitation convenient for all hands.

Control your water supply. Purify drinking water by accepted techniques. Establish and plainly mark separate water points for washing, cooking, and human consumption. Locate washing points downstream from points used for human consumption.

Give particular care to location, maintenance, and cleanliness of heads and urinals. Follow prescribed designs in construction. *Flyproof every head.* Locate heads and urinals conveniently to living areas but away from the galley, messhall, and water supply. Never locate a head uphill on a drainage line leading down toward a water source. When a head goes out of use, it must be filled and covered, and then marked with a sign, "HEAD CLOSED (Date)."

Sanitary conditions in the galley are as important as in the head. Galley, garbage house, and, if possible, the mess itself must be flyproof. Garbage must be kept covered and must be removed to garbage pits at least once daily. Empty food containers should be either burned or buried, both for camouflage and to prevent flies from swarming. For any but the most temporary bivouac, a grease trap must be built for disposal of waste grease and greasy water. Most important of all, the galley area must include facilities so that each man's mess gear (plus all pots and food containers) can be thoroughly washed down in boiling soapy water, and then rinsed twice in boiling clear water.

Wage ceaseless war on insects and pets. The principal enemies are: flies (enteric diseases); mosquitoes (malaria and yellow fever); lice, ticks, and mites (typhus); cockroaches; and all rodents.

The simplest way to control flies is to cut off their nourishment by screening heads, galleys, and messes. This keeps flies away from food and thus from poisoning you. Watch for young flies, particularly *inside* a screened structure. The presence of small young flies means that flies are breeding nearby, usually inside.

Drainage of standing water, coupled with oiling of stagnant pools and low, swampy spots, kills mosquito larvae as they breed.

Clearing and burning tall grass, brush, and undergrowth help to reduce the danger from ticks and mites. Human cleanliness and rodent control stop lice.

Cockroach control is a stubborn problem and requires constant effort. Cleanliness, discovery and attack of hiding places, and insecticides are the prime essentials (but insecticides alone are a mere palliative).

All insect control problems can be reduced in a large camp area if aerial dusting with insecticides is carried out immediately before occupation of the site.

1706. FEEDING IN THE FIELD. The sanitary aspects of your field mess and galley have just been discussed. This section supplements the foregoing with a few hints on feeding in the field.

The simplest type of field rations are the components packaged for individual or small-group consumption without being prepared by a galley. Although field rations can be eaten without heating, their edibility increases considerably with heating, which may be carried out either in the can or in mess gear. If you heat rations in the can, you may immerse the can in hot water, or warm it over an open flame. In the latter case *open the can before heating,* or it will explode with dangerous violence. Aside from an open fire, the usual methods of heating rations are heat tablets, sterno (solidified alchohol), or a gasoline stove. This lightweight, collapsible stove is an excellent investment for any staff NCO.

During the Korean War, hungry Marines line up at a field
kitchen for a hot meal.

If you find yourself in a situation which permits a little "housekeeping," you will find that field rations—although well seasoned
for the average palate—can be improved by such condiments as
tabasco, garlic salt, curry powder, paprika, and bouillon cubes.

The next step up the subsistence scale from individual rations is a

"B" ration, which is a garrison ration in which fresh components requiring refrigeration have been replaced by equivalent canned items. The "B" ration, of course, is prepared and served on a unit basis through the mess, and thus requires a galley.

The essential features and requisites of a galley in the field are:

1. Shelter from the elements and, if necessary, from enemy fire and observation.
2. Access for ration vehicles or carrying parties
3. Water supply for cooking and washing, plus a pot-walloping area nearby.
4. Ration storage safe from human, rodent, and insect incursions.
5. Fuel storage for stoves and lanterns. (*Note:* The gasoline field range is a versatile and durable stove, but requires expert maintenance and cleaning. Establish a preventive-maintenance area for stoves in conjunction with the refueling point.)
6. Refrigeration and electric power are the ultimate refinements of a galley in the field. Although not necessities, both are luxuries which every mess officer and mess sergeant should try to get.

Note: For the foxhole chef, *The Charlie Ration Cookbook,* originated by a Marine, BrigGen W. S. McIlhenny, is highly recommended. This entertaining pamphlet contains over 20 gourmet recipes based on C-ration components. Any Marine can write McIlhenny Company, Avery Island, Louisiana, 70313, and get a free copy.

1707. HINTS FOR TROPICAL SERVICE. Disease and climate are enemies which all soldiers in the tropics must fight. Both enemies can be conquered by common sense, plus heightened attention to the precautions which you would take anywhere.

The most serious tropical disease are insect-borne. These are malaria, dengue fever, yellow fever, elephantiasis, and the various dysenteries. In addition, humid climates beget fungus complaints on a scale unknown elsewhere. Control of all these (except fungus) is a function of insect control and sanitation, plus rigid observance of prophylactic measures prescribed by your surgeon. Fungus in the tropics, as anywhere else, thrives on heat, dampness, insufficient ventilation, and negligence at its inception.

Tropical climates may be dry and hot, or hot and humid. Of these, the dry climate is of course the more healthful.

In dry, hot regions, such as Arabia or the Persian Gulf, protection against the direct rays of the sun is paramount. Always remain covered. Do not overexpose large skin areas to sunburn. If possible, wear light-colored uniform, such as khaki, which reflects heat, rather than dark-colored, heat-absorbent clothing. Use sunglasses made of light-polarizing material or you may be blinded by glare. Beware of heat exhaustion and keep your salt balance up by use of salt tablets. Do not overheat if you can help it.

In hot and humid climates, special attention to sanitation and personal hygiene is called for. Here, too, dehydration and heat exhaustion must be guarded against. Dampness constitutes an enemy both to you and to your equipment, which will quickly deteriorate under the ravages of rust, rot, and mildew. Clean and oil your weapon and its magazines more frequently. Bathe as often as you can, with special attention to your feet and body areas where perspiration naturally collects. (Soap, incidentally, is often a good fungicide.) If you have been operating in paddy or swamp, get your feet dry whenever you can, change socks (wool, *not* cotton, the kind you can rinse, wring out, and, if necessary, wear damp).

The essential items of clothing are shirt, trousers, and shoes—just those. If necessary or if you prefer, you can do without socks and drawers or undershirts. A mosquito headnet and heavy cotton gloves, tight enough to prevent bites at night, can be godsends. Hang your shirttail out, not tucked in, to allow body ventilation. Under no circumstances continue the self-defeating garrison practice of shining field boots. (The original concept of the World War II field shoe was expressly to allow open pores in the leather for passage of air and essential ventilation of feet—a practical fact which was quickly forgotten.)

Travel light. Hang gear from your shoulders or waist, rather than your back. A poncho and items slung from your belt are better than a pack. But a heavy knife, such as the Marine Corps combat (or "Kabar") knife, is essential.

Avoid excessive use of strong drink. Expose yourself as little as possible to biting insects, and try to hold down the biting area of your body they can get access to. After nightfall, try to keep under cover or, if available, behind screening. Mosquitoes have killed more men in the jungle than armed enemies. If possible, sleep, and keep your gear, off the ground. Another good reason for keeping off the ground, in Southeast Asia, is snakes. However, remember that snakes, carnivorous animals, even fire ants, and other such fierce insects are more concerned with avoiding than attacking you.

1708. COLD WEATHER HINTS. Survival and military efficiency in extreme cold weather constitute very severe tests of NCO leadership. Severe cold renders the most simple operations difficult, prolonged, and clumsy, and enervates, paralyzes, and numbs the individual. In winter warfare, compared to the tropics, disease plays a minor role, while climate is the major problem. Cold is largely overcome by intelligent use of cold-weather clothing designed for military operations. It is your job, as a leader, not only to see that your men *know* how to wear cold-weather clothing, but (much more difficult) that they take the pains to do so. Frostbite, when not fatal, is crippling; the paraplegic amputees from the early Korean winter campaigns were virtually all the result of severe frostbite (and, behind that, of incompetent leadership). *Frostbite is not only avoidable, but, if it occurs, is reprehensible and usually warrants disciplinary action.*

The rule for cold-weather survival is the word, "C-O-L-D":

C: Keep yourself and clothing Clean.
O: Avoid Overheating.
L: Wear clothing and equipment Loosely.
D: Keep Dry.

To avoid frost-bitten feet or toes (ususally the result of wet or sweaty socks while marching), tuck wet socks next to your stomach under your loose clothing, and rotate the resulting dry pair with those on your feet at each halt. It is also good practice to switch right and left socks to the opposite foot.

Other problems of cold-weather operations are danger from fires due to overheated stoves, carbon monoxide poisoning in improperly ventilated shelters, and temporary blindness resulting from snow or ice glare. All these can be prevented by leadership and supervision.

Before you go into the field in arctic or subarctic climates, the Marine Corps will probably send you through cold-weather indoctrination. If unable to obtain such training, be sure to get the effective manual on cold-weather operations and survival.

There is nothing magical or even superhuman about successful warfare in extreme cold. It is a technique which can be learned, and, for your own sake and your men's, you must learn it.

1709. BREAK CAMP. The main points to be remembered in vacating a camp site are as follows:

1. *Always leave the site in better condition than you found it.* Good camping grounds are rare; think of the next unit. Every individual and every unit, from squad up, must police its area prior to vacating.
2. *The site must be left completely sanitary.* Heads and garbage pits must be filled and properly marked. Trash must be collected and disposed of.
3. *Gear adrift must be collected and salvaged.* There is no worse reflection on an organization than a miscellaneous accumulation of jettisoned or forgotten property and equipment on a former campsite. Nothing useful should be left behind. No documents of any sort (especially if classified) should be lying about.
4. *Fires must be extinguished.*
5. *Officers and NCOs must inspect their areas prior to vacating.* In most instances, a rear party under officer command should be detailed for final police; check for property left behind and closely inspect all areas. The officer should be required to report to the commanding officer on the condition of the campsite when finally vacated.

It is unworthy of the Marine Corps and is an inexcusable mark of disorganization, low morale, and defective leadership for a unit to leave a crummy camp area behind. Whenever possible, you should try to leave an area in *better* condition than when you found it. (This last emphatically applies in garrison, too.)

1710. CARE OF FIELD GEAR. *Your helmet,* next to your weapon, is your most important piece of combat equipment. It may seem practically indestructible, but even helmets can be abused.

Don't use it for cooking or expose it to flame. This weakens or destroys its temper and thus reduces its protective strength.

If you employ the helmet as an intrenching tool or for any kind of digging, you will scratch off its dull, camouflage coating.

Helmets are nonmagnetic so that the steel won't interfere with your compass. However, if the helmet is badly scraped, scratched, or dented, this may remagnetize it.

Protect the liner from being cracked or deformed by rough use.

Don't sit on the helmet or you may break the chin strap loops.

Canteens should be thoroughly dried out after use, or else they will collect corrosion and/or unpleasant taste. If you have one of the old-type canteen covers with felt liner, hang onto it; this feature is designed so that, when the felt is dampened, it keeps the canteen nicely cooled. Once a canteen is dried out, screw on the cap so that the cork liner won't shrink, dry up, or dry out.

Mess gear. The most important rule regarding mess gear is to keep it clean and sanitary. Careful drying will avert corrosion.

1711. USEFUL ARTICLES FOR FIELD SERVICE. A lot of items are nice to have when in the field, but their necessity has to be weighed (literally) against the fact that most Marines can't afford to have what they can't carry by themselves. As General R. S. Ewell, of the Confederate Army, once remarked, "The path to glory cannot be followed with much baggage." On the other hand, when in a nontactical or static situation, a few added items can make a great deal of difference.

USEFUL ARTICLES FOR FIELD SERVICE

Wrist watch (luminous dial)
Jackknife (should have corkscrew)
Miniature can opener (get from C-ration can, and carry with your dog tags)
* Pliers
* Medium screwdriver
* Wire coat-hanger(s)
* Double socket
Flashlight, waterproof
Stove, individual, gasoline
* Lantern, pressure, gasoline
Sunglasses (made of light-polarizing material)
Tennis shoes (wear at night, so you can remove field boots but still turn out in a hurry)
Foot powder
Insect powder and insect repellant
* Shower clogs
Housewife
Steel mirror

Multicolor automatic pencil (Norma)
Pocket notebook
Air mattress
Plastic bags (those used to pack radio batteries can be cumshawed from battalion or company radiomen; they are particularly useful for keeping things dry, such as socks, map, pistol, etc.).
Sponge (practically weightless supplement to towel or substitute for washcloth in warm climate with limited laundry facilities; carry in helmet liner).
* For static situation or nontactical camp only.

As you lay in your stock of such items, try to ascertain which may be available by issue (air mattress or flashlight, for example). Avoid purchasing what you can be sure of being able to draw. Especially avoid buying nonregulation combat equipment or weapons, such as fancy pistols or knives. The Government spends millions a year to make certain that the combat gear issued to you is the finest and most reliable. You merely make a fool of yourself and set a poor example if you are not content with regulation equipment and weapons.

P.S.—When you you go into the field, take a pocket edition of some good book with you. You will be amazed how often it can chase monotony and provide relaxation when most needed.

. . . that no persons be appointed to offices, or enlisted into said battalions, but such as are good seamen, or so acquainted with maritime affairs as to be able to serve to advantage by sea.

—Resolution of the Continental Congress
to raise Marines, 10 November 1775.

A ship without Marines is like a coat without buttons.

—David G. Farragut

18 Service Afloat

Sea duty is the oldest and original duty of Marines, dating from the Athenian fleets of the 5th century B.C., and carrying on through Roman times when separate legions of *milites classiarii* ("soldiers of the Fleet") were assigned to duty afloat. In the seventeenth century, when the British and Dutch organized the first modern corps of Marines, it was for duty as ships' detachments, and it was for this same purpose that U. S. Marines were first raised in 1775. And the anchor in our Marine Corps emblem symbolizes today that the Marine is first and foremost a maritime soldier who wages war on and from the sea.

Since World War II and the Korean War (and with even greater manpower pressures resulting from WestPac requirements), the great permanent expansion of the Marine Corps has unfortunately been accompanied by a corresponding reduction in the number of ships of the Navy carrying Marine detachments, with the result that sea duty is a much rarer tour for the young Marine than in the past. Thus when you receive orders to report on board the USS *Tuscarora* for duty, you are not only embarking upon a tour that previous experience has little prepared you for, but you may not even be able to get advice from anyone you know unless he has had sea duty. Nonetheless, sea duty is one of the most rewarding tours that can come your way. (Some old-timers will say you aren't a real Marine until you have served in a ship's detachment.) It is an opportunity and a professional privilege.

1801. SEA-DUTY TRAINING AND INDOCTRINATION. Because the Navy forms its opinions of the Marine Corps to a large extent from observation of seagoing Marines and because ships' detachments represent the Corps "in every clime and place," Marines detailed for sea duty are carefully selected. On each coast —at Norfolk Navy Yard (Portsmouth, Virginia) and at San Diego —are the East and West Coast Sea Schools. These schools indoctrinate Marines of the rank of corporal and below who are ordered to sea duty. Sergeants and higher, however, are detailed directly to their prospective ships and are thus responsible for picking up their own indoctrination, so to speak, on the run.

Although, as just stated, the sea schools have as their primary job the training of junior Marines, they are of course prepared to help indoctrinate senior NCOs on an informal basis to whatever extent permitted by time, mutual convenience, or individual orders and travel plans.

So your first step, on receiving orders to sea, should be to get in touch, either in person or by letter, with the officer-in-charge of the nearest Sea School (and, since Fleet practices vary, preferably with the one which provides replacements for your prospective ship). In addition, if time is available, first sergeants and gunnery sergeants going to sea should also visit the Ships Detachment Supply Officer (either at Portsmouth or San Diego) who supports their detachment, for essential information on fiscal and supply matters peculiar to service afloat.

By way of background reading and reference publications, the nominal cost of a current *Bluejackets' Manual,* (U. S. Naval Institute, Annapolis) will repay itself many times. In addition, obtain a copy of the Marine Corps Development and Education Command's Education Command Publication ECP 1-17, *Service Afloat.*

The Ship and Shipboard Life

> *The words Marine and Mariner differ by one small letter only; but no two races of men, I had well nigh said no two animals, differ from one another more completely.*
>
> *—Captain Basil Hall, RN, 1832*

1802. REPORTING ABOARD. Your orders, in case of sea duty, will direct you to report to a ship for duty and, in peacetime, will ordinarily state the port in which you are to report. When this is impossible for security reasons, you will be directed to report to some shore command, such as a naval operating base, a naval shipyard, or a naval district. This headquarters will further direct you where and when to join your ship. Arrive in the specified port at least as early as the night before you are expected to report.

Ships in port, anchored out, periodically send boats to the regular fleet landings. Plan to have your baggage and yourself at the landing by 0730. Better still, if you know your ship is in port, go to the landing and take the next boat; that way you will run no risk of missing ship, which is a very serious dereliction.

The uniform for Marine reporting for sea duty is undress blue or, in warm climes or places, tropical khaki.

As you reach the top of the gangway or accommodation ladder, come to a halt, face aft, and salute the Colors. Then face and salute the officer of the deck (OOD), saying, "I request permission to come aboard, sir. I am Staff Sergeant Basilone reporting aboard for duty."

The OOD will return your salute and will probably welcome you aboard. He will ask for a copy of your orders for the log. The OOD's messenger or a sideboy will take you below to the Marine detachment office, where the first sergeant will check you in, orient you, size you up, and present you to the detachment commander, usually a captain. You will then be assigned berthing space in the Marine compartment, or, if a staff NCO, probably in the chief petty officers' (CPO) quarters.

> *Note:* Navy CPOs are in pay grades E-7 and higher, whereas, as you know, we split our NCO groups one grade lower, commencing the staff NCO bracket at staff sergeant. Aboard some ships this may lead to friction, as staff sergeants are by *Navy Regulations* entitled to the privileges of the CPO Mess. In most instances, especially where the Marines concerned have shown tact and common sense (plus recognition, after all, that the ship and the mess and the rules belong to the Navy), staff sergeants will be made welcome by the CPOs. But watch your step, and don't barge in; take your cues from the first sergeant.

1803. SHIP'S ORGANIZATION. One of your first tasks should be to study the ship's organization. Each ship prepares its own organization book, which varies somewhat from those of other ships, but all have certain essentials in common.

The Captain of a naval ship, the senior line officer assigned to the ship's company, has full command and responsibility for his ship, and he exercises authority and precedence over all persons serving aboard. He is also charged with the supervision, safety, and good order of all persons temporarily embarked in the ship. His authority, responsibility, and duties are described in *Navy Regulations.*

The Executive Officer is the executive arm of the commanding officer. As such, he is the Captain's direct representative and is responsible for the prompt and efficient execution of his orders. The executive officer works through the heads of departments, who assist him in organization, administration, operation, and fighting the ship. In addition to his general responsibilities just mentioned, the "exec" directly oversees such administrative functions as morale, welfare, berthing, training, personnel administration, religious, and legal matters.

DEPARTMENTS AND ACTIVITIES. Under the executive officer, the tasks of the ship are divided among the departments and activities and then further subdivided into divisions.

Most ships have the following departments:

Weapons	Medical/Dental
Operations	Supply
Navigation	Engineering

SUPPORT DEPARTMENTS

SUPPLY DEPARTMENT

General supply
Disbursing of monies
Operation of general mess
Operation of ship's stores
Maintenance of store rooms

REPAIR DEPARTMENT

Preparation of repair schedules
Repair and service to ships
(as assigned)
Maintenance of repair
machinery

TRANSPORTATION DEPARTMENT

Embarkation and debarkation
of passengers
Berthing, messing, and
direction of passengers
Liaison with shore loading
authorities (ships without
combat cargo officer)

MEDICAL DEPARTMENT

Treatment of the sick and
wounded
Health, sanitation, and
hygiene
First aid instructions

ORDNANCE REPAIR DEPARTMENT

Preparation of repair schedules
Repair and service to submarine ordnance
Maintenance of ordnance
repair machinery

DENTAL DEPARTMENT

Dental treatment
Oral hygiene instruction
Photo dosimetry

*Fig. 18-1: Shipboard departments. (The Marine
Detachment is always part of the Weapons Department.)*

COMMANDING OFFICER

EXECUTIVE OFFICER — EXECUTIVE STAFF

COMMAND DEPARTMENTS

NAVIGATION DEPARTMENT

Navigation and piloting
Care and maintenance of
  navigating equipment

AIR DEPARTMENT

Aircraft landing, launching,
  and handling
Aircraft services (fueling and
  arming)
Handling of aviation fuels
Handling of aviation ammunition (outside of magazines)
Maintenance and repair of
  aircraft (when maintenance
  personnel are not em-
  barked with squadrons)

ENGINEERING DEPARTMENT

Operation and maintenance
  of ship's machinery
Damage and casualty control
Repair of hull and machinery
Power lighting and water
  maintenance
Upkeep and maintenance of
  underwater fittings

AIR GROUP

(Embarked command)

OPERATIONS DEPARTMENT

Preparation of operation plans
Preparation of operational
  training schedules
Visual and electronic search
Intelligence
Operational Evaluation
Combat information
Operational control of air-
  borne aircraft
Electronic countermeasures
Radio and visual communica-
  tions
Issuance control of RPS-
  distributed publications
Repair of assigned electronics
  equipment

WEAPONS DEPARTMENT

Operation, maintenance, and
  repair of armament
Antisubmarine search and
  attack
Mine warfare
Deck seamanship
Maintenance of ship's exterior
  hull
Handling and stowage of
  ammunition and explosives
Handling and stowage of
  cargo
Operation and maintenance
  of assigned electronics
  equipment
Launching and recovery of
  aircraft (ships without air
  department)
Marine detachment
Guided missiles
Nuclear weapons

The Weapons (or *Gunnery*) *Department* includes all the ship's weapons and the people required to fight and maintain them. In combatant ships the Marine detachment forms part of this department.

In ships primarily concerned with offense through missiles, guns, or aircraft, gunnery includes the activities of the deck department, and the *first lieutenant* ("first lieutenant" is the traditional title for an important billet among the ship's officers; it is not a rank) is an assistant to *the gunnery officer.* In ships not primarily concerned with offense, the deck department includes air operations and gunnery, and the air officer and the gunnery officer assist the first lieutenant. Deck functions are those having to do with deck seamanship and ground tackle, with the rigging, masts, and superstructure and exterior of the hull, and with the operation and upkeep of all boats.

The Operations Department is responsible for collection, evaluation, and dissemination of combat and operational information required to enable the ship to perform her assigned missions and tasks. The two principal divisions in this department are communications and CIC (combat information center).

The Navigation Department, headed by *the navigator,* is responsible for the safe navigation and piloting of the ship. The navigator will usually be senior to all watch and division officers.

The Engineering Department operates and maintains all propulsion and auxiliary machinery and electrical equipment and is responsible for the repair or control of emergency or battle damage.

The Supply Department is charged with all logistic functions for the ship (procurement, stowage, issue, and accounting of supplies and equipment) plus disbursing and operation of the general mess (crew's mess) and ship's store. The ship's supply officer is responsible for stocking and supplying Marine Corps clothing (requisitioned from Marine supply sources) for his ship's detachment. Responsibility for Marine Corps equipment, as distinct from clothing, rests with the Commanding Officer of the Marine detachment.

The Medical Department has its normal responsibilities for the ship's sanitation and hygiene and for the health of all hands.

Other Departments. According to function and mission, certain ships will also have *Air Departments* (aircraft carriers, helicopter assault ships, etc.), *Dental Departments* (when a dental officer is assigned), *Repair Departments* (repair ships and tenders), and *Military Departments* (on transports manned by civilians and permanently assigned to the Military Sea Transport Service, or MSTS).

1804. SHIP'S REGULATIONS. Usually in one binder with the Ship's Organization, Ship's Regulations (which are the Captain's standing orders to all hands) contain indispensable information as to the ship and the department and division to which you are assigned. The Marine detachment office will have a copy of Ship's Organization and Ship's Regulations that you can examine. Study them carefully; these regulations will answer many questions and save much embarrassment.

Study the ship's plans. Supplement these by a tour of the ship. Visit the bridge, forecastle, combat information center, crew's quarters, galley, central station, plotting rooms, all directors, one mount or turret in each battery, ship control stations, the engine room, and one fireroom.

The Plan of the Day (POD) is an important document, issued daily by the executive officer, giving the next day's schedule of routine work or operations and any variations or unusual additions. The Plan of the Day promulgates the orders of the day, drills and training, duty and liberty sections, working parties, and movies or recreational events.

The Boat Schedule is promulgated when in port and not lying alongside a dock or pier. Obtain a copy and keep it with you, especially when going ashore.

1805. THE QUARTERDECK. The quarterdeck is a portion of the ship's main deck (or occasionally a prescribed area on another deck) set aside by the Captain for official and ceremonial functions. Certain parts of the quarterdeck (usually the starboard side) are reserved for the Captain or for an admiral if embarked. The remainder is reserved for the ship's officers. The quarterdeck is out of bounds at all times to enlisted men except when engaged in ship's work thereon or on duty. The detachment parade of the Marines is either on or immediately adjoining the quarterdeck. The rules, traditions, and etiquette of the quarterdeck are among the most venerable in the service, and their strict observance by all hands is the mark of good sea manners.

Never appear on the quarterdeck unless in the uniform of the day, except when crossing to enter or leave a boat, or when otherwise required by duty.

Do not be seen on the quarterdeck with hands in pockets or uncovered.

Salute the quarterdeck every time you set foot on it, even from other parts of the ship.

Do not smoke, whistle, or skylark on the quarterdeck.

Remain clear of those portions of the quarterdeck reserved for Captain or Admiral.

1806. THE CPO MESS. For Marines entitled to the privileges of the Chief Petty Officers' Mess, here are a few pointers and rules which will smooth your way. The CPO mess is your home—and your club. Here you meet and get to know some of the most important people in the ship's company, the "Chiefs." It's up to you to make them shipmates. With their help, you can get just about anything done aboard ship that is legal or worth doing.

As in all Navy messes, tradition is important and seniority draws a great deal of water, possibly even more so than ashore. For example, seating at meals runs by seniority; you will be assigned your rightful place, and there you sit.

Unless you are on duty under arms, remove your cap when entering the mess. Never unsheathe your sword in a mess. Save your quarrels for elsewhere.

This does not mean that the silence of a library need be maintained. A noisy mess is often the sign of a happy mess. Between meals, you gather in the mess for a moment of relaxation, discussion of problems, a game of acey-deucey or cribbage, or a cup of coffee. It is also often a place for fun, when wives and sweethearts are entertained, or on the occasion of a ship's party. It can be all these things, or it can be just a place to eat. It depends upon you and upon the other members of the mess.

CPO messes are organized as business concerns, with a mess fund to which you contribute your share on joining. Monthly assessments are made, from which costs of extras, periodicals, decorations, and other essentials and conveniences are paid. This fund is administered by a mess treasurer. In addition, aboard some ships a junior member—it could be you—is designated as "mess caterer" and put in charge of menu planning, detailed supervision of meal service, etc. A good way to get this job is to complain about any of these matters. Avoid doing so unless you have better ideas.

Like a staff NCO mess ashore, the CPO mess is out of bounds to more junior enlisted men. See that they have little occasion to enter the CPO mess. When they do, require that they uncover (unless under arms), keep quiet, and refrain from profane language.

Be punctual for meals. If unavoidably delayed, express your regrets to the senior member. If necessary to leave a meal before it is over, ask to be excused.

Do not lounge about the mess out of uniform. Some latitude may be allowed during "all-hands" evolutions which require working uniform, but be certain that whatever you do is in accord with the local ground rules.

Introduce guests to as many as possible, and *always* to the senior member. Entertain only such guests as your messmates and their families will be happy to meet.

Each guest is considered a guest of the mess. Be friendly and sociable with all guests.

When a visiting chief or staff NCO enters, extend the courtesies of the mess, and try to help him in any way you can.

Gambling, drinking, and possession of liquor aboard ship, except for medical purposes, are serious offenses.

Pay your bills promptly.

When necessary, admit ignorance. People in the Navy respect a frank admission and detest bluff. But spare no effort to find out what you did not know.

As a Marine, you can expect considerable good-natured bantering (but remember that—in their hearts—almost all sailors deeply respect and admire the Corps, and it is your responsibility to live up to their private picture of a model Marine). Get to know your mess-mates and, if possible, to like them. In cramped quarters in a ship, it requires a nice adjustment to live in harmony with a number of other positive personalities.

Make a definite effort to get along. It's a matter of give-and-take; be sure you give more than you take.

The Marine Detachment

Every battleship, large aircraft carrier, and cruiser (together with certain amphibious ships), normally has its detachment of Marines. In addition, each major amphibious force ship (LPA, LKA, LPH, LPD) carries Marine combat cargo or Marines, and, in the case of certain ships on which Marine aircraft are to be based, Marine air crews. Moreover, to meet special security requirements, nuclear submarine tenders carry Marine guards, too.

Marines aboard a man-of-war are a distinct and integral part of the ship's company. On board a combatant ship, the Marine detachment is one of the gunnery divisions, ususally in the antiaircraft battery. Shipboard Marines do the following jobs.

1. Provide the trained backbone of the ship's landing force as a whole, as well as an independent force for limited operations ashore;
2. Form provisional battalions of Marines, together with other ships' detachments, for landing operations by the Fleet;
3. Man guns and fire control instruments aboard ship;
4. Provide internal security (guard and orderly) services for the ship.

In addition, Marine officers frequently serve as the ship's gunnery air spotters.

Marine detachments aboard large carriers (support, attack, and nuclear-powered aircraft carriers) include, on the average, two officers and about 55 enlisted Marines. Aboard cruisers the detachment has two officers and approximately 40 enlisted Marines. In addition, each admiral's headquarters has a special detachment called a "flag allowance." Marine detachments on board amphibious command ships (LCCs) consist entirely of communication personnel and do amphibious communication duties only.

The Marine detachment is always a separate division. Marines participate in such all-hands evolutions as taking on ammunition, and provisioning ship. In port, when moored to a pier, Marine sentries guard the brows and dock as required. The detachment commander performs a dual role. He is, in effect, head of department with respect to internal administration and security duties of the Marines; but since the Marine detachment is also a division, the Marine officer is a deck or gunnery division officer as well.

The commanding officer of Marines is responsible to the Captain for the efficiency, shipboard administration, and total performance of the detachment. He is responsible to the Commandant of the

Marine Corps for the detachment's personnel administration, its training in military subjects (ITEM), and the Marine Corps property in his charge. He is responsible to his head of department for the gunnery training of the Marines and bluejackets (if any) under his supervision and for upkeep and operation of ship's equipment, supplies, and spaces assigned to the Marine detachment.

1807. SHIPBOARD DUTIES AND RESPONSIBILITIES OF MARINE NCOs. The shipboard duties of Marine NCOs are basically much the same as ashore because, internally speaking, a ship's detachment tends to operate much like any other small Marine unit. However, because there are very few experienced Marines to turn to for supervision and instruction, young NCOs find themselves called on more often and in more varied circumstances to exercise their responsibilities.

Not only for the sake of the detachment but because Marines are often required to instruct members of the seaman guard or landing force, every Marine NCO aboard ship should be expert in all general military subjects and all T/O weapons. If not already a competent, well-qualified instructor (see Chapter 12), the seagoing noncommissioned officer must become one in short order. Training aids, films, and facilities are sharply limited aboard ship. Only imagination and instructor initiative can compensate to produce well trained Marines.

> *Note:* Because Navy landing forces are still equipped with the WW II and Korean War family of infantry weapons (i.e., M1 rifle, BAR, and M1919A4 light machine gun—all good weapons that won two wars, incidentally), ships' Marine detachments must be so armed, too. Therefore, Marine NCOs going to sea should brush up particularly on this family of weapons.

Besides the foregoing duties, a Marine NCO afloat will usually supervise at least part of the care, cleaning, and upkeep of the battery and fire-control gear entrusted to the Marine detachment.

Keeping the *Watch, Quarter, and Station Bill* may be included in the seagoing NCO's duties. This is a chart which lists every man in the detachment by name, rank, bunk and locker assignment, cleaning station, watch and liberty section, and battle station. This bill is arranged in standard tabular form for each division (including the Marines) and, when up-to-date, gives a graphic picture of what every man in the detachment does, and when.

Guard Duty Afloat

1808. SHIPBOARD GUARD. Marines perform all guard duty aboard ships possessing Marine detachments. This is the oldest mission of Marines.

The same regulations and routine prevail for guard duty afloat—subject to shipboard conditions—as pertain on shore. For instructions specifically applicable to guard duty on board ship, consult the *Landing Party Manual,* Chapter 5, Section VII. The ship's Captain has the same responsibilities for the interior guard as the commanding officer ashore. The *officer of the deck* has the same general relationship toward interior guards as the officer of the day ashore. For shipboard guard duty and security, the *commanding officer of Marines* functions much like the provost marshal on a shore station and, for this purpose, is a "head of department," directly responsible to the Captain. General and special orders for the guard are promulgated by the commanding officer of Marines, but must be approved and countersigned by the Captain.

A ship's detachment is often called "the ship's guard." One of the guard's important duties is to render honors as prescribed in *Navy Regulations.* For this purpose, the Marine detachment maintains a *"guard of the day,"* from which routine guard details are provided. The guard of the day, which functions directly under the officer of the deck, remains ready between Morning and Evening Colors to turn out immediately, in prescribed uniform, on the quarterdeck to render honors. The guard of the day is paraded by the sergeant of the guard, *not* by the detachment officers. The *"full guard,"* so called, consists of the entire complement of Marines, less men detailed to other duties, and is commanded by an officer. Ordinarily, the band turns out on occasions when the full guard is required.

Aside from honors, the guard of the day ordinarily parades for an informal guard mount (see *Landing Party Manual,* Chapter 5, Section IV), and for Morning and Evening Colors when the ship is in port (but not underway). Informal guard mounting may be combined with Morning Quarters, when the entire Marine Detachment parades. Formations for Colors take place on the ship's fantail, in sight of the flagstaff. Guard mounting, Quarters, and other routine formations of the Marine detachment take place at the detachment parade, which is located on or as near the quarterdeck as the ship's topside arrangement permits.

1809. SHIPBOARD POSTS MAINTAINED BY MARINES. The security posts maintained for the safety and good order of the ship correspond to similar posts on shore, although some general orders (such as that pertaining to challenging) are relaxed or modified. Certain shipboard guard duties are peculiar to sea duty, however:

Special weapons security: Aboard carriers and Polaris submarine tenders (or any other ship carrying nuclear weapons) the Marine detachment provides security guards—operating under very stringent special orders—to protect the weapons in question.

Life-buoy watch: When required, this watch is posted in the vicinity of the ship's life buoy(s) when underway. The life-buoy sentry keeps a bright lookout for any person falling overboard or alert for the cry, "Man overboard!"; he releases the life buoy and keeps the man in the water in sight.

Communication orderly: Delivers radio messages (dispatches) or signals to officers concerned. This duty demands intelligence, knowledge of the ship, and knowledge by name, face, stateroom,

382   and duty, of all officers aboard.

Orderlies: Flag officers and the Captain of the ship are authorized by *Navy Regulations* to have personal orderlies. In addition, if the detachment's commitments permit, it is customary to assign an orderly to the executive officer, as well as to any embarked senior Navy or Marine officer who is not a member of the ship's company. Shipboard orderlies not only perform the usual personal services associated with orderly duty, but act as messengers and as receptionists for the officer to whom assigned.

The qualities required for orderly duty are high, and only the best Marines in the detachment should be detailed as orderlies. In selecting and training orderlies, look for intelligence, alertness, discretion, tact, neatness, military bearing, and knowledge of the ship and the ship's company. The closest contact that most naval officers have with the Marine detachment is through its orderlies. Put your best in the show window.

Brig Watch: The CO of the Marine detachment is responsible to the Captain for the operation of the ship's brig. The sergeant of the guard performs duties as brig warden, and the corporal of the guard acts as turnkey. Although the Captain is ultimately responsible for enforcement of standards prescribed in *The Brig Manual,* all Marines performing duties in connection with the brig should be thoroughly conversant with this publication.

The Marine orderly takes post behind the Commanding Officer on the bridge.   *Richard Mowrey*

1810. GUARD DUTY IN EMBARKED MARINE CORPS UNITS. When a Marine Corps unit *not* part of the ship's company goes to sea, the guard duty required is a combination of that maintained ashore and that described above for a Marine detachment.

Bear in mind two principles of command relations: *first,* the Captain of a ship has paramount authority and responsibility for safety, good order, and discipline over everyone embarked in his ship, whether or not under his military command; *second,* the commanding officer of troops embarked in a ship retains his military command authority and responsibility for his officers and men, subject only to the overriding authority and responsibility of the Captain. The CO of Troops is the senior troop commander embarked in the ship, and is ordinarily specifically designated as commanding officer of troops by higher troop authority.

Consistent with the foregoing principles, the Captain of the ship can call upon the embarked troop units to establish a guard to assist in maintaining the security and safety of the ship by manning such posts as lifebuoy, by control of circulation of passengers, by providing communication orderlies, and by performing any other necessary guard duties. For internal order, security, and control of embarked units, the troop commander (Commanding Officer of Troops), with the concurrence of the Captain, may establish any posts he considers necessary. In general, he organizes his guard like an interior guard ashore, providing an Officer of the Day as his direct representative for supervising the troop guard and for carrying out troop orders, ship's regulations, and special instructions of the ship's Captain.

All orders to troops embarked in a ship, including instructions for the troop guard, are transmitted through the Commanding Officer of Troops.

1811. STATUS, AUTHORITY, AND RESPONSIBILITY OF THE OFFICER OF THE DECK. When on watch as officer of the deck, an officer is the direct representative of the Captain; every person in the ship who is subject to the orders of the commanding officer is subordinate to the officer of the deck and must carry out his lawful orders. While on watch, the OOD is responsible for the safety of the ship and for execution of the ship's routine.

No person may board the ship without permission of the OOD or his representative. When leaving the ship, all persons must report to the OOD or his representative, giving their authority.

Courtesy, Etiquette, and Honors

1812. SHIPBOARD COURTESY AND ETIQUETTE. On many occasions during your career, you will find yourself serving or embarked in naval vessels, as part of the ship's Marine detachment or as a passenger. Because of this and because, as a Marine, you are a member of the Naval Services, you must comply meticulously with the courtesies and customs practiced on board men-of-war.

Ladders and Gangways. The starboard accommodation ladder is

Leatherneck Magazine.

Informal guard mount is conducted aboard a cruiser by the Corporal of the Guard.

reserved for officers; if there are two starboard ladders, the after ladder is for flag and general officers. The port ladder is for enlisted men. When a ship is alongside a pier, the officers' gangway is usually aft and leads to the quarterdeck; the enlisted men's gangway is forward.

Most ships have a prescribed traffic pattern for all ladders, such as "Starboard ladders—Forward and down." "Port ladders—Aft and up." No matter what the traffic pattern on a given ladder, *always give way to seniors.*

Coming on Board and Leaving a Man-of-War. As a Marine, whether on duty or as a visitor, you will always be welcome on board a Navy ship. In fact, you should seize every opportunity to visit each type and class of ship so that you may increase your fund of seagoing knowledge. The Navy is rightly flattered by such visits and will do everything possible to make your stay instructive as well as pleasant. Always pay your respects to the first sergeant when visiting a warship that has a Marine detachment.

If the ship is moored to a pier, there will be little complication. If the ship is anchored in the stream, obtain permission from the ship's senior officer present at the landing (or from the boat coxswain, if no officer is on hand) to go out in one of the ship's boats. If no boats are at the landing, ask the shore patrol representative when the next boat is due.

Observe boat etiquette (see below). Defer to seniors in the boat, officer and enlisted, Marine and Navy.

On reaching the quarterdeck, either from the gangway or an accommodation ladder, halt, face aft (or toward the National Ensign), and salute the Colors. Immediately afterward, render a second, distinct salute to the officer of the deck or junior officer of the deck, and say, "Sir, I request permission to come on board." When the time comes to leave the ship, render the same courtesies in reverse order, saying, "Sir, I request permission to leave the ship."

Boat Etiquette. When boarding a small boat, juniors embark first and sit forward, leaving the sternsheets for seniors, who embark last. The most senior officer in the boat sits farthest aft, at the centerline, or elsewhere as he wishes. When debarking, officers do so in order of rank. In embarking liberty parties aboard ship, CPOs and staff NCOs embark first, then other petty officers and NCOs, then nonrated men. Officers or enlisted men in the boat rise and salute when a more senior officer boards or debarks.

When another boat passes close aboard with a senior officer embarked and in view or when a senior officer passes close aboard on shore, the senior officer and the coxswain in each boat render hand salutes. Coxswains rise unless to do so would be dangerous or impracticable. When a boat is crowded, juniors rise and yield seats to seniors. If there are not enough seats, take the next boat.

Marine officers (although line officers) and officers of the Navy staff corps, when senior in a boat, receive and return salutes and

386

Fig. 18-2: Boat Etiquette: On embarking, juniors board first and sit forward.

Fig. 18-3: Boat Etiquette: On disembarking, seniors board first.

Fig. 18-4: Boat Etiquette: On coming alongside, senior officer and coxswain render hand salutes.

are otherwise accorded the deference due individuals of their seniority, *but* the senior Navy line officer or petty officer in the boat, regardless of how junior he may be, is in charge of the boat and is responsible for its navigation and for the safety of personnel and material embarked.

During Colors, boats underway within sight or hearing lie to or, if necessary, proceed at slowest safe speed. The coxswain (or boat officer, if embarked) stands and salutes unless dangerous to do so. Other persons embarked remain in place and do not salute.

Shipboard Amenities and Saluting. While in general the amenities and rules for saluting set forth in Chapter 15 apply aboard ship, the following special points should be observed.

Men at work, at games, or at meals are not required to rise when an officer other than the Captain or a flag or general officer or an officer senior to the Captain passes, unless attention is called, or when passageway must be cleared. It is customary to uncover when entering a sick bay or space in which food is being prepared or served; when a senior officer does so, this indicates that he does not desire men present to be brought to attention.

Juniors give way to seniors in ship's passageways and particularly when going up and down ladders.

"Gangway!" is a command given by anyone who sees an officer or civilian dignitary approaching a gangway, ladder, or passage which is blocked. Never use "Gangway!" except for an officer or senior civilian. For others, "Coming through!" is appropriate. The senior officer, NCO, or petty officer present must clear the passage after "Gangway!" has been given.

The ship's Captain, any officer senior to the Captain, all flag and general officers, the executive officer, and inspecting officers are saluted at every meeting except in officers' country, heads, and messing compartments.

On the first meeting of the day, salute each officer; thereafter, salutes are dispensed with except when an officer is directly addressed by a subordinate or in the cases of senior officers listed above.

Sentries at gangways salute all officers coming aboard or leaving the ship. Sentries posted on the topside also salute officers passing close aboard in boats.

When passing honors (see below) are being exchanged between men-of-war or when ruffles and flourishes are sounded on the quarterdeck, all personnel on weather decks, not in formation, come to attention and salute.

Navy (*but not Marine*) formations on board ship are dismissed with the command, "Leave your quarters," whereupon all members of the formation salute, the officer in charge returns the salute, and all hands fall out.

Ship's sentries posted on the pier, when a ship is moored alongside, carry out normal saluting procedures for sentinels ashore.

1812a. PASSING HONORS. "Passing honors" are the courtesies (equivalent to exchange of salutes between individuals) rendered by passing warships to each other. Basically, passing honors involve the junior ship (i.e., whose captain or embarked admiral is junior) rendering certain honors, and the acknowledgment of those honors by the senior ship (that whose captain or embarked admiral is the senior). The procedure also applies between warships of friendly foreign powers.

With precise timing, the exchange of passing honors between two men-of-war, each with a flag officer aboard, is a stirring example of naval courtesy in action. As the bows of the two ships (approaching on opposite course) pass, the officer-of-the-deck on the bridge of the junior ship orders the field music (or Navy bugler) of the watch to sound "Attention to Starboard (Port)" ("Attention" followed by one (two) short blasts on the bugle). The senior ship responds in like manner. The junior ship must then render the appropriate ruffles and flourishes—in time for the senior ship to return the salute with appropriate bugle commands—before the two ships are abeam of each other. The senior ship then sounds "Carry on", followed immediately by the junior ship.

This brief, effective, and precisely timed ceremony requires coordination between OOD, field music, band, and Marine guard (if paraded), but if well done leaves a lasting impression.

Housekeeping and Administration Aboard Ship

A ship's detachment has dual administrative and housekeeping responsibilities, both to the ship and her Captain and of course to the Commandant of the Marine Corps. In the Navy, the military term, "housekeeping," with which we are familiar ashore, has no exact equivalent. The following paragraphs, however, will describe the way certain administrative and housekeeping functions are discharged aboard ship, and how the Marine detachment fits in.

1813. POINTERS ON HOUSEKEEPING. *Police.* "Police," in the Navy sense, means the ship's police force. Under the Chief Police Petty Officer (or "Chief Master-at-Arms," to use the old Navy title), each division, other than the Marines, details a police petty officer ("master-at-arms" or "jimmy-legs") whose job is to act as a kind of ship's policeman in enforcing good order and ship's regulations. It is a popular misconception that Marines perform this function and act as "the Navy's police force" on board ship. Nothing could be further from the truth.

Within the Marine detachment, however, the term "police" has its normal meaning, and the detachment police sergeant performs the duties usually associated with that title anywhere in the Corps.

Subsistence and Mess Management. Like "police" (in the Navy sense), subsistence and mess management are functions of the ship's executive officer. The supply officer and his assistants perform the duties which ashore would fall to the post mess officer. In most ships, a central enlisted mess is operated on a cafeteria basis. Chief petty officers have a separate mess; as you have seen, staff NCOs of the Marine detachment subsist in the CPO mess.

Messmen are detailed from privates and Pfcs of the Marine detachment on the basis provided by *Navy Regulations.* For obvious reasons, it is highly undesirable to detail even a junior NCO as a messman. Should it become necessary, however, the most junior man is detailed first. If the detachment includes a rated cook, he should be assigned to duty in the ship's galley. *But never lose sight of him as a Marine.*

Clothing and Small Stores. As already noted, the ship's supply officer stocks Marine Corps clothing for the detachment.

Marines may likewise avail themselves—for cash purchases—of the ship's "Clothing and Small Stores," where many items of regulation (Navy) clothing may be bought at considerable saving over shoreside prices—such articles as hankerchiefs, socks, underwear, etc. Obviously, the Marine officers and NCOs must prevent Marines from improper wearing of Navy articles of uniform in lieu of prescribed Marine items of similar type.

Working Details. Marines participate only in working parties directly concerned with the detachment, or in all-hands evolutions (such as ammunitioning, provisioning, etc.). Otherwise, Marines are *not* part of the general labor pool for ship's work.

Pay. Payday for the Marines is held on the regularly scheduled Navy paydays for the ship's crew. When Marines are paid, the first sergeant and clerk assist, and the junior Marine officer may be called on for his share of duty among the other junior officers as a pay-call witnessing officer, just as he would on shore.

Ship's Store. The ship's store is the seagoing equivalent of the post exchange ashore. It is still sometimes called "Ship's Service Store." The ship's store is operated by the supply officer. It stocks stationery, candy, toilet articles, insignia, and the usual selection of post exchange supplies, including, in most ships, "pogey bait" and soda fountain ("geedunk") delicacies such as are found ashore.

Ship's Welfare and Recreation. Aboard ship, Welfare and Recreation embraces the activities associated with Special Services on the beach. Both as individuals and as a division, Marines take part in the ship's athletic and recreation programs. A ship's *welfare officer* administers the funds provided for these purposes.

1814. SHIPBOARD CLEANLINESS AND UPKEEP. As its "part of the ship," the Marine detachment usually has a berthing compartment, a storeroom, an office, several guns, a gunnery control station, and adjacent topside deck space. The cleanliness and upkeep of these spaces and structures are the responsibility of the Marine detachment's CO in his capacity as a division officer. Each division performs its own minor repairs; more extensive repair, when needed, is the job of the shipfitters and "repair gangs," based on "work requests" submitted by the division officer (detachment commander).

As ashore, your detachment will have a police sergeant. Instead of his police shed, though, he will have a *gear locker.* In lieu of a police gang—career men in their field—the police sergeant will call on every Marine in the detachment to keep the ship's "Marine country" a model space, spic and span, an example to the blue-jackets. Each noncommissioned officer in the detachment is usually assigned a "cleaning station"—a portion of the Marine detachment's spaces for whose structural upkeep and cleanliness he and the men under him are responsible.

Sea Duty Hints and Pointers

1815. SHIPBOARD POINTERS. Learn to be as salty (in a military way) as any sailor. Never lean on the lifelines; always know which is the lee side; learn what the different boatswains' calls mean. Make yourself into a true seagoing man-of-warsman.

Know which NCO is responsible for each cleaning station; know who the Marine gun captains and key members of gun crews are.

Keep a sharp eye on the corners, out-of-way areas, tops of angle irons and beams, under lockers, and behind and under gear. The center of the deck takes care of itself.

Give special attention to gaskets, knife edges, and dogs on hatches, scuttles, ports, and doorways. The condition of these items is a direct measure of the watertight integrity of the ship.

Timely, energetic scrubbing prevents wasting paint to cover up dirt. Paint not only costs money, but greatly increases danger from fire.

Know your whole ship; know every nut, rivet, and detail in your own spaces.

Ship's detachments are justly noted for the splendid appearance of rifles. By applying several coats of a preparation of olive oil and orange shellac to previously scraped rifle stocks and bayonet grips, the grain of the wood can be brought out in a beautiful gloss-like finish. This work should preferably be done by a single individual, such as the detachment armorer, who can master the technique and mix and thus get very best results.

If your detachment has chrome-plated bayonets, make sure that all fingerprints are wiped off, as sweat will corrode the chrome. If bayonets have wooden grips, sand and finish them the same color as rifle stocks (as suggested above).

Smart and uniform appearance of web rifle slings is important. Position all sling keepers below the trigger guard near the small of the stock. This gives the troops a uniform appearance as well as taut slings. If keeper is loose or bent, wedge part of a matchbook inside the keeper to prevent slippage and loose sling.

Enlisted dress buttons, issued with a very thin layer of gold plate, can be stripped down for polishing by working over with women's nail-polish remover. This gives a button which can be brought to a fine, high polish with jeweler's rouge or any good-quality bright-work polish.

Be scrupulously neat and clean. A self-respecting noncommissioned officer never appears unshaven before his shipmates and his men. If you find one of your people unshaven, make him shave immediately.

Salute admiral, captain, executive officer, and any other officer of the rank of commander or above, whenever you meet them about the ship, except when standing watch on the bridge. Salute whenever making reports. Salute all officers when you meet them for the first time during the day, and give them a cheerful, "Good morning, sir."

Try to get as much accomplished during normal working hours as you can, so that your men get the benefit of their free time. But work as long as a job remains to be done, working hours or not.

Most Navy men at all levels have a high regard for Marines, which usually lasts as long as the Marines continue to function at the level of professional competence which the Navy has a right to expect of them. Relationships between Navy and Marines on board ship are therefore generally healthy and rewarding. If you cannot adjust yourself to cooperating and working with those whose methods admittedly differ from our own, you have no business on sea duty.

Be alert for (and don't hesitate to suggest to the gunnery sergeant) opportunities to get ashore for training, even if no more than close-order drill on the dock. If your ship is at a base that includes a Marine barracks, possibly arrangements can be worked out to have the detachment take part in weekly parades and other ceremonies or drills along with the barracks troops. Bases whose terrain permits, such as Guantanamo Bay, Oahu, Guam, Panama, or Roosevelt Roads, may provide a chance for all or part of the detachment to get ashore for a day's hiking and field training. If you run into another ship's detachment or unit ashore—or troops of a foreign country being visited—who would like some rifle or pistol competition, be sure to pass the word along.

Finally, never neglect to establish informal liaison with the local Marines ashore; they can always give you help and support.

1816. POINTERS ON FOREIGN LIBERTY. This section owes much to the Bureau of Naval Personnel's famous "Overseasman," Mr. David Rosenberg, whose briefings throughout the Fleet combine sell-out entertainment with down-to-earth advice. If you get a chance to attend one, don't miss it.

The most common advice to people going on foreign liberty centers on how to avoid various diseases and stay out of trouble. The following pointers, while hopefully contributing to both of the foregoing objectives, are also designed to help you get the most out of every foreign liberty you make.

When a civilian visits a foreign country, he may cut up a little and be able to get away with it. After all, he's probably wearing a tweed jacket or a beach-boy shirt. But when a Marine goes ashore in blues, he enjoys no margin for misbehavior; nobody can miss what he is and what he stands for. At any given time and place, he is an American ambassador.

Just because you have a very limited margin for misbehavior doesn't mean you can't have fun in acceptable ways. Instead of looking for girls in dockside gin mills (which are much the same in Panama as they are in Amsterdam or Yokohama), you can find them uptown in libraries, department stores, and restaurants. For example, teachers, telephone operators, nurses, and cashiers all have patience and are used to talking to strangers.

Don't be afraid to strike out into a foreign city. If possible, get a pocket map (most bookstores stock these). Get out of the waterfront areas; there's where most of the trouble starts. Look for a really good restaurant and buy yourself a well-prepared local meal or just a top-quality steak. Either is a better buy than some junky souvenir. Furthermore, by getting to know the local food, you get to know local people.

Keep asking questions. Not only does this get you needed information, but it helps you meet people and it flatters them to be asked. It also makes you look like a down-to-earth human being who is trying to find out things about their town.

Organizations are great for lonely men on liberty. Going to church ashore may lead to Sunday dinner and a date. If your father is a Rotarian at home, go to the local Rotary meeting and introduce yourself. If you were an Eagle Scout, look up the local Scout organization. If one of your friends is a corpsman, suggest that you pay a visit to a local hospital (preferably one with a school for student nurses).

While you obviously can't speak the language everywhere you go, you can readily pick up some of the "instant language"—a shrug, a smile, clasped hands, etc. Furthermore, with a very few words or phrases, you can get around remarkably. The first phrases you should learn are "Hello . . . Goodbye . . . Please . . . Thank you . . .", followed closely by "Where? . . . How much (many)? . . . Where is the men's room?" Then learn to count up to ten, and you are practically an interpreter. On the other hand, watch out for words or gestures which may seem innocent to Americans but are unacceptable elsewhere.

(For example, in Spain, whistling shows contempt; or, in reverse, it is good manners in China or Japan to burp loudly after dinner to show appreciation.)

Try to meet people who have things in common with you or your background before you became a Marine. And of course, if you are in a country that has a Marine Corps, try to scrape acquaintances with the local Marines. You will be pleased to discover the special comradeship and mutual respect that exist between Marines of all the various nations.

Learn to recognize and distinguish between the different foreign military uniforms and to spot the insignia and badges of rank and corps. These are all instant conversation-makers.

Naturally, you must be prepared to take care of fellow Marines or shipmates at any time. This includes "preventive maintenence" if you see them taking a drink too many or snuggling up to some "bad news" that Mom or Sis might not wholly approve of. If a group of you and your fellow NCOs are planning a big liberty, include a nondrinker in the crowd. He will always know the way back to the ship and when the last boat leaves.

Glossary for Seagoing Marines

Here you will find a glossary of commonly used shipboard terms and phrases that every Marine should know. By using and understanding these, you will prove to Navy shipmates that Marines can be, and are, just as salty as any sailor.

ABAFT: behind or farther aft; astern or toward the stern.

ABEAM: at right angles to the centerline of and outside a ship.

ABOARD: on or in a vessel. *Close aboard* means near a ship.

ABSENTEE PENNANT: special pennant flown to indicate absence of commanding officer, admiral, his chief of staff, or officer whose flag is flying (division, squadron, or flotilla commander).

ACCOMMODATION LADDER: a portable flight of steps down a ship's side.

ADRIFT: loose from moorings, or out of place.

AFT: in, near, or toward the stern of a vessel.

ALONGSIDE: by the side of a ship or pier.

AGROUND: resting on or touching the ground or bottom.

AHEAD: forward of the bow.

AHOY: term used to hail a boat or a ship, as "Boat ahoy!"

ALL HANDS: entire ship's company, both officers and enlisted personnel.

ALL NIGHT IN: having no night watches.

ALOFT: above the ship's uppermost solid structure; overhead or high above.

AFTERNOON WATCH: the 1200–1600 watch.

AMIDSHIPS (OR MIDSHIPS): in middle portion of ship, along the line of the keel.

ANCHORAGE: suitable place for a ship to anchor. Area of a port or harbor.

ANCHOR'S AWEIGH: said of an anchor when just clear of the bottom.

ANCHOR BALL: black shape hoisted in forepart of a ship to show that ship is anchored in a fairway.

ANCHOR BUOY: a small buoy secured by a light line to anchor to indicate position of anchor on bottom.

ANCHOR CABLE: wire or line running between anchor and ship.

ANCHOR CHAIN: heavy stud-linked chain used as above.

ANCHOR DETAIL: group of men who handle ground tackle when the ship is anchoring or getting underway.

ANCHOR WATCH: detail of men standing by at night as a readiness precaution while ship is in port.

ASHORE: on the beach or shore.

ASTERN: toward the stern; an object or vessel that is abaft another vessel or object.

ASW: anti-submarine warfare.

ATHWART, ATHWARTSHIPS: at right angles to the fore and aft or center-line of a ship. Pronounced "A'thort".

AVAST: a command to cease or desist from whatever is being done.

AWASH: so low in the water that the water is constantly washing across the surface.

AWEIGH: position of an anchor just clear of the bottom.

AYE, AYE: acknowledgment to an order or command to indicate that it is understood and will be carried out. ("Aye, aye, sir," to officers.)

BACKSTAY: a stay supporting a mast from aft.

BACKWASH: water thrown aft by turning of ship's propeller.

BACK WATER: command given to oarsmen to reverse usual rowing motion.

BAIL: to dip water out of a boat with a bucket. A hoop or ring; a half hoop or yoke.

BALLAST: heavy weight in the hold of a vessel to maintain proper stability, trim, or draft. A ship is *in ballast* when she carries no cargo, only ballast.

BARBETTE: heavily armored cylinder within which turret rotates; extends from upper part of a turret down to the lowest armored deck.

BARGE: craft used to haul material, as a coal barge; a power boat used by flag officers, as admiral's barge.

BARNACLE: small marine animal that attaches itself to side and bottoms of hulls and to piers.

BATTEN: long strip of steel or wood that wedges the edge of a tarpaulin against the hatch.

BATTEN DOWN: to cover and fasten down; to close off a hatch or watertight door.

BATTLE LANTERN: battery-powered portable electric lights for emergency use.

BATTLE LIGHTS: dim red lights that furnish sufficient light for personnel during darken-ship period.

BEACON: conspicuous mark or structure used to guide ships.

BEAM: width; breadth; greatest athwartships width of a vessel.

BEAR: to lie in a certain direction from the observer.

BEAR A HAND: speed up the action; lend a helping hand.

BEARING: direction of an object, expressed in degrees either as *relative* or *true* bearing.

BECKET: circular metal fitting on a block; a rope eye or grommet.

BELAY: to cancel an order; to stop; to firmly secure a line.

BELOW: short for *below decks;* below the main deck.

BEND: a general class of knots used to join two lines together.

BEND ON: to secure one thing to another, as bend a flag onto a halyard.

BERTH: space assigned a vessel for anchoring or mooring.

BIGHT: middle part of a line as distinguished from the end and the standing part; a single complete turn of line; bend in a river or coastline.

BILGE: lower part of vessel where waste water and seepage collect.

BILLET: allotted sleeping space; a man's position in the ship's organization.

BINNACLE: large stand used to house a magnetic compass and its fittings.

BINNACLE LIST: sick list of men excused from duty; in old days it was posted on or near the binnacle.

BITT: strong iron post on ship's deck for working or fastening lines; almost invariably in pairs.

BITTER END: the free end of a line, wire or chain.

BLACK GANG: slang for engine-room force.

BLINKER: lamp or set of lamps, triggered to a telegraph key; used for sending flashing light message.

BLOCK: an item of deck gear made of one or more grooved sheaves, a frame (casing or shell), supporting hooks, eyes or straps; may be metal or wood.

BLUEJACKET: a Navy enlisted man below the grade of CPO; a "white hat."

BOATS: small open or decked-over craft propelled by oars, sails, or some type of engine. This term also applies to larger vessels built to navigate rivers and inland waters; calling a *ship* a *boat* is not good Navy talk.

BOAT BOOM: a boom to which boats secure. It is swung out from the side when the ship is anchored or moored.

BOAT CHOCK: a strong deck fitting that supports one end of a boat that is resting on deck.

BOAT FALL: rigging used to hoist or lower a ship's boats.

BOAT GRIPE: lashing used at sea to secure against the strongback a boat hanging from the davits and away from the ship's side.

BOATHOOK: wooden staff with metal hook and prod at one end; used to fend off or hold on.

BOAT PAINTER: line attached to the stem ringbolt of a boat; used for securing it. Also a short piece of rope secured in the bow of a boat; used for towing or making fast. Not to be confused with the sea-painter, which is a much longer line.

BOAT SKID: heavy wood and metal frame on ship's boat deck used to support a boat's keel.

BOAT SLING: rope or chain sling used for hoisting or lowering larger-size boats with a single davit or crane.

BOAT STATION: allotted place of each person when boat is being lowered.

BOATSWAIN: warrant officer in charge of deck work. Pronounced "bosun."

BOATSWAIN'S CALL: See BOATSWAIN'S PIPE.

BOATSWAIN'S CHAIR: line-secured board on which a man sits as he works aloft or over the side.

BOATSWAIN'S LOCKER: compartment where deck gear is stowed.

BOATSWAIN'S PIPE: small, shrill silver whistle used by boatswain's mate to pass a call or pipe the side. Never say "boatswain's whistle."

BOLLARD: wooden or iron post on a pier or wharf to which mooring lines are secured.

BOOM: projecting spar or pole that provides an outreach for extending the foot of sails, or for mooring boats, handling cargo, and so on. Rigged horizontally or nearly so.

BOOT TOPPING: surface of the outside plating of ship or boat's side between light and load lines.

BOW: forward section of a vessel.

BOWER ANCHOR: either of the two anchors usually carried at the ship's bow. Most ships anchor by using one of the bowers.

BOWLINE: one of the most used knots; used to make a temporary eye in the end of a line.

BOX PAINTER: See BOAT PAINTER.

BOXING THE COMPASS: naming all the compass points and quarter points in their proper order, from noth, east, south, through west.

BREAK: to unfurl a flag with a quick motion. In ship construction, an abrupt change in the fore-and-aft contour of a ship's main deck.

BREAKER: a small container for stowing drinking water carried by boats or rafts; a wave that breaks into form against the shore.

BREAK OUT: to unstow or prepare for use.

BREAKWATER: a structure used to break the force of the waves.

BREAST LINE: a mooring line running at right angles from the ship's fore-and-aft line.

BRIDGE: raised platform from which ship is steered, navigated, and conned; usually located in forward part of the ship.

BRIDLE: span of rope or chain with both ends secured.

BRIGHTWORK: metalwork that is kept polished rather than painted.

BROAD COMMAND PENNANT: personal command pennant of an officer, not a flag officer, commanding a major unit of ships or aircraft.

BROAD ON THE STARBOARD BEAM OR PORT BEAM: bearing 090° or 270° relative to the bow of the ship.

BROAD ON THE STARBOARD OR PORT BOW: bearing 045° or 315° relative to the bow of the ship

BROAD ON THE STARBOARD OR PORT QUARTER: bearing 135° or 225° relative to the bow of the ship.

BROADSIDE: simultaneous firing of all main-battery guns on one side of a warship.

BROADSIDE TO: at right angles to the fore-and-aft line of a ship.

BROW: large gangplank leading from a ship to a pier, wharf, or float; usually equipped with rollers on the bottom and hand rails on the side.

BULKHEAD: one of the vertical wall-like structures enclosing a compartment.

BULL NOSE: a closed chock at the head of the bow on the forecastle deck.

BULWARK: raised plating or woodwork running along the side of a vessel above the weather deck. Helps keep decks dry and prevents men and gear from being swept overboard.

BUMBOAT: small boats used in port to sell merchandise.

BUNKER: storage space for fuel.

BUNTING: cloth used to make signal flags.

BUOY: floating marker anchored by a line to the bottom, which by shape and color conveys navigational information; may be lighted or unlighted. Pronounced "boo-ee."

BURGEE: swallow-tailed flag.

BURGEE COMMAND PENNANT: personal command pennant of an officer not a flag officer, commanding a division of minor war vessels or major subdivision of an aircraft wing.

BY THE HEAD: ship's appearance with a greater draft forward than aft.

BY THE STERN: opposite of *by the head.*

CABIN: captain's living quarters; covered compartment of a boat.

CABLE: See ANCHOR CABLE.

CALL: series of notes played on boatswain's pipe indicating commands.

CALKING, CAULKING: burring or driving up the edges of steel plates along riveted seams to make them water-tight; forcing a quantity of sealing material into the seams of a deck or ship's side to make them watertight. Pronounced "kawking."

CAMEL: large fender float used for keeping vessel off wharf, pier, or quay; usually consists of one or more heavy timbers.

CAN BUOY: cylindrical, flat-topped metal buoy.

CAPSTAN OR CAPSTAN HEAD: that part of vertical shaft windlass around which a working line is passed.

CARDINAL POINT: one of the four principal points of the compass— north, east, south, and west.

CARGO NET: heavy, square, rope net used for slinging cargo.

CARGO WHIP: rope or chain used with a boom and which is used for handling cargo. One end has a heavy hook; the other end is rove through a block and taken to the winch. Also called *cargo hoist, cargo rope.*

CARRY AWAY: to break loose, tear loose, or wash overboard.

CARRY ON: an order to resume work or duties.

CAST: act of heaving the lead into the sea to determine depth of water; to direct the ship's bow in one direction or another when getting underway.

CAST LOOSE: to let go a line or lines.

CAST OFF: to throw off; to let go; to unfurl.

CATAPULT: shipboard mechanism for launching aircraft or drones.

CATCH A CRAB: striking a boat's oar at the wrong angle in the water during recovery, thereby losing control.

CAT'S PAW: a quickly formed twist in the bight of a line by which two eyes are formed.

CATWALK: elevated walkway between bridges; commonly found on tankers. Also called *fore and aft bridge, connecting bridge,* and *monkey bridge.*

CAULK: See CALK.

CENTERLINE: imaginary line running from ship's bow to stern.

CHAFE: wearing away the surface of a line, spar, or chock by rubbing.

CHAFING GEAR: guard of canvas or rope around spars, hawsers, chocks, or rigging to prevent chafing.

CHAIN LOCKER: compartment in which chain cable is stowed.

CHAIN CABLE: See ANCHOR CABLE.

CHAIN GRAB: Same as *Wildcat.*

CHAIN PIPE: heavy steel pipe that leads the chain cable through the deck to the chain locker.

CHAINS: platform or a general area on either side of forward part of a ship where leadsman stands as he takes soundings.

CHAIN STOPPER: short length of chain fitted with a pelican hook and secured to an eyebolt on the forecastle; used for quickly letting go the anchor or for securing the anchor in stowed position.

CHARLEY NOBLE: galley smokepipe.

CHART: nautical map used as an aid to navigation.

CHARTHOUSE OR CHARTROOM: compartment on or near the bridge for handling and stowage of navigational equipment.

CHECK: to slack off slowly; to stop a vessel's way gradually by a line fastened to some fixed object or to an anchor on the bottom; to ease off a line a little, especially with a view to reducing the tension; to stop or regulate the motion, as of a cable when it is running out too fast.

CHIPPING HAMMER: small hammer with a sharp peen and face set at right angles to each other; used for chipping and scaling metal surfaces.

CHOCK: steel deck member, either oval or U-shaped, through which mooring lines are passed. Usually paired off with bitts.

CHOCKABLOCK: completely full; full to the top.

CHRONOMETER: an especially accurate timepiece, set to Greenwich time; used for navigation.

CLAMP DOWN: going over a deck with damp swabs; a lesser form of swabbing down.

CLAP ON: to clap on a rope means to catch hold in order to haul on it; to clap on a stopper or tackle means to put on a stopper or tackle; to clap on canvas means to put on more sail.

CLEAR HAWSE: to disentangle anchor cables when they are twisted around one another.

CLEAT: a small deck fitting of metal with horns; used for securing lines; also called *belaying cleat.* Short piece of wood nailed to brow or gangplank to give surer footing.

CLINOMETER: bridge and engine-room instrument that indicates amount of a ship's roll or degree of list.

CLOSE ABOARD: nearby.

CLOSE UP: a flag or pennant is close up when it is all the way up on its halyard. (equals "Two-blocked")

CLOTHES STOP: small cotton lanyard used for fastening clothes to a line after washing them, or for securing clothes that are rolled up.

CLOVE HITCH: a knot much used for fastening a line to a spar or stanchion. A clove hitch will not slip.

COAMING: raised framework around deck or bulkhead openings and cockpits of open boats to prevent entry of water.

COCKPIT: well or sunken space in a boat for the use of the boat crew or passengers; the pilots compartment in an airplane.

COIL: laying down line in circular turns, usually one turn atop the other.

COLLISION MAT: a mat used to temporarily close a hole in a ship's hull below the waterline.

COMMISSION PENNANT: long, thin, 7-star pennant flow by a ship to indicate that the ship is commissioned in the U. S. Navy.

COMPANIONWAY: set of steps or ladders leading from one deck to another.

COMPARTMENT: space enclosed by bulkheads, deck, and overhead, corresponds to a room in a building.

COMPASS: instrument to indicate geographic directions.

COMPASS ROSE: diagram of a compass card on a chart, assists navigator in laying out courses and directions on chart.

CONDENSER: device for converting exhaust steam from engines into water for re-use in the boilers.

CONN: to direct the helmsman as to movement of helm, especially when navigating in narrow channels on heavy traffic.

CONNING TOWER: heavily armored structure just forward of and slightly below the bridge, for conning the ship in battle. Found on larger warships.

CONVOY: a number of merchant ships sailing under the escort of warships and patrol craft.

CORDAGE: general term for rope and line of all kinds.

COUNTER: part of the ship's side at the stern.

COUNTRY: the general area occupied by living quarters, such as officers' country, wardroom country, CPO country.

COURSE: direction steered by a ship.

COW'S-TAIL: frayed end of a rope.

COXCOMBING: a type of fancy ropework used around tiller handles, boat hooks, stanchions.

COXSWAIN: enlisted man in charge of a boat; usually acts as helmsman. Pronounced "coksun."

CPO: chief petty officer.

CRADLE: a stowage rest for a ship's boat.

CROSSING THE LINE: crossing the earth's equator.

CROSSTREE: superstructure member at top of a low mast or between two such masts; runs athwartships.

CROWS NEST: lookout's stand high on a mast or crosstrees.

CUT OF THE JIB: general appearance of a vessel or of a person.

COUPLING: metal fitting at the ends of a length of fire hose.

CURRENT: continuous movement of water in a horizontal direction.

CUTTER: type of sailing vessel; a transom-sterned boat, at present in little use.

CUTWATER: forward edge of the stem at and below the waterline.

DAMAGE CONTROL: measures necessary to keep ship afloat, fighting, and in operating condition.

DAVIT: shipboard crane that can be swung out over the side; used for hoisting and lowering boats and weights. Often found in pairs. Pronounced 'day-vit."

DAVY JONES'S LOCKER: the bottom of the sea.

DAY'S DUTY: tour of duty on shipboard lasting 24 hours.

DEAD AHEAD: directly ahead of the ship's bow, bearing 000° relative.

DEAD IN THE WATER: said of an underway ship that is making neither headway nor sternway.

DEADLIGHT (VENTILATING DEADLIGHT): an arrangement of baffles to permit air while preventing the passage of light. Usually seen on Navy ships as a circular device that fits into ports.

DEAD RECKONING: navigator's estimate of ship's position from the course steered and the distance run.

DEADWEIGHT TONNAGE: difference between a ship's light and loaded displacement.

DECK: on a ship corresponds to the floor of a building on land.

DECK GANG: men of the ship's deck and gunnery department; all the deck force.

DECKHAND: seaman of the deck department.

DECKHOUSE: structure built on an upper or weather deck; it does not extend over the full breadth of the ship. Deckhouses are typical of smaller vessels.

DECK SEAMANSHIP: branch of seamanship embracing the practical side, from the simplest rudiments of marlinespike seamanship up to navigation; includes small-boat handling, ground tackle, steering, heaving the lead, signaling, etc.

DECK TREADS: thin abrasive mats held to the deck by an adhesive compound; furnish a better foothold, especially on wet decks.

DEEP: the distance in fathoms between two successive marks on a lead line, as "By the deep, four."

DEEPS: in a lead line, the fathoms which are not marked on the line.

DEEP SIX: a term meaning to dispose of by throwing over the side.

DEGAUSSING GEAR: electrical gear which sets up neutralizing magnetic fields to protect the ship from magnetic-action mines. Pronounced "de-gow'sing."

DEPTH CHARGE: explosive charge used against submarines.

DERELICT: abandoned vessel at sea, still afloat.

DINGHY: small, handy boat, 16 to 20 feet in length, propelled either by oars or sail.

DIP: lowering a flag part way in salute or in answer, and hoisting it again. A flag is "at the dip" when it is flown at about two-thirds the height of the halyards.

DIRECTOR: electro-mechanical device for directing and controlling gunfire.

DISPLACEMENT: weight of water displaced by a ship.

DITTY BAG, DITTY BOX: small container used by sailors for stowage of personal articles or toilet articles.

DIVISION: in an organization of ship or plane groups, the unit between sections and squadrons. In shipboard organization, a number of men and officers grouped together for command purposes.

DOCK: artificial basin for ships, fitted with gates to keep in or shut out water; water area between piers.

DOG: small, bent metal fitting used to secure watertight doors, hatch covers, scuttles, etc.

DOGWATCH: one of the two-hour watches from 1600 to 2000.

DOLDRUMS: areas on both sides of the equator where light and variable breezes blow.

DOLPHIN: cluster of piles for mooring.

DOOR: opening between compartments; see *hatch*.

DORY: small, double-ended, flat-bottomed pulling boat, used chiefly by fishermen.

DOUBLE-BOTTOMS: watertight sub-divisions of ship, next to the keel and between outer and inner bottoms.

DOUBLE UP: to increase the number of ship-to-pier-to-ship turns of a mooring line.

DOWSE: to take in or lower a sail; to put out a light; to cover with water.

DOWNHAUL: line or wire that pulls something downward.

DRAFT: depth of water from the surface to the ship's keel: a detail of men.

DRAFT MARKS: numeral figures on either side of the stem and sternpost, used to indicate the amount of the ship's draft.

DRESSING SHIP: to display the national ensign at all mastheads and the flagstaff; *full dressing* further requires a rainbow of flags bow to stern over the mastheads.

DRIFT LEAD: sounding lead and line dropped over side of a ship to detect dragging of the vessel.

DUNNAGE: loose material placed in holds for cargo to rest on, or jammed between the cargo to wedge it.

DUCTS: large sheet metal pipes that lead air from blowers to enclosed spaces.

EASE HER: a command to reduce the amount of rudder or helm.

EASE OFF: to ease a line; slacken it when taut.

EASY: carefully, gently, handsomely.

EBB TIDE: tide falling or flowing out.

EDDY: a small whirlpool.

EMBARK: to go on board a ship preparatory to sailing.

END FOR END: reversing position of an object or line.

END ON: head-to-head or stem-to-stem.

ENGINE-ORDER TELEGRAPH: signaling gear for transmitting speed and direction orders from bridge to engine room.

ENSIGN: colors, national flag. Also, junior commissioned officer in the Navy. Pronounced "en'sin."

ESCAPE HATCH: in general any hatch, usually small, that permits men to escape from a compartment when ordinary means of egress are blocked.

EVEN KEEL: floating level; no list.

EYEBOLT: a metal bolt ending in an eye.

EYEBROW: curved metal arc mounted above a porthole, used to shed water.

EYES: foremost part of weatherdeck in the bow of the ship.

FAG: Frayed or untwisted end of rope.

FAIRLEAD: an eye, block, or fitting furnishing a clear lead for a line. Pronounced "leed."

FAIR TIDE: tidal current running in same direction as the ship.

FAIRWAY: in inland waters, an open channel or midchannel.

FAIR WIND: a favoring wind.

FAKE DOWN: Coiling down a line in long flat bights so that each run of line overlaps the one underneath and makes the line clear for running.

FALL: entire length of rope in a tackle; the end secured to the block is called the *standing part;* the opposite part, the *hauling part.* Also, the line used to lower and hoist a boat.

FALSE KEEL: thin covering secured to lower side of main keel of ships; affords more protection.

FANCYWORK: intricate, symmetrical rope work used for decorative purposes.

FANTAIL: main deck section in the after part of a flush-deck ship.

FAST: snugly secured; said of a line when it is fastened securely.

FATHOM: a six-foot unit of length.

FEATHER: turning the blade of an oar horizontally at the finish of a stroke to reduce resistance of air or water; changing the pitch of a variable pitch propeller on an airplane to vary amount of bite into the air.

FENDER: canvas, wood, rope gear or old rubber tire used over the side to protect a ship from chafing when alongside a pier or another ship.

FEND OFF: to push away; pushing away from a pier or another ship when coming alongside, to prevent damage or chafing.

FIBER ROPE: general term for cordage made of vegetable fibers such as hemp, Manila, flax, cotton, or sisal.

FID: a wooden marlinspike used in separating the strands for splicing.

FIELD DAY: general cleaning day aboard ship; usually the day before inspection.

FIFE RAIL: a wood or metal rail bored with holes to take belaying pins; seen on Navy ships at head of flag bags.

FIGURE-EIGHT FAKE: method of coiling rope in which the turns form a series of overlapping figure-eights advancing about one or two diameters of the rope for each turn; ususally done over the lifelines.

FIGURE-EIGHT KNOT: knot forming a large knob; easily tied.

FIRE CONTROL: shipboard system of directing and controlling gunfire or torpedo fire.

FIRE CONTROL TOWER: may be either a separate structure or a part of the conning tower containing fire control equipment; typical of major warships.

FIRE MAIN: system of pipes which furnish water to fireplugs.

FIRST LIEUTENANT: officer in charge of cleanliness and general upkeep of a ship or shore station. This is a duty, not a rank.

FIRST WATCH: the 2000-2400 watch.

FISH HOOKS: jagged ends of wire protruding from a wire rope.

FIX: determination of a ship's position by using one or more navigational methods.

FLAG BAG: container for stowage of signal flags and pennants; rigged with different slots to take the flags' snaps and rings.

FLAG OFFICER: an officer of the rank of commodore or above; so called because he is entitled to fly his personal flag which, by stars, indicates his rank.

FLAGSTAFF: small vertical spar at the stern on which the ensign is hoisted when the ship is moored or anchored.

FLANK SPEED: a certain prescribed speed increase over standard speed; faster than full speed, but less than emergency full speed.

FLARE: outward and upward curving sweep of a ship's bow; outward curve of the side from waterline to deck level. Also, a blaze to illuminate or attract attention.

FLASH BURN: burn received from the heat of explosion of a projectile or bomb or inflammable liquid.

FLASH PLATE: protective metal plate over which the anchor cable rides. It is a part of the forecastle deck.

FLAT-TOP: slang for aircraft carrier.

FLEET: organization of ships and aircraft under one commander; normally includes all types of ships and aircraft necessary for major operations. Also to draw the blocks of a tackle apart.

FLEMISH: to coil line flat on deck in a clockwise direction, each fake outside the other, all laid snugly side by side; begins in the middle and works outward.

FLIGHT DECK: deck on an aircraft carrier on which planes take off and land.

FLOOD TIDE: tide rising or flowing toward land.

FLOTSAM: floating wreckage. See JETSAM.

FLUKE: flat end of an anchor which bites into the ground.

FLUSH DECK: continuous upper deck extending from side to side and from bow to stern.

FLYING BRIDGE: a bridge extending out from the control tower.

FORE AND AFT: running in the direction of the keel.

FORECASTLE: upper deck in the forward part of the ship. Pronounced "foke'-sul"; abbreviated fo'c'sle.

FORECASTLE DECK: partial deck over the main deck at the bow.

FOREMAST: on a two-masted ship, the first mast abaft the bow.

FORENOON WATCH: the 0800-1200 watch.

FORESTAY: a stay supporting a mast from forward.

FORWARD: toward the bow; opposite of *aft*.

FOUL: jammed; not clear for running.

FOUL ANCHOR: anchor with its cable twisted around it.

FOXTAIL: small hand brush.

FOUNDER: to sink.

FRAME: ribs of a vessel; numbered from forward to aft, they serve as reference points.

FRAPPING LINES: lines passed around the boat falls to steady them.

FREEBOARD: height of a ship's sides from waterline to main deck.

FULL SPEED: a prescribed speed that is greater than standard speed but less than flank speed.

FUNNEL: ship's smokestack; stack.

FURL: fathering up and securing a sail or awning; opposite of *spread*.

GAFF: small spar abaft the mainmast from which the national ensign is flown when the ship is underway.

GALE: a wind between a strong breeze and a storm; wind force 28 to 55 knots.

GALLEY: the ship's kitchen.

GANGPLANK: See BROW.

GANGWAY: opening in the bulwarks or the rail of the ship to give entrance; an order to stand aside and get out of the way.

GATHER WAY: to gain headway.

GEAR: general term for lines, ropes, blocks, fenders, etc.; personnel effects.

GENERAL ALARM: sound signals used for general quarters and other emergencies.

GENERAL QUARTERS: battle stations for all hands.

GIG: one of the ship's boats designated for commanding officer's use.

GIMBALS: a pair of rings, one within the other, with axes at right angles to each other; supports the compass and keeps it horizontal despite the ship's motion.

GIPSEY, GIPSY: cathead; drum on a horizontal shaft windlass or winch for working lines.

GLASS: barometer or quartermaster's spyglass.

GLASSES: binoculars.

GO ADRIFT: to break loose.

GRAB-ROPE: a rope secured above a boat boom or gangplank; used to steady oneself.

GRANNY KNOT: a knot similar to square knot; does not hold under strain.

GRAPNEL: small anchor with several arms; used for dragging for lost objects or for anchoring skiffs or dories.

GRATINGS: wooden or iron openwork covers for hatches, sunken decks, etc.

GRIPES: metal fastenings for securing a boat in its cradle; canvas bands fitted with thimbles in their ends and passed from the davit heads over and under the boat for securing for sea.

GROMMET: ring of rope formed by a single strand laid three times around; a metal ring set in canvas, cloth, or plastic.

GROUND: to run ashore; to strike the bottom through ignorance, violence, or accident.

GROUND TACKLE: term referring to all anchor gear.

GUN MOUNT: a gun structure with 1 to 4 guns; may be open or enclosed in a steel shield. Enclosed mounts are not as heavily armored as *turrets* and carry no gun larger than 5-inch.

GUNWALE: upper edge or rail of a ship or boat's side. Pronounced "gunnel."

GUY: a line used to steady and support a spar or boom in a horizontal or inclined position. See STAY.

GYROCOMPASS: compass used to determine true directions by means of gyroscopes.

GYROCOMPASS REPEATERS: compass cards electrically connected to gyrocompass and repeating the same readings.

GYROPILOT: automatic steering device connected to the repeater of a gyrocompass; designed to hold a ship on its course without a helmsman. Also called *automatic steerer, iron mike, iron quartermaster.*

HAIL: to address a nearby boat or ship. Also a ship or man is said to *hail from* such and such a home port or home town.

HALFDECK: partial deck below the main deck and above the lowest complete deck.

HALF HITCH: usually seen as two half hitches; a knot used much for the same purposes as a clove hitch.

HALF-MAST: position of the ensign when hoisted halfway; usually done in respect to a deceased person.

HALYARD OR HALLIARD: line used for hoisting flags or sails.

HAND LEAD: a lead weighing from 7 to 14 pounds, secured to a line and used for measuring the depth of water or for obtaining a sample of the bottom. Pronounced "led."

HAND RAIL: metal or wood rail on brow, ladder, etc.

HAND ROPE: See GRAB-ROPE.

HANDSOMELY: to ease off a line gradually; to execute something deliberately and carefully, but not necessarily slowly.

HANDY BILLY: small, portable, powerdriven water pump.

HANGFIRE: gun charge that does not fire immediately upon closing the firing key, but some time later.

HATCH: an opening in the ship's deck, for communication or for handling stores and cargo.

HAUL: to pull.

HAULING PART: that part of the fall of a tackle to which power is applied.

HAWSEPIPES AND HAWSEHOLES: the steel castings in the bow through which anchor cables run are hawsepipes; the openings are hawseholes.

HAWSER: heavy line, 5 inches or more in circumference, used for heavy work such as towing or mooring.

HEAD: compartment of a ship or plane having toilet facilities.

HEADROOM: clearance between decks.

HEADWAY: forward motion of a ship.

HEAVE: to throw or toss; to pull on a line.

HEAVE AWAY: an order to start heaving on a capstan or windlass, or to pull on a line.

HEAVE IN: an order to haul in a line or the anchor cable.

HEAVE 'ROUND: to revolve the drum of a winch or windlass so as to pull in a line or anchor cable.

HEAVE SHORT: an order to heave in on anchor chain until the ship is riding nearly over her anchor.

HEAVE TO: to bring the ship's head into the wind or sea and hold her there by the use of engines and rudder.

HEAVE THE LEAD: to employ the lead line.

HEAVING LINE: a small line with a weight on one end; weighted end is thrown to another ship or to a pier so that a larger line may be passed.

HEEL: to list over.

HELM: the helm proper is the *tiller,* but the term is often used to mean the rudder and the gear for turning it.

HELMSMAN: the man at the wheel; the man who steers the ship.

HIGH LINE: line running between ships that are replenishing.

HIGH-LINE TRANSFER: method of sending men, supplies, etc., from one ship to another while underway.

HITCH: general class of knots by which a line is fastened to another object, either directly or around it.

HOIST: display of signal flags on halyard. The end of a flag or pennant to which the halyard is secured. Also, to raise a piece of cargo or gear.

HOISTING PAD: metal piece bolted to boat's keel; has an eye to which hoisting rod is bolted.

HOISTING ROD: vertical metal rod bolted to hoisting pad; hoisting shackle is bolted to its upper end.

HOLD: space below decks for storage of ballast, cargo, etc.

HOLIDAY: an imperfection or vacant space in an orderly arrangement; spots in painting or cleaning left unfinished.

HOLIDAY ROUTINE: routine followed aboard ship on authorized holidays and Sundays.

HORNS: horizontal arms of a cleat or chock; projecting timbers of a stage to which rigging lines are secured.

HOUSE: to stow or secure in a safe place; to run an anchor's shank up into the hawsepipe.

HOUSING ANCHOR: anchor having one stock; houses itself in hawse-pipe when hove in.

HOVE TAUT: pulled tight.

HUG: to keep close. A vessel might *hug* the shore.

HULK: a worn-out and stripped vessel unable to move under her own power.

HULL: framework of a vessel, together with all her decks, deckhouses, inside plating, or planking, but exclusive of masts, rigging, guns, and all superstructure items.

HULL DOWN: said of a distant vessel when only her stack-tops and mast are visible above the horizon.

INTERIOR COMMUNICATION (I.C.): telephone or communication systems inside a ship.

IDLER: member of ship's company who does not stand night watches.

INBOARD: toward the ship's centerline.

INHAUL: line used to haul an object in to a ship.

INSHORE: toward land.

INTERCARDINAL POINTS: the four points midway between the cardinal points of the compass: northeast, southeast, southwest, northwest.

IRISH PENNANT: unseamanlike, dangling loose end of a line or piece of bunting.

ISLAND: superstructure on an aircraft carrier; contains conning tower, navigation bridge, etc.

JACK: flag similar to the union of the national ensign; flown at the jackstaff when in port; plug for connecting an electrical appliance to a power or phone line.

JACKBOX: fitting on a bulkhead into which telephone or power lines are plugged.

JACK-O'-THE-DUST: enlisted man serving as assistant to the ship's cooks.

JACKSTAFF: small vertical spar at the bow of a ship from which the jack is flown.

JACOB'S LADDER: light ladder made of rope or chain with metal or wooden rungs; used over the side and aloft.

JETSAM: goods, cast overboard to lighten a ship in distress. See FLOTSAM.

JETTISON: to throw goods overboard.

JETTY: breakwater built to protect a harbor entrance of river mouth.

JIGGER: light handy tackle for general work about the deck.

JURY RIG: makeshift rig of mast and sail or of other gear, as jury anchor, jury rudder; any makeshift device.

KAPOK: water-resistant fiber stuff packed into life jackets to make them buoyant.

KEDGE: anchor used for kedging; that is, moving a ship a short distance at a time by taking one of the anchors out in a boat, letting it go, and then hauling the ship up to it. If this is done merely to change the heading of the ship, it is called *warping*. See **WARP**.

KEEL: backbone of a ship, running from stem to sternpost at the bottom.

KEELHAUL: to reprimand severely.

KEELSON: timber or steel fabrications bolted on top of a keel to strengthen it.

KING POST: short mast supporting a boom.

KNIFE EDGE: smooth, polished edge of the coaming against which the rubber gaskets of watertight doors and scuttles press when closed; furnishes better watertight integrity.

KNOCK OFF: to cease what is being done; to stop work.

KNOT: one nautical mile (6080.2 feet) per hour. (Never say "knots per hour." This would be the same as saying "miles per hour per hour.") Also, a tie or fastening formed with rope.

LACING: line used to secure canvas by passing through eyelets or grommets in the canvas.

LADDER: in a ship, corresponds to stairs in a building.

LANDFALL: first sighting of land at the end of a sea voyage.

LANDING PARTY: force of infantry from ship's crew detailed for emergency, riot or parade duty ashore.

LANDLUBBER: seaman's term for one who has never been to sea.

LANDMARK: any conspicuous object on shore, used for piloting.

LANYARD: a line made fast to an article for securing it; for example, a *knife lanyard, bucket lanyard.*

LASH: to tie or secure by turns of line.

LAY: the direction of the twist of strands of a rope.

LEAD OR SOUNDING LEAD: weight used for soundings; that is, for measuring the depth of the water.

LEAD LINE: line secured to the lead used for soundings.

LEADSMAN: seaman detailed to heave the sounding lead.

LEE: direction away from the wind.

LEE HELMSMAN: assistant or relief helmsman.

LEEWARD: in a lee direction. Pronounced "lu'ard."

LEEWAY: drift of a vessel to leeward.

LET GO BY THE RUN: allowing a line to run free.

LIE OFF: order to a boat to await word from the OOD to come alongside.

LIE TO: said of a vessel when underway with no way on.

LIFE BUOY OR LIFE RING: a ring or U-shaped buoy of cork or metal to support a person in the water.

LIFEJACKET OR LIFE PRESERVER: a belt or jacket of buoyant or inflatable material; worn to keep a person afloat.

LIFELINE: line secured along the deck to lay hold of in heavy weather; line thrown on board a wreck by a rescue crew; knotted line secured to the span of lifeboat davits for the use of the crew when hoisting and lowering.

LIFELINES: lines or metal pipes stretched fore and aft along the weather decks to furnish shipboard personnel safety against falling or being washed overboard.

LIFERAFT: float constructed either with a metallic tube covered with cork and canvas, or made of balsa wood or other suitable material.

LIGHTER: small vessel used for working (loading and unloading cargo) ships anchored in harbor.

LIGHTSHIP: small ship equipped with a distinctive light and anchored near an obstruction to navigation or in shallow water to warn shipping.

LINE: seagoing term for rope; the equator.

LIST: inclination or heeling over of a ship to one side.

LOCK: compartment in a canal for lowering or lifting vessels to different levels.

LOCKER: small metal or wooden stowage space; either a chest or closet.

LOG: instrument for measuring a ship's speed through the water. Also, a short term for *logbook.*

LOGBOOK: a book containing the official record of a ship's activities and of other pertinent or required data.

LOG ROOM: engineers' shipboard record room.

LOOKOUT: seaman assigned duties involving watching and reporting to the OOD any objects of interest; the lookouts are "the eyes of the ship."

LORAN (*lo*ng *ra*nge *n*avigation): a navigational system that fixes the position of a ship by measuring the difference in the time of reception of two synchronized radio signals.

LUBBER'S LINE: line marked on inner surface of compass bowl to indicate direction of ship's bow.

LUCKY BAG: locker for stowage of personal gear found adrift.

MACNAMARA LACE: fancywork and trimming, chiefly used on boats; formed of threads of unlaid canvas.

MAGAZINE: compartment used for stowage of ammunition and explosives.

MAIN BATTERY: the largest caliber guns carried by a warship.

MAIN DECK: highest complete deck extending from stem to stern and from side to side.

MAINMAST: second mast from bow of a ship that has two or more masts. If a ship has but one mast, that mast is considered the mainmast.

MANHOLE: round or oval hole cut in deck, bulkhead, or tank top to provide access.

MAN-OF-WAR: fighting ship; warship.

MANROPE: side rope to a ladder used as a handrail; rope used as a safety line anywhere on deck; rope hanging down on the side of a ship to assist in ascending the ship's side.

MARK: call used in comparing watches, compass readings, or bearings; fathoms in a lead line that are marked. Also, a model or type of a piece of equipment, as Mark XIV torpedo.

MARLINSPIKE: pointed iron instrument used in splicing line or wire.

MARRY: placing two lines together, as in hoisting a boat; to sew together temporarily the ends of two lines for rendering through a block.

MAST: upright spar supporting signal yard and antennas in a naval ship. Also the seagoing equivalent of CO's office hours in the Marine Corps.

MEAL FLAG: Echo Flag, which is hoisted from port yardarm of a Navy ship at anchor when crew is at mess, sometimes called "the bean rag."

MESS: to eat; group of men eating together.

MESSMAN (OR SLANG, MESSCOOK): enlisted man who performs duties in mess hall or galley.

MESSENGER: light line used for hauling over a heavier rope or cable; for example, the messenger is sent over from the ship to the pier by the heaving line and then used to pull the heavy mooring lines across. Also, an enlisted man who runs errands for the OOD.

MIDWATCH: the 0000-0400 watch.

MIDSHIPMAN: A man in training at the U.S. Naval Academy; a student officer.

MISFIRE: powder charge that fails to fire when the firing key has been closed.

MONKEY FIST: a knot, with or without a weight enclosed, worked in the end of a heaving line to form a heavy ball to facilitate throwing the line.

MOORING: securing a ship to a pier, buoy, or another ship; or anchoring with two anchors.

MOORING BUOY: a large, well anchored buoy to which one or more ships moor.

MOORING LINE: one of the lines used for mooring a ship to a pier, wharf, or another ship.

MORNING WATCH: 0400-0800 watch.

MORSE CODE: code of dots and dashes used in radio and visual signaling.

MOTOR LAUNCH: large, sturdily-built powerboat used for liberty parties and heavy workloads.

MOTOR WHALEBOAT: a 26-foot powerboat pointed at both ends.

NAUTICAL MILE: 6,080.2 feet, or about a sixth longer than a land mile.

NEST: two or more vessels moored alongside one another; boat stowage in which one boat nests inside another.

NETTING OR SNAKING: small stuff criss-crossed and strung around the forecastles and fantails of many ships. Extending up about two feet from the deck, it furnishes a life-saving device to exposed personnel.

NOTHING TO THE RIGHT (LEFT): order to the helmsman not to let the ship go to the right (left) of the designated course.

NUN BUOY: cone-shaped buoy used to mark channels; it is anchored on the right side, entering from seaward, and is painted red.

OAKUM: a calking material made of old, tarred, hemp rope fiber.

OARLOCK: device to hold oars when pulling a boat; also called *rowlock*.

OFFICER OF THE DECK (OOD): the officer on watch in charge of the ship, equivalent to the Officer of the Day ashore.

OFFICER OF THE WATCH: See WATCH OFFICER.

OILER: a tanker—a vessel especially designed to carry fuel oil.

OIL KING: petty officer in charge of fuel oil storage.

OILSKINS: waterproof clothing.

OLD MAN: seaman's term for the captain of a ship or other naval activity.

ON THE BOW: bearing of an object ahead somewhere within 45° to either side of the bow.

ON THE QUARTER: bearing of an object somewhere astern of the ship, 45° to either side of the stern.

OOD: officer of the deck.

ORLOP: partial deck below the lower deck; also the lowest deck in a ship having four or more decks.

OUTBOARD: toward the side of the vessel, or outside the vessel entirely.

OUT OF BOUNDS: buildings or areas off limits to military personnel.

OVERHANG: projection of ship's bow or stern beyond the stem or sternpost.

OVERHAUL: to separate the blocks of a tackle; to overtake a vessel; to clear or repair anything for use.

OVERHEAD: on a ship, equivalent to the ceiling of a building ashore; ships have *overheads* rather than *ceilings*.

PAD EYE: metal eye permanently secured to deck or bulkhead.

PAINTER: a line in the bow of a boat for towing or making fast.

PALM AND NEEDLE: sailor's thimble made of leather, and a large needle; used for sewing heavy canvas or leather.

PARAVANES: torpedo-shaped devices towed on either side of ship's bow to deflect and cut moored mines adrift.

PARCELING: wrapping a rope spirally with long strips of canvas, following the lay of the rope and overlapping like the shingles on a roof to shed moisture.

PART: to break, snap, or carry away a line.

PASSAGEWAY: corridor or hallway on a ship.

PASS A LINE: to carry or send a line to or around an object, or to reeve through and make fast.

PASS THE WORD: to repeat an order or information to all hands.

PATENT LOG: device for measuring ship's speed through the water. See TAFFRAIL LOG.

PAY OFF: to turn the bow away from the wind.

PAY OUT: to increase the scope of anchor cable; to ease off or slack a line.

PEACOAT: a short, heavy blue coat worn by enlisted men below the grade of CPO.

PEAK: topmost end of the gaff; from this point the ensign is flown while the ship is underway.

PELICAN HOOK: hinged hook held in place by a ring; when the ring is knocked off, the hook swings open.

PELORUS: navigational instrument used in taking bearings; consists of two sight vanes mounted on a hoop revolving about a dumb compass or a gyro repeater.

PENDANT: length of rope with a block or thimble at the end.

PENNANT: three-sided flag, swallow-tail flag, or four-sided flag that tapers off toward the end.

PERISCOPE: optical instrument used to observe at a level above eye level.

PIER: a harbor structure projecting out into the water with sufficient depth alongside to accommodate vessels.

PIGSTICK: a small spar that projects above top of mainmast; commission pennants are usually mounted on this.

PILE: pointed spar driven into the bottom and projecting above the surface of water; when driven at the corners of a pier or wharf, they are termed *fender piles.*

PILOT: an expert who comes aboard ships in harbors or dangerous waters to advise the captains as to how the ship should be conned; also a man at the controls of an aircraft.

PINTLES: pivot pins on which a rudder turns.

PIPE DOWN: an order to keep silent; also used to dismiss the crew from an evolution.

PIPE THE SIDE: ceremony at the gangway in which sideboys are drawn up and the boatswain's pipe is blown when a high-ranking officer or distinguished visitor comes aboard.

PITCH: the heaving and plunging vertical motion of a vessel at sea.

PIVOT POINT: point in a ship about which she turns.

PLAN OF THE DAY: schedule of day's routine and events ordered by executive officer; published daily aboard ship or at a shore activity.

PLANK OWNER: a person who served aboard ship from its commissioning.

PLATFORM DECK: partial deck below lowest complete deck; called first, second, etc., from the top where there is more than one.

PLIMSOLL MARK: a mark on the side of merchant ships to indicate allowed loading depths.

POINTER: member of gun crew who controls vertical elevation of a gun in aiming at a target; that is, he positions the gun up and down. See TRAINER.

POLLYWOG: person who has never crossed the Line (the equator).

POOP DECK: partial deck at the stern over the main deck.

PORT: left side of ship facing forward; a harbor; an opening in the ship's side, such as a *cargo port.* The usual opening in the ship's side for light and air is also a *port.* The glass set in a brass frame that fits against it is called a *port light.*

PREVENTER: line used for additional safety and to prevent loss of gear under heavy strain or in case of accident.

PRICKER: small marlinspike.

PROTECTIVE DECK: deck fitted with heaviest protective plating.

PUDDING: bulky rope fender attached to a strongback, or to a boat or tug's stem or gunwales.

PUNT: rectangular, flat-bottomed boat usually used for painting and other work around waterline of a ship.

QUADRANTAL CORRECTORS OR SPHERES: two iron balls secured at either side of the binnacle; help compensate for ship's magnetic effect on compass. Also known as "the Navigator's balls."

QUARTER: that part of ship's side within 45 degrees on either side of the stern.

QUARTERDECK: that part of the main (or other) deck reserved for honors and ceremonies and as the station of the OOD in port.

QUARTERS: living space; assembly of the crew; all hands assembled at established stations for muster, drills, or inspection.

QUAY: a wharf; a landing place for receiving and discharging cargo. Pronounced "key."

RADAR PICKET: ship stationed at a distance from the main force for the purpose of picking up by radar the approach of an enemy.

RADIO DIRECTION FINDER (RDF): apparatus for taking bearings on the source of radio transmissions.

RAIL: top pipe of the lifeline pipes that extend along various outboard sections of weather decks; uppermost edge of a bulwark.

RAIL LOADING: loading a davit- or crane-supported boat while it is swung out and even with the deck.

RAKE: angle of a vessel's masts and stacks from the vertical.

RAKISH: having a rake to the masts; smart, speedy appearance.

RATE: enlisted rank in the Navy. A rate identifies a man by pay grade or level of advancement, within a *rating,* a rate reflects levels of aptitude, training, experience, knowledge, skill, and responsibility. See RATING.

RAT GUARD: a sheet metal disk constructed in conical form with a hole in the center and slit from the center to the edge. It is installed over the mooring lines to prevent rats from boarding ship from the shore over the mooring lines.

RATED MAN: Any petty officer, or noncommissioned officer of Marines, as distinct from seaman and privates.

RATING: seagoing equivalent of an MOS. Men in pay grades E-1, E-2, and E-3 are not considered as possessing ratings.

RATLINE: short length of small stuff running horizontally across shrouds; used for a step.

READY ROOM: compartment on aircraft carriers in which pilots assemble for flight orders.

REDUCER: metal fitting between fire main outlet and hose coupling of smaller diameter.

REEF: chain or ridge of rocks, coral, or sand in shallow water.

REEFER: refrigerator vessel for carrying chilled or frozen foodstuffs.

REEVE: to pass the end of a rope through any lead, such as a sheave or fairlead.

RELIEVING (THE WATCH, THE DUTY, ETC.): to take over the duty and responsibilities, as when one sentry or lookout relieves another. Those who relieve are *reliefs.*

RENDER: to pass through or around, as a cargo whip renders through the head block.

REQUEST MAST: mast held by captain or executive officer to hear special requests for leave, liberty, etc.

RIG: general description of a ship's upper works; to set up, fit out, or put together.

RIGGING: general term for all ropes, chains, and gear used for supporting and operating masts, yards, booms, gaffs, and sails. Rigging is of two kinds: *standing rigging,* or lines that support but ordinarily do not move; and *running rigging,* or lines that move to operate equipment.

RIG SHIP FOR VISITORS: word passed as a warning to all hands to have ship and their persons in neat order for expected visitors.

RISER: a pipe running vertically between decks with branch connections or off-shoots.

ROLL: the side-to-side motion of a ship at sea.

ROPE: general term for cordage over one inch in diameter. If smaller, it is known as cord, twine, line or string; if finer still, as thread or double yarn. It is constructed by twisting fibers or metal wire. The size is designated by the diameter (for wire rope) or by the circumference (for fiber rope). The length is given in fathoms or feet.

ROPEYARN SUNDAY: a time for repairing clothing and other personal gear. (Usually Wednesday afternoon at sea.)

RUDDER: a flat, vertical, mobile structure at the stern of a vessel; used to control vessel's heading.

RUFFLES: roll of the drum used in rendering honors.

RUNNING BOWLINE: bowline made over the standing part of its own line so that it forms a free-sliding noose.

RUNNING LIGHTS: lights required by law to be shown by ship or plane when underway between sunset and sunrise.

SALLY SHIP: evolution in which the crew runs from side to side together to cause the ship to list, used to help free a grounded ship.

SALVAGE: to save a ship or cargo from danger; to recover a ship or cargo from disaster and wreckage.

SAMSON POST: in small craft, a single bitt amidships or in the bow.

SCOPE: length of anchor cable out.

SCOW: large, open, flat-bottomed boat for transporting sand, gravel, mud, etc.

SCREW: the propeller; the rotating, bladed device the propels a vessel through the water.

SCULL: to propel a boat by working an oar from side to side over the stern; to propel oneself in the water by working hands and forearms in a figure-eight motion.

SCUPPER: opening in side of ship to carry off water from waterways.

SCUTTLE: small opening through hatch, deck, or bulkhead to provide access; similar hole in side or bottom of ship; cover for such an opening; to sink a ship intentionally by boring holes in the bottom or by opening seacocks.

SCUTTLEBUTT: container of drinking water, or a drinking fountain. Also, a rumor, usually of local importance.

SEA BAG: large canvas bag for stowing a man's gear and clothing.

SEA CHEST: sailor's trunk; intake between ship's side and sea valve or seacock.

SEACOCK: valve in a pipe connected to the sea; a vessel may be flooded by opening the seacocks.

SEA LADDER: rope ladder, usually with wooden steps, for use over the side. Also known as a Jacob's ladder.

SEA LAWYER: enlisted man who likes to argue; usually one who thinks he can twist the regulations and standing orders around to favor his personal inclinations.

SEA MARKER: dye for brightly coloring the water to facilitate search and rescue.

SEA PAINTER: a long line running from well forward on the ship and secured by a toggle over the inboard gunwale in the bow of a boat.

SEAWORTHY: capable of putting to sea and meeting usual sea conditions.

SECOND DECK: complete deck below the main deck.

SECTION: a unit of a division or watch.

SECURE: to make fast; to tie; recall on completion of a drill or exercise.

SECURE FOR SEA: extra prescribed lashings on all movable objects.

SEIZE: to bind with small rope.

SEMAPHORE: code indicated by the position of the arms; hand flags are used to increase readability.

SENNET, SENNIT: ornamental, braided, fancy ropework, formed by plaiting (inter-weaving) a number of strands.

SERVING: additional protection over parcelling, consisting of continuous round turns of small stuff.

SET: direction of the leeway of a ship or of a tide or current.

SET TAUT: an order to take in the slack and take a strain or running gear before heaving it in.

SET THE COURSE: to give the helmsman the desired course to be steered.

SET THE WATCH: the order to station the first watch.

SHACKLE: U-shaped piece of iron or steel with eyes in the ends through which a bolt passes to close the U.

SHAFT ALLEY: spaces within a ship surrounding the propeller shaft.

SHAKEDOWN CRUISE: cruise of newly-commissioned ship to test and adjust all machinery and equipment and to train the crew as a working unit.

SHEER: longitudinal upward curve of a deck; amount by which the deck at the bow is higher than the deck at the stern. Also, a sudden change of course.

SHEER OFF: to turn suddenly away.

SHELL: casing of a block.

SHELLBACK: man who has crossed the equator and been initiated.

SHELL ROOM: compartment for stowage of projectiles.

SHIFT COLORS: to shift the ensign from the gaff to the flagstaff upon mooring or anchoring; from the flagstaff to the gaff upon getting underway.

SHIFT THE RUDDER: an order to swing the rudder an equal distance in the opposite direction.

SHIP: a general term for large ocean-going craft or vessels; to enlist (*ship in*) or reenlist, as to *ship over.*

SHIP'S COMPANY: all the officers and men serving in, and attached to, a ship; *all hands.*

SHIPSHAPE: neat, orderly.

SHORE PATROL: Petty and noncommissioned officers detailed to maintain discipline, to aid local police in handling naval personnel on liberty or leave, and to assist naval personnel in difficulties ashore.

SHORE UP: to prop up.

SHORT STAY: when anchor chain has been hauled in until amount of chain out is only slightly greater than depth of water and ship is riding almost directly over the anchor.

SHOVE OFF: to leave; an order to a boat to leave a landing or a ship's side.

SHROUD: side stay of hemp or wire running from masthead to rail to give athwartship support to the mast.

SICKBAY: ship's hospital or dispensary.

SIDEBOYS: non-rated men manning the side when visiting officers or distinguished visitors come aboard.

SIDE LIGHTS: red and green running lights carried on port and starboard sides respectively.

SINGLE UP: to reduce the number of mooring lines out to a pier preparatory to sailing; that is, to leave only one easily cast-off line in each place where mooring lines were doubled up for greater security.

SKIDS: beams fitted over decks for stowage of heavy boats.

SLACK: the part of a line hanging loose; to ease off; state of the tide when there is no horizontal motion. See STAND.

SLINGS: fitting for hoisting a boat or other heavy lift by crane or boom; consist of a metal ring with four pendants. Two of these pendants are for athwartships steadying lines, the other two shackle to chain bridles permanently bolted to the keel of the boat.

SLIP: to let go by unshackling, as an anchor cable; space between two piers; waste motion of a propeller.

SLUSH: to apply a protective, greasy substance to wire rope; the stuff applied is *soogy.*

SMALL CRAFT: generally, all vessels less than small-ship size.

SMALL STUFF: small cordage designated by the number of threads (nine-thread, twelve-thread, etc.) or by special names, such as marline, ratline stuff, etc.

SMART: snappy, seamanlike.

SMOKING LAMP: a lamp aboard oldtime ships used by men to light their pipes; now used in phrase "The smoking lamp is lighted (or out)" to indicate when men are allowed (or forbidden) to smoke.

SNATCH BLOCK: single-sheaved block with a hinged strap. It can be quickly opened to take the bight of a line.

SNUB: to check suddenly.

SNIPES: slang for members of the engineering department.

SONAR: (*so*und *n*avigation *a*nd *r*anging): device for locating objects under water by emitting vibrations similar to sound and measuring the time taken for these vibrations to bounce back from anything in their path.

SOUND: to measure depth of water by means of a lead line. Also, to measure the depth of liquids in oil tanks, voids, blisters, and other compartment or tanks.

SOUND-POWERED PHONE: shipboard telephone powered by voice alone.

SPANNER: tool for coupling hoses.

SPAR: steel or wood pole serving as a mast, boom, gaff, pile, etc.

SPAR BUOY: long, thin, wooden spar used to mark channels.

SPEED CONE: cone-shaped, bright-yellow signal used when steaming in formation to indicate engine speeds.

SPITKIT: derisive term for small, unseaworthy vessel.

SPLICE: to join two lines by tucking the strands of each into the other.

SPLINTER SCREEN: protective plating around a gun mount.

SPRING: mooring line leading at an angle of about 45° off centerline of vessel; to turn a vessel with a line.

SQUALL: sudden gust of wind.

SQUARE AWAY: to get things settled down or in order.

SQUILGEE: drier for wooden decks made of a flat piece of wood with a rubber blade and a long wooden handle. Pronounced "squeegee."

STACK: ship's smoke pipe. See FUNNEL.

STACK COVER: canvas secured over the top of a stack when it is not in use.

STADIMETER: instrument for measuring distance from an object.

STAGE: platform rigged over ship's side for painting or repair work.

STANCHION: wood or metal upright used as a support.

STAND: condition of tide when there is no vertical motion. See SLACK.

STAND BY: preparatory order meaning "Get ready," or "Prepare to."

STANDARD SPEED: speed set as basic speed by officer in command of a unit.

STARBOARD: right side of a ship looking forward.

STATEROOM: officer's shipboard bedroom.

STATION KEEPING: the art of keeping a ship in its proper position in a formation of ships.

STAY: piece of rigging, either wire or fiber, used to give fore-and-aft support to a mast; See *Guy*.

STEADY: order to steersman to hold ship on course.

STEERAGE WAY: slowest speed at which a ship can be steered.

STERN FAST: line used to secure a boat's stern.

STEM: upright post or bar at most forward part of the bow of a ship or boat. It may be a casting, forging welding, or made of wood.

STERN: after part of a ship.

STERN SHEETS: space in a boat abaft the after thwart.

STERNWAY: backward movement of a ship.

STOPPER: short length of rope or chain firmly secured at one end; used in securing or checking a running line.

STOVE: broken in; crushed in.

STOW: to put gear in its proper place.

STRAND: part of a line or rope made up of yarns.

STRIKER: enlisted man in training for a particular rating.

STRIP SHIP: to prepare ship for battle action by getting rid of any unnecessary gear.

STRONGBACK: spar lashed to a pair of boat davits; acts as a spreader for the davits and provides a brace for more secure stowage of lifeboat at sea.

SURVEY: examination by authorized competent personnel to determine whether a piece of gear, equipment, stores, or supplies should be discarded or retained.

SUPERSTRUCTURE: all equipment and fittings, except armament, extending above hull.

SUPERSTRUCTURE DECK: partial deck higher than the main, forecastle, and poop deck, and not extending to the ship's sides.

SWAB: a rope or yarn mop.

SWAMP: to sink by filling with water.

SWEEPERS: men who use brooms in cleaning ship when "clean sweep down" is ordered.

SWING SHIP: moving the ship through the compass points to check the magnetic compass on different headings and make up a deviation table.

SWIVEL: metal link with an eye at one end, fitted to revolve freely and thus keep turns out of a chain.

TACKLE: arrangement of ropes and blocks to give mechanical advantage; to purchase, that is, a rig of lines and pulleys to increase available hauling force. Pronounced "take-el."

TACKLINE: short length of line used to separate flags in a hoist.

TAFFRAIL: a rail at the stern of a ship.

TAFFRAIL LOG: device which indicates the speed of the ship through the water. It is trailed on a line from the taffrail and consists of a rotator and a recording instrument.

TAKE A TURN: to pass a turn around a cleat, bitts, or bollard and hold on.

TALKER: man who handles a sound-powered phone during drills or combat.

TARPAULIN: heavy canvas used as protective covering.

TAUT: with no slack. Also, strict as to discipline.

TEND: to man; direction and cable leads when ship is anchored.

TENDER: an auxiliary vessel that supplies and repairs ships or aircraft.

THIMBLE: iron ring grooved on outside for rope grommet.

THWART: crosspiece used as a seat for a boat. Pronounced "thort".

TIDE: the vertical rise and fall of the sea caused by gravitational effect of sun and moon.

TILLER: short handle of metal or wood used to turn a boat's rudder.

TOGGLE: wooden or metal pin in a becket for rapid release.

TOMPION: plug placed in muzzle of gun to keep dampness and foreign objects out. Pronounced "tompkin."

TOP: platform at top of mast; to *top a boom* is to lift up its end.

TOPSIDE OR TOPSIDES: above decks.

TOW: to pull through the water; vessels so towed. The usual towing vessels in Navy talk are *tugs,* not *towboats.*

TRACK: path of a vessel or aircraft.

TRADES: generally steady winds of the tropics that blow toward the equator, NE in the northern hemisphere, and SE in the southern.

TRAIN: to traverse a gun horizontally onto a target.

TRAINER: gun crew member who controls horizontal movement of gun in aiming it at a target.

TRANSOM: athwartship piece bolted to sternpost; planking across stern of square-sterned boat.

TRICE UP: to hitch up or hook up, such at trice up a shipboard bunk.

TRICK: period of time a helmsman is at the wheel, as "to take a trick at the wheel."

TRIM: angle to the horizontal at which a ship rides; that is, how level the ship sits in the water; shipshape.

TRUCK: flat, circular piece secured at top of mast or at top of flagstaff and jackstaff. Also, uppermost part of a mast.

TURN TO: an order to begin work.

TURNBUCKLE: metal appliance with a thread and screw capable of being set taut or slacked and used for setting up standing rigging.

TURRET: heavily armored housing containing a grouping of main battery guns. It extends downward through decks and includes ammunition handling rooms and hoists. See GUN MOUNT.

TWO-BLOCKED: when two blocks of a tackle have been drawn as closely together as possible. The official term is now *Close-up.*

UNBEND: to cast adrift or to untie.

UNCOVER: to remove headgear.

UNDERWAY: a ship is underway when not at anchor, made fast to the shore, or aground. She need not be actually moving; she is underway as long as she lies free in the water.

UNION: inner upper corner of a flag. See JACK.

UNSHIP: to remove from place; to take apart.

UP ANCHOR: the order to weight anchor and get underway.

UP AND DOWN: perpendicular (pertaining to the anchor cable).

UP END: to stand an object on one of its ends.

UPPER DECK: partial deck amidships above main deck.

UPTAKE: enclosed truck connecting the boiler(s) to the stack.

VEER: to slack off, to let anchor cable, line, or chain run out by its own weight. Also, when the wind changes direction clockwise or to the right, it is said to veer.

VERY WELL: reply of a senior (or officer) to a junior (or enlisted man) to indicate that information given is understood, or that permission is granted.

VESSEL: inclusive term for *ships, small craft,* and *boats.*

WAKE: the track left in the water behind a ship.

WALK BACK: an order to keep the gear in hand but to walk back with it toward the belaying point.

WARDROOM: officers' mess and lounge aboard a ship.

WARP: to move a vessel by a line or laid-out anchor, as "Warp the ship into the slip." See KEDGE.

WATCH: a period of duty, usually of four hours' duration.

WATCH AND WATCH: alternating four hours on watch with four hours off watch. Most off-watch periods are of 8 to 12 hours' duration.

WATCHCAP: knitted wool cap worn by enlisted men below CPO in cool or cold weather; canvas cover placed over a stack when not in use.

WATCH OFFICER: an officer regularly assigned to duty in charge of a watch or of a portion thereof; for example, the OOD, or the engineering officer of the watch.

WATCH, QUARTER, AND STATION BILL: a large chart showing every man's location in the ship's organization and his station in the various shipboard drills.

WATER BREAKER: drinking-water cask or container carried in boats.

WATERLINE: point to which ship sinks in water; line painted on hull showing point to which ship sinks in water when properly trimmed.

WATER-LOGGED: filled or soaked with water but still afloat.

WATERTIGHT INTEGRITY: system of keeping ship afloat by maintaining water-tightness.

WATERWAY: gutter at side of ship's deck to carry water to scuppers.

WEATHER: exposed to wind and rain: to the windward, as "to face the weather," or "to weather a storm."

WEATHER CLOTH: canvas spread for protection from wind and weather.

WEATHER DECK: portion of main, forecastle, poop, and upper deck exposed to weather.

WEATHER EYE: to keep a weather eye is to be on the alert.

WEIGH: to lift the anchor off the bottom.

WELL DECK: a low weather deck.

WHALEBOAT: sharp-ended lifeboat, pulled by oars and/or fitted with sails; when equipped with an engine it is called a *motor whaleboat*.

WHARF: harbor structure alongside which vessels moor. A *wharf* generally is built along the water's edge; a *pier* extends well out into the harbor.

WHEELHOUSE: pilothouse; the topside compartment where on most ships the OOD, helmsman, quartermaster of the watch, etc., stand their watches.

WHERE AWAY?: answering call requesting location of object sighted by lookout.

WHIPPING: keeping the ends of a rope from unlaying, by wrapping with turns of twine and tucking the ends.

WILDCAT: sprocket wheel on windlass for taking the links of the chain cable.

WINCH: hoisting engine secured to the deck; used to haul lines by turns around a horizontally driven drum or gypsey.

WINDLASS: anchor engine used for heaving in the anchor.

WINDWARD: into the wind; toward the direction from which wind is blowing; opposite of *leeward.*

WIND SCOOP: metal scoop fitted into a port to direct air into the ship for ventilation.

WIND SHIP: to turn a ship end for end, usually with lines at a pier. Pronounced "wined."

WIRE ROPE: rope made of wire strands, as distinguished from *fiber rope;* sometimes called a *cable,* in error.

WITH THE SUN: in clockwise direction; the proper direction in which to coil a line; right-handed.

WORK A SHIP: to handle ship by means of engines and other gear; for example, to work a ship into a slip using engines, rudder, and lines to docks.

YARD: spar attached at the middle to a mast and running athwartships; used as a support for signal halyards or signal lights; also a place used for shipbuilding and as a repair depot, as Boston Naval Shipyard.

YARDARM: either side of a yard.

YARDARM BLINKER: signal lights mounted above the end of a yardarm and flashed on and off to send messages.

YARN: twisted fibers used for rough seizings, which may be twisted into strands; also, a story, as to "spin a yarn," meaning to tell a story not necessarily true.

YAW: zigzagging motion of a vessel as it is carried off its heading by strong overtaking seas. This motion swings the ship back and forth across the intended course.

1817. NAVY RATING ABBREVIATIONS. The Navy's system of ratings (i.e., petty officer ranks and specialties) with its many different abbreviations may at first appear confusing but is something seagoing Marines must understand. The list below gives the basic abbreviations and their titles. Rank is shown in the following way by suffixes to the basic rating:

Suffix	Denotes rank as	Example
CM	Master chief PO (E-9)	GMCM
CS	Senior CPO (E-8)	HMCS
C	Chief, or CPO (E-7)	BMC
1	1st Class PO (E-6)	YN1
2	2nd Class PO (E-5)	DT2
3	3d Class PO (E-4)	QM3

Note: Abbreviations for E-3, E-2, and E-1 carry no grade suffix as above.

Abbr	Title
AA	Airman Apprentice
AB	Aviation Boatswain's Mate
AC	Air Controlman
AD	Aviation Machinist's Mate
AE	Aviation Electrician's Mate
AFCM	Master Chief Aircraft Maintenanceman
AG	Aerographer's Mate
AK	Aviation Storekeeper
AM	Aviation Structural Mechanic
AN	Airman
AO	Aviation Ordnanceman
AQ	Aviation Fire Control Technician
AR	Airman Recruit
AS	Aviation Support Equipment Technician
AT	Aviation Electronics Technician
AVCM	Master Chief Avionics Technician
AX	Aviation ASW Technician
AZ	Aviation Maintenance Administrationman
BM	Boatswain's Mate
BR	Boilermaker
BT	Boilerman
BU	Builder
CA	Construction Apprentice
CE	Construction Electrician
CM	Construction Mechanic
CN	Constructionman
CR	Construction Recruit
CS	Commissaryman
CT	Communications Technician
CYN	Communications Yeoman
DA	Dental Technician Apprentice
DC	Damage Controlman

Abbr	Title
DK	Disbursing Clerk
DM	Illustrator Draftsman
DN	Dental Technician (E-3)
DP	Data Processing Technician
DR	Dental Technician Recruit
DS	Data Systems Technician
DT	Dental Technician
EA	Engineering Aid
EM	Electrician's Mate
EN	Engineman
EO	Equipment Operator
EQCM	Master Chief Equipmentman
ET	Electronics Technician
FA	Fireman Apprentice
FN	Fireman
FR	Fireman Recruit
FT	Fire Control Technician
GM	Gunner's Mate
HA	Hospital Corpsman Apprentice
HM	Hospital Corpsman
HN	Hospital Corpsman (E-3)
HR	Hospital Corpsman Recruit
IC	Interior Communications Electrician
IM	Instrumentman
JO	Journalist
LI	Lithographer
MA	Machine Accountant
ML	Molder
MM	Machinist's Mate
MN	Mineman
MR	Machinery Repairman
MT	Missile Technician
MU	Musician
OM	Opticalman
PC	Postal Clerk
PH	Photographer's Mate
PICM	Master Chief Precision Instrumentman
PM	Patternmaker
PN	Personnelman
PR	Aircrew Survival Equipmentman
PT	Photographic Intelligenceman
QM	Quartermaster
RD	Radarman
RM	Radioman
SA	Seaman Apprentice
SD	Steward
SF	Shipfitter
SH	Ship's Serviceman

Abbr	Title
SK	Storekeeper
SM	Signalman
SN	Seaman
SPCM	Master Chief Steam Propulsionman
SR	Seaman Recruit
ST	Sonar Technician
SW	Steelworker
TA	Steward Apprentice
TD	Tradevman
TM	Torpedoman's Mate
TN	Stewardsman
TR	Steward Recruit
UT	Utilitiesman
YN	Yeoman

He is best secure from dangers who is on his guard even when he seems safe.

—Publilius Syrus: Sententiae, c 50 B.C.

19 Embassy Guard Duty

The Marine Corps has no responsibility in which individual quality and outstanding performance are of higher importance than the Marine Security Guard program which the Corps administers and operates for the Department of State.

Under this program, more than a thousand carefully selected Marines maintain the internal security of over a hundred American embassies, legations, missions, and consulates throughout the world. All but a handful of these vitally important security posts are under the independent command of staff noncommissioned officers. With the possible exception of recruiting duty and drill instruction at the recruit depots, the Corps has no other program which depends so directly and singly on the loyalty, devotion to duty, military character, and good sense of its noncommissioned officers.

Past History
1901. MARINE SECURITY GUARDS OF THE PAST. The first State Department security guard duty performed by the Marine Corps was in 1801, when President Jefferson directed that the Marine Corps provide security guards for the State, War, and Navy Departments in the infant capital city of Washington, founded in 1800. In the same year, on request of the Secretary of State, a Marine guard was provided for the Washington legation of the Bey of Tripoli.

From 1894 until 1905 (when Japan finally annexed Korea), a platoon-sized guard was maintained to provide for the security of the American Legation at Seoul. The first commanding officer of this guard was Captain G. F. Elliott, later to become tenth Commandant of the Marine Corps.

Shortly before outbreak of the Boxer Uprising in China in 1900, a legation guard made up of Marine detachments from USS *Newark* and *Oregon* was organized and sent to Peking, where its members won two Medals of Honor and played a leading role in the defense of the Legation Quarter throughout the summer of 1900. After the relief of the legations, on unilateral order of the U.S. Army commanding general in China, the Peking legation guard duty was taken over by Army troops and held until 1904, when the Department of State requested that the Marine Corps again furnish the Peking guard, which it did until the outbreak of World War II in 1941.

In 1903, a Marine guard was assigned to escort the first American Minister to Ethiopia and provide protection and security during establishment of the legation in Addis Ababa.

Meanwhile, from 1912 until 1925, a company-sized security guard was maintained by the Marine Corps at the American Legation in Managua, Nicaragua.

In 1934, when diplomatic relations were established between the USSR and the United States, President Franklin D. Roosevelt personally directed establishment of a Marine security guard, consisting of eight carefully selected enlisted men and a captain. This guard was maintained through the 1930s but lapsed after outbreak of war in Europe.

1902. THE MODERN SECURITY GUARD PROGRAM. The need for some type of more reliable embassy guards than the civilian watchmen (often local nationals) then employed became evident with the beginning of the Cold War in late 1945. The State Department's initial reaction to the heightened security problems of its overseas establishment was to request the War Department (then headed by Former Secretary of State Stimson) to provide security detachments at certain key posts. Unfortunately this arrangement broke down, culminating in the defection to the communists of a senior noncommissioned officer assigned to code-room security at our Moscow embassy, and a number of lesser but nonetheless serious failures.

As a result, language was written into the Foreign Service Act of 1946, restoring to the Marine Corps its historic role of State Department security duties. Based on the provisions of this act, by 1948 the State and Navy Departments had worked out a permanent Marine security guard program resulting in initial selection, training, and overseas deployment of 303 officers and men. The first posts taken over by Marines were Bangkok and Tangier. At the outset, the Marine Corps administered the security guards through Headquarters Battalion, HQMC, first under Casual Company, later under Company F (activated for the program), and finally by the Marine Security Guard Battalion, which superseded Company F on 10 February 1967.

Within five years after its establishment in 1948, the Marine commitment more than doubled in strength and number of missions covered. In 1954, the size and important responsibilities of the program resulted in establishment at Henderson Hall of the Marine Security Guard School, which is now the training institution for all officers and men assigned.

In its first two decades, the Marine Corps/State arrangement has functioned with outstanding success. Marine guards have done their duty under trying and dangerous conditions often approximating those of combat. The detachments in Budapest during the Hungarian Revolution, in Seoul when the North Koreans attacked, in Cairo when mobs tried to burn our embassy, in Taiwan, in Saigon during the Tet offensive, and in many other hot spots, have amply advertised to the world that *Semper Fidelis* means what it says.

Functions and Organization

1903. MISSION AND FUNCTIONS. The fundamental mission of Marine security guards in the Foreign Service Establishment is to prevent compromise of classified material vital to the security of the United States. The secondary mission of Marine security guards is, as might be expected, protection of U.S. Government property at Foreign Service posts.

Within the two foregoing missions, Marine security guards carry out the following functions.

Enforce security regulations and controls as directed;
Provide entry and exit control for U.S. buildings containing classified material;
Destroy classified material when directed;
Execute special orders for such emergency situations as fire, mob violence, persons seeking political asylum, etc.;
Provide security guard services at regional or international conferences of classified character;
Assist in guarding the President, Vice President, and Secretary of State when outside the limits of the United States.

On the other hand, here are certain duties to which Marine guards will *not* be assigned: courier, receptionist, disbursing officer's bodyguard, janitor, switchboard operator, mail clerk, vehicle dispatcher, or any other duty not pertaining primarily to security.

1904. MARINE SECURITY GUARD BATTALION. The Marine Corps side of the program (which is what concerns readers of this *Handbook*) comes under the Marine Security Guard Battalion at Henderson Hall. This unit trains and screens all Marines for State Department duty, provides logistic support, and, through its companies, administers and supervises the Marine security guards throughout the world.

Company A, with headquarters at Frankfurt, Germany, comprises all guards in Europe; Company B, with headquarters in Beirut, guards all American embassies in Africa and the Middle East; Company C, with headquarters in Manila, takes care of the Far East; Company D, with headquarters in Panama, handles Central America, the West Indies, and South America. Company E, stationed in Saigon, is the one nonregional company; this unit protects the American Embassy and is responsible for the safety and security of the American Ambassador in Saigon. The one embassy guard re-

Company C guards all the American embassies in the Far East. The Staff Sergeant points out Rangoon, Burma on the Henderson Hall map.

porting directly to battalion headquarters company is that in Ottawa, because of its proximity to Washington.

In addition to the various embassy guards overseas throughout the globe, the battalion also includes the Special Security Detail, or "SSD," which is responsible for aiding the State Department in protecting foreign heads of state when in this country. The Marines who mount guard at Blair House in Washington during state visits of foreign chiefs of state are from the SSD.

Aside from headquarters and support functions for what is certainly the most widely deployed battalion in the Corps, one of the most important responsibilities of the Marine Security Guard Battalion is to operate and conduct the Marine Security Guard School at Henderson Hall. The battalion CO has a second hat as director of this school.

1905. COMPANY FUNCTIONS. The headquarters of each of the regional companies is colocated with the office of the State Department's Regional Security Supervisor for that area. The company commander also carries the title of Regional Marine Officer (RMO). The duties of the RMO consist of the normal command functions of administration, personnel accounting, logistic support, inspection (at least semiannually), discipline, training, and morale over the Marine security guards assigned to the company. In addition, the company commander acts as an advisor to the Regional Security Supervisor mentioned above.

1906. TOURS OF DUTY. Tours of duty for enlisted Marines at specific State Department posts vary according to local conditions, but the basic tour in the program is 24 months. As in the Marine Corps as a whole, certain assignments permit accompaniment by dependents; others do not. No unaccompanied tour is greater than 15 months for NCOinC.

Selection and Training

1907. ASSIGNMENT AND SCREENING. To be accepted for embassy guard duty, you must be an outstanding, mature Marine who is not afraid of hard work. More specifically, here are the current criteria:

Be a lance corporal or above, with at least 30 months to do or be willing to extend or ship over;
Must have a minimum of 18 months' active service;
Be unmarried (Sgt or below) and remain unmarried until completion of tour;
Average proficiency and conduct marks (Cpl and LCpl only) 4.4 or higher)
Be interviewed and recommended by commanding officer;
Be eligible for Top Secret clearance.

If you are selected, your organization gives you a special physical examination, requests initiation of your security background investigation, and orders you to the Marine Security Guard School for the next course.

1908. MARINE SECURITY GUARD SCHOOL. The course at Henderson Hall normally runs six weeks for a 125-man class. Among the subjects taught, both by Marine Corps and State Department instructors, are: watchstanding; communist techniques of espionage and subversion; sabotage prevention and detection; riots and civil disturbances; health, sanitation, and hygiene abroad; weapons familiarization and firing with .38 caliber revolver and riot gun; review of general military subjects; security of classified material; and protection of dignitaries.

One of the easiest things to do at this school is to flunk out. Students are under continuing evaluation throughout the course, and, in addition, each must appear at least twice before a screening board made up of Marine and State Department Officers. At the same time, just as at the Sea School, heavy emphasis is placed on correct and immaculate wearing of the uniform, blues especially.

When you receive your diploma (sometimes from the Secretary of State himself), you will have completed a demanding course of academic training, your administrative processing will be finished, and your physical and dental readiness assured. You will receive an official passport and orders to proceed to your new post.

1909. UNIFORMS AND CLOTHING. The basic uniform for State Department Marines is dress blue B, and every Marine in the program is issued a complete set of blues. In addition, depending on local climate and requirements, you also get an allowance for civilian clothing.

1910. A TYPICAL GUARD. The typical Marine security guard consists of six to eight watchstanders and the noncommissioned-officer-in-charge (NCOinC), who is a staff NCO. During working hours, a static exit and entry control post is usually maintained at the Chancery (embassy headquarters offices). This post—very much in the public eye, both of U.S. officials and of every American and foreign visitor to the embassy—can be likened to a main gate watch, where the Marine on guard is in the show window. Outside of working hours, this post is usually backed up by a roving security patrol which may also provide security control over cleaning details within the building.

The most important man you deal with—and one you must strive to please in every way—is the American Ambassador. He holds civilian rank equal to a Marine general officer and should be accorded the same respect, military courtesy, and instant obedience you would give to a general or admiral.

Other senior and important officials are the Deputy Chief of Mission, or "DCM", who is in effect the Ambassador's chief of staff; the political officer; the consul (or consul general); the chiefs of our Military Assistance Advisory Group (MAAG) or military or naval missions; and the AID Mission Chief.

The Marine guard's immediate supervisor is the *embassy security officer,* who is frequently also embassy administrative officer.

1911. THE NONCOMMISSIONED-OFFICER-IN-CHARGE. The NCOinC is the senior Marine of the detachment. Effectively speaking, he is and functions as a small-unit commander, with all the responsibilities of command—accomplishment of a mission, troop welfare and morale, discipline, administration, training, co-ordination of workload, and liaison between the Marine guard and the Foreign Service officers and agencies it deals with.

As you will realize, an NCOinC is serving on one of the most important tours that can befall a noncommissioned officer. He is the keystone and backbone of the entire embassy guard program, and he enjoys independence, responsibilities, and prerogatives which are probably greater than those of any other NCO in the Corps. Successful completion of such a tour is a splendid accomplishment to have on your record.

> *Note:* One delicate area of the NCOinC's duties pertains to his relations with military officers assigned to the embassy or the MAAGs or missions. On the one hand, as a member of the armed forces, you owe them respect and military deference, but, on the other, you are in a special relationship to the Department of State and are operating under special orders (approved by your Marine Corps superiors) which exempt you from *the command authority* of other than your State and Marine Corps superiors. Here is where tact, maturity, and common sense come in.

1912. LOCAL TRAINING. The main areas of local training for embassy guards are general military subjects, MCI correspondence training (which is required for all sergeants and below), language training, and physical readiness (including a tough weight-control program).

The foregoing training is closely monitored by regional Marine officers and by the battalion headquarters at Henderson Hall. In addition, any Marine in the program who has not completed high school is strongly encouraged to take the GED test.

1913. QUARTERS. The guard's quarters, or "Marine House" as it is often called, is essentially a small-size sergeants' mess set up in a U.S. Government-leased or -owned building, usually a large private house. Certain basic items of furniture are provided and certain expenses are borne by the State Department and by the Marine Corps. For the remainder, you will pay a mess bill covering meals, servants, extras, etc., and will pay a share in such items as TV sets, mixers and blenders, bar and bar supplies, etc. The NCOinC, like any commanding officer, will designate one member of the guard as mess treasurer or caterer in addition to his regular duties.

At the Marine House, you can usually expect a room of your own (though in some posts junior men may have to double up). The general atmosphere, the decorations, the standard of living are *up to you.* Make them what you want, and of course always live up to what the Marine Corps could be proud of.

1914. TEN COMMANDMENTS FOR MARINE SECURITY GUARDS. Herewith, in abridged form, are ten so-called commandments for Marine security guards, which have been compiled in the *Marine Security Guard Handbook,* a joint State-Marine Corps publication.

Learn the customs of the country. Understand and adhere to them closely. You will thus avoid offense to local inhabitants.

Avoid suggestions of American superiority. Try to meet foreign nationals on a footing of mutual respect for cultural and racial characteristics and differences. Be friendly and easy in manner. Be open, engaging, and unpretentious in the American style.

Look for aspects of the country and people that interest you and that you can like. Avoid unfavorable comparisons to the United States. Lean over backward in this respect when serving in small new, less-developed countries, where sensitivites are high.

Conduct yourself with propriety, discretion, and common sense. Strict honesty in all transactions and incorruptible integrity are admired (even if not always followed) the world over. Your personal conduct as a representative of the Marine Corps abroad is not your private business: you cannot engage in any activity or behavior which might lessen respect for Corps or country.

Do not associate exclusively with any one local class or faction. Remember that *ins* eventually become *outs,* and vice versa.

Avoid ostentation or unnecessary display. Don't be a flashy spender, especially in a poor country. Don't embarrass local nationals by gifts or hospitality it will be difficult or impossible for them to repay.

People like you better when they can associate with you on even terms.

Stand up firmly for your country and its rights. You don't have to carry a chip on your shoulder, but you don't have to go to the other extreme and accept unfair or uninformed criticism of the United States, or infringement on its rights. (Remember Stephen Decatur—*"My Country! may she ever be right, but—my Country, right or wrong!"*)

Sheer off from conflicts with local government or people. If conflicts arise, first be sure you are right; then try to win by firmness, patience, and reason, and always try to leave room for the other party to back down without losing face.

You are a guest of the country where you are stationed. As a guest, make yourself agreeable to your hosts, rather than ignoring them and associating exclusively with other Americans. If you do turn your back on the locals, whatever the reason, they will quickly infer that you think you are too good for them.

Avoid financial transactions and obligations, except of the most open and routine character, with individual foreign nationals or companies. Pay bills promptly and openly. Specifically avoid any type of corner-cutting, such as currency speculation, kickbacks, black market, etc. Regardless of what you may see a few others doing, these practices are reprehensible in a Marine.

Note: None of the foregoing, however important, can supersede your first and foremost rule of conduct, which is simply to be, at all times and in all places and situations, *a thoroughly squared-away Marine.*

Three things come not back: the arrow that is flown, the spoken word—and lost opportunities.

—Omar Ibn, 581-644.

20 Personal Affairs

Your first responsibilities as a Marine are to Corps and country. Hardly second, however, are your responsibility to your family and your responsibility to organize your affairs so that they can continue undisturbed through all the ups and downs in a service career.

Sudden death is only one contingency you must anticipate. What if you are captured? Prematurely retired? Ordered overseas where your family cannot follow?

Put your house in order. *Keep* it in order.

Your Estate

Most noncommissioned officers transfer to the Fleet Reserve or retire between the ages of 45 and 60. Thus a Service career is shorter than any other profession. While virtually every Fleet Reservist or retired Marine finds some second career, you should nevertheless start early in laying the foundations of a balanced estate, however modest. Your estate—which you will leave to your dependents when you go—consists of your savings, investments (such as "E" Bonds or sound mutual funds), and other property (house, car, etc.). Life insurance, though not technically part of your estate as such, is in reality one of its most important foundations.

Besides being something you leave to your dependents, your estate can be a living thing, from which you realize returns, which helps pay for children's education, and which buys a new and better house. While an estate is not so important for a bachelor, statistics show that most senior Marine noncommissioned officers end up married, so you would be wise to begin saving and planning now.

2001. SURVIVOR BENEFITS. Current laws provide a structure of benefits for eligible survivors of all officers and men who die on active service or after separation from active service if, in the latter case, death results from a condition incurred or aggravated on active service. These benefits are described in this chapter as follows: Federal Government insurance (Section 2002), Social Security (Section 2003), Retired Serviceman's Family Protection Plan (Section 2005), death benefits (including back pay, death gratuity, dependency and indemnity compensation, pension for non-service-connected death, compensation for unused leave), Section 2023, and other benefits (Section 2024).

2002. LIFE INSURANCE. From the moment you take out life insurance, you create a cash estate of the amount of that policy, an estate whose proceeds are not taxable under the inheritance laws of most states. Life insurance provides an estate while you are in a low-income bracket and it protects the future of your wife and family during your younger years against the occupational hazards of your profession. Finally, some types of life insurance give a modest return on your investment and can help maintain your standard of living after retirement.

TYPES OF POLICIES. On a *straight life policy* you pay premiums over a lifetime. It is the most widely used type of insurance because it provides lifetime protection at less cost than any other permanent insurance.

Term insurance, which has no cash value and only gives temporary protection over a certain period, is the cheapest of all. On it, you pay premiums for a set term—usually from one to 15 years—and its protection ends at the end of that period.

Limited payment policies provide lifetime protection and contain cash values just as straight life policies do. It is more expensive than straight life, however, because it is designed to give you a paid-up policy at the end of a certain number of years or at a certain age. After that, you are still fully protected, but you no longer have preminums to pay.

Endowment policies are essentially a form of insured savings. This type of policy provides for the payment of its face value to you at a future date elected by you. If you die before that date, the face value goes to your beneficiary. Premiums on endowment policies are higher than on any other insurance since the emphasis is on savings rather than protection.

YOUR LIFE-INSURANCE PROGRAM. A sound life-insurance program varies with income, age and number of your children, your own age, and your probable number of years remaining upon the active list. Periodically, you must overhaul your program, considering carefully the number of years your children will remain dependent, their educational requirements, your outside income, your wife's employment capabilities, your income after retirement, and any experience qualifying you for civil employment.

Consider your probable income and the needs of your family five, ten, twenty years from now. Think about retirement income, education, and cash for the down payment on a house. Contrary to some opinion, not all endowment policies are bad; neither are short-term policies. Short-term policies cost more in the long run, but you buy them while receiving full pay; when you retire, they are paid up.

But first *by all means join the Group Insurance Plan of the Marine Corps Association,* which pays an active-duty death benefit of $10,000. Details on the MCA Group Insurance Plan are given below.

Try to get a good start on an insurance program by the time you have served ten years, so that a 20-year plan can be paid out before retirement. As soon as a child is born, take out an education policy for it, either an endowment policy on the life of the child or on your own life; if on the child, arrange for a policy which guarantees continuation of premiums should you die. Consider an education policy on your own life, either endowment or retirement-income plan. If you do not need the money for children's education, let the policy mature and receive it either as a lump-sum payment or as retirement income at the age of 60 or 65.

At least every five years, review your program. You may well find that changes in income or employment and a different family situation indicate modifications. Look through a sound guide on insurance, and consult your unit insurance officer.

GOVERNMENT LIFE INSURANCE. There are three types of U. S. Government life insurance, one currently open to all hands on active duty and two others of earlier vintage that are still in force for those who hold and for most but not all of those who have held, policies established under their provisions.

Servicemen's Group Life Insurance (SGLI) provides up to $10,000 term life insurance, in addition to any other Government insurance carried, for all persons on active duty from 29 September 1965. Your pay is checked two dollars per month for this coverage, and you are covered for the full amount until and unless you cancel all or part of your coverage or until (as the law permits) you convert this term insurance into permanent protection with one of many fine insurance companies. Such conversion of SGLI to an individual commercial insurance policy may be effected, *without medical examination,* at any time within 120 days of your retirement or separation from the Corps. Death claims are handled by Marine Corps Headquarters and by the commercial company which is the prime insurer.

> NOTE: Under no circumstances should you cancel any part of this marvelous insurance protection; nor should you cancel any other insurance you may carry. Instead, you should consider SGLI as extra protection above and beyond your permanent insurance plan.

In addition to SGLI, just described, which is current, the other two Government life insurance plans are these:

1. *United States Government Life Insurance* (USGLI) established during World War I and continued until World War II.
2. *National Service Life Insurance* (NSLI) established during World War II and continued until the Korean War.

Neither program is open except to those previously insured thereunder. If, however, you had a policy, either USGLI or NSLI, which was in force on or before 25 April 1951, which you have allowed to lapse or surrendered for cash while on active duty before 1 January 1957, you may replace or reinstate this policy at any time while you remain on active duty or within 120 days after active duty terminates. This is a most valuable privilege and should be taken advantage of. As long as such Government insurance can be had, it constitutes by far the cheapest and the best.

In addition to the foregoing, postservice nonparticipating insurance for service-connected disability is still available for regulars and reservists who are disabled while on continuous active duty. It is also open to reservists disabled under certain conditions when on active duty for training.

If eligible on separation from the service, be sure to take advantage of this opportunity. *You cannot get a better insurance bargain,* unless it be SGLI described above.

On Government insurance matters, refer also to the *Handbook for Retired Marines,* published by Headquarters, U. S. Marine Corps, and frequently updated.

MARINE CORPS ASSOCIATION INSURANCE. *Marine Corps Association (MCA) Group Insurance* is a plan designed and operated by Marines. It is open to any member of the Marine Corps Association on active duty or in the Class II Reserve under age 65. The benefit is $10,000 for all participants under age 60; (there is an expanded $20,000 option, with the feature of automatic insurance for spouse and children as well); from age 60 to age 65, the benefit is $6,000. On reaching either age 60, 65, or 75, you may convert to any permanent life insurance or endowment policy then being issued by the insuring company, an old-line commercial firm which has been in business since 1845. Rates are minimum, and premiums are automatically paid if you are disabled before age 60. One of the attractive features of this plan is that, unlike most group insurance schemes, you may, even after separation or retirement, continue your low-cost protection until age 75, so long as you retain your MCA membership. To inquire, or better, to join, address:

Administrator, Marine Corps Association
    Group Insurance Plan
P.O. Box 3712, Grand Central Station
New York City.

NOTES ON LIFE INSURANCE. If you hold Government insurance, don't let it lapse. In service or out of, it it the *best* insurance you can get.

Don't take out insurance haphazardly. Follow a program.

Keep your beneficiaries up-to-date. Name contingent beneficiaries. Remember to include the phrase ". . . or to the survivor or survivors thereof," which is all-inclusive. If a beneficiary dies, make a prompt change in beneficiary. Consider the effect if both beneficiary and you should die in the same accident.

Will your wife have funds immediately after your death?

Pay premiums by allotment. Regulations permit indefinite allotments for insurance premiums which continue after retirement. Payment by allotment prevents lapse of policies. On the other hand, annual (rather than monthly) payment of premiums saves money.

Don't overload yourself with insurance against remote dangers, but be sure your policies protect against all expected military hazards. Many insurance companies have restrictions as to war, flying hazards as pilot or crew of a military aircraft, etc.

Do not place all your insurance with any one company. Protection is enhanced by diversification among several good companies.

Although insurance is something you should attend to promptly, be wary before you start signing. Avoid fly-by-night companies and insurance agents. Deal with sound, well-known companies, and seek advice from your unit insurance officer.

2003. SOCIAL SECURITY. Contributory Social Security coverage is extended to all hands in uniform. Your contribution is made through an automatic checkage of a percentage of your basic pay. In addition to your military retirement pay and any disability compensation paid by the Veterans Administration, Social Security provides monthly income for:

You, on reaching age 65 (or age 62, if you apply to receive the smaller payments due at that time);
Your wife, if you die and your minor children remain in her care;
You, your wife, and children, if you should be totally disabled;
Your wife or widow, if not entitled earlier, on attaining age 62;
Your children under 18, or older if incapable of self-support, after your death or while you are disabled; also, children between 18 and 22, if bona fide students;
Your dependent parents.

The payments for a family group may go as high as the legal maximum even though you have only paid into the Social Security program through taxation of your basic pay for a few years. The amount of your Social Security benefits is determined by your "average monthly wage" during the years you were contributing. The exact amount differs in almost every case and must be worked out. If you are eligible for any or all of the Social Security benefits just mentioned, you must apply for them, since benefits are not paid automatically. You must file an application, and it must be in the hands of the Social Security Administration before they can pay you. File immediately when you become eligible, since back payments are limited by law. The local post office can furnish you with the address of the nearest Social Security district office. You should get in touch with them on attaining age 65, or when your wife reaches 62, or at any time if disabled before reaching age 65. When you die, your next to kin should check with the Social Security office to see if there is an entitlement to survivor's insurance.

An application must be filed with the Social Security Administration (or with a U. S. Foreign Service officer, if outside the United States) to start payments.

You need not have wage credits for military service added to your record currently. These credits are recorded when a claim is made for retirement or survivor's insurance payments.

Your Social Security number is important both for you and your dependents to know. It can be found in your service record book and must, of course, accompany claims or inquiries. Moreover, it is your basic number for income tax purposes and is used by the Bureau of Internal Revenue in connection with all your tax returns and related records. You should memorize this number and, as a precaution, record it not only in your notebook, but also with any emergency papers you keep, such as insurance policies, etc.

To assist in computing where you stand under Social Security, the Social Security Administration encourages every insured individual —you—to request a Statement of Wages every three years from the Social Security Administration, Baltimore, Maryland. In this way you can determine whether their records are complete and you are getting credit for all earnings on which Social Security tax has been paid.

You can get full information on these and other matters of interest usually by applying to the nearest Social Security Administration office or from your unit personal affairs officer. Before retirement, investigate your Social Security rights and credits, and be sure your wife is acquainted with her rights under this law.

2004. INSURANCE DEATH CLAIMS. *Government Insurance* death claims should be submitted as follows:

ON ACTIVE DUTY:

Beneficiary will be mailed forms by the Veterans Administration. The VA is notified by Marine Corps Headquarters; no further proof of death is required. Beneficiary must fill out the form and return it.

RETIRED OR SEPARATED FROM SERVICE:

Beneficiary should apply to the nearest VA Regional Office for necessary forms or see the legal assistance or personal affairs officer at the nearest Navy or Marine Corps station, and if these are inaccessible, the beneficiary should seek assistance from his nearest state or other service organization. Proof of death must be furnished; beneficiary should get certified copies of public death record, coroner's report, death certificate of attending physician, or death certificate of naval hospital. If one of these is not available, beneficiary should obtain an affidavit from persons who viewed the body and knew the deceased when living.

Veterans Administration central and regional offices will be helpful, but because of a backlog of claims, there may be appreciable delay before payment.

Beneficiary should hold your Government policy until claim is paid; do not send it with claim.

On commercial insurance policies, death claims should be submitted as follows:

Beneficiary should consult local representatives of each company or write direct to the home office. Take the following steps:

Give insured's name.

Give insurance policy numbers.

Request necessary forms to make a death claim.

Return *by certified mail* the accomplished forms, with return receipt requested.

Send a certified copy of death certificate, affidavit of death as described above, or, if death occurred at sea or abroad, a certified copy of the official notification of death. (Next of kin may and should request extra copies from HQMC of the official notification of death. These qualify as official death certificates and are accepted as such by commercial insurance companies.)

You yourself should list the commercial insurance companies which insure your life, in the Record of Emergency Data (DD From 93-1) in your service record book; Marine Corps Headquarters will notify the companies in case of death. Most companies accept such notification as proof of death.

Some companies require submission of policy before paying claim.

Your insurance agent will help your beneficiary complete all this paperwork, and, in any case, whether you die on the active or retired list, a Casualty Assistance Officer will be assigned to help your next of kin in obtaining all benefits to which entitled.

> *Note:* In general it is unwise for your dependents to put claims for Government benefits in the hands of private attorneys, as this may simply cause unnecessary delay and will certainly entail added expense.

2005. RETIRED SERVICEMAN'S FAMILY PROTECTION PLAN (RSFPP). This plan permits you to elect to receive a reduced amount of retired pay so that your surviving wife and/or children may receive a Government annuity following your death in retired pay status.

An important advantage to RSFPP is that *you may elect to participate regardless of your health.* You do not have to take or pass a physical examination to qualify.

If you decide to elect RSFPP prior to the 19th anniversary of your pay-entry base date (PEBD), you become immediately eligible for this protection at any time thereafter, should you retire or transfer to the Fleet Reserve. If you elect the RSFPP *after* the 19th anniversary, you must continue on active duty for at least two years thereafter. Regardless of when you make your decision, however, you elect one or a combination of three basic options provided by the Plan, and at the same time you may designate a specific amount or percentage of your retired pay which will be payable to your dependents after your death. Here are the options:

Option 1: Annuity for your widow—payable to her until her death or remarriage.

Option 2: Annuity for a child or children—payable to a child or surviving children until there ceases to be at least one surviving child unmarried and under age 23. Unmarried children 18 through 22 years of age qualify for annuity benefits provided they are attending a recognized educational institution, full-time. (An unmarried child incapacitated prior to age 18 and incapable of self-support receives the annuity until marriage, death, or recovery.)

Option 3: Annuity for both—payable to both widow and surviving children, until death or remarriage of widow, or until there are no surviving children under 18, unmarried or incapacitated.

Besides the foregoing three options, all participants now automatically have what was formerly Option 4, i.e., a rider to cover the contingency of the beneficiary's dying before you do, in which case no further deductions will be made from your retired pay.

Participants are allowed to reduce their protection or get out of the plan entirely, on six months' notice.

If already retired, a participant may elect (subject to approval by the Secretary of the Navy) coverage for his wife only (Option 1) in place of the family option (Option 3) if he does not have an eligible child beneficiary. Children between ages 18 and 23 will not be considered eligible beneficiaries if their father wants to shift to a wife-only coverage.

The decision to elect or not to elect the Contingency Option Plan of RSFPP is a big one. It is not a substitute for life insurance (while not taxable as an annuity, you have no equity in the plan, and you cannot cash it in or borrow against it). Whether it is best for you depends on your personal situation. Basically, if you have a long life expectancy on retirement, are well-fixed, with adequate life insurance and a solid estate, the plan has the disadvantages that you will probably receive reduced retired pay for many years, your widow may remarry or die soon (at which time payments cease), and she would receive little benefit. On the other hand, if you are in such poor health that you cannot obtain additional insurance, it could be an excellent means of augmenting insurance and other survivor benefits, at a relatively small cost.

Detailed information on RSFPP can be found in the pamphlet, *Retired Serviceman's Family Protection Plan* (NAVMC-2506-).

2006. OTHER KINDS OF INSURANCE. *Automobile Insurance.* Your car can cause you much grief if not properly insured.

Auto insurance is available to cover liability for bodily injury, property damage, medical payments, collision or upset, fire and lightning, and transportation, theft, windstorm, earthquake, explosion, hail, or water damage. Awards for bodily injury are high, so you should have not less than $10,000 to $20,000 under this coverage.

Property damage coverage for $5,000 should be carried. Since collision or upset coverage is very expensive, you would be well advised to take out a "deductible" policy—$50 deductible for each accident or, better, $25, if you can afford the premium, as nearly ever accident costs upward of $25. This coverage protects you against heavy damage to or total loss of your car.

Fire Insurance and Personal Liability Insurance. Take out fire insurance on any house or other real property of your own. Another valuable coverage is personal liability insurance, which protects you against claims for injuries by persons visiting your home or by servants or workmen, or for damage done by pets, children, wife or self (usually including damage arising out of sports) or for damage done to the property of others by such accidents as falling trees, or fire originating on your property. This insurance is inexpensive, but invaluable when trouble comes.

2007. REAL ESTATE. As you get older and have children, you may agree with many noncommissioned officers that it is advantageous to own your own home. Marines have some advantage in this, as there are a few localities where they may be ordered to duty over and over again. For example, a ground NCO would serve most of his stateside duty in the vicinity of Camp Lejeune, Washington-Quantico, and San Diego or Pendleton; an aviation NCO would have maximum service in the vicinity of El Toro, Washington-Quantico, and Cherry Point.

Some find it financially advantageous to buy a house where they have duty and are not assigned quarters, then sell or rent when ordered to other shore duty, or else leave the family in their own home while on sea or expeditionary service. While absentee landlord is certainly a difficult role, it is worthwhile to have a home available when you return, and you can approach retirement with something besides cancelled checks and rent receipts. When retirement comes, you have an asset which will permit you to buy a house wherever you decide to settle, if the city where you already own a house does not suit you. And if you die on active duty, your family will have a home or an income from the real estate you leave. Moreover, the Federal Housing Authority (FHA) will in most cases be able to grant you a low-interest long-term mortgage which will facilitate purchase or construction of the home you want or purchase of a second home, providing your first FHA-sponsored home had to be disposed of because of military orders.

When you sell a home, money realized in appreciation of the property is considered a capital gain (profit) by the IRS and therefore taxable. However, if you reinvest within a given period in another home, you are exempt from this tax. Check this carefully.

Consider carefully the terms of ownership of any real property you buy, before the deed is prepared. Consult the legal assistance officer. Joint ownership or transfer of property to your spouse by deed may offer material advantage to your estate. Leave with your valuable papers a list of your real estate holdings, giving: description and location of all holdings; location of deeds, mortgages, or other papers; original cost, depreciated cost, estimated present value, and present ownership status.

2008. CONTROL OF PROPERTY. An individual may use or control his estate himself or through an agent acting for him under power of attorney. Remote control of one kind or another is often necessary during a service career.

Joint Ownership. To facilitate use of property and to provide for its disposition on death, an individual may arrange for most property to be held in joint tenancy (with his wife or other beneficiary) with right of survivorship, thus enabling his joint tenant to use and control the property jointly during his lifetime, and after his death to obtain full title as survivor without the property being part of his estate, subject to probate and inheritance taxes. Property held jointly cannot be disposed of by will if your joint tenant survives you, but it is wise to include provision for its disposal should your joint tenant die before you do.

The advantages of joint tenancy are less expense, less inconvenience, and less time required to dispose of property after a death. But there are also disadvantages. The provisions of the Soldiers' and Sailors' Civil Relief Act exempting military personnel from state or municipal taxation do not apply to your wife's interest in property.

Real estate is not the only property that may be held in joint tenancy. Joint bank accounts and joint ownership of securities, with right of survivorship, have some advantages.

Note that joint ownership of Government savings bonds, if held in safekeeping with the Treasury Department, does not necessarily insure flexibility. Such a bond cannot be withdrawn by a joint owner unless the purchaser has registered with the safekeeping agency a sample of the co-owner's signature, along with written authority to withdraw the bond.

Automobiles. Joint ownership of the family car also has advantages. Serious loss may result if your wife or another family member drives your individually owned car after your death. The best plan is to hold the title to the car in joint tenancy. The certificate of title and the insurance policy should bear the names of the *joint* owners.

While joint ownership of automobiles is desirable, the wife's interest in this personal property is taxable. Payment of taxes in a state where you live temporarily may be avoided under Section 514 of the Soldiers' and Sailors' Civil Relief Act of 1940, if the car is registered in your name, in your own state of legal residence. A power of attorney to your wife, however, will enable her to transfer title, secure registration, sell, or buy a car during your lifetime.

If, as sometimes happens, you or your wife should have to dispose of your car in a direct sale to some other person, the following guidelines are generally used in figuring fair depreciation on automobile for resale as used cars. During the first year of ownership, a car loses 25 percent of its initial purchase price; for each succeeding year, it depreciates 20 percent of its current value. Taking the case of a new car which cost $1,800, the following would be its sale prices:

During first year after purchase $1,350
During second year after purchase 1,080
During third year after purchase 864
During fourth year after purchase 692

Naturally, the foregoing scale is flexible and always depends on the condition of the car, existing market, etc.

Joint Bank Accounts. If suddenly ordered to expeditionary service, or upon his sudden death, a Marine who carries his bank account in his own name only may deprive his dependents temporarily of access to funds at a time when most needed. Investigate the advantages of joint accounts—at least during times when you are separated from your family.

2009. INVESTMENTS. The first time you buy an "E" Series Savings Bond, you become an investor, because you are thereby investing in your own future and that of the U.S. Government. As you advance in rank, you should continue to allot a part of every paycheck to purchase of U.S. Savings Bonds. (*However, when serving overseas, you should put every single surplus dollar on the books at 10 percent—an unmatched opportunity to make your savings grow.* You accomplish this by pay-record checkage which will, as just stated, draw 10 percent interest and do so until 90 days after your return Stateside.)

As soon as you have an emergency backlog of Government bonds (say, $1,000 at maturity value), you should consider putting your savings into a good mutual fund. A "mutual fund" is a company which receives your money, along with that of many other small investors, and invests it expertly in diversified, high-quality stocks, keeping track of them and enabling you to share in the resulting profits and dividends. Needless to say, you should only select your particular fund by and with the advice of a reputable U.S. bank. Do not, under any circumstances, speculate or "play the market" unless you have a lot of money you can afford to lose.

2010. BORROWING MONEY AND LOANS. The best words on this subject are found in Shakespeare, "Neither a borrower nor a lender be . . ." Avoid loan-sharks, and equally avoid private loans to brother NCOs, however deserving the case may appear; particularly avoid acting as comaker to any note—this makes you just as liable as the borrower.

Interest Rates. The amount of interest you pay on a loan is a matter of vital concern and often a source of confusion. This is because most lenders charge different rates than they quote. There are four ways of quoting interest: (1) monthly ($\frac{1}{2}$ of 1% per month);

(2) add-on rate (6% per year); (3) discount rate (6% per year); (4) simple annual rate (6% per year). Only the last—simple annual interest—is quoted in *true* terms.

To convert quoted rates to simple annual interest, and thus to *true* interests,

Multiply a monthly rate by 12
Multiply "add-on" or "discount" rate by 2.

Whenever you borrow, ask what kind of interest is being charged—add-on, discount, monthly, or simple. Convert the quoted rate to true annual interest. Then compare interest costs and other charges to determine which lender offers you the terms which are truly best.

If you need credit, investigate the *Navy Federal Credit Union.* Both for borrowing and saving, whether by mail or in person, this non-profit organization is tailored to the needs of noncommissioned officers, and its charges are very low, while dividends are generous. Navy Federal Credit also covers loans with life insurance at no extra cost which is of great benefit to a young noncommissioned officer.

Should you find yourself in debt, however, send each of your creditors something each month, no matter how little. Those who have given you goods on your credit as a Marine NCO are entitled to this consideration, which will show that you have not forgotten them and that your obligations will be paid.

> *Note:* Never forget that there is a direct relationship, as seen by staff NCO selection boards, between your credit rating and your promotability. *One indebtedness letter can slow your advancement to a snail's pace.*

2011. ALLOTMENTS. Upon receipt of orders to sea, expeditionary, or foreign service, allot all pay which you will not actually need. *Be sure that allotments to dependents, to a bank for dependents, and for insurance are so described in your pay account.* This is vital, because if a Marine becomes a prisoner or is missing in action, allotments are continued in force under supervision of the Secretary of the Navy, who has authority to start, stop, increase, or decrease allotments for any proper purpose, or as requested by the next of kin.

When a Marine has been missing for 12 months and no official report of death or of his being a prisoner or interned has been received, the Navy Department reviews the case. If the facts do not warrant a finding of death, missing status may be continued. Without allotments, although your right to receive and accumulate pay would not be impaired, your insurance premiums might not be paid, and your family might suffer hardship.

2012. SAFEGUARDING PERSONAL FUNDS. Here are some ways to safeguard personal funds while in combat or serving under hazardous conditions:

Allot most of your pay to a dependent or to your bank for support of dependents. Even if an allotment is for your personal use, make it a joint account with your other dependents, naming the dependent on the allotment request; for example, "First National Bank, Quantico, Virginia, a/c Sara Stockham." The allotment will continue without interruption if you are missing or become prisoner.

If serving overseas, designate all your spare pay for pay-record checkage and deposit with the Government at 10 percent interest (see Section 2009). Draw only enough money to take care of immediate expenses. If you continue to purchase savings bonds, however, they may be retained in safekeeping by the Bond Allotment Office, Marine Corps Finance Center, Kansas City, Missouri.

Do not accumulate cash in the field. Bank or deposit extra money and pay bills by check, saving important cancelled checks. If field records are lost, it may be difficult to establish claim for more pay than would be normally due after the disbursing officer closes his accounts for a pay period.

In any case, consider a safe-deposit box in your bank for important papers and valuables. Your wife or attorney should have access to the box through joint tenancy or power of attorney.

Taxes

2013. INCOME TAXES. *Federal Income Taxes.* The bulk of your U.S. income taxes are collected by withholding, as described in Section 1139. With this information you fill out your return, which is due on 15 April, payable to either the District Director of Internal Revenue in whose area you are stationed or (if you are out of the U. S.) the Director of International Operations, IRS, Washington, D.C. 20225. Your Director of Internal Revenue can provide the necessary returns and instructions, but it is usual for the paymaster to keep a supply of these, and you can find answers to most of your tax problems in the pay office. Here you should ask for a copy of the pamphlet issued periodically by the Judge Advocate General of the Navy (*Federal Income Tax Information for Service Personnel*), covering income tax problems and exemptions applicable to Navy and Marine personnel. In general, members of the armed forces are taxed in the same way as civilian wage earners, including credits on portions of retired pay. In time of war or emergency, however, as in the case of Vietnam, tax exemptions are granted on pay earned in specific combat zones prescribed by executive order of the President, as well as on pay earned while hospitalized as a result of wounds sustained in action. See Chapter 11. If in a combat zone, you are also allowed generous delays without penalty in filing and payment of returns. Up-to-date information on this, too, can be obtained from your disbursing officer.

It goes without saying that you should keep copies of your income tax returns, and the cancelled checks with which you paid any taxes above those withheld as well as checks, receipts, or vouchers covering all deductions claimed.

State Income Taxes.—Under the provisions of the Soldiers' and

Sailors' Civil Relief Act, you are only liable for income (and other) taxes of the state of which you are a citizen, regardless of whether or not you may be stationed in another state. This law, however, does not exempt retired and retainer pay, the separate income of a spouse or of your family, your income derived from business, investments, rents, and income earned through outside employment or other sources. Although the provisions and intent of this Act are clear, some states, counties, and municipalities try to impose local taxes on all military personnel on duty within their jurisdiction, even though these may be citizens of other states. Do not pay state or local taxes of this type until you obtain competent verification of your liability from your legal assistance officer. See the paragraph below.

2014. SOLDIERS' AND SAILORS' CIVIL RELIEF ACT. This legislation is designed to relieve officers and men of the armed forces from worry over certain civil problems and obligations.

The Civil Relief Act—as it is sometimes short-titled—temporarily suspends enforcement of some civil liabilities of military personnel on active duty, but only if your inability to meet your obligations results from your military status. It does not release you from your obligations, which you still have to meet. However, the law provides machinery for the postponement of legal actions that might be taken against you. The act also provides that in most cases, if you are a legal resident of one state but are stationed in another, *you may not be subjected* to certain taxes imposed by the latter state. Included are personal property taxes and state income taxes. It applies to auto licenses only if you purchase home-state tags. No state tax exemption is applicable to your dependents.

Two other provisions of the act which may be useful for you to know are: (1) You are entitled to court protection while on active duty if you are unable to pay charges on household effects in storage; moreover, the storage company cannot sell your property over charges, except with a court order. (2) If your dependents are renting quarters for $150 a month or less and the rent is not paid, they can be evicted only after court hearing under the act.

Legal technicalities are frequently involved in any application of the Civil Relief Act, so *legal advice is necessary in each case.* Remember that the act is designed to provide a shield against hardship, not a device to evade civil liabilities. Information and advice may be obtained from your legal assistance officer.

Note: In the case of debt, invoking the act may increase the total amount you owe, since interest charges up to six percent are authorized on the postponed payments.

Powers of Attorney and Wills

2015. POWERS OF ATTORNEY. A power of attorney authorizes someone else to act in your name in the same manner and extent as you yourself could act. The power permits your representative to do only acts expressly stated therein.

In days not many years back, it was customary for married officers and NCOs to execute general powers of attorney to their wives or next of kin. Today, with assured rapid worldwide communications, the occasions when a power of attorney may be required have diminished sharply. On the other hand, a general power of attorney is a very dangerous legal instrument in the hands of persons lacking business experience, of those of unstable temperament, or, for example, of a spouse when the marriage is heading for the rocks.

Therefore, before you sign a power of attorney as if it were a change-of-address card, ask yourself a few questions.

How often—*within a few hours*—will you, while overseas or in the field, have to decide to "collect, sue for, compromise, or otherwise dispose of any claim, debt, or rent . . . "?

Or—*on a moment's notice*—how often will your wife need to "buy, lease, sell, insure, transfer, mortgage, pledge, exchange, acquire, recover, or dispose of property"—such, for example, as your home at Oceanside?

The above transactions, which are only examples of things a general power of attorney permits your dependents to do (on the spur of the moment if they feel like it), are in fact usually those where some time for reflection, while you are being consulted, pays off.

On the other hand, it may well make sense for you to execute a power of attorney valid *only after* you have been declared missing in action. Such an arrangement—conferring powers only if you are officially missing in action—may provide your survivors with legal authority to perform essential acts they might otherwise be powerless to do.

Whether general or limited or conditional, your power of attorney should always include a cutoff date after which (usually two or three years after signature), it ceases to be effective. This protects you against giving away these potentially dangerous powers and having them used long after you have forgotten about them.

In addition, to permit your dependents to transact routine business with the Government in such matters as shipment of effects, etc., virtually any Marine's power of attorney should include phraseology as follows:

> To execute vouchers in my behalf for any and all allowances and reimbursements payable to me by the United States, including, but not restricted to, allowances and reimbursement for transportation of dependents or shipment of household effects as authorized by law or Navy or other regulations; to receive, endorse, and collect the proceeds of checks payable to the order of the undersigned drawn on the Treasurer of the United States for whatever account, and to execute in the name and on behalf of the undersigned, all bonds, indemnities, applications, or other documents, which may be required by law or regulation to secure the issuance of duplicates of such checks, and to give full discharge of same.

Such a power of attorney for Governmental transactions should be executed in the presence of three witnesses and acknowledged before a notary public or, if outside the United States, by any officer of the United States authorized to administer oaths. For purposes other than those given, each specific power must be mentioned to be effective.

Finally, remember two things. First, a power of attorney is not a will or equivalent to one. Its effect ceases the moment you die (which is when a will starts to act). Second, a power of attorney is revocable, like any other legal document. If you should want to revoke yours, see your legal assistance officer.

2016. YOUR WILL. Considering occupational hazards of our profession, it is important that you have a will. A will simplifies settlement of your estate, reduces expenses, conserves assets, and enables your last wishes to be carried out.

Every Marine should devote serious thought to making a will. Whatever your age and however few your belongings may be, a will eliminates problems for your survivors and insures that your effects and property go where you want them to go. Otherwise, the law of the state where you have legal residence, or the law of a state where you may have property, will do the deciding.

DEFINITIONS. A *will* is the legal document by which an individual leaves instructions for disposition of his property after death. A *holographic will* is entirely in the handwriting of the testator.

Intestate is a person who dies without a will.

A *testator* is a person who leaves a will.

Settling an estate is a general term used to denote the entire process of collecting assets, filing inventories and accounts, paying claims, distributing assets in accordance with the will or laws of descent and distribution, and filing final accounting with the court.

An *executor* (*executrix*) is appointed by your will to execute its provisions after your death.

A *codicil* adds to or qualifies a will; it revokes the will only to the extent that it is inconsistent therewith. Will and codicil are construed together. A codicil is drawn in the same way as a will. When possible, the best procedure is to make a new will rather than to add a codicil to an old will.

Probating a will consists in presenting the will for record to the proper authority in the county where the deceased had *legal* residence.

DRAWING A WILL. The most important advice to anybody who wants to draw a will is to consult a lawyer. In your case, you should, as a minimum, consult the legal assistance officer.

In the absence of a lawyer or legal assistance officer, here is a short form of will which you can use on your own responsibility (but, as soon as opportunity presents itself, you should later review any such will with legal help).

The number of witnesses required for a will varies from none (for

I, _____ legal resident of _____
     (Name of testator)   (City, town, or county)

_____, United States of America, now in the active mili-
     (State or district)

tary service as a _____, (Service No. _____), in
                 (Grade)

the United States Marine Corps, do hereby make, publish and declare this instrument as my last WILL and TESTAMENT, in manner following, that is to say:

1. I hereby cancel, annul, and revoke all wills and codicils by me at any time
heretofore made;

2. I hereby give, devise, and bequeath to _____
                                (Name of person or persons who are to

_____ now residing in _____
inherit, with relationship, if any)   (City, town, or county)

_____, all my estate and all of the property
     (State or district)   (Country)

of which I may die seized and possessed, and to which I may be entitled at the
time of my decease, of whatsoever kind and nature, and wheresoever it may be
situated, be it real, personal, or mixed, absolutely;

3. I hereby nominate, constitute, and appoint _____
                                     (Name of executor,

_____ of _____ _____
with relationship, if any)   (City, town, or county)   (State or district)

United States of America, as my executor (executrix) and request that he (she) be
permitted to serve without bond or without surety thereon;

4. I hereby authorize and empower my executor (executrix) in his (her) absolute
discretion to sell, exchange, convey, transfer, assign, mortgage, pledge, invest or
reinvest the whole or any part of my real or personal estate.

In WITNESS WHEREOF, I have hereunto set my hand and seal to this my

last WILL AND TESTAMENT, at _____, this _____
                         (Place of execution)

day of _____, 19____

                   _____ (seal)
                         (Signature of testator)

                     _____
                         (Name printed or typed)

Signed, sealed, published, and declared by the above-named testator, _____

_____ to be his last WILL and TESTAMENT in the
     (Name of testator)

presence of all of us at one time, and at the same time we, at his request and in
his presence and in the presence of each other, have hereunto subscribed our names
as witnesses, and to hereby attest to the sound and disposing mind of said testator

and to the performance of the aforesaid acts of execution at _____

_____ this _____ day of _____ 19____
(Place of execution)   (Street, town, State)

          WITNESSES   PERMANENT ADDRESSES

_____
            (Signature)

_____
(Name, rank, and permanent
address, printed or typed)

_____   _____
            (Signature)   (Street, town, State)

_____
(Name, rank, and permanent
address, printed or typed)

_____
            (Signature)

_____   _____
(Name, rank, and permanent   (Street, town, State)
address, printed or typed)

Fig. 20-1: Sample of Last Will and Testament.

a holographic will—that is, a will *entirely* in your own handwriting) to three; *have three witnesses* to your will, and be safe. Sign in their presence, so that they see you sign and understand that it is your will you are signing. Witnesses, then, in your presence and in the presence of each other, sign the attestation. Be sure that none of the witnesses is mentioned in the will; attestation by an interested witness may invalidate the will, or the witness may lose his legacy. A witness should write opposite his signature his place of residence. Since the authenticity of signatures must be proven in court at the time of probating, care should be exercised to select witnesses who can be located.

A Simple Will. The following short form of a simple, holographic will has been used by many. To be effective, this must be entirely in your own handwriting.

> All my estate I devise and bequeath to my wife, for her own use and benefit forever, and I hereby appoint her my executrix, without bond, with full power to sell, mortgage, lease, or in any other manner dispose of the whole or any part of my estate.
>
> JOHN GLOWIN (Seal)
>
> Dated October 15, 1970.
>
> Subscribed, sealed, published, and declared by John Glowin, testator above named, as and for his last will in the presence of each of us, who at his request and in his presence, in the presence of each other, at the same time, have hereto subscribed our names as witnesses this fifteenth day of October, 1970 at Nuoc Mam, Republic of Vietnam.

(Signatures and addresses of witnesses, *preferably three in number.* Be sure that the word "Seal" is written in parenthesis after each signature as shown above.)

A Simple Codicil. If possible, write a codicil on the same sheet of paper as the will; if the codicil is written on a separate sheet, fasten the two together securely. Here is a simple form of codicil. **This also must be completely in your own handwriting.**

> I, John Glowin, of Washington, District of Columbia, make this codicil to my last will dated October 15, 1970, hereby ratifying said will in all respects save as changed by this codicil. Whereas, by said will I gave Robert Anderson Glowin, my son, a legacy of $5,000, I now give him a second legacy of $10,000, making $15,000 in all.

(Then follow the testator's signature and seal, the attestative clause, and the witnesses' signatures and seals.)

If you decide to modify your will, once it is executed, do not make alterations or interlineations. Consult your legal assistance officer on what to do.

Probate. If executed according to law of your legal domicile, a will made anywhere in the world will be admitted to probate in the jurisdiction of your domicile without question.

Probate establishes the validity of the will and evidences the right of beneficiaries to succeed to title to property in the estate. The place of probate is usually the county and state in which you are domiciled at the time of death; the will must also be probated in any other county and state where you own real property.

WHEN TO MAKE A NEW WILL. During your lifetime, you will probably make a new will several times. Certain milestones indicate when to reconsider your will and bring it up-to-date:

Change of legal residence
Removal of executor to another state, or his death
Radical change in your estate
Sale of property mentioned in your will
Major changes in tax laws
Marriage, divorce, or remarriage
Birth or death of child
Death of spouse

Check your will on changing legal residence (*not* change of station) to another state, as the provisions of your will may not be legal in that state and your executor may not be able to function there.

2017. VALUABLE PAPERS. Besides wills and powers of attorney, you will accumulate important papers, most of which you should retain permanently. As a very minimum, keep them together in your footlocker. Later, when you make staff NCO and marry, you should rent a safe-deposit box in a bank either in your permanent hometown or near one of the major Marine Corps stations where you may already have purchased a home. The cost of a safe-deposit box runs about $6 a year; its value far exceeds that small sum.

PAPERS YOU SHOULD STOW IN SAFE-DEPOSIT BOX. You should keep all the following in safe-deposit: will, insurance policies, stock certificates or bonds, auto title and bill of sale, real estate deed, birth certificate, marriage license, children's birth certificates, and military discharge certificates.

PAPERS TO RETAIN. The following papers or records should be kept securely in one place, readily accessible, even though not warranting safe-deposit stowage: bankbook; copies of tax returns (keep five years); social security card; guarantees (until date of expiration); employment record (list of every job held, with dates and employers); cancelled checks which substantiate payment of important debts or obligations; list of all credit cards, driver's permit, and other documents carried in billfold, with numbers (in case of loss or theft of billfold); promotion warrants; and school certificates or diplomas.

Death and Burial

2018. BURIAL ARRANGEMENTS. *When Death Occurs Near a Navy or Marine Activity.* When a Marine on active duty dies at or near his station, the commanding officer takes charge and arranges for shipment of the body at Government expense or for local burial. (For burial in Arlington, see Section 2020 and *Marine Corps Personnel Manual,* Chapter 12).

In case of death in a naval hospital, the hospital authorities handle the arrangements (again, see *Marine Corps Personnel Manual,* Chapter 12).

Death at a Remote Place. When a Marine on active duty dies at some distance from a Marine Corps or Naval station or hospital, the next of kin should contact the nearest Marine Corps or Navy activity for aid. If unable to contact a local activity, they should telegraph the deceased's commanding officer or the Commandant of the Marine Corps, Washington, D.C., giving the deceased's full name, rank, and service number; the date, place, and cause of his death; and the place where burial is desired. The telegram should request instructions as to burial arrangements and should give the address to which a reply may be sent. A telephone report may be made to Marine Corps Headquarters (OXford 4-1787 or 4-1788 or, if neither of the foregoing answers, to OXford 4-2645 (HQMC Duty Officer).

Death in a Naval, Military, or Veterans' Hospital (while in Inactive Status). Where death of a veteran or a retired or inactive Marine occurs in a Naval or military hospital or in a Veterans' Administration facility, the hospital authorities will make necessary arrangements upon request of the next of kin.

> *Note:* Marine Corps Headquarters (Code DNA) has an outstanding pamphlet, *Information for Survivors of Deceased U.S. Marine Corps Personnel,* which is available on request. Obtain a copy of this and keep it with your important papers, as it is a complete checklist of essential information and actions required. Your wife should know of this pamphlet.

2019. BURIAL EXPENSES. The expenses of burial or shipment of the remains of Marines who die on active duty, which are borne by the widow or another individual, may be reimbursed within limits allowed by the Government. When the place of death is remote from a Marine Corps or Naval station or hospital and it is impossible to obtain instructions from Marine or Navy authorities, the widow may employ a local undertaker and, if necessary, arrange shipment of the body to the place of burial, but in such cases *she should obtain itemized bills.* In the case of a regular or reserve Marine who dies on active duty in an area where an armed forces contract is available and not used, the limit of reimbursement is an amount not to exceed what such authorized services and supplies would have cost the Navy; or where an Armed Forces contract is not available, an amount is not to exceed $500.00. In the case of an honorably discharged, inactive, or retired veteran of any war, the limit of disbursement is $250 (payable by the Veterans' Administration). In addition, Social Security will pay a death payment up to $255 if the deceased was covered. This claim must be filed with the nearest Social Security office.

Generally, no expenditure is authorized for shipping the remains of a Marine who dies on inactive duty. There is no interment expense for burial in a Federal cemetery.

If the remains of a Marine who dies on active duty are forwarded to the next of kin for private burial, the expenses of preparation, encasement, and transportation will be borne by the Department of the Navy; and after the body has arrived, the Department will allow a total of not over $500.00 (for burial in a private cemetery), or $250.00 (for remains consigned to a funeral prior to burial in a National or Naval Cemetery), or $75 (for remains consigned directly to a National or Naval Cemetery for burial), for one or more of the following items: hearse; transportation of immediate relatives to the cemetery; undertaker, clergyman (fee not to exceed $5); cost of a single grave site in a private cemetery when burial plot is not already owned by relatives of the deceased; and digging and closing of grave.

If funeral expenses have been paid, claim for reimbursement should be submitted on DD Form 1375 (Request for Payment of Funeral and/or Interment Expenses), in quintuplicate, to the Commandant of the Naval District in which burial was made. The correct address is contained on the application form. Any transportation charges necessary to deliver the remains to the first place designated by the next of kin will be paid by the Government. Where transportation charges were incurred by next of kin or other persons to deliver the remains to the place designated by the next of kin, reimbursement will be made therefor in an amount not to exceed what the transportation would have cost the Government.

Application may be made for reimbursement of transportation charges paid to a common carrier by submitting to the Commandant of the Naval District in which burial takes place, a receipted bill, in triplicate, from an appropriate official of the carrier which furnished transportation. Claims for reimbursement or payment of transportation expenses incurred outside the United States should be forwarded to the Chief, Bureau of Medicine and Surgery (Code 454), Washington, D.C., 20390.

(All claims for burial expenses must be submitted within two years after permanent burial or cremation.)

If remains are claimed at the place of death for private burial and the service of the Government is refused, the next of kin thereby relieves the Government of any obligation for funeral or transportation expenses.

2020. PLACE OF BURIAL. You may be buried at the place of death, in a private cemetery near your home, or in an open National Cemetery. Leave written instructions as to your choice. If burial is to be in a National Cemetery, your widow or undertaker should telegraph the Superintendent of the National Cemetery selected; if your family lives near the selected National Cemetery, the next of kin may request burial directly from the cemetery superintendent.

Remains are cremated only on written request from the next of kin.

When practicable, should burial at sea be desired, arrangements may be initiated via either the Marine Corps Headquarters funeral director or local naval authorities. However, burial at sea is not a right but a privilege which it may not be feasible to accord.

Military Funerals, Arlington National Cemetery. Funeral arrangements for burial in Arlington National Cemetery are made with the Superintendent by the shipping activity, undertaker, or next of kin. Headquarters, Marine Corps (Casualty Branch) can make hotel reservations for family and friends, can meet trains or planes, can explain the different types of military funeral, can assist in selection of honorary pallbearers and furnish transportation therefor, and can select an undertaker if desired. Headquarters, Marine Corps will also put the widow in touch with veterans organizations which can assist in preparing applications for pensions, compensation, or other claims on the Government. However, these details are usually handled by an appointed Casualty Assistance Officer.

After the next of kin has received confirmation from Arlington of the request for burial, he or she should telegraph Arlington (with an information copy to Headquarters Marine Corps), stating the number in the funeral party; the means of transportation, and date and hour of arrival; and whether local transportation and hotel reservations are required. The phone number of the Office of the Superintendent, Arlington National Cemetery, is area code 202— JAckson 5-2700, ext 64215/64216; or OXford 7-3509; or OXford 5-0540.

Note: Under regulations recently adopted, burial in Arlington Cemetery has, in general, been restricted to armed forces personnel who die on active duty or who were retired in pay status. Before planning an Arlington burial solely on the basis of previous honorable service, you should obtain confirmation of eligibility from the cemetery superintendent.

2021. OTHER INFORMATION. *Funeral Flag.* A United States flag accompanies the remains and may be retained by the family. When death is remote from a naval or Marine activity, the postmaster of the county seat may furnish a flag.

Honors. When practicable and if requested, military honors will be provided at the funeral of a Marine. See *Marine Corps Manual,* Chapter 5. But at cemeteries remote from Marine Corps or naval stations, military honors are not practicable, and relatives must make their own arrangements for funeral services. Veterans organizations usually can assist.

Gravestones. The Government will provide a standard white headstone inscribed with the name, grade, and branch of service of the deceased. If burial is in a National Cemetery, do not order a private monument until the design, material, and inscription have been approved by the Chief, Support Services, U. S. Army (who administers this phase of National Cemeteries). The superintendent of the National Cemetery concerned should be informed of plans for the headstone when you apply for the burial lot, since many National Cemeteries allow private markers only in certain areas. The Chief,

Support Services, of the Army will furnish a Government headstone prepaid to the consignee of your choice as recorded on DD Form 1330 (Application for Headstone or Marker).

Government headstones are provided for dependents buried in National Cemeteries.

Transportation for family. One person may escort the body of a Marine who dies on active duty to the place of burial. The escort may be a relative or friend (not in the service), with the Government providing transportation in kind. If private burial is desired, a military escort accompanies the remains.

Household Effects. The household and personal effects of a Marine who dies on active duty may be shipped from his last duty station or place of storage to the place the next of kin selects as home. Arrangements are made in the usual manner with the local supply officer, but shipment must take place within a year of death.

Death Certificates. For a death on inactive duty, the undertaker will obtain as many certificates as may be requested, at a nominal cost ($1 to $2 each, depending on the locality). They are needed for each insurance company, for the will, for each claim, for the Commandant of the Marine Corps, for the pay office carrying your accounts, and for the transfer of each security held in joint ownership. For deaths on active duty, Marine Corps Headquarters, Code DNA, furnishes five copies of official Report of Casualty (DD Form 1300) which will serve as a legal death certificate. Additional copies may be obtained on request.

The next of kin should also ask two brother Marines or other friends, who knew her husband, to identify his remains. These witnesses will then be prepared, if required, to furnish the affidavit of death sometimes demanded by commercial insurance companies.

Burial Privileges for Dependents. The wife, husband, widow, widower, minor child, and (if approved by the Secretary of the Army) unmarried adult child of any Marine or former Marine whose service ended honorably is entitled to burial in a National Cemetery. If this is desired, telegraph the Superintendent of the National Cemetery selected, requesting burial arrangements.

2022. SURVIVOR BENEFITS CHECKOFF LIST. This section lists applications which should be made by next of kin to insure participation in principal survivor benefits. This list is up to date as of publication; remember that such provisions are subject to change (frequently to the advantage of surviving dependents), and double-check what you see here with current, official sources.

Application for Dependency and Indemnity Compensation from Veterans Administration. Submit, to nearest VA office, VA Form 21-534 for widow and/or children, or VA Form 21-535 for parents.

Application for Survivors Benefits from Social Security Administration (*widow, children, and parents*). Submit, to nearest Social Security Office, VA Form OA-C24.

Claim for Death Benefits, Servicemen's Group Life Insurance

(*SGLI*) (*persons eligible or designated as beneficiary*). Use VA Form 29-8283 and submit to:

Office of Servicemen's Group Life Insurance,
212 Washington Street,
Newark, New Jersey, 07102.

Application for Headstone or Marker (*Primary next of kin only*). Use DD Form 1330 and submit to:

Chief of Support Services,
(Attn: Memorial Division),
Department of the Army,
Washington, D.C., 20315.

Request for Payment of Funeral and/or Burial Expenses. Use DD Form 1375 and submit to Commandant, appropriate Naval District.

Claim for Six Months, Death Gratuity. Use DD Form 397 and submit to:

Commandant of the Marine Corps (Code DNA),
Washington, D.C., 20380.

Claim for Unpaid Pay and Allowances (*Arrears of Pay*). Use Standard Form 1174 and submit to:

Commandant of the Marine Corps (Code DNA),
Washington, D.C., 20380.

Application for Identification and Privilege Card (*widows, certain dependent children, and dependent parents*). Use DD Form 1172 and apply to nearest Marine or Navy activity.

Survivor Benefits and Assistance

2023. DEATH BENEFITS. *Back Pay.* Pay and allowances to the credit of a deceased Marine are payable to the persons he designated on his Record of Emergency Data to receive them. If he does not make such a designation or if the person designated dies first, this payment is made to his widow, or if he is not survived by a widow, to his children, then his parents, and so on. Headquarters Marine Corps will send the necessary form to the person(s) eligible to receive this payment.

Death Gratuity to Active Personnel. When death occurs on active duty, six months' pay (including flight and hazardous duty pay), in an amount not less than $800 nor more than $3,000 is payable to the widow of the deceased, or if he has no widow, to children; if not survived by children, then to any of his parents or brothers and sisters he designated. Payment to the widow or children is mandatory and is not affected by designations. *This gratuity cannot be checked to liquidate overpayment or any debt to the United States and is nontaxable.* In most cases, payment by the cognizant commander is proper and authorized and in fact should be paid within 24 hours after receipt of notification of death. In all other cases, Headquarters

Marine Corps will institute the claim for death gratuity to the eligible beneficiary upon notification of death of a Marine; therefore, it is not necessary for your next of kin to request this benefit. In case of financial distress, your widow may apply to the nearest Marine command for help. The Navy Relief Society will also help with either a grant or loan. The death gratuity just described is also paid if death occurs within 120 days after retirement or separation from the service provided death is due to disease or injury incurred or aggravated while on active duty.

DEPENDENCY-INDEMNITY COMPENSATION. If you die in line of duty on the active list or on reserve training, your widow, surviving children, or parents (in that order), receive monthly compensation from the Veterans Administration based on a flat rate plus a percentage of your pay at time of death. This "compensation" payment is nontaxable.

PENSION. If your survivors are not entitled to Dependency-Indemnity Compensation (see above), because your death (1) did not occur on active duty, or (2) did not result from a service-connected condition, if you served honorably in World Wars I or II, or in the Korean War or Vietnam, even though retired or separated, your dependents may be entitled to pension payments.

If, for example, you served honorably in World Wars I or II, or the Korean War or Vietnam, your unremarried widow and unmarried children under 18 (21, if attending an approved school), are eligible for pension. So would be any children over 18 if permanently incapable of self-support. If your widow has other income of given categories, this may reduce or terminate her pension during periods when she receives income in disqualifying amounts.

Payment of pension commences as of the day following death of the veteran, *if a claim is filed within a year following death;* otherwise, it commences from the date of receipt of the application. Claims should be filed with Dependents' Claims Service, Veterans' Administration, Washington, D.C., 20420. Considerable investigation is required before a pension claim can be approved, and the following evidence must accompany a claim.

Proof of death. Death of a veteran in active service, on the retired list, or in a Government hospital does not need to be proved.
Proof of marriage of the claimant to the veteran. If either has been married previously, proof of death or divorce of the former spouse is required.
Proof of date of birth of children.
Proof of birth of veteran (showing filial relationship, if a parent makes the claim).

If claimant qualifies under more than one rate, the maximum rate is awarded.

WIDOWS' SOCIAL SECURITY. Widows under age 62 with children are entitled to substantial Social Security benefits. If, at the time of death, you are considered under Social Security rules to be "insured" (by virtue of having made pay-deduction payments during any period of approximately 18 months during the three years previous to death), your widow receives monthly payments, tax-exempt, based on your pay rate. If your children are orphaned, they are also covered under Social Security.

UNUSED LEAVE COMPENSATION. Your surviving dependent is eligible to claim and receive compensation for any unused leave to your credit, should you die on active duty.

2024. OTHER BENEFITS. HOSPITAL AND MEDICAL CARE. Dependent parents, widows, and children under 21, of Marines are in general eligible for admission to armed forces hospitals and may receive outpatient medical service where such service is available. In addition, dependents of deceased Marines, both active and retired, are covered by CHAMPUS (Civilian Health and Medical Program for the Uniformed Services) or Medicare, whose application to retired Marines and their survivors is covered in Section 2027.

EDUCATIONAL ASSISTANCE FOR CHILDREN OF MARINE CORPS PERSONNEL. From time to time, the Bureau of Naval Personnel publishes a list of schools, colleges, universities, and other organizations which grant concessions and scholarships to service children. For this information, write to the Commandant of the Marine Corps (Code DNC).

Navy Relief Educational Loans. The Navy Relief Society will lend up to $1,000 per year, *interest-free,* for college or vocational education above high school or for preparatory work to enter a state or service academy, to eligible dependents (not over age 23) of active or retired regular Navy or Marine Corps officers or men, and to children of reservists on extended active duty. Information on this valuable privilege may be obtained from the national headquarters of the Navy Relief Society, Room 1030, Munitions Building, Washington, D.C. 20380.

Society of Sponsors Scholarships. The Society of Sponsors of the U. S. Navy awards scholarships to preparatory schools to enable young men to prepare for the Naval Academy. Eligible are sons of active-duty, retired, and deceased members of the Marine Corps, Navy, and Coast Guard. Information on this may be obtained from the Chief of Naval Personnel.

War Orphans' Educational Assistance Act. This act provides up to 36 months' schooling, within rates prescribed by law, for the child of any member of the armed forces or veteran whose death or total disability occurred in line of duty and resulted from service during a period of war (including Korea), or an "induction period" defined as follows:

1. From 16 September 1940 to 6 December 1940; from 1 January 1947 to 26 June 1950. *Or*
2. From 1 February 1955 to the day before the first day on which all persons are no longer liable for induction under the Universal Military Training and Service Act.

EXCHANGE AND COMMISSARY PRIVILEGES. Armed forces exchange and commissary privileges are available to the families of Marine Corps personnel upon presentation of a valid Dependents Identification Card. Before going overseas be sure that these ID cards are current for each dependent and that members of your family over 10 years old have their own cards.

EMPLOYMENT. Important Civil Service preference benefits are granted to service widows, not remarried, in connection with examinations, ratings, appointments, and reinstatements under Civil Service and in connection with Government reductions in force. Interested widows should apply also to the nearest U. S. Employment Service office for information concerning job opportunities administered by that agency.

2025. MARINE CORPS CASUALTY PROCEDURES. Unless you specifically request otherwise, the next of kin recorded on your Record of Emergency Data is notified in case you are seriously injured, wounded, killed, or missing. Your next of kin is kept advised of your condition while you are on the critical list.

When a Marine dies or is missing in action, a Casualty Assistance Officer is appointed from a nearby Marine Corps organization to provide advice and assistance to the survivors. The Casualty Assistance Officer outlines rights and benefits of survivors, and helps prepare claims, etc. (See *Marine Corps Personnel Manual,* Chapter 12.)

The Chaplain. The survivors of a deceased Marine (active or retired) should not fail to seek assistance from the chaplain of the nearest Marine Corps or Naval activity. Not only can chaplains minister spiritually at this difficult time, but they are also ready to help with burial arrangements, transportation, and all the problems which arise after the death of the head of the family. Chaplains will likewise arrange for burial in Government or civilian cemeteries and will conduct the funeral service.

Marine Officials. The nearest Marine commanding officer, recruiting officer, or inspector-instructor is competent and glad to assist families of deceased Marines with their problems.

2026. AID FROM ORGANIZATIONS. Dependents of deceased Marines can get advice and assistance from several organizations listed below:

American Red Cross. This organization assists dependents with all types of Government claims as well as other problems. Proof of dependency is necessary; dependents should consult the Red Cross field director at the post or station or the Red Cross chapter in their town.

Navy Relief Society. This organization provides aid to members of the Naval Services and their dependents. Aid includes financial assistance (loan or gratuity); services of the Navy Relief Nurse; help with transportation and housing; and securing information about dependency allowances, pensions, and Government insurance; locating and communicating with naval personnel; and advising about community service available locally. Apply to the Navy Relief Society, Navy Department, Washington, D.C. 20360 or to nearest local chapter.

Veterans' Groups. The American Legion, Veterans of Foreign Wars, Disabled American Veterans, and other veterans' groups may also render aid to surviving dependents of Marine veterans.

Retired Benefits

When you retire, you rate various Marine Corps benefits and perquisites by virtue of your retired status, and you may also be entitled to various veterans' benefits if you apply and qualify for them. Some of these have already been mentioned, and this section sums up the most important ones remaining. In connection with most veterans' benefits, it is important to know that, although your retired pay is taxable, it is not classed as "other income," and thus does not bar you from receipt, or limit the extent, of benefits for which you are otherwise eligible, except that, if you receive disability compensation from the VA, your retired pay is reduced by the amount of the VA disability payment.

2027. MEDICAL CARE AND HOSPITALIZATION. Retired Marines and their surviving dependents (except parents) are eligible under CHAMPUS (Civilian Health and Medical Program for the Uniformed Services) for civilian hospitalization and for outpatient care from civilian medical facilities or by civilian doctors.

Under the hospitalization or inpatient formula for retired Marines or their dependents, and the dependents of deceased Marines (but in neither case including surviving dependent parents), the retired Marine or dependent has to pay 25 percent of the cost with the Government paying 75 percent of the cost, including doctor's bills. This means that for a hospital bill of $1,000, you would pay the first $250, and the Government would pick up the remaining $750.

Under the outpatient program, you pay the first $50 per person per year (but not to exceed $100 for your entire family) and 25 percent of the remaining outpatient cost. The Government then pays the 75 percent that remains. For example, if two or more members of your family use outpatient CHAMPUS services during a 12-month period, and the total bill is $200, you would pay the first $100 (equals first $50 per person, for 2 persons), plus $25 of the remaining $100, or a total payment by you of $125. The Government would then pay $75.

At age 65 (the age at which civilians become eligible for Social Security Medicare), your eligibility for CHAMPUS ceases, and you come under the Social Security coverage just mentioned. This does not, however, affect your continuing eligibility for care at military medical facilities, described below.

CARE IN MILITARY MEDICAL FACILITIES. Any retired Marine eligible for retired or retainer pay is entitled to medical and dental care in

Uniformed Services medical facilities on an availability of space and capabilities of the medical staff. Their dependents are also eligible on this basis, except for dental care.

For blindness, neuropsychiatric disorders, tuberculosis, and other chronic disorders, you must obtain treatment from Veterans Administration hospitals only, if care at Government expense is desired. In addition to the hospitalization just mentioned, retired personnel (who are also veterans) are also entitled to outpatient treatment.

2028. ELIGIBILITY FOR U. S. NAVAL HOME. Aged and infirm retired regular noncommissioned officers are eligible for admission to the U. S. Naval Home, Philadelphia, on approval by the Secretary of the Navy (see *Marine Corps Personnel Manual,* Chapter 11). Residence at the Home does not entail forfeiture of retired pay.

2029. VETERANS' PRIVILEGES. As a veteran of World Wars I and II, of Korea, and of Vietnam, you have certain privileges. Some of these are subject to expiration, while Congress adds others from time to time. The most important now current are:

The Veterans Administration(VA) affords a multitude of special benefits, such as care for the blind; allowance to purchase specially equipped automobiles for severely disabled veterans; special housing for wheelchair invalids; special hospitalization and domiciliary care; vocational rehabilitation if handicapped; and admission to VA hospitals for some types of care not always available from Navy medical resources. In addition, it may sometimes be advantageous to receive VA disability compensation instead of a portion of your retired pay. Consult the nearest VA field office.

Home Loans. The National Housing Act (P.L. 83-560), as well as PL. 89-117, establishes an FHA mortgage insurance program to assist members of the armed forces and veterans in buying or building homes. This program is a continuing one and has no date of expiration. See your banker.

Homesteads. World War I or II veterans get special preferences under various homesteading laws which open public lands in the U. S. and Alaska to settlement, but very little good land remains in the public domain. You can get details on this from the Bureau of Land Management, Department of the Interior, Washington 25, D.C.

U.S. Employment Service. Both the U. S. Employment Service and all state employment offices have counseling and placement facilities for veterans, to which you are entitled.

Education Assistance. Courses may be pursued at college and university level and at correspondence, vocational and business schools. For those who need secondary school training classes, accelerated or regular courses are available under certain conditions if they lead to specific vocational goals. In certain cases, correspondence courses or courses at foreign institutions may be permitted.

2030. OPTIONS ON DISABILITY RETIREMENT. If wounded

or otherwise seriously disabled and therefore facing separation from active service, you have a choice of taking military retirement or accepting Veterans Administration compensation. Naturally you will want to choose the alternative that brings you most money.

Military retirement is in general aimed at senior noncommissioned officers or officers with over 20 years' service. People of lower rank and short service receive relatively small amounts when computing retirement benefits on this basis. Moreover, although some disability retirements, especially for wounds, may result from disabilities up to 100 percent, the highest retired pay is 75 percent of active-duty pay.

VA compensation is not based on active-duty pay or longevity (as is military retirement) but rather on percent of disability and (under high degree of disability) number of dependents. The VA compensation also has a number of special allowances for special or aggravated types of disability. Computed on 1969 rates, a veteran gravely disabled by war wounds with a large family *could* receive as much as $850 per month. All VA compensation is tax-exempt.

Your choice will depend on many individual factors. However, before you opt for military disability retirement—if you are junior in rank and have a high disability—submit an application for VA compensation. This will enable you to find out which is most advantageous. Then you can make the best choice.

2031. INFORMATION FOR RETIRED MARINES. Marine Corps Headquarters issues from time to time updated editions of *Handbook for Retired Marines,* a comprehensive guide and compendium on benefits, privileges, and special provisions affecting retired Marine Corps personnel. A copy of this handbook will be furnished you on retirement. In addition, the Bureau of Naval Personnel has three excellent booklets, all of which may be had on application: *The Rights and Privileges of Navy Men and Their Dependents* (NavPers 11885A), *Navy Guide for Retired and Fleet Reserve Personnel* (NavPers 15891), and *Your New Career* (NavPers 15895A).

> *Note:* When and after you retire, you are required to keep the Commandant of the Marine Corps (Code DGH) informed of your current address. All correspondence concerning retired, retainer, and survivor annuity payments should go to Retired Pay Division, Marine Corps Finance Center, Kansas City, Missouri, 64197. You are also required to keep this activity advised *by letter* of your current address.

For Benefit of Your Dependents

2032. FOR BENEFIT OF YOUR DEPENDENTS. Secure *at once* copies of the following, certified by the seal of the issuing official:

Marriage certificate

Decree of divorce or annulment of former marriage of either your spouse or yourself

Death certificate of any previous spouse of your wife or yourself
Birth or baptismal certificates for your wife, children, and yourself
Your retirement orders (when you retire).

Have photostatic copies made of these certificates, and then have the copies certified by a notary public. Place these certificates, along with your will and other valuable papers, in an envelope and stow them in your safe-deposit box. Discuss these papers and the plans they represent, with your wife and anyone else who will have to act upon them.

Record of Emergency Data (Form NAVMC-10526 PD). Should you die while on active duty, your Emergency Data Form, which is filed in your service record book, becomes the most important document in your entire official files. The information you have furnished on this form indicates the person or persons to: (1) be notified of your death; (2) be paid death gratuity; and (3); be paid arrears of pay.

In addition, your record of emergency data enables you to designate anyone in your immediate family who, due to ill health, *should not* be notified of your death. Moreover, there are spaces in which you indicate the commercial insurance (and policy numbers) that you carry, as well as all Government insurance. The latter item becomes important to your next of kin when Marine Corps Headquarters prepares an official Marine Corps Report of Death and sends a copy to all such insurance companies you may have listed.

In short, every item of information on your Emergency Data Form is important to your wife, your children, and/or your next of kin. It is your responsibility to them to make certain that this form is kept current and in accordance with your desires. *If you die tomorrow, the most important thing you did today* will have been to bring your Emergency Data Form up to date.

> *Note:* If you hold USGLI or NSLI remember that Emergency Data Form does not of itself effect designation or change of beneficiary, which is a separate transaction between you and the VA. If in doubt, query the Veterans Administration, Insurance Center, P.O. Box 8079, Philadelphia, Pa., 19101.

2033. FOREIGN DIVORCES. Medical care, quarters allowances, and other dependents' benefits have been denied in the cases of military personnel who have obtained foreign divorces, usually Mexican, and later attempted to marry some other person. In almost all instances in which both parties to foreign divorce are U. S. citizens, the validity of the divorce and any later marriage is not recognized for allowances or for many other administrative purposes.

2034. INSTRUCTIONS CONCERNING YOUR PERSONAL AFFAIRS. Death is always unexpected. Even in peacetime one Marine dies every day. Thus it is essential that you gather together all information and instructions concerning your personal affairs and record this in suitable form for use by your surviving dependents. *Handbook for Retired Marines* contains an excellent form for recording your personal affairs record. As a minimum, collect and file in one place the following in up-to-date form:

Burial information and instructions
Official letters and correspondence with Government agencies
Will (location and any supplementary instructions)
Various important certificates (death, birth, marriage, discharge, etc.)
Safe-deposit box (location, key, inventories)
Bank deposit records and insurance policies
Income taxes
Money your beneficiary will receive from the Government (back pay, death gratuity, pension, etc.)
Inventory of real estate, securities, valuable personal property, etc.

On the blank pages, you should list: debts or outstanding obligations which will have to be paid by your estate; other assets (debts owed you, and any other interest or investment which has value); notes or advice which may be useful to your dependents in management of your estate after death.

Date and sign your record of personal affairs. Show it to your wife; tell your lawyer and your executor where this record and your will are.

Your family has the right to expect long-range planning and consideration from you. Don't procrastinate! *Do it now!*

*We are all members of the same great family.
. . . On social occasions the formality of
strictly military occasions should be relaxed,
and a spirit of friendliness and good will
should prevail.*

—*John A. Lejeune*

21 Social Life

Marines hold a special place in the military establishment for many
well-known reasons. Because of the high standing the Corps enjoys,
every Marine owes it to himself and to the Corps to be a model
not only in combat and on parade, but on social occasions as well.
Being a Marine (and having been selected to be a noncommissioned
officer) therefore puts you in a very special group. Like most special
groups, the corps of noncommissioned officers has its own well-
established rules, customs, and privileges that in effect add up to
a code of social behavior for you, and for your family, too.

This code shouldn't make you feel that rigid conformity is required
everywhere and in every detail. As a matter of fact, there is probably
no military group in the world where social and professional individuality are more appreciated, than among Marine NCOs. In the
good sense of the phrase, a Marine need never be afraid of developing into "a character"—which really means not being afraid to be
yourself.

The sections which follow will therefore cover some of the social
rules and customs which are followed in the corps of noncommissioned officers, and will also set out a few social rules and precautions
which may be helpful to younger NCOs.

Social Occasions

2101. THE MARINE CORPS BIRTHDAY. As every Marine
knows, the Corps was founded on 10 November 1775. From that
day to this, the Tenth of November has been the climax of the
Marine Corps year. November Tenth is the top social occasion of
the Corps.

The Birthday of the Marine Corps is celebrated officially and
socially by all Marines throughout the world. Not only do Marine
units carry out the prescribed ceremony, but wherever one or more

Marines are stationed—aboard ship, at posts of other services, even in the field—November 10th is habitually celebrated.

How a Command Observes November 10th. For a Marine command, the Birthday includes prescribed or customary features which are observed as circumstances permit. For Marines with other services, many of these items cannot be fulfilled exactly, but this list may serve as a guide:

1. A troop formation (preferably a parade) for publication of the article from the *Marine Corps Manual.* The uniform should be dress blue A (which includes medals). If blues cannot be worn, medals should be prescribed on the service uniform for this occasion. On shipboard, hold a special formation of the Marine detachment and get permission from the Captain to pipe the birthday article over the public-address system. If you are with some other service, and only a few Marines are present, you may defer publishing the article until the evening social function.
2. Holiday rations and, if the recreation fund can stand it, beer for the troops.
3. Maximum liberty and minimum work consistent with the missions of the command.
4. Memorial service at the Post Chapel for Marines who have died in the service of the nation. This service should follow the military ceremony and should be attended by the Commanding Officer, officers, and—if practicable—the command in a body.
5. A birthday ball at which a cake-cutting ceremony takes place.
6. At any schools or instruction scheduled for 10 November, you should emphasize the traditions and the history of the Corps.

The Birthday Ball. It is up to you to arrange the annual birthday ball with pride, forethought, and care. Every Marine command must have one. If on detached service away from the Corps, the senior Marine present must arrange a suitable birthday ball, and it is up to you to chip in to support it.

The birthday ball is formal, which means dress blues with medals. If you do not possess blues, wear service uniform with medals. For the ladies, formal dresses, of course.

Should November 10th fall on a Sunday, the custom is to hold the birthday ball on the Saturday night preceding, with the ceremony timed so that reading of the traditional Article takes place at 0001.

The birthday ball is a command performance. Unless duty prevents, you attend. If resources permit, appropriate civilian guests and noncommissioned officers from the other services may be invited, but not too many. Be sure that retired Marines and any foreign Marine NCOs who may be present are included.

The procedure for a birthday ball ceremony is described in Chapter 3, *Landing Party Manual.* This procedure, of course, is a guide, and details may vary according to facilities, number of guests, and local traditions. There is only one ironclad rule for the birthday ball: *Make it a good one.*

2102. MESS NIGHT. A Mess Night is a formal stag dinner in mess by all members, or by the noncommissioned officers of a particular post or unit. Ladies do not attend. This may cause some irritation, but must cheerfully be accepted as one of the many hardships a soldier's wife must bear.

Mess nights may be held periodically, for example, to celebrate special anniversaries (such as that of a battle in which the unit has participated); to "dine out" NCOs being detached; or to honor guests from another unit, service, or country.

PLANS AND PREPARATIONS. The first step in preparing for a mess night is to designate the noncommissioned officer who will act as *Vice President* (or "Mr. Vice", as he is traditionally called). In some messes or organizations, the vice president is the junior staff sergeant present. However, it is good practice to rotate the job among all staff sergeants on board so that all may gain experience. In any case, the function of the vice president—at least beforehand—is to undertake all preliminary arrangements, i.e., guest list (to be approved by the mess president), seating diagram (also to be approved), menu and catering, music, decorations, etc. The success of the evening depends on the vice president.

Subject to local or unit customs and to facilities which are available, here are specific arrangements which should be made for a mess night.

1. After approval of the guest list, invitations should be prepared and mailed or delivered at least two weeks in advance of the Mess Night. Each guest, regardless of organization or of sponsor in the host unit, is a guest of the Mess and should be so treated.
2. The table is set with complete dinner service—wine glasses, candles, and flowers. Unit or post silver and trophies should be used as ornaments on the table or in places where they will show to advantage. Naturally, they should be in a high state of polish.
3. Unless the post or unit sergeant major or the president of the staff NCO mess desires to preside, a sergeant major is detailed as *President of the Mess* for the occasion. As stated before, a junior staff sergeant acts as Vice President.
4. Uniform is dress blues (or, at tropical stations, white-blue-whites). Civilians invited to a mess night should wear black tie with miniature medals (if they rate them) or dark suit and tie with large medals (if they rate them). Noncommissioned or petty officer guests from other services should wear equivalent uniforms. Retired NCOs who are invited may either attend in uniform or wear civilian clothes with medals, as above.
5. The National Color and the Marine Corps Color are placed behind the president's chair. At organizational mess nights, guidons of companies and batteries can be banked behind the top table. Drums can also be used to good effect, if pyramided up. Another idea is to place all barracks caps of those present on bandstands or a trestle, in a row or rows in rear of the vice

468   president's place. Stacks of rifles in each corner of the room (out of the way, of course) are another touch.

6. The mess president sits at the head of the table, the vice president at the foot. Other guests and members take seat by rank except that guests of honor are on the right and left of the president. A seating diagram should be posted in advance, and place cards and menu cards prepared. All preliminary arrangements are supervised by the vice president.

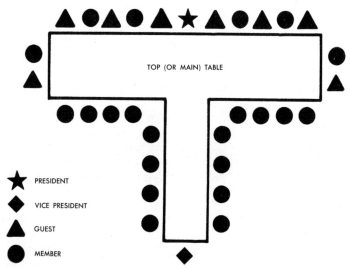

Fig. 21-1: Typical layout of seating for a mess night.

7. If available, a three- or four-piece military string orchestra should be detailed to provide dinner music, and should know the national anthems and regimental marches of guests. If suitable "live" music is not available, a good-quality public-address system with taped or recorded selections will serve as a substitute. The musical program should be checked and timed by the vice president, and should always include *Semper Fidelis* and the unit song or march of each guest. If live music is available, coordinate all these and other musical arrangements with the bandmaster.

8. Advance planning with the mess includes arrangements as to cost, menu (usually roast beef), wine (a good rosé goes with any menu), and the 1775 rum punch which is often used as the traditional drink for the toasts. Give the mess manager at least two weeks for his own planning, based on a tentative attendance figure from you, being sure sufficient private space is available for cocktails, dinner, and drinks afterward. A week beforehand, give the mess manager a final figure on who is coming.

9. The vice president should be at the mess early on the morning of the dinner with a working party to assist in final preparations. Decorations and trophies are placed, table is set, and place cards are checked against the seating diagram, which should be posted in the mess lobby or cocktail lounge. If the toasts are being drunk in traditional rum punch, the punch bowl is positioned for best service.

10. The vice president should be on hand a half hour before the appointed hour for cocktails. This provides time for a last-minute check of details.

PROCEDURE. Staff NCOs and guests assemble punctually 45 minutes before dinner for cocktails. This allows time for all to arrive, *but not too much time for preliminary drinks* (remember, there will be a long stretch ahead). The cocktail hour should be the occasion for all SNCOs to speak to each guest and make him feel welcome; also for the mess president to welcome each guest on board individually. In addition, the younger NCOs should take this occasion to pay their respects informally on sergeants major and first sergeants and senior chief petty officers; this is much appreciated by the older men.

If possible, a section from the unit band should provide semiclassical or light musical background, but, if there is nothing better, a record player or tape recorder will do.

Dinner is announced in accordance with local custom. If a field music is available, the preferred way is to have him sound the old-time *First Sergeants' Call.* Then music can follow, such as *Semper Fidelis* or (for drum and bugle corps) *Sea Soldiers.* Another variation, for fife and drum, is *The Roast Beef of Old England* (which used to be played aboard ship as "Officers' Mess Gear" or for all hands when a holiday ration was to be served). When playing any of the foregoing, musics usually strike up in the mess proper, march through the cocktail lounge, back into the mess, around the table, and return to the lounge, where they halt and continue to play.

Depending on local ground rules, members and guests proceed informally to their places; or, where more formality is the custom, those seated at the top table enter in a body after all others are in place waiting to sit down. In any case, neither drinks nor cigarettes should be carried in from the lounge, as a courtesy to those members and guests at the dining table. When going in, each guest should be escorted by a member of the mess. Grace is said by the chaplain, if present, otherwise by the president. All hands then take seats. The ranking guest, seated at the mess president's right, is served first, then the president, and so on counterclockwise without further regard to seniority. Appropriate wines are served with each course (however, remember that chilled rosé goes with all food combinations, has a light, pleasant taste, and is inexpensive; in other words, you don't have to be a wine snob to run a good mess night). There should be no smoking during dinner, and no noncommissioned officer may leave the table until after the toasts, except by permission from the president. (If for any reason, official or otherwise, you arrive late, you should express your regrets to the mess president before taking your seat.)

In some organizations, when roast beef is the entrée, the head waiter rolls on the beef, halts behind the president, cuts him a small but choice piece and lays it before him on a plate. The president then tastes it and, if satisfied, pronounces, "This beef is tasty and fit for human consumption."

Dinner then proceeds. When the president and senior guests have finished, the table is cleared. The president raps for attention with gavel or spoon (but not on a glass; if crystal it might shatter), and says or obtains silence for the chaplain to say a short concluding Grace. *Note for Chaplains:* don't make a sermon out of Grace.)

On some occasions, port is drunk with the toasts after dinner, in the English fashion. If so, here are certain traditional rules:

Don't drink toasts bottoms-up.
Port is served from decanters passed *clockwise* from the president and vice president.
Never drink a toast from an empty glass, or worse, in water.

If toasts are drunk in the 1775 rum punch (see below for recipe), there are no decanters to pass, and it is up to waiters to keep glasses or punch cups charged during intervals between toasts.

In any case, when port decanters have made their rounds or all cups have been charged with 1775 rum punch, the president raps for silence. If a foreign military, naval, or other official guest is present, the president rises, lifts his glass, and says, "Mr. Vice, His Majesty, King————of————." The vice president then rises, glass in hand, waits until all have risen, and gives the toast. "Gentlemen, His Majesty, King————of————." The orchestra plays the foreign national anthem, following which all say, "King————of————," drink, and resume seats. After about a minute, the president again raps for silence, the senior foreign officer rises, and says "Gentlemen, the President of the United States," and the orchestra plays the National Anthem. This toast is called "The Loyal Toast." If no foreign guests are present, the first toast is to the President of the United States, and—in any case—the *concluding* toast is to the Marine Corps, during which, if music is available, "The Marines' Hymn" is played. The wording of this toast should be, *"Mr. Vice, Corps and Country,"* and the custom has grown up that the vice president replies in words taken from a Revolutionary War recruiting poster of the Continental Marines—*"Long live the United States, and success to the Marines!"* If the guest of honor be a Marine, he may take this occasion to proceed to a few remarks. If the guest of honor is from another service, a toast to his service is in order. He may respond and speak.

Before leaving the subject of toasts, note that toasts may be divided into four classes, and that they are given in the following order:

Toasts of Protocol: Toasts to foreign governments or chiefs of state; toast to the President of the United States.

Official Toasts: Toasts to other services, military organizations, Government departments, agencies, or institutions.

Traditional Toast: "Corps and Country."

Personal Toasts: Toasts to individuals (distinguished guests, officer being dined out, etc.)

> *Note:* To make 1775 rum punch, mix four parts dark rum; two parts lime juice; and one part pure maple syrup. Add small amount of grenadine syrup to taste. Ice generously and stir well. The maple syrup, incidentally, was originally used because of the British blockade which cut off supplies of West Indies sugar cane.

The traditional toast ends the formal part of the evening. Personal toasts and speeches may follow at a suitable interval afterward, as described below.

Following the toasts, coffee is served, the president announces, "The smoking lamp is lighted," (never say "lit"), and individual drinks or liqueurs may be ordered. At this point or whenever the orchestra is released, the president may send for the bandmaster, and offer him a drink. If speeches are planned (other than remarks associated with toasts), they are made now. In "dining out" a departing messmate, the president makes brief, usually humorous remarks, whereupon the noncommissioned officer being honored replies in the same vein. In some messes the orchestra remains and plays the regimental march of each guest, during which the individual stands. When speeches are over, the top table guests rise, following which the remainder of the party adjourn individually to the bar and anteroom, where songs are generally sung and sea stories recounted. All hands should remain until the ranking guest and the president leave, after which anyone may secure at discretion.

Circumstances will frequently not permit a mess night with all formalities as to uniform, catering, and table service that are outlined herein, or it may not be desired. This should not deter an organization from making the effort. The idea is to do the best you can with what you have, and let the spirit of the occasion take care of the rest. *Do not, in particular, let yourself be overcome by the apparent formality of mess nights; the object is the pleasure and comradeship of all hands.*

As to timing, it is better not to schedule mess nights regularly. It is much preferable that people begin asking when the next one will take place. Thus a mess night will be looked forward to with anticipation and never as a burden.

> *Note:* The costs of a mess night, like other "chip-in" Marine Corps functions, should be prorated by rank so that people who make the most, pay the most. Here is the formula for prorating by rank, which, even though complicated-looking, is actually quite simple:

Rank	Base Pay	Number Participating
SgtMaj	x	δ
1stSgt	y	σ
GySgt	z	ν
SSgt	α	ϕ

$$K = \text{total cost of the function}$$
$$E = x\delta + y\sigma + z\nu + \alpha\phi$$

$$\text{SgtMaj share} = \frac{\delta K}{E} \qquad \text{1stSgt share} = \frac{\sigma K}{E}$$

$$\text{GySgt share} = \frac{\nu K}{E} \qquad \text{SSgt share} = \frac{\phi K}{E}$$

2103. MILITARY WEDDINGS. As a Marine, you enjoy the privilege of having a military wedding. A military wedding is simply a formal wedding with traditional service embellishments. The characteristic features and ground rules of a military wedding are as follows:

Uniform. Marine members of the wedding party wear dress blue A with sword. Dress A uniforms call for medals, not ribbons. Even though wearing sword and thus under arms, the groom should not wear gloves, whereas the ushers should wear gloves throughout the ceremony.

Needless to say, all members of the wedding party wear the same uniform. If noncommissioned or petty officers from other services are included, they wear their nearest equivalent uniform.

Best Man and Ushers. Since your wedding is to be military, your best man and ushers should be in the Service, too. Inactive reserves may don uniform for the occasion. It is usual but not necessary for ushers to be the same rank as the groom. The senior usher coordinates the military side of the ceremony and gives commands or signals for movements by the ushers and for the arch of swords.

The best man looks out for the groom. It is the best man's job to get the groom to the altar, on time and clean and sober. He should be prepared to render quick and effective help in seeing that the groom's uniform and gear are in top condition.

If the wedding takes place away from the bride's home and her parents or near relatives cannot attend—as is sometimes the case in the service—it is appropriate for you to ask your commanding officer, or some senior NCO friend, such as your first sergeant or sergeant major, to give away the bride.

Bachelor Dinner. The night before the wedding, the best man and ushers should give the groom a send-off party known as "the bachelor dinner." The best man and senior usher attend to arrangements. This party is designed to keep up the groom's spirits rather than, as is sometimes thought, to bend him out of shape.

The Clergyman. You may choose either a chaplain or a civilian clergyman. A chaplain performs the ceremony in uniform or in vestments, according to the customs of the denomination. In some denominations (such as the Episcopal Church) ministers, whether chaplain or civilian, are permitted to wear military ribbons on their vestments and will do so if you request. Your best man should see to this.

Do not pay a chaplain for officiating at a military wedding. If you have a civilian clergyman, follow civilian custom regarding fees. Again, this is something your best man should attend to. The same applies to fees for organist and music at the church.

Wedding Under the Colors. If you wish and if your denomination permits, the National Color and Marine Corps Color of your unit may be crossed above and in rear of the chaplain, or displayed during the ceremony in the chancel of the church. This is known as "A wedding under the Colors." It is an old tradition.

Handling the Colors for this ceremony is the responsibility of the senior usher, who, with designated ushers, receives the Colors (cased) from the adjutant, places them before the ceremony, and removes, cases, and returns them immediately afterward.

Arch of Swords. The "Arch of Swords" is probably the best-known feature of a military wedding. It is carried out in this fashion:

After the ceremony, the senior usher forms the ushers in column of twos, and places them *immediately outside* the exit of the church, facing inboard. As the newly married couple pass through the portal, the senior usher commands: 1. DRAW; 2. SWORDS. At the command of execution, ushers carry out *only* the first count of the movement leaving their swords raised, with tips touching, to form an arch under which the couple pass. After the newlyweds have passed, swords are returned on command by the senior usher.

Cutting the Wedding Cake. The wedding cake is cut by the bride and groom together, using the groom's sword. If a Marine Corps daughter is being married to a civilian, it is proper to use her father's sword. After the cake has been cut, the best man proposes a toast to the bride and groom, and, as the guests drink, the orchestra plays "Auld Lang Syne."

2104. CHRISTENINGS. It is customary to celebrate the christening of a service child with a party after the ceremony. As a minimum, invite the child's sponsors in baptism, the officiating clergyman, and friends of the family. Like weddings, christenings too may be performed "under the Colors," as described in Section 2103. At a christening party, one of the godparents proposes the health of the child.

2105. DANCES. In most commands it is usual to have occasional formal dances, either dinner or buffet, at which you wear uniform. The appropriate uniform on these occasions is blue dress. During the course of such an evening, you should try to dance with each lady at your table, and make it a point to dance with the wife of your first sergeant and sergeant major. After the last dance, to indicate the official end of the evening, the orchestra should play the National Anthem.

2106. "BOSSES' NIGHT." At periodic intervals, according to mess or unit customs, the staff noncommissioned officers of a company, battery, squadron, headquarters unit or detachment, invite the officers of the unit (or sometimes officers of individual choosing) to the Staff NCO Mess (see below) for an evening get-together known as "Bosses' Night." This is the time when, in General Lejeune's words that head this chapter, "the formality of strictly military occasions should be relaxed, and a spirit of friendliness and goodwill should prevail."

Some important ground rules that make for a good "Bosses' Night" are as follows:

Always set a time limit. This prevents overloading, which is particularly undesirable on such an occasion.

Don't turn "Bosses' Night" into a grievance session.

Pay special attention to new or junior officers; nobody will overlook the Old Man.

If you are one of the junior men in the mess, don't be too free to barge in on the sergeant major or first sergeant, when they and the captain or the major are having a drink.

Obviously, the guests cannot be permitted to spend a cent or buy a round. (This means no poker dice or other such contests.)

Clubs and Messes

As you know, in large posts or organizations, there are separate NCO clubs, one for the staff noncommissioned officers, the other for sergeants and corporals. Smaller posts generally consolidate these into a single club. What follows is primarily written at the level of the Staff NCO Mess, but is of course generally applicable to the sergeants' mess as well.

2107. CLUB AND MESS ORGANIZATION. Staff NCO clubs are organized and run in the following way.

Major policies, overall supervision, and representation of the membership as a whole are the functions of the *board of governors*. This is normally headed by the base sergeant major as chairman, with a member representing each regiment, separate battalion, or other major organization. The board usually meets once a month, at which time new ideas, complaints, special expenditures, policy changes, etc. are considered.

Below the board of governors, the operating organization of the mess is headed by a *club manager* (often a retired or FMCR NCO) who has had experience with such work. The manager is usually backstopped by one or more assistant (or, at large clubs, nightly duty) managers, who represent him whenever the club is open. Secretaries and waitresses are usually civilian employees, while

475 bartenders, barmen-waiters, and other male employees are usually off-duty Marines.

2108. RULES AND GROUND RULES FOR THE NCO MESS.
Here are some general rules and ground rules of conduct which have maintained the tone and atmosphere of the best NCO clubs and messes.

Remember that the mess belongs to the members who support it. As a guest, defer to their ways and rules; as a member, assume responsibility for it and support it as *your* mess.

Attend public mess meetings whenever they are held. You have no right to complain about the way a club is run if you are unwilling to attend meetings and voice your ideas at the proper time.

Dress conservatively and correctly at "the club." You can't go wrong, ordinarily, if you wear full uniform of the day or complete civilian clothes, including coat and suitable neckwear. Most messes publish and post their uniform rules. You, your guest, and your dependents must abide by these if you expect to use the club.

Pay club bills promptly, sign chits legibly and accurately, and always be sure your checking account is in shape to meet any checks you write. Disregard of your obligations will destroy your personal standing, weaken your mess, force irksome restrictions on other members, and bring swift retribution which will mar your record.

Do not tip mess employees unless club rules expressly so authorize and encourage (and be very leery, as a club member, of giving approval to any such relaxation of rules; individual tipping at a club is a sure way to tarnish both service and attitude of servants).

When you are a *guest* in a club or mess, do not attempt to stand drinks. If you are on temporary additional duty and become a member of the mess, however, you pay for your fair share. If, as a member, you see a strange noncommissioned officer alone in your mess, introduce yourself and extend him all hospitality, remembering that a guest of any member is a guest of the mess.

When you bring guests to the mess, be sure they are those you would entertain in your own home.

A staff NCO mess is a place for relaxation and pleasant enjoyment of the company of your brother noncommissioned officers. Although, so to speak, you leave your chevrons at the door, it is wise to remember that you are still a Marine and to remember where you stand.

In particular, avoid making yourself the center of attention as a result of taking one drink too many or for any other reason. Your contemporaries and many others will always be judging you by your actions.

If officer or civilian guests are present, make sure they don't stand around with empty glasses. If you have a lady guest, don't leave her for prolonged periods of time.

Should you have reason to complain about service, or any other club arrangements, if possible hold off your complaint and make it in writing, preferably in the form of a suggestion as to how things can be improved. If the matter requires immediate action, take it to the duty manager, not to the world at large, and especially don't take it on yourself to call down club employees. This is the manager's job.

When a new noncommissioned officer has reported in, or a man has just joined the staff or noncommissioned ranks, he should be taken to the appropriate club as part of his reporting-aboard or promotion procedure. This is a responsibility for NCOs of his unit. On such occasions, all hands extend a special effort to make new-comers feel welcome and at home.

In general, except on "Bosses' Night," you should be rather con-servative in inviting officers to the club. But do not forget to call the club manager and get his permission before you do so. This is a throwback to the old-time unwritten rule that no officer (other than the CO) could enter an NCO mess without express invitation from the senior noncommissioned officer of the command. This is no longer literally observed, but it is a good old custom to remember. By obtaining prior clearance from the club manager when you plan to bring in special guests (officers, senior NCOs from other services or foreign countries, distinguished civilians, etc.) you insure that the club will have its best foot forward when they appear.

Don't forget that, if your conduct should warrant, the club's board of governors can deprive you of the privileges of the mess for given periods, usually not more than six months (anything calling for a longer deprivation usually results in permanent loss of privileges of that particular club).

Finally, if in doubt as to some nicety or ground rule, simply do the gentlemanly thing. You will never go far wrong.

Social Customs

2109. MARINE SOCIAL CUSTOMS AND TRADITIONS. Cer-tain social customs and traditions are observed throughout the Corps and deserve mention here.

WETTING DOWN YOUR WARRANT. Whenever you are promoted, you are obligated to hold a "wetting-down party." At this affair your new warrant (which is usually displayed at some conspicuous but safe vantage point) is said to be "wet down." When several noncommissioned officers are promoted together, you may join in a single wetting-down party.

CIGARS. If you are either newly promoted or a new father, you distribute cigars to all NCOs of your unit. If you are a newly pro-moted woman NCO, candy (unless you happen to smoke cigars!) is an acceptable substitute.

FIVE ACES. Any member who rolls five aces when throwing dice for refreshments in a mess is obliged by tradition to buy a complete round for all messmates present. In large messes this custom is eased to the extent that you have to buy drinks only for your own party.

ENTERING A MESS COVERED. Unless you are on duty and under arms, if you enter a mess covered, you are liable to buy a round of drinks. Most messes adhere to and post the old rule: "He who enters covered here buys the house a round of cheer." In fact, some even have a bell and lanyard which may be rung by anyone present who spots an offender against this rule, thus signaling a free round.

DRAWING YOUR SWORD IN A MESS. The seagoing rule that anyone who unsheathes his sword in the wardroom must buy a round also applies on shore, if you are so unwary as to draw sword in any mess. The custom goes back to the days of duelling, when this was one method of restricting indiscreet sword-play.

WELCOME ON BOARD. Whenever a new unit arrives at a post or a transport brings in an appreciable number of Marines or Marine dependents, the local Marine commanding officer or his representative, together with the sergeant major and the post band, greets the newcomers.

DEPARTURE FROM A POST. When a unit or a draft leaves, the commanding officer, sergeant major, band, and friends see them off. If the move is routine, the band plays "Auld Lang Syne" as aircraft embarkation is completed, or as the transport casts off her last line or the train gets under way. If the unit is on war or expeditionary service, "The Marines' Hymn" is the send-off. In either case, the departing unit should be played down to the airfield, dock, or loading platform by "Semper Fidelis."

CHRISTMAS CARDS. At Christmas time, it is customary for the mess to reserve special display space for individual Christmas cards. All families affix personal greeting cards on this board. This not only adds Christmas color to the mess but constitutes an exchange of greetings among all who participate.

HAPPY HOUR. During set hours on Monday and Friday evenings, and just before payday, it is customary for the NCO club to reduce the price of drinks.

Good Manners

A Marine stands out sharply anywhere, and a noncommissioned officer is even more conspicuous. Good conduct, courtesy, and basic good manners are expected of every Marine. The following rules should be of particular usefulness to the new and younger noncommissioned officer as he makes his way upward and ahead.

2110. CONDUCT TOWARD AND WITH WOMEN. Until the laws of biology are repealed, women will always be the weaker sex, and it is up to men to protect them. Most social customs spring from this fact.

On the street, a man walks on the curb side, outboard of a lady, thus sheltering her. In a crowd, when she needs assistance, or in heavy traffic, or going up steps, the man gives her his arm. Aboard train, aircraft, or bus, she gets the window seat. On bus or street car, a Marine always gets up and offers his seat to a woman with packages or children, an elderly lady, or a pregnant woman.

When you are with a lady, don't embarrass her by off-color jokes, loud talking, violent gestures, or other actions that may attract undue attention. When you are out with a lady, don't look over every other passing woman.

Except in crowded situations where the man obviously has to "run interference," you should let the lady precede you, as when boarding a bus or going down a theater aisle.

If a lady seems to need help you should offer your assistance. But don't presume on your act of courtesy or helpfulness by imposing on the lady or trying to strike up an unwanted acquaintance with her.

At table, men remain standing until the ladies are seated. In this, each man helps the lady to his right into her place by pulling out her chair for her and then gently pushing it toward the table as she sits down. When the ladies at table rise, so do you (except in the case of the hostess, who often has to get up and down in connection with the meal).

2111. MANNERS AT MEALS. Basic table manners are very simple. Don't eat in a sloppy or slurpy way, don't shovel down your food, wait until everyone is served before you start in, and take time out from eating for appropriate conversation.

In addition to the foregoing, however, here are a few other pointers.

Keep your elbows off the table and sit up straight.

Don't pick your teeth in public, even though there may be toothpicks on the table.

If in doubt as to which fork or other implement to use, watch your hostess and follow her choice.

Put your napkin in your lap, not around your neck or in the collar of your blouse or shirt.

If you have to cough or sneeze, do so into your handkerchief, and turn your head away from table or others present.

Should you be one of a group going out to a restaurant, it is a good idea to phone ahead for a reservation if your party numbers more than four. When time comes to pay, one man should take care of the entire check, while the others settle up promptly and privately with him afterward. For large parties, the one who attends to the check should excuse himself and take care of it with the waiter or cashier to one side.

2112. MISCELLANEOUS POINTERS. Always remember that you are a Marine, and use correct military titles when introducing or referring to other military people. (See Chapter 15.) Similarly, under circumstances when a civilian would raise his hat (as in greeting a lady), a man in uniform, if covered, salutes with a slight bow. *Never tip your cap to anybody when in uniform.*

In making introductions, always pronounce the names of both parties distinctly. Men are always introduced to ladies; younger people to older people; juniors to seniors. Examples:

"Mrs. Nicholson, I would like to introduce First Sergeant Bond."
"Drum Major Oeser, may I present my son, Robert?"
"Sergeant Major Sweet, this is First Sergeant Lee."

When introduced, shake hands firmly but don't try to Indian-wrestle (only shake hands with a lady when she first extends her hand). Look your new acquaintance in the eye when acknowledging, and pronounce his name as you do so. The best way to acknowledge an introduction, either to another man or to a lady, is to say, "How do you do?" Steer clear of "Pleased, I'm sure . . . Hiya . . . Pleasedta meetcha . . ." or other such catchphrases.

Be punctual. It is never wrong to arrive exactly on time for a date or an invitation.

Never speak ill of your Corps or of any fellow Marine in the presence of outsiders, civilians, or members of any other service. And remember insofar as public utterances are concerned, an American soldier has no politics and espouses no political party or cause.

Polite society is no place to play "the tough Marine." Courtesy and personal modesty are never more becoming than in a NCO. Rudeness, gory tales of blood and guts, and coarse language usually show up the greenhorn or counterfeit, and certainly the ill-bred.

Remember that your wife does not and cannot wear your rank. Be certain that she understands this clearly and does not put herself ahead of the wives of juniors or subordinates. This will only belittle your rank in the eyes of others. Insist, however, that your wife, as a lady, receive the courtesy due her from all.

"Courtesy is the lubricant of life."

Appendices

1. Commandants of the Marine Corps
2. The Importance of Being Inspected
3. Brother Marines
4. Marine Veterans' Associations
5. Simple Exhibition Drills

Appendix 1

Commandants of the Marine Corps

Major Samuel Nicholas, 1775–1781
Lieutenant Colonel William Ward Burrows, 1798–1804
Lieutenant Colonel Franklin Wharton, 1804–1818
Lieutenant Colonel Anthony Gale, 1819–1820
Brigadier General Archibald Henderson, 1820–1859
Colonel John Harris, 1859–1864
Brigadier General Jacob Zeilin, 1864–1876
Colonel Charles G. McCawley, 1876–1891
Major General Charles Heywood, 1891–1903
Major General George F. Elliott, 1903–1910
Major General William P. Biddle, 1910–1914
Major General George Barnett, 1914–1920
Major General John A. Lejeune, 1920–1929
Major General Wendell C. Neville, 1929–1930
Major General Ben H. Fuller, 1930–1934
Major General John H. Russell, Jr., 1934–1936
Lieutenant General Thomas Holcomb, 1936–1944
General Alexander Archer Vandegrift, 1944–1948
General Clifton B. Cates, 1948–1952
General Lemuel C. Shepherd, Jr., 1952–1956
General Randolph McC. Pate, 1956–1960
General David M. Shoup, 1960–1964
General Wallace M. Greene, Jr., 1964–1968
General Leonard F. Chapman, Jr., 1968–

Appendix 2

The Importance of Being Inspected

(This appendix consists of a slightly abridged version of an article of the same title, by Lieutenant Colonel W. C. Stoll, which appeared in the May 1955 *Marine Corps Gazette,* and is now reprinted by kind permission of the *Gazette.* As a compilation of highly practical advice, even though written mainly for officer readers, this article can be of great value to every NCO.)

Inspections have a very important significance in every Marine officer's career. It is by inspections that the efficiency, morale, discipline, training, and leadership of a unit are often determined. Quite often a superior has little opportunity to observe certain subordinates. Thus, he often must rely on inspections to evaluate that officer's efficiency for reporting purposes, causing an inspection to be a very serious and important event.

Through numerous Inspector General, Fleet Marine Force, Division, Force Troops and Commanding Officer's Inspections, it has become obvious that most junior officers and staff NCOs do not prepare their units properly for these important events.

Why is this? In search of an answer to this $64 question I have observed many inspections and made many queries with an attempt to correlate results of inspections with preinspection preparation, procedures, and planning.

As a result, I am of the opinion that many competent leaders do not have a follow-through program of checks and double checks to insure that all discrepancies are corrected. The following five-step program for improving inspection results is offered, and excellent results are guaranteed if these steps are meticulously followed. Perhaps outstanding inspection results may be obtained without actually performing the below-listed steps, but why gamble when you can take a guaranteed course of action?

STEP 1: *Check-Off List.* A detailed check-off list is a must. This list must not only be available to officers and NCOs but must be disseminated to all hands. If the paper supply permits, issue one copy to every man in your unit so that he can actually inspect himself as well as others.

STEP 2: *Proper Inspection.* Instruction on how to prepare for inspections, including what and how to inspect, should be held periodically and included in the regular training schedule. Each Marine should be trained to inspect himself first and then others. Practice inspections should be held with Marines in ranks and certain discrepancies noted. Every other Marine is then given the opportunity to inspect and jot down the discrepancies. This not only gives each man valuable experience and sharpens his observation, but it also gives him interest in an otherwise dull subject.

STEP 3: *Routine Weekly or Monthly Inspection.* The routine inspection must include all hands. Those persons on leave, in the hospital, on working parties, or otherwise absent from an inspection, must be inspected either in a special group or individually as appropriate after their return. Often a man will miss a routine inspection and therefore has discrepancies which are allowed to continue without correction. Measures must be taken to insure that inspections are thorough and that all men with discrepancies are reinspected and discrepancies are corrected.

STEP 4: *The Preliminary Inspection.* When an inspection is announced beforehand, as most Inspector General, Commanding General or Commanding Officer's inspections are, a detailed preliminary inspection by subordinate commanders should be held immediately after the announcement is made so that maximum time will be available to correct all discrepancies beforehand.

STEP 5: *Last-Minute Inspection.* It is always irritating and infuriating to a commanding officer to make an inspection and find troops with buttons unbuttoned, shoes not shined, fingernails dirty, cartridge belts not properly adjusted, hats not properly placed on heads, field scarves not properly tied and other numerous discrepancies that take but a moment to remedy on the spot. A thorough inspection administered a half an hour or so before the superior's inspection will correct these discrepancies.

If the program outlined below is followed, step-by-step, by all officers and NCOs in charge of units, the results of inspections will improve considerably and the efficiency, morale, discipline, and leadership of the units will improve proportionally.

Uniform

1. Is each item of regulation material?
2. Is each item tailored correctly?
3. Does each item fit?
4. Is item neat, clean, pressed (if applicable), and properly marked?
5. Is each item in good repair, free from frayed edges, holes, and tears?
6. Are shoes shined and in good repair? Soles and heels not worn down?
7. Do shoe laces match shoes?
8. Are socks regulation color and material?
9. Are field boots clean, in good repair, and properly shined? Evenly worn, indicating rotation?
10. Headgear worn properly?
11. Garrison cap sewed properly?
12. Are chevrons and hashmarks worn properly?
13. Visibly bulging pockets?
14. Neckties (field scarves) knotted properly?
15. Collar neat in appearance and unfrayed?
16. Proper insignia worn, and worn properly?
17. Emblems proper color, and neither shiny nor corroded?
18. Buckle and tip of belt shined?
19. Current authorized marksmanship badge worn in proper place?
20. Authorized ribbons worn in correct sequence, clean, unfrayed, positioned in accordance with *Uniform Regulations,* battle stars pointed correctly?
21. All insignia worn properly, anchors on collar emblems pointed inboard, cap emblem pointed correctly?
22. Is belt proper length of overlap (two to four inches)?
23. Trousers proper length?
24. Are nonregulation items showing?
25. Are nonregulation markings showing?

Weapon

1. Is weapon clean and does it function properly?
2. Are magazines clean and functioning properly?
3. Bayonet clean and bayonet ring turned properly? Does release operate smoothly?
4. Does each man know the number of his weapon, name of weapon, safety device, nomenclature of principal parts, and field-stripping procedures?
5. Does each man know the zero of his weapon and his windage and elevation rules?
6. Rifle: Is sling properly placed and cared for, is stock properly cared for and combination tool and thong case present?
7. Is inspection arms executed correctly and uniformly throughout unit?

8. Has man fired T/O weapon, at least for familiarization?

Miscellaneous

1. Satisfactory posture?
2. Hair cut neatly, face shaven and mustache, if authorized and worn, neatly trimmed?
3. Hands, face, and fingernails clean?
4. Web equipment clean, serviceable, in good repair, and uniformly placed?
5. All items on cartridge belts worn uniformly?
6. Leather holsters shined?
7. Identification tags and regulation chain?
8. I.D. card up-to-date and not cracked?
9. Does man hold up-to-date personal immunization card?
10. Eyeglasses, if required? (two pairs).
11. (When helmet is worn) Helmet cover skintight, right color out, and is chin strap properly adjusted and on exact point of chin?

Clothing and Equipment on Bunk

1. Display neat, regulation and uniform with other displays throughout unit?
2. Is all clothing displayed, regardless of required amount?
3. Clothing clean, in good repair and marked in accordance with regulations?
4. Missing clothing accounted for by a laundry, cleaning, or cobbler's chit and certified by platoon leader?
5. Equipment all present and uniformly displayed?
6. Canteen corks serviceable?
7. Extra shoelaces present?
8. Are all improper markings on clothes blocked out neatly?
9. Has shelter half all buttons, tie-down loops, and no holes?
10. Tent pins, poles, and line, in serviceable condition?
11. All snaps (e.g., first-aid pouch and canteen cover) working easily, but holding firmly?
12. All metal ends on web straps present and not deformed?
13. Do hooks for D-rings have spring catch?
14. Does mess gear close tightly and is it free of dirt or corrosion?
15. Canteen cup free of rust and dirt?
16. Is entrenching tool clean and does locking nut move freely?
17. First-aid packet present and unopened?

Field Display

1. Does each individual know proper method of laying out equipment?
2. Is display uniform throughout unit and in accordance with the LPM?
3. Are all items present?
4. Does first-aid packet have necessary component items?
5. Canteen cork serviceable?

6. All equipment serviceable?
7. Identification tags present?

Other Items

1. Locker boxes, locker, and other personal gear neatly stowed in accordance with local requirements?
2. Name tag on bunk?
3. Sheets, bedding, and blankets clean and in serviceable condition?
4. Bunk in good repair, all parts present and double-deck bunks secured?

Check-List for Junior Troop Leaders

1. Does each unit leader in a company know each and every man by name?
2. Does each platoon leader or section leader keep a record with pertinent data on each of his men?
3. Is each subordinate leader thoroughly familiar with messing of troops, and do they visit troop mess halls frequently?
4. Do subordinate leaders know location and time of operation of all recreation and post exchange facilities available to the troops?
5. Are subordinates familiar with liberty transportation schedules?
6. Does each leader know how many men are enrolled in MCS/MCI correspondence courses and which; and what recent disenrollments and why?
7. Article 137, UCMJ, being fully complied with and carried out?
8. Do all of the NCOs know capabilities, use and characteristics of all weapons and equipment in their charge?
9. Do they keep a record of people absent from formations, where orders are promulgated or important information is put out? If a record is kept, are plans made to get this information to absentees as soon as possible?
10. Does each NCO have a personal interest in basic training of his troops? Does he keep a personal record of troop training other than the record kept by the companies?
11. Do the subordinates give personal attention to their troops and make themselves available to troops for instructions after hours when special instruction is needed?
12. Do subordinates comply with spirit of request-mast rights of troops and make it easy for a man to see his commanding officer without a lot of red tape?
13. Does each subordinate leader know how many troops he has, exactly where they are and what they are supposed to be doing?
14. Does each leader know what equipment or supplies his unit should have but is unserviceable or missing, and has he initiated action to remedy the situation?
15. Are all needs for repairs, supplies, or shortages of personnel covered in writing by appropriate work requests, requisitions, or personnel requests?

16. Are any men on mess duty in violation of current regulations?
17. Are all pertinent regulations and orders affecting troops repromulgated regularly to individuals just joining the command?
18. Are all men joining the organization properly indoctrinated by their NCOs in a planned program?
19. Are people in brig being paid health and comfort allowances; are hospital patients visited by their company officers regularly?
20. Are all hands aware of various benefits of a Marine Corps career?
21. Do troops have access to all pertinent regulations, chart instructions for marking clothes, and uniform regulations?
22. Do all troops and leaders know meaning of various security classifications?

Appendix 3

Brother Marines

The bonds of professional comradeship which knit most of the Marine Corps in existence today are unusually strong. As a member of the world's largest (though not oldest) Marine Corps, you should know of the distinguished bodies of Marines under other flags, with which our Corps has associations.

THE ROYAL MARINES.

I never knew an appeal to their courage or loyalty that they did not more than realize my expectations. If ever the hour of real danger should come to England, the Marines will be found the country's sheet-anchor.
—*Lord St. Vincent*

Britain's Royal Marines were 111 years old in 1775 when our own Corps was founded. From inception, the American corps was modeled after its British prototype, and many of the traditions of our Corps today can be traced to the Royal Marines.

As a result, despite early fallings-out (as in 1775, at Bunker Hill, and in 1814, when Royal Marines burned Washington after the Bladensburg fight), the camaraderie between U.S. and British Marines is a tradition of both Corps, and knowledge of the Royal Marines is part of every U.S. Marine's fund of information.

The Royal Marines perform much the same duties as U.S. Marines, with certain variations. They do not, for example, provide security personnel for naval stations, nor do they have a Fleet Marine Force although the Commando Brigade, Royal Marines, units of which are always embarked in "commando ships" (LPH), performs many similar functions. Royal Marines provide all bands for the British Navy, and the Corps has the combat mission of maintaining commando, or amphibious raiding, troops for the British armed forces. Although amphibious warfare is not a primary mission or

490

responsibility for the Royal Marines, but rather (in the United Kingdom) a joint, inter-service affair, the British Marines have, through tradition and background, always played a major role in England's long amphibious history.

The Royal Marines' badge, like our own, is the globe, though in this case the half shown is the eastern rather than the western hemisphere. Their right to wear "the Great Globe itself" as their emblem was conferred in 1827 by King George IV. Surrounding the globe is a laurel wreath, which was won in 1761, in recognition of the Royals' storming of Belle Isle. The motto of the Royal Marines is truly descriptive: *Per Mare, Per Terram* ("By Land and by Sea"). Like all Royal regiments, they are entitled to display the Lion and Crown as part of their Corps device and on their Colors.

The uniforms of the Royal Marines are much like our own. Aboard ship and on certain shore duties, they wear blues. Their ranks, rank insignia, and field and undress uniforms are those of the British Army, but the color of the service uniform is forest green. All Royal Marines wear a blue beret as one type of headgear, but members of commando units wear green berets, since green has always been the traditional commando color.

The official colors of the Corps are scarlet, yellow, green, and blue. These colors appear on the Royal Marines necktie, which is worn with civilian clothing by all members of the Corps, in the same way as our own Corps necktie.

The "Birth of the Corps Day," which corresponds to our November 10th, is 28 October of each year. The Royal Marines were organized in 1664.

The Sovereign, or a member of the royal family, is Captain-General of the Corps. At present this post is filled by the Duke of Edinburgh, husband of Queen Elizabeth.

The principal stations of the Royal Marine are the two major barracks (Eastney and Stonehouse) at Portsmouth and Plymouth; Commando School, Bickleigh; Infantry Training Center, Lympstone; Amphibious School, Poole; and a recruit depot and school of music at Deal.

Although U. S. and British Marines have served side by side on many occasions, both Corps particularly cherish associations stemming from the Boxer Uprising and from the Korean War. In the Boxer Uprising, U. S. and Royal Marines formed the backbone of the band of Western troops who defended the Legation Quarter in Peking throughout a long and bloody siege in 1900. In addition, in the International Brigade which finally relieved both Peking and Tientsin, U. S. and British Marines were formed side by side. Fifty years later, the 41 Commando, Royal Marines, was attached to the 1st Marine Division in Korea and served with the Division throughout the Chosin Reservoir campaign. And it was at Suez, in 1956, that the Royal Marines conducted the first carrier-based helicopter assault landing ever executed in combat.

ROYAL NETHERLANDS MARINES (KORPS MARINIERS). The *Korps Mariniers*—as the Dutch Marines are officially entitled—were founded on 10 December, 1665 in the Dutch Wars which caused the British to form the Royal Marines. One of the most important early operations of the Netherlands Marines was the amphibious raid up the Thames in 1666, one of the few occasions when foreign troops have landed in Great Britain since the Norman Conquest. Subsequently the *Korps Mariniers* performed normal sea duty and garrison duty throughout the Dutch empire. During World War II, when Holland was overrun by the Germans, several thousand Dutch Marines were trained at Camp Lejeune as the basis for reconstitution of the Corps, and the relationship between our two Corps has since been close. *Qua Patet Orbis* ("To the Ends of the World") is the Dutch Marines' motto; their uniforms, both service and dress, are similar to those of the Royal Marines and of our own Corps.

Today, the *Korps Mariniers* numbers about 4,000 officers and men, serving in ships' detachments, in colonial garrison duty, and at the Corps depot, Marine Barracks, Doorn. In addition to Doorn, the Dutch Marines have an amphibious training center at Texel and another marine barracks at Rotterdam, where Netherlands Marine Corps Headquarters is also located.

The basic tactical formation of the *Korps Marieniers* is the QPO Company (standing for the words in the Corps motto, *Qua Patet Orbis*). A QPO Company is a heavily reinforced rifle company with added crew-served weapons, an amphibious reconnaissance element, and headquarters and service personnel for independent operations. These units, which are stationed in Holland and abroad, comprise the force-in-readiness of the Netherlands Marines.

The ceremonial functions of the Corps are to provide the Netherlands Marine Band and to act as ceremonial troops for the Dutch government. Marines are the only Dutch troops authorized to have fifes and drums, and this music is the Marine trademark in Holland.

SPANISH MARINES (INFANTERIA DE MARINA ESPAÑOLA). Dating from the *Tercios de la Armada Naval* of Spanish Armada days and earlier, Spain's *Infanteria de Marina* can claim four centuries of service. Its men fought at Lepanto (1571), with the Armada in 1588, defended Cartagena (1741), took Sardinia in 1748, served gallantly in the Peninsular War, in Cuba, the Philippines, Guam, Morocco, Cochin China, and the Spanish Civil War.

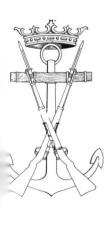

The missions of the Spanish Marines are to provide ships' detachments and garrison and defense forces for the naval districts and bases of Spain and to maintain a BLT-scale expeditionary landing force.

With a strength of approximately 8,000 officers and men, the *Infanteria de Marina* today, maintains *Tercios* (light infantry regiments) at El Ferrol, Cartagena, and Cadiz, together with separate battalions in Madrid and the Canary Islands. The Cadiz *Tercio* is part of the so-called "Special Group" including the Marine Corps School, school troops, and research and development activities. The major general commandant of the Corps, officially titled "Inspector General of the Marine Corps," has his headquarters at Madrid.

Spanish Marine officers uniforms are those of the Navy, with distinguishing badges; enlisted Marines wear dress blue similar to those of the Royal Marines, and combat/utility uniforms resembling those of our own Corps. The emblem of the *Infanteria de Marina* is an anchor (up-and-down) with crossed rifles, surmounted by the crown of Spain.

The Spanish Marines' motto is "Valiant on Land and Sea." Since 1701 the traditional colors of the Corps have been red and blue. As in the case of our own Corps, Horse Marines are both a tradition and a joke with the Spanish, dating from the fact that, during the 19th century guerrilla operations in Cuba, "Navy Cavalry" mounted units were formed of Marines.

ARGENTINE MARINE CORPS. The origin of the Argentine Marines goes back to 1807 when a naval battalion was organized to defend Buenos Aires against British attack. Subsequently, during Argentina's War of Independence, Marines served aboard warships and conducted landing operations. In 1879, a Marine artillery battalion was formed, to man coast defenses at Argentina's seaports and naval bases. In 1947, following World War II, the Corps was reorganized along modern amphibious lines, and a U.S. Marine advisor was provided.

The major operating units of the Argentine Marine Corps (which numbers about 8,000) are in the 1st and 2d Marine Forces. The former includes a cold-weather center garrisoned by a battalion in Patagonia, a riverine battalion on the River Plate delta, and another battalion at Rio Santiago naval base. The 2d Marine Force includes the Marine Brigade, an amphibious RLT, based at Puerto Belgrano.

The uniforms and ranks of the Corps are similar to those of our own. The annual birthday ceremonies are held on "Day of the Marine Corps," 19 November.

BRAZILIAN MARINE CORPS (CORPO DE FUSILEIROS NAVAIS). The *"Fusileiros"*, as the Marines are known throughout Brazil, date their lineage back to the Portuguese Marines, which were founded in 1797. Units of this organization first came to Brazil in 1808, and March 7, the date of their landing, is the birthday of the Corps in Brazil, which was then an overseas dominion of Portugal and subsequently separated amicably from the mother country.

Brazilian Marines fought in their country's wars throughout the 19th century, including major riverine operations along the River Paraguay. The most recent expeditionary service of the *Fusileiros* was as part of the Inter-American Peace Force, which kept order in the Dominican Republic for 15 months in 1965 and 1966, side by side with U.S. Marines during part of that time.

The Brazilian Marine Corps is divided into operating forces (which include a Fleet Marine Force and security forces and ships' detachments) and a supporting establishment which functions in the

same way as our own. The *Fusileiros'* headquarters and FMF (shaped around a divisional nucleus) are located at Rio de Janeiro.

COLOMBIAN MARINE CORPS. The first combat landing by Colombian Marines took place on 11 November 1811, less than a year after their organization during their country's War of Independence. Throughout the 19th century the Corps had its ups and downs, but was permanently constituted as amphibious and expeditionary troops in 1936. Ever since 1948, during Colombia's prolonged struggle to win over communist banditry, the Corps has been continually engaged in riverine, amphibious, and pacification duties. Like our own Corps, the Colombian Marines carry out operations in both the Atlantic and Pacific. With a strength of about 2,000 it includes one tactical battalion. Virtually all its officers today are graduates of Basic or Amphibious Warfare Schools at Quantico, and many of its NCOs are also graduates of U.S. schools.

VENEZUELAN MARINE CORPS (INFANTERIA DE MARINA VENEZOLANA). The Venezuelan Marine Corps was formed on 22 July 1822—as in the case of most of the other South American Marines—during their country's War of Independence. During the 19th century, however, it became inactive and was not officially reconstituted until 1938.

The missions of the Venezuelan Marines include amphibious operations, counterguerrilla and pacification duties, and naval base security. The Corps regularly conducts BLT-level landing exercises, and over a third of all its officers are graduates of Marine Corps Schools.

The Venezuelan Marine Corps is made up of three battalions, based at Puerto Cabella and Maiquetia, with headquarters at Caracas. All these units have been active in Venezuela's defense against Castro-communist guerrillas and seaborne infiltrations from Cuba.

REPUBLIC OF KOREA MARINE CORPS (ROKMC). The Korean Marine Corps, which has fought side by side with U.S. Marines in two wars—Korea and Vietnam—was founded on 15 April 1949, at Chinhae, destined to become the Quantico of Korea. Within less than two years, the 1st Korean Marine Regiment had become an integral part of the 1st U.S. Marine Division and played an outstanding part in the three years of hard fighting.

The primary mission of the ROKMC is to conduct amphibious landings as part of the national mobile striking force and to serve as a portion of the national force in readiness. In addition, like our Corps, they perform security duty for the naval shore establishment and are responsible for the development of amphibious warfare doctrine, tactics, techniques, and materiel.

In addition to maintaining a brigade in the main line of resistance at Kimpo and the renowned "Blue Dragon" brigade in Vietnam, the ROKMC has two Marine Corps Bases, Chinhae and Pohang. Marine garrisons or security units are found at Seoul, Paeng Yong Do, Cheju-Do, Pusan, Muk-Ho, Inchon, and Mok Po.

The uniforms of the ROKMC are similar to those of the U.S.

Marine Corps. The official color of the Korean Marine Corps is scarlet. The creed of the Corps, which serves as its motto, is as follows:

Loyal to the nation
Be ever victorious
Unite as a family
Honor is worth more than life
Love your fellow countrymen.

CHINESE MARINE CORPS. The Marine Corps of the Republic of China—at the time of writing, the second largest Corps of Marines in the free world—dates from 1917. It has a combat record extending throughout China's anti-Japanese war up to the defense and resupply of the Kinmen Islands in 1958, for which units of the Chinese Marine Corps were awarded the Banner of Honor.

The missions of the Corps closely resemble those of our own Corps, and are threefold:

1. To provide a Fleet Marine Force for the conduct of amphibious landing operations.
2. To provide security forces for naval shore bases.
3. To develop doctrine, tactics, technique, and equipment for amphibious operations.

Chinese Marine Corps Headquarters, FMF Headquarters, Schools, Reserve Training Center, and a Marine brigade are grouped at Tsoying on Taiwan. The 1st Chinese Marine Division and the Recruit Depot are located in the vicinity of Fang-Shan.

The colors of the Chinese Marines are scarlet and gold. The Corps has a Chinese motto which is translated *Semper Fidelis.*

VIETNAMESE MARINE CORPS. The Republic of Vietnam Marine Corps dates from 1 October 1954, but, in the best tradition of Marines everywhere, has seen combat in every year since its founding. Originally formed as a so-called Marine Group for riverine operations, with no units above company level, it now is grouped around a strong Marine brigade.

The mission of the Vietnamese Marine Corps is to conduct amphibious operations and to be prepared to take part in ground operations as directed. It is part of the national General Reserve.

The motto of the Corps is "Honor and Country." The Corps colors are scarlet (symbolizing fighting spirit); yellow (symbolizing the tradition that the Vietnamese people are descended from dragons); and green (the symbolic color of brave death).

Brigade headquarters and headquarters of the Corps are located in Saigon. The Vietnamese Marine Training Center is at Gia Dinh, and the tactical units of the brigade are deployed in the field.

ROYAL THAI MARINE CORPS. The Royal Thai Marine Corps was founded in 1932. Its missions are amphibious operations, naval base security, counterinsurgency, and support, when required, of the Thai

Army. Because it is part of the Navy, the Corps uses naval rank and rating titles.

The principal operating unit of the Thai Marines is the Marine brigade, composed of three rifle battalions, an artillery battalion, and supporting headquarters and service units.

Sattahip, on the Gulf of Thailand, is the main base of the Thai Marines, but Chantaburi, near the Cambodian frontier is the secondary base. In addition to being headquarters for the Corps, Bangkok is also the home station for a Marine garrison.

Appendix 4

Marine Veterans' Associations

ORGANIZATION
First Marine Division Association
Capt E. C. Clarke,
Executive Secretary,
PO Box 84, Alexandria,
Virginia, 22313.

Second Marine Division Association
Mr. John R. Hruska, Jr.,
President,
7505 Halleck Street, S.E.
Washington, D.C., 20028

Third Marine Division Association
LtCol C. L. Jenson,
Executive Secretary,
PO Box 7154,
San Diego, California, 92107

Fourth Marine Division Association
Mr. D. E. Sullivan,
President,
36 Campbell Street,
Waldwick, New Jersey, 07436

Fifth Marine Division Association
Mr. Joseph J. Roma,
President,
1328 West 6th Street,
Brooklyn, N.Y., 11204

First Marine Aviation Force Veterans Association
LtGen Karl S. Day,
Commander,
25 Summit Avenue,
East Williston, N.Y., 11596

Edson's Raiders
Mr. Francis C. Pettus,
Executive Secretary,
PO Box 980,
Washington, D.C., 20044

Marine Corps Combat
Correspondents Association
Secretary and Librarian,
663 Fifth Avenue,
New York City, 10022.

Marine Corps Newsmen's
Association
LtCol Clement J. Stadtler,
6087 Sunset Boulevard,
Los Angeles, California,

Montford Point Marine Association
Mr. Arthur F. Earley,
President,
1501 Chestnut Street, Suite 300,
Philadelphia, Pennsylvania, 19102

Marine Corps League
Mr. Claude H. Downing,
National Commandant,
939 North Kenmore Street,
Arlington, Virginia, 22201.

Women Marines Association
Mrs. Helen Moore,
President,
PO Box 206,
Rushville, Indiana, 46173

498

Appendix 5
Simple Exhibition Drills

This appendix gives several well-tested, reasonably simple exhibition-drill sequences, manuals, movements, and formations, based on compilations by First Sergeant E. P. Bond, Jr. All these can be worked up and performed by experienced Marines on fairly short notice. Do not regard what is given here as limiting. There is ample room in these evolutions for added features suggested by your own or your men's imagination and inventiveness.

THE FACING MOVEMENTS

The facing movements are in slightly more detail than the normal movements, to add to the color of the move by exaggeration of what would hardly be noticed otherwise . . . The position of *trail arms*. In this *new* position the right arm is held out straight and the rifle is inclined so that the rifle is at an angle of thirty degrees with the heel of the butt pointed just to the right of the right toe.

The movement of *right face* is executed in the following manner: in four counts:

1. Bring the piece to the above mentioned *trail arms*.
2. Turn to the right in the normal manner, keeping the rifle at this exaggerated position.
3. The left heel is brought up beside the right with distinct audible movement.
4. The rifle is brought back to the order.

Left face is executed in the same fashion except to the other direction.

Movements are executed from positions other than the order in two counts.

About face is the same as right and left faces if the rifle is at the order.

The famed Silent Drill Platoon from historic Marine Barracks, Washington, D.C., performs its ten-minute drill sequence without verbal commands.

SEVENTEEN COUNT MANUAL

The command is given while at the position of *order arms.* At the command 1. SEVENTEEN COUNT MANUAL 2. MOVE, bring the rifle to the position of *port arms,* tap the rifle with the right hand at the small of the stock and execute the *Cossack Spin,* (see below), go to the position of *right shoulder,* return to *port,* tap the rifle and execute another Cossack spin, then to *left shoulder,* back to *port,* another Cossack spin and a repeat. Then to *order arms.* Then assume the position of *parade rest* and come back to attention and the movement is complete.

TWENTY-THREE COUNT MANUAL

The "twenty-three count manual" is *a marching manual.* Although it no longer has the original twenty-three counts, the name is the same. The manual starts at *right shoulder arms* and proceeds as follows: *Right shoulder* to *port,* tap and *cossack spin, left shoulder arms, left shoulder* to *port arms,* tap and *cossack spin, carry arms,* tap sling twice—left leg twice—sling twice again, *port arms,* tap and spin, left shoulder, *port arms,* tap and *cossack spin,* then to the position of *right shoulder* completing the movement.

When the movement is completed, the march is continued; remember that it is executed on the march at the cadence of 120 steps per minute.

THE COSSACK SPIN

With the rifle at *port arms,* left hand grasping the piece, the right hand PALM UP, grasp the weapon just behind the trigger housing. Then the piece is swung sharply, counter-clockwise, back to its original position, and the right hand returns from the inverted position to the small of the stock. The final position is *port arms.*

1. RIGHT SHOULDER 2. ARMS: You are at *order arms*. On the first count, kick the inside part of the rifle butt, so as to make it swing back approximately 30 degrees. Then, using your wrist along with the momentum of the swinging rifle, bring the piece forward. In bringing it forward, thrust your right forearm and palm outward. In doing this, the piece should be turned over. Therefore, when grasping it with your left hand, your hand should grasp the piece under the rear part of the bolt, directly behind the trigger guard. At this point, the piece, with your left hand holding it, should be parallel to the deck. A count of three should have elapsed. From this position, let go of the rifle with your right hand, thus allowing it to swing forward. As it is swinging forward, grasp the butt plate with your right hand and, using the momentum and strength of your right hand, allow the piece to fall in the correct position on your right shoulder. Your left hand is still grasping the underside of the butt. A count of five should have elapsed in getting the rifle to this position. Finally, to complete the movement, smartly cut your left hand away to your side. This movement requires a total of six counts.

1. LEFT SHOULDER 2. ARMS: You are at *order arms*. With your right foot, shove the piece about 30 degrees to the right. As it starts to fall back, using your right wrist and the piece's momentum, swing it up. Now, in swinging it up, allow your right hand to turn so as to have the palm facing up. In doing this, the swing brings the piece up in front of you with the bolt handle facing outward away from you. As the piece swings up in front of you, grab it with your left hand. Now, it is important to grasp it palm up and on the bolt. In grasping it in this fashion, a count of three should have elapsed. Then, let go of the rifle with your right hand and slap it in the same area. The piece will then swing off your left hand. The momentum created by hitting it will carry it (that is, the butt of the rifle) across to the right side. As it approaches your right side, with your right hand placed palm up, grab the piece right behind the trigger guard; your thumb is extended across the hollowed part of the butt. Simultaneously, as you grab the piece with the right hand, take your left hand (palm up) and grasp the piece at the balance so as to balance it. Then, letting go of the piece with your left hand, allow it to fall. Using both your right wrist and the momentum of the rifle, allow it to make a complete spin, returning to the same position as when you let it go. As it again arrives to that position, grab it again in the same place with your left hand (on the balance). Now, in allowing it to spin around, your right hand will be twisted outward from your right side. *It is important not to let go of the piece until it is secured by your left hand.* Once it is secured, take your right hand and grab the butt behind the bolt (in the hollowed part of the butt). Then from this position, with your right hand, place the piece on your left shoulder, allowing your left hand to fall off, and grasp the butt plate of the piece as it arrives on your left shoulder. Finally,

cut your right hand away smartly to your side. There are nine counts to this movement.

    1. PORT 2. ARMS: This movement is very similar to *left shoulder arms* in procedure. In referring to the *left shoulder arms* movement, note that at the point when you place your right hand in the hollowed part of the butt, after having spun the rifle around, you are now at *port arms*. The rifle should be at 45 degrees with the vertical and approximately four inches from your body. This movement, therefore, is nothing more than the *left shoulder arms* movement minus the actual placing of the piece on the left shoulder. Consequently, there are two less counts to this maneuver, a total of seven.

CLOSE-MARCH

1. On the command of execution the platoon halts.
2. While the first squad stands fast, the second, third, and fourth squads take one right or left step *toward* the first squad.
3. The second squad halts; the third and fourth squads take another step toward the first squad.
4. The third squad halts, and the fourth squad takes another side step toward the first squad, and comes to a halt.
5. The entire platoon then continues to march.

    Each rank at this time should be marching shoulder to shoulder at right shoulder arms. The distance from front to rear should be the same as when marching at regular interval.

EXTEND-MARCH

1. On the command of execution the platoon halts.
2. The first squad again stands fast while the second, third, and fourth squads take the same number of side steps as described above *away* from the first squad.
3. When the fourth squad has completed its side steps, the platoon continues to march.

PINWHEEL-MARCH

1. This movement is performed *only* at *close march*. For the first turn the man on the right is the pivot man, and the entire rank does a 90-degree right turn in eight counts.
2. The next two counts are mark-time steps.
3. The pivot then shifts to the left man, and the entire rank does a 90-degree left turn in eight counts.
4. The next two counts are mark-time steps.
5. The pivot then shifts back to the right man, and the entire rank does a 180-degree right turn in 16 counts.
6. The next two counts are mark-time steps.
7. The pivot again shifts to the left man, and the entire rank does a 180-degree left turn in 16 counts.

502

8. The next two counts are mark-time steps.

9. The entire platoon steps out.

COUNTER-RIGHT STEP

When four squads are marching in column formation and the command 1. COUNTER RIGHT STEP 2. MARCH is given, the four squad leaders immediately execute a right flank and come to a halt. Immediately on the next count, they begin the movement of *right step*. Each rank does exactly the same when it comes to the pivot point of the respective squad leaders. Finally all squads will be executing *right step*. When the command 1. FORWARD 2. MARCH is given as the right foot hits the deck, every man comes to a halt. On the next count, each man executes a right face, comes to a halt, and ten steps off with his left foot.

Fig. E-1: Counter-March.

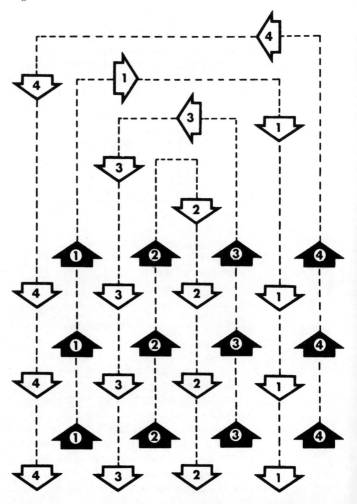

When the squads are marching in column formation and the command 1. COUNTER 2. MARCH is given, the second squad leader immediately executes two right flanks, takes one full step and begins to half-step. Each member of the second squad then follows him, pivoting at the same points of the squad leader. The third squad leader takes one extra step and then executes two left flanks. Each member of the third squad follows him and also pivots in the pivot points of the squad leader. The third squad leader then marches until he is abreast of the second squad leader. Each member should then be abreast of his rank members. The fourth squad leader takes two extra steps, executes a left flank, takes two steps, and executes a left flank. The fourth squad members follow him and also pivot in his same pivot spots. The fourth squad goes outside the third and first squads. The first squad leader leads his squad right in between the fourth and third squad using oblique right flanks until he is marching in the direction of the other squads. It is very important that the first squad members pivot in their squad leaders pivot points. The leaders must wait until they are all abreast of their respective ranks before they step out and march at the correct distance. The member of each rank should also be abreast when they step out.

PLAN "T"

The entire platoon halts on the command 2. MARCH. The first squad then exercises the following movements: *left face,* one step forward, *right face.* Simultaneously the fourth squad executes the following movements: *right face,* one step forward, *left face.*

The entire platoon takes one step forward.

The first squad now executes these movements: *Right face,* one step forward and *left face.* Simultaneously the fourth squad executes

Fig. E-2: Plan "T": Phase One.

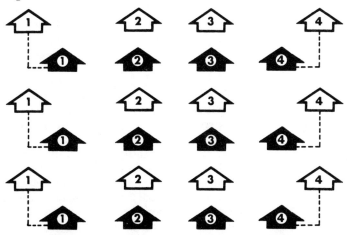

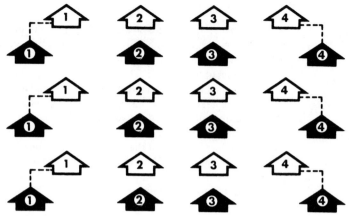

Fig. E-3: Plan "T": Phase Two.

right face, one step forward, and *right face.*

The entire platoon then steps off into the original direction.

During the entire manuever the second and third squads are stationary except for the one step forward that the entire platoon takes.

There are no counts between the individual movements.

PLAN "T–C"

Plan "T–C" is an exibition drill evolution requiring 20 counts for its completion.

With the platoon marching in a column of files, the command 1. PLAN "T–C" 2. MARCH is given. The entire platoon will come to an immediate halt in the usual two-count manner, and will begin to execute the evolution in the following manner.

The men of the first and fourth squads in the first rank, third rank, and fifth rank execute four distinct steps in an outboard direction from the platoon.

At the same time the second and fourth ranks of these squads execute four distinct steps in an outboard direction from the platoon and then two steps inboard, returning to their original position.

While the first and fourth squads are executing the above movements, the second and third squads execute the following: the first, third, and fifth ranks of the second squad and the second and fourth ranks of the third squad, execute four right-faces. The first, third, and fifth ranks of the third squad and the second and fourth ranks of the second squad execute four left-faces.

Next the entire platoon takes one step forward.

The process is then reversed. The men in the second and third squads who faced right, now face left. Those who previously faced left, now face right. The men who took four steps outboard from the platoon now take four steps inboard. The remaining men now take two steps outboard and inboard exactly as they did before.

The platoon now resumes the march.

505   During the entire manuever the first and fourth squads remain faced in the direction in which they were halted.

All men move simultaneously.

The entire movement is executed without delay after halting or before resuming the march.

Fig. E-4: Plan "T-C": Phase One.

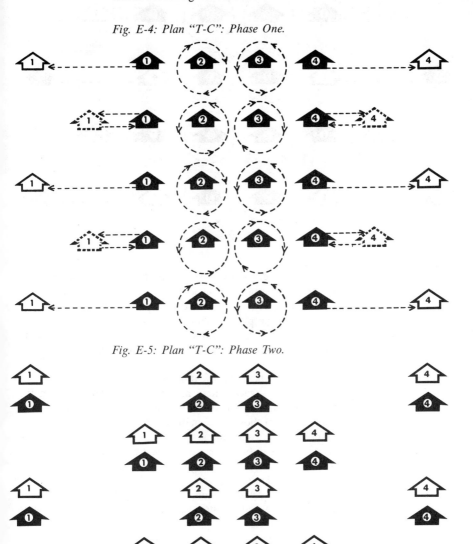

Fig. E-5: Plan "T-C": Phase Two.

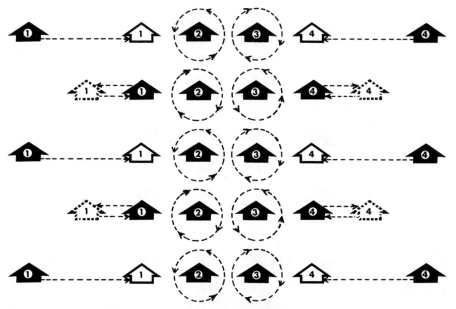

Fig. E-6: Plan "T-C": Phase Three.

The following diagrams illustrate the individual movements.
First phase: The platoon opens ranks.
Second phase: The platoon takes one pace forward.
Third phase: The platoon closes ranks.
Remember that the first and fourth squads execute the same movements EXCEPT that the directions will be OPPOSITES.

RIGHT (LEFT) FLANK, PLATOON HALT

As the names suggest, these movements are derived from the common right and left flanks in marching and have been altered only slightly from those basic marching movements.

The preparatory command is given on the foot in which direction the movement is to be made, i.e., to the right flank, the command of execution is given on the right foot; and to the left flank, the command of execution is given on the left foot.

On the command of execution, HALT, the foot not in the direction of the turn is advanced one step. From this position execute a facing movement, resulting in the pivot foot being at 90 degrees to the original front. Do not advance the pivot foot from this position, rather bring the other foot smartly to the side of the advanced foot.

This movement leaves you facing in a direction 90 degrees from the original line of march, at a halt, and at attention.

LEAP FROG

On the command 1. LEAP FROG 2. MARCH, the platoon comes

to a full halt. Without delay the even ranks take one side-step right coming to a halt, then take three forward steps (Left-right-left) coming to a complete halt, then taking one side step left back into position. The odd ranks now repeat this movement, when they reach position the entire platoon steps out.

RANKS TO THE REAR

Ranks to the rear is a movement designed to obtain an extended distance between ranks and to re-form at the normal distance. This is accomplished through a succession of *to-the-rear marches* executed by each rank independently. The initial extended distance is obtained by each rank, beginning with the rear rank, delaying four counts in the execution of *to-the-rear, march.*

On the command of execution, MARCH, the last rank executes the movement immediately. The next to the last rank delays four counts and executes the movement on the fifth count after the command. The next rank executes the movement on the ninth count, the next on the thirteenth, etc.; each rank delays four counts from the preceding rank executing the movement.

Immediately upon completion of their first *to-the-rear,* each rank takes two steps and executes another *to-the-rear* on the third count. This is repeated two more times until an overall total of four *to-the-rears* have been completed. The platoon will then be in a normal marching arrangement and be marching to the original direction.

IN PROGRESSION-HALT

This command is given on the march and is a combination of movements. It includes a *halt,* the proper faces, a rifle manual involving an exchange of arms, and a *forward march.*

On the command of execution 2. HALT, the ranks counting from the rear rank halt on even counts— the rear rank halts in the normal manner; the next rank halts in four; the next on six; etc. As each rank halts, it independently performs the following movements:

1. Delay.
2. Bring the rifle off the right shoulder, catching it with the left hand at the balance.
3. Tap the piece at the small of the stock with the right hand.
4. Grasp the rifle at the small of the stock with the right hand, palm up.
5. Spin the piece counterclockwise, letting go with the left hand.
6. Re-grasp the piece with the left hand at the balance.
7. Grasp the piece above the upper sling-swivel with the right hand.
8. Place the rifle in the position of *trail arms* bracing it just below the stacking swivel.
9. Cut away the left hand smartly while simultaneously placing the piece in the position of *order arms.*

10. Come to the position of an exaggerated *trail arms.*
11. If in first or third squads, perform first count of *right face;* if in second or fourth squads, perform the first count of *left face.*
12. Perform the second count of the facing movement.
13. Bring the rifle back to the position of *order arms.*
14. Move the rifle diagonally across the body grasping it at the balance with the left hand.
15. Tap the piece at the small of the stock.
16. Cossack spin (See above).
17. Re-grasp the piece at the balance with the left hand.
18. With the right hand grasp the heel of the butt.
19. Place the rifle on the right shoulder bracing it with the left hand at the small of the stock.
20. Cut away the left hand, slapping the left hand away audibly.
21. Bring the rifle off the right shoulder catching it at the balance with the left hand.
22. Tap.
23. Cossack Spin (See above).
24. Re-grasp.
25. With the right hand grasp the rifle at the small of the stock.
26. Place the piece on the left shoulder, grasping the heel of the butt with the left hand.
27. Cut away the right hand audibly, striking the right side.
28. With the right hand grasp the small of the stock.
29. Take the rifle off the left shoulder and catch it with the left hand at the balance.
30. Tap.
31. Cossack spin (See above).
32. Re-grasp.
33. Move the right hand to the small of the stock, palm down.
34. Let go of the rifle with the left hand, holding it perpendicular to the deck, sling toward the person standing across from you at arms length. Simultaneously, with the left hand, grasp the piece of the other individual at the balance.
35. Let go of your piece and move the piece of the other man to the normal *port arms* position.
36. Tap.
37. Cossack spin (See above).
38. Re-grasp.
39. Move right hand to small of stock, palm down.
40. Put the piece on the left shoulder.
41. Cut away right hand, slapping the right side.
42. Move right hand to small of stock.
43. Take rifle off left shoulder and grasp at the balance with the left hand.
44. Tap.
45. Cossack spin (See above).
46. Re-grasp.

509

47. Move right hand to the heel of the butt
48. Place on right shoulder, bracing with left hand at small of stock.
49. Cut away left hand and audibly slap the left side.
50. Move the rifle off right shoulder and grasp at balance with left hand.
51. Tap.
52. Cossack spin (See above).
53. Re-grasp.
54. With right hand, grasp rifle above upper sling-swivel.
55. Move the piece to *trail arms* bracing it with left hand.
56. Move rifle to *order arms,* cutting away left hand to left side.
57. Throw rifle to the left side of the opposite man to enable him to catch it at the balance about chest-high. Simultaneously, catch at the balance with your left hand, the piece which the other man is tossing to you.
58. Bring rifle to position of *port arms.*
59. Tap.
60. Cossack spin (See above).
61. Re-grasp.
62. Grasp small of stock with right hand.
63. Place rifle on left shoulder.
64. Cut away right hand and slap right side audibly.
65. Grasp rifle at small of the stock with the right hand.
66. Take the rifle off the left shoulder, holding it at the balance with the left hand.
67. Tap.
68. Cossack spin (See above).
69. Re-grasp.
70. Place right hand on heel of butt.
71. Put piece on right shoulder, bracing it with left hand at small of the stock.
72. Cut away left hand and audibly slap left side
73. Bring rifle off right shoulder, catching it at the balance with left hand.
74. Tap.
75. Cossack spin (See above).
76. Re-grasp.
77. Grasp the rifle above the upper sling-swivel with the right hand.
78. Move rifle to *trail arms,* bracing it with the left hand just below the stacking swivel.
79. Place the rifle in *order arms* position, cutting away the left hand.
80. Execute *trail arms.*
81. First and third squads execute first count of *left face;* second and fourth squads execute the first count of *right face.*
82. Complete the facing movement.
83. Bring rifle back to *order arms.*
84. Move the rifle diagonally across the body and grasp rifle at the balance with the left hand.

85. Tap.

86. Cossack spin (See above).

87. Re-grasp.

88. Place the right hand on heel of butt.

89. Put piece on right shoulder, bracing it with the left hand at the small of the stock.

90. Cut the left hand away and slap the side audibly.

91. Step out with the left foot and continue marching.

"O'GRADY SEZ" COMPETITION

When it is desired to hold a competitive drill to test the alertness and reactions of individual Marines, an "O'Grady Sez . . ." drill provides considerable amusement for spectators and participants.

The commands, movements, and manual of close-order drill under arms are used by the officer or NCO conducting the competition, *but no command is to be obeyed unless prefaced with the preliminary command,* **1. O'Grady Sez . . .**

When any command is given *without* the prefatory "O'Grady Sez", all hands stand fast. Any Marine who moves or flinches in any way toward execution of a command *not* prefaced by "O'Grady Sez", must come to *port arms* and fall out.

The winner of the contest is the last Marine remaining in ranks.

DRILL-TEAM POINTERS

Members of drill teams should be individually selected by the team commander. They should be Marines of good appearance, high motivation, team spirit, and excellent discipline. Physically, they should correspond in height and in build as much as possible.

Since exhibition drills involve many additions to, or deviations from, normal close-order drill, the team commander's word must be law and his decisions final.

Eight hours' drill a week is the minimum time required to keep a team up to the mark.

Each team should (and will) develop its own style of marching and performing evolutions. Marching with clenched fists, for example, and perceptible pauses when executing flank and to-the-rear marchings, convey such a style.

Index

Academic reports. *See* Fitness reports
Access to record, 187
Accrued leave, 208
Actions against the Creeks and Seminoles, 69
Active duty, 172
    for training, 172
Address, 304-308
Address while on leave, 209
Administrative duty, 172
Advance, travel, 226
Advance leave, 208
Advance pay, 215
Advanced Base
    Force, 74
    School, 74
Adverse marginal reports. *See* Fitness reports
Air Force, Department of the, 16–17
    mission, 16
    Secretary, 16
    structure, 16–17
    women in, 17
Albany, Ga. (MCSC), 57, 149–150
Allotments, 232–233, 444
    and taxes, 232–234
Allowances
    clothing, 215–216
    Cost-of-Living (COLA), 216
    dependents, 213
    dislocation, 230
    Family Separation (FSA), 216–217
    Interim Housing (IHA), 216

Allowances (*cont.*)
 overseas, 216
 per diem, 225
 quarters, 214
 Station Housing (HOLA), 216
 Temporary Lodging (TLA), 216
 trailer, 230
Amphibious Development, Quantico, 79
Amphibious pioneering, 78–80
 East Coast Expeditionary Force, 79
 Equipment Board, 79
 Landing Operations Doctrine (FTP-167), 79
 Tentative Landing Operations Manual, 79
Amphibious Warfare School, 54
Annual leave, 208
Annual training duty, 172
Appointment, certificate of, 6–7
Appointments, temporary, for WMs, 196
Appropriate duty, 171
Appurtenances of flags and streamers, 106
Armed Forces Institute (USAFI), 242
Army, Department of the, 13–16
 mission, 13
 National Guard, 15–16
 Secretary, 13
 special branches, 15
 structure, 13–16
 women in, 16
Atomic Energy Commission (AEC), 8
Automated Service Center, Marine Corps, 166
Aviation, Marine Corps, 58–60
 aircraft, Fleet Marine Forces, 60
 Air-Ground team, 58
 Aviation Supporting Establishment, 60
 Cunningham, Major A. A., 77
 Defense of Wake Island, 58
 Deputy Chief of Staff (Air), 59
 first enlisted pilot, 77
 founding of, 77
 organization, 59
 primary function, 59
 Wing organization, 51
 See also Marine Air-Ground Task Force
Awards, 91–112

Band, Marine, 98–100
Bandsmen, Marine, promotion of, 197
Bars to promotion, 197
Barstow, California (MCSC), 57, 151-153
Basic School, Quantico, 54

Battle color of the Marine Corps, 107–108
Beaufort, S.C. (MCAS), 57–149
Benefits
 retired, 460–464
 survivor, 456–459
Birthday of the Corps, 96, 465–466
Blazers, Marine Corps, 128
Blues, 132
Bonus
 reenlistment, 218–219
 variable, 219
Boot Camp. *See* Marine Corps Recruit Depots
Boxer Rebellion, 72–73
Bureau of Medicine and Surgery (BuMed), 22
Bureau of the Budget, 8
Bureau of Naval Personnel (BuPers), 22
Burial, death and, 451–454
Burrows, Major William W., 65
Bus travel, 228

Camp Elmore, Va. (MCB), 57, 145
Camp Garcia, Vieques, Puerto Rico, 57
Camp Lejeune, N.C. (MCB), 57, 146–147
Camp Pendleton, Calif (MCB), 57, 153–156
Camp Smedley D. Butler, Okinawa, 57, 157–158
Campaign medals, 539
Canton Bell, 98
Career, 235–260
 assignment, 237
 balanced experience, 235
 correspondence courses, 239–242
 formal schools, 239
 hints on studying, 242–243
 independent duty and special programs, 238–239
 Military Occupational Specialty (MOS), 236–237
 pointers for professionals, 258–260
 preference for duty, 238–239
 professional reading, 244
 public relations, 258
 schooling and study, 239–244
 sea and foreign shore duty, combat duty, and FMF overseas, 237–238
 tuition assistance and instructor-hire program, 242
Carmick, Major Daniel, 67
Casualty procedures, 459

513   Categories of reserve, training and instruction, 171–172
Central Intelligence Agency (CIA), 8
Ceremonial Evening Parade. *See* Evening Parade
Ceremonies, 335–345
    escort of the color, 337
    guard mounting, 338
    honors, 331–335
    honors pointers, 332–335
    morning and evening colors, 330-331
    parade, 336
    pointers, 342–345
    pointers for color guard, 341–342
    precedence, 339–340
    rendering honors, 331–332
    review, 335–336
    traditional elements and terms in a Marine Corps parade, 338–339
Certificate of Appointment, 6–7
Charge of quarters, 300–301
Cherry Point, N.C. (MCAS), 57, 145–146
Chinese Communist forces, 86
Chosin Reservoir, 86
Christenings, 473
Chulai, 90
Citations, 108–110
Civil War, 71
Class "E" message. *See* Personal radio traffic
Classified matter, security of, 206–207
Cleanliness and upkeep, shipboard, 389–390
Clothing allowances, 215–216
Clubs and messes, 474–476
Coast Guard, 30–32
    Commandant, 21
Collar emblems, 98
Color guard, 341–342
Colors, flags, and standards, 104–108
    displaying, 327–329
    escort of the, 337
    garrison flag, 105
    guidons, 105
    Marine Corps, 94–95, 105
    miscellaneous flags, 106
    National Color or Standard, 104
    National Ensign, 104
    personal flags, 106
    post flags, 105
    preventing capture, 104
    storm flag, 105
    "the flag is a jealous mistress," 104

types of flags, 104
    See also Ceremonies *and* Military Courtesy and Ceremonies
Commandant (CMC), 20–21
    appointment of, 43
    principle duties, 43
Commandant's license plate, 100
Commander of the Guard, duties of, 297–298
Commands, specified, 12–13
Commissary, 138–139
    privileges for Reserve, 175
Commuted rations. *See* Subsistence
Composite scores, 192–193
Concurrent reports. *See* Fitness reports
Conduct in action, 103
Correspondence courses, 239–242
Correspondence and messages, 202–205
    official, 202
    personal, 204–205
Cost-of-living allowance (COLA), 216
Courtesy, 383–388. *See also* Military courtesy and ceremonies
Courts-martial, 353–358. *See also* Military law
Cuban Crisis, 88
Cunningham, Major A. A., 77
Customs
    social life, 476–477
    traditions and, Marine Corps, 93–104
Cutting and composite scores, 192–193

Danang, 90
Dances, 473–474
Dead horse. *See* Advance pay
Death and burial, 451–454
Decorations and medals, 91–112, 108
    initiating an award, 110–111
    reserve, 175
    unit, 109
    wearing, 111–112
Defense, Department of, 10–13
    boards, committees, offices, 10–11
    Defense Supply Agency (DSA), 56
    Joint Chiefs of Staff, 11–12
    National Security Act, 10–11
    Office of the Secretary, 11
    other agencies, 12
    unified and specified commands, 12–13
Defense Establishment, 8–32
Department of Air Force. *See* Air Force, Department of

514

Department of the Army. *See* Army, Department of

Department of the Navy. *See* Navy, Department of

Dependents for allowances, defined, 213

Dependents' identification and privilege cards, 138, 211

Dependents' medical care, 136–138

Detachment, Marine, 379–380

Discharges,
 bad conduct, 200
 dishonorable, 200
 general, 199
 honorable, 199
 reasons for, 200
 release from active duty, 199
 separations, 199
 undesirable discharge, 199

Dislocation allowance, 230

Distinguished unit emblem (Army-Air Force), 110

Divine services, at, 103

Diving pay, 215

Division of reserve, 165

Dog tags. *See* Identification tags

Drill Instructor School, 54–55

Drills, regular, 171

Duty
 annual training, 172
 appropriate, 171
 preference for, 238–239
 ROTC, 172–173
 sea, foreign shore, and combat, 237–238

Early Years, 65
 assault of the fortress of Derna, Tripoli, 66
 First Lieutenant Presley N. O'Bannon, 66
 Major William W. Burrows, 65
 SgtMaj Archibald Summers (1st Sgt-Maj), 65
 re-creation of the Corps, 65

Earned leave, 208

Educational facilities, 140

Eighth and Eye (MB), 57, 141–142

El Toro (Santa Ana), Calif (MCAS), 57, 156

Embassy Guard Duty, 425–432
 duties and routine, 430–432
 functions and organization, 427–429
 history, 425–427
 NCOIC, 430
 selection and training, 429
 ten commandants, 431–432
 tours, 428–429

Emblems, collar, 98

Emergency leave, 208

Employment, off-duty, 210–211

Enlisted promotion system, 190–192

Equivalent instruction or duty, 171

Esprit de corps, 36

Estates, 433–445

Etiquette, 308–310, 383–388

Evening parade, 100

Excess leave, 208

Exchanges, Marine Corps, 139–140
 privileges for Reserve, 175

Expeditionary Force, East Coast, 79

Expeditions between wars, 77
 Marines in Nicaragua, 77–78

Expenses, reimbursable, 225

Explosion in Santo Domingo, 88

Extension School (MCDEC, Quantico), 240–241

Extensions, 198

Fair rental, 214

Family Separation Allowance (FSA), 216–217
 FSA-1, 217
 FSA-2, 217

Field, life in the, 359–370
 break camp, 368
 care of field gear, 369
 cold-weather hints, 367–368
 feeding, 364–366
 hints for tropical service, 366–367
 individual hygiene, 363
 living under canvas, 361–363
 make camp, 359–361
 sanitation, 363–364
 useful articles, 369–370

File, personal, 187

First on foot and right of the line, 96

First to fight, 97

Fitness reports, 188–191

Flags, 91–112. *See also* Colors, flags, and standards
 appurtenances of, 106

Fleet Marine Corps Reserve, 167. *See also* Reserve
 transfer into, 200–201

Fleet Marine Forces (FMF), 47–49
 overseas, 237

Foreign duty pay, 216

515

Foreign leave, 209
Fortitudine, 95
French Fourragère, 109
Funerals. *See* Military funerals

Gamble, Captain John M., 66
Garrison flag, 105
Geneva Convention Card, 211
Gillespie, Archibald, 1stLt, 69
Globe and Anchor, history of, 93–94
Glossary for seagoing Marines, 393–424
Good manners, 477–479
Green, 1stLt Israel, 71
Grog, issue of, 100
Guadalcanal, 80–81
Guard, interior, 290–295
Guard duty aboard ship, 383
Guard mounting, 338
Guarding the mails, 78
Guidons, 105

Haiti, Marines off, 88
Halls of Montezumas, 69
Hawaiian area, 156–157
Hazard and incentive pay, 214–215
Headgear, 98
Headquarters (HIMC), 43
Health record. *See* Staff returns
Henderson, Colonel, rescues the Corps, 68
Henderson Hall, 57
Hints for
    cold weather, 367–368
    I&I NCOs, 170
    Military Police and Shore Patrol, 302
    tropical service, 366–367
    official letter writers, 203
History of the Reserve, 160–164
History of the uniform, 113
Honors, rendering, 331–332. *See* Ceremonies
Hostile-fire pay, 215
Household goods
    checkoff list, 231–232
    prohibited articles, 230
    shipment, 229
    storage, 229–230
    transit insurance, 230–231
    transportation of, 228–232
    weight allowance, 229
Housekeeping, pointers on, 388–389
How to express time in writing, 203
Hymn, Marines', 95–96

Identification card, 211
Iceland, occupation of, 80
Identification tags, 211
Imjin River, 87
Inchon landing, 86
Income tax, 233
Individual administration, 186–211
Inspector General, 46
Inspector Instructor (I & I), 169–170
Inspector Instructor staff, noncommissioned, 170
Institute, Marine Corps (MCI), 241–242
Instruct, how to, 245–253
    applicatory instruction, 248–249
    delivery of instruction, 251
    how to build a sand table, 250–251
    learning process, 245–246
    lesson plan, 246–248
    preparations for instructing, 246
    things to avoid, 252
    tips for instructors, 252–253
    training aids, 249
Instructor-hire program, 242
Insurance, 434–441
Interim Housing Allowance, (IHA), 216
Interior Guard, 290–295
    daily routine, 294–295
    duties, 291–294
Inventory Control Point (ICP), 55
Investments, 443
Iwakuni, Japan (MCAS), 57, 157–158

Joint Chiefs of Staff, 11–12
Judge Advocate General (JAG), office of, 22
Junior NCO Ranks, 92–93
    grade of Cpl, 92–93
    grade of LCpl, 93
    grade of Sgt, 92

Korea, 84–87
    1st Provisional Marine Brigade, 84
    capture of Seoul, 86
    Chinese Communists forces, 86
    Chosin Reservoir, 86
    Imjin River, 87
    Inchon landing, 86
    Punchbowl sector, 87
    Pusan perimeter, 84
    Spring Offensive of 1951, 86–87
    Yudam-Ni, 86

516   *Landing Operations Doctrine* (*FTP-167*), 79

Last to leave the ship, 102

Leadership, 261–287
  attributes, 262–265
  chain of command, 267–268
  combat, 283–286
  developing techniques, 269–272
  discipline, 265–266
  heritage of, 261
  indicators, 279–281
  inspections, 281–283
  maxims, 286–287
  noncommissioned leaders, 267
  praise and reprimand, 276–277
  principles, 261–262
  relations with seniors, 278–279
  subordinates, 272–276

Leatherneck, 97

Leave
  annual, 208
  computing, 208–209
  earned, 208
  emergency, 208
  excess, 208
  foreign, 209
  and liberty, 207–210
  unused, compensation, 219

Leave of absence, 207–208

Lebanon, Marines in, 88

Lesson plan, 246–248

Letter reports. *See* Fitness reports

Letters, official, 202–204

Liberty, 210
  foreign, pointers on, 391–393

Liberty card, 211

Lost original orders, 226–227

Mail, official, 204

Mameluke sword, 96

Manners, good, 477–479

Marine Air-Ground Task Force
  Air Group, 49
  Battalion Landing Team, (BLT), 49
  Expeditionary Brigade, 49–53
  Expeditionary Unit, 49–53
  Marine Air Reserve Training Command (MARTC), 804
  Regimental Landing Team, 49
  typical organization, 53

Marine Band, 98–100

Marine Corps
  Assistant Chief of Staff, G-1, 44–45
  Assistant Chief of Staff, G-2, 45
  Assistant Chief of Staff, G-3, 45
  Assistant Chief of Staff, G-4, 45
  Assistant Commandant, 43
  Chief of Staff, 44
  Colors, 94–95
  Commandant (CMC), 20–21, 43
  countries maintaining, 33
  Deputy Chief of Staff, 44
  Director, Administrative Division, 45
  Director, Command Center, 46
  Director, Data Systems Division, 46
  Director, Information, 45
  Director, Personnel, 46
  Director, Policy Analysis Division, 45
  Director, Reserve, 46
  Director, Women Marines, 44
  discipline, 36
  Districts, 165
  Division, 49–50
  Fiscal Director, 47
  Fleet Marine Force, Aviation, 49
  Force Logistics Command, 49
  formation of, 33
  Headquarters (HQMC), 43
  Inspector General, 46
  Legislative Assistant to the Commandant, 44
  Liaison Officer with CNO, 43
  loyalty and faithfulness, 36
  mission and roles, 18–19, 37–39
  Organization of, 18–19, 40–43
  professionalism, 37
  quality and competence, 36
  Quartermaster, General (QMG), 46
  relations between officers and men, 36–37
  Secretary of the General Staff, 44
  Sergeant Major, 44–47
  status of, 39–40
  strength of, 19
  table of equipment, 49
  table of organization, 49
  the individual, 36
  the volunteer, 36
  traditions, 37
  what it stands for, 36–37
  valor, 36

Marine Corps Association, 176

Marine Corps Automated Service Center, 166

Marine Corps Aviation. *See* Aviation, Marine Corps

517   Marine Corps Development and Education Command (MCDEC)
Amphibious Warfare School, 54
Basic School, 54
Command and Staff College, 54
Communication Officer School, 54
Computer Sciences School, 54
Extension School, 54
Instructor Training School, 54
Officer Candidate School (OCS), 54
Optical Instrument Repairman, 54
Ordnance School, 54
Physical Fitness Academy, 54
Women NCO Leadership Course, 54
Women Officer School, 54
Marine Corps Exchanges ("PX"), 139–140
Marine Corps Institute (MCI), 241–242
Marine Corps March, 95–96
Marine Corps Memorial Chapel, Quantico, 104
Marine Corps, Mid-20th Century, 87–88
Cuban Crisis, 88
Marines in Lebanon, 88
Marines Land at Alexandria, Suez, 88
Marines Off Haiti, 88
Marine Corps Mottoes, 95
By sea and by land, 95
Fortitudine, 95
From the Halls of Montezumas to the Shores of Tripoli, 95
Semper Fidelis, 95
Marine Corps Museums, 103
Marine Corps Operating Forces. See Operating Forces, Marine Corps
Marine Corps, Postwar, 83
Douglass-Mansfield Bill (1952), 83
National Security Act of 1947, 83
Marine Corps Recruit Depots, 54
Marine Corps Reserve. See Reserve, Marine Corps
Marine Corps Reserve Units. See Reserve Units, Marine Corps
Marine Corps Reservists. See Reservists, Marine Corps
Marine Corps Staff Organization and Procedures. See Staff Organization and Procedures, Marine Corps
Marine Corps story, 64–90
Marine Corps Supply. See Supply, Marine Corps
Marine Expeditionary Force (MEF), 47–49

Marines' Hymn and Marine Corps March, 95–96
Marines in the Revolution, 64
Continental Marines, 64
First Objective, 64
Nicholas, Captain Samuel, 64
Recruiting at Tun Tavern, 64
Marine Junior ROTC, 173
Marines "Over There," 75–76
Marinettes, 178
Marquesas Islands, 66
Mascot, Marine Corps, 101–102
Medal of Honor, 109
Medals, 91–112
Medical care, dependents', 136–138
reserve, 175
wearing, 111–112
Meritorious Promotions, 196
Meritorious Unit Commendation, 110
Mess
clubs and messes, 474–476
CPO, 377–379
Mess night, 467–472
Military courtesy and ceremonies, 303–345
address, 304–308
conduct toward members of other services, 303
etiquette pointers, 308–310
displaying colors, 327–329
phraseology, 304–308
salutes and saluting, 310–322
Military funerals. See also Personal Affairs, 433
escorts, 324
general information
Military law, 346–358
civil and military, 347
courts-martial, 353–358
NCO authority, 349–350
nonjudicial punishment, 350–353
nonjudicial punishment limits, 352–353
Office Hours, 351–352
sources, 346–347
UCMJ, 347–349
Military Occupational Specialty (MOS), 236–237
Military Police and Shore Patrol, 301
hints on, 302
Military Standby. See Travel by commercial air
Mission and roles, Marine Corps, 18–19, 37–39

518

Mottoes, Marine Corps, 95
Museums, Marine Corps, 103

National Aeronautics and Space Administration (NASA), 8
National ensign, 104
National objectives, 9
National Security Act, 10–11
National Security Council (NSC), 8
Naval Air Systems Command (NavAir), 21
Naval Districts. *See* Naval Shore Establishment
Naval Electronics Systems Command (NavElecs), 21
Naval Executive Assistants, 20
Naval Facilities Engineering Command (NavFacEng), 22
Naval Ordnance Systems Command (NavOrd), 21–22
Naval Personnel (NavPers) Boards, 20
Naval Research, Office of (ONR), 22
Naval Ship Systems Command (NavShip), 21
Naval Shore Establishment, 23
Naval Supply Systems Command (NavSup), 22
Naval Supporting Establishment, 21
Naval Tactical Data System (NTDS), 21
Navy, Department of the, 16–23
  executive assistants, 20–21
  mission, 18–19
  Secretary, 19–20
Navy Department, 17–18
  Chief of Naval Operations (CNO), 20
  mission of, 18–19
  Secretary and Assistants, 19–20
Navy Unit Commendation, 110
Noncommissioned Officer (NCO), 3–7
  in charge (NCOIC), 430
  distribution, 192
  Junior, 92–93
  the Marine NCO, 5
  origins, 4–5
  precedence among, 197
  ranks and traditions, 91–93
  sword, 325–327
  Women Marines, 183–184
Nonjudicial punishment, 350–353. *See also* Military law
Norfolk, Virginia, Marine activities, 145

O'Bannon, First Lieutenant Presley N., 66
Obligated service and training, 172

Off-duty employment, 210–211
Office Hours, 351–352
Officer, becoming an, 253–257
  general requirements, 253
  Limited Duty Officers (LDO), 256–257
  Navy Enlisted Scientific Program (NESEP), 256–257
  Officer Candidate School (OCS), 257
  roads to your commission, 253–257
  U. S. Naval Academy, 256
  Warrant Officers, 257
  Women Officer Candidates Course (WOCC), 257
Officer of the Day, 295
  duties, 296–297
  hints for, 298–300
Officer of the Deck, 383
Official correspondence, mail, and letters, 202–204
Official record, 186–187
Operating Forces, Marine Corps, 47–52
  Fleet Marine Forces, 47–49
  Force Troops, 48
  Forces on other assignment, 52
  Forces with Naval Establishment Shore Activities, 52
  Forces with Operating Forces of the Navy, 47
Operating Forces of the Navy
  components of, 23–24
  Regular Navy, 24–27
  "task force principle," 28–29
Orders, lost original, 226–227
Organization
  Marine Corps, 18–19, 40–43
    table of, 49
  posts of the Marine Corps, 134–135
  reserve, Marine Corps, 164
  ships, 373–376
Organized Marine Corps Reserve, 167–168
  Medal, 175
Overseas allowance, 216

Parade, traditional elements and terms, 338–339
Parris Island, S.C., (MCRDep), 57, 147–149
Pay
  foreign duty, 216
  hazard and incentive, 214–215
  hostile fire, 215

519 Pay (*cont.*)
proficiency, 218
reserve, 174
separation travel, 219
severance, 219
special, 215
Pay record. *See* Staff returns
Per diem allowances, 225
in U. S., 225
outside U. S., 225
Permanent Change of Station (PCS), 221
Personal Affairs, 433–464
allotments, 444
death and burial, 451–454
estates, 433–445
insurance, 434–441
investments, 443
powers of attorney and wills, 446–451
real estate, 441–442
retired benefits, 460–464
Retired Serviceman's Family Protection Plan (RSFPP), 439–440
social security, 437–438
Soldiers and Sailors Civil Relief Act, 446
survivor benefits, 456–459
taxes, 445–446
Personal and Unit Citations in Order of Precedence, list of, 108–109
Personal correspondence, 204–205
Personal file, 187
Personal radio traffic, 205
Physical retirement, 201–202
Platt Amendment, 73
"Plug Uglies," 70
Post-Civil War, 71
Post Exchange. *See* Marine Corps Exchanges
Post flag, 105
Posts of the Marine Corps, 133–159
Camp Smedley D. Butler, Okinawa, 157–158
Commissary, 138–139
dependents' medical care, 136–138
educational facilities, 140
exchanges, 139–140
facilities and services, 135
Hawaiian area, Marine activities in the, 156–157
Marine Barracks, Eighth and Eye, 141–142
Marine Corps Air Station, Beaufort, S.C., 149

Marine Corps Air Station, Cherry Point, N.C., 145–146
Marine Corps Air Station, El Toro, Calif., 156
Marine Corps Air Station, Yuma, Arizona, 150–151
Marine Corps Base, Camp Lejeune, N.C., 146–147
Marine Corps Base, Camp Pendleton, Calif., 153–156
Marine Corps Base, Twentynine Palms, Calif., 151
Marine Corps Development and Education Command (MCDEC), 142–143
Marine Corps Recruit Depot, Parris Island, S.C., 147–149
Marine Corps Recruit Depot, San Diego, Calif., 153
Marine Corps Supply Activity, Philadelphia, Pa., 144
Marine Corps Supply Center, Albany, Ga., 149–150
Marine Corps Supply Center, Barstow, Calif., 151–153
Medical and dental care, 135–136
Norfolk area, Marine activities in, 145
organization, 134–135
public quarters, 140–141
recreation, 140
smaller posts, 158–159
typical post, 134
welfare activities, 140. *See also* Chapter 20
Powers of attorney and wills, 446–451
Precedence among NCOs, 197
Precept, Staff NCO Selection Boards, 193–194
Presidential Unit Citation (PUC) 109–110
Presidents Own, 98–100
Proceed. *See* Travel orders
Proficiency Pay, 218
Promotion
bandsmen, Marine, 197
bars to, 197
basic qualifications for NCO, 195–196
meritorious, 196
of POWs and missing, 196
remedial, 197
special provisions, 196–197
Staff NCO, 197
Public quarters, 140–141
Public relations, 258

Punchbowl sector, 87
Pusan perimeter, 84

Qualifications, basic, for NCO promotion, 195–196
Quantico, Va. (MCDEC), 57, 142–143
Quarterdeck, 377
Quarters Allowance (BAQ), 214
Quarters, Charge of, 300–301
Quick, Sergeant John H., 72

Radio traffic, personal, 205
Ranks and traditions, NCO, 91–93
    Centurion's duties, 91
    maniple, 91
    Vegetius, Roman Centurion, 91
Rations, commuted. See Subsistence
Ready Reserve, 168
Real estate, 441–442
Record, official, 186–187
Records and returns, 186–198
Recreation, 140
Recruit Depots, Marine, 54
Recruiting service, 55
Reductions in rank, 197
Reenlistment, 198
    bonus, 218–219
    broken, 198
    classes of, 197
    continuous, 197
    immediate, 198
Regular drills, Reserve, 171
Regular Reports. See Fitness reports
Regulations, ships, 376–377
Reimbursable expenses, 225
Reimbursement, 224
    travel, 226
Release from active duty. See Discharges
Remedial promotion, 197
Remote Storage Activities (RSA), 56
Removing stains, singes, and "shine," 125–126
Rental, fair, 214
Repeated training duty, 172
Reporting aboard, 372–373
Reporting seniors. See Fitness reports
Reserve, Marine Corps, 160–177
    categories for active duty, 168–169
    composition of, 167
    decorations and medals, 175
    employment protection, 176
    exchange and commissary privileges, 175
    history, 160–164

miscellaneous, 173–177
    organization of, 164
    organized, 167–168
    pay, 174
    promotion opportunities, 175
    Ready, 168
    regular drills, 171
    repeated training duty, 172
    retirement, 176–177
    ribbon, 176
    special commendation ribbon, 175
    standby, 168
    training, 169–172
    training opportunities, 170–171
    transfer into, 172–173
    uniforms, 175
Reserve Units, Marine Corps, 166
    organized aviation units, 166
    organized ground units, 166
    staff groups, 167
    volunteer training units, 167
Reservists, Marine Corps,
    privileges and perquisites, 174–176
    Women Marines, 168, 182–183
Retired and retainer pay, 219–220
    computation, 220
    miscellaneous provisions, 220
Retired benefits, 460–464
Retired Reserve, 168–169
Retired Serviceman's Family Protection Plan (RSFPP), 439–440
Retirement
    basic definitions, 199
    disability, temporary, 201
    Reserve, 176–177
    and separation, 199
Review, 335–336
Revolutionary War, Marines in, 64
ROTC duty, 172–173
    hints for, 173
    NCOs with, 173
ROTC, Junior, 173
Rum on New Year's Day, 100
Russell, Major General John H., 47

Salutes and saluting, 310–322. See also Military Courtesy and Honors
San Diego, Calif. (MCRDep), 57, 153
Sand table, 250–251
Sanitation, field, 363–364
Savings deposits. See Allotments
Scarlet trouser stripe, 97
Schools, formal, 239

Sea power, 90
Seagoing Marines, 52
Seal, Marine Corps, 94
Seas, beyond the, 77
Security of
    classified matter, 206–207
    information, 205–207
Selection boards, Staff NCO, 193–195
Selective Service System, 8
Semper Fidelis (March), 95–96
Semper Fidelis (Motto), 95
Separation travel pay, 219
Separations. *See* Discharges *and* Retirement
Sergeant Major, 44–47, 184
    first, 65
Serial numbers, 197–198
Seringapatam, HMS, 66
Service afloat, 371–393
    courtesy, etiquette, and honors, 383–388
    CPO mess, 377–379
    glossary for seagoing Marines, 393–424
    guard duty in embarked Marine Corps units, 383
    Marine detachment, 379–380
    officer of the deck, 383
    pointers on foreign liberty, 391–393
    pointers on housekeeping, 388–389
    quarterdeck, 377
    reporting aboard, 372–373
    sea-duty training and indoctrination, 371–372
    shipboard cleanliness and upkeep, 389–390
    shipboard guard, 380–382
    shipboard pointers, 390–391
    ship's organization, 373–376
    ship's regulations, 376–377
Service creditable for pay purposes, 213
Service and training, obligated, 172
Severance pay, 219
Sewing, 126–127
Shipboard duty and life. *See* Service afloat
Shipment of household goods, 229
    check-off list, 231–232
Shipment of pets, 231
Ship's bell, 101–102
Shore Patrol, Military Police and, 301–302
Social Life, 465–472
    christenings, 473
    clubs and messes, 474–476
    customs, 476–477
    dances, 473–474

good manners, 477–479
Marine Corps Birthday, 465–466
mess night, 467–472
weddings, 472–473
Social Security, 233–234, 437–438
Soldiers and Sailors Civil Relief Act, 446
Space available, military air travel, 227–228
Spatterdashes. *See* Uniforms, early Marine
Special Reports. *See* Fitness reports
Specified commands, 12–13
Spit and polish, 130–132
Staff NCO promotions, 193
    Selection boards, precept, 193–194
Staff NCO ranks, 92
    grade of 1stSgt, 92
    grade of MSgt, 92
    grade of SgtMaj, 92
Staff NCO selection boards and procedures, 193–195
Staff Organization and Procedures, Marine Corps
    Aviation Staff Function, 63
    General Staff, 61
    Personal Staff, 62–63
    Special Staff, 61–62
    Staff Organization, 60–61
Staff returns, 187
Standard Written Agreement (SWAG), 172
Standards. *See* Colors, flags, and standards
Standby reserve, 168
Station Housing Allowance (HOLA), 216
Storage
    of household goods, 229–230
    nontemporary, 229–230
    of prohibited articles, 230
    temporary, 230
Storm flag, 105
Streamers, appurtenances of, 106
Study, schooling and, 239–244
Subsistence, 213–214
Suez, Alexandria, Marines in, 88
Summers, SgtMaj Archibald, 65
Supply, Marine Corps, 55–57
    Alternate Inventory Control Point (ICP), MCSC, Albany, Ga., 55
    Aviation Supply, 57
    cataloging, 55
    Defense Supply Agency (DSA), 56
    Inventory Control Point, MCSA, Philadelphia, Pa., 55

Supply (*cont.*)
   logistic support, 55
   Marine Corps Unified Materiel Management System (MUMMS), 55
   organization, 55
   provisioning, 55–56
   publication support, 56
   Remote Storage Activities (RSA), 56
   sources, 57
   technical services, 56
Supporting Establishment
   Marine Corps, 52–58
   Naval, 21
Swagger stick, 102
Sword, 96
   Mameluke, 96
   Manual, 326–327
   NCO, 325–327

Talk and terminology, 98
Tax exemptions, 234
Taxes, 445–446
"Tell it to the Marines!", 102–103
Temporary Additional Duty (TAD), 222
Temporary appointments for WMs, 196
Temporary disability retirement, 201
Temporary Lodging Allowance (TLA), 216
Temporary Storage, 230
Tentative Landing Operations Manual, 79
Time, expressed in writing, 203
Ties, Marine Corps, 128
Traditions,
   and customs, 93–104
   flags, decorations, and medals, 91–112
Trailer Allowance, 230
Training
   aids, 249
   duty, annual, 172
   duty, repeated, 172
   and indoctrination, sea duty, 371–372
Transfer into Marine Corps Reserve, 173–174
Transfer to Fleet Marine Corps Reserve, 200–201
Transportation of dependents and household goods, 228–232
   on permanent change of station, 228
Travel Advance, 226
Travel by
   commercial air, 228
   government conveyance, 226
   military air, 227–228

train, 228
Travel expense and mileage, 220
Travel hints, 226
Travel orders, 220–222
   authority to issue, 221
   blanket or repeat orders, 222
   how to comply, 222–223
   Permanent Change of Station (PCS), 221
   proceed, 221
   proceed immediately, 221
   proceed time, 221
   proceed without delay, 221
   Temporary Additional Duty (TAD), 222
   temporary duty, 222
Travel pay, separation, 219
Travel reimbursement, 226
Travel status, 220
Travel time, 223
   air travel, 223–224
   commercial land travel, 223
   government and commercial vessel travel, 224
   private conveyance travel, 223
Traveling while on leave, 227
Tripoli, Derna, 66
Trouser stripe, scarlet, 97
Tuition assistance, 242
Tun Tavern, 64
Twentynine Palms, Calif (MCB), 57, 151

Uncommon valor, 80–83
Unified commands, 12–13
Unified Material Management System, Marine Corps (MUMMS), 55
Uniform Code of Military Justice (UCMJ), 347–349
   See also Military Law
Uniforms, 113–132
   accessories, wearing of, 120–121
   care of footgear, 124
   care and maintenance, 123–124
   civilian clothes, 127
   early Marine, 113
   fit and marking, 122–123
   grooming, 128–130
   history, 113–116
   types and combinations, 118–119
   your own blues, 132
   wearing, 117
Unit decorations, 109

523   Unused leave compensation, 219
      USAFI, 242

      Variable bonus, 219
      Veterans Administration, 9
      Vietnam, 89–90
         Chulai, 90
         Danang, 90
         First Marine Aircraft Wing, 89
         First Marine Division, 89
         Third Marine Division, 89
         Walt, Lewis, General, 90
      Volunteer Marine Corps Reserve, 168

      Walt, General Lewis, 90
      War of 1812, 66–68
         Carmick, Major Daniel, 67
         Gamble, Captain John M., 66
         HMS *Seringapatam,* 66
         Marquesas Islands, 66
      War with Spain, 71–72
      Wars, between the, 69–70

      Watchstanding, 290
      Weddings, 472–473
      Welfare activities, 140. *See also* Chapter 20
      Wills, power of attorney and, 446–451
      Women Marines, 178–185
         Director, 44, 181
         duties, 181–182
         first director, 180
         history, 178–181
         NCO Leadership, 184–185
         NCOs, 183–184
         officer school, 54
         organization and composition, 181
         Reservists, 168, 182–183
         SgtMaj, 184
         strength, 181
         top two grades, 184
      Women's Reserve. *See* Women Marines,
         history

      Yudam-Ni, 86
      Yuma, Arizona (MCAS), 57, 150–151